CIMA

MANAGEMENT

PAPER P2

ADVANCED MANAGEMENT ACCOUNTING

S T U D Y   T E X T

Our text is designed to help you study **effectively** and **efficiently**.

In this edition we:

- **Highlight** the **most important elements** in the syllabus and the **key skills** you will need
- **Signpost** how each chapter links to the syllabus and the learning outcomes
- Use **overview and summary diagrams** to develop understanding of interrelations between topics
- **Provide** lots of **exam alerts** explaining how what you're learning may be tested
- **Include examples** and **questions** to help you apply what you've learnt
- **Emphasise key points** in **section summaries**
- **Test your knowledge** of what you've studied in **quick quizzes**
- **Examine your understanding** in our **practice question bank**

SUITABLE FOR EXAMS IN 2017

PUBLISHED NOVEMBER 2016

BPP
LEARNING MEDIA

ii

Third edition 2016

ISBN 9781 5097 0687 7
e-ISBN 9781 5097 0731 7

British Library Cataloguing-in-Publication Data
A catalogue record for this book
is available from the British Library

Published by

BPP Learning Media Ltd
BPP House, Aldine Place
London W12 8AA

www.bpp.com/learningmedia

Printed by Wheatons Exeter Ltd

Hennock Road
Marsh Barton
Exeter
EX2 8RP

Your learning materials, published by BPP
Learning Media Ltd, are printed on paper sourced
from sustainable, managed forests.

We are grateful to the Chartered Institute of
Management Accountants for permission to
reproduce past examination questions. The
suggested solutions in the exam answer bank have
been prepared by BPP Learning Media Ltd.

BPP
LEARNING MEDIA

Contents

How our Study Text can help you pass

Streamlined studying	• We show you the best ways to study efficiently • Our Text has been designed to ensure you can easily and quickly navigate through it • The different features in our Text emphasise important knowledge and techniques
Exam expertise	• **Studying P2** on page xv introduces the key themes of the syllabus and summarises how to pass • We highlight throughout our Text how topics may be tested and what you'll have to do in the exam • We help you see the complete picture of the syllabus, so that you can answer questions that range across the whole syllabus • Our Text covers the syllabus content – no more, no less
Regular review	• We frequently summarise the key knowledge you need • We test what you've learnt by providing questions and quizzes throughout our Text

Our other products

BPP Learning Media also offers these products for the P2 Objective Test exams and the integrated case study (ICS) exams:

i-Pass	Providing computer-based testing in a variety of formats, ideal for self-assessment
Exam Practice Kit	Providing helpful guidance on how to pass the objective test and more question practice
Passcards	Summarising what you should know in visual, easy to remember, form
ICS Workbook	Providing help with exam skills and question practice for the Integrated Case Study exam

You can purchase these products by visiting www.bpp.com/cimamaterials

Online Learning with BPP

BPP's online learning study modes provide flexibility and convenience, allowing you to study effectively, at a pace that suits you, where and when you choose.

Online Classroom Live	Through live interactive online sessions it provides you with the traditional structure and support of classroom learning, but with the convenience of attending classes wherever you are
Online Classroom	Through pre-recorded online lectures it provides you with the classroom experience via the web with the tutor guidance & support you'd expect from a face to face classroom

You can find out more by visiting www.bpp.com/cima

Features in our Study Text

Chapter Overview Diagrams illustrate the connections between the topic areas you are about to cover

 Section Introductions explain how the section fits into the chapter

KEY TERM

Key Terms are the core vocabulary you need to learn

KEY POINT

Key Points are points that you have to know, ideas or calculations that will be the foundations of your answers

 Exam Alerts show you how subjects are likely to be tested

 Exam Skills are the key skills you will need to demonstrate in the exam, linked to question requirements

LEARN

Formulae To Learn are formulae you must remember in the exam

EXAM

Exam Formulae are formulae you will be given in the exam

 Examples show how theory is put into practice

 Questions give you the practice you need to test your understanding of what you've learnt

CASE STUDY

Case Studies link what you've learnt with the real-world business environment

 Links show how the syllabus overlaps with other parts of the qualification, including Knowledge Brought Forward that you need to remember from previous exams

 Website References link to material that will enhance your understanding of what you're studying

 Further Reading will give you a wider perspective on the subjects you're covering

Section Summary Diagrams allow you to review each section

Streamlined studying

What you should do	In order to
Read the Chapter and Section Introductions and look at the Chapter Overview Diagram	See why topics need to be studied and map your way through the chapter
Go quickly through the explanations	Gain the depth of knowledge and understanding that you'll need
Highlight the Key Points, Key Terms and Formulae To Learn	Make sure you know the basics that you can't do without in the exam
Focus on the Exam Skills and Exam Alerts	Know how you'll be tested and what you'll have to do
Work through the Examples and Case Studies	See how what you've learnt applies in practice
Prepare Answers to the Questions	See if you can apply what you've learnt in practice
Review the Chapter Summary Diagrams	Remind you of, and reinforce, what you've learnt
Answer the Quick Quiz	Find out if there are any gaps in your knowledge
Answer the Question(s) in the Practice Question Bank	Practice what you've learnt in depth

Should I take notes?

Brief notes may help you remember what you're learning. You should use the notes format that's most helpful to you (lists, diagrams, mindmaps).

Further help

BPP Learning Media's *Learning to Learn Accountancy* provides lots more helpful guidance on studying. It is designed to be used both at the outset of your CIMA studies and throughout the process of learning accountancy. It can help you **focus your studies on the subject and exam**, enabling you to **acquire knowledge**, **practice and revise efficiently and effectively**.

Syllabus and learning outcomes

Paper P2 Advanced Management Accounting

The syllabus comprises:

Topic and Study Weighting

		%
A	Cost planning and analysis for competitive advantage	25
B	Control and performance management of responsibility centres	30
C	Long-term decision making	30
D	Management control and risk	15

Learning Outcomes On completion of their studies, students should be able to:		
Lead	**Component**	**Indicative syllabus content**
A Cost planning and analysis for competitive advantage		
1 Evaluate techniques for analysing and managing costs for competitive advantage.	(a) Evaluate activity-based management	• Activity-based costing to derive 'long-run' costs appropriate for use in decision making.
		• Activity-based management and its use in improving the efficiency of repetitive overhead activities.
		• Direct and activity-based cost methods in tracing costs to 'cost objects', such as customers or distribution channels, and the comparison of such costs with appropriate revenues to establish 'tiered' contribution levels, as in the activity-based cost hierarchy.
		• Direct customer profitability and distribution channel profitability.
	(b) Evaluate total quality management (TQM) techniques	• The impacts of just-in-time (JIT) production, the theory of constraints and total quality management on efficiency, inventory and cost.
		• The benefits of JIT production, total quality management and theory of constraints and the implications of these methods for decision making in the contemporary manufacturing environment.
		• Kaizen costing, continuous improvement and cost of quality reporting.
		• Process re-engineering and the elimination of non-value adding activities and reduction of activity costs.
	(c) Discuss techniques for enhancing long-term profits	• Target costing and the determination of target costs from target prices.
		• Value analysis and quality function deployment.
		• The Value Chain and the management of contribution/profit generated throughout the chain.
		• Life cycle costing and its implications for marketing strategies.
	(d) Apply learning curves to estimate time and cost for activities, products and services.	• Learning curves and their use in predicting product/service costs, including derivation of the learning rate and the learning index

Learning Outcomes On completion of their studies, students should be able to:		
Lead	**Component**	**Indicative syllabus content**
B	**Control and performance management of responsibility centres**	
1 Discuss decision making in responsibility centres.	(a) Discuss the information needed for decision making in different organisational structures	• Relevant cost information for cost centre managers: controllable and uncontrollable costs and budget flexing. • Relevant revenue and cost information for profit and investment centre managers: cost variability, attributable costs, controllable costs and identification of appropriate measures of profit centre 'contribution'. • Alternative measures of performance for responsibility centres.
	(b) Prepare reports to inform decisions.	• Performance reports: recognising issues of controllable/uncontrollable costs, variable/fixed costs and tracing revenues and costs to particular cost objects.
2 Discuss issues arising from the use of performance measures and budgets for control.	(a) Prepare performance reports for the evaluation of projected and actual performance	• Key metrics for the assessment of financial consequences including profitability, liquidity and asset turnover ratios, return on investment, residual income and economic value. • Benchmarking. • Analysis of reporting by dimension (e.g. segment, product, channel).
	(b) Discuss traditional and non-traditional approaches to performance measurement	• Non-financial performance indicators. • Balanced Scorecards (BSC).
	(c) Discuss the criticisms and behavioural aspects of budgeting in responsibility centres.	• Behavioural issues in budgeting: participation in budgeting and its possible beneficial consequences for ownership and motivation; participation in budgeting and its possible adverse consequences for 'budget padding' and manipulation; setting budget targets for motivation; implications of setting standard costs etc. • Criticisms of budgeting and the arguments for and against 'beyond budgeting'.

Learning Outcomes On completion of their studies, students should be able to:		
Lead	**Component**	**Indicative syllabus content**
3 Evaluate issues arising from the division of the organisation into responsibility centres.	(a) Discuss the likely behavioural consequences of performance measurement within an organisation	• The behavioural consequences of performance management and control in responsibility centres. • The behavioural consequences arising from divisional structures: internal competition and internal trading.
	(b) Discuss transfer pricing systems	• The theory of transfer pricing, including perfect, imperfect and no market for the intermediate good. • Negotiated, market, cost-plus and variable cost-based transfer prices. Dual transfer prices and lump sum payments as means of addressing some of the issues that arise.
	(c) Evaluate the effects of transfer prices.	• The motivation of divisional management. • Divisional and group profitability. • The autonomy of individual divisions.

Learning Outcomes On completion of their studies, students should be able to:		
Lead	Component	Indicative syllabus content
C Long-term decision making		
1 Evaluate information to support project appraisal.	(a) Analyse information for use in long-term decision making (including consideration of tax, inflation and other factors)	• Relevant cash flows taking account of tax, inflation and other factors, and the use of perpetuities to derive 'final' project value where appropriate. • The identification and integration of non-financial factors in long-term decisions.
	(b) Discuss the financial consequences of dealing with long-run projects, in particular the importance of accounting for the 'time value of money'	• The process of investment decision making, including origination of proposals, creation of capital budgets, go/no go decisions on individual projects (where judgements on qualitative issues interact with financial analysis). • Discounting, including the use of annuities in comparing projects with unequal lives and the profitability index in capital rationing situations. • Capital investment real options (i.e. to make follow-on investment, abandon or wait).
	(c) Evaluate investment appraisal techniques and explain their results.	• The strengths and weaknesses of: payback, discounted payback, accounting rate of return (ARR), net present value (NPV), internal rate of return (IRR) and modified internal rate of return (based on a project's terminal value). • Prioritisation of projects that are mutually exclusive, and/or are subject to single-period capital rationing, and/or have unequal lives.
2 Discuss pricing strategies and their consequences.	(a) Discuss pricing strategies and their consequences.	• Pricing decisions for profit maximising in imperfect markets. Note: tabular methods of solution are acceptable. • Pricing strategies and the financial consequences of market skimming, premium pricing, penetration pricing, loss leaders, product bundling/optional extras and product differentiation to appeal to different market segments.

Learning Outcomes On completion of their studies, students should be able to:		
Lead	**Component**	**Indicative syllabus content**
D Management control and risk		
1 Analyse information to assess its impact on long-term decisions.	(a) Apply sensitivity analysis	• Sensitivity analysis to identify the input variables that most affect the chosen measure of project worth (payback, ARR, NPV or IRR).
	(b) Analyse risk and uncertainty.	• Quantification of risk. • Probabilistic models and interpretation of distribution of project outcomes. • Decision trees. • Bayes Theorem. • Decision making in conditions of uncertainty.
2 Discuss management's responsibilities with regard to risk.	(a) Discuss risk management	• Upside and downside risk. • The TARA framework – transfer, avoid, reduce, accept. • Business risks. • Ethical implications and the public interest.
	(b) Discuss the risks associated with the collection and use of information.	• Costs and benefits associated with investing in information systems. • Big Data.

Studying P2

1 What's P2 about

1.1 Cost planning and analysis for competitive advantage

We look at the various techniques that can be used for **cost planning and analysis** in this section. Cost analysis covered in Chapter 1 – focuses on such techniques as ABC, direct product profitability and customer profitability analysis. Cost management techniques such as JIT, total quality management (TQM) and outsourcing are also covered in this chapter. Techniques for enhancing long term profits such as target costing and value chain analysis are examined in chapter 2. In chapter 3 we look at cost planning techniques such as learning curves, and life cycle costing.

1.2 Control and performance management of responsibility centres

We look at measuring performance in divisionalised organisations in chapters 5 to 7. After understanding different types of **responsibility centres**, we focus on measures of performance such as residual income and return on investment. This section also deals with the use of flexible budgets for evaluation and control purposes and then looks at the behavioural aspects of budgeting. There is also considerable focus on financial and non-financial performance indicators as well as the Balanced Scorecard.

In this section the main focus is on **interpretation and analysis** rather than on mechanical calculations which have been covered at P1 level (although you may need to perform numerical calculations before moving onto the discussion elements).

The effects of **transfer pricing strategies** on divisional performance are also considered.

1.3 Long term decision making

This part of the syllabus looks at long term decision making. The issue of **Pricing** was covered in chapter 4. You are expected to understand and apply techniques for **evaluating long-term proposals** which are covered in chapters 8 and 9. This includes identifying relevant cash flows, using investment appraisal techniques (including DCF and ARR) and factoring in inflation and taxation, ranking the projects and applying sensitivity analysis.

1.4 Management control and risk

This part of the syllabus looks at techniques for **measuring risk and evaluating uncertainty**. These techniques include expected values, sensitivity analysis and decision trees. You need to be familiar with the techniques and their application across a variety of decision making tools such as relevant cash flows, DCF and CVP analysis. Finally the topic of 'Big Data' and its role in risk management is introduced.

2 What's required

You will be expected to demonstrate knowledge and understanding of various techniques as well as the ability to apply these techniques to different scenarios. Key higher skills include evaluation, interpretation and analysis.

The examiners are looking for

- Clear layout and labelling of workings
- Ability to apply knowledge to given scenarios rather than the production of generic answers
- Understanding of key techniques
- Ability to analyse and discuss data and information rather than just production of the numbers

3 How to pass

3.1 Study the whole syllabus

You need to be comfortable with **all areas of the syllabus**, as questions in the objective test exam will cover all syllabus areas. **Wider reading** will help you understand the main risks businesses face, which will be particularly useful in the Integrated Case Study exam.

3.2 Lots of question practice

You can **develop application skills** by attempting questions in the Practice Question Bank. While these might not be in the format that you will experience in your exam, doing the full question will enable you to answer the exam questions. However, you should practice OT exam standard questions, which you will find in the BPP Exam Practice Kit.

However, you should practice OT exam standard questions, which you will find in the BPP Exam Practice Kit.

4 Brought forward knowledge

The examiner may test knowledge or techniques you've learnt at lower levels. As P2 is part of the Performance pillar, the content of Paper P1 will definitely be significant.

Remember that brought forward knowledge will only be useful if it is linked to the learning outcomes of Paper P2. For example, you might not be asked to produce a detailed budget but you might be required to comment on how budgets can affect individuals' behaviour in the workplace.

5 The Integrated Case Study and links with other exams

The Integrated Case Study exam is based on the expectation that students are developing a pool of knowledge. When faced with a problem students can appropriately apply their knowledge from any syllabus. Students will avoid a historical problem of partitioning their knowledge and accessing, for example, their knowledge of IFRS only when faced with a set of financial statements.

Performance measurement techniques such as ratio analysis may be useful in any paper. The effectiveness of management accounting systems, particularly the information provided and how useful they are as control mechanisms, could impact upon any of the papers.

6 What the examiner means

The table below has been prepared by CIMA to help you interpret the syllabus and learning outcomes and the meaning of questions.

You will see that there are 5 levels of Learning objective, ranging from Knowledge to Evaluation, reflecting the level of skill you will be expected to demonstrate. CIMA Certificate subjects only use levels 1 to 3, but in CIMA's Professional qualification the entire hierarchy will be used.

At the start of each chapter in your study text is a topic list relating the coverage in the chapter to the level of skill you may be called on to demonstrate in the exam.

Learning objectives	Verbs used	Definition
1 Knowledge		
What are you expected to know	• List	• Make a list of
	• State	• Express, fully or clearly, the details of/facts of
	• Define	• Give the exact meaning of
2 Comprehension		
What you are expected to understand	• Describe	• Communicate the key features of
	• Distinguish	• Highlight the differences between
	• Explain	• Make clear or intelligible/state the meaning or purpose of
	• Identify	
	• Illustrate	• Recognise, establish or select after consideration
		• Use an example to describe or explain something
3 Application		
How you are expected to apply your knowledge	• Apply	• Put to practical use
	• Calculate/ compute	• Ascertain or reckon mathematically
		• Prove with certainty or to exhibit by practical means
	• Demonstrate	
	• Prepare	• Make or get ready for use
	• Reconcile	• Make or prove consistent/compatible
	• Solve	• Find an answer to
	• Tabulate	• Arrange in a table
4 Analysis		
How you are expected to analyse the detail of what you have learned	• Analyse	• Examine in detail the structure of
	• Categorise	• Place into a defined class or division
	• Compare and contrast	• Show the similarities and/or differences between
		• Build up or compile
	• Construct	• Examine in detail by argument
	• Discuss	• Translate into intelligible or familiar terms
	• Interpret	• Place in order of priority or sequence for action
	• Prioritise	• Create or bring into existence
	• Produce	
5 Evaluation		
How you are expected to use your learning to evaluate, make decisions or recommendations	• Advise	• Counsel, inform or notify
	• Evaluate	• Appraise or assess the value of
	• Recommend	• Propose a course of action

Competency Framework

CIMA has developed a competency framework detailing the skills, abilities and competencies that finance professionals need. The CIMA syllabus has been developed to match the competency mix as it develops over the three levels of the professional qualification. The importance of the various competencies at the management level is shown below.

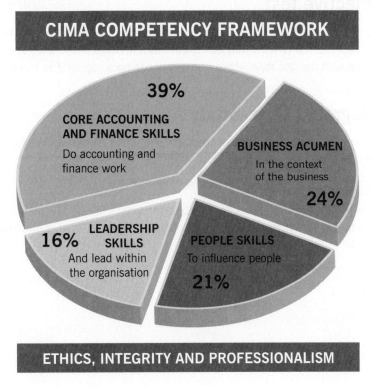

CIMA COMPETENCY FRAMEWORK

39%
CORE ACCOUNTING AND FINANCE SKILLS
Do accounting and finance work

BUSINESS ACUMEN
In the context of the business
24%

16% LEADERSHIP SKILLS
And lead within the organisation

PEOPLE SKILLS
To influence people
21%

ETHICS, INTEGRITY AND PROFESSIONALISM

BPP
LEARNING MEDIA

Assessment

The CIMA assessment is a two-tier structure with objective tests for each subject and an Integrated Case Study at each level.

Objective test

The objective tests are computer based and can be taken on demand. The student exam preparation on the CIMA website (www.cimaglobal.com) has additional information and tools to help you become familiar with the test style. Make sure you check back regularly as more information may be added.

Integrated Case Study

Candidates must pass or receive exemptions from the three objective tests at each level, before attempting the Integrated Case Study exam for that level.

The Integrated Case Studies are available four times a year.

The Integrated Case Study exams combine the knowledge and learning from all the pillars. They will be set in the context of a preseen fictional organisation based on a real industry.

COST PLANNING AND ANALYSIS FOR COMPETITIVE ADVANTAGE

Part A

INTRODUCTION – A REVISION OF BASIC COST ACCOUNTING CONCEPTS AND TECHNIQUES

 Before you start your P2 studies, read through this chapter to remind yourself of basic cost accounting concepts and techniques. These areas were introduced at Certificate level but are fundamental to your understanding of many topics covered in the P2 syllabus.

If you are confident you understand the contents of this chapter, have a go at the questions and then feel free to move on to Chapter 1. If you are a bit rusty, read the chapter in full and attempt the questions as you go along. You can also continue to refer to this introduction as you move through the P2 syllabus.

topic list	learning outcomes	syllabus references	ability required
1 Some basic cost accounting concepts	Revision	n/a	knowledge
2 The problem of overheads	Revision	n/a	application
3 Revision of absorption costing	Revision	n/a	application
4 Overhead absorption	Revision	n/a	analysis
5 Revision of marginal costing	Revision	n/a	analysis
6 Revision of variance analysis	Revision	n/a	analysis
7 Reconciling profit figures	Revision	n/a	analysis

1 Some basic cost accounting concepts

Introduction

This section reviews a number of key terms that you must be familiar with.

KEY POINTS

- **Costs** can be **classified** according to their **nature** or according to their **purpose** (inventory valuation/profit measurement, decision making, control).

- **Costs** can **behave** in **variable, fixed, semi-variable/semi-fixed/mixed** or **stepped** fashion in relation to changes in activity level.

- **Semi-variable costs** can be **analysed** using the **high-low** or **scattergraph methods**.

Knowledge brought forward from earlier studies

Cost units and cost centres

Cost unit

- Anything that is measurable and useful for cost control purposes

- Can be tangible (such as a tonne of coal) or intangible (such as an hour of accountant's time)

- Composite cost units are made up of two parts (such as the passenger/kilometre (the cost of transporting one passenger for one kilometre) for a bus company)

Cost centre

- Act as collecting places for costs before they are analysed further

- Examples: a production department, a service location such as the canteen, a function such as a sales representative, an activity such as quality control or an item of equipment such as a key production machine

Cost classification

According to their nature

- Into materials, labour, expenses and then further subdivided (such as raw materials, components, consumables)

According to their purpose

- For **inventory valuation and profit measurement**, costs might be classified as **product costs and period costs, direct costs and indirect costs/overheads,** or they might be **classified by function** (production/manufacturing, administration, marketing/selling and distribution)

- For **decision making**, costs are **classified by behaviour** (see below) or as **relevant and non-relevant**

- **Classification for control** involves dividing costs into those that are **controllable** and those that are **uncontrollable,** or into **normal and abnormal costs**

Cost behaviour

Variable costs

- Tend to **vary directly with the level of output** (so that there is a **linear relationship** between **variable cost per unit and output**)

- Variable cost per unit is the **same amount for each unit produced** but **total variable cost increases as volume of output increases** (for example, materials)

Fixed costs

- Tend to be **unaffected by increases or decreases in the level of output**

- Relate to a span of time and so are a **period charge** (as the **time span increases so too will the cost**)

- Only **constant** at all levels of output **within the relevant range** of output (the range of output at which the organisation has had experience of operating in the past and for which cost information is available)

- Examples: local government taxes for commercial properties (rates) and UK road fund licence

Semi-variable (or semi-fixed or mixed) costs

- Made up of a **fixed cost element** and a **variable cost element** and so **partly affected by changes in the level of activity**

- Can be **analysed** using the **high-low method** or the **scattergraph method**

Stepped costs

- **Behave like fixed costs within certain ranges of activity**

- Example: rent (of an organisation's one factory) may be a fixed cost if production remains below 1,000 units a month, but if production exceeds 1,000 units a second factory may be required and the cost of rent (on two factories) would go up a step

- Do not behave like variable costs and so, continuing the example above, if monthly output is 1,500 units, 2 factories are required – not 1.5 factories

---

Section summary

Costs can be **classified** according to their **nature** or according to their **purpose** (inventory valuation/profit measurement, decision making, control).

Costs can **behave** in **variable, fixed, semi-variable/semi-fixed/mixed** or **stepped** fashion in relation to changes in activity level.

Semi-variable costs can be **analysed** using the **high-low** or **scattergraph** methods.

---

2   The problem of overheads

Introduction

Traditionally, the view has been that a fair share of overheads should be added to the cost of units produced. This fair share will **include a portion of all production overhead expenditure** and possibly administration and marketing overheads too. This is the view embodied in the principles of **absorption costing**.

2.1 Using absorption costing to deal with the problem of overheads

The **theoretical justification** for using absorption costing is that all production overheads are incurred in the production of the organisation's output and so each unit of the product receives some benefit from these costs. Each unit of output should therefore be charged with some of the overhead costs.

2.1.1 Practical reasons for using absorption costing

(a) **Inventory valuations**

   Inventory in hand must be valued for two reasons.

   (i)   For the **closing inventory** figure in the balance sheet (statement of financial position)
   (ii) For the **cost of sales** figure in the income statement (statement of comprehensive income)

(b) **Pricing decisions**

   Many companies attempt to set selling prices **by calculating the full cost of production or sales** of each product, and then adding a margin for profit. 'Full cost plus pricing' can be particularly useful for companies which do jobbing or contract work, where each job or contract is different, so that a standard unit sales price cannot be fixed. Without using absorption costing, a full cost is difficult to ascertain.

(c) **Establishing the profitability of different products**

   This argument in favour of absorption costing states that if a company sells more than one product, it will be difficult to judge **how profitable each individual product is**, unless overhead costs are shared on a fair basis and charged to the cost of sales of each product.

2.2 Using marginal costing to deal with the problem of overheads

Advocates of **marginal costing** take the view that only the variable costs of making and selling a product or service should be identified. **Fixed costs should be dealt with separately** and treated as a cost of the accounting period rather than shared out somehow between units produced. Some overhead costs are, however, variable costs which increase as the total level of activity rises and so the marginal cost of production and sales should include an amount for variable overheads.

Section summary

The traditional approach to dealing with overheads is **absorption costing**. It is recommended in financial accounting, but in some situations the information it provides can be **misleading**.

3   Revision of absorption costing

Introduction

This section acts as a reminder of how to calculate cost per unit using absorption costing and the terminology used in this costing technique.

KEY TERM

ABSORPTION COSTING is 'A method of costing that, in addition to direct costs, assigns all, or a proportion of, production overhead costs to cost units by means of one or a number of overhead absorption rates'.

(CIMA Official Terminology)

Knowledge brought forward from earlier studies

Absorption costing

- Product costs are built up using absorption costing by a process of **allocation**, apportionment and **overhead absorption**.

- **Allocation** is the process by which whole cost items are charged directly to a cost unit or cost centre. **Direct costs are allocated directly to cost units. Overheads clearly identifiable with cost**

centres are allocated to those cost centres but costs which **cannot be identified with one particular cost centre** are **allocated to general overhead cost centres**. The cost of a warehouse security guard would therefore be charged to the warehouse cost centre but heating and lighting costs would be charged to a general overhead cost centre.

- The **first stage of overhead apportionment** involves sharing out (or apportioning) the overheads within **general overhead cost centres** between the other cost centres using a fair basis of apportionment (such as floor area occupied by each cost centre for heating and lighting costs).

- The **second stage of overhead apportionment** is to apportion the costs of **service cost centres** (both directly allocated and apportioned costs) to production cost centres.

- The **final stage** in absorption costing is the **absorption into product costs** (using overhead absorption rates) of the overheads which have been allocated and apportioned to the production cost centres.

3.1 Calculating the cost per unit

The diagram below illustrates the procedures you should follow when trying to calculate the cost per unit using absorption costing. Note the process of **allocating, apportioning** and **reapportioning** indirect costs to cost centres and ultimately production centres.

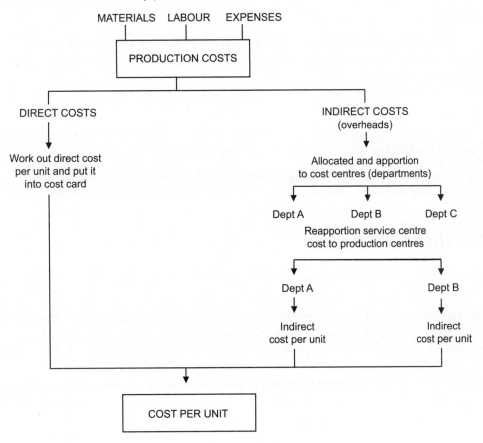

Question 1   Apportionment

A company is preparing its production overhead budgets and determining the apportionment of those
overheads to products. Cost centre expenses and related information have been budgeted as follows.

	Total $	Machine shop A $	Machine shop B $	Assembly $	Canteen $	Maintenance $
Indirect wages	78,560	8,586	9,190	15,674	29,650	15,460
Consumable materials	16,900	6,400	8,700	1,200	600	–
Rent and rates	16,700					
Buildings insurance	2,400					
Power	8,600					
Heat and light	3,400					
Depreciation (machinery)	40,200					
Value of machinery	402,000	201,000	179,000	22,000	–	–
Power usage (%)	100	55	40	3	–	2
Direct labour (hours)	35,000	8,000	6,200	20,800	–	–
Machine usage (hours)	25,200	7,200	18,000	–	–	–
Area (sq ft)	45,000	10,000	12,000	15,000	6,000	2,000

Required

Using the direct apportionment to production departments method and bases of apportionment which you
consider most appropriate from the information provided, calculate overhead totals for the three
production departments.

Section summary

The three stages of absorption costing are **allocation**, **apportionment** and **absorption**.

4 Overhead absorption

Introduction

Having allocated and/or apportioned all overheads, the next stage in absorption costing is to add them to,
or absorb them into, the cost of production or sales.

KEY TERM

ABSORBED OVERHEAD is 'Overhead attached to products or services by means of absorption rates'.

(CIMA Official Terminology)

4.1 Use of a predetermined absorption rate

KEY TERM

OVERHEAD ABSORPTION RATE is 'A means of attributing overhead to a product or service, based for
example on direct labour hours, direct labour cost or machine hours'.   *(CIMA Official Terminology)*

Knowledge brought forward from earlier studies

 The overhead likely to be incurred during the coming year is estimated.

 The total hours, units or direct costs on which the overhead absorption rates are based (activity levels) are estimated.

 Absorption rate = estimated overhead ÷ budgeted activity level.

4.2 Choosing the appropriate absorption base

The choice of an absorption basis is a **matter of judgement and common sense**. There are no strict rules or formulae involved. The ease of collecting the data required for the chosen rate is a major factor. But the basis should realistically reflect the characteristics of a given cost centre, avoid undue anomalies and be 'fair'. It is generally accepted that **time-based bases** should be used if possible as many overheads, such as rent and rates, increase with time. The **choice will be significant in determining the cost of individual products, but the total cost of production overheads is the budgeted overhead expenditure, no matter what basis of absorption is selected**. It is the relative share of overhead costs borne by individual products and jobs which is affected.

Question 2	Bases of absorption

List as many possible bases of absorption (or 'overhead recovery rates') that you can think of, and give their advantages and disadvantages.

Question 3	Absorption rates

Using the information in and the results of **Question 1: apportionment** (in Section 3), determine budgeted overhead absorption rates for each of the production departments using appropriate bases of absorption.

4.3 Under and over absorption of overheads

KEY POINT

Under-/over-absorbed overhead occurs when overheads incurred do not equal overheads absorbed.

The rate of overhead absorption is based on **estimates** (of both numerator and denominator) and it is quite likely that either one or both of the estimates will not agree with what actually occurs.

- **Over absorption** means that the **overheads charged to the cost of sales are greater than the overheads actually incurred**.

- **Under absorption** means that **insufficient overheads have been included in the cost of sales**.

KEY TERM

UNDER- OR OVER-ABSORBED OVERHEAD (or UNDER- OR OVER-RECOVERED OVERHEAD) is 'The difference between overhead incurred and overhead absorbed, using an estimated rate, in a given period'.

(CIMA Official Terminology)

Suppose that the budgeted overhead in a production department is $80,000 and the budgeted activity is 40,000 direct labour hours; the overhead recovery rate (using a direct labour hour basis) would be $2 per direct labour hour. Actual overheads in the period are, say, $84,000 and 45,000 direct labour hours are worked.

	$
Overhead incurred (actual)	84,000
Overhead absorbed (45,000 × $2)	90,000
Over absorption of overhead	6,000

In this example, the cost of production has been charged with $6,000 more than was actually spent and so the cost that is recorded will be too high. The over-absorbed overhead will be an adjustment to the income statement at the end of the accounting period to reconcile the overheads charged to the actual overhead.

Question 4
Under and over absorption

The total production overhead expenditure of the company in **Question: apportionment and Question: absorption rates** (in Sections 3 and 4) was $176,533 and its actual activity was as follows.

	Machine shop A	Machine shop B	Assembly
Direct labour hours	8,200	6,500	21,900
Machine usage hours	7,300	18,700	–

Required

Using the information in and results of the two questions mentioned above, what is the under or over absorption of overheads?

4.3.1 The reasons for under-/over-absorbed overhead

The overhead absorption rate is predetermined from budget estimates of overhead cost and activity level. Under or over recovery of overhead will occur in the following circumstances.

- Actual overhead costs are different from budgeted overheads.
- The actual activity level is different from the budgeted activity level.
- Actual overhead costs **and** actual activity level differ from those budgeted.

Question 5
Reasons for under/over absorption

Elsewhere Ltd has a budgeted production overhead of $180,000 and a budgeted activity of 45,000 machine hours.

Required

Fill in the blanks and choose the correct terms from those highlighted in the following statements.

(a)   If actual overheads cost $170,000 and 45,000 machine hours were worked, **under-absorbed/over-absorbed** overhead will be $ .... because
....
....

(b)   If actual overheads cost $180,000 and 40,000 machine hours were worked, **under-absorbed/over-absorbed** overhead will be $ .... because ....
....

(c)   If actual overheads cost $170,000 and 40,000 machine hours were worked, **under-absorbed/over-absorbed** overhead will be $ .... because ....
....

4.3.2 Accounting for under-/over-absorbed overheads

If overheads are **under-absorbed**, the cost of units sold will have been understated and therefore the under absorption is charged to the income statement for the period. It is not usually considered necessary to adjust individual unit costs and therefore inventory values are not altered.

Any **over absorption** is credited to the income statement for the period.

4.3.3 The problems caused by under/over absorption of overheads

If **under absorption** occurs, product prices may have been set too low as managers have been working with unit rates for overheads that are too low. This could have a significant impact on profit levels.

If overhead rates have been unnecessarily high (**over absorption**), it is likely that prices have been set too high which could significantly reduce sales of the product.

Section summary

After apportionment, overheads are absorbed into products using an **appropriate absorption rate based on budgeted costs and budgeted activity levels**.

Under-/over-absorbed overhead occurs when overheads incurred do not equal overheads absorbed.

5   Revision of marginal costing

Introduction

This section acts as a reminder of the marginal costing technique that was covered in your previous studies. Make sure you read the 'knowledge brought forward' to ensure you are familiar with the terminology and the differences between a marginal costing income statement and one used for absorption costing.

KEY TERMS

MARGINAL COST is 'The part of the cost of one unit of a product or service which would be avoided if that unit were not produced, or which would increase if one extra unit were produced'.

CONTRIBUTION is 'Sales value less variable cost of sales'.

MARGINAL COSTING is 'The accounting system in which variable costs are charged to cost units and fixed costs of the period are written off in full against the aggregate contribution. Its special value is in recognising cost behaviour, and hence assisting in decision-making.'   (*CIMA Official Terminology*)

Knowledge brought forward from earlier studies

Marginal costing

*   In **marginal costing**, closing **inventories are valued at marginal (variable) production cost** whereas, in **absorption costing**, inventories are **valued at their full production cost** which includes absorbed fixed production overhead.

*   If the opening and closing inventory levels differ, the **profit reported** for the accounting period **under the two costing systems will therefore be different**.

- But **in the long run, total profit for a company will be the same** whichever is used because, in the long run, total costs will be the same by either method of accounting. Different accounting conventions merely affect the profit of individual periods.

Income statements

- **Absorption costing**

	$	$
Sales		X
Opening inventory (at full cost)	X	
Full production cost	X	
Less closing inventory (at full cost)	X	
Cost of sales	X	
Under-/over-absorbed overhead	X	
Total cost		X
Gross profit		X
Less non-manufacturing costs		X
Net profit		X

- **Marginal costing**

	$	$
Sales		X
Opening inventory (at variable cost)	X	
Production cost (variable costs)	X	
Less closing inventory (at variable cost)	X	
Cost of sales		X
Contribution		X
Less fixed production costs		X
Gross profit		X
Less non-manufacturing fixed costs		X
Net profit		X

Question 6   Marginal costing and absorption costing

RH makes and sells one product, which has the following standard production cost.

		$
Direct labour	3 hours at $6 per hour	18
Direct materials	4 kilograms at $7 per kg	28
Production overhead	Variable	3
	Fixed	20
Standard production cost per unit		69

Normal output is 16,000 units per annum. Variable selling, distribution and administration costs are 20 per cent of sales value. Fixed costs are $180,000 per annum. There are no units in finished goods inventory at 1 October 20X2. The fixed overhead expenditure is spread evenly throughout the year. The selling price per unit is $140. Production and sales budgets are as follows.

	Six months ending 31 March 20X3	Six months ending 30 September 20X3
Production	8,500	7,000
Sales	7,000	8,000

Required

Prepare profit statements for each of the six-monthly periods, using the following methods of costing.

(a)   Marginal costing   (b)   Absorption costing

Section summary

In **marginal costing**, inventories are valued at **variable (marginal) production cost** whereas in **absorption costing** they are valued at their **full production cost**.

If **opening and closing inventory levels differ**, **profit** reported under the two methods will be **different**.

In the **long run, total profit** will be the **same** whatever method is used.

6   Revision of variance analysis

Introduction

Variance analysis reconciles actual to budgeted costs, revenue or profit. It is a way of explaining the difference between actual and budgeted results. They can either be favourable (F), better than expected or adverse (A), worse than expected.

You should remember the variances summarised below from your previous studies.

Variance	Favourable	Adverse	Calculation	
Material price	– Unforeseen discounts received – Greater care in purchasing – Change in material standard	– Price increase – Careless purchasing – Change in material standard	Price Based on actual purchases What should it have cost? What did it cost?	$ X (X) X
Material usage	– Material used of higher quality than standard – More efficient use of material – Errors in allocating material to jobs	– Defective material – Excessive waste or theft – Stricter quality control	Usage Based on actual production What should have been used? What was used? Difference valued at standard cost per kg	Kg X (X) X $X
Labour rate	– Use of workers at a rate of pay lower than standard	– Wage rate increase	Rate Based on actual hours paid What should it have cost? What did it cost?	$ X (X) X

Variance	Favourable	Adverse	Calculation
Idle time	– The idle time variance is always adverse	– Machine breakdown – Illness or injury to worker	Idle time Hours Hours worked X Hours paid (X) Difference valued at $X standard rate per hour
Labour efficiency	– Output produced more quickly than expected because of worker motivation, better-quality materials etc – Errors in allocating time to jobs	– Lost time in excess of standard – Output lower than standard set because of lack of training, sub-standard materials etc – Errors in allocating time to jobs	Efficiency Hours Based on actual production How long should it have taken? X How long did it take? (X) X Difference valued at $X standard rate per hour
Variable overhead expenditure	– See fixed overhead expenditure (below)	– See fixed overhead expenditure (below)	Based on actual hours worked $ What should it have cost? X What did it cost? (X) X
Variable overhead efficiency	– See labour efficiency (above)	– See labour efficiency (above)	Based on actual production Hours How long should it have taken? X How long did it take? (X) X Difference valued at standard rate per hour $X

Note. This assumes variable overheads are incurred per labour hour.

Fixed overhead expenditure	– Savings in costs incurred – More economical use of services	– Increase in cost of services used – Excessive use of services – Change in type of service used	$ Budgeted expenditure X Actual expenditure (X) X

Overhead expenditure variances ought to be traced to the individual cost centres where the variances occurred.

Fixed overhead volume	Production or level of activity greater than budgeted	Production or level of activity less than budgeted	Units Budgeted units X Actual units (X) X Difference valued at $X OAR per unit

Remember that where inputs can be substituted for one another, the efficiency/usage variance can be subdivided. Material and labour variances can both be split into mix and yield (or output) components.

Variance	Description	Calculation
Yield	Measures the effect on costs of inputs yielding more or less than expected.	Calculated as the difference between the expected output and the actual output, valued at the standard cost per unit.
Mix	Measures whether the actual mix is cheaper or more expensive than the standard.	Calculated as the difference between the actual total quantity used in the standard mix and the actual quantity used in the actual mix, valued at the standard input price of each material.

Planning and operational variances are summarised below.

Variance	Description	Calculation	
Planning variance	A planning variance arises because of inaccurate planning or faulty standards.	Original standard Revised standard Difference valued at standard rate	Hours X (X) $X
Operational variance	An operational variance compares actual results with the revised (or ex-post) standard.	How long should it have taken? How long did it take? Difference valued at standard rate	Hours X (X) $X

Section summary

Whilst you are unlikely to be required to calculate a number of variances in the exam, you should understand how different variances are interlinked and be able to discuss potential causes of variances.

7 Reconciling profit figures

Introduction

Now that you can calculate profits using absorption costing and marginal costing, the final issue is how to reconcile the profits. You might be required to reconcile profits calculated using the two methods. Alternatively you might be asked to reconcile profits for different periods calculated using the same method.

7.1 Reconciling the profit figures given by the two methods

KEY POINT

The **difference in profits** reported using marginal costing and absorption costing is **due** to the **different inventory valuation methods** used.

(a)   **Inventory levels increase during the period**

Absorption costing will report the higher profit. Some of the fixed production overhead incurred during the period will be carried forward in closing inventory (which reduces cost of sales) to be set against sales revenue in the following period instead of being written off in full against profit in the period concerned.

(b)   **Inventory levels decrease during the period**

Absorption costing will report the lower profit. As well as the fixed overhead incurred, fixed production overhead which had been carried forward in opening inventory is released and is also included in cost of sales.

Example: reconciling profits

The profits reported for the six months ending 31 March 20X3 in the previous question would be reconciled as follows.

	$'000
Marginal costing profit	191
Adjust for fixed overhead in inventory (inventory increase of 1,500 units × $20 per unit)	30
Absorption costing profit	221

Question 7   Profit reconciliation

Reconcile the profits reported for the six months ending 30 September 20X3 in **Question 6: marginal costing and absorption costing**.

Question 8   Differences between absorption costing and marginal costing profits

D&M report an absorption costing profit of $112,500 for the year to 31 December 19X0. Opening inventory consisted of 58,000 units, closing inventory 43,000 units. The fixed overhead absorbed per unit is $19.50.

Required

Fill in the blank in the following statement.

The marginal costing profit for the period would be $ ....

7.2 Reconciling the profits for different periods

KEY POINTS

When **marginal costing** is used, differences in profits in different periods are **due to changes in sales volume**.

When **absorption costing** is used differences are **due to changes in sales volumes and adjustments made for over-/under-absorbed overhead.**

Example: reconciling marginal costing profit with absorption costing profit

Look back at the information in **Question 6: marginal costing and absorption costing**.

Reconcile the marginal costing profits for the two periods and also the absorption costing profits for the two periods.

For marginal costing

The difference in profits in the two periods is due entirely to **changes in units sold** (everything else has remained the same). Higher sales volume means higher contribution and thus greater profits.

Contribution per unit

	$
Selling price	140
Less: direct labour	((18)
direct materials	(28)
variable production overhead	(3)
variable selling and other costs (20% × $140)	(28)
Contribution	63

The **marginal costing profit figures** can be reconciled as follows.

	$'000
Marginal costing profit for 6 months to 31 March 20X3	191
Increase in contribution in second 6-month period due to increase in sales volume	
((8,000 – 7,000) × $63)	63
Marginal costing profit for 6 months to 30 September 20X3	254

For absorption costing

Profit per unit

	$
Selling price	140
Less: standard production cost	(69)
variable selling and so on costs	(28)
Profit	43

The **absorption costing** profit figures can be reconciled as follows.

	$'000
Absorption costing profit for 6 months to 31 March 20X3	221
Increase in profit in second 6-month period due to increase in sales volume	
((8,000 – 7,000) × $43)	43
Adjustments for under/over absorption	
Six months to 31 March 20X3	(10)
Six months to 30 September 20X3	(20)
Absorption costing profit for 6 months to 30 September 20X3	234

The **over absorption** in the first six months must be **deducted** in the reconciliation because it made that period's profit higher (and we are reconciling from the first six months' figure to the second six months'). The **under absorption** in the second six months must also be **deducted**, however, as it made that period's profits lower than the first six months'.

This is a bit confusing so go over the paragraph above until you have the reasoning clear in your mind. Then try the following question.

Question 9	Reconciliation of profits for different periods

In a reconciliation of the absorption costing profits of 20X0 to those of 20X1, there was under absorption of fixed production overhead in both periods. How should the under-absorbed overhead figures be dealt with in the reconciliation?

	20X0 figure	20X1 figure
A	Add	Add
B	Deduct	Add
C	Add	Deduct
D	Deduct	Deduct

Section summary

When **marginal costing** is used, differences in profits in different periods are **due to changes in sales volume**.

When **absorption costing** is used differences are **due to changes in sales volumes and adjustments made for over-/under-absorbed overhead**.

Chapter Roundup

✓   Costs can be **classified** according to their **nature** or according to their **purpose** (inventory valuation/profit measurement, decision making, control).

✓   **Costs** can **behave** in **variable, fixed, semi-variable/semi-fixed/mixed** or **stepped** fashion in relation to changes in activity level.

✓   **Semi-variable costs** can be **analysed** using the **high-low** or **scattergraph methods**.

✓   The traditional approach to dealing with overheads is **absorption costing**. It is recommended in financial accounting, but in some situations the information it provides can be **misleading**.

✓   The three stages of absorption costing are **allocation, apportionment** and **absorption**.

✓   After apportionment, overheads are absorbed into products using **an appropriate absorption rate based on budgeted costs and budgeted activity levels**.

✓   **Under-/over-absorbed overhead** occurs when overheads incurred do not equal overheads absorbed.

✓   In **marginal costing**, inventories are valued at **variable (marginal) production cost** whereas in **absorption costing** they are valued at their **full production cost**.

✓   If **opening and closing inventory levels differ**, **profit** reported under the two methods will be **different**.

✓   In the **long run**, **total profit** will be the **same** whatever method is used.

✓   When **marginal costing** is used, differences in profits in different periods are **due to changes in sales volume**.

✓   When **absorption costing** is used differences are **due to changes in sales volumes and adjustments made for over-/under-absorbed overhead**.

Quick Quiz

1   The behaviour of fixed costs depends on whether marginal costing or absorption costing is used. *True or false?*

2   How is an overhead absorption rate calculated?

    A   Estimated overhead ÷ actual activity level
    B   Estimated overhead ÷ budgeted activity level
    C   Actual overhead ÷ actual activity level
    D   Actual overhead ÷ budgeted activity level

3   Over absorption means that the overheads charged to the cost of sales are greater than the overheads actually incurred. *True or false?*

4   *Fill in the blanks in the statements about marginal costing and absorption costing below.*

    (a)   If inventory levels .... between the beginning and end of a period, absorption costing will report the higher profit.

    (b)   If inventory levels decrease, ... costing will report the lower profit.

5   *Fill in the following blanks with either 'marginal' or 'absorption'.*

    (a)   Using .... costing, profits can be manipulated simply by changing output and inventory levels.

    (b)   Fixed costs are charged in full against the profit of the period in which they are incurred when .... costing is used.

    (c)   .... costing fails to recognise the importance of working to full capacity.

    (d)   .... costing could be argued to be preferable to .... costing in management accounting in order to be consistent with the requirements of SSAP 9.

    (e)   .... costing should not be used when decision-making information is required.

6   What are the three practical reasons cited in the chapter for using absorption costing?

    (a)   ....

    (b)   ....

    (c)   ....

Answers to Quick Quiz

1   False. The behaviour of fixed costs remains the same regardless of the costing system being used.

2   B. Actual figures are **not** used.

3   True

4   (a)   Increase
    (b)   Absorption

5   (a)   absorption
    (b)   marginal
    (c)   marginal
    (d)   absorption, marginal
    (e)   absorption

6   (a)   Inventory valuation
    (b)   Pricing decisions
    (c)   Establishing profitability of different products

Answers to Questions

1 Apportionment

	Total $	A $	B $	Assembly $	Canteen $	Maintenance $	Basis of apportionment
Indirect wages	78,560	8,586	9,190	15,674	29,650	15,460	Actual
Consumable materials	16,900	6,400	8,700	1,200	600	–	Actual
Rent and rates	16,700	3,711	4,453	5,567	2,227	742	Area
Insurance	2,400	533	640	800	320	107	Area
Power	8,600	4,730	3,440	258	–	172	Usage
Heat and light	3,400	756	907	1,133	453	151	Area
Depreciation	40,200	20,100	17,900	2,200	–	–	Val of mach
	166,760	44,816	45,230	26,832	33,250	16,632	
Reallocate	–	7,600	5,890	19,760	(33,250)	–	Direct labour
Reallocate	–	4,752	11,880	–	–	(16,632)	Mach usage
Totals	166,760	57,168	63,000	46,592	–	–	

2 Bases of absorption

(a) **Percentage of direct materials cost**. It is safe to assume that the overhead costs for producing brass screws, say, are similar to those for producing steel screws. The cost of brass is, however, very much greater than that of steel. Consequently, the overhead charge for brass screws would be too high and that for steel screws too low, if a percentage of cost of materials rate were to be used.

(b) Using **prime cost** as the absorption base would lead to anomalies because of the inclusion of the cost of material, as outlined above.

(c) **Percentage of direct labour cost**. If the overhead actually attributable to units was incurred on, say, a time basis, but one highly paid employee was engaged on producing one item, while a lower-paid employee was producing another item, the overhead charged to the first item using a percentage of wages rate might be too high while the amount absorbed by the second item might be too low. This method should therefore only be used if similar wage rates are paid to all direct employees in a production department. A direct labour hour rate might be considered 'fairer'.

(d) A **direct labour** hour basis is most appropriate in a **labour intensive** environment.

(e) A **machine hour** rate would be used in departments where production is controlled or dictated by **machines**. This basis is becoming more appropriate as factories become more heavily automated.

(f) A **rate per unit** would be effective only if all units were identical.

3 Absorption rates

Machine shop A:	$57,168/7,200	= $7.94 per machine hour
Machine shop B:	$63,000/18,000	= $3.50 per machine hour
Assembly:	$46,592/20,800	= $2.24 per direct labour hour

4 Under and over absorption

		$	$
Actual expenditure			176,533
Overhead absorbed			
Machine shop A	7,300 hours × $7.94	57,962	
Machine shop B	18,700 hours × $3.50	65,450	
Assembly	21,900 hours × $2.24	49,056	
			172,468
Under-absorbed overhead			4,065

Option B is incorrect because actual expenditure was greater than overhead absorbed. Not enough overhead was therefore absorbed.

Options C and **D** are based on absorption using direct labour hours for the two machine shops. Their overheads are incurred in line with machine hours.

---

5 Reasons for under/over absorption

The overhead recovery rate is $180,000/45,000 = $4 per machine hour.

		$
(a)	Actual overhead	170,000
	Absorbed overhead (45,000 × $4)	180,000
	Over-absorbed overhead	10,000

Reason: Actual and budgeted machine hours are the same but actual overheads cost less than expected.

		$
(b)	Actual overhead	180,000
	Absorbed overhead (40,000 × $4)	160,000
	Under-absorbed overhead	20,000

Reason: Budgeted and actual overhead costs were the same but fewer machine hours were worked than expected.

		$
(c)	Actual overhead	170,000
	Absorbed overhead (40,000 × $4)	160,000
	Under-absorbed overhead	10,000

Reason: A combination of the reasons in (a) and (b).

---

6 Marginal costing and absorption costing

(a) **Income statements for the year ending 30 September 20X3: Marginal costing basis**

	Six months ending 31 March 20X3		Six months ending 30 September 20X3	
	$'000	$'000	$'000	$'000
Sales at $140 per unit		980		1,120
Opening inventory	–		73.5	
Std. variable prod. cost (at $49 per unit)	416.5		343.0	
	416.5		416.5	
Closing inventory (W1)	73.5		24.5	
Cost of sales		343		392
		637		728
Variable selling and so on costs		196		224
Contribution		441		504
Fixed costs: production (W2)		160		160
Gross profit		281		344
Fixed costs: selling and so on		90		90
Net profit		191		254

(b)   **Income statements for the year ending 30 September 20X3: Absorption costing basis**

	Six months ending 31 March 20X3		Six months ending 30 September 20X3	
	$'000	$'000	$'000	$'000
Sales at $140 per unit		980		1,120
Opening inventory	–		103.5	
Std. cost of prod. (at $69 per unit)	586.5		483.0	
	586.5		586.5	
Closing inventory (W1)	103.5		34.5	
Cost of sales	483.0		552.0	
(Over-)/under-absorbed overhead (W3)	(10.0)		20.0	
Total costs		473		572
Gross profit		507		548
Selling and so on costs				
Variable	196		224	
Fixed	90		90	
		286		314
Net profit		221		234

Workings

1

	Six months ending 31 March 20X3	Six months ending 30 September 20X3
	Units	Units
Opening inventory	–	1,500
Production	8,500	7,000
	8,500	8,500
Sales	7,000	8,000
Closing inventory	1,500	500
Marginal cost valuation (× $49)	$73,500	$24,500
Absorption cost valuation (× $69)	$103,500	$34,500

2   Budgeted fixed production o/hd = 16,000 units × $20 = $320,000 pa = $160,000 per 6 months

3

	Six months ending 31 March 20X3		Six months ending 30 September 20X3	
Normal output (16,000 ÷ 2)	8,000	Units	8,000	Units
Budgeted output	8,500	Units	7,000	Units
Difference	500	Units	1,000	Units
× std. fixed prod. o/hd per unit	× $20		× $20	
(Over-)/under-absorbed overhead	(($10,000)		$20,000	

7 Profit reconciliation

	$
Marginal costing profit	254
Adjust for fixed overhead in inventory (inventory decrease of 1,000 units × $20 per unit)	(20)
Absorption costing profit	234

8 Differences between absorption costing and marginal costing profits

The correct answer is $405,000.

	$
Absorption costing profit	112,500
Adjust for fixed overhead in inventory	
(inventory decrease of 15,000 × $19.50 per unit)	292,500
Marginal costing profit	405,000

9 Reconciliation of profits for different periods

The correct answer is C.

The under absorption in 20X0 made the 20X0 profit lower and so it should be added. The under absorption in 20X1 made the 20X1 profit lower than the 20X0 profit and so it should be deducted.

Now try the question from the Practice Question Bank

Number	Marks	Time
Q1 Restaurant	10	18 mins

ANALYSING AND MANAGING COSTS

 This chapter considers activity based management (ABM) and quality management techniques.

Section 1 sets the scene by discussing costs in the modern business environment, while **Section 2** looks at **activity based costing (ABC)**, a topic you may have encountered in your earlier studies.

Activity based management (covered in **Section 3**) is basically the cost management application of ABC.

Sections 4 and 5 look at how ABC can be used to determine the **profitability** of products, customers and distribution channels. **Section 6** onwards looks at relatively modern techniques such as total quality management, just-in-time (JIT), Kaizen costing, quality reporting and process re-engineering.

topic list	learning outcomes	syllabus references	ability required
1 The nature of costs	A1(a)	A1(a)(i)	analysis
2 Activity based costing (ABC)	A1(a)	A1(a)(i)	analysis
3 Activity based management (ABM)	A1(a)	A1(a)(ii)	analysis
4 Direct product profitability (DPP)	A1(a)	A1(a)(iv)	analysis
5 Customer profitability analysis (CPA)	A1(a)	A1(a)(iv)	analysis
6 Distribution channel profitability	A1(a)	A1(a)(iv)	analysis
7 Activity based profitability analysis	A1(a)	A1(a)(iii)	analysis
8 Pareto analysis	A1(a)	A1(a)(iv)	analysis

topic list	learning outcomes	syllabus references	ability required
9 Total quality management (TQM)	A1(b)	A1(b)(i)	analysis
10 Cost of quality and cost of quality reports	A1(b)	A1(b)(iii)	analysis
11 Continuous improvement	A1(b)	A1(b)(iii)	analysis
12 Kaizen costing	A1(b)	A1(b)(iii)	analysis
13 Just-in-time (JIT)	A1(b)	A1(b)(i)	analysis
14 Theory of constraints	A1(b)	A1(b)(ii)	analysis
15 Throughput accounting (TA)	A1(b)	A1(b)(ii)	analysis
16 Business process re-engineering (BPR)	A1(b)	A1(b)(iv)	analysis

Chapter Overview

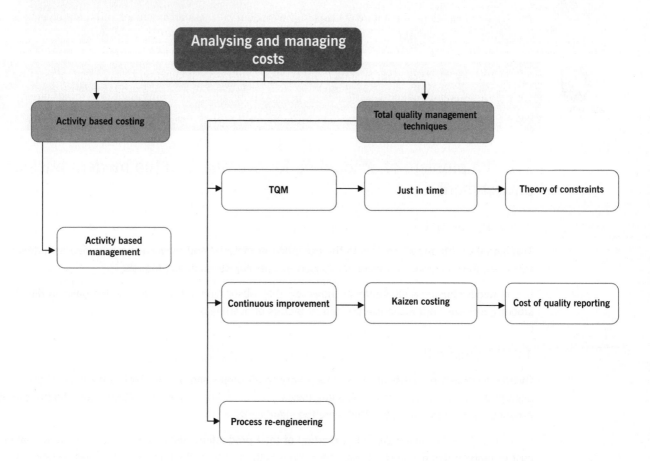

1 The nature of costs

Introduction

This section focuses on the nature of costs in the modern business environment and the problems of accounting for these costs.

KEY POINT

In the **modern business environment**, most costs can be analysed into **short-term variable costs** (that vary with the volume of production) and **long-term variable costs** (that are fixed in the short term and vary not with volume of production but with a different measure of activity).

1.1 The problem of accounting for overheads in the modern business environment

1.1.1 Problem 1

Traditionally, **virtually all costs** with the **exception of material and labour** were classified as **indirect** expenses, meaning that they were not caused by cost objects such as products.

In the **modern business environment**, however, their absorption into products on the **basis of direct labour hours does not recognise the causal factors** of overheads.

1.1.2 Problem 2

Overheads or indirect costs accounted for a **very small proportion of total cost** in the **past**. Their **absorption** into products using **misleading bases** such as in line with direct labour hours **did not therefore produce errors** in product costs that were **too significant**.

Such costs have become a **greater proportion of total production costs**, however, and the **direct labour cost proportion has declined**, in some cases to less than 10% of the total cost. This has resulted in a large volume of costs being spread on the basis of the behaviour of a small volume of costs, thereby producing **misleading** and **even inaccurate cost information**.

1.1.3 Problem 3

Nowadays, **most costs are fixed in the short term** rather than variable, and so **marginal costing is not a particularly appropriate** costing convention to use. The majority of companies prefer to use some method of absorption costing – hence the development of activity based costing (ABC) and the other systems described in this chapter.

1.2 Cost analysis in the modern business environment

Most costs can be analysed between the following.

(a)   **Short-term variable costs**, that vary with the volume of production

(b)   **Long-term variable costs**, that are fixed in the short term and do **not** vary with the volume of production, but that do **vary with a different measure of activity**

It has been suggested that **long-term variable costs** are **related** to the **complexity** and **diversity of production** rather than to simple volume of output. For example, costs for support services such as set-ups, handling of inventory, expediting (progress chasing) and scheduling do not increase with the volume of output. They are fixed in the shorter term but they vary in the longer term according to the range and complexity of product items manufactured. If **another product** or product variation is added to the range,

the **support activities** will become more **complex**. If a **single product** is made, **some support activities**, such as production scheduling, will **not exist**.

The problem of producing a **small number of products in volume** against producing a **large variety of products in small runs** is known as **volume versus variety** and can be expressed graphically.

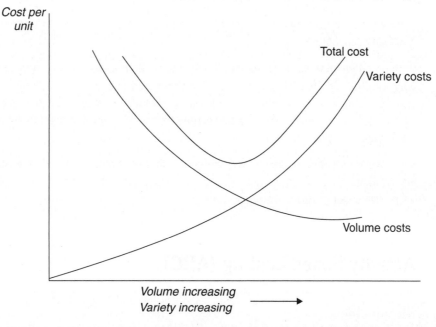

Long production runs (volume) reduce some costs; short production runs (variety) increase some costs. Research has shown that when volume doubles, the average cost per unit decreases by 15% to 25% (the experience curve effect). Stalk and Hout (1990) found that when the variety of products manufactured doubles, the average unit costs rise by 20% to 35%.

When a company adopts the **modern philosophy** and **manufactures in variety, costs of support activities** therefore **increase**, and **emphasis is inevitably put on controlling these costs**, such as minimising production scheduling and set-up costs. In **order to control costs, some attempt must be made to relate these costs to products via their causal factors in as accurate a way as possible**.

1.3 Traditional vs modern manufacturing philosophy

1.3.1 Traditional manufacturing philosophy

Traditional manufacturing philosophy focuses on the need to continue to **use valuable resources** (such as manufacturing equipment) to their **full capacity** and to **maximise** the length of production runs. The main features of the traditional approach to manufacturing are as follows.

(a)   **Labour** and **manufacturing equipment** are so valuable they should **not be left idle**.

(b)   Resulting **inventory** not needed should be **stored** (thus **hiding** inefficient and uneven production methods).

(c)   To increase efficiency and reduce production cost per unit, **batch sizes** and **production runs** should be **as large as possible**.

(d)   It is concerned with **balancing** production run costs and inventory holding costs.

1.3.2 Modern manufacturing philosophy

The main features of the modern approach to manufacturing are as follows.

(a)   **Smooth, steady** production flow (**throughput**)

(b) **Flexibility**, providing the customer with exactly what is wanted, exactly when it is wanted (making the organisation a more complex affair to manage), so as to achieve **competitive advantage**

(c) **Volume versus variety** – greater variety in volumes required by customers

(d) **Just-in-time** – that is, little or no inventory

Section summary

In the **modern business environment**, most costs can be analysed into **short-term variable costs** (that vary with the volume of production) and **long-term variable costs** (that are fixed in the short term and vary not with volume of production, but with a different measure of activity). **Costing systems** have evolved to reflect a **manufacturing philosophy** that is based on the need to achieve **competitive advantage**.

- Flexibility and the ability to respond quickly to customer demands are vital.
- Product life cycles are shorter and products must be brought to the market quickly.
- New technology has been introduced.

2 Activity based costing (ABC)

Introduction

Activity based costing (ABC) has been developed as an **alternative costing system** to traditional overhead absorption costing. This section focuses on the **features** of this system, the **calculations** involved in cost allocation and **wider applications** of ABC.

KEY TERM

ACTIVITY BASED COSTING (ABC) is 'An approach to the costing and monitoring of activities which involves tracing resource consumption and costing final outputs. Resources are assigned to activities and activities to cost objects based on consumption estimates. The latter use **cost drivers** to attach activity costs to outputs'.
(CIMA Official Terminology)

ABC was developed to improve the cost allocation process as traditional techniques assumed that costs were only driven by volume (for example, costs may have been absorbed on a rate per machine hour basis).

Production overheads are **not necessarily driven by volume**, therefore allocation using traditional methods is not necessarily meaningful. With ABC, **multiple overhead absorption rates (OARs)** are calculated based on the different activities that **cause** the costs to **change**.

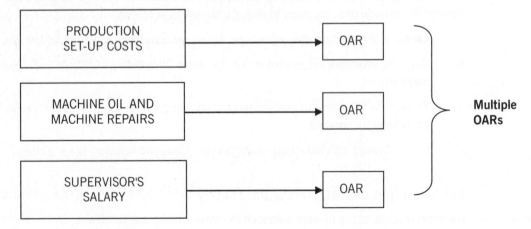

2.1 Cost drivers and cost pools

KEY TERM

A COST DRIVER is a 'factor influencing the level of cost. Often used in the context of ABC to denote the factor which links activity resource consumption to product outputs; for example, the number of purchase orders would be a cost driver for procurement cost'.   (*CIMA Official Terminology*)

2.1.1 Examples of cost drivers

Support department costs	Possible cost driver
Set-up costs	Number of production runs
Production scheduling	Number of production runs
Material handling	Number of production runs
Inspection costs	Number of inspections or inspection hours
Raw materials inventory handling etc	Number of purchase orders delivered
Despatch costs	Number of customer orders delivered

All of the costs associated with a particular cost driver (for example production runs) would be grouped into **cost pools**.

In order to understand how ABC operates in detail, we need to look at two types of cost driver.

KEY TERMS

A RESOURCE COST DRIVER is a measure of the quantity of resources consumed by an activity. It is used to assign the cost of a resource to an activity or cost pool.

An ACTIVITY COST DRIVER is a measure of the frequency and intensity of demand placed on activities by cost objects. It is used to assign activity costs to cost objects.

An **example** of a **resource cost driver** is **area**, which can be used to assign office occupancy costs to purchasing, the accounts department and so on.

An **example** of an **activity cost driver** is **number of customer orders**, the number of orders measuring the consumption of order entry activities by each customer.

In **traditional absorption costing**, overheads are first related to **cost centres** and then to **cost objects** (products). In **ABC**, overheads are first related to **activities** or grouped into **cost pools** (depending on the terminology preferred) and then related to the **cost objects**. (Unlike traditional absorption costing, ABC has other cost objects, such as customers. This will be discussed later.) **The two processes** are therefore **very similar**, but the first stage is different, as ABC uses activities instead of cost centres (functional departments).

Proponents of **ABC** therefore claim that it gives a **more realistic picture of cost behaviour**.

(a)   Costs collected into cost pools tend to behave in the same way (they have the same cost driver).
(b)   Costs related to cost centres might behave in different ways.

Like traditional absorption costing rates, **ABC rates** are **calculated in advance**, usually for **a year ahead**.

2.2 Stages in ABC calculations

  Group overheads into cost pools, according to how they are driven. This involves gathering overheads that are caused by the **same activity** into one group and is done by means of **resource cost drivers** (see the definition in Section 2.1.1 above).

 Identify the cost drivers for each activity (that is, what causes the activity to be incurred). Examples of cost drivers are given in Section 2.1.1 above.

Calculate a cost per unit of cost driver. This is done in a similar way to the calculation of traditional OARs:

$$\text{Cost driver rate} = \frac{\text{total cost of activity}}{\text{Cost driver}}$$

 Absorb activity costs into production based on the usage of cost drivers – for example, rate per production set-up multiplied by number of production set-ups. The **cost driver rate** can be used to **cost products**, as in traditional absorption costing, but it can also cost **other cost objects** such as **customers** or groups of customers.

Example: ABC

The following example illustrates how traditional cost accounting techniques could result in a misleading and inequitable division of costs between low-volume and high-volume products, and demonstrates that ABC may provide a more meaningful allocation of costs.

Suppose that Cooplan manufactures four products, W, X, Y and Z. The direct labour cost per hour is $5. Other output and cost data for the period just ended are as follows.

	Output units	Number of production runs in the period	Material cost per unit $	Direct labour hours per unit	Machine hours per unit
W	10	2	20	1	1
X	10	2	80	3	3
Y	100	5	20	1	1
Z	100	5	80	3	3
		14			

Overhead costs			$
Short-run variable costs	3,080	Expediting and scheduling costs	9,100
Set-up costs	10,920	Materials handling costs	7,700

Required

Prepare unit costs for each product using traditional costing and ABC.

Solution

Using a **conventional absorption costing approach** and an absorption rate for overheads based on either direct labour hours or machine hours, the product costs would be as follows.

	W $	X $	Y $	Z $	Total $
Direct material	200	800	2,000	8,000	
Direct labour	50	150	500	1,500	
Overheads*	700	2,100	7,000	21,000	
	950	3,050	9,500	30,500	44,000
Units produced	10	10	100	100	
Cost per unit	$95	$305	$95	$305	

*$30,800 ÷ 440 hours = $70 per direct labour or machine hour.

Using **ABC** and assuming that the number of production runs is the cost driver for set-up costs, expediting and scheduling costs and materials handling costs, and that machine hours are the cost driver for short-run variable costs, unit costs would be as follows.

	W $	X $	Y $	Z $	Total $
Direct material	200	800	2,000	8,000	
Direct labour	50	150	500	1,500	
Short-run variable overheads (W1)	70	210	700	2,100	
Set-up costs (W2)	1,560	1,560	3,900	3,900	
Expediting, scheduling costs (W3)	1,300	1,300	3,250	3,250	
Materials handling costs (W4)	1,100	1,100	2,750	2,750	
	4,280	5,120	13,100	21,500	44,000
Units produced	10	10	100	100	
Cost per unit	$428	$512	$131	$215	

Workings

1	$3,080 ÷ 440 machine hours	=	$7 per machine hour
2	$10,920 ÷ 14 production runs	=	$780 per run
3	$9,100 ÷ 14 production runs	=	$650 per run
4	$7,700 ÷ 14 production runs	=	$550 per run

Summary

Product	Traditional costing unit cost $	ABC unit cost $	Difference per unit $	Difference in total $
W	95	428	+333	+3,330
X	305	512	+207	+2,070
Y	95	131	+36	+3,600
Z	305	215	−90	−9,000

The figures suggest that the traditional volume-based absorption costing system is flawed.

(a)   It **under-allocates overhead costs to low-volume products** (here, W and X) and **over-allocates overheads to higher-volume products** (here, Z in particular).

(b)   It **under-allocates overhead costs to smaller-sized products** (here, W and Y with just one hour of work needed per unit) and **over-allocates overheads to larger products** (here, X and particularly Z).

ABC traces the appropriate amount of input to each product. However, it is **important** to realise that although **ABC should be** a **more accurate** way of relating overheads to products, **it is not a perfect system** and **product costs** could still be **inaccurate**, as ABC is based on a number of assumptions.

2.3 The merits and criticisms of activity based costing

2.3.1 Merits

As the above example illustrates, there is nothing difficult about ABC. Once the necessary information has been obtained, it is similar to traditional absorption costing. This **simplicity** is part of its appeal. Further merits of ABC are as follows.

(a)   ABC **recognises the increased complexity** of modern businesses with its **multiple cost drivers**, many of which are transaction based rather than volume based.

(b)   ABC is **concerned with all overhead costs**, including such 'non factory floor' costs as quality control and customer service, and so it takes cost accounting beyond its 'traditional' factory floor boundaries.

(c)   ABC gives a meaningful analysis of costs which should provide a suitable basis for decisions about pricing, product mix, design and production.

(d)   ABC helps with **cost reduction** because it provides an insight into causal activities and allows organisations to consider the possibility of **outsourcing particular activities**, or even of **moving to different areas in the industry value chain**. This is discussed later in the chapter, under activity based management.

(e)   ABC can be **used in conjunction with customer profitability analysis (CPA)**, discussed later in this chapter, to determine more accurately the profit earned by serving particular customers.

(f)   ABC can be used by **service and retail organisations**. This will be discussed later in the chapter. Many service and retail businesses have characteristics very similar to those required for the successful application of ABC in modern manufacturing industry.

      (i)   A highly **competitive** market

      (ii)   **Diversity** of products, processes and customers

      (iii)   **Significant overhead costs** which are not easily assigned to individual products

      (iv)   **Demands placed on overhead resources** by individual products and customers, which are **not proportional to volume**

If ABC were to be used in a hotel, for example, attempts could be made to identify the activities required to support each guest by category and the cost drivers of those activities. The cost of a one-night stay midweek by a businessperson could then be distinguished from the cost of a one-night stay by a teenager at the weekend. Such information may prove invaluable for CPA.

Exam alert

An assessment question could ask you to calculate differences in fees charged by a business using activity based costing.

2.3.2 Criticisms

ABC has some serious flaws, and concern is now growing that ABC is seen by many as a panacea for management accounting ills, despite the fact that its suitability for all environments remains unproven.

(a)   The **cost** of obtaining and interpreting the new information may be considerable. **ABC should not be introduced unless it can provide additional information** for management to use in planning or control decisions.

(b)   Some arbitrary **cost apportionment** may still be required at the cost pooling stage for items like rent, rates and building depreciation. If an ABC system has many cost pools, the amount of apportionment needed may be greater than ever.

(c)   Many **overheads relate neither to volume nor to complexity**. The ability of a **single cost driver** to fully explain the cost behaviour of all items in its associated pool is **questionable**.

(d)   There will have to be a **trade-off between accuracy, the number of cost drivers and complexity**.

(e)   ABC tends to **burden low-volume (new) products** with a punitive level of overhead costs and hence threatens opportunities for successful innovation if it is used without due care.

(f)   Some people have questioned the fundamental assumption that activities cause cost; they suggest **that decisions cause cost or the passage of time causes cost** – or that there may be **no clear cause of cost**.

2.4 Wider uses of ABC

2.4.1 Planning

Before an ABC system can be implemented, management must **analyse** the **organisation's activities**, determine the **extent of their occurrence**, and establish the **relationship between activities, products/services and their cost**. This can be used as a basis for **forward planning and budgeting**.

2.4.2 Control

Knowledge of activities also provides an **insight into the way in which costs are structured and incurred in service and support departments**. Traditionally, it has been difficult to control the costs of such departments because of the lack of relationship between departmental output levels and departmental cost. With ABC, however, it is possible to **control or manage the costs by managing the activities that underlie them** using a number of key performance measures which must be monitored if costs and the business generally are to be controlled.

2.4.3 Decision making

Many of **ABC's supporters** claim that it can **assist with decision making** because it provides accurate and reliable cost information. This is a **contentious issue** among accountants. Many 'purists' consider that **marginal costing** alone provides the correct information on which to **make short-term decisions such as the following**.

(a)   Pricing
(b)   Make or buy decisions
(c)   Promoting or discontinuing products or parts of the business
(d)   Developing and designing changed products

ABC establishes a long-run product cost and, because it provides data that can be used to evaluate different business possibilities and opportunities, it is particularly suited for the types of decision listed above. Those decisions have long-term strategic implications and **average cost** is probably **more important** than **marginal cost** in many circumstances. **An ABC cost is an average cost**, but it is **not always a true cost** because some costs, such as depreciation, are usually arbitrarily allocated to products. An ABC cost is therefore **not a relevant cost for all decisions**.

2.4.4 ABC and long-term decisions

ABC is **particularly suited for long-term and strategic decisions** (such as long-run pricing, capacity management and product mix decisions) for a number of reasons.

(a)   It assumes all costs are **variable** in relation to product choice or production-level decisions.

(b)   It has strategic relevance because it allows for a **full understanding of activities** and their resource consumption.

(c)   **Short-run changes in consumption do not translate into changes in spending** (as real cash savings or expenditure are not made/incurred in the short run).

Question 1.1   Using ABC

Learning outcome A1(a)

(a)   List the features of organisations that would find ABC particularly useful for product costing.

(b)   Briefly explain the reasons why ABC is particularly suitable in a modern business environment, and describe any situations where it is not appropriate.

2.5 Pricing and ABC

Example: activity based costing and pricing

ABP makes two products, X and Y, with the following cost patterns.

	Product X $	Product Y $
Direct materials	27	24
Direct labour at $5 per hour	20	25
Variable production overheads at $6 per hour	3	6
	50	55

Production fixed overheads total $300,000 per month and these are absorbed on the basis of direct labour hours. Budgeted direct labour hours are 25,000 per month. However, the company has carried out an analysis of its production support activities and found that its 'fixed costs' actually vary in accordance with non volume related factors.

Activity	Cost driver	Product X	Product Y	Total cost $
Set-ups	Production runs	30	20	40,000
Materials handling	Production runs	30	20	150,000
Inspection	Inspections	880	3,520	110,000
				300,000

Budgeted production is 1,250 units of product X and 4,000 units of product Y.

Required

Given that the company wishes to make a profit of 20% on full production costs, calculate the prices that should be charged for products X and Y using the following.

(a)   Full cost pricing

(b)   Activity based cost pricing

Solution

(a)   The **full cost and mark-up** will be calculated as follows.

	Product X $	Product Y $
Variable costs	50.00	55.00
Fixed prod o/hds ($300,000/25,000 = $12 per direct labour hr)	48.00	60.00
	98.00	115.00
Profit mark-up (20%)	19.60	23.00
Selling price	117.60	138.00

(b)   Using **activity based costing**, overheads will be allocated on the basis of cost drivers.

	X $	Y $	Total $
Set-ups (30:20)	24,000	16,000	40,000
Materials handling (30:20)	90,000	60,000	150,000
Inspections (880:3,520)	22,000	88,000	110,000
	136,000	164,000	300,000
Budgeted units	1,250	4,000	
Overheads per unit	108.80	41.00	

The price is then calculated as before.

	Product X $	Product Y $
Variable costs	50.00	55.00
Production overheads	108.80	41.00
	158.80	96.00
Profit mark-up (20%)	31.76	19.20
	190.56	115.20

(c)   Commentary

The results in (b) are radically different from those in (a). On this basis it appears that the company has **previously been making a huge loss** on every unit of product X sold for $117.60. If the market will not accept a price increase, it may be worth considering ceasing production of product X entirely. It also appears that there is scope for a reduction in the price of product Y, and this would certainly be worthwhile if demand for the product is elastic.

2.5.1 The pricing implications of activity based costing

Many modern companies produce and sell **large volumes** of a **standard product** and a number of variants of the basic product that sell in low volumes at a higher price. Such companies absorb fixed overheads on a conventional basis, such as direct labour hours, and price their products by adding a **mark-up** to full cost.

This means that the **majority of the overheads** would be allocated to the **standard** range, and only a small percentage to the up-market products. The result would be that the **profit margin** achieved on the standard range would be much lower than that on the up-market range.

Although the traditional costing system might suggest that the company should concentrate on the lower-volume, higher-profit margin products, it should be borne in mind that a large quantity of the overhead costs are likely to be related to the up-market products – for example, production scheduling and marketing and distribution costs. Such costs should therefore be **absorbed by the products that cause them** rather than the standard product.

The problem arises with **marginal cost-plus** approaches as well as with absorption cost based approaches, particularly in a modern manufacturing environment, where a relatively small proportion of the total cost is variable. The implication in both cases is that conventional costing should be abandoned in favour of ABC.

2.6 Using ABC in service and retail organisations

ABC was **first introduced in manufacturing organisations** but it can equally well be used in **other types of organisation**. For example, the management of the Post Office in the US uses ABC. They analysed the activities associated with cash processing as follows.

Activities	Examples	Possible cost driver
Unit level	Accept cash	Number of transactions
	Processing of cash by bank	Number of transactions
Batch level	'Close out' and supervisor review of clerk	Number of 'close outs'
	Deposits	Number of deposits
	Review and transfer of funds	Number of accounts
Product level	Maintenance charges for bank accounts	Number of accounts
	Reconciling bank accounts	Number of accounts

Question 1.2   ABC and retail organisations

Learning outcome A1(a)

What activities and drivers might be used in a retail organisation?

Section summary

The ABC approach is to relate costs to the factors that cause or 'drive' them to be incurred in the first place and to change subsequently. These factors are called '**cost drivers**'.

ABC relates overhead/resource costs to the activities that cause or drive them. This is done using **resource cost drivers**. The costs of activities are related to cost units using **activity cost drivers**.

The **information** provided by **analysing activities** can support the management functions of **planning, control and decision making**, provided it is used carefully and with full appreciation of its implications.

3 Activity based management (ABM)

Introduction

Recently, the emphasis has switched away from using activity based approaches for product costing to using it to improve cost management. This section covers the cost management version of ABC – that is, activity based management (ABM). Make sure you know the differences between the two systems and how ABM can be used by companies to gain competitive advantage.

3.1 What is ABM?

There are a great many different **definitions** of activity based management. We focus on the CIMA official definitions below.

KEY TERMS

ACTIVITY BASED MANAGEMENT (ABM):

OPERATIONAL ABM. Actions based on activity driver analysis, that increase efficiency, lower costs and improve asset utilisation.

STRATEGIC ABM. Actions based on activity based cost analysis, that aim to change the demand for activities so as to improve profitability.

                                                (*CIMA Official Terminology*)

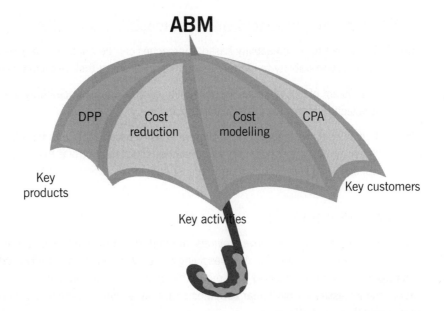

ABM acts as an 'umbrella' for a number of techniques – such as **CPA**, which will be covered later in this chapter – thus focusing the company's attention on key products, activities and customers. It uses the information generated by ABC to **control or reduce cost drivers** and also to **reduce overheads**. By doing so, the company can gain competitive advantage.

3.2 Cost reduction and process improvement

ABM analyses costs on the basis of cross-departmental activities and thus provides management with information on why costs are incurred and on the output of the activity in terms of cost drivers. **By controlling or reducing the incidence of the cost driver, the associated cost can also be controlled or reduced.**

This difference is illustrated in the example below of a customer order processing activity.

Traditional analysis

	$
Salaries	5,700
Stationery	350
Travel	1,290
Telephone	980
Equipment depreciation	680
	9,000

ABC analysis

	$
Preparation of quotations	4,200
Receipt of customer orders	900
Assessment of customer creditworthiness	1,100
Expedition of orders	1,300
Resolution of customer problems	1,500
	9,000

Suppose that the analysis above showed that it cost $250 to process a customer's order. This would indicate to sales staff that it may not be worthwhile chasing orders with a low sales value. By eliminating lots of small orders and focusing on those with a larger value, demand for the activities associated with customer order processing should fall, with spending decreasing as a consequence.

3.2.1 Problems associated with cost reduction and ABM

(a) The extent to which activity based approaches can be applied is very dependent on an organisation's ability to **identify** its main activities and their associated cost drivers.

(b) If a system of 'conventional' responsibility centres has been carefully designed, this may already be a reflection of the key organisational activities.

(c) In some circumstances, the 'pooling' of activity based costs and the identification of a single cost driver for every cost pool may even hamper effective control if the cost driver is not completely applicable to every cost within that cost pool.

3.3 Activity analysis

The activity based analysis above provides information not available from a traditional cost analysis – for example, why was $1,500 spent on resolving customer orders? An **activity analysis** usually **surprises managers** who had not realised the amount being spent on certain activities. This leads to **questions** about the **necessity for particular activities** and, if an activity is required, whether it can be carried out more effectively and efficiently.

Such questions can be answered by classifying activities as value-added or non value added (or as core/primary, support or diversionary/discretionary).

3.3.1 Value-added and non value added activities

KEY TERM

An activity may increase the worth of a product or service to the customer; in this case the customer is willing to pay for that activity and it is considered VALUE-ADDED. Some activities, though, simply increase the time spent on a product or service but do not increase its worth to the customer; these activities are NON-VALUE-ADDED.   (Rayborn, Barfield and Kinney, *Managerial Accounting*)

As an example, **getting luggage on the proper flight is a value-added activity** for airlines; **dealing with the complaints from customers whose luggage gets lost is not**.

The **time** spent on **non value added activities** creates additional costs that are unnecessary. If such activities were **eliminated**, **costs** would **decrease without affecting the market value or quality of the product or service**.

KEY POINT

Two questions can be used to **assess whether an activity adds value**.

- Would an external customer encourage the organisation to do more of the activity?
- Would the organisation be more likely to achieve its goals by performing the activity?

If both answers are yes, the activity adds value.

The processing **time** of an organisation is made up of four types.

(a) **Production** or **performance time** is the actual time that it takes to perform the functions necessary to manufacture the product or perform the service.

(b) Performing quality control results in **inspection time**.

(c) Moving products or components from one place to another is **transfer time**.

(d) Storage time and time spent waiting at the production operation for processing are **idle time**.

Production time is value added. The other three are not. The time from receipt of an order to completion of a product or performance of a service equals production time plus non value added time.

Sometimes **non value added activities** arise because of inadequacies in existing processes and so they **cannot be eliminated unless these inadequacies are addressed**.

One of the **costliest** things an organisation can do is to **invest in equipment and people to make non value added activities more efficient**. The objective is to **eliminate them altogether** or subject them to a major overhaul, not make them more efficient!

3.4 Cost management of activities

Costs are assigned using cost driver rates (calculated on the basis of available resource) to cost objects on the basis of the objects' demand for an activity or consumption of a resource.

But the amount of resource available in a period is not necessarily the same as the amount of resource consumed by cost objects.

If the staff of a purchasing department are **fully occupied**, **all costs** of the department will be **assigned**, via a cost driver rate based on, say, number of orders, to cost objects. Unlike inventories of material, however, **unused capacity** in the purchasing department **cannot be stored** for the future. Management must therefore **control the provision of activities and the associated resources if costs are to be kept to a minimum**.

However, a **change in the level of demand for an activity does not necessarily lead to a change in the level of provision of that activity**.

(a) If the demand for orders increases, the existing purchasing department staff may be able to meet this extra demand with overtime working, but in the medium to long term additional staff would be required. It is not usually possible to take on and get rid of staff at short notice, however, and so there is usually a delay between changes in demand for activity and change in the availability of resource for that activity.

(b) If the demand for orders decreases, the purchasing department staff are not likely to bring to management's attention the fact that they now have slack in their working hours. A traditional absorption costing system would not highlight this situation for management attention, either. If ABC is used, however, the drop in demand for the resource/activity will be obvious as the cost driver rate will be applied to fewer orders/units of output.

The application of **ABC** therefore offers the possibility of **turning costs that were deemed to be fixed into variable costs**: variability is a function of managers' decisions about levels of expenditure and the speed at which the supply of resources should be changed as requirements change.

Whereas **absorption costing aims to recover costs, ABC aims to highlight inefficiencies,** and so cost drivers should be based on the possible level of activity rather than the expected level of activity. If the cost driver rate is $100 per order and 50 orders are handled in a month, the cost assigned is $5,000. If budgeted expenditure is $6,000, the cost of unused capacity is $1,000.

ABC therefore enables management to **identify resources that are not being fully utilised**.

3.5 Design decisions

In many organisations today, roughly 80% of a product's costs are committed at the product design stage, well before production begins. By **providing product designers with cost driver information**, they can be encouraged to **design low cost products that still meet customer requirements**.

The identification of appropriate cost drivers and tracing costs to products on the basis of these cost drivers has the potential to **influence behaviour to support the cost management strategies of the organisation**.

A product that is designed so that it uses fewer components will be cheaper to produce. A product using standard components will also be cheaper to produce. Management can **influence the action of designers** through OARs if overheads are related to products on the basis of the number of component parts they contain. Hitachi's refrigeration plant uses this method to influence the behaviour of their product designers and ultimately the **cost of manufacture**.

3.6 Cost driver analysis

Exam alert

It is important that you learn the four classification levels (shown below) and that you understand their applications to specific organisations.

KEY TERM

The **ABC** cost hierarchy (or manufacturing cost hierarchy) categorises costs and activities as **unit** level, **batch** level, **product** level and **facility sustaining** level.

To reflect today's more **complex business environment**, recognition must be given to the fact that **costs are created and incurred because their cost drivers occur at different levels**. **Cost driver analysis investigates, quantifies and explains the relationships between cost drivers and their related costs**.

Activities and their related costs fall into four different categories, known as the **manufacturing cost hierarchy**. The **categories determine the type of activity cost driver required**.

Classification level	Cause of cost	Types of cost	Cost driver
Unit level	Production/acquisition of a single unit of product or delivery of single unit of service	Direct materials Direct labour	Units produced
Batch level	A group of things being made, handled or processed	Purchase orders Set-ups Inspection	Batches produced
Product level	Development, production or acquisition of different items	Equipment maintenance Product development	Product lines produced
Facility sustaining level	Some costs cannot be related to a particular product line; instead they are related to maintaining the buildings and facilities. These costs cannot be related to cost objects with any degree of accuracy and are often excluded from ABC calculations for this reason.	Building depreciation Organisational advertising	None – supports the overall production or service process

Traditionally, it has been assumed that if costs did not vary with changes in production at the unit level, they were fixed rather than variable. The analysis above shows this assumption to be false, and that costs vary for reasons other than production volume. To determine an accurate estimate of product or service cost, **costs should be accumulated at each successively higher level of costs**.

Unit level costs are allocated over number of units produced, batch level costs over the number of units in the batch, and product level costs over the number of units produced by the product line. These costs are all related to units of product (merely at different levels) and so can be gathered together at the product level to match with revenue. Organisational level costs are not product related, however, and so should simply be deducted from net revenue.

Such an approach gives a far greater insight into product profitability.

Question 1.3	Classification of activities

Learning outcome A1(a)

A food processing company operates an ABC system. Which of the following would be classified as a facility sustaining activity?

(a) General staff administration
(b) Plant management
(c) Technical support for individual products and services
(d) Updating of product specification database
(e) Property management

3.7 Performance evaluation

ABM **encourages and rewards employees** for developing new skills, accepting greater responsibilities and making suggestions for improvements in plant layout, product design and staff utilisation. Each of these improvements reduces non value added time and cost. In addition, by focusing on activities and costs, ABM is better able to provide more appropriate measures of performance than are found in more traditional systems.

KEY POINT

To monitor the effectiveness and efficiency of activities using ABM, performance measures relating to volume, time, quality and costs are needed.

(a) Activity **volume** measures provide an indication of the throughput and capacity utilisation of activities. For example, reporting the number of times an activity such as setting-up is undertaken focuses attention on the need to investigate ways of reducing the volume of the activity and hence future costs.

(b) To increase customer satisfaction, organisations must provide a speedy response to customer requests and reduce the time taken to develop and bring a new product to the market. Organisations must therefore focus on the **time** taken to complete an activity or sequence of activities. This time can be reduced by eliminating (as far as is possible) the time spent on non value added activities.

(c) A focus on value chain analysis is a means of enhancing customer satisfaction. The value chain is the linked set of activities from basic raw material acquisition all the way through to the end-use product or service delivered to the customer. By viewing each of the activities in the value chain as a supplier-customer relationship, the opinions of the customers can be used to provide useful feedback on the **quality** of the service provided by the supplying activity. For example, the quality of the service provided by the processing of purchase orders activity can be evaluated by users of the activity in terms of the speed of processing orders and the quality of the service provided by the supplier chosen by the purchasing activity. Such qualitative evaluations can be supported by quantitative measures such as percentage of deliveries that are late.

(d) **Cost** driver rates (such as cost per set-up) can be communicated in a format that is easily understood by all staff and can be used to motivate managers to reduce the cost of performing activities (given that cost driver rate × activity level = cost of activity). However, their use as a measure of performance can induce dysfunctional behaviour. By splitting production runs and therefore having more set-ups, the cost per set-up can be reduced. Workload will be increased, however, and so in the long run costs could increase.

3.8 Implementing ABM

In an article in *Financial Management* in 2001 ('Tool of the trade'), Stephanie Gourdie provided the following 'Tips for ABM'.

(a)   Get the support of senior management.

(b)   Recognise that ABM requires a major investment in time and resources.

(c)   Know what ABM can achieve and what information you want from the system.

(d)   Decide which model to use.

(e)   Choose the model approach that emphasises the operational understanding of all activities in the business.

(f)   Involve people in the field.

(g)   Transfer ownership of cost management from the accounts department to the departments and processes where costs are incurred.

(h)   Do not underestimate the need to manage the change process.

(i)   Link ABM to corporate objectives in the form of increased product profitability and added value for customers.

In 'Voyage of discovery' (*Financial Manager*, May 2002), Selvan Naidoo describes the key decisions to be made and the major pitfalls to be avoided when implementing ABM.

(a)   Decide on whether results are to be used at a strategic level or for cost management, as this will affect the level of analysis of activities required.

(b)   Establish if implementation will be in certain areas only, such as head office, or across the organisation.

(c)   Agree the acceptable level of accuracy.

(d)   Decide on the products and services to be costed. (**BPP note**. Pareto analysis could be applied. See Section 8.)

(e)   Involve operational staff from the start of the project.

(f)   Gain full support from senior management.

(g)   Manage expectations. ABC will not solve all of an organisation's problems.

(h)   Implement effective project management.

(i)   Provide regular progress reports for management.

(j)   Do not underestimate the effort needed to obtain the information required in the correct format.

(k)   Consider using a pilot implementation if ABC is being implemented across a number of sites.

(l)   Be wary of running ABC and another project with similar deadlines and demands on resources in a business unit.

3.9 Problems with ABM

ABM is not a 'cure for all ills', however.

(a)   The **amount of work** in setting up the system and in data collection must be considered.

(b)   Organisational and behavioural consequences. Selected activity cost pools may not correspond to the formal structure of cost responsibilities within the organisation (the purchasing activity may spread across purchasing, production, stores, administrative and finance departments) and so determining 'ownership' of the activity and its costs may be problematic. We have already mentioned the behavioural impact of some performance measures.

Section summary

Activity based management (ABM) is **operational ABM**. Actions based on activity driver analysis that increase efficiency, lower costs and improve asset utilisation.

Strategic ABM. Actions based on activity based cost analysis that aim to change the demand for activities so as to improve profitability.

Two questions can be used to **assess whether an activity adds value**.

- Would an external customer encourage the organisation to do more of the activity?
- Would the organisation be more likely to achieve its goals by performing the activity?

If both answers are yes, the activity adds value.

The **manufacturing cost hierarchy** categorises costs and activities as **unit** level, **batch** level, **product** level and **facility sustaining** level.

To monitor the effectiveness and efficiency of activities using **ABM, performance measures** relating to **volume, time, quality** and **costs** are needed.

4 Direct product profitability (DPP)

Introduction

We have been mainly focusing on manufacturing organisations so far in this chapter. Direct product profitability is a costing system used by retail businesses and focuses on the resource consumption of individual products.

KEY TERMS

DIRECT PRODUCT PROFITABILITY **(DPP)** is 'Used primarily within the retail sector, [and] involves the attribution of both the purchase price and other indirect costs (eg distribution, warehousing, retailing) to each product line. Thus a net profit, as opposed to a gross profit, can be identified for each product. The cost attribution process utilises a variety of measures (eg warehousing space, transport time) to reflect the resource consumption of individual products.'   *(CIMA Official Terminology)*

DIRECT PRODUCT PROFIT is the contribution a product category makes to fixed costs and profits. It is calculated by deducting direct product costs (such as warehousing and transport) from the product's gross margin.

4.1 Calculation of direct product profit

Direct product profit is calculated as follows:

	$	$
Sales price		X
Less purchase cost		(X)
Gross margin		X
Less: direct product costs		
warehouse direct costs	(X)	
transport direct costs	(X)	
store direct costs	(X)	(X)
Direct product profit		(X)

KEY POINT

Any costs that are **general** to the organisation (but not specific to any particular product) should be **ignored** when calculating direct product profit.

4.1.1 What are direct product costs?

These can be **directly attributed** to the handling and storing of individual products.

Direct product cost	Examples
Warehouse direct costs	Offloading, unpacking, picking and sorting, space costs, inventory financing costs
Transport direct costs	Fuel, depreciation of vehicle, driver's salary, vehicle servicing
Store/supermarket direct costs	Receiving and inspecting, moving, shelf filling, space costs, inventory financing costs

Direct product costs may include other product-specific costs such as retailer brand development costs.

In general, warehouse, transport and store costs will tend to be spread across the different goods sold in relation to volume or area occupied, as most costs increase in proportion to the volume of the good or the space it occupies.

Rather confusingly, direct product cost also contains **part of the indirect cost** that can be **apportioned** to the product, **based on one or more product characteristics**. For example, the **cost of shelf space** is apportioned by means of the **physical volume** of the product. All other costs, for example Head Office costs, are not included.

In practice, each product would be charged with a number of different costs but the following example deals only with the space costs in a store.

Example: DPP

A supermarket group has estimated that its store space cost is $0.50 per cubic metre per day.

Its product range includes the following products.

(a)   Six-packs of fizzy pop – volume: 0.01 cubic metres, days in store: 5
(b)   Detergent – volume: 0.005 cubic metres, days in store: 4
(c)   Double roll of kitchen paper – volume: 0.185 cubic metres, days in store: 3

Solution

The space costs would be allocated as follows.

Fizzy pop $0.50 × 0.01 × 5   = $0.025 per pack
Detergent $0.50 × 0.005 × 4   = $0.01 per pack
Kitchen paper $0.50 × 0.185 × 3 = $0.278 per pack

The results show the need to achieve a high turnover with bulky low price goods. Refrigerated items would carry a higher space cost due to the cost of refrigeration.

4.2 Benefits of using DPP

(a)   Detailed information is provided on the **performance** of an **individual product**.

(b)   Products can be **ranked** according to product profitability.

(c)   **Diagnostic capabilities**. Why did a product underperform? Was the inventory turn acceptable?

(d)   Profitable product lines can be identified and given more **prominent shelf space**.

(e)   Leads to a **mutual understanding** of **product and supply chain** costs and **improves supplier/retailer relationships**.

(f)   **Better pricing decisions**.

(g)   **Improved management of store** and **warehouse space**.

4.3 DPP software systems

These allow 'what if?' analysis to be carried out. A number of key variables can be changed to analyse different scenarios.

(a)   **Prices at which products are bought and sold.** The higher the selling price relative to other retailers, the slower the likely inventory movement.

(b)   **Rate of selling.** This is a key variable and needs to be as high as possible to minimise warehouse and store space costs, and to ensure that interest on money tied up in inventory is not lost.

(c)   **Size of stockholding.** In line with JIT principles, inventory should be kept to a minimum but stock-outs avoided.

(d)   **Size of the product.** This variable requires consideration as it is one of the drivers of space cost per item.

(e)   **Configuration of pallets.** The handling cost per unit falls as the number of cases on a pallet increases.

(f)   **Ordering cost.** A balance has to be found because ordering only occasionally will mean ordering costs are minimised but inventory levels are higher.

(g)   **Distribution routes.** The software can model whether direct delivery to the store or the use of a central warehouse offers the cheaper option. It is likely to be the latter.

Section summary

DPP is a **costing system used by retail businesses.**

Any costs that are **general** to the organisation (but not specific to any particular product) should be **ignored** when calculating direct product profit.

5   Customer profitability analysis (CPA)

Introduction

Customer profitability analysis uses ABC principles to identify the most profitable customers or groups of customers to allow marketing efforts to be directed at attracting and retaining these customers.

KEY TERM

CUSTOMER PROFITABILITY ANALYSIS (CPA) is 'the analysis of the revenue streams and service costs associated with specific customers or customer groups'.   (*CIMA Official Terminology*)

5.1 Analysing customers

Profitability can vary widely between different customers because various **overhead costs** are, to some extent, **variable and customer driven**.

- Discounts
- Sales force
- Quality control
- Merchandising

- Distribution
- Promotions
- Financing costs
- Enquiries

Suppose a hotel offers a number of services such as a swimming pool, a gym and a nightly dinner dance.

(a) Older guests may attend the dinner dance.

(b) Families may use the swimming pool.

(c) People without children may appreciate the gym.

By charging services to the guests using them, a cost per bed night can be calculated for each guest group. **Strategies for attracting the most profitable guest group** can then be adopted.

Whether individual customers or groups of customers are costed largely depends on the number of customers.

(a) A manufacturing company supplying six companies would cost each customer separately.

(b) A supermarket or bank would cost groups of similar customers. UK banks divide their customers into categories such as single and around 30 years of age, married with young children, and older couples with spending money.

Marketing departments should be aiming to **attract and retain profitable customers**, but in order to do this they need to **know which customers are profitable** and **how much can be spent on retaining them**. The **costing system** should **provide the necessary answers**.

CPA provides important information that allows an organisation to determine both **which classes of customers it should concentrate on** and the **prices it should charge for customer services**. Its use ensures that those customers **contributing sizeably to the profitability** of the organisation receive a **comparable amount of attention** from the organisation.

5.2 Customer revenues

Customer revenues are cash flows from customers. They are influenced by different factors, mainly **allowances and discounts**.

(a) Some types of customer **store and distribute goods** (eg wholesalers) or **promote** the goods in return for an **allowance**.

(b) By giving a **discount**, a company may **encourage bulk orders**, which may be cheaper to provide and may result in higher sales volume. However, studies on customer profitability have found large price discounting to be a key explanation for a group of customers being below expected profitability. Sales representatives may have given customers large price discounts unrelated to their current or potential value to the company, perhaps to meet bonuses dependent on sales

volumes. Two customers may be purchasing the same volumes but the price discount given to one may make it unprofitable, while the other is profitable.

CASE STUDY

The US company General Electric (GE), which manufactures and sells refrigerators and so on, used to give substantial discounts to customers who placed large orders. This did not result in customers buying more products. Instead, GE's sales orders bunched in particular weeks of the year. In turn this led to an uneven production and distribution flow, which increased costs. The company found that, by removing the discounts while at the same time guaranteeing swift delivery, order size decreased and profits increased.

5.3 Customer costs and ABC

The creation of cost pools for activities in **ABC** systems allows organisations to arrange costs in a variety of different ways. Because different customers use different amounts of activities, it is possible to **build up costs for individual customers or groups of customers** on an activity basis so that their **relative profitability** can be assessed.

Examples of the build-up of customer costs using an activity based system

Activity	Cost driver
Order taking	Number of orders taken
Sales visits	Number of sales visits
Emergency orders	Number of rushed orders
Delivery	Miles travelled

CASE STUDY

Drury cites the case of Kanthal, a Swedish company that sells electric heating elements. Customer-related selling costs represented 34% of total costs. In the past, Kanthal had allocated these costs on the basis of sales value when customer profitability studies were carried out. The company then introduced an ABC system in order to determine the resources consumed by different customers.

An investigation identified two cost drivers for the resources used to service different customers.

(a) **Number of orders placed**. Each order had a large fixed cost, which did not vary with the number of items ordered. A customer ordering 10 items 100 times cost more to service than a customer placing a single order for 1,000 items.

(b) **Non-standard production items**. These cost more to manufacture than standard items.

The cost per order and the cost of handling standard and non-standard items were calculated and a CPA carried out on the basis of the previous year's sales. The analysis showed that only 40% of customers were profitable, and a further 10% lost 120% of the profits. In other words, 10% of customers incurred losses equal to 120% of Kanthal's total profits. Two of the most unprofitable customers were actually in the top three in terms of total sales volume but made many small orders of non-standard items.

Unprofitable customers identified by CPA should be persuaded to **alter their buying behaviour** so they become profitable customers. In the Kanthal example above, unprofitable customers should be discouraged from placing lots of small orders and/or from buying non-standard products.

The **activity based approach** also **highlights where cost reduction efforts should be focused**. Kanthal should concentrate on reducing ordering cost and the cost of handling non-standard items.

Activity based CPA allows an organisation to adopt a more **market-orientated approach** to management accounting.

Question 1.4   CPA

Learning outcome A1(a)

BB manufactures components for the heavy goods vehicle industry. The following annual information regarding three of its key customers is available.

	P	Q	R
Gross margin	$897,000	$1,070,000	$1,056,000
General administration costs	$35,000	$67,000	$56,000
Units sold	4,600	5,800	3,800
Orders placed	300	320	480
Sales visits	80	50	100
Invoices raised	310	390	1,050

The company uses an activity based costing system and the analysis of customer-related costs is as follows.

Sales visits	$420 per visit
Order processing	$190 per order placed
Despatch costs	$350 per order placed
Billing and collections	$97 per invoice raised

Using customer profitability analysis, in which order would the customers be ranked?

5.4 Customer profitability statement

There is no set format, but it would normally be similar to the one below. Note that financing costs have been included.

	$'000	$'000
Revenue at list prices		100
Less discounts given		8
Net revenue		92
Less cost of goods sold		50
Gross margin		42
Less: customer-specific costs (such as those listed above)	28	
financing costs:		
credit period	3	
customer-specific inventory	2	
		33
Net margin from customer		9

Question 1.5   Profitable customers

Learning outcome A1(a)

Seth supplies shoes to Narayan and Kipling. Each pair of shoes has a list price of $50 and costs Seth $25. As Kipling buys in bulk, it receives a 10% trade discount for every order for 100 pairs of shoes or more. Narayan receives a 15% discount irrespective of order size, because that company collects the shoes, thereby saving Seth any distribution costs. The cost of administering each order is $50 and the distribution cost is $1,000 per order. Narayan makes 10 orders in the year, totalling 420 pairs of shoes, and Kipling places 5 orders for 100 pairs.

Required

The most profitable customer for Seth is ....

5.5 Costing customers

Not all customers cost the same to serve, even if they require the same products. Customers will cost more to serve if they are based a long way from the factory (delivery costs increase), or place rush orders (production scheduling is interrupted, special transport is required), or require a high level of after-sales service and technical assistance.

In order to analyse different customers, it may therefore be useful to review **non-financial data**.

	Customer		
	X	Y	Z
Number of purchase orders	10	20	30
Number of sales visits	5	5	5
Number of deliveries	15	20	55
Distance per delivery	50	20	70
Number of emergency orders	1	0	4

Customer Y may be the cheapest to serve because of the number of deliveries per order, the lower distance travelled and the lack of emergency orders.

5.6 Customers and life cycle costing

Customers can also be **costed over their expected 'life cycle'** and expected future cash flows relating to the customer may be discounted. It is rarely possible to predict accurately the life cycle of a particular customer unless contracts are awarded for a specific time period. Nevertheless, the information is valuable as **the longer the customer remains with the organisation**, the **more profitable** the customer becomes. This is valuable information and may show the **importance of creating and retaining loyal customers**.

| Question 1.6 | CPA and competitive advantage |

Learning outcome A1(a)

Explain how customer profitability analysis can enhance an organisation's competitive advantage.

Section summary

Customer profitability analysis uses an activity based approach to relate revenues and costs to groups of customers in order to assess their relative profitability.

6 Distribution channel profitability

Introduction

As well as focusing on individual customers or groups of customers (in terms of revenue, number of transactions and so on), a similar analysis can be carried out on different distribution channels. This section looks at distribution channel profitability and why it is so important to manage these channels. It is linked to ABC and ABM, which were covered earlier in this chapter.

6.1 Traditional approach to determining distribution channel profitability

Product costs are **allocated** to distribution channels **based on standard costs and the product mix** sold through the channel.

Sales, general and administrative costs are typically **allocated** to distribution channels on the **basis of sales volume or net revenue** for each channel.

This approach is shown diagrammatically below.

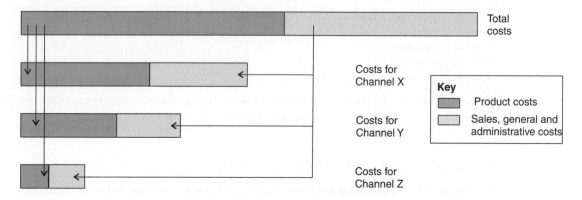

Such an approach may provide **useful information if the organisation is structured on the basis of distribution channels**, but structures tend to be based around regions, product lines or manufacturing locations, making allocation of costs to channels difficult. The approach also obviously has all the **disadvantages associated with the traditional approach to product costing**.

6.2 The ABC approach to determining distribution channel profitability

Material costs and activity costs are allocated direct to products to produce product-related costs, which are **then allocated** to distribution channels on the **basis of the mix of products sold** in each channel.

This approach, which carries with it all the **advantages of ABC**, should result in **more accurate** information.

The main **disadvantage** to this approach is that the allocation is based on the **assumption** that **all costs are driven by the production of particular products** and hence must be allocated to products. For most organisations, however, the **products** they produce is just **one of a range of cost drivers**.

6.3 A refined ABC approach to determining distribution channel profitability

This approach is based on the **assumption** that **costs are driven** not only by **products produced**, but also by the **customers served** and the **channels through which the products are offered**. This allows managers to see the effect on the costs of channels of all three categories.

6.3.1 Developing accurate costs for distribution channels

Separate the organisation's costs into activity related costs and costs not related to activities

Identify all costs within the two classifications as product related, customer related or channel related

(a)   Activity costs for a manufacturing organisation might include production scheduling (product related), collection of bad debts (customer related) and advertising brand X (channel related).

(b)   Costs not related to activities might include material costs (product related), customer rebates (customer related) and trade discounts (channel related).

Trace these costs to individual products, customers and channels
Cost drivers can be used to trace activity related costs. Direct allocation to the product, customer or channel that caused them should be possible for other costs.

Link the product-related and customer-related costs to channels
Split total product costs across customers by analysing customer purchases on a product by product basis. Then split total customer costs across channels by analysing this customer data on a channel by channel basis.

Obviously revenue information for the same products, customers and distribution channels also needs to be captured.

6.4 Comparison of the two ABC approaches

The traditional product-related ABC approach fits in with the way in which most organisations are formed around product lines and product groups.

However, nowadays customers are being served through a variety of distribution channels (distributors, catalogues, megastores, direct mail and so on). Understanding the cost and profitability of using different distribution channels will therefore become increasingly important for good business decision making.

Section summary

Just as **ABC** can be used in conjunction with CPA, it can also be used to determine the relative **profitability of different distribution channels**.

---

7   Activity based profitability analysis

Introduction

Activity based profitability analysis can be linked to ABC techniques that were covered earlier in this chapter.

7.1 Extending activity based techniques to profitability analysis

The hierarchical classification of activities can be extended by applying it to profitability analysis. This is illustrated in the following diagram, which is based on one in Drury adapted from an approach advocated by Kaplan ('Contribution margin analysis: no longer relevant', *Journal of Management Accounting Research (USA)*, Fall, 1990).

Unit-level product contributions

Product contributions after deducting
batch-related expenses

Product contributions after deducting
product-sustaining expenses

Product-line contributions after deducting
product-line sustaining expenses

Plant profit after deducting facility-sustaining
expenses

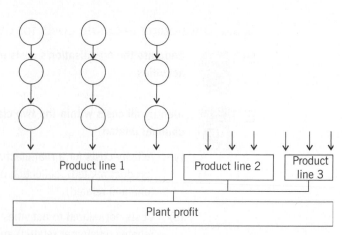

At the point at which **product-level contribution margins for each individual product in the product line** have been calculated, there has been **no cost allocation. Some costs incurred at the product-line level**, such as research and development, advertising and distribution, are common to all products in the product line, however, and within this analysis they are **traced to product lines** rather than individual products within the line.

The resulting product-line contribution margin is the sum of the individual product-level contributions sold within the line and shows whether the products sold within the line earn enough contribution to cover the costs of activities required to sustain the line.

Plant profit is arrived at by deducting facility-sustaining costs from the sum of the product-line contributions.

7.2 Using this approach for customers and distribution channels

This approach should not be limited to analysing the profitability of products and product lines. Customers and distribution channels should also be considered, by **summing the product-level contribution margins of the products sold to each customer or through each distribution channel**, and **then deducting costs incurred for individual customers or distribution channels**.

7.3 Dealing with marketing and distribution costs

These costs should be **included** within such an analysis and dealt with in a similar way to production costs. The activity based analysis therefore assigns the costs to the appropriate level in the hierarchy (depending on whether a cost is incurred in relation to an activity that supports a product, product line/customer/distribution channel) and then aggregates the costs down the hierarchy to determine contribution margins by product, product line, customer and distribution channel.

Section summary

By comparing the costs of products, customers and distribution channels with revenues, a **tier of contribution levels** can be established by applying the concept of the activity based cost hierarchy.

8 Pareto analysis

Introduction

In this section of the chapter, we look at the concept of Pareto analysis which is based on the general principle that 80% of wealth is owned by 20% of the population. This links to ABM and CPA in that 20% of customers could be viewed as providing 80% of the profit.

KEY TERM

PARETO ANALYSIS is based on the observations of the economist Vilfredo Pareto, who suggested that 80% of a nation's wealth is held by 20% of its population (and so the remaining 80% of the population holds only 20% of the nation's wealth).

8.1 What is Pareto analysis?

Pareto analysis is the **80/20 rule** and it has been applied to many other situations.

(a) In inventory control, where 20% of inventory items might represent 80% of the value

(b) In product analysis, where 80% of company profit is earned by 20% of the products

Example: Pareto analysis and products

(a) A company produces ten products which it sells in various markets. The revenue from each product is as follows.

Product	Revenue
	$'000
A	231
B	593
C	150
D	32
E	74
F	17
G	1,440
H	12
I	2
J	19
	2,570

(b) Rearranging revenue in descending order and calculating cumulative figures and percentages gives us the following analysis.

Product	Revenue	Cumulative revenue (W1)	% (W2)
	$'000	$'000	
G	1,440	1,440	56.0
B	593	2,033	79.1
A	231	2,264	88.1
C	150	2,414	93.9
E	74	2,488	96.8
D	32	2,520	98.1
J	19	2,539	98.8
F	17	2,556	99.5
H	12	2,568	99.9
I	2	2,570	100.0
	2,570		

Workings

1   This is calculated as follows:

1,440 + 593 = 2,033
2,033 + 231 = 2,264   and so on.

2   (1/2,570 × 1,440 × 100)% = 56.0%
(1/2,570 × 2,033 × 100)% = 79.1%   and so on.

(Enter 1/2,570 into your calculator as a constant – do the calculation and then tap the multiplication button twice until 'k' appears on the screen – and then simply enter each cumulative revenue figure and press the 'equals' button to get the percentage as a decimal.)

(c)   In this case the Pareto rule applies – almost 80% of revenue is brought in by just two products, G and B. The point of Pareto analysis is to highlight the fact that the effort that is put into a company's products is often barely worth the trouble in terms of the sales revenue generated.

KEY POINT

You should not expect that the 80/20 rule will always apply as precisely as in the above example. It may be that, say, 25% of products will account for 90% of revenue. **The basic principle is that a small number of products often yields a high proportion of income**.

It does not necessarily follow that the products generating the highest income are the most profitable. The costs of producing the products need to be taken into account. It may be, for example, that products G and B both cost more to produce than the income they bring in, whereas products A, C and E cost virtually nothing. In other words, **Pareto analysis can be carried out for costs and contribution as well as for sales**.

Poor performers could also be new products which are establishing themselves in the market and which have more profitable futures.

8.2 Further analysis

Suppose the figures you are given provide some additional information, and you are asked to analyse them and comment on them in a way that will be useful to management.

Product	Revenue	Profit
	$'000	$'000
A	231	46
B	593	108
C	150	52
D	32	7
E	74	16
F	17	4
G	1,440	202
H	12	8
I	2	1
J	19	8
	2,570	452

An analysis might take the following form.

(a)   The revenue figures can be **ranked** and **expressed as percentages** and in **cumulative terms** (as before), and profit can be ranked and analysed in the same way.

The figures are pretty self-explanatory, but make sure that you understand how all of them are calculated, because you may well have to do this yourself in an exam.

Product	Revenue $'000	Rev. %	Cum. revenue $'000	Cum. %	Product	Profit $'000	Profit %	Cum. profit $'000	Cum. %
G	1,440	56.0	1,440	56.0	G	202	44.7	202	44.7
B	593	23.1	2,033	79.1	B	108	23.9	310	68.6
A	231	9.0	2,264	88.1	C	52	11.5	362	80.1
C	150	5.8	2,414	93.9	A	46	10.2	408	90.3
E	74	2.9	2,488	96.8	E	16	3.5	424	93.8
D	32	1.2	2,520	98.1	H	8	1.8	432	95.6
J	19	0.7	2,539	98.8	J	8	1.8	440	97.4
F	17	0.7	2,556	99.5	D	7	1.5	447	98.9
H	12	0.5	2,568	99.9	F	4	0.9	451	99.8
I	2	0.1	2,570	100.0	I	1	0.2	452	100.0
	2,570					452			

This shows us that, whereas the top ranking products are G, B and A in revenue terms, G, B and C are the top three in terms of profit. In **revenue terms** product C produces under 6% of the overall total but in **profit terms** it produces over 10%. Four products each produce 10% or more of the overall **profit**, but only 3 products individually produce more than 9% of **revenue**.

(b)   We can also calculate the **profit margin** (the profit divided by the revenue expressed as a percentage) for individual products and overall. The figures shown below indicate that while most of the products vary slightly around the overall profit margin of 17.6%, some have much higher margins, notably products H, I and J, although these are relatively insignificant in overall revenue terms. The product that provides the greatest amount of revenue and profit, product G, actually has the lowest profit margin of all.

Product	Revenue $'000	Profit $'000	Profit margin %
A	231	46	19.9
B	593	108	18.2
C	150	52	34.7
D	32	7	21.9
E	74	16	21.6
F	17	4	23.5
G	1,440	202	14.0
H	12	8	66.7
I	2	1	50.0
J	19	8	42.1
	2,570	452	17.6

Your overall recommendations to management might be to make efforts to **save costs** to **improve the profit margin** of product G, and to put **extra marketing effort** into products C, H, I and J where the potential returns are greatest. Obviously what can be done depends on the nature of the products themselves: the smaller revenue items may be specialist add-ons that are only ever likely to be purchased by a few people.

8.3 Analysing customers

Instead of analysing products, customers can be analysed to determine their relative profitability.

When a **CPA** is first carried out it is often found that something close to **Pareto's rule** applies. This is illustrated in the following diagram where **20 of the 100** customers generate approximately **80%** of the

company's total margin. As 50 of the 100 customers generate 100% of the total margin, resources appear to be wasted serving the remaining 50 customers.

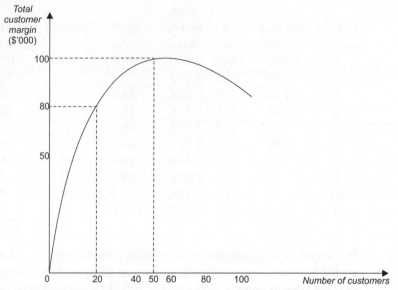

In order to produce a chart such as that above, customers need to be **ranked** according to their **relative profitability** to the company. A bar chart, such as that below, produces an alternative view and may prove more useful for the marketing department.

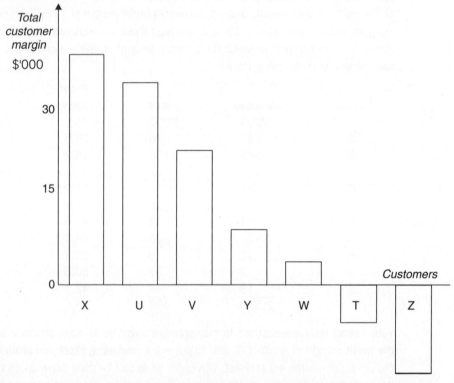

The more evenly customers contribute to profit, the better, as the position of the organisation is stabilised. If customers do not contribute evenly, the loss of two key customers could be disastrous for an organisation.

8.4 Analysing inventory

Pareto analysis can be used to improve inventory control.

(a)   15% of inventory volume might represent 80% of inventory value and so control should be concentrated on that 15%.

(b)   10% of inventory might require 75% of storage space (so that storage costs are particularly high). A just-in-time system could therefore be used for this 10%, saving money and space.

8.5 Analysing overheads

If an organisation uses activity based costing, a Pareto analysis of cost drivers or activities might show that, say, 15% of cost drivers or activities are responsible for 80% of total cost. Analysing, monitoring and controlling these cost drivers or activities will provide improved cost control and increased understanding of the way in which costs behave.

8.6 Pareto diagrams and quality

The term 'Pareto diagram' usually refers to a **histogram or frequency chart on product quality**, following research in the 1950s which showed that a **few causes of poor quality usually accounted for most of the quality problems** – hence the name Pareto. Such diagrams highlight the area or areas to which attention should be given to produce the best returns.

Section summary

Pareto analysis is used to highlight the general principle that 80% of value (inventory value, wealth, profit and so on) is concentrated in 20% of the items in a particular population.

9   Total quality management (TQM)

Introduction

The modern business environment has been progressively switching emphasis from quantity to quality as competition intensifies for customers. This section looks at how total quality management is employed within modern businesses to achieve the best possible quality. The technique is linked with continuous improvement, which is the focus of Section 9 below.

9.1 Management of quality

Quality means 'the **degree of excellence of a thing**' – how well made it is, or how well performed if it is a service, how well it serves its purpose, and how it measures up against its rivals. These criteria imply two things.

(a)   That quality is something that **requires care on the part of the provider**
(b)   That quality is largely **subjective** – it is in the eye of the beholder, the **customer**

The **management** of quality is the process of:

(a)   Establishing **standards of quality** for a product or service

(b)   Establishing **procedures or production methods** that ought to ensure that these required standards of quality are met in a suitably high proportion of cases

(c)   **Monitoring** actual quality

(d) Taking **control action** when actual quality falls below standard

Take the postal service as an example. The postal service might establish a standard that 90% of first class letters will be delivered on the day after they are posted, and 99% will be delivered within 2 days of posting.

(a) Procedures would have to be established for ensuring that these standards could be met (attending to such matters as frequency of collections, automated letter sorting, frequency of deliveries and number of staff employed).

(b) Actual performance could be monitored, perhaps by taking samples from time to time of letters that are posted and delivered.

(c) If the quality standard is not being achieved, management should take control action (employ more postmen or advertise the use of postcodes again).

9.2 TQM

Quality management becomes **total (total quality management (TQM)) when it is applied to everything a business does**.

KEY TERM

TOTAL QUALITY MANAGEMENT **(TQM)** is 'an integrated and comprehensive system of planning and controlling all business functions so that products or services are produced which meet or exceed customer expectations. TQM is a philosophy of business behaviour, embracing principles such as employee involvement, continuous improvement at all levels and customer focus, as well as being a collection of related techniques aimed at improving quality, such as full documentation of activities, clear goal setting and performance measurement from the customer perspective'. (*CIMA Official Terminology*)

9.2.1 Get it right, first time

One of the basic principles of TQM is that the **cost of preventing mistakes is less than the cost of correcting them** once they occur. The aim should therefore be **to get things right first time**. Every mistake, delay and misunderstanding directly costs an organisation money through **wasted time and effort**, including time taken in pacifying customers. The **lost potential for future sales because of poor customer service must also be taken into account**.

9.2.2 Continuous improvement

A second basic principle of TQM is dissatisfaction with the *status quo*: the belief that it is **always possible to improve** and so the aim should be to '**get it more right next time**'. TQM should foster a consistent, systematic approach to continuous improvement that involves every aspect of the organisation.

9.3 Key elements of TQM

There are nine key elements of TQM.

(a) Acceptance that the only thing that matters is the **customer**.

(b) Recognition of the all-pervasive nature of the **customer-supplier relationship**, including internal customers: passing sub-standard material to another division is not satisfactory or acceptable.

(c) A move from relying on inspecting to a predefined level of quality to **preventing the cause** of the defect in the first place.

(d) Personal responsibility for each operative or group of operatives for defect-free production or service in their domain. TQM requires an awareness by **all personnel** of the quality requirements compatible with supplying the customer with products of the agreed design specification.

(e)   A move away from 'acceptable' quality levels. **Any** level of defects is **unacceptable**. TQM aims towards an environment of **zero defects** at minimum cost.

(f)   An aim to **eliminate waste**, where waste is defined as anything other than the minimum essential amount of equipment, materials, space and workers' time.

(g)   Obsessive attempts by **all departments** to get things right first time: this applies to misdirected telephone calls and typing errors as much as to production.

(h)   Introduction of **quality certification** programmes.

(i)   Emphasis on the **cost of poor quality**: good quality generates savings.

Exam alert

An assessment question could ask you to discuss the importance of a TQM system within a just-in-time environment.

9.4 Quality assurance procedures

Because TQM embraces every activity of a business, quality assurance procedures **cannot be confined to the production process** but must also cover the work of sales, distribution and administration departments, the efforts of external suppliers, and the reaction of external customers.

9.4.1 Quality assurance of goods inwards

The quality of output depends on the quality of input materials, and so quality control should include **procedures for acceptance and inspection of goods inwards and measurement of rejects**. Each supplier can be given a 'rating' for the quality of the goods they tend to supply, and preference with purchase orders can be given to well-rated suppliers. This method is referred to as 'vendor rating'.

Where a **quality assurance scheme** is in place, the supplier guarantees the quality of goods supplied and allows the customers' inspectors access while the items are being manufactured. The **onus is on the supplier to carry out the necessary quality checks**, or face cancellation of the contract.

Suppliers' quality assurance schemes are being used increasingly, particularly where extensive sub-contracting work is carried out, for example in the motor industries. One such scheme is **BS EN ISO 9000** certification. A company that gains registration has a certificate testifying that it is operating to a structure of written policies and procedures that are designed to ensure that it can consistently deliver a product or service to meet customer requirements.

9.4.2 Inspection of output

This will take place at various key stages in the production process and will provide a continual check that the production process is under control. The aim of inspection is **not** really to sort out the bad products from the good ones after the work has been done. The **aim is to satisfy management that quality control in production is being maintained**.

The **inspection of samples** rather than 100% testing of all items will keep inspection costs down, and smaller samples will be less costly to inspect than larger samples. The greater the confidence in the reliability of production methods and process control, the smaller the samples will be.

9.5 Monitoring customer reaction

Some sub-standard items will inevitably be produced. Checks during production will identify some bad output, but other items will reach the customer, who is the ultimate judge of quality. **Complaints should be monitored**, whether they arrive in the form of complaint letters, returned goods, claims under guarantee, or requests for visits by service engineers. Some companies survey customers on a regular basis.

9.6 Internal customers and internal suppliers

The work done by an internal supplier for an internal customer will eventually affect the quality of the product or service to the external customer. In order to satisfy the expectations of the external customer, it is therefore also necessary to satisfy the expectations of the internal customer at each stage of the overall operation. Internal customers are therefore linked in **quality chains**. Internal customer A can satisfy internal customer B, who can satisfy internal customer C, who in turn can satisfy the external customer.

The management of each 'micro operation' within an overall operation has the responsibility for managing its internal supplier and internal customer relationships. They should do this by specifying the requirements of their internal customers, for example in terms of quality, speed, dependability and flexibility, and the requirements for the operation itself (for example, in terms of cost).

The **concept of internal supplier-customer relationships in a series of micro-operations** helps to **focus attention on the 'up-stream' activities in an operation**, several stages removed from the external customer. Failure at an early stage of the operation, for example in new product design, has an adverse impact on all the supplier-customer relationships down the line to the external customer. The **cost of rectifying an error** becomes **more expensive the further it goes down the 'supply chain'** without rectification.

Some organisations **formalise the internal supplier-internal customer concept** by requiring each internal supplier to make a **service level agreement** with its internal customer. A service level agreement is a statement of the standard of service and supply that will be provided to the internal customer and will cover issues such as the range of services supplied, response times and dependability. Boundaries of responsibility and performance standards might also be included in the agreement.

Service level agreements have been criticised, however, for over-formalising the relationship between the internal supplier and internal customer, and so creating barriers to the development of a constructive relationship and genuine co-operation between them.

9.7 Employees and quality

Employees often have a poor attitude towards quality, as a system imposed 'from outside' by non-operational staff and as an implication of lack of trust in workers to maintain quality standards or to apply a control system with objectivity themselves.

Attitudes to quality control and the management of it have, however, been **undergoing changes**.

(a)   As the pace of change in the environment has increased, so attention to quality and a commitment to quality standards has become a **vital factor for organisational adaptation and survival**.

(b)   It is being recognised that **workers can be motivated by a positive approach to quality**: producing quality work is a tangible and worthwhile objective. Where responsibility for quality checking has been given to the individual worker (encouraging self-supervision), **job satisfaction may be increased**: it is a kind of job enrichment, and also a sign of trust and respect, because imposed controls have been removed.

(c)   **Non-aversive ways of implementing quality control** have been devised. **Cultural orientation** (the deep 'belief' in quality, filtered down to all operatives) can be enlisted. **Inter-group competition** to meet and beat quality standards, for example, might be encouraged. **Quality circles** may be set up, perhaps with responsibility for implementing improvements that they identify.

Problems can therefore be overcome by **changing people's attitudes** rather than teaching them new tricks. The key issue is to instil **understanding of, and commitment to, working practices that lead to quality**.

Empowerment has two key aspects.

(a)   Allowing workers to have the **freedom to decide how to do** the necessary work, using the skills they possess and acquiring new skills as necessary to be an effective team member

(b)   Making workers **responsible** for achieving production targets and for quality control

However, it is important to **question the value of these developments**.

'Do employees and management really find "empowerment" to be liberating? Empirical studies suggest that "empowerment" often amounts to the delegation of additional duties to employees. Limits have to be placed on what employees can do, so empowerment is often associated with rules, bureaucracy and form-filling. That apart, many employees find most satisfaction from outside work activities and are quite happy to confine themselves to doing what they are told while at work. The proponents of TQM are often very work-centred people themselves and tend to judge others by their own standards.

Do teams contribute to organisational effectiveness? Just calling a group of people who work in the same office "a team" does not make it a team. A team requires a high level of co-operation and consensus. Many competitive and motivated people find working in a team environment to be uncongenial. It means that every time you want to do anything you have to communicate with and seek approval from fellow team members. In practice, this is likely to involve bureaucracy and form-filling.

... it can be argued that TQM merely moves empowerment from management to employees. It has been argued that the latter cannot be expected to succeed where the former have failed.'

(Scarlett, B. 'Quality Streak'. *CIMA Insider*)

9.8 Design for quality

A TQM environment aims to get it right first time, and this means that **quality, not faults, must be designed into the organisation's products and operations from the outset**.

Quality control happens at various stages in the process of designing a product or service.

(a)   At the **product design stage**, quality control means trying to design a product or service so that its specifications provide a suitable balance between price and quality (of sales and delivery, as well as manufacture) which will make the product or service competitive. Modern manufacturing businesses use **computer aided design (CAD)** to identify or rectify design features. This might involve:

   (i)   Reducing the **number of parts** in a product overall. The fewer the number of parts, the less parts there are to go wrong.

   (ii)   Using parts or materials that are **already used** (or could be used) by other products. The more common parts overall, the less chance there is of a product failing to meet quality standards due to a rogue supplier of just one of many components. For example, if a car with electric windows can be designed to use the same glass as a cheaper model with manually wound windows, there will only be one glass supplier to keep a check on.

   (iii)   Improving **physical characteristics** such as shape, size or positioning of controls to make the product more user friendly.

(b)   **Production engineering** is the **process of designing the methods for making a product** (or service) **to the design specification**. It sets out to make production methods as efficient as possible, and to avoid the manufacture of sub-standard items.

(c)   **Information systems** should be designed to get the required information to the right person at the right time; **distribution systems** should be designed to get the right item to the right person at the right time; and so on.

9.9 Quality control and inspection

A distinction should be made between **quality control** and **inspection**.

(a)   **Quality control** involves setting controls for the process of manufacture or service delivery. It is aimed at **preventing the manufacture of defective items** or the provision of defective services.

(b)   **Inspection** is a technique of **identifying when defective items are being produced at an unacceptable level**. Inspection is usually carried out at three main points.

    (i)   Receiving inspection – for raw materials and purchased components

    (ii)   Floor or process inspection for work in progress (WIP)

    (iii)   Final inspection or testing for finished goods

 | **Question 1.7** | Quality

Learning outcome A1(b)

Read the following extract from an article in the *Financial Times*, then list the features and methods of a quality information system that Lloyds Bank might have devised to collect information on the impact of the 'service challenge' described here.

'If you phone a branch of Lloyds Bank and it rings five times before there is a reply; if the person who answers does not introduce him or herself by name during the conversation; if you are standing in a queue with more people in it than the number of tills, then something is wrong.

If any of these things happen then the branch is breaching standards of customer service set by the bank ... the "service challenge" was launched in the bank's 1,888 branches after being tested in 55 branches ... Lloyds already has evidence of the impact. Customers were more satisfied with pilot branches than with others.'

9.10 Benefits of TQM

(a)   Elimination of waste

(b)   Elimination of non value adding activities and processes

(c)   Reduced costs

(d)   Increased profitability

(e)   Greater competitive advantage

(f)   Reduction in the variability in processes and outputs to ensure customer satisfaction

(g)   Increased staff morale, leading to greater productivity and efficiency

(h)   Increased customer loyalty and hence more repeat purchases

9.11 Is TQM too expensive?

In the **current economic climate**, companies are trying to eliminate **unnecessary costs** as much as possible. Some people have argued that strategies to improve quality are **too expensive** to implement and run. Training employees is expensive and any changes to quality procedures means additional costs. All quality programmes must be managed, which is another costly requirement.

As shareholders are often looking for a **quick return** – and will also be focusing on ways in which management could **reduce costs** – any long-term investment in TQM might be unpopular. Also, if the company is operating in a market with **little competition** it can be tempting to ignore quality issues.

 | **Question 1.8** | Ignoring quality issues

Learning outcome A1(b)

Why do you think it would be wrong for companies to cut spending on quality in an economic downturn?

Section summary

In the context of **total quality management**, 'quality' means getting it right first time, and improving continuously.

The **main focus** of TQM is **100% satisfaction** of both internal and external customers through the **continuous improvement** of all activities and processes.

Key elements of TQM include preventing the cause of defects in the first place (rather than relying on inspecting to a predefined level of quality) and aiming towards an environment of zero defects at minimum cost.

TQM promotes the concept of the **internal customer** and **internal supplier**.

Workers themselves are frequently the best source of information about how (or how not) to improve **quality**.

10   Costs of quality and cost of quality reports

Introduction

Linked with TQM are the costs of quality and cost of quality reports. Make sure you understand the concept that good quality saves money and poor quality costs money.

KEY POINT

When we talk about quality-related costs you should remember that a concern for **good quality saves money**; it is **poor quality that costs money**.

10.1 Costs of quality

Cost of quality reports highlight the total cost to an organisation of producing products or services that do not conform to quality requirements. Four categories of cost should be reported: prevention costs, appraisal costs, internal failure costs and external failure costs.

KEY TERMS

The COST OF QUALITY is 'the difference between the actual cost of producing, selling and supporting products or services and the equivalent costs if there were no failures during production or usage'. The cost of quality can be analysed into the following.

- COST OF PREVENTION – 'the costs incurred prior to or during production in order to prevent substandard or defective products or services from being produced'

- COST OF APPRAISAL – 'costs incurred in order to ensure that outputs produced meet required quality standards'

- COST OF INTERNAL FAILURE – 'the costs arising from inadequate quality which are identified before the transfer of ownership from supplier to purchaser'

- COST OF EXTERAL FAILURE – 'the cost arising from inadequate quality discovered after the transfer of ownership from supplier to purchaser'

(CIMA Official Terminology)

External failure costs are the costs of failing to deliver a quality product externally. The sum of internal failure costs, prevention and appraisal costs is the cost of failing to deliver a quality product internally.

Quality-related cost	Example
Prevention costs	Quality engineering Training in quality control
Appraisal costs	Acceptance testing Inspection of goods inwards
Internal failure costs	Failure analysis Losses from failure of purchased items
External failure costs	Administration of customer complaints section Cost of repairing products returned from customers

10.2 Views on quality costs

10.2.1 View 1

KEY TERMS

COST OF CONFORMANCE is 'The cost of achieving specified quality standards'.

COST OF NON-CONFORMANCE is 'The cost of failure to deliver the required standard of quality'.

(CIMA Official Terminology)

Exam alert

Ensure you are able to explain quality conformance costs and quality non-conformance costs and the relationship between them.

The **cost of conformance** is a **discretionary** cost which is incurred with the intention of **eliminating the costs of internal and external failure**. The **cost of non-conformance**, on the other hand, can **only be reduced by increasing the cost of conformance**. The **optimal investment in conformance costs** is when **total costs of quality reach a minimum** (which may be below 100% quality conformance). This is illustrated in the following diagram.

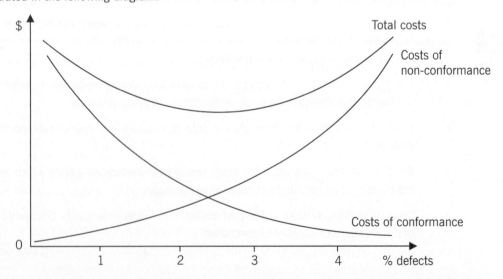

To achieve **0% defects, costs of conformance must be high**. As a **greater proportion of defects are accepted**, however, these costs can be **reduced**. At a level of **0% defects, costs of non-conformance** should be **nil** but these will **increase** as the **accepted level of defects rises**. There should therefore be an **acceptable level of defects** at which the **total costs of quality are at a minimum**.

10.2.2 View 2

A 'traditional' approach to quality management (view 1) is that there is an **optimal level of quality effort, that minimises total quality costs**, and there is a point beyond which spending more on quality yields a benefit that is less than the additional cost incurred. Diminishing returns set in beyond the optimal quality level.

The **TQM philosophy** is different.

(a)   Failure and poor quality are unacceptable. It is **inappropriate to think of an optimal level of quality** at which some failures will occur, and the **inevitability of errors is not something that an organisation should accept**. The target should be zero defects.

(b)   Quality costs are difficult to measure, and failure costs in particular are often seriously underestimated. The **real costs of failure include** not just the cost of scrapped items and reworking faulty items, but also the **management time spent sorting out problems** and the **loss of confidence** between different parts of the organisation whenever faults occur.

(c)   A TQM approach does not accept that the prevention costs of achieving zero defects become unacceptably high as the quality standard improves and goes above a certain level. In other words, **diminishing returns do not necessarily set in**. If everyone in the organisation is involved in improving quality, the cost of continuous improvement need not be high.

(d)   If an organisation **accepts an optimal quality level** that it believes will minimise total quality costs, there will be **no further challenge** to management to improve quality further.

The **TQM quality cost model** is based on the view that:

(a)   **Prevention costs and appraisal costs** are **subject to management influence** or control. It is **better to spend money on prevention**, before failures occur, than on inspection to detect failures after they have happened.

(b)   **Internal failure costs and external failure costs** are the **consequences of the efforts spent on prevention and appraisal**. Extra effort on prevention will reduce internal failure costs and this in turn will have a knock-on effect, reducing external failure costs as well.

In other words, **higher spending on prevention will eventually lead to lower total quality costs**, because appraisal costs, internal failure costs and external failure costs will all be reduced. The emphasis should be on 'getting things right first time' and 'designing in quality' to the product or service.

Question 1.9	Quality costs

Learning outcome A1(b)

LL designs and makes a single product, the X4, used in the telecommunications industry. The organisation has a goods received store, which employs staff who carry out random checks to ensure materials are of the correct specification. In addition to the random checks, a standard allowance is made for failures due to faulty materials at the completion stage, and the normal practice is to charge the cost of any remedial work required to the cost of production for the month. Once delivered to the customer, any faults discovered in the X4 during its warranty period become an expense of the customer support department.

At the end of each month, management reports are prepared for the board of directors. These identify the cost of running the stores and the number of issues, the cost of production and the number of units manufactured, and the cost of customer support.

Required

(a) Briefly discuss why the current accounting system fails to highlight the cost of quality.

(b) Identify four general categories (or classifications) of LL's activities where expenditure making up the explicit cost of quality will be found, and provide an example of a cost found within each category.

(c) Give one example of a cost of quality not normally identified by the accounting system.

Section summary

Quality costs can be analysed into **prevention**, **appraisal**, **internal failure** and **external failure** costs and should be detailed in a **cost of quality report**.

11 Continuous improvement

Introduction

As the name suggests, continuous improvement aims to constantly improve all aspects of customer value, while lowering costs at the same time. This section focuses on the essential factors for continuous improvement and the benefits it brings to an organisation.

11.1 The concept of continuous improvement

In today's highly competitive environment, performance against static historical standards is no longer appropriate, and successful organisations must be **open to change** if they are to **maintain their business advantage**. Being **forward looking** and **receptive to new ideas** are **essential elements of continuous improvement**. The concept was popularised in Japan, where it is known as Kaizen, and many of Japan's economic advances over the past 20 years have been attributed to it.

KEY TERM

CONTINUOUS IMPROVEMENT is an 'ongoing process that involves a continuous search to reduce costs, eliminate waste, and improve the quality and performance of activities that increase customer value or satisfaction'.

(Drury, *Management and Cost Accounting*)

The implementation of continuous improvement does not necessarily call for significant investment, but it does require a great deal of **commitment and continuous effort**.

Continuous improvement is often associated with **incremental changes** in the day to day process of work **suggested by employees** themselves. This is not to say that continuous improvement organisations do not engage in radical change. **Quantum leaps in performance** can occur when cumulative improvements synergise, the sum of a number of small improvements causing a profound net effect greater than the sum of all the small improvements.

The process must be ongoing, and sustained success is more likely in organisations that regularly review their business methods and processes in the drive for improvement.

11.2 Essential factors for continuous improvement

(a)   Total **commitment from senior management**.

(b)   The **opportunity for all employees to contribute** to the continuous improvement process. Tactical and operational level staff, rather than senior management, usually have the information required. The most successful continuous improvement programmes are the ones that have the highest staff involvement.

(c)   Good, objective **information about the organisation's environment** so that its outcomes (what it does) and its processes (how it does it) can be evaluated.

(d)   **Employees' awareness of their role** in the achievement of the organisation's strategy.

(e)   **Management of the performance and contribution of employees**.

(f)   **Good communications** throughout the organisation.

(g)   Implementation of **recognised quality management systems and standards**.

(h)   **Measurement and evaluation of progress against KPIs and benchmarks**. Some organisations have found that simply displaying productivity and quality data every day or week raises production and quality because staff can tell when they are doing things right, and so find themselves in a personal continuous improvement cycle.

It is claimed that if these areas are **regularly reviewed**, change can be managed effectively and **continuous improvement becomes a natural part of the organisational processes**. It should create steady growth and development by keeping the organisation focused on its aims, priorities and performance.

11.2.1 Quality circles

A quality circle consists of a **group of employees**, often from different areas of the organisation, who meet regularly to **discuss problems of quality and quality control** in their area of work, and perhaps to suggest **ways of improving quality**. It is also a way to **encourage innovation**. The aim of quality circles is to **improve employee development and morale** so as to create a **sense of ownership of the quality** of products and services.

Teamwork, in the form of quality circles and **group problem-solving activities**, is the cornerstone of continuous improvement.

11.3 Benefits of continuous improvement

(a)   Better performance, which produces increased profits

(b)   Improvements in customer satisfaction

(c)   Increases in staff morale

(d)   Improvement on a continual, step by step basis is more prudent than changing things all at once

(e)   Better communication within the organisation

(f)   Improvements in relations with suppliers

(g)   Better use of resources

(h)   More efficient planning

CASE STUDY

The continuous improvement process has been shown to bring significant benefits to all types of organisation in a variety of sectors. The Customer Service Excellence standard is a well-established government award scheme promoting and recognising public sector excellence in customer service. Continuous improvement is a key principle of the Customer Service Excellence standard. The principle requires that organisations continually look for ways to improve their services and the facilities they offer. They do this by:

(i)   Promoting innovation, creativity and striving for excellence

(ii)   Recognising that, no matter how good, service can always improve

(iii)   Adopting the latest technologies to change the way business is done

Section summary

The essence of **continuous improvement** is the use of an organisation's human resources to produce a constant stream of improvements in all aspects of customer value, including quality, functional design, and timely delivery, while lowering cost at the same time.

12 Kaizen costing

Introduction

Kaizen costing aims to reduce current costs by using such tools as value analysis and functional analysis.

12.1 The Kaizen costing process

KEY TERM

KAIZEN COSTING focuses on obtaining small incremental cost reductions during the production stage of the product life cycle.

Kaizen costing has been used by some Japanese firms for over 20 years and is now widely used in the electronics and automobile industries, for example. 'Kaizen' translates as **continuous improvement**. It is based on the idea of an ongoing process of reviewing how the business operates in order to identify and implement cost savings. Each individual action may result in a small cost saving, but these are incremental and can add up to a material saving.

Kaizen costing has become more important in the modern business environment following a shift from cost-plus pricing to target costing. Traditionally, companies set the price using cost-plus pricing techniques; however, in today's market, companies have less control over the price and have to accept the market price. As a result, target costing has become increasingly used.

Functional analysis is applied at the design stage of a new product, and a **target cost for each function** is set. The functional target costs are added together and the total becomes the **product target cost**.

Once the product has been in production for a year, the **actual cost of the first year becomes the starting point for further cost reduction**.

It is this **process of continuous improvement, encouraging constant reductions by tightening the 'standards'**, during the production phase that is known as Kaizen costing. The cultural requirements of Kaizen costing are that the whole workforce should be involved, as suggestions for improvements can come from anyone.

The following Kaizen costing chart is based on one used at Daihatsu, the Japanese car manufacturer owned in part by Toyota, and reported in Monden and Lee's 'How a Japanese Auto Maker Reduced Costs' (*Management Accounting* (US Version), 2002).

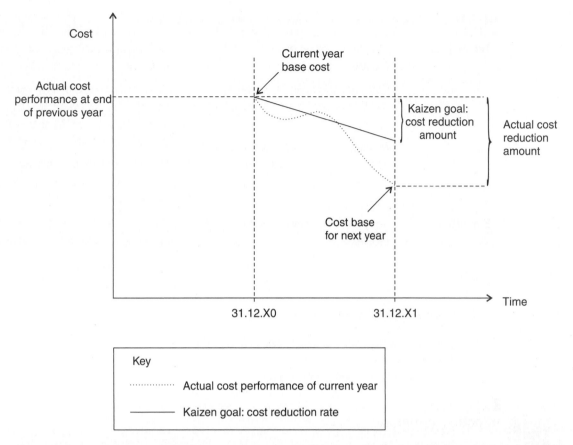

The previous year's actual production cost serves as the cost base for the current year's production cost. A reduction rate and reduction amount are set (**Kaizen cost goals**). **Actual performance** is **compared** to the **Kaizen goals** throughout the year and **variances are monitored**. At the end of the current year, the current actual cost becomes the cost base for the next year. New (lower) Kaizen goals are set and the whole process starts again.

12.2 Kaizen costing vs standard costing

Standard costing is used in conjunction with management by exception (management's attention is directed towards situations where actual results differ from expected results). The expected results are based on standards that have been derived from the capability of current organisational processes. **Standard costing** therefore **reflects current levels of performance** and **fails to provide any motivation to improve**.

The following table sets out the **principal differences between Kaizen costing and standard costing techniques**.

	Standard costing	Kaizen costing
Concepts	It is used for cost control.	It is used for cost reduction.
	It assumes that current manufacturing conditions will stay the same.	It assumes continuous improvement.
	The cost focus is on standard costs based on static conditions.	The cost focus is on actual costs assuming dynamic conditions.
	The aim is to meet cost performance standards.	The aim is to achieve cost reduction targets.

	Standard costing	Kaizen costing
Techniques	Standards are set every 6 or 12 months.	Cost reduction targets are set and applied monthly.
	Costs are controlled using variance analysis based on standard and actual costs.	Costs are reduced by implementing continuous improvement (Kaizen) to attain the target profit or to reduce the gap between target and estimated profit.
	Management should investigate and respond when standards are not met.	Management should investigate and respond when target Kaizen amounts are not attained.
Employees	They are often viewed as the cause of problems.	They are viewed as the source of, and are empowered to find, the solutions.

(Adapted from Monden and Lee)

12.3 How are Kaizen goals met?

(a) Reduction of non value added activities and costs
(b) Elimination of waste
(c) Improvements in production cycle time

Section summary

The aim of **Kaizen costing** is to reduce current costs by using various tools such as value analysis and functional analysis.

13   Just-in-time (JIT)

Introduction

This section covers a technique that should be familiar to you from your CIMA P1 studies. Make sure you are familiar with the just-in-time (JIT) philosophy and techniques and how this technique can eliminate non value added costs.

13.1 Overview of JIT

In **traditional** manufacturing, where there is a production process with several stages, management seek to **insulate each stage** in the process from disruption by another stage, by means of **producing for**, and **holding, inventory**.

With JIT, a **disruption at any point in the system becomes a problem for the whole operation to resolve**. Supporters of JIT management argue that this will improve the likelihood of the problem being resolved, because it is in the interests of everyone to resolve it. They also argue that **inventories** help to **hide problems** within the system, so that problems go unnoticed for too long.

KEY TERMS

JUST-IN-TIME (JIT) is a system whose objective is to produce or to procure products or components as they are required (by a customer or for use) rather than for inventory. A JIT system is a 'pull' system, which responds to demand, in contrast to a 'push' system, in which inventories act as buffers between the different elements of the system, such as purchasing, production and sales.

JUST-IN-TIME PRODUCTION is a production system that is driven by demand for finished products whereby each component on a production line is produced only when needed for the next stage.

JUST-IN-TIME PURCHASING is a purchasing system in which material purchases are contracted so that the receipt and usage of material, to the maximum extent possible, coincide.   (*CIMA Official Terminology*)

13.2 Operational requirements of JIT

High quality	Disruption in production due to errors in quality will reduce throughput and also the dependability of internal supply
Speed	Throughput in the operation must be fast so that customer orders can be met by production rather than from inventory
Reliability	Production must be reliable and not subject to hold-ups
Flexibility	Production must be flexible, and in small batch sizes, to respond immediately to customer orders
Lower cost	High-quality production, faster throughput and elimination of errors will result in reduced costs

A consequence of JIT is that if there is **no immediate demand for output**, the operation **should not produce goods for inventory**. Average capacity utilisation could therefore be low (lower than in a traditional manufacturing operation). With a traditional manufacturing system, however, a higher capacity utilisation would only be achieved by producing for inventory at different stages of the production process. Supporters of JIT argue that there is no value in producing for inventory and, as suggested above, it could damage the overall efficiency of an operation. So whereas **traditional manufacturing systems** are **'push'** systems (a delivery from a supplier pushes products through production), **JIT systems** are **'pull'** systems (demand from a customer pulls products through production).

'Push' systems	**'Pull' systems**
Supplier → production → customer	Supplier ← production ← customer

13.3 The JIT philosophy

JIT can be regarded as an approach to management that encompasses a **commitment to continuous improvement** and the **search for excellence** in the **design and operation of the production management system**. Its aim is to streamline the flow of products through the production process and into the hands of customers.

The JIT philosophy originated in Japan in the 1970s, with companies such as the car manufacturer Toyota. At its most basic, the philosophy is:

(a)   To do things well, and gradually do them better (**continuous improvement**)
(b)   To **squeeze waste out** of the system

A criticism of JIT, in its extreme form, is that having no inventory between any stages in the production process ignores the fact that some stages, by their very nature, could be less reliable than others, and more prone to disruption. It could therefore be argued that some inventory should be held at these stages to provide a degree of extra protection to the rest of the operation.

13.3.1 Three key elements in the JIT philosophy

Elimination of waste	**Waste** is defined as **any activity that does not add value**. Examples of waste identified by Toyota were:
	• **Waiting time**. Waiting time can be measured by labour efficiency and machine efficiency.
	• **Transport**. Moving items around a plant does not add value. Waste can be reduced by **changing the layout of the factory floor so as to minimise the movement of materials**.
	• **Inventory**. The target should be to eliminate all inventory by tackling the things that cause it to build up.
The involvement of all staff in the operation	JIT is a cultural issue, and its philosophy has to be embraced by everyone involved in the operation if it is to be applied successfully. Critics of JIT argue that management efforts to involve all staff can be patronising.
Continuous improvement	The ideal target is to meet demand immediately with perfect quality and no waste. In practice, this ideal is never achieved. However, the JIT philosophy is that an organisation should **work towards the ideal**.

13.4 JIT techniques

13.4.1 Management techniques

JIT is not just a philosophy, it is also a **collection of management techniques**. Some of these techniques relate to basic working practices.

(a) **Work standards**. Work standards should be established and followed by everyone at all times.

(b) **Flexibility in responsibilities**. The organisation should provide for the possibility of expanding the responsibilities of any individual to the extent of their capabilities, regardless of the individual's position in the organisation. Grading structures and restrictive working practices should be abolished.

(c) **Equality of all people working in the organisation**. Equality should exist and be visible. For example, there should be a single staff canteen for everyone, without a special executive dining area; and all staff, including managers, might be required to wear the same uniform. An example of where such practices occur is the car manufacturer Honda.

(d) **Autonomy**. Authority should be delegated to the individuals directly responsible for the activities of the operation. Management should support people on the shop floor, not direct them. For example, if a quality problem arises, an operative on the production line should have the authority to bring the line to a halt. Gathering data about performance should be delegated to the shop floor and the individuals who use it. Shop floor staff should also be given the first opportunity to solve problems affecting their work, and expert help should only be sought if it is needed.

(e) **Development of personnel**. Individual workers should be developed and trained.

(f) **Quality of working life**. The quality of working life should be improved, through better work area facilities, job security, involvement of everyone in job-related decision making, and so on.

(g) **Creativity**. Employees should be encouraged to be creative in devising improvements to the way their work is done.

13.4.2 Other JIT techniques and methodologies

(a) **Design for manufacture**. In many industries, the way that a product is designed determines a large proportion of its eventual production costs. Production costs can therefore be significantly reduced at the design stage, for example by reducing the number of different components and sub-assemblies required in the product.

(b)   **Use several small, simple machines**, rather than a single large and more complex machine. Small machines can be moved around more easily, and so offer greater flexibility in shop floor layout. The risk of making a bad and costly investment decision is reduced, because relatively simple small machines usually cost much less than sophisticated large machines.

(c)   **Work floor layout and work flow**. Work can be laid out to promote the smooth flow of operations. Work flow is an important element in JIT, because the work needs to flow without interruption in order to avoid a build-up of inventory or unnecessary downtimes. Machines or workers should be grouped by product or component instead of by type of work performed. The non value added activity of materials movement between operations is therefore minimised by eliminating space between work stations. Products can flow from machine to machine without having to wait for the next stage of processing or return to stores. Lead times and WIP are thus reduced.

(d)   **Total productive maintenance (TPM)**. TPM seeks to eliminate unplanned breakdowns and the damage they cause to production and work flow. Staff working on the production line are brought into the search for improvements in maintenance, and are encouraged to take ownership of their machines and carry out simple repairs on them. This frees up maintenance specialists to use their expertise to look for higher-level ways to improve maintenance systems, instead of spending their time on fire fighting repairs and maintenance jobs.

(e)   **Set-up reductions**. Set-up is the collection of activities carried out between completing work on one job or batch of production and preparing the process or machine to take the next batch. Set-up time is non-productive time. An aim in JIT is to reduce set-up times, for example by pre-preparing set-up tasks that can be done in advance. Alternatively, set-up time can be reduced by undertaking some tasks previously not done until the machines had stopped while the machines are running.

(f)   **Total people involvement**. Staff are encouraged to take on more responsibility for using their abilities for the benefit of the organisation. They are trusted and given authority for tasks such as:

    (i)   Monitoring and measuring their own performance

    (ii)   Reviewing the work they have done each day

    (iii) Dealing directly with suppliers about quality issues and to find out about materials delivery times

    (iv)   Dealing with customer problems and queries

    (v)   Selecting new staff to work with them

(g)   **Visibility**. The workplace and the operations taking place in it are made more visible, through open plan work space, visual control systems (such as Kanbans, described later), information displays showing performance achievements, and signal lights to show where a stoppage has occurred.

(h)   **JIT purchasing**. With JIT purchasing, an organisation establishes a close, long-term relationship with trusted suppliers, and develops an arrangement with the supplier for being able to purchase materials only when they are needed for production. The supplier is required to have a flexible production system capable of responding immediately to purchase orders from the organisation. Responsibility for the quality of goods lies with the supplier. If an organisation has confidence that suppliers will deliver material of 100% quality, on time, so that there will be no rejects, returns and hence no production delays, usage of materials can be matched exactly with delivery of materials and inventories can be kept at near zero levels.

13.5 Elimination of non value added costs

As you know, value is only added while a product is actually being processed. While it is being inspected for quality, moving from one part of the factory to another, waiting for further processing and held in store, value is not being added. **Non value added activities** (or diversionary activities) **should therefore be eliminated**.

Question 1.10

Non value added activities

Learning outcome A1(b)

Solo produces one product, the P. Parts for the product are quality inspected on arrival and stored in a warehouse until needed. They are then moved from the warehouse to the machine room where they are machined to the product specification. This work is then inspected and, if satisfactory, the machined parts are moved to the assembly area. Once this processing is complete, the finished product is inspected and tested. This is then passed to the despatch department, where employees pack it in an attractive box with a printed instruction sheet. Finished goods are stored back in the warehouse until despatched to customers.

Required

Eliminate the non value added activities from Solo's current activities listed below to produce the set of activities that would take place under a JIT approach. Comment on your answer.

Parts received	Machined parts assembled
Parts quality inspected	Finished product inspected and tested
Parts stored in warehouse	Finished goods passed to despatch department
Parts moved to machine room	Finished goods packaged
Parts machined	Packed goods moved back to warehouse
Machined parts inspected	Packed goods stored
Machined parts moved to assembly area	Packed goods despatched to customer

Question 1.11

Value-added activity

Learning outcome A1(b)

Which of the following is a value-added activity?

A   Setting up a machine so that it drills holes of a certain size
B   Repairing faulty production work
C   Painting a car, if the organisation manufactures cars
D   Storing materials

CASE STUDY

The following extract from an article in the *Financial Times* illustrates how 'just-in-time' some manufacturing processes can be. The emphasis is BPP's.

'Just-in-time manufacturing is down to a fine art at Nissan Motor Manufacturing (UK). **Stockholding of some components is just ten minutes** – and the holding of all parts bought in Europe is less than a day.

'Nissan has moved beyond just-in-time to **synchronous supply** for some components, which means manufacturers deliver these components directly to the production line minutes before they are needed.

'These manufacturers do not even receive an order to make a component until the car for which it is intended has started along the final assembly line. Seat manufacturer Ikeda Hoover, for example, has about 45 minutes to build seats to specification and deliver them to the assembly line a mile away. It delivers 12 sets of seats every 20 minutes and they are mounted in the right order on an overhead conveyor ready for fitting to the right car.

'Nissan has **close relationships with this dozen or so suppliers** and deals exclusively with them in their component areas. It involves them and even their own suppliers in discussions about future needs and other issues. These companies have generally established their own manufacturing units close to the Nissan plant.

'Other parts from further afield are collected from manufacturers by Nissan several times a month at fixed times. This is more efficient than having each supplier making individual haulage arrangements.'

13.6 JIT planning and control with Kanban

Holding inventories is one source of waste in production. Not having materials or parts when they are needed is another. In other words, both having inventory when it is not needed and not having it when it is needed is wasteful practice.

Kanban is the Japanese word for card or signal. A **Kanban control system** is a system for **controlling the flow of materials between one stage in a process and the next**. In its simple form, a card is used by an 'internal customer' as a signal to an 'internal supplier' that the customer now requires more parts or materials. The card will contain details of the parts or materials required.

Kanbans are the only means of authorising a flow of materials or parts. The receipt of a card from an internal customer sets in motion the movement or production or supply of one unit of an item, or one standard container of the item. The receipt of two cards will trigger the movement, production or supply of two units or two standard containers, and so on.

There are variants on the basic Kanban system. For example, a production system might use **Kanban squares**. A space is marked out on the work shop floor. When the space is empty, it acts as a signal for production to start at the previous stage. When it is full, it acts as a signal that production at the previous stage should be halted.

13.7 JIT in service operations

The JIT philosophy can be applied to service operations as well as to manufacturing operations. Whereas JIT in manufacturing seeks to eliminate inventories, JIT in service operations **seeks to remove queues of customers**.

Queues of customers are wasteful because:

(a)   They **waste customers' time**
(b)   Queues require **space for customers to wait in**, and this **space is not adding value**
(c)   **Queuing lowers the customers' perception of the quality of the service**

The application of JIT to a service operation calls for the **removal of specialisation of tasks**, so that the workforce can be **used more flexibly and moved from one type of work to another**, in response to demand and work flow requirements.

CASE STUDY

Queue management systems in supermarkets seek to allocate staff according to the customer need. There may be times during the day when there is an influx of shoppers and times when there are few people in the store. Since the timing of these peaks and troughs can be difficult to predict, the 'on duty' checkout staff may be overwhelmed at some times and underutilised at others.

To avoid both lengthy queues and idle staff, minimal levels of checkout staff are in place and shop floor staff are reallocated to the tills as needed.

Teamwork and flexibility are difficult to introduce into an organisation because people might be more comfortable with clearly delineated boundaries in terms of their responsibilities. Customers are usually not interested in the company organisation structure, however, because they are more interested in receiving a timely service.

In practice, service organisations are likely to use a **buffer operation** to minimise customer queuing times. For example, a hairdresser will get an assistant to give the client a shampoo to reduce the impact of waiting for the stylist.

Question 1.12	JIT

Learning outcome A1(b)

At the end of the Second World War, Toyota was making losses and was prevented from increasing prices by the weak Japanese car market. It also suffered from major strike action in 1950.

The individual credited with devising JIT in Toyota from the 1940s was Taiichi Ohno, and JIT techniques were developed gradually over time. The Kanban system, for example, was devised by Toyota in the early 1950s, but was only finally fully implemented throughout the Japanese manufacturing operation in 1962.

Ohno identified seven wastes.

(a)   Overproduction
(b)   Waste caused by transportation
(c)   Waiting
(d)   Waste caused by physical movement of items
(e)   Overprocessing
(f)   Waste caused by inventory
(g)   Defects/corrections

He worked to eliminate them from operations in Toyota. Measures that were taken by the company included the following.

(a)   The aim of reducing costs was of paramount importance in the late 1940s.

(b)   The company aimed to level the flow of production and eliminate unevenness in the work flow.

(c)   The factory layout was changed. Previously all machines, such as presses, were located in the same area of the factory. Under the new system, different types of machines were clustered together in production cells.

(d)   Machine operators were retrained.

(e)   Employee involvement in the changes was seen as being particularly important. Teamwork was promoted.

(f)   The Kanban system was eventually introduced, but a major problem with its introduction was the elimination of defects in production.

Required

Explain how each of the changes described above came to be regarded as essential by Toyota's management.

13.8 Problems associated with JIT

JIT should not be seen as a fix for all the underlying problems associated with Western manufacturing. It might not even be appropriate in all circumstances.

(a)   It is **not always easy to predict patterns of demand**.

(b)   JIT makes the organisation **far more vulnerable to disruptions in the supply chain**.

(c)   JIT was designed at a time when all of Toyota's manufacturing was done within a 50 km radius of its headquarters. Wide geographical spread, however, makes this difficult.

Question 1.13	JIT manufacturing environment

Learning outcome A1(b)

Batch sizes within a JIT manufacturing environment may well be smaller than those associated with traditional manufacturing systems.

What costs might be associated with this feature of JIT?

1   Increased set-up costs

2   Opportunity cost of lost production capacity as machinery and the workforce reorganise for a different product

3   Additional materials handling costs

4   Increased administrative costs

13.9 Modern versus traditional inventory control systems

There is no reason for the newer approaches to supersede the old entirely. A restaurant, for example, might find it preferable to use the traditional economic order quantity approach for staple non-perishable food, but adopt JIT for perishable and 'exotic' items. In a hospital, a lack of inventory could, quite literally, be fatal, and JIT would be quite unsuitable.

13.10 Manufacturing cycle efficiency

13.10.1 Customer response time (CRT)

As product life cycles shorten and customers demand quick response to orders, organisations are seeking to improve **customer response time (CRT)** (the length of time between an order being placed and delivery of goods/services to the customer) and **on-time delivery rate**.

CRT is a measure of an organisation's ability to respond to a customer's request and is in general determined by internal factors (delay between order and work starting, length of time the order spends in the production process), both of which are linked to the length of the manufacturing cycle.

13.10.2 Manufacturing cycle time (MCT)

Manufacturing cycle time (MCT) is the length of time between starting and finishing the production of an order and is typically made up of:

(a)   Processing time
(b)   Waiting time
(c)   Moving time
(d)   Inspection time

Manufacturing cycle efficiency (MCE) shows (in ratio form) the proportion of time during which value is being added during the production process, and is calculated as:

Processing time/(processing time + waiting time + moving time + inspection time)

The closer the ratio is to 1, the **more efficient the production operation**. As the **ratio increases**:

(a) **WIP investment will fall** (with all the associated benefits). For example, if an organisation has an annual cost of goods sold of $5,000,000 and the MCT reduces from 20 days to 15 days, the average value of WIP will fall by $((20 - 15)/365) \times \$5,000,000 = \$68,493$.

(b) An organisation's ability to act **flexibly** and **respond to rush orders** or sudden market changes is improved.

(c) **Production throughput** can be **increased** without increasing plant capacity. The need for overtime may fall or additional production may be possible without increasing fixed production costs.

Reducing MCT links well with TQM (see Section 7) because of the need to reduce reworking and inspection.

However, **improving MCE will increase costs**. A reduction in cycle times may require the manufacturing process to be redesigned or investment in new machinery. The net benefits will very much depend on the circumstances under consideration. Will the investment required be justified by the increase in volumes or reduction in costs? Relevant costing can be used: the proportion of, say, stockholding costs which would be avoidable can be determined, perhaps by using activity based costing. If the reduction in cycle time produces X extra additional saleable units, the opportunity cost of a cycle hour can be calculated and used to assist in the decision of whether or not to invest in reducing cycle time.

13.10.3 MCT and JIT

(a) The reduction in MCT is a key phase in the introduction of JIT.

(b) JIT has advantages in certain manufacturing environments, but the benefits of increasing MCE apply to all organisations, irrespective of whether they also use JIT.

(c) Just as JIT can be applied to the supply chain, so too can the concept of MCE. For example, by requiring a guaranteed level of quality from suppliers, inspection time can be reduced.

Section summary

Just-in-time is an approach to operations planning and control based on the idea that **goods and services should be produced only when they are needed,** and neither too early (so that inventories build up) nor too late (so that the customer has to wait).

Just-in-time systems challenge 'traditional' views of manufacturing.

JIT consists of **JIT purchasing** and **JIT production**.

Elimination of waste, involvement of all staff and **continuous improvement** are the three key elements in the JIT philosophy.

JIT aims to **eliminate all non value added costs.**

14 Theory of constraints (TOC)

Introduction

Another cost management technique is theory of constraints (TOC), whose aim is to ensure that production flows evenly and works as effectively as possible. This section links closely with Section 13 on throughput accounting.

14.1 The concept of the theory of constraints

The use of a JIT operating system, whether in a manufacturing or a service organisation, requires a particular type of costing system. **Throughput accounting** is a technique that has been developed to deal with this. The name was first coined in the late 1980s, when Galloway and Waldron developed the system in the UK. Throughput accounting is based on the concept of the **theory of constraints (TOC)** which was formulated by Goldratt and Cox in the US in 1986. Its key financial concept is to **turn materials into sales as quickly as possible**, thereby maximising throughput and the net cash generated from sales. This is to be achieved by striving for **balance in production processes**, and so **evenness of production flow** is an important aim.

KEY TERMS

THEORY OF CONSTRAINTS (TOC) is 'Procedure based on identifying bottleneck (constraints), maximising their use, subordinating other facilities to the demands of the bottleneck facilities, alleviating bottlenecks and re-evaluating the whole system'.

BOTTLENECK is a 'facility that has lower capacity than preceding or subsequent activities, and restricts output based on current capacity'.   (*CIMA Official Terminology*)

One process will inevitably act as a bottleneck (or limiting factor) and constrain throughput – this is known as the **binding constraint** in TOC terminology. The important concept behind TOC is that the production rate of the entire factory is set at the pace of the bottleneck. (Goldratt advocates a **drum – buffer – rope system**, with the bottleneck as the drum.) Steps should therefore be taken to remove this bottleneck.

(a)   Buy more equipment
(b)   Provide additional training for slow workers
(c)   Change a product design to reduce the processing time on a bottleneck activity
(d)   Eliminate idle time at the bottleneck (eg machine set-up time)

But ultimately there will always be a binding constraint, unless capacity is far greater than sales demand or all processes are totally in balance, which is unlikely even if it is a goal to be aimed for.

Output through the binding constraint should never be delayed or held up, otherwise sales will be lost. To avoid this happening **a buffer inventory should be built up immediately prior to the bottleneck** or binding constraint. **This is the only inventory that the business should hold**, with the exception of possibly a very small amount of finished goods inventory and raw materials that are consistent with the JIT approach. (This is Goldratt's **buffer** in the drum – buffer – rope system.)

Operations prior to the binding constraint should operate at the same speed as the binding constraint, otherwise WIP (other than the buffer inventory) will be built up. (Here the **rope** links all upstream operations to the pace of the bottleneck.) According to TOC, **inventory costs money** in terms of storage space and interest costs and so inventory is **not desirable**. In a **traditional** production system an **organisation will often pay staff a bonus to produce as many units as possible**. **TOC** views this as **inefficient** since the organisation is paying extra to build up inventory which then costs money to store until it is required.

Example: An illustration of the theory of constraints

Machine X can process 1,000 kg of raw material per hour, machine Y 800 kg. Of an input of 900 kg, 100 kg of processed material must wait on the bottleneck machine (machine Y) at the end of an hour of processing.

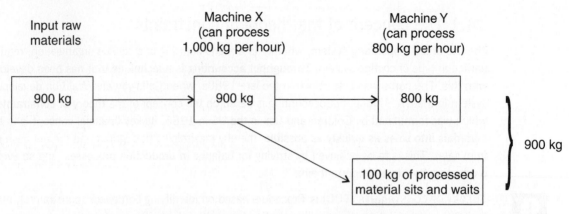

The **traditional view** is that **machines should be working, not sitting idle**. So if the desired output from the above process were 8,100 kg, **machine X would be kept in continual use** and all 8,100 kg would be processed through the machine in 9 hours. However, there would be a **backlog** of 900 kg [8,100 − (9 hours × 800)] of processed material in front of machine Y. All this material **would require handling** and **storage space** and **create the additional costs related to these non value added activities**. Its **processing would not increase throughput contribution**.

14.2 Key measures

To apply TOC ideas, Goldratt and Cox recommend the use of three key measures.

KEY TERMS

THROUGHPUT CONTRIBUTION (THE RATE AT WHICH PROFIT IS GENERATED THROUGH SALES) = SALES REVENUE − DIRECT MATERIAL COST

CONVERSION COSTS (OTHER OPERATIONAL EXPENSES) = ALL OPERATING COSTS EXCEPT DIRECT MATERIAL COST

INVESTMENTS (INVENTORY) = INVENTORIES + RESEARCH AND DEVELOPMENT COSTS + COSTS OF EQUIPMENT AND BUILDINGS

The aim is to maximise throughput contribution while keeping inventory and operational expenses to a minimum. If a strategy for increasing throughput contribution is being considered, it will therefore only be accepted if operational expenses and inventory increase by a lower amount than contribution. TOC considers the short term and assumes operating expenses to be fixed costs.

14.3 Bottlenecks and quality control

Quality control points should be placed before bottlenecks: 'Make sure the bottleneck works only on good parts by weeding out the ones that are defective. If you scrap a part before it reaches the bottleneck, all you have lost is a scrapped part. But if you scrap the part after it's passed through the bottleneck, you have lost time that cannot be recovered.'

(Goldratt and Cox, *The Goal*)

KEY POINT

It is important to realise that TOC is not an accounting system but a **production** system.

CASE STUDY

TOC is not just applicable in manufacturing organisations, but can be applied successfully in the service sector too. The binding constraint in the service sector is often skilled labour.

Using the 'Theory of Constraints' methodology to improve response rates to emergency services in the UK.

Why was the initiative launched?

The UK Police Force was seeking innovative ways to tackle a long-standing problem: how to improve the response rate to emergency calls in an affordable way.

Problems

IA large proportion of calls to the 999 emergency number in the UK are not emergencies. These calls block the lines and take up valuable phone operator time, which delays the response to genuine emergency calls. **Using the TOC approach, non-emergency calls need to be weeded out before they get to the operator.** Within the system these calls were 'defective parts' that place excess demand on the bottleneck and need to be eliminated.

Solutions

Diverting the non-emergency numbers to other operators frees up the 999 operators. For the new number, a short, easily memorable number that everyone could use was chosen, 101. There was concern about whether there would be public acceptance and the demands that it would place on the 101 operators if demand exceeded the existing resources.

Tips for success

(a)   Remember TOC is a thinking process and not a list of possible solutions.

(b)   Success is more likely if the methodology is embraced by a core group of senior people in the organisation.

(c)   Involve all staff levels in finding solutions.

(d)   Watch the use of language because the jargon of TOC is not necessary for everyone.

(e)   Don't think of TOC as yet another expensive management tool. It is a relatively simple set of basic principles that are accessible to all.

(f)   Don't allow historical tradition, 'we've always done it this way', to inhibit innovation.

Section summary

Theory of constraints (TOC) is a set of concepts which aim to identify the binding constraints in a production system and which strive for evenness of production flow so that the organisation works as effectively as possible. No inventory should be held, except prior to the binding constraint.

15   Throughput accounting (TA)

Introduction

This section is closely linked with Section 12 on the theory of constraints. Make sure you understand what is meant by 'throughput' and how this technique differs from other management accounting systems.

15.1 A definition

KEY TERM

'THROUGHPUT ACCOUNTING (TA) is an approach to accounting which is largely in sympathy with the JIT philosophy. In essence, TA assumes that a manager has a given set of resources available. These comprise existing buildings, capital equipment and labour force. Using these resources, purchased materials and parts must be processed to generate sales revenue. Given this scenario, the most

appropriate financial objective to set for doing this is the maximisation of throughput (Goldratt and Cox, 1984) which is defined as: sales revenue **less** direct material cost.'

(Tanaka, Yoshikawa, Innes and Mitchell, *Contemporary Cost Management*)

Throughput accounting (TA) is different from all other management accounting systems because of what it **emphasises**.

(a) Firstly **throughput**
(b) Secondly minimisation of inventory
(c) Thirdly **cost control**

15.2 TA concepts

KEY POINT

TA is based on three concepts.

- In the short run, most costs in the factory (with the exception of materials costs) are fixed.
- The ideal inventory level is zero.
- Profitability is determined by the rate at which sales are made.

15.2.1 Concept 1

Because TA differentiates between fixed and variable costs, it is often compared with marginal costing and **some people argue that there is no difference between marginal costing and TA**. In marginal costing, direct labour costs are usually assumed to be variable costs. Years ago this assumption was true, but employees are not usually paid piece rate today and they are not laid off for part of the year when there is no work, and so labour cost is not truly variable. If this is accepted, the two techniques are identical in some respects, but **marginal costing is generally thought of as being purely a short-term decision-making technique**, while **TA, or at least TOC, was conceived with the aim of changing manufacturing strategy to achieve evenness of flow. It is therefore much more than a short-term decision-making technique.**

Because **TA combines all conversion costs** together and does not attempt to examine them in detail, it is particularly **suited to use with ABC**, which examines the behaviour of these costs and assumes them to be variable in the long run.

15.2.2 Concept 2

In a JIT environment, all inventory is a 'bad thing' and the **ideal inventory level is zero**. Products should not be made unless there is a customer waiting for them. This means **unavoidable idle capacity must be accepted in some operations**, but not for the operation that is the bottleneck of the moment. There is one exception to the zero inventory policy, being that a buffer inventory should be held prior to the bottleneck process.

15.2.3 Concept 3

Profitability is determined by the rate at which 'money comes in at the door' (that is, sales are made) and, in a JIT environment, this depends on how quickly goods can be produced to satisfy customer orders. Since the goal of a profit-orientated organisation is to make money, inventory must be sold for that goal to be achieved.

The buffer inventory and any other WIP or finished goods inventory should be **valued at material cost only** until the output is eventually sold, so that **no value will be added and no profit earned until the sale takes place**. Producing output just to add to WIP or finished goods inventory creates no profit, and so should not be encouraged.

| Question 1.14 | TA vs conventional cost accounting |

Learning outcome A1(b)

How are these concepts a direct contrast to the fundamental principles of conventional cost accounting?

15.3 Bottleneck resources

The aim of **modern manufacturing** approaches is to match production resources with the demand for them. This implies that there are **no constraints, termed bottleneck resources** in TA, within an organisation. The throughput philosophy entails the **identification** and **elimination** of these bottleneck resources. Where they **cannot be eliminated, production must be limited to the capacity of the bottleneck resource in order to avoid the build-up of WIP**. If a rearrangement of existing resources (such as moving a machine) or buying in resources does not alleviate the bottleneck, investment in new equipment may be necessary. However, the **elimination of one bottleneck is likely to lead to the creation of another** at a previously satisfactory location. The **management of bottlenecks** therefore becomes a **primary concern** of the manager seeking to increase throughput.

(a)   There is nothing to be gained by measuring and encouraging the efficiency of machines that do not govern the overall flow of work.

(b)   Likewise, there is little point in measuring the efficiency of production staff working on non-bottleneck processes.

(c)   Bonuses paid to encourage faster working on non-bottleneck processes are wasted and could lead to increased storage costs and more faulty goods.

Other factors that might limit throughput other than a lack of production resources (bottlenecks):

(a)   The existence of a non-competitive selling price

(b)   The need to deliver on time to particular customers, which may disrupt normal production flow

(c)   The lack of product quality and reliability, which may cause large amounts of rework or an unnecessary increase in production volume

(d)   Unreliable material suppliers, which will lead to poor-quality products that require rework

15.4 Throughput measures

15.4.1 Return per time period

In a TA environment, the overall **focus of attention** is the **rate at which the organisation can generate profits**. To monitor this, the return on the throughput **through the bottleneck resource** is monitored using:

$$\textbf{Return per time period} = \frac{\text{sales revenue} - \text{material costs}}{\text{time period}}$$

This measure shows the **value added** by an organisation during a particular time period. Time plays a crucial role in the measure, so **managers** are strongly **encouraged to remove bottlenecks that might cause production delays**.

15.4.2 Return per time period on bottleneck resource

In TA, the limiting factor is the bottleneck. The return per time period measure can be adapted and used for **ranking products to optimise production** in the **short term**.

$$\textbf{Product return per minute} = \frac{\text{sales price} - \text{material costs}}{\text{minutes on key / bottleneck resource}}$$

Ranking products on the basis of throughput contribution per minute (or hour) on the bottleneck resource is **similar in concept to maximising contribution per unit of limiting factor**. Such product rankings are for **short-term production scheduling only**. In TA, bottlenecks should be eliminated and so rankings may change quickly. Customer demand can, of course, cause the bottleneck to change at short notice too.

Rankings by TA product return and by contribution per unit of limiting factor may be different. Which one leads to profit maximisation? The correct approach depends on the variability or otherwise of labour and variable overheads, which in turn depends on the time horizon of the decision. Both are short-term profit maximisation techniques and given that labour is nowadays likely to be fixed in the short term, it could be argued that TA provides the more correct solution. An analysis of variable overheads would be needed to determine their variability.

KEY POINT

Bear in mind that the huge majority of organisations cannot produce and market products based on short-term profit considerations alone. Strategic-level issues such as market developments, product developments and stage reached in the product life cycle must also be taken into account.

15.4.3 TA ratio

Products can also be ranked according to the **throughput accounting ratio (TA ratio)**.

LEARN

$$\text{TA ratio} = \frac{\text{throughput contribution or value added per time period}}{\text{conversion cost per time period}}$$

$$= \frac{(\text{sales} - \text{material costs}) \text{ per time period}}{(\text{labour} + \text{overhead}) \text{ per time period}}$$

This measure has the **advantage** of **including the costs involved in running the factory**. **The higher the ratio, the more profitable the company**.

Here's an example.

	Product A $ per hour	Product B $ per hour
Sales price	100	150
Material cost	(40)	(50)
Conversion cost	(50)	(50)
Profit	10	50
TA ratio	$\frac{60}{50} = 1.2$	$\frac{100}{50} = 2.0$

Profit will be maximised by manufacturing as much of product B as possible.

Exam skills

If conversion cost cannot be directly allocated to products (because it is not a unit-level manufacturing cost), the TA ratio cannot be calculated and products have to be ranked in terms of throughput contribution per hour or minute of bottleneck resource.

15.4.4 Effectiveness measures and cost control

Traditional efficiency measures such as standard costing variances and labour ratios are **unsuitable** in a TA environment because traditional efficiency should not be encouraged (as the **labour force should not produce just for inventory**).

Effectiveness is a **more important** issue. The **current effectiveness ratio** compares current levels of effectiveness with the standard and is calculated as:

$$\frac{\text{standard minutes of throughput achieved}}{\text{minutes available}}$$

Generally adverse variances are not considered to be a good thing. In a TA environment, however, if overtime is worked at the bottleneck to increase throughput, an adverse labour rate variance would arise. However, provided the increase in value added was greater than the extra labour cost, this would be a good thing.

15.5 TA and non value added activities

Like JIT, TA aims to minimise production time. In order that **process time approaches lead time**, **all non value added activities need to be minimised or eliminated**. Set-up time, waiting time, inspection time and so on should therefore be minimised or eliminated.

15.6 Is it good or bad?

TA is seen by some as **too short term**, as all costs other than direct material are regarded as fixed. This is not true. But TA does **concentrate on direct material costs** and does nothing for the control of other costs. These characteristics make TA a **good complement for ABC**, as ABC focuses on labour and overhead costs.

TA attempts to maximise throughput, whereas traditional systems attempt to maximise profit. By trying to maximise throughput an organisation could be producing more than the profit-maximising output.

Where TA helps direct attention:

(a)   Bottlenecks
(b)   Key elements in making profits
(c)   Inventory reduction
(d)   Reducing the response time to customer demand
(e)   Evenness of production flow
(f)   Overall effectiveness and efficiency

A **global measure of throughput** at factory level can produce an insight into the effectiveness of factory management, especially in a multi-product, multi-process organisation in which product demand is unpredictable and prices are set by negotiation between supplier and buyer. With a given level of resources (employees, machines, buildings and so on), an increase period by period in the level of throughput would indicate an improvement in the flow of products through the factory to the customer. If bottleneck resources are highlighted, management can focus their attention on removing factors limiting the profitability of the factory as a whole (as opposed to subunits or product lines).

Example: Throughput accounting

Corrie produces three products, X, Y and Z. The capacity of Corrie's plant is restricted by process alpha. Process alpha is expected to be operational for 8 hours per day and can produce 1,200 units of X per hour, 1,500 units of Y per hour, and 600 units of Z per hour.

Selling prices and material costs for each product are as follows.

Product	Selling price $ per unit	Material cost $ per unit	Throughput contribution $ per unit
X	150	70	80
Y	120	40	80
Z	300	100	200

Conversion costs are $720,000 per day.

Requirements

(a) Calculate the profit per day if daily output achieved is 6,000 units of X, 4,500 units of Y and 1,200 units of Z.

(b) Calculate the TA ratio for each product.

(c) In the absence of demand restrictions for the three products, advise Corrie's management on the optimal production plan.

Solution

(a) Profit per day = throughput contribution – conversion cost

= [($80 × 6,000) + ($80 × 4,500) + ($200 × 1,200)] – $720,000
= $360,000

(b) TA ratio = throughput contribution per factory hour/conversion cost per factory hour

Conversion cost per factory hour = $720,000/8 = $90,000

Product	Throughput contribution per factory hour	Cost per factory hour	TA ratio
X	$80 × (60 ÷ 0.05 mins) = $96,000	$90,000	1.07
Y	$80 × (60 ÷ 0.04 mins) = $120,000	$90,000	1.33
Z	$200 × (60 ÷ 0.10 mins) = $120,000	$90,000	1.33

(c) An attempt should be made to remove the restriction on output caused by process alpha's capacity. This will probably result in another bottleneck emerging elsewhere. The extra capacity required to remove the restriction could be obtained by working overtime, making process improvements or product specification changes. Until the volume of throughput can be increased, output should be concentrated upon products Y and Z (greatest TA ratios), unless there are good marketing reasons for continuing the current production mix.

Now try a question for yourself.

Question 1.15   Performance measurement in throughput accounting

Learning outcome A1(b)

Growler manufactures computer components. Health and safety regulations mean that one of its processes can only be operated 8 hours a day. The hourly capacity of this process is 500 units per hour. The selling price of each component is $100 and the unit material cost is $40. The daily total of all factory costs (conversion costs) is $144,000, excluding materials. Expected production is 3,600 units per day.

Required

Calculate:

(a)   Total profit per day
(b)   Return per factory hours
(c)   Throughput accounting ratio

15.7 TA in service and retail industries

Sales staff have always preferred to use a marginal costing approach so that they can use their discretion on discounts, and **retail organisations** have traditionally thought in terms of sales revenue less the bought-in price of goods. The TA approach is therefore **nothing new** to them.

TA can be used very effectively in **support departments and service industries** to **highlight and remove bottlenecks**. For example, if there is a delay in processing a potential customer's application, business can be lost or the potential customer may decide not to proceed. Sometimes credit rating checks are too detailed, slowing the whole procedure unnecessarily and delaying acceptance from, say, 24 hours to 8 days.

A similar problem could occur in hospitals where work that could be done by nurses has to be carried out by doctors. Not only does this increase the cost of the work, but it may well also cause a bottleneck by tying up a doctor's time unnecessarily.

Question 1.16   Product costing vs TA

Learning outcome A1(b)

Here are some statements about traditional product costing. Provide the equivalent statements about throughput accounting.

Statement 1:   Inventory is valued in the financial statements at full production cost.
Statement 2:   Labour, material and variable overheads are treated as variable costs.
Statement 3:   A process is deemed efficient if labour and machine time are fully utilised.
Statement 4:   Value is added when a unit of product is produced.

15.8 Differences between TA and traditional product cost systems

Traditional product costing	Throughput accounting
Labour costs and 'traditional' variable overheads are treated as variable costs.	They are not normally treated as variable costs.
Inventory is valued in the income statement and balance sheet at total production cost.	Inventory is valued at material cost only.
Variance analysis is employed to determine whether standards were achieved.	Variance analysis is used to determine why the planned product mix was not produced.
Efficiency is based on labour and machines working to full capacity.	Efficiency requires schedule adherence and meeting delivery dates.
Value is added when an item is produced.	Value is added when an item is sold.

Section summary

The concept of **throughput accounting (TA)** has been developed from TOC as an alternative system of cost and management accounting in a JIT environment.

TA is based on three concepts.

- In the short run, most costs in the factory (with the exception of materials costs) are fixed.
- The ideal inventory level is zero.
- Profitability is determined by the rate at which sales are made.

The TA philosophy entails the identification and elimination of **bottleneck resources**.

Throughput measures include **return per time period, return per time period on the bottleneck resource** and the **TA ratio.**

16 Business process re-engineering (BPR)

Introduction

Business process re-engineering looks at how processes can be redesigned to improve efficiency. Note the link between all these techniques – they are all focused on **improvements**.

16.1 An overview of BPR

Business process re-engineering (BPR) **can** lead to fundamental changes in the way an organisation functions. In particular, it has been realised that processes which were developed in a paper-intensive processing environment may not be suitable for an environment that is underpinned by IT.

KEY TERM

BUSINESS PROCESS RE-ENGINEERING (BPR) is the fundamental rethinking and radical redesign of business processes to achieve dramatic improvements in critical contemporary measures of performance, such as cost, quality, service and speed.   (Hammer and Champy, *Reengineering the Corporation*, 1993)

The key words here are **fundamental, radical, dramatic** and **process**.

(a) **Fundamental** and **radical** indicate that BPR is somewhat akin to zero base budgeting: it starts by asking basic questions such as 'why do we do what we do', without making any assumptions or looking back to what has always been done in the past.

(b)   **Dramatic** means that BPR should achieve 'quantum leaps in performance', not just marginal, incremental improvements.

(c)   **Process**. BPR recognises that there is a need to change functional hierarchies.

A PROCESS is a collection of activities that takes one or more kinds of input and creates an output.

For example, order fulfilment is a process that takes an order as its input and results in the delivery of the ordered goods. Part of this process is the manufacture of the goods, but under **BPR** the **aim** of **manufacturing** is **not merely to make** the goods. Manufacturing should aim to **deliver the goods that were ordered**, and any aspect of the manufacturing process that hinders this aim should be re-engineered. The first question to ask might be 'Do they need to be manufactured at all?'.

A **re-engineered process** has certain **characteristics**.

(a)   Often several jobs are **combined** into one.

(b)   Workers often **make decisions**.

(c)   The **steps** in the process are performed in **a logical order**.

(d)   **Work** is performed where it **makes most sense**.

(e)   Checks and controls may be reduced, and **quality 'built in'**.

(f)   One manager provides a **single point of contact**.

(g)   The advantages of **centralised and decentralised** operations are combined.

Based on a problem at a **major car manufacturer**.

A company employs 25 staff to perform the standard accounting task of matching goods received notes with orders and then with invoices. About 80% of their time is spent trying to find out why 20% of the set of three documents do not agree.

One way of improving the situation would have been to computerise the existing process to facilitate matching. This would have helped, but BPR went further: why accept any incorrect orders at all? What if all the orders are entered onto a computerised database? When goods arrive at the goods inwards department they either agree to goods that have been ordered or they don't. It's as simple as that. Goods that agree to an order are accepted and paid for. Goods that are not agreed are sent back to the supplier. There are no files of unmatched items and time is not wasted trying to sort out these files.

The re-engineering of the process resulted in gains for the company: less staff time wasted, quicker payment for suppliers, lower inventory and lower investment in working capital.

16.2 Principles of BPR

Seven principles of BPR (Hammer)

(a)   Processes should be designed to achieve a desired **outcome rather than** focusing on existing **tasks**.

(b)   **Personnel who use** the **output** from a process should **perform the process**. For example, a company could set up a database of approved suppliers; this would allow personnel who actually require supplies to order them themselves, perhaps using online technology, thereby eliminating the need for a separate purchasing function.

(c)   **Information processing** should be **included in the work which produces the information**. This eliminates the differentiation between information gathering and information processing.

(d)   **Geographically dispersed resources** should be **treated** as if they are **centralised**. This allows the benefits of centralisation to be obtained; for example, economies of scale through central negotiation of supply contracts, without losing the benefits of decentralisation, such as flexibility and responsiveness.

(e)   **Parallel activities** should be **linked rather than integrated**. This would involve, for example, co-ordination between teams working on different aspects of a single process.

(f)   **'Doers'** should be allowed to be **self-managing**. The traditional **distinction** between **workers** and **managers** can be **abolished**: decision aids such as expert systems can be provided where they are required.

(g)   **Information** should be **captured once** at **source**. Electronic distribution of information makes this possible.

16.2.1 Examples of BPR

(a)   A move from a traditional functional plant layout to a JIT cellular product layout is a simple example.

(b)   **Elimination of non value added activities**. Consider a materials handling process which incorporates scheduling production, storing materials, processing purchase orders, inspecting materials and paying suppliers.

This process could be re-engineered by sending the production schedule direct to nominated suppliers with whom contracts are set up to ensure that materials are delivered in accordance with the production schedule and that their quality is guaranteed (by supplier inspection before delivery). Such re-engineering should result in the elimination or permanent reduction of the non value added activities of storing, purchasing and inspection.

Section summary

Business process re-engineering involves focusing attention inwards to consider how business processes can be redesigned or re-engineered to improve efficiency.

Chapter Summary

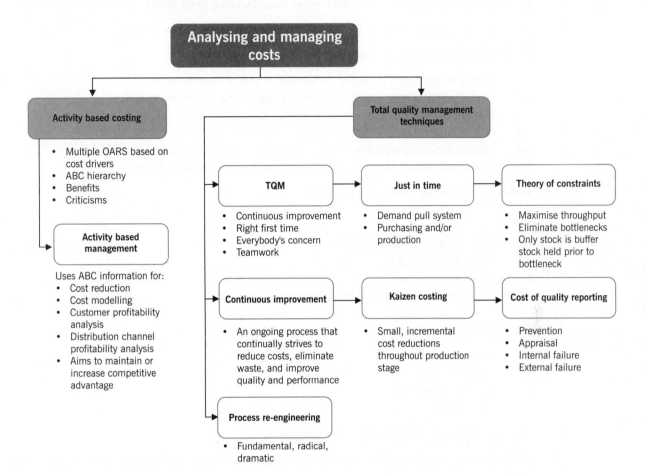

Analysing and managing costs

Activity based costing

- Multiple OARS based on cost drivers
- ABC hierarchy
- Benefits
- Criticisms

Activity based management

Uses ABC information for:
- Cost reduction
- Cost modelling
- Customer profitability analysis
- Distribution channel profitability analysis
- Aims to maintain or increase competitive advantage

Total quality management techniques

TQM

- Continuous improvement
- Right first time
- Everybody's concern
- Teamwork

Just in time

- Demand pull system
- Purchasing and/or production

Theory of constraints

- Maximise throughput
- Eliminate bottlenecks
- Only stock is buffer stock held prior to bottleneck

Continuous improvement

- An ongoing process that continually strives to reduce costs, eliminate waste, and improve quality and performance

Kaizen costing

- Small, incremental cost reductions throughout production stage

Cost of quality reporting

- Prevention
- Appraisal
- Internal failure
- External failure

Process re-engineering

- Fundamental, radical, dramatic

Quick Quiz

1   What four key words/phrases describe modern manufacturing philosophy?

2   The cost of inspecting a product for quality is a value-added cost. True or false?

3   Which of the following is/are correct?

   (a)   Cost of conformance = cost of prevention + cost of internal failure
   (b)   Cost of conformance = cost of internal failure + cost of external failure
   (c)   Cost of non-conformance = cost of internal failure + cost of external failure
   (d)   Cost of conformance = cost of appraisal + cost of prevention
   (e)   Cost of non-conformance = cost of prevention + cost of appraisal
   (f)   Cost of non-conformance = cost of appraisal + cost of external failure

4   Match the cost to the correct cost category.

Costs

   (a)   Administration of quality control
   (b)   Product liability costs
   (c)   Acceptance testing
   (d)   Losses due to lower selling prices for sub-quality goods

Cost categories

   •   Prevention costs
   •   Appraisal costs
   •   Internal failure costs
   •   External failure costs

5   Choose the appropriate words from those highlighted.

JIT purchasing requires **small, frequent/large, infrequent** deliveries **well in advance of/as near as possible to** the time the raw materials and parts are needed.

In a JIT environment, the responsibility for the quality of goods lies with the **supplier/purchaser**.

6   Fill in the blanks in the statements below, using the words in the box. Some words may be used twice.

   (a)   The theory of constraints is an approach to production management which aims to maximise (1)............. less (2)......... . It focuses on factors such as (3)................ which act as (4).....................

   (b)   Throughput contribution = (5)............. minus (6) ....

   (c)   TA ratio = (7) .... per factory hour ÷ (8) ....per factory hour

     •   bottlenecks
     •   material costs
     •   sales revenue
     •   throughput contribution
     •   constraints
     •   conversion cost

7   Put a tick in the boxes of those statements that relate to Kaizen costing, and a cross for statements about standard costing.

☐   Employees are often viewed as the cause of problems.

☐   Costs are reduced by implementing continuous improvement.

☐   The aim is to meet cost performance targets.

☐   The aim is to achieve cost reduction targets.

☐   It is assumed that current manufacturing conditions remain unchanged.

8   Continuous improvement organisations never engage in radical change. True or false?

9   Fill in the right-hand side of the table below, which looks at the differences between throughput accounting and traditional product costing.

Traditional product costing	Throughput accounting
Labour costs and 'traditional' variable overheads are treated as variable costs.	
Inventory is valued in the income statement and balance sheet at total production cost.	
Variance analysis is employed to determine whether standards were achieved.	
Efficiency is based on labour and machines working to full capacity.	
Value is added when an item is produced.	

10   BPR can be likened to continuous budgeting. True or false?

11   On the axes below, sketch and label correctly a Pareto curve to demonstrate a situation where 75% of an organisation's profit is derived from 25% of its retail outlets.

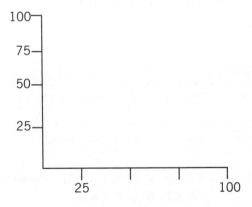

12   A wholesaler has estimated that its store space cost is $1.00 per cubic metre per day.

Its product range includes the following products.

(a)   Six-packs of fizzy pop – volume: 0.02 cubic metres, days in store: 5
(b)   Bleach – volume: 0.01 cubic metres, days in store: 4
(c)   Packs of toilet rolls – volume: 0.37 cubic metres, days in store: 3.

State how space costs would be allocated to the products using direct product profitability.

Answers to Quick Quiz

1   (a)   Smooth, steady production flow (throughput)
    (b)   Flexibility
    (c)   Volume versus variety
    (d)   JIT

2   False

3   (c) and (d) are correct.

4   (a)   Prevention costs
    (b)   External failure costs
    (c)   Appraisal costs
    (d)   Internal failure costs

5   small, frequent
    as near as possible to
    supplier

6   1   sales revenue
    2   material costs
    3   bottlenecks
    4   constraints
    5   sales revenue
    6   material costs
    7   throughput contribution
    8   conversion cost

7   ✗   Employees are often viewed as the cause of problems.

    ✓   Costs are reduced by implementing continuous improvement.

    ✗   The aim is to meet cost performance targets.

    ✓   The aim is to achieve cost reduction targets.

    ✗   It is assumed that current manufacturing conditions remain unchanged.

8   False. Quantum leaps in performance can occur.

9

Traditional product costing	Throughput accounting
Labour costs and 'traditional' variable overheads are treated as variable costs.	They are not normally treated as variable costs.
Inventory is valued in the income statement and balance sheet at total production cost.	It is valued at material cost only.
Variance analysis is employed to determine whether standards were achieved.	It is used to determine why the planned product mix was not produced.
Efficiency is based on labour and machines working to full capacity.	Efficiency requires schedule adherence and meeting delivery dates.
Value is added when an item is produced.	It is added when an item is sold.

10   False. It is somewhat akin to ZBB.

11

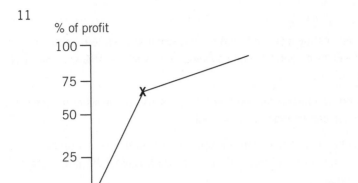

12 The space costs would be allocated as follows.

Fizzy pop $1.00 × 0.02 × 5 = $0.1 per pack

Bleach $1.00 × 0.01 × 4 = $0.04 per pack

Packs of toilet rolls $1.00 × 0.37 × 3 = $1.11 per pack

The results show the need to achieve a high turnover with bulky low price goods such as toilet paper. Refrigerated items would carry a higher space cost due to the cost of refrigeration.

 # Answers to Questions

1.1 Using ABC

(a) Here are our suggestions.

(i) Production overheads are a high proportion of total production costs.
(ii) The product range is wide and diverse.
(iii) The amounts of overhead resources used by products varies.
(iv) Volume is not the primary driver of overhead resource consumption.

(b) **Reasons for suitability**

(i) Most modern organisations tend to have a **high level of overhead costs**, especially relating to **support services** such as maintenance and data processing. ABC, by the use of carefully chosen cost drivers, traces these overheads to product lines in a more logical and less arbitrary manner than traditional absorption costing.

(ii) The determination and use of cost drivers helps to measure and improve the **efficiency and effectiveness of support departments**.

(iii) Many costs included in general overheads can actually be traced to specific product lines using ABC. This **improves product costing** and **cost management** because the costs are made the responsibility of the line manager.

(iv) ABC forces the organisation to ask such searching questions as 'What causes the demand for the activity?', 'What does the department achieve?', and 'Does it add value?'.

(v) ABC systems may **encourage reductions** in throughput time and inventory and improvements in quality.

Unsuitable situations

(i) A number of businesses have recently been split into several **small autonomous sections**. In this situation there may be no need for a sophisticated costing system such as ABC because staff should be aware of cost behaviour.

(ii) ABC can **work against modern manufacturing methods** such as JIT. JIT seeks to reduce set-up time so that very small batches can be made economically.

(iii) The aim of set-up time reduction is to allow more set-ups, not just to reduce set-up costs. The use of a cost driver based on the number of set-ups will therefore **work against JIT principles** as it will tend to encourage larger batches.

1.2 ABC and retail organisations

Activities	Possible cost driver
Procure goods	Number of orders
Receive goods	Number of orders or pallets
Store goods	Volume of goods
Pick goods	Number of packs
Handle returnables/recyclables	Volume of goods

1.3 Classification of activities

The correct answer is options (a), (b) and (e). Options (c) and (d) would be **product level** activities. The level of **internal** support cost would be driven by the degree of **variety** between different products, not by production volume. If item (iii) refers to **external** technical support, this cost would most probably be driven by the fact that the product is too complicated for its market or the instructions provided (product packaging) are inadequate.

1.4 CPA

	P $'000	Q $'000	R $'000
Gross margin	897.00	1,070.00	1,056.00
Less: Customer specific costs			
Sales visits (80/50/100 × $420)	(33.60)	(21.00)	(42.00)
Order processing (300/320/480 × $190)	(57.00)	(60.80)	(91.20)
Despatch costs (300/320/480 × $350)	(105.00)	(112.00)	(168.00)
Billing and collections (310/390/1,050 × $97)	(30.07)	(37.83)	(101.85)
	671.33	838.37	652.95
Ranking	2	1	3

1.5 Profitable customers

The correct answer is Narayan.

It can be shown that Seth earns more from supplying Narayan, despite the larger discount percentage.

	Kipling $	Narayan $
Revenue	25,000	21,000
Less discount	2,500	3,150
Net revenue	22,500	17,850
Less: cost of shoes	(12,500)	(10,500)
customer transport cost	(5,000)	–
customer administration cost	(250)	(500)
Net gain	4,750	6,850

The difference on a unit basis is considerable.

Number of pairs of shoes sold	500	420
Net gain per pair of shoes sold	$9.50	$16.31
Net gain per $1 of sales revenue	$0.19	$0.33

1.6 CPA and competitive advantage

By **focusing on the way in which costs are allocated to customers** rather than to the products and services sold, CPA attempts to provide answers to the following types of question.

(a) What profit or contribution is the organisation making on sales to the customer, after taking account of all costs which can be specifically identified with the customer?

(b) What would be the financial consequences of losing the customer?

(c) Is the customer buying in order sizes that are unprofitable to supply?

(d) What is the return on investment on any plant that is used specifically for this customer?

(e) Is any inventory held specifically for this customer and what period of credit do they require?

(f) Are there any other specific costs involved in supplying this customer, such as technical and test facilities, R&D facilities, dedicated sales or administrative staff?

(g) What is the ratio of the customer's net contribution to the investment made on the customer's behalf?

The technique **enhances an organisation's competitive advantage** because it considers the profits generated by customers and **allows the organisation to focus its efforts on those customers who promise the highest profit**. The organisation is also in a better position to **rationalise its approach** to customers who demonstrate a low potential for generating profit.

1.7 Quality

A wide variety of answers is possible. The article goes on to explain how the bank is actually going about monitoring the impact of the initiative.

(a) It has devised a 100 point scale showing average satisfaction with branch service.

(b) It conducts a 'first impressions' survey of all new customers.

(c) There is also a general survey carried out every 6 months which seeks the views of a weighted sample of 350 customers per branch.

(d) A survey company telephones each branch anonymously twice a month to test how staff respond to enquiries about products.

(e) One-quarter of each branch's staff answer a monthly questionnaire about the bank's products to test their knowledge.

(f) Groups of employees working in teams in branches are allowed to set their own additional standards. This is to encourage participation.

(g) Branches that underperform are more closely watched by 24 managers who monitor the initiative.

1.8 Ignoring quality issues

In an economic downturn companies are **anxious to hold onto existing business** and perhaps secure new business from competitors. **Quality** becomes even **more important** as it is very much a **customer's market** – if customers are not happy with any aspect of the product or service they can go elsewhere.

Although maintaining and improving quality is expensive, it should be seen as an **investment** in the company's long-term future. If companies lose contracts due to reductions in quality their reputation will be damaged (particularly if they were previously known for excellent quality). Ultimately they could go out of business altogether.

1.9 Quality costs

(a) **Failure of the current accounting system to highlight the cost of quality**

Traditionally, **the costs of scrapped units, wasted materials and reworking** have been **subsumed within the costs of production** by assigning the costs of an expected level of loss (a normal loss) to the costs of good production, while accounting for **other costs of poor quality** within **production or marketing overheads**. Such costs are therefore not only considered as **inevitable** but are not **highlighted** for management attention. Moreover, traditional accounting reports tend to **ignore the hidden but real costs of excessive inventory levels** (held to enable faulty material to be replaced without hindering production) and the facilities necessary for storing that **inventory**.

(b) **Explicit costs of quality**

There are four recognised categories of cost identifiable within an accounting system which make up the cost of quality.

(1) **Prevention costs** are the costs of any action taken to investigate, prevent or reduce the production of faulty output. Included within this category are the costs of training in quality control and the cost of the design/development and maintenance of quality control and inspection equipment.

(2) **Appraisal costs** are the costs of assessing the actual quality achieved. Examples include the cost of the inspection of goods delivered and the cost of inspecting production during the manufacturing process.

(3) **Internal failure costs** are the costs incurred by the organisation when production fails to meet the level of quality required. Such costs include losses due to lower selling prices for sub-quality goods, the costs of reviewing product specifications after failures and losses arising from the failure of purchased items.

(4) **External failure costs** are the costs which arise outside the organisation (after the customer has received the product) due to failure to achieve the required level of quality. Included within this category are the costs of repairing products returned from customers, the cost of providing replacement items due to sub-standard products or marketing errors and the costs of a customer service department.

(c) **Quality costs not identified by the accounting system**

Quality costs which are not identified by the accounting system tend to be of two forms.

(1) Opportunity costs such as the loss of future sales to a customer dissatisfied with faulty goods

(2)   Costs which tend to be subsumed within other account headings such as those costs which result from the disruption caused by stockouts due to faulty purchases

1.10 Non value added activities

The correct answer is:

Parts received	Machined parts assembled
~~Parts quality inspected~~	~~Finished product inspected and tested~~
~~Parts stored in warehouse~~	~~Finished goods passed to despatch department~~
~~Parts moved to machine room~~	Finished goods packaged
Parts machined	~~Packed goods moved back to warehouse~~
~~Machined parts inspected~~	~~Packed goods stored~~
~~Machined parts moved to assembly area~~	Packed goods despatched to customer

Comment

The JIT approach has 5 value-added activities, compared with 14 activities under the traditional approach – 9 non value added activities have been eliminated.

Receipt of parts, their machining, assembly, packaging and despatch to the customer are essential activities that increase the saleability of the product.

Solo needs to negotiate with its suppliers to guarantee the delivery of high-quality parts to eliminate the need for quality inspection on arrival.

Storage and movement of parts, work in progress and finished goods do not add value; rather they introduce unnecessary delays. The machining, assembly and packaging areas should be in close proximity to avoid excessive movement, and ordering and processing should be scheduled so that there is no need to store parts before they go into production. Similarly, production should be scheduled to finish goods just as they are needed for despatch to avoid storage of finished goods.

Proper maintenance of machinery and good staff training in quality production procedures should ensure finished goods of a consistently high quality, removing the need for inspection and testing.

Thus the JIT approach eliminates all wastage of time in the storage of goods, unnecessary movement of goods and all quality checks, resulting in one continuous string of value-added activities.

1.11 Value-added activity

The correct answer is C. The other activities are non value adding activities.

1.12 JIT

(a)   **Cost reduction**. Toyota was losing money, and market demand was weak, preventing price rises. The only way to move from losses into profits was to cut costs, and cost reduction was probably essential for the survival of the company.

(b)   **Production levelling**. Production levelling should help to minimise idle time whilst at the same time allowing the company to achieve its objective of minimum inventories.

(c)   The **change in factory layout** was to improve the work flow and eliminate the waste of moving items around the work floor from one set of machines to another. Each cell contained all the machines required to complete production, thus eliminating unnecessary materials movements.

(d)   With having **cells of different machines**, workers in each work cell would have to be trained to use each different machine, whereas previously they would have specialised in just one type of machine.

(e)   A **change of culture** was needed to overcome the industrial problems of the company. Employee involvement would have been an element in this change. Teamwork would have helped with the elimination of waste: mistakes or delays by one member of a team would be corrected or dealt with by others in the team. The workforce moved from a sense of individual responsibility/blame to collective responsibility.

(f)   The **Kanban system** is a 'pull' system of production scheduling. Items are only produced when they are needed. If a part is faulty when it is produced, the production line will be held up until the fault is corrected. For a Kanban system to work properly, defects must therefore be eliminated.

1.13 JIT manufacturing environment

The correct answer is: 1, 2, 3 and 4.

1.14 TA vs conventional cost accounting

Conventional cost accounting	Throughput accounting
Inventory is an asset.	Inventory is **not** an asset. It is a result of unsynchronised manufacturing and is a barrier to making profit.
Costs can be classified either as direct or as indirect.	Such classifications are no longer useful.
Product profitability can be determined by deducting a product cost from selling price.	Profitability is determined by the rate at which money is earned.
Profit is a function of costs.	Profit is a function of throughput as well as costs.

1.15 Performance measurement in throughput accounting

(a)   Total profit per day
$$= \text{Throughput contribution} - \text{Conversion costs}$$
$$= (3{,}600 \times (100 - 40) - 144{,}000)$$
$$= \$72{,}000$$

(b)   Return per factory hour
$$= \frac{\text{Sales} - \text{direct material costs}}{\text{Usage of bottleneck resource in hours (factory hours)}}$$
$$= \frac{100 - 40}{1/500}$$
$$= \$30{,}000$$

(c)   Throughput accounting ratio
$$= \frac{\text{Return per factory hour}}{\text{Total conversion cost per factory hour}}$$
$$= \frac{30{,}000}{144{,}000/8}$$
$$= 1.67$$

1.16 Product costing vs TA

1   Inventory is valued at material cost only (ie variable cost).
2   Only direct material is treated as a variable cost.
3   Effectiveness is measured in terms of schedule adherence and meeting delivery dates.
4   Value is added when an item is sold.

Now try the question from the Practice Question Bank

Number	Marks	Time
Q2 Objective test questions	10	18 mins
Q3 ABC	10	18 mins
Q4 ABC systems	10	18 mins
Q5 Abkaber plc	30	54 mins
Q6 CPA	18	10 mins
Q7 Just-in-time	25	45 mins

TECHNIQUES FOR ENHANCING LONG-TERM PROFITS

 This chapter looks at techniques for deriving competitive advantage and enhancing long-term profits. The syllabus specifically mentions target costing, value analysis and the value chain.

Target costing (Section 1) aims to control and manage costs of production at the product design stage, rather than when production starts.

Value analysis (Section 2) looks at how a product can be produced (or a service delivered) more economically without reducing its value to the customer or user.

Functional analysis (Section 3) uses the functions of a product as the basis for cost management purposes.

Section 4 looks at the **value chain**. This is the sequence of business activities which add value to products or services.

Supply chain management, outsourcing, and gain-sharing arrangements are covered in Sections 5 to 7.

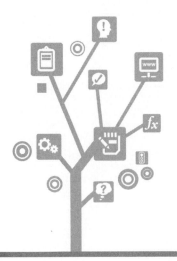

topic list	learning outcomes	syllabus references	ability required
1 Target costing	A1(c)	A1(c)(i)	analysis
2 Value analysis	A1(c)	A1(ii)	analysis
3 Functional analysis	A1(c)	A1(c)(ii)	analysis
4 The value chain	A1(c)	A1(c)(iii)	analysis
5 Supply chain management	A1(c)	A1(c)(iii)	analysis
6 Outsourcing	A1(c)	A1(c)(iii)	analysis
7 Partnering, incentives and gain-sharing arrangements	A1(c)	A1(c)(iii)	analysis

Chapter Overview

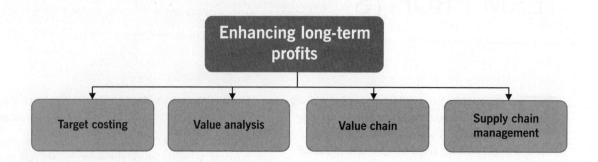

1   Target costing

Introduction

The cost planning technique, target costing, is the focus of this section. Target costing works in the opposite way to normal methods of pricing, by setting a selling price and then working backwards to find the target cost.

1.1 The importance of product design

In order to compete effectively in today's competitive market, organisations need to **redesign their products continually**, with the result that **product life cycles** have become much **shorter**. The **planning, design and development stages of a product's cycle** are therefore **critical to an organisation's cost management process**. Cost reduction at this stage of a product's life cycle, rather than during the production process, is one of the most important ways of reducing product cost.

CASE STUDY

General Motors estimates that 70% of the cost of manufacturing truck transmissions is determined in the design stage. Estimates for other companies and products often exceed 80%.

1.1.1 Factors that build in costs at the design stage

(a)   **The number of different components.** Production time increases as the number increases.

(b)   **Whether the components are standard or not.** Standard components are reliable and reduce inventory and handling costs.

(c)   **The number of extra features** (included as a standard or paid for separately).

(d)   **Type of packaging.** The aim is to protect the product and minimise handling costs by not breaking pallets or cases during distribution.

1.2 What is target costing?

Japanese companies developed **target costing** as a response to the problem of managing **costs over the product life cycle**.

KEY TERM

'TARGET COSTING is an activity which is aimed at reducing the life-cycle costs of new products, while ensuring quality, reliability, and other consumer requirements, by examining all possible ideas for cost reduction at the product planning, research and development, and the prototyping phases of production. But it is not just a cost reduction technique; it is part of a comprehensive strategic profit management system.'   (Kato, 1993)

CASE STUDY

When Toyota developed the Lexus to compete with BMW, Mercedes and Jaguar, it employed two basic concepts: reverse engineering and target costing. In essence, it sought to produce a car with BMW 7-series attributes at a BMW 5-series price. Cost was the dominant design parameter that shaped the development of the Lexus, as it was later with Nissan's Infiniti.

The response from Mercedes Benz, one of the competitors which lost market share through this strategy, was to acknowledge that its cars were over-engineered and too expensive and to change its product development process to determine target product costs from competitive market prices.

Target costing requires managers to think differently about the relationship between cost, price and profit.

(a)   The **traditional approach** is to **develop a product, determine the expected standard production cost** of that product and **then set a selling price** (probably based on cost) with a resulting profit or loss. Costs are controlled through monthly variance analysis.

BPP
LEARNING MEDIA

(b)   The **target costing approach** is to develop a **product concept** and the primary specifications for performance and design and then to **determine the price customers would be willing to pay** for that concept. The **desired profit margin is deducted from the price, leaving a figure that represents total cost**. This is the target cost and the product must be capable of being produced for this amount, otherwise the product will not be manufactured. **During the product's life the target cost will constantly be reduced** so that the **price can fall. Continuous cost reduction techniques** must therefore be employed.

TARGET COST is 'A product cost estimate derived by subtracting a desired profit margin from a competitive market price.'   (*CIMA Official Terminology*)

Because it **encourages cost consciousness** and **focuses on profit margins**, target costing is a **useful tool for strengthening an organisation's competitive position**.

1.3 Setting the target price

Products that are **varieties of existing products** or **new brands of existing products** enter an already established market and therefore a competitive **price should be fairly easy to set**. There is no existing market price for **new products**, however, and so **market research** will probably be used to assist in price setting. Many Japanese companies use **functional analysis** and **pricing by function** in such circumstances. We cover functional analysis in Section 3 of this chapter.

Selling price will also be **affected by factors such as the stage in the product life cycle, expected sales volume and the price charged by rivals** in the market.

1.4 Setting the target profit requirement

This should **not be simply a standard mark-up** but instead should be **based on strategic profit plans**. Procedures used to derive the target profit must be agreed by all staff responsible for achieving it and it must be seen as something more than just an expectation. In this way **staff will both accept responsibility for achieving it** and **be committed to achieving it**.

1.5 The target costing process

Analyse the external environment to ascertain what customers require and what competitors are producing. Determine the **product concept**, the **price** customers will be willing to pay and thus the **target cost**.

Split the total target cost into broad cost categories, such as development, marketing, manufacturing and so on. **Then split up the manufacturing target cost per unit across the different functional areas of the product. Design the product so that each functional product area can be made within the target cost.** If a functional product area cannot be made within the target cost, the targets for the other areas must be reduced, or the product redesigned or scrapped. The product should be developed in an atmosphere of **continuous improvement** using **value engineering techniques** (see Section 2 of this chapter) and **close collaboration with suppliers** to enhance the product (in terms of service, quality, durability and so on) and reduce costs.

Once it is decided that it is feasible to meet the total target cost, **detailed cost sheets** will be prepared and **processes formalised**.

It is possible that management may decide to go ahead and manufacture a product whose target cost is well below the currently attainable cost, determined by current technology and processes. If this is the case, management will **set benchmarks for improvement** towards the target costs, by specified dates.

Options available to reduce costs:

(a)   **Training** staff in more efficient techniques
(b)   Using **cheaper staff**
(c)   Acquiring new, more **efficient technology**
(d)   Cutting out **non value added activities**

Even if the product can be produced within the target cost, the story does not end there. **Once the product goes into production, target costs will gradually be reduced.** These reductions will be incorporated into the budgeting process. This means that cost savings must be actively sought and made continuously. Value analysis will be used to reduce costs if and when targets are missed. Value analysis is covered in Section 2 of this chapter.

1.5.1 Cost tables

Cost tables are useful value engineering tools. They are **high volume, computerised databases of detailed cost information based on various manufacturing variables**. They are a source of information about the effect on product costs of using different resources, production methods, designs and so on.

CASE STUDY

Swedish retailer IKEA continues to dominate the home furniture market.. The 'IKEA concept', as defined on the company website www.ikea.com, is 'based on offering a wide range of well-designed functional home furnishing products at prices so low as many people as possible will be able to afford them'.

IKEA is widely known for pricing products at 30–50% below the price charged by competitors. Extracts from the website outline how the company has successfully employed a strategy of target pricing:

'While most retailers use design to justify a higher price, IKEA designers work in exactly the opposite way. Instead they use design to secure the lowest possible price. IKEA designers design every IKEA product starting with a functional need and a price. Then they use their vast knowledge of innovative, low-cost manufacturing processes to create functional products, often co-ordinated in style. Then large volumes are purchased to push prices down even further.

Most IKEA products are also designed to be transported in flat packs and assembled at the customer's home. This lowers the price by minimising transportation and storage costs. In this way, the IKEA concept uses design to ensure that IKEA products can be purchased and enjoyed by as many people as possible.'

1.6 The target cost gap

When a product is first planned, its estimated cost will often be higher than its target cost. The aim of target costing is then to find ways of closing this target cost gap, and producing and selling the product at the target cost.

The **target cost gap** is the estimated cost less the target cost. Increasing the selling price **will not** close the cost gap. In a system of target costing, **the total target cost is split into broad cost categories**, such as development, marketing and manufacturing. **Then the manufacturing target cost per unit is split up across the different functional areas of the product. The product is designed so that each functional product area can be made within the target cost.** If a functional product area cannot be made within the target cost, so that a **cost gap** exists between the currently achievable cost and the target cost, the targets for the other areas must be reduced, or the product redesigned or scrapped. The product should be developed in an atmosphere of **continuous improvement** using **value engineering techniques** and **close collaboration with suppliers** to enhance the product (in terms of service, quality, durability and so on) and reduce costs.

Management can then set **benchmarks for improvement** towards the target cost, by improving production technologies and processes. Various techniques can be employed.

•   Reducing the **number of components**
•   Using **cheaper staff**

- Using **standard components** wherever possible
- Acquiring new, more efficient **technology**
- **Training** staff in more efficient techniques
- Cutting out **non value added activities**
- Using **different materials** (identified using **activity analysis** etc)

However, as stated earlier, the most effective time to eliminate unnecessary cost and reduce the expected cost to the target cost level is during the product design and development phase, not after 'live' production has begun.

1.7 Target costing support systems

Target costing cannot operate in isolation. **Information** to enable it to operate successfully is needed from a wide range of support systems.

(a) **Sales pricing support systems**, which can, for example, break down product functions into sub-functions and provide information on that basis, and can convert the value placed on each function into a price

(b) **Target profit computation support systems**, which can, for example, calculate the optimal product mix in the future (product portfolio planning system)

(c) **Research and development support systems**, which include computer-aided design and computer-aided engineering

(d) Support systems for **infusing target costs** into products, which include **value engineering** and **variety reduction**

(e) **Human resource management systems**, which are particularly important when an organisation uses target costing for the first time

1.8 Target costing versus standard costing

You should have covered standard costing in your earlier studies.

	Standard costing	Target costing
How costs are controlled	Costs must be kept within predetermined standard costs. Variances are calculated to check that this has happened.	There is no cost slashing but continual pressure to ensure costs are kept to a minimum.
Relationship between product concept, cost and price	Predetermined product design ↓ Cost ↓ Price	Product design concept ↓ Selling price ↓ Target cost ↑ Profit margin
Link with strategic plans	None. The approach is short-term cost control through variance analysis.	The product concept and target profit margin take into account medium-term strategic plans.
Time frame for cost control	Standards are usually revised annually.	Continual cost reduction. Target costs are revised monthly.

1.9 Possible adverse effects of target costing

(a) Longer product development times because of numerous changes to designs and costings

(b) Employee demotivation because of pressure to meet targets

(c)   Organisational conflict between designers who try to reduce costs and marketing staff who give away promotional items costing even more

| Question 2.1 | | Standard costing vs target costing |

Learning outcomes A1(c)

Fill in the blank spaces ((a) to (d)) in the table below to show how standard costing and target costing differ.

Stage in product life cycle	Standard costing approach	Target costing approach
Product concept stage	No action	(a)
Design stage	(b)	Keep costs to a minimum
Production stage	Costs are controlled using variance analysis	(c)
Remainder of life	(d)	Target cost reduced, perhaps monthly

Section summary

Target costing is a proactive cost control system. The target cost is calculated by deducting the target profit from a predetermined selling price based on customers' views. Functional analysis, value engineering and value analysis (covered in the next two sections) are used to change production methods and/or reduce expected costs so that the target cost is met.

2   Value analysis

Introduction

Value analysis embraces many of the techniques already mentioned in this Study Text. It looks at trying to reduce costs without reducing the value to the customer.

2.1 What is value analysis?

KEY TERMS

VALUE ANALYSIS is 'A systematic inter-disciplinary examination of factors affecting the cost of a product or service, in order to devise means of achieving the specified purpose most economically at the required standard of quality and reliability'.   (*CIMA Official Terminology*)

The **value of the product must therefore be kept the same or else improved, at a reduced cost.**

VALUE ENGINEERING is 'Redesign of an activity, product or service so that value to the customer is enhanced while costs are reduced (or at least increase by less than the resulting price increase)'.

(*CIMA Official Terminology*)

The distinction between value engineering and value analysis is not clear cut but, in general, **value engineering is cost avoidance or cost prevention before production**, whereas **value analysis is cost reduction during production**.

2.2 What is different about value analysis?

There are two features of value analysis that distinguish it from other approaches to cost reduction.

(a)   It **encourages innovation** and a more radical outlook for ways of reducing costs because ideas for cost reduction are **not constrained by the existing product design**.

(b)   It **recognises the various types of value** which a product or service provides, **analyses** this value, and then **seeks ways of improving** or maintaining aspects of this value, but at a lower cost.

Conventional cost reduction techniques try to achieve the lowest production costs for a specific product design, whereas value analysis tries to find the least-cost method of making a product that achieves its desired function, not the least-cost method of accomplishing a product design to a mandatory and detailed specification.

2.3 Value

KEY TERMS

- COST VALUE is the cost of producing and selling an item.
- EXCHANGE VALUE is the market value of the product or service.
- USE VALUE is what the article does; the purposes it fulfils.
- ESTEEM VALUE is the prestige the customer attaches to the product.

(a)   Value analysis seeks to **reduce** unit costs, and so cost value is the one aspect of value to be reduced.

(b)   Value analysis attempts to provide the same (or a better) use value at the lowest cost. **Use value** therefore involves considerations of the **performance and reliability** of the product or service.

(c)   Value analysis attempts to maintain or enhance the **esteem value** of a product at the lowest cost.

Question 2.2   Value

Learning outcomes A1(c)

Below are three features of a product.

(a)   The product can be sold for £27.50.
(b)   The product is available in six colours to suit customers' tastes.
(c)   The product will last for at least ten years.

What are the correct classifications of the features using the types of value in the key terms above?

2.4 The scope of value analysis

Any commercial organisation should be continually seeking lower costs, better products and higher profits. These can be achieved in any of the following ways:

(a)   Cost elimination or cost prevention
(b)   Cost reduction
(c)   Improving product quality and so selling greater quantities at the same price as before
(d)   Improving product quality and so being able to increase the sales price

Value analysis can achieve all four of these objectives.

| Question 2.3 | Benefits of a VA programme |

Learning outcomes A1(c)

In addition to the above, what other benefits of a VA programme can you think of?

Three areas of special importance are as follows.

Area	Method
Product design	At the design stage, value analysis is called value engineering. The designer should be cost conscious and avoid unnecessary complications. Simple product design can avoid production and quality control problems, thereby resulting in lower costs.
Components and material costs	The purchasing department should beware of lapsing into habit with routine buying decisions. It has a crucial role to play in reducing costs and improving value by procuring the desired quality materials at the lowest possible price.
Production methods	These ought to be reviewed continually, on a product by product basis, especially with changing technology.

2.5 Carrying out a value analysis

2.5.1 Typical considerations in value analysis

(a) **Can a cheaper substitute material be found** which is as good, if not better, than the material currently used?

(b) **Can unnecessary weight or embellishments be removed** without reducing the product's attractions or desirability?

(c) **Is it possible to use standardised components** (or to make components to a particular standard), thereby reducing the variety of units used and produced? Variety reduction through standardisation facilitates longer production runs at lower unit costs.

(d) **Is it possible to reduce the number of components**, for example could a product be assembled safely with a smaller number of screws?

The origins of value analysis were in the engineering industry, but it **can be applied to services, or aspects of office work, or to management information systems** (for example the value of information, reports and so on).

2.5.2 The steps in value analysis

A value analysis study should be carried out by a team of experts, preferably with varying backgrounds, which blends experience, skill and imagination.

 Selecting a product or service for study. The product selected should be one which accounts for a high proportion of the organisation's costs, since the greatest cost savings should be obtainable from high cost areas. The choice should also take into account the stage of its 'life cycle' that it has reached. A product reaching the end of its marketable life is unlikely to offer scope for substantial savings.

 Obtaining and recording information. The questions to be asked include: What is the product or service supposed to do? Does it succeed? Are there alternative ways of making or providing it? What do these alternatives cost?

Analysing the information and evaluating the product. Each aspect of the product or service should now be analysed. Any cost reductions must be achieved without the loss of use or esteem value (or, at least, cost savings must exceed any loss in value suffered, and customers would then have to be compensated for the loss in use or esteem value in the form of a lower selling price). The types of questions asked in a value analysis include:

(a) Are all the parts necessary?
(b) Can the parts be obtained or made at a lower cost?
(c) Can standardised parts be used?
(d) Does the value provided by each feature justify its cost?

 Considering alternatives. From the analysis, a variety of options can be devised. This is the 'new ideas' stage of the study, and alternative options would mix ideas for eliminating unnecessary parts or features or standardising certain components or features.

 Selection of the least cost alternative. The costs (and other aspects of value) of each alternative should be compared.

 Recommendation. The preferred alternative should then be recommended to the decision makers for approval.

 Implementation and follow-up. Once a value analysis proposal is approved and accepted, its implementation must be properly planned and co-ordinated. The VA team should review the implementation and, where appropriate, improve the new product or method in the light of practical experience.

To be successful, **value analysis programmes must have the full backing of senior management.**

 Section summary

Value analysis is a planned, scientific approach to cost reduction which reviews the material composition of a product and production design so that modifications and improvements can be made which do not reduce the value of the product to the customer or to the user.

Value engineering is the application of value analysis techniques to new products.

Four aspects of value should be considered in value analysis (**cost value, exchange value, use value, esteem value**).

---

3 Functional analysis

 Introduction

Functional analysis is a cost management technique which has similarities with value analysis. This section looks at the basic steps involved in this technique and compares and contrasts the technique with value analysis.

3.1 Basic steps

KEY TERM

FUNCTIONAL ANALYSIS is 'An analysis of the relationships between product functions, their perceived value to the customer and their cost of provision'.

(CIMA Official Terminology)

The technique involves the following nine steps, some of which are similar to those required in value analysis.

 Choose the object of analysis (such as product, service or overhead area). If it is not a new product, **a high volume** product with a complex design and relatively large production costs is often an ideal candidate.

 Select members for the functional analysis team. The team will usually consist of six to eight members from a number of different departments (such as accounting, production, purchasing, engineering, design and marketing).

 Gather information. This will include information both from inside the organisation (detailed design, manufacturing and marketing information, for example) and from outside the organisation (such as information about new technologies).

 Define the functions of the object. The various functions of the product should be defined in terms of a verb and a noun. Functions should be classified as basic or secondary in terms of the importance of that particular function for the product.

 Draw a functional family tree. The functions identified in Step 4 should be arranged in a logical order in a family-tree diagram. A table illustrating the relationship between the functions and the parts of the product, as well as relevant existing costs, should also be drawn up. An extract for a propelling ballpoint pen is shown below.

Part number	Name of part	Function Verb	Function Noun	Cost $
5	ink	put	colour	0.03
9	clip	prevent	loss	0.02

 Evaluate the functions. The relative value of each function to a total target cost from the customers' point of view has to be estimated (either using market research or by each member of the team placing values and a consensus being reached for each function). This relative value provides a target cost for each function.

 Suggest alternatives and compare these with the target cost. Alternatives might include the use of new materials or parts or a different method of manufacturing the product.

 Choose the alternatives for manufacturing. The alternatives must be assessed and a final choice made of those to implement.

 Review the actual results. An audit or review of the changes implemented should be conducted promptly and the findings reported to senior management. This will prevent over-optimistic assessments of the functional analysis exercise and provide feedback so that future functional analysis can be improved.

3.2 Advantages

(a)   Competitive advantage resulting from improved, cost-effective design or redesign of products

(b)   Probably of most benefit during the planning and design stages of new products (because up to 90% of the costs of many products are committed by the end of the design stage)

(c)   Flexible application (has been applied to services, particular overhead areas, organisational restructuring and corporate strategy) because it views objects in abstract (service potential) terms rather than in physical (parts and people) terms

(d)   Information about product functions and about the views of customers is integrated into the formal reporting system

3.3 Comparison of value and functional analysis

The differences between the two techniques can be summarised as follows:

	Value analysis	Functional analysis
When used	During production	Prior to production
Focus on	Process to reduce cost	Customer value
Involves	Reducing cost without reducing value	Adding features to improve profits

Value analysis focuses on **cost reduction** through a **review of the processes** required to produce a product or service. **Functional analysis** focuses on the **value to the customer of each function** of the product or service and then makes a decision as to whether cost reduction is necessary.

Quality function deployment is the term given to a structured approach to defining customer needs or requirements and translating them into specific plans to produce products to meet those needs.

3.4 Functional analysis and ABC

An activity based costing (ABC) system will provide useful information about what drives specific overheads in the organisation. These **cost drivers** can then be used to **link overhead costs to individual functions or groups of functions** so that when a **function is changed**, a basis for ascertaining the **effect (if any) on the overheads** is available. ABC was explained in detail in Chapter 1.

Section summary

Functional analysis is concerned with improving profits by attempting to reduce costs and/or by improving products by adding new features in a cost-effective way that are so attractive to customers that profits actually increase.

4 The value chain

Introduction

This section focuses on the value chain which is a model of the activities of an organisation.

4.1 Basic concepts

According to Porter, the **activities of any organisation** can be divided into nine types and **analysed into a value chain**. This is a model of the activities (which procure inputs, process them and add value to them in some way, to generate outputs for customers) and the relationships between them.

KEY TERM

The VALUE CHAIN is 'The sequence of business activities by which, from the perspective of the end user, value is added to the products and services produced by an entry'.　　　*(CIMA Official Terminology)*

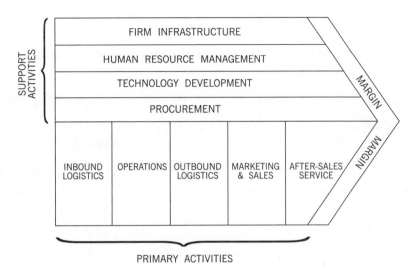

4.2 Activities

KEY TERM

ACTIVITIES are the means by which an organisation creates value in its products.

It is important to realise that **business activities are not the same as business functions**.

(a)   Functions are the familiar departments of an organisation (production, finance and so on). They reflect the formal organisation structure and the distribution of labour.

(b)   Activities are what actually goes on, and the work that is done. A single activity can be performed by a number of functions in sequence. Activities are the means by which an organisation creates value in its products (they are sometimes referred to as value activities). Activities incur costs and, in combination with other activities, provide a product or service that earns revenue.

For example, most organisations need to secure resources from the environment. This activity can be called procurement. However, procurement will involve more departments than just purchasing; the accounts department will certainly be involved and possibly production and quality assurance.

4.2.1 Primary activities

Primary activities are directly related to production, sales, marketing, delivery and service.

	Comment
Inbound logistics	Receiving, handling and storing inputs to the production system (warehousing, transport, inventory control and so on)
Operations	Converting resource inputs into a final product. Resource inputs are not only materials. 'People' are a 'resource', especially in service industries.
Outbound logistics	Storing the product and its distribution to customers (packaging, warehousing, testing and so on)
Marketing and sales	Informing customers about the product, persuading them to buy it, and enabling them to do so (advertising, promotion and so on)
After-sales service	Installing products, repairing them, upgrading them, providing spare parts and so on

4.2.2 Support activities

Support activities provide purchased inputs, human resources, technology and infrastructural functions to support the primary activities.

	Comment
Procurement	Acquiring the resource inputs to the primary activities (such as purchase of materials, subcomponents equipment)
Technology development	Designing products, improving processes and/or resource utilisation
Human resource management	Recruiting, training, developing and rewarding people
Firm infrastructure	Planning, finance, quality control (Porter believes they are crucially important to an organisation's strategic capability in all primary activities)

4.3 The value chain in non-manufacturing environments

The diagram below shows an alternative value chain in non-manufacturing environments.

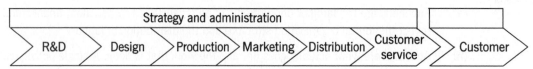

The value chain asserts that whilst excellence in manufacturing is essential for success, it is not sufficient to guarantee success.

All business factors should still add value and can run consecutively and concurrently. Value can also be added by the way in which these activities are **linked**.

(a) R&D – new ideas for products, services or processes
(b) Design – planning and engineering
(c) Production – co-ordination and assembly of resources to produce a product
(d) Marketing – teaching customers about products and persuading them to purchase
(e) Distribution – delivery to customers
(f) Customer service – support to customers

4.4 Creating value

An organisation is profitable if the realised value to customers exceeds the collective cost of performing the activities.

(a) **Customers 'purchase' value**, which they measure by comparing an organisation's products and services with similar offerings by competitors.

(b) **An organisation 'creates' value** either by carrying out its activities more efficiently than other organisations, or by combining them in such a way as to provide a unique product or service. We return to this point below.

Question 2.4	Creating value

Learning outcome A1(c)

Outline different ways in which a restaurant can 'create' value.

4.5 The focus of the value chain

This contrasts with **traditional management accounting**, which takes a value-added perspective and which has a focus largely **internal** to the organisation, each organisation being viewed in relation to its purchases, its processes, its functions, its products and its customers.

4.6 Value system

Activities that add value do not stop at the organisation's boundaries. For example, when a restaurant serves a meal, the quality of the ingredients – although they are chosen by the cook – is determined by the grower. The grower has added value, and the grower's success in growing produce of good quality is as important to the customer's ultimate satisfaction as the skills of the chef. An **organisation's value chain** is **connected** to what Porter calls a **value system**.

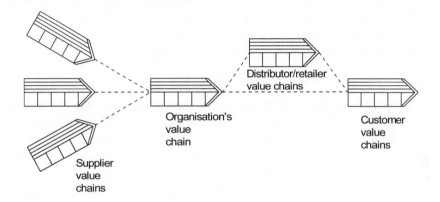

4.7 Linkages

Linkages **connect the activities of the value chain**. Linkages might be with suppliers or with customers, or within the organisation itself.

(a)   Activities in the value chain affect one another.

    (i)   More costly product design or better-quality production might reduce the need for after-sales service and post-purchase costs for customers. Designing a product to reduce post-purchase costs can be a major weapon in **capturing competitive advantage**.

    (ii)   Just-in-time (JIT) requires close partnerships with suppliers. Its introduction might save an organisation storage costs, say, but production schedule instability for suppliers might cause them to raise their prices.

(b)   Linkages require **co-ordination**. Unlike the value-added concept, value chain analysis explicitly recognises the fact that various activities within an organisation are **interdependent**. There is little point in a fast-food chain running a promotional campaign (one value activity) if there is insufficient capacity within 'production' (another value activity) to cope with the increased demand. These linked activities must be co-ordinated if the full effect of the promotion is to be realised.

Beneficial linkages are linkages with customers or suppliers that are managed in such a way that all parties benefit.

4.8 The value chain and competitive advantage

According to Porter, an organisation can develop sustainable competitive advantage by following one of two strategies.

(a)   **Low-cost strategy.** Essentially this is a strategy of cost leadership, which involves achieving a lower cost than competitors via, for example, economies of scale and tight cost control. Hyundai

(in cars) and Timex (wrist watches) are examples of organisations that have followed such a
strategy.

(b)   **Differentiation strategy.** This involves creating something that customers perceive as being unique
via brand loyalty, superior customer service, product design and features, technology and so on.
Mercedes Benz (in cars) and Rolex (wrist watches) are examples of organisations that have
followed such a strategy.

As **competitive advantage** is gained either from providing **better customer value for equivalent cost** or
equivalent customer value for lower cost, value chain analysis is essential to determine **where in an
organisation's value chain costs can be lowered or value enhanced**.

4.8.1 Strategic cost management and the value chain

Shank and Govindarajan explained how an organisation's value chain can be used with a view to lowering
costs and enhancing value: '... the value chain framework is a method for breaking down the chain – from
basic raw materials to end-use customers – into strategically relevant activities to understand the
behaviour of costs and the sources of differentiation'.

They suggest a three-step approach.

Build up the industry's value chain to determine the various activities in the value chain
and to allocate operating costs, revenues and assets to individual value activities. (It is vital
to understand the entire value chain, not just the portion of the chain in which the
organisation participates. Suppliers and distribution channels have profit margins that
impact on an organisation's cost or differentiation positioning, because the final customer
has to pay for all the profit margins throughout the value chain.)

Establish the cost drivers of the costs of each value activity, which are one of two types.

(a)   **Structural cost drivers.** These are derived from an organisation's decisions about its
underlying economic structure and include:

     (i)   Scale of operations (giving rise to economies or diseconomies of scale)
     (ii)   Scope (degree of vertical integration)
     (iii)   Experience (has the organisation climbed the learning curve?)
     (iv)   Technology used in the value chain
     (v)   Complexity (number of products/services being sold)

(b)   **Executional cost drivers.** These relate to an organisation's ability to deliver the
product/service successfully to the customer. According to Shank and Govindarajan,
the 'more' of these cost drivers there is, the better. Basic examples include:

     (i)   Employee participation
     (ii)   TQM
     (iii)   Capacity utilisation
     (iv)   Plant layout efficiency
     (v)   Product configuration
     (vi)   Linkages with suppliers or customers

**Develop sustainable competitive advantage by controlling these drivers better than
competitors or by configuring the value chain.** For each value activity, **sustainable
competitive advantage can be developed by reducing costs whilst maintaining value
(sales) and/or increasing value (sales) whilst maintaining costs**.

(a)   **Cost reduction.** Compare the value chain of the organisation with the value chain of
one or two major competitors, then identify the action required to manage the
organisation's value chain better than competitors manage theirs.

(b)   **Increasing value.** Identify where in the value chain payoffs could be significant.

4.8.2 Example: using the value chain in competitive strategy

The examples below are based on two supermarket chains, **one concentrating on low prices**, the **other differentiated on quality and service**. See if you can tell which is which.

(a)

	INBOUND LOGISTICS	OPERATIONS	OUTBOUND LOGISTICS	MARKETING & SALES	SERVICE
Firm infrastructure	Minimum corporate HQ				
Human resource management		De-skilled store operatives	Dismissal for checkout error		
Technology development	Computerised warehousing		Checkouts simple		
Procurement	Branded only purchases Big discounts	Low cost sites			Use of concessions
	Bulk warehousing	1,000 lines only Price points Basic store design		Low price promotion Local focus	Nil

(b)

	INBOUND LOGISTICS	OPERATIONS	OUTBOUND LOGISTICS	MARKETING & SALES	SERVICE
Firm infrastructure	Central control of operations and credit control				
Human resource management	Recruitment of mature staff	Client care training	Flexible staff to help with packing		
Technology development		Recipe research	Electronic point of sale	Consumer research and tests	Itemised bills
Procurement	Own label products	Prime retail positions		Adverts in quality magazines	
	Dedicated refrigerated transport	In store food halls Modern store design Open front refrigerators Tight control of sell-by dates	Collect by car service	No price discounts on food past sell-by dates	No quibble refunds

The two supermarkets represented are based on the following:

(a)   The value chain in (a) is similar to that of Lidl, a 'discount' supermarket chain which sells on price. This can be seen in the limited product range and its low-cost sites.

(b)   The value chain in (b) is based on Marks & Spencer, which seeks to differentiate on quality and service. Hence the 'no quibble' refunds, the use of prime retail sites and customer care training.

CASE STUDY

'By comparing two organisations from the computer retail sector we can observe the strategic choices that organisations make. Dell chooses to use the Internet and telesales as the main channels for its marketing and sales activity, and uses distributors to fulfil its outbound logistics. PC World uses shops as well as the Internet. Both firms employ sales staff, but PC World, consistent with its decision to use retail outlets, has identified that its target customers value the personal touch, so it has chosen to employ trained staff (HR management activity) who can deal with them face to face. Its TV advertising (marketing and sales activity) emphasises this expert personal service as a benefit (differentiating factor) of shopping at PC World.

'Compare this approach with that of a retailer such as Ikea, which believes that its target customers do not place a high value on personal customer service and has therefore decided against employing large numbers of sales staff. This allows it to keep employment costs down, supporting its low-cost strategy and its position in the market. Note that competitive advantage and what the customer values are the factors that have driven the decision.'

(Graham Pitcher, 'The Missing Link', *CIMA Insider*)

Question 2.5
Value chain analysis v conventional management accounting

Learning outcome A1(c)

Compare and contrast value chain analysis with conventional management accounting by completing the table below.

	Traditional management accounting	Value chain analysis
Focus		
Perspective		
Cost driver concept		
Cost containment philosophy		
Insights for strategic decisions		

Section summary

The **value chain model**, developed by Michael Porter, offers a bird's eye view of an organisation, of what it does and the way in which its business activities are organised.

Activities or **value activities** can be categorised as **primary** or **support**.

The ultimate **value** an organisation creates is measured by the amount customers are willing to pay for its products and services above the cost of carrying out value activities.

The **focus of the value chain** is **external to the organisation**, each organisation being viewed in the context of the overall chain of value-creating activities of which it is only a part, from basic raw materials to end-use consumers.

An organisation's ability to develop and sustain **cost leadership** or **product differentiation**, and hence **gain competitive advantage**, depends on how well it manages its own value chain relative to competitors.

5 Supply chain management

Introduction

This section focuses on how and where a business operates in the supply chain and the ways in which the supply chain can be managed.

5.1 The supply chain

A SUPPLY CHAIN is a network of facilities and distribution options that performs the functions of procurement of materials, transformation of these materials into intermediate and finished products and the distribution of these finished products to customers.

(Ganeshan and Harrison, *Supply Chain Management*).

Within a supply chain, many processes might take place between the origination of raw materials to the eventual delivery of the finished product or service to the end customer. For each organisation inside a supply chain, some of the processes are carried out by the organisation itself, and others are carried out by suppliers or by other organisations further down the supply chain.

For example, a company manufacturing motor vehicles might have a plant where the vehicles are assembled and finished. It might manufacture some parts itself and produce the car body work, but most sub-assemblies and the tyres will be purchased from outside suppliers. The suppliers of sub-assemblies might make some components themselves, but will also purchase many of their components from other suppliers. The manufacturer, suppliers and sub-suppliers might all purchase raw materials, such as steel, from other suppliers. The manufacturer will also purchase capital equipment from equipment suppliers, who are another part of the supply chain. The finished cars will not be sold directly to the end customer, but to distributors, and the distributors will sell to the end customer.

5.2 The concept of supply chain management

If there is a **given amount of profit** in a particular market for a finished product, this profit will be **shared out between all the organisations involved in the supply chain**. In this sense, suppliers and their customers **compete** with each other for **a bigger share of the available profit**. This 'traditional' **adversarial arm's length** attitude is evident in negotiations between an organisation and its suppliers, and efforts by the organisation to get the best terms possible and the lowest prices in their purchasing negotiations.

This view of the supply chain is **challenged by** the concept of **supply chain management**.

SUPPLY CHAIN MANAGEMENT looks at the supply chain as a whole, and starts with the view that all organisations in the supply chain collaborate to produce something of value for the end customer.

This has two advantages.

(a)   By **adding value** within the supply chain, **customer satisfaction** will be **improved** and **customers** will **pay more** for what they buy.

(b)   **Organisations can also benefit collectively by reducing waste and inefficiency**. A lot of **wasteful activity** (activity that does not add any value to the final product) **occurs at the interface between organisations within the supply chain**. For example, a supplier might spend money on checking outwards supplies for quality, and the same goods will be checked by the organisation buying them when they are delivered. Inspection costs could be reduced by closer collaboration between the organisations, both to improve quality and to reduce inspection activities.

By looking at the supply chain as a collaborative effort, managers can look for ways of enhancing the profitability of the supply chain as a whole, so that everyone, including the end customer, benefits.

5.2.1 Developing relationships

Developing strong relationships is not an easy task, however. The arm's length supplier–purchaser relationship has been based on both sides winning as much short-term gain as possible, and so sharing sensitive information and developing long-term ties is often difficult.

There are a number of practices which can be used to foster improved relationships with key suppliers.

(a) **Power balancing** occurs if the proportion of a supplier's total output that is sold to a customer roughly equals the proportion of total purchases acquired by the customer from that supplier. Maintaining relative dependence between suppliers and buyers increases the likelihood that both parties will have a vested interest in the success of the other.

(b) **Codependency.** When a supplier commits substantial specialised resources to meeting the demands of a purchaser and the purchaser chooses to single-source from that supplier, both parties have a vested interest in the success of the purchaser.

(c) **Target costing.** Suppliers can be rewarded when targets are reached.

(d) **Personal ties.** The establishment of teams of employees from both supplier and purchaser helps foster good working relationships and develop trust.

CASE STUDY

'To design vehicle and production systems [for the M-class], Mercedes Benz US International used *function groups* that included representatives from every area of the company.... The role of these function groups was to develop specifications and cost projections.

Mercedes included suppliers early in the design stage of the vehicle. By including suppliers as members of the function groups, Mercedes was able to take advantage of their expertise and advice on matters such as supplier capability, cost and quality. The synergy generated by these cross-function groups also allowed the groups to solve larger design issues, such as how to more efficiently and economically switch from manufacturing left-side-drive vehicles to right-side-vehicles. Significant time savings were recognised because of the design improvements implemented by the function groups. Because supplier personnel were at the Mercedes plant on a full-time basis during the launch, other issues (such as quality problems or slight modifications to the product) could be addressed in a more timely fashion.'

(Albright and Davis, 'The Elements of Supply Chain Management',
International Journal of Strategic Cost Management)

KEY TERM

SUPPLY CHAIN MANAGEMENT (or PIPELINE MANAGEMENT or VALUE STREAM MANAGEMENT) views all the buyers and sellers in this chain as part of a continuum, and the aim should be to look at the supply chain as a whole and seek to optimise the functioning of the entire chain. In other words, a company should look beyond its immediate suppliers and its immediate customers to add value, for example by improving efficiency and eliminating waste.

5.2.2 Adding value

The overall supply chain can be thought of as a **sequence of operations, each of which should add value**. An activity has value if it gives the customer something that the customer considers worth having (ie values), but an activity only adds value if the amount of value added exceeds the cost of creating it. Value is therefore added by making something worth more (in terms of the price the customer will pay, or the quality the customer perceives) or by reducing the cost of the operation (without sacrificing quality).

5.3 Elements of supply chain management

To apply the concept of supply chain management fully, there has to be **close collaboration** between organisations within the supply chain. A company must be able to work constructively with its suppliers. At the same time, it should continually **look for ways of improving the supply chain structure**, and this could involve switching to **different suppliers**, or selling **output through new channels**. The **internet** has opened up new possibilities for identifying new suppliers worldwide and for **selling direct to customers** instead of through distributors.

There is no single model for the ideal supply chain, and supply chain management can involve:

(a) Decisions about improving collaboration with suppliers by sharing information and through the joint development of new products

(b)   Switching to new suppliers by purchasing online

(c)   Outsourcing some activities that were previously performed in-house

5.4 Issues facing supply chain managers

5.4.1 Production

The customer often wants suppliers to respond to their particular requirements, and to customise orders to their specific needs. A supply chain that can **respond quickly to individual customer requirements** is known as an **'agile' supply chain**.

Issues for management include deciding **what** products or components to make, and **where** to make them. Should the production of components, sub-assemblies or even the final product be done in-house or by external suppliers?

Management **focus** is on **capacity**, **quality** and **order volume**. Production has to be scheduled so as to provide a sufficient workload for the production resources, and to achieve workload balance (so as to avoid both production bottlenecks and under-utilisation of resources). Quality control is an issue, because producing poor-quality output has implications for both cost and customer dissatisfaction.

The **challenge** is to **meet customer orders immediately**, **without** having to invest heavily in **inventories** of finished goods, which are wasteful and expensive.

5.4.2 Supply

Most manufacturing companies cannot make everything themselves and still keep the quality of their output high. Decisions have to be made about how much should be purchased from 'outside'. Some companies have chosen to **close in-house production facilities** and **switch to external suppliers**, so that they can **concentrate on their 'core competences' where they add most value**.

In choosing external suppliers, management need to consider the capabilities of the supplier, and the extent to which a close collaboration will be necessary. (Collaboration is much more important for key supplies, and much less important for low-cost general supplies that can be purchased from numerous sources.) **Distinctive competences** of supplier and the organisation should be **similar**. An organisation selling 'cheap and cheerful' goods will want suppliers which are able to supply 'cheap and cheerful' subcomponents. The management focus should be on the **speed, quality and flexibility of supply**, as well as on cost.

5.4.3 Inventory

If a firm holds large amounts of inventory, it should be able to meet many customer orders immediately out of inventory and should not suffer hold-ups due to inventory shortages. Holding inventory is expensive, however, and there is no certainty that finished goods inventories will ever find a customer, unless they have been made to satisfy specific customer orders. **Ideally, inventory levels should be minimised, but without damaging the ability of the firm to meet customer orders quickly or holding up work flow due to a stockout of key supplies**.

In managing inventory levels, organisations need to know, with as much certainty as possible, the **lead time** for delivery of supplies and for the production of goods. Unknown lead times increase the chance of too little or too much inventory, both of which are costly for organisations.

5.4.4 Location

Decisions need to be made about where to locate production facilities and warehousing facilities. Cost and tax issues might result in production facilities being constructed in **emerging market economies**.

5.4.5 Transportation

Logistics management is another aspect of supply chain management. Supplies need to be delivered to a firm's premises and finished goods delivered to customers **efficiently, reliably** and at a **low cost**.

5.4.6 Information

Information resources throughout the supply chain need to be **linked together**, for speed of information exchange and to reduce wasteful paperwork. Some firms link their computer networks, or share information through the internet.

5.4.7 Overall management

Managing the supply chain therefore calls for an **understanding of** and **knowledge about**:

(a) **Customer demand patterns**
(b) **Service level requirements** (speed of delivery expectations, quality expectations, and so on)
(c) **Distance considerations** (logistics)
(d) **Cost**

5.5 Using information and technology

A firm can **share** its **information** about expected customer demand and orders in the pipeline, so that the **suppliers can get ready** themselves for orders that might come to them from the firm. 'Modern' supply chain management uses the **internet** to share information as soon as it is available. A firm might have an integrated **enterprise resource planning (ERP)** system sitting on a website or on a server running on the internet. The ERP system runs the supply chain database, holding information about a wide range of items, such as customer orders, inventory levels and pricing structures.

The use of EDI, internet technology and software applications means that **suppliers know what a customer needs before the customer asks**. A supplier that 'knows' what its customers want does not have to guess or wait until the customer places an order. It will be able to **better plan its own delivery systems**. Technology has made the concept of the **'seamless' supply chain** a reality. The development of creative links with suppliers and customers provides organisations with the chance of **competitive advantage over competitors unwilling or unable to invest the time and resources in improving their supply chains**.

A critical issue for successful supply chain management is the **speed** with which activities can be carried out and customer demands met. If a firm, helped by its suppliers and sub-suppliers in the chain, can **respond quickly and flexibly** to customer requirements, the benefits will come from **lower inventories, lower operating costs, better product availability and greater customer satisfaction**.

CASE STUDY

Supply chain management and customisation of orders

Personal computer production provides an interesting example of how supply chain management can be used to provide fast delivery of customised products, thereby creating a 'flexible' or 'agile' supply chain.

When customers expect fast delivery of their orders for personal computers, and at the same time want PCs produced to their individual specifications, the parts needed to deliver the item to the customer must exist somewhere within the supply chain. A PC manufacturer operating in a build to order market relies on suppliers keeping inventory available, so that the manufacturer can minimise its own inventories without compromising the time needed to deliver the order to the customer. In the case of Dell Computers (reported in a *Financial Times* supplement on supply chain management), Dell itself held about five days' supply and other firms in the supply chain held about ten days' inventory of supplier-owned items. Replenishment of inventories took between 12 hours and 2 days.

'Build-to-order involves balancing what is available with what the customers want and Dell has become expert in gently massaging both these factors. Any shortage in a particular component is immediately countered by offering other available products on promotion.... By monitoring component inventory availability in real time, Dell and its suppliers can quickly see problems with any particular part. A first step is to increase lead time, informing customers that their preferred configuration will take eight to 10 days to deliver rather than the usual five. If that does not slow up demand, then would-be customers are offered a more expensive upgrade for the same price. "Everyone wins," [says Dell's vice president in the US]. "Our customers get a better deal, the suppliers get business and we can satisfy demand."'

The efficiency of the Dell build to order system depends on data sharing between Dell and its suppliers, and the integrity of the information databases. All systems throughout the supply chain are integrated, with common parts numbers and automated order processing and parts management.

Section summary

A **supply chain** is the network of suppliers, manufacturers and distributors that is involved in the process of moving goods for a customer order from the raw materials stage through the production and distribution stages to the customer. Every organisation operates somewhere within a supply chain.

A **commonly held view** by management is that **to improve profitability** it is necessary to **get the lowest prices from suppliers** and to **obtain the best prices from the customers** next in line down the supply chain.

Supply chain management looks at the supply chain as a whole, and starts with the view that all organisations in the supply chain collaborate to produce something of value for the end customer.

Supply chain managers need to consider **production, supply, inventory, location, transportation and information.**

The **internet** and **software applications** have had a huge impact on supply chain management.

6 Outsourcing

Introduction

A significant trend in recent years has been for organisations and government bodies to **concentrate on their core competences** – what they are really good at (or set up to achieve) – and **turn other activities over to specialist contractors**. This section looks at reasons for this trend and how outsourcing is likely to move forward in the future.

KEY TERM

OUTSOURCING is 'The use of external suppliers as a source of finished products, components or services. This is also known as **contract manufacturing** or **sub-contracting**.'   *(CIMA Official Terminology)*

6.1 Reasons for this trend

(a)   Frequently the decision is made on the grounds that **specialist contractors** can offer **superior quality** and **efficiency**. If a contractor's main business is making a specific component it can invest in the specialist machinery and labour and knowledge skills needed to make that component. However, this component may be only one of many needed by the contractor's customer, and the complexity of components is now such that attempting to keep internal facilities up to the standard of specialists detracts from the main business of the customer. For example, Dell Computers buys the Pentium chip for its personal computers from Intel because it does not have the know-how and technology to make the chip itself.

(b)   Contracting out manufacturing **frees capital** that can then be invested in core activities such as market research, product definition, product planning, marketing and sales.

(c)   **Contractors** have the **capacity** and **flexibility** to start production very quickly to meet sudden **variations in demand**. In-house facilities may not be able to respond as quickly, because of the need to redirect resources from elsewhere.

CASE STUDY

'... chocolate confectionery companies in the UK will sell Easter eggs promoting their brands and products every spring. Mars, for instance, will provide chocolate eggs containing mini Mars products, or in packaging highlighting Mars products around the egg. The reason that you might be tempted to buy one of these eggs is because it has Mars products associated with it. Mars therefore doesn't have to produce the egg itself – that activity can be outsourced. After all, it would be expensive to maintain production facilities for chocolate eggs for only a couple of months a year.

However, you might buy a Cadbury's Easter egg because it is made of Cadbury's chocolate. Therefore Cadbury's needs the operational capability to produce Easter eggs. The company has focused on marketing and sales activities to develop the Cadbury's Creme Egg into a product that is sold all year round, thereby making the operation viable. The decision whether or not to outsource can often be bound strongly to an organisation's competitive strategy and focuses on how strategic the activity is to the organisation.'

(G Pitcher, 'The Missing Link', *CIMA Student*)

6.2 Internal and external services

In administrative and support functions, too, organisations are increasingly likely to use specialist companies. **Decisions** such as the following are now common.

(a)   Whether the **design and development of a new computer system** should be entrusted to in-house data processing staff or whether an external software house should be hired to do the work

(b)   Whether **maintenance and repairs** of certain items of equipment should be dealt with by in-house engineers, or whether a maintenance contract should be made with a specialist organisation

Even if you are not aware of specialist 'facilities management' companies such as Securicor, you will be familiar with the idea of office cleaning being done by contractors.

6.3 Choosing the activities to outsource

Within the value chain, both primary activities and support activities are candidates for outsourcing, although many can be **eliminated** from the list immediately either **because the activity cannot be contracted out or because the organisation must control it to maintain its competitive position**. Coca-Cola does not outsource the manufacture of its concentrate to safeguard its formula and retain control of the product.

Of the remaining activities, an organisation **should carry out only those that it can deliver on a level comparable with the best organisations in the world**. If the organisation cannot achieve benchmarked levels of performance, the activity should be outsourced so that the organisation is **only concentrating on those core activities that enhance its competitive advantage**.

A differential cost analysis should then be carried out on outsourcing possibilities. Some argue that this analysis should be over the long term, using discounted cash flow analysis.

6.4 Advantages and disadvantages

The **advantages** of outsourcing are as follows.

(a)   It **frees up time** taken by existing staff on the contracted-out activities.

(b)   It allows the company to **take advantage of specialist expertise and equipment** rather than investing in these facilities itself and underutilising them.

(c)   It **frees up time spent supporting the contracted-out services** by staff not directly involved, for example supervisory staff, personnel staff.

(d)   It may be **cheaper**, once time savings and opportunity costs are taken into account.

(e)   It is particularly **appropriate** when an organisation is **attempting to expand in a time of uncertainty**, because it allows the use of facilities on a short-term (readily cancelled) basis which

would only otherwise be available via the relatively long-term investments of a permanent employee and the training he or she requires. In other words, it is a way of gaining all the benefits of extra capacity without having to find the full cost.

However, there are also a number of **disadvantages**.

(a)   Without monitoring there is **no guarantee** that the service will be **performed to the organisation's satisfaction**.

(b)   There is a good chance that contracting out will be **more expensive** than providing the service in-house.

(c)   By performing services itself the organisation retains or develops **skills** that may be needed in the future and will otherwise be **lost**.

(d)   Contracting out any aspect of information-handling carries with it the possibility that **commercially sensitive data will get into the wrong hands**.

(e)   There may be some **ethical reservations**, such as exploitation of staff and inadequate pay and conditions.

(f)   There will almost certainly be **opposition from employees** and their representatives if contracting out involves redundancies.

CASE STUDY

Albright and Davis ('The Elements of Supply Chain Management') describe the extreme outsourcing approach adopted by Mercedes.

Instead of contracting with suppliers for parts, Mercedes outsourced the modules making up a completed M-class to suppliers who purchase the subcomponents and assemble the modules for Mercedes.

This has led to a reduction in plant and warehouse space needed, and a dramatic reduction in the number of suppliers used (from 35 to 1 for the cockpit, for example).

At the beginning of the production process Mercedes maintained strict control in terms of quality and cost on both the first tier suppliers (who provide finished modules) and the second tier suppliers (from whom the first tier suppliers purchase parts). As the level of trust grew between Mercedes and the first tier suppliers, Mercedes allowed them to make their own arrangements with second tier suppliers.

Benefits of this approach for Mercedes

(i)   Reduction in purchasing overhead

(ii)   Reduction in labour and employee-related costs

(iii)   Higher level of service from suppliers

(iv)   Supplier expertise in seeking ways to improve current operations

(v)   Suppliers working together to continuously improve both their own module and the integrated product

6.5 Current trends in outsourcing

Improvements in technology and telecommunications and more willingness for managers to manage people they can't see have fuelled this trend.

Before taking the decision to outsource overseas, a number of points should be **considered**.

(a)   **Environmental** (location, infrastructure, risk, cultural compatibility, time differences)
(b)   **Labour** (experience in relevant fields, language barriers, size of labour market)
(c)   **Management** (remote management)
(d)   **Bad press** associated with the perception of jobs leaving the home country

CASE STUDY

Call centres

The inside of a call centre will look virtually the same wherever it is in the world; similar headsets, hardware and software being used, for example. With pressure to provide adequate customer service at low cost, many organisations have closed call centres in parts of Western Europe and relocated to low-cost countries and regions, such as India and South Africa.

It is claimed that savings on call centre costs range from 35% to 55% for near shore outsourcing and 50% to 75% for offshore outsourcing.

Section summary

Any activity is a candidate for outsourcing unless the organisation **must control it to maintain its competitive position** or if the organisation can **deliver it on a level comparable with the best organisations in the world**.

To minimise the risks associated with outsourcing, organisations generally enter into **long-run contracts** with their suppliers that specify costs, quality and delivery schedules. They build **close partnerships** or **alliances** with a few key suppliers, collaborating with suppliers on design and manufacturing decisions, and building a culture and commitment for quality and timely delivery.

7 Partnering, incentives and gain-sharing arrangements

Introduction

Other techniques that focus on external relationships are partnering, incentives and gain-sharing arrangements. Each of these techniques are considered in this section.

7.1 Partnering

KEY TERM

'The term 'PARTNERING' is used about a type of collaboration in a construction project based on DIALOGUE, TRUST, OPENNESS and with EARLY PARTICIPATION from all actors. The project is carried out under a MUTUAL AGREEMENT expressed by MUTUAL ACTIVITIES and based on MUTUAL ECONOMIC INTERESTS.'

Guidelines for partnering, National Agency for Enterprise and Construction, Copenhagen (2004)

Partnering is therefore a **structured management approach** to **facilitate team working across the boundaries of contracts**. It is widely used in the construction industry and within government departments such as the Ministry of Defence.

7.1.1 Fundamental components of partnering

(a) Mutual interdependence and trust (as opposed to a blame culture)
(b) Identification of common goals for success
(c) Agreed decision-making and problem-solving procedures
(d) Commitment to continuous improvement
(e) Team working down the entire product and supply chain
(f) Gain share and pain share arrangements (incentives)
(g) Open book accounting
(h) Targets that provide continuous measurable improvements in performance

7.1.2 Claimed benefits of partnering

(a) Cost savings

(b) Improved profit margins

(c) Reduction in project times

(d) More predictability of costs and quality

(e) Increased customer satisfaction

(f) Improved quality and safety

7.1.3 When to use partnering

For partnering arrangements to be successful, they need the full and visible **support from very senior management** of each organisation. Partnering is not just a bolt-on extra that delivers results through one partnering workshop. It is a **continuous process** that needs **sustained effort** by all of the parties to deliver measurable benefits. Partnering arrangements are likely to fail if efforts to contribute to their success are not sustained.

Partnering is **particularly suitable in the following circumstances**.

(a) If significant input is required from specialist contractors or subcontractors (such as in the construction of a new airport terminal)

(b) If there is a rapid expansion of a programme of construction (say, if a supermarket chain opens lots of new branches)

(c) If time is a critical factor

(d) If projects are repetitive and based upon a set of standard designs (such as the construction of McDonald's restaurants)

(e) If there is a particular construction problem which is best solved by a team of experts (such as the construction of oil rigs)

Partnering is **less suitable in the following circumstances**.

(a) If it is important that costs can be predicted with certainty

(b) If the project is a one-off, commissioned by a one-off customer

(c) If the customer has little knowledge of the construction process

The table below gives examples of where partnering has been used and the motives for and concerns about the partnering arrangements.

Context	Example	Motives	Concerns
Industry and channel partnering	Star Alliance - international passenger air travel	• Customer demands a global service but governments and regulators prevent consolidation • Economies of scale	• Delivering a similar service using different carriers • Firm rivalry • Cultural differences
Project partnering	Civil engineering projects in the UK water sector	• Poor industry profitability • Threat of external competition	• Managing hard contract relationship at the same time as partnering • Internal cultures
Channel and customer partnering	Linking social services and mental health services to provide care in the community through Health Partnerships	• Better health outcomes • Cost savings	• Difficult to work in practice due to poor systems and the lack of investment • Political and professional rivalry
Supply Chain	Internal partnering North Sea Fields	• Cost savings • Limited asset base	• Changing industry mindsets
Integrated Strategic Partnering Strategy (TIPS)	Automotive General Motors	• Cost reduction • Customer value	• Mindsets

7.1.4 Types of partnering

Two key types of partnering arrangement exist.

(a)   **Strategic partnering** (longer-term partnering for agreements involving more than one project)

(b)   **Project specific partnering**

The Reading Construction Forum report 'The Seven Pillars of Partnering' notes that strategic partnering has been known to deliver cost savings of 40% and time savings of more than 50%. In comparison, the cost savings for project specific partnering lie in the range 2% to 10%.

The **greater benefits from strategic partnering** arrangements arise because the lessons learnt from one project can be applied to further similar projects through a process of continuous improvement. Strategic partnering arrangements should be adopted in preference to project specific partnering arrangements wherever possible.

Irrespective of the type of partnering relationship that the customer enters into with a primary supplier (such as the main contractor or main consultant), significant benefits (in achieving overall value for money) can be obtained where a primary supplier has entered into strategic partnering arrangements with secondary suppliers (such as sub-contractors or sub-consultants). Supply chain relationships of this type are essential to obtain the maximum benefits from partnering.

7.1.5 Partnering contracts

A contract is required to ensure that all parties are certain of their risks and responsibilities. This encourages **openness and trust**.

An effective partnering contract must be able to deal with any problems in the project and a team-based solution found.

The **defensive attitude embodied in traditional contracts** is a major **obstacle** to the partnering process, however, and so a new form of contractual arrangement is required.

7.2 Incentivisation

Incentives should be **included** in contracts or in **partnering arrangements**, to encourage designers, constructors and/or other suppliers to **provide benefits** to the client significantly **beyond those contracted for** (by using innovation or different working practices to deliver the same or better service whilst yielding cost savings) and **rewarding them for doing so**.

Incentives should **encourage the parties to work together to eliminate wasteful activities that do not add value to the client** and to **identify and implement process improvements, alternative designs, working methods and other activities that result in added value.**

Incentives should **not be given merely for doing a good job** (in other words, meeting the contractual requirements) nor should they be made for improvements in performance that are of no value to the client (such as completing a building contract three months early when the client is still committed to paying rent, rates and other charges on the existing premises).

Here are some examples of features of project performance that can be considered for incentivisation.

- Cost
- Time
- Quality
- Operational efficiency
- Productivity
- Value for the customer
- Safety

Savings can also be **shared amongst members of the supply chain, based on pre-agreed proportions**, so that profits for contractors and suppliers are increased. Alternatively, cost savings can be used by the customer to commission additional work from the partnering team, which again increases the profitability of the supply chain.

Incentive schemes can **also operate 'negatively'**, with the costs of unforeseen risks and problems being shared.

7.2.1 Examples of incentivisation

(a) **Better fee structure**

This applies if the timing and scope of payments deliver a better or lower priced contract.

CASE STUDY

The Highways Agency sets a target completion date for major road maintenance contracts. If contractors 'beat' this date, a bonus is paid. Failure to meet the target date results in a reduction in baseline fees (subject to a maximum figure).

(b) **Enhanced performance and quality**

This applies if a contractor provides a better or faster service than would be delivered under a traditional contract.

CASE STUDY

In a contract for facilities management at one of its sites, HM Revenue & Customs benchmarked the service required against similar contracts, studied the performance required, and established the degree of risk and extent of the profit and savings that might accrue. Fees and costs were fixed and incentives for sharing savings were established. Open book accounting regimes were agreed. Savings were achieved and at the conclusion of each year these savings became a base line for future years. HM Revenue & Customs makes a 50/50 payment share of increased margin to the contractor.

(c) **Target cost incentive scheme**

This applies where a target cost is set based on a given set of parameters. If this fixed target is exceeded or undercut, the outcome is split between the contractor and the customer. These are also known as gain-sharing arrangements.

7.3 Gain-sharing arrangements

In pain/gain-sharing arrangements, **all cost overruns and cost savings are shared between the customer and the contractor**. A target cost is negotiated and agreed. If the actual cost is less than the target cost, the customer and contractor (and sometimes the contractor's supply chain) split any savings between them in agreed proportions. Likewise any cost overruns are shared by both parties. Sometimes the contractor's share of any cost overrun is up to a pre-arranged limit, and there may be time limits for the gain to be realised.

This does not mean that contractors or suppliers get extra for doing what they are basically contracted to do, but for exceeding those targets. Cost savings should not be seen as incentives to be shared if the scope or standard of work is simply reduced.

Cost savings might be generated from reducing the cost of raw materials, implementing new technologies or suggesting and implementing improvements in operations. The Ministry of Defence sees gain sharing as 'a reward for innovative thinking by the contractor'.

Because the resulting benefits from a gain-sharing arrangement are shared, there is an incentive for both parties to look for cost-cutting opportunities.

Many contracts involving these arrangements have **emphasis on greater openness** and **shared development and improvement**.

The Ministry of Defence, for example, is committed to gain sharing as a method of improving the efficient use of the defence procurement budget.

7.3.1 What are the gains?

The gain, benefit or advantage to be shared is **not necessarily financial**, although financial benefits are likely to occur frequently. The Ministry of Defence, for example, will not necessarily take cost savings in the form of a lower contract value but might require a higher specification.

7.3.2 Where might gain-sharing opportunities exist?

Gain-sharing opportunities can exist in various areas of a contract and the associated supply chain.

(a)   Through advances in technology, changes to **technical specifications or levels of performance** may be negotiated.

(b)   Revised **delivery** times may lead to reduced costs and/or improved performance.

(c)   Opportunities for the generation of an **income stream** from the use of the customer's assets by or for a **third party** could emerge or be developed.

(d)   Opportunities may be found **within the supply chain**.

Question 2.6	Gain-sharing arrangements

Learning outcome A1(c)

The Prime Contracting Initiative marks an innovation in the approach adopted by the Defence Estates on behalf of the Ministry of Defence (MoD) in the UK for the procurement of its capital and maintenance construction work. The Defence Estates arm of the MoD spends well in excess of $1 billion a year and its portfolio ranges from simple structures to complex airfields, garrisons and naval bases.

Required

Describe briefly what you think could be the main features of Prime Contracting.

Note. You are not required to know the specifics of the initiative. You should simply set out some general principles for supply contracts between contractors and the MoD.

Section summary

In some situations, normal competitive pressures do not apply in relationships between customers and contractors. This might be because of the size of the project (say in the construction or civil engineering industries), because there are a limited number of contractors or because of security issues (as in defence work). In such circumstances, **partnering**, **incentives** and **gain-sharing arrangements** are required.

Chapter Summary

```
                    ┌─────────────────────────┐
                    │  Enhancing long-term     │
                    │        profits           │
                    └─────────────────────────┘
```

Target costing	Value analysis	Value chain	Supply chain management
• Externally focused approach • Considers what the customer is prepared to pay • Desired margin is deducted from selling price to arrive at a target cost • Cost gap is the difference between the target and expected cost	• Looks to maintain or improve value whilst reducing cost • Non value added activities should be eliminated • Five stages in process • Analyses existing products	• Analyses activities through which firms can create value and competitive advantage	• Outsourcing • Gain-sharing arrangements

Quick Quiz

1 Put the three terms below in the correct order to represent (a) the target costing process and (b) the traditional costing process.

- Selling price
- Cost
- Profit

2 Choose the correct words from those highlighted.

Value **engineering/analysis** is cost avoidance or cost prevention before production whereas value **engineering/analysis** is cost reduction during production.

3 Match the terms to the correct definitions.

Terms
Cost value
Exchange value
Use value
Esteem value

Definitions

(a) The prestige the customer attaches to the product
(b) The market value of the product
(c) What the product does
(d) The cost of producing and selling the product

4 Fill in the action to take at each step in a value analysis.

STEP ① ....

STEP ② ....

STEP ③ ....

STEP ④ ....

STEP ⑤ ....

STEP ⑥ ....

STEP ⑦ ....

5   Fill in the blanks.

Functional analysis is an analysis of the relationships between ...., their
.... and their ....

6   Complete the following diagram of the value chain.

7   Choose the correct term from those highlighted.

If the proportion of a supplier's total output that is sold to a customer roughly equals the proportion of total purchases acquired by the customer from that supplier, this is known as **power balancing/ target balancing/codependency/power ties**.

8   Activities that are a source of competitive advantage should be outsourced. True or false?

9   List in the spaces below six features of project performance that can be considered for incentivisation.

1   3   5   ....

2   4   6   ....

Answers to Quick Quiz

1 (a) Selling price, profit, cost
   (b) Cost, selling price, profit

2 First term should be value engineering, the second term value analysis.

3 Cost value   (d)
   Exchange value   (b)
   Use value   (c)
   Esteem value   (a)

4

 Select a product or service for study

 Obtain and record information

 Analyse the information and evaluate the product

 Consider alternatives

 Select the least cost alternative

 Make a recommendation

STEP 7 Implement and follow up

5 Functional analysis is an analysis of the relationships between product functions, their perceived value to the customer and their cost of provision.

6

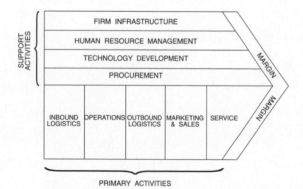

7   The correct answer is power balancing.

8   False. These are the activities an organisation should keep in-house.

9   You could have listed cost, time, quality, operational efficiency, productivity, value for the customer or safety.

Answers to Questions

2.1 Standard costing vs target costing

(a) Set the selling price and required profit and determine the resulting target cost
(b) Set standard cost and a resulting standard price
(c) Constant cost reduction
(d) Standards usually revised annually

2.2 Value

(a) Exchange value
(b) Esteem value
(c) Use value

2.3 Benefits of a VA programme

(a) Improved product performance and product reliability

(b) Improved product quality

(c) An increased product life, in terms of both the marketable life of the product (for the company) and the usable life of each product unit (for the customer)

(d) Possibly, shorter delivery 'lead times' to customers because of a shorter production cycle

(e) The increased use of standard parts and components which contribute to lower costs for the customer

(f) A more economic use of scarce resources

(g) Encouraging employees to show innovation and creative ideas

2.4 Creating value

Here are some ideas. Each of these options is a way of organising the activities of buying, cooking and serving food in a way that customers will value.

(a) It can become more efficient by automating the production of food, as in a fast food chain.

(b) The chef can develop commercial relationships with growers, so he or she can obtain the best quality fresh produce.

(c) The chef can specialise in a particular type of cuisine (such as French or Thai).

(d) The restaurant can be sumptuously decorated for those customers who value 'atmosphere' and a sense of occasion, in addition to a restaurant's purely gastronomic pleasures.

(e) The restaurant can serve a particular type of customer (such as celebrities).

2.5 Value chain analysis vs conventional management accounting

	Traditional management accounting	Value chain analysis
Focus	Internal	External
Perspective	Value-added	Entire set of linked activities from suppliers to final-use customers
Cost driver concept	Single driver (volume) Applied at organisational level	Multiple cost drivers (structural and executional) Unique cost drivers for each value activity
Cost containment philosophy	'Across the board' cost reductions	By regulating cost drivers Exploit linkages with customers and suppliers Spend to save
Insights for strategic decisions	None readily apparent	Develop cost/differentiation advantage by controlling drivers better than competitors or by reconfiguring the value chain For each value activity, consider make versus buy, forwards/backwards integration and so on Exploit linkages with customers and suppliers

(Adapted from Shank and Govindarajan)

2.6 Gain-sharing arrangements

Here are some of the actual principles of and details about the Prime Contracting Initiative, taken from 'Prime Contracting – the UK experience and the way forward' by David M Jones, an external adviser to the Defence Estates and a member of the small working party empowered to deliver Prime Contracting. Obviously you are unlikely to have come up with this level of detail but you should have mentioned some of the basic points.

(a) **Collaborative working**. 'The intention behind the Prime Contracting Initiative in facilitating best value to the customer is to foster a more collaborative and less adversarial relationship between the MoD and the Prime Contractor..... The Core Conditions give opportunities throughout the contract period for collaboration and discussion between the Defence Estates Project Manager (DEPM) for each contract and the Prime Contractor..... There are opportunities for continual adjustment and improvement within the relationship, not least to provide good feedback among the contract members. This will be vital to develop trust, to work on upgrading performance and to add value...... and having a common interest and willingness to co-operate to meet mutual goals.'

(b) **Gain-sharing arrangement**. 'Of importance, the Core Conditions include a Target Cost pricing mechanism and a pain/gain-sharing arrangement between the MoD and the Prime Contractor for both cost under-runs and over-runs up to a Maximum Price Target Cost (MPTC). In the most important area, therefore, there is significant sharing and incentives on both parties...... This arrangement is considered to provide the strongest incentive for industry to improve performance and innovate thereby increasing value to the MoD and providing an opportunity for the Prime Contractor's level of profit to increase to reflect his improved performance.... It is expected that Prime Contractors will be entitled to a fair profit margin, bringing tangible benefits from the Prime Contracting approach, which should be passed down through the Supply Chain.'

(c) **Open book accounting**. 'Throughout the entire contract period the Prime Contractor will be required to operate an "Open Book" accounting regime providing the MoD with access to such relevant financial information as may reasonably be required to, amongst other things:

  (i) Monitor actual incurred costs against Target Cost;
  (ii) Substantiate claims for payment against milestones;
  (iii) Agree changes to the Target Cost to reflect additions/deletions from scope of contract;
  (iv) Assess final out-turn costs and final price payable;
  (v) Consider impact of innovative proposals.'

(d) **Project teams**. 'One of the critical success factors of Prime Contracting will be the Authority's ability to become a better-informed client. To achieve this, Prime Contracts will be managed by an MoD Integrated Project Team (IPT) consisting of full-time members with all the necessary skills and functions required to deliver the project supported, as appropriate, by specialist advice from industry. Any such support provided will be an integral part of the IPT. Throughout the bidding process organisations will be given the opportunity for greater access to the IPT to ensure that a full understanding of the project can be gained. There will in future be a direct MoD/Prime Contractor interface. After contract award the Prime Contractor will become a full member of the IPT along with his supply chain.'

(e) **Innovative solutions**. 'Throughout the entire Prime Contract process, ie from advertising the requirement through selection and evaluation and ultimately to delivery of the requirement, Prime Contractors will be encouraged to think of innovative ways of delivering the requirements which demonstrate improved value for money and continuous improvement.'

(f) **Size and length of contract**. 'Prime Contracts because of their size (they will be substantially concerned with geographical areas rather than single sites) and their duration (often five to seven years) will offer better value for money to both the MoD and the Prime Contractor than traditional procurement contracts. They represent long-term commitment and application by both participants and provide an opportunity for shared learning and development.'

Now try these questions from the Practice Question Bank

Number	Marks	Time
Q8 Objective test questions	10	18 mins
Q9 Cost reduction	25	45 mins

COST PLANNING

 Learning curve theory (Section 1) is concerned with the reduction in unit labour times (and hence cost) with the repetition of complex, labour-intensive activities. Clearly this has an impact on forecasting future costs of products and services.

Life cycle costing (Section 2) is a technique for reviewing and hence managing the costs of a product (or service or customer) for its entire life, not just during the production stage.

topic list	learning outcomes	syllabus references	ability required
1 The learning curve	A1(d)	A1(d)(i)	application
2 Life cycle costing	A1(c)	A1(c)(iv)	analysis

Chapter Overview

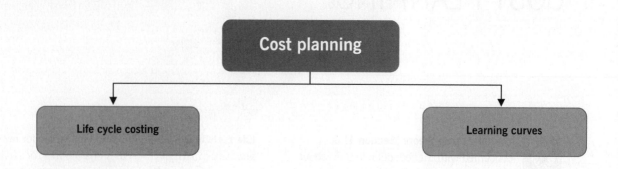

1 The learning curve

KEY TERM

Introduction

In this section we look at learning curve theory, when it is used and how to calculate rates of learning. By having an idea of how quickly labour efficiency improves, management are better placed to plan how much a product is likely to cost and how long it will take to produce.

LEARNING CURVE THEORY is used to measure how, in some industries and some situations, the incremental cost per unit of output continues to fall for each extra unit produced.

1.1 When does learning curve theory apply?

Labour time should be expected to get shorter, with experience, in the production of items which exhibit any or all of the following features.

(a) **Made largely by labour effort** rather than by a highly mechanised process
(b) **Brand new** or relatively **short-lived** product (the learning process does not continue indefinitely)
(c) **Complex** and **made in small quantities for special orders**

1.2 The learning curve theory

KEY TERM

The **LEARNING CURVE** is 'The mathematical expression of the commonly observed effect that, as complex and labour-intensive procedures are repeated, unit labour times tend to decrease. The learning curve models mathematically this reduction in unit production time'.   (*CIMA Official Terminology*)

More specifically, the learning curve theory states that the **cumulative average time per unit** produced is assumed to **decrease by a constant percentage every time total output of the product doubles**.

For instance, where an **80% learning effect or rate** occurs, the **cumulative average time required per unit of output is reduced to 80% of the previous cumulative average time when output is doubled**.

KEY POINT

By cumulative average time, we mean the average time per unit for all units produced so far, back to and including the first unit made.

The **doubling of output** is an **important feature** of the learning curve measurement. With a 70% learning curve, the cumulative average time per unit of output will fall to 70% of what it was before, every time output is doubled.

1.2.1 Example: an 80% learning curve

If the first unit of output requires 100 hours and an 80% learning curve applies, the production times would be as follows.

Cumulative number of units produced		Cumulative average time per unit Hours		Total time required Hours	Incremental time taken		
					Total hours		Hours per unit
1		100.0	(× 1)	100.0			
2*	(80%)	80.0	(× 2)	160.0	60.0	÷ 1	60.0
4*	(80%)	64.0	(× 4)	256.0	96.0	÷ 2	48.0
8*	(80%)	51.2	(× 8)	409.6	153.6	÷ 4	38.4

* Output is being doubled each time.

Notice that the incremental time per unit at each output level is much lower than the average time per unit.

1.3 Graph of the learning curve

This learning effect can be shown on a **graph** as a learning curve, either for **unit times (graph (a))** or for **cumulative total times or costs (graph (b))**.

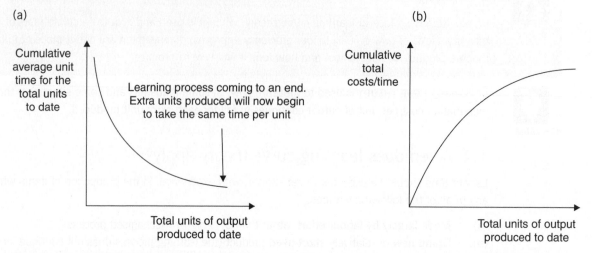

(a)

Cumulative average unit time for the total units to date

Learning process coming to an end. Extra units produced will now begin to take the same time per unit

Total units of output produced to date

(b)

Cumulative total costs/time

Total units of output produced to date

The curve on graph (a) becomes horizontal once a sufficient number of units have been produced. At this point the learning effect is lost and production time should become a constant standard, to which a standard efficiency rate may be applied.

Example: The learning curve effect

Captain Kitts has designed a new type of sailing boat, for which the cost and sales price of the first boat to be produced has been estimated as follows.

	$
Materials	5,000
Labour (800 hours × $5 per hour)	4,000
Overhead (150% of labour cost)	6,000
	15,000
Profit mark-up (20%)	3,000
Sales price	18,000

It is planned to sell all the yachts at full cost plus 20%. An 80% learning curve is expected to apply to the production work. Only one customer has expressed interest in buying the yacht so far, but he thinks $18,000 is too high a price to pay. He might want to buy two, or even four of the yachts over the next six months.

He has asked the following questions.

(a)   If he paid $18,000 for the first yacht, what price would he have to pay later for a second yacht?

(b)   Could Captain Kitts quote the same unit price for two yachts, if the customer ordered two at the same time?

(c)   If the customer bought two yachts now at one price, what would be the price per unit for a third and fourth yacht, if he ordered them both together later on?

(d)   Could Captain Kitts quote a single unit price for the following numbers of yachts if they were all ordered now?

    (i)   Four yachts
    (ii)   Eight yachts

Assuming there are no other prospective customers for the yacht, how would the questions be answered?

Solution

Number of yachts		Cumulative average time per yacht		Total time for all yachts to date		Incremental time for additional yachts
		Hours		Hours		Hours
1		800.0		800.0		
2	(× 80%)	640.0	(× 2)	1,280.0	(1,280 – 800)	480.0
4	(× 80%)	512.0	(× 4)	2,048.0	(2,048 – 1,280)	768.0
8	(× 80%)	409.6	(× 8)	3,276.8	(3,276.8 – 2,048)	1,228.8

(a)   *Separate price for a second yacht*

	$
Materials	5,000
Labour (480 hours × $5)	2,400
Overhead (150% of labour cost)	3,600
Total cost	11,000
Profit (20%)	2,200
Sales price	13,200

(b)   *A single price for the first two yachts*

	$
Materials cost for 2 yachts	10,000
Labour (1,280 hours × $5)	6,400
Overhead (150% of labour cost)	9,600
Total cost for 2 yachts	26,000
Profit (20%)	5,200
Total sales price for 2 yachts	31,200
Price per yacht (÷ 2)	15,600

(c)   *A price for the third and fourth yachts*

	$
Materials cost for 2 yachts	10,000
Labour (768 hours × $5)	3,840
Overhead (150% of labour cost)	5,760
Total cost	19,600
Profit (20%)	3,920
Total sales price for 2 yachts	23,520
Price per yacht (÷ 2)	11,760

(d)   *A price for the first four yachts together and for the first eight yachts together*

		First four yachts		First eight yachts
		$		$
Materials		20,000		40,000
Labour	(2,048 hours)	10,240	(3,276.8 hours)	16,384
Overhead	(150% of labour cost)	15,360	(150% of labour cost)	24,576
Total cost		45,600		80,960
Profit (20%)		9,120		16,192
Total sales price		54,720		97,152
Price per yacht	(÷ 4)	13,680	(÷ 8)	12,144

Question 3.1 Learning curves

Learning outcomes A1(d)

A 90% learning curve applies to the manufacture of product X. If the time taken for the first unit is three hours, what will be the average time per unit for units 5 to 8?

1.4 A formula for the learning curve

EXAM

The formula for the learning curve shown in Section 1.3(a) is $Y_x = aX^b$

Where Y = cumulative average time per unit to produce X units
a = the time required to produce the first unit of output
X = the cumulative number of units
b = the learning coefficient or the index of learning/learning index

By calculating the value of b, using logarithms or a calculator, you can calculate expected labour times for certain work.

1.4.1 Logarithms

We need to take a look at logarithms because they appear in the definition of b, the learning coefficient.

KEY TERM

The LOGARITHM of a number is the power to which ten has to be raised to produce that number.

If you have never learnt how to use logarithms, here is a brief explanation.

The **logarithm of a number, x, is the value of x expressed in terms of '10 to the power of'.**

$10 = 10^1$ The logarithm of 10 is 1.0
$100 = 10^2$ The logarithm of 100 is 2.0
$1,000 = 10^3$ The logarithm of 1,000 is 3.0

Your **calculator** will provide you with the logarithm of any number, probably using the **button marked log 10^x**. For example, to find log of 566 using a calculator, you will probably press the log button then type in 566 and the close brackets and '=', to get 2.7528, which means that $10^{2.7528} = 566$.

Logarithms are useful to us for two main reasons.

(a) The logarithm of the product of two numbers is the sum of their logarithms: **log (c × d) = log c + log d**.

(b) The logarithm of one number (say, f) to the power of another number (say, g) is the second number multiplied by the logarithm of the first: **log (f^g) = g log f**.

Logarithms can therefore be used to derive non-linear functions of the form $Y = aX^n$.

If $Y = aX^n$, the logarithm of y and the logarithm of ax^n must be the same and so **log y = log a + nlog X. This gives us a linear function similar to Y = a + nX**, the only difference being that in place of Y we have to use the logarithm of Y and in place of X we must use the logarithm of X. **Using simultaneous equations, we can get a value for n and a value for log a**, which we can convert back into a 'normal' figure using antilogarithms (the button probably marked 10^x on your calculator).

For example, suppose the relationship between x and y can be described by the function $Y = aX^n$, and suppose we know that if X = 1,000, Y = 80,000 and if X = 750, Y = 63,750.

Substitute these value into log Y = log a + n log X.

log 80,000 = log a + n log 1,000
4.9031 = log a + 3n
∴ 4.9031 – 3n = log a   (1)

log 63,750 = log a + n log 750
4.8045 = log a + 2.8751n   (2)

Sub (1) into (2).

4.8045 = 4.9031 – 3n + 2.8751n
∴ 0.1249n = 0.0986
∴ n = 0.7894

Sub value of n into (1)

4.9031 – (3 × 0.7894) = log a
2.5349 = log a
∴ 342.69 = a
∴ Our function is **Y = 342.69X $^{0.7894}$**

This technique will be useful when we come to look at the derivation of the learning rate in Section 1.4.3.

1.4.2 Logarithms and the value of b

When $Y_x = aX^b$ in learning curve theory, the value of **b = log of the learning rate/log of 2**. The learning rate is expressed as a proportion, so that for an 80% learning curve the learning rate is 0.8, and for a 90% learning curve it is 0.9, and so on.

For an 80% learning curve, b = log 0.8/log 2.

Using the button on your calculator marked log 10^x

$$b = \frac{-0.0969}{0.3010} = -0.322$$

Question 3.2   Learning curve formula

Learning outcomes A1(d)

The value of b when a 90% learning curve applies is –0.0458. True or false?

Example: Using the formula

Suppose, for example, that an 80% learning curve applies to production of item ABC. To date (the end of June) 230 units of ABC have been produced. Budgeted production for July is 55 units.

The time taken to produce the very first unit of ABC, in January, was 120 hours.

Required

Calculate the budgeted total labour time for July.

Solution

To solve this problem, we need to calculate three things:

(a)   The cumulative total labour time needed so far to produce 230 units of ABC

(b)   The cumulative total labour time needed to produce 285 units of ABC; that is, adding on the extra 55 units for July

(c)   The extra time needed to produce 55 units of ABC in July, as the difference between (b) and (a)

Calculation (a)

$Y_x = aX^b$ and we know that for 230 cumulative units, a = 120 hours (time for first unit), X = 230 (cumulative units) and b = –0.322 (80% learning curve) and so $Y = (120) \times (230^{-0.322}) = 20.83$.

So when X = 230 units, the cumulative average time per unit is 20.83 hours.

Calculation (b)

Now we do the same sort of calculation for X = 285.

If X = 285, $Y = 120 \times (285^{-0.322}) = 19.44$

So when X = 285 units, the cumulative average time per unit is 19.44 hours.

Calculation (c)

Cumulative units	Average time per unit	Total time
	Hours	Hours
230	20.83	4,791
285	19.44	5,540
Incremental time for 55 units		749

Average time per unit, between 230 and 285 units = 749/55 = 13.6 hours per unit approx

Instead of the formula you can use the **graphical methodology** (Section 1.3) to determine cumulative average time per unit but you will need considerable drawing skill to obtain an accurate result.

1.4.3 Derivation of the learning rate

The approach to derive the learning rate very much depends on the information given in the question. If you are provided with **details about cumulative production levels of 1, 2, 4, 8 or 16 (etc) units**, you can use the **first approach** shown below. If details are given about other levels, however, you need to use the second approach, which involves the use of logarithms.

Question 3.3	Calculation of the percentage learning effect

Learning outcomes A1(d)

BL is planning to produce product A. Development tests suggest that 60% of the variable manufacturing cost of product A will be affected by a learning and experience curve. This learning effect will apply to each unit produced and continue at a constant rate of learning until cumulative production reaches 4,000 units, when learning will stop. The unit variable manufacturing cost of the first unit is estimated to be $1,200 (of which 60% will be subject to the effect of learning), while the average unit variable manufacturing cost of 4 units will be $405.

Required

Calculate the rate of learning that is expected to apply.

| Question 3.4 | Calculation of percentage learning effect using logs |

Learning outcomes A1(d)

XX is aware that there is a learning effect for the production of one of its new products, but is unsure about the degree of learning. The following data relate to this product.

Time taken to produce the first unit	28 direct labour hours
Production to date	15 units
Cumulative time taken to date	104 direct labour hours

What is the percentage learning effect?

| Question 3.5 | Using the learning curve formula |

Learning outcomes A1(d)

Sciento Products manufactures complex electronic measuring instruments for which highly skilled labour is required.

Analysis of production times has shown that there is a learning curve effect on the labour time required to manufacture each unit and it has been decided to allow for this in establishing future forecast times and costs. Records have been kept of the production times for one particular instrument, the V8, an extract of which follows.

Cumulative production Units	Cumulative time Hours	Average time per unit Hours
1	200	200.0
2	360	180.0
4	648	162.0
8	1,166	145.8

The labour time analyses have shown that the learning curve follows the general form $Y = aX^b$

Where Y = average labour hours per unit   X = cumulative number of units
     a = number of labour hours for first unit   b = the learning index

Sciento Products is planning to produce a new version of the V8, the V8II, and believes that the same learning effect will apply to its production.

The company wishes to forecast the cost per V8II in a future period, to which the following data applies.

Estimated cumulative production at start of period	528 units
Estimated production in period	86 units
Estimated overheads	$150,903
Estimated labour cost	$10 per hour
Estimated material cost per unit	$250

Required

(a)   Calculate an estimated cost for the V8II in the period in question.
(b)   Discuss the usefulness of allowing for the learning effect in forecasting future labour costs and times.
(c)   Discuss the limitations of the learning effect.

1.5 Incremental time model

The model described so far is the cumulative average time model and is the one most commonly encountered. An alternative is the incremental (**or marginal or direct**) model. This model uses the same formula as the cumulative average time model but Y represents the time required to produce the final unit.

Exam alert

When learning curve theory is incorporated in an assessment question, you can assume that the cumulative average time model is applicable unless explicit instructions are given to the contrary.

1.6 The practical application of learning curve theory

What costs are affected by the learning curve?

(a) Direct labour time and costs.

(b) Variable overhead costs, if they vary with direct labour hours worked.

(c) **Materials costs** are usually **unaffected** by learning among the workforce, although it is conceivable that materials handling might improve, and so wastage costs be reduced.

(d) **Fixed overhead expenditure** should be **unaffected** by the learning curve (although in an organisation that uses absorption costing, if fewer hours are worked in producing a unit of output, and the factory operates at full capacity, the **fixed overheads recovered or absorbed per unit** in the cost of the output will decline as more and more units are made).

1.7 The relevance of learning curve effects in management accounting

1.7.1 Situations in which learning curve theory can be used

(a) To **calculate the marginal (incremental)** cost of making extra units of a product

(b) To **quote selling prices for products/services**, where prices are calculated at cost plus a percentage mark-up for profit

(c) To **prepare realistic production budgets**

(d) To design more **efficient production schedules**

(e) To **prepare realistic standard costs** for cost control purposes

1.7.2 Experience curves

The learning curve effect can be applied more broadly than just to labour. There are also efficiency gains in other areas:

(a) As methods are standardised **material wastage and spoilage** will decrease.

(b) Machine costs may decrease as **better use is made of the equipment**.

(c) **Process redesign may take place.** As understanding of the process increases, improvements and shortcuts may be developed.

(d) Learning curve labour efficiency will have a knock-on effect on the **fixed cost per unit**.

1.7.3 Further considerations

Further considerations that should be borne in mind	Detail
Sales projections, advertising expenditure and delivery date commitments	Identifying a learning curve effect should allow an organisation to plan its advertising and delivery schedules to coincide with expected production schedules. Production capacity obviously affects sales capacity and sales projections.
Budgeting with standard costs	Companies that use standard costing for much of their production output cannot apply standard times to output where a learning effect is taking place. This problem can be overcome in practice by establishing standard times for output once the learning effect has worn off or become insignificant and introducing a 'launch cost' budget for the product for the duration of the learning period. Alternatively, a standard average time per unit can be estimated for a budgeted volume of output, which makes allowance for the expected learning rate.
Cash budgets	Since the learning effect reduces unit variable costs as more units are produced, it should be allowed for in cash flow projections.
Work scheduling and overtime decisions	To take full advantage of the learning effect, idle production time should be avoided and work scheduling/overtime decisions should take account of the expected learning effect.
Pay	Where the workforce is paid a productivity bonus, the time needed to learn a new production process should be allowed for in calculating the bonus for a period.
Recruiting new labour	When a company plans to take on new labour to help with increasing production, the learning curve assumption will have to be reviewed.
Market share	The significance of the learning curve is that by increasing its share of the market, a company can benefit from shop-floor, managerial and technological 'learning' to achieve economies of scale.

1.8 Cessation of the learning effect

Improvements in the learning effect will not continue indefinitely. There will come a time when no further improvements can be made (known as a **steady state**). There are practical reasons for this cessation.

1.8.1 Machine efficiency

Machinery only has a **certain capacity of production** it can cope with. Once that capacity has been reached there can be **no further improvements** in efficiency (and thus no further improvements in time taken to produce each unit). If attempts are made to exceed capacity, efficiency could actually **decline**.

1.8.2 Workforce capacity

In a similar manner to machinery, the workforce **can only physically produce a certain amount**. Once they have reached their limit, there can be no further improvements in the time they take to produce each unit. Again, any attempts to push them beyond their capacity could have an **adverse effect** on efficiency.

1.8.3 'Go slow' agreements

Workers might agree to work no faster than a certain rate. Regardless of production conditions and potential for improvements, learning rates will **not increase** if this is the case.

1.9 Problems with applying learning curve theory

(a)   The learning curve phenomenon is **not always present**.

(b)   It **assumes stable conditions at work** which will enable learning to take place. This is not always practicable (for example because of labour turnover).

(c)   It must also **assume a certain degree of motivation** amongst employees.

(d)   **Breaks** between repeating production of an item must not be too long, or **workers will 'forget'** and the learning process would have to begin all over again.

(e)   It might be difficult to **obtain enough accurate data** to determine the learning rate.

(f)   **Workers might not agree** to a gradual reduction in production times per unit.

(g)   **Production techniques might change**, or product design alterations might be made, so that it **takes a long time for a 'standard' production method to emerge**, to which a learning effect will apply.

Section summary

Learning curve theory is used to measure how, in some industries and some situations, the incremental cost per unit of output continues to fall for each extra unit produced.

The theory is that the **cumulative average time per unit produced is assumed to fall by a constant percentage every time total output of the product doubles**. Cumulative average time is the average time per unit for all units produced so far, back to and including the first unit made.

The formula for the learning curve is $Y_x = aX^b$, where b, the learning coefficient or learning index, is defined as (log of the learning rate/log of 2).

2 Life cycle costing

Introduction

Life cycle costing is another technique used in cost planning. This section focuses on the concept of life cycle costing and how life cycle costs are linked with marketing strategies at various stages of the product life cycle.

2.1 What are life cycle costs?

Product life cycle costs are incurred **from the design stage through development to market launch, production and sales, and their eventual withdrawal from the market**.

Component elements of a product's cost over its life cycle:

(a)   **Research and development (R&D) costs:** design, testing, production process and equipment

(b)   **Technical data cost:** cost of purchasing any technical data required

(c)   **Training costs** including initial operator training and skills updating

(d)   **Production costs**

(e)   **Distribution costs:** transportation and handling costs

(f)   **Marketing costs:** customer service, field maintenance, brand promotion

(g)   **Inventory costs:** holding spare parts, warehousing and so on

(h)   **Retirement and disposal costs:** costs occurring at the end of the product's life

Life cycle costs can **apply** to **services** as well as to physical **products**, and to **customers** and **projects**.

Traditional management accounting systems are based on the financial accounting year and tend to dissect the product's life cycle into a series of annual sections. This means that management accounting systems do not accumulate costs over the entire life cycle. They **do not**, therefore, **assess a product's profitability over its entire life** but rather on a periodic basis.

Life cycle costing, on the other hand, **tracks and accumulates actual costs and revenues** attributable to each product **over the entire product life cycle**. Hence the total profitability of any given product can be determined.

KEY TERM

LIFE CYCLE COSTING is 'the profiling of cost over a product's life, including the pre-production stage'.

Life cycle costs of a product or service

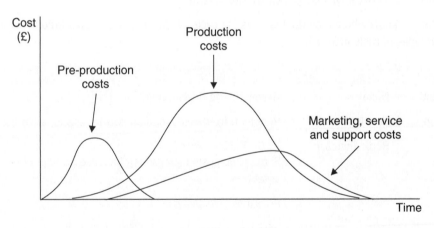

(*CIMA Official Terminology*)

2.2 The product life cycle

Every product goes through a life cycle, the curve of which resembles the generic curve in the following diagram.

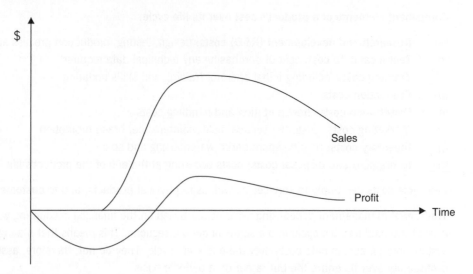

The product represented in the diagram above had an R&D stage prior to production.

The horizontal axis measures the duration of the **life cycle**, which **can last** from, say, **18 months to several hundred years**. Fad products have very short lives, while some products, such as binoculars (invented in the 18th century), can last a very long time.

2.2.1 Characteristics of the product life cycle

It is important to know where a product is in its life cycle as this will affect **expectations** regarding sales volume and types of costs incurred.

Stage	Sales volume	Costs
Development	None	Research and development
Introduction	Very low levels	Very high fixed costs (eg non-current assets, advertising)
Growth	Rapid increase	Increase in variable costs Some fixed costs increase (eg increase number of non-current assets)
Maturity	Stable High volume	Primarily variable costs Variable cost per unit stabilises as economies of scale are achieved and the learning curve may cease to apply
Decline	Falling demand	Primarily variable costs (now decreasing) Some fixed costs (eg decommissioning costs)

Where the product is in its life cycle will also **affect the returns** that are expected.

Performance measure	Stage in the life cycle			
	Introduction	Growth	Maturity	Decline
Cash	Net user	Net user	Generator	Generator
Return on capital	Not important	Not important	Important	Important
Growth	Vital	Vital	Grow with new uses	Negative growth
Profit	Not expected	Important	Important	Very important

If a product is in the **introductory or growth stages**, it **cannot be expected to be a net generator of cash**, as all the cash it generates will be used in expansion through increased sales and so on. As the product moves from **maturity towards decline**, it is of **prime importance** that the product still **generates a profit and cash** and that its **return on capital** is **acceptable**.

2.3 Problems with traditional accounting systems

Traditional accounting systems **do not tend to relate R&D costs to the products that caused them**. Instead they **write off** these costs on an **annual basis against the revenue generated by existing products**. This makes the **existing products seem less profitable** than they really are and there is a danger that they might be **scrapped** too quickly. If R&D costs are not related to the causal product, the true profitability of that product cannot be assessed.

Traditional management accounting systems usually **total all non-production costs** and record them as a **period expense**. With **life cycle costing**, these costs are **traced to individual products** over complete life cycles.

2.4 Maximising the return over the product life cycle

2.4.1 Design costs out of products

Between 70% and 90% of a product's life cycle costs are determined by decisions made early in the life cycle, at the design or development stage. Careful design of the product and manufacturing and other processes will keep cost to a minimum over the life cycle.

2.4.2 Minimise the time to market

This is the time from the **conception** of the product to its **launch**. If an organisation is launching a new product, it is **vital** to get it to the marketplace as soon as possible. This will give the product as long a period as possible without a rival in the marketplace and should mean **increased market share** in the long run. Furthermore, the life span may not proportionally lengthen if the product's launch is delayed and so sales may be permanently lost. It is not unusual for the product's overall profitability to fall by 25% if the launch is delayed by 6 months. This means that it is usually worthwhile incurring extra costs to keep the launch on schedule or to speed up the launch.

2.4.3 Minimise breakeven time (BET)

A **short** breakeven time (BET) is very important in keeping an organisation **liquid**. The sooner the product is launched, the quicker the R&D costs will be repaid, providing the organisation with funds to develop further products.

2.4.4 Maximise the length of the life span

Product life cycles are **not predetermined**; they are set by the actions of **management** and **competitors**. Once developed, some products lend themselves to a number of different uses; this is especially true of materials, such as plastic, PVC, nylon and other synthetic materials. The life cycle of the material is then a series of individual product curves nesting on top of each other, as shown below.

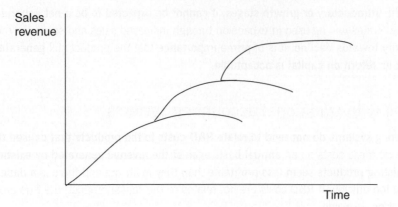

By entering different national or regional markets one after another, an organisation may be able to **maximise revenue**. This allows resources to be better applied. On the other hand, in today's fast-moving world, an organisation could lose out to a competitor if it failed to establish an early presence in a particular market.

2.4.5 Minimise product proliferation

If products are updated or superseded too quickly, the life cycle is cut short and the product may just cover its R&D costs before its successor is launched.

2.4.6 Manage the product's cash flows

Hewlett-Packard developed a return map to manage the life cycle of their products. Here is an example:

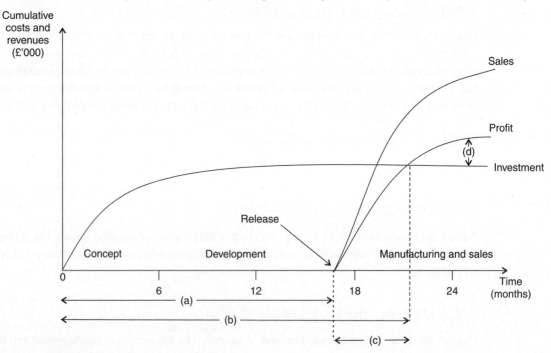

Key time periods are measured by the map:

(a)   Time to market
(b)   Breakeven time
(c)   Breakeven time after product launch
(d)   Return factor (the excess of profit over the investment)

Changes to planned time periods can be incorporated into the map (for example, if the development plan takes longer than expected) and the resulting changes to the return factor at set points after release highlighted.

2.5 Service and project life cycles

A service organisation will have services that have life cycles. The only difference is that the **R&D stages will not exist in the same way and will not have the same impact on subsequent costs**. The **different processes that go to form the complete service** are important, however, and **consideration should be given in advance as to how to carry them out and arrange them so as to minimise cost**.

Products that **take years to produce** or **come to fruition** are usually called **projects**, and **discounted cash flow calculations** are invariably used to **cost them over their life cycle in advance**. The projects need to be **monitored** very carefully **over their life** to make sure that they **remain on schedule and that cost overruns are not being incurred**.

2.6 Customer life cycles

Customers also have life cycles, and an organisation will wish to **maximise the return from a customer over their life cycle**. The aim is to **extend the life cycle of a particular customer** or decrease the 'churn' rate, as the Americans say. This means **encouraging customer loyalty**. For example, some supermarkets and other retail outlets issue **loyalty cards** that offer discounts to loyal customers who return to the shop and spend a certain amount with the organisation. As existing customers tend to be more profitable than new ones, they should be retained wherever possible.

Customers become more profitable over their life cycle. The profit can go on increasing for a period of between approximately 4 and 20 years. For example, if you open a bank account, take out insurance or invest in a pension, the company involved has to set up the account, run checks and so on. The initial cost is high and the company will be keen to retain your business so that it can recoup this cost. Once customers get used to their supplier, they tend to use them more frequently, and so there is a double benefit in holding on to customers. For example, you may use the bank to purchase shares on your behalf, or you may take out a second insurance policy with the same company.

The projected cash flows over the full lives of customers or customer segments can be analysed to highlight the worth of customers and the importance of customer retention. It may take a year or more to **recoup the initial costs of winning a customer**, and this could be referred to as the **payback period** of the investment in the customer. The investment in the customer and the consequent returns can be analysed in the same way as an investment in a capital project, a topic that we will look at later in this Study Text.

2.7 Life cycle costs and marketing strategies

As a product progresses through its life cycle, it faces different challenges and opportunities which require changes in the marketing mix (product, price, distribution and promotion) and alternative marketing strategies.

2.7.1 Introduction stage

(a)   The principal aim during this stage is to establish a market and build demand.

(b)   Some organisations may market a product before it is actually introduced, but this will alert competitors and remove any element of surprise.

(c)   Advertising costs are usually high so as to increase customer awareness of the product and to target early adopters.

(d)   Costs associated with the initial distribution of the product are likely to be incurred.

(e)   **Implications for the marketing mix:**

    (i)   **Product**. There are one or two, relatively undifferentiated products.

    (ii)   **Price**. Prices are generally high, on the assumption that a market-skimming strategy is adopted in order to earn a high profit margin from early adopters and recoup development

costs quickly. If a penetration pricing policy is adopted, introductory prices will be low to gain market share.

(iii) **Distribution**. This will be selective and scattered.

(iv) **Promotion**. This is aimed at building brand awareness. Early adopters may be offered samples or trial incentives.

2.7.2 Growth stage

(a) The aim during this stage is to gain consumer preference and increase sales.

(b) Revenue grows rapidly.

(c) More customers become aware of the product and additional market segments are targeted.

(d) As customers begin asking for the product, more retailers will want to carry it.

(e) Expansion of distribution channels may be required at this point.

(f) As competitors enter the market, promotional costs may increase (to convince consumers of the superiority of the organisation's version of the product) or price competition may occur.

(g) **Implications for the marketing mix:**

(i) **Product**. There will be improvements in the quality of the product, new product features may be introduced and alternative packaging options may be considered.

(ii) **Price**. Prices will be high if demand is high, but will be reduced if demand needs stimulating.

(iii) **Distribution**. This becomes more intensive.

(iv) **Promotion**. In order to build a preference for the brand, there may be increased advertising.

2.7.3 Maturity stage

(a) The aim during this, the most profitable stage, is to maintain market share and extend the product's life cycle.

(b) The rate of increase in sales slows down.

(c) Advertising expenditure is reduced as brand awareness should be strong.

(d) Market share and/or prices may fall as competition increases.

(e) Product differentiation will become increasingly difficult given the similarity of competitors' offerings.

(f) Marketing efforts are focused on finding new customers, encouraging customers to switch from competitors and increasing volumes of purchases per customer.

(g) Sales promotions may be used to encourage retailers to give the product more shelf space than competitors' products.

(h) **Implications for the marketing mix:**

(i) **Product**. To differentiate the product from those of competitors, modifications are made and features are added.

(ii) **Price**. In the face of competition and to avoid a price war, prices may be cut.

(iii) **Distribution**. New distribution channels may be sought. Incentives may be given to maintain shelf space.

(iv) **Promotion**. The product will need to be differentiated from those of competitors. Brand loyalty should be built. Incentives can be given to entice competitors' customers to switch.

2.7.4 Decline stage

An organisation usually has three options:

(a)   Keep the product on the market in the hope that competitors will remove theirs. Reduce costs and find new uses for the product.

(b)   Reduce marketing support and let the product continue until profits dry up.

(c)   Discontinue the product when profits dry up or a replacement product is available.

Implications for the marketing mix:

(a)   **Product**. The number of products in a product line may need to be reduced. Remaining products could be rejuvenated.

(b)   **Price**. Prices of products to be discontinued may need to be reduced to get rid of remaining inventory.

(c)   **Distribution**. Unprofitable channels are no longer used.

(d)   **Promotion**. Expenditure is reduced and focuses on reinforcing the brand image of remaining products.

2.7.5 Advantages and disadvantages of the product life cycle concept for marketing strategies

The life cycle curves of different products vary immensely and so the concept is **not always an accurate tool** for sales forecasting purposes.

It has been suggested that the product life cycle may become **self-fulfilling**: if it is thought that a product is in the decline stage and the advertising budget is cut, the product will decline further.

The product life cycle does offer a framework within which alternative marketing strategies can be planned, however, which will address the various challenges products are likely to face.

It also offers a means for comparing performance with products with similar life cycles.

Section summary

Life cycle costing involves a number of techniques that assist in the planning and control of a product's life cycle costs by monitoring spending and commitment to spend during a product's life cycle. Its aim is to minimise cost and maximise sales revenue over the life of the product.

Chapter Summary

Cost planning

Life cycle costing

- Considers the whole life of the product from development to decline
- Aims to maximise return over product's life
- Implications for marketing strategies

Learning curves

- As output doubles, the cumulative average time per unit falls to a fixed % of the previous cumulative average time per unit
- $Y = axb$
  Where:
  y = cumulative average time or cost per unit
  a = time or cost for 1st unit
  x = cumulative number of units
  $b = \dfrac{\log \text{learning rate}}{\log 2}$
- Steady state is the point at which no further improvements are possible

Quick Quiz

1   In the formula for the learning curve, $Y_x = aX^b$, how is the value of b calculated?

    A   Log of the learning rate/log of 2
    B   Log of 2/learning rate
    C   Learning rate × log of 2
    D   Log of learning rate/2

2   A company is about to commence work on a repeat order for a customer. The item to be manufactured is identical to the first order, and it is expected that a 90% learning curve will apply to the labour operations. The time taken to produce the first item was 100 hours. If labour is paid at the rate of $7 per hour, the labour cost of manufacturing the second item will be:

    A $560
    B $630
    C $700
    D $1,260

3   T plc has developed a new product, the TF8. The time taken to produce the first unit was 18 minutes. Assuming that an 80% learning curve applies, the time allowed for the fifth unit (to 2 decimal places) should be:

    A   5.79 minutes
    B   7.53 minutes
    C   10.72 minutes
    D   11.52 minutes

    Note. For an 80% learning curve $Y = aX{-}0.3219$

4   Life cycle costing is the profiling of cost over a product's production life. True or false?

5   Draw a curve of a typical product life cycle.

Answers to Quick Quiz

1   A. Make sure you can use the log function on your calculator.

2   A.

Average time per unit for first two units = 100 × 90% =	90 hours
∴ Total time for first two units = 90 × 2 =	180 hours
Less time taken for first unit	100 hours
Time taken for second unit	80 hours
Labour cost at $7 per hour	$560

3   B $Y = aX{-}0.3219$

a = 18 minutes

If the cumulative number of units (X) = 5, the cumulative average time per unit (Y) = 18 × 5-0.3219 = 10.722

Total time for 5 units = 10.722 × 5 = 53.61 minutes

If the cumulative number of units (X) = 4, the cumulative average time per unit (Y) = 18 × 4-0.3219 = 11.520

Total time for 4 units = 11.520 × 4 = 46.08 minutes

Time for fifth unit = 53.61 – 46.08 = 7.53 minutes

4   False. It includes development costs and so on prior to production and any costs such as dismantling costs when production has ceased.

5

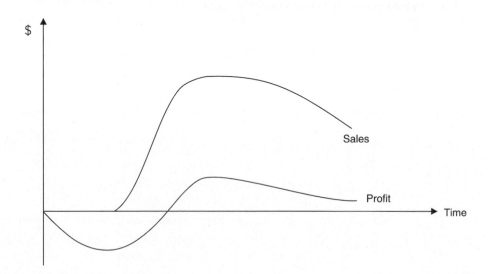

Answers to Questions

3.1 Learning curves

Cumulative number of units produced		Cumulative average time per unit Hours	Total time Hours
1		3	
2	(90%)	2.7	
4	(90%)	2.43	9.720
8	(90%)	2.187	17.496
Time taken for units 5 to 8			7.776
Average time per unit (÷ 4)			1.944 hours

3.2 Learning curve formula

The correct answer is –0.152 and so the statement is false.

b = log 0.9/log 2 = –0.0458/0.3010 = –0.152

3.3 Calculation of the percentage learning effect

Let the rate of learning be r.

Cumulative production	Cumulative average cost $
1	720*
2	720 × r
4	$720 \times r^2$

∴ $720r^2$ = £405

     r^2 = £405/£720 = 0.5625

     r = 0.75

∴ The rate of learning is 75%.

* $1,200 × 60%

3.4 Calculation of percentage learning effect using logs

Average time taken per unit to date = (104 ÷ 15) = 6.933 hours

Since Y_x = aX^b

     6.933 = $28(15)^b$

     15^b = 6.933 ÷ 28 = 0.2476

Taking logs   b log15 = log 0.2476

Since   log15 = 1.1761 (using log 10^x on your calculator)

And $\qquad \log 0.2476 = \quad -0.6062$

$$b = \frac{\log 0.2476}{\log 15} = \frac{-0.6062}{1.1761} = -0.515$$

$$b = \frac{\log \text{ of learning rate}}{\log 2}$$

$$-0.515 = \frac{\log \text{ of learning rate}}{0.3010}$$

Log of learning rate $\qquad = \quad -0.515 \times 0.3010 = -0.155$

Using the button on your calculator probably marked 10^x, -0.155 converts back to a 'normal' figure of 0.70. Thus the learning rate is 70%.

3.5 Using the learning curve formula

You need to start with a working that provides you with an **average time per unit for the units actually produced within the period**. This means that you need to determine **the number of hours worked in the period**. By calculating the average time per unit for the units produced up to the beginning of the period, you can work out the number of hours worked in total before the beginning of the period by multiplying the average time by the total output. The same calculations can then be performed but for the output produced by the end of the period. The difference between the two total times is the number of hours worked in the period, from which the period average can be calculated.

It might be tempting to take the **average time as an average of the two averages you calculate** $((77.124 + 75.375)/2 = 76.25$ hours per unit). This would be **wrong**, however, since this average would include the time taken for the first unit (200 hours) and the second, third, fourth and so on, whereas we should really be wanting a 'standard' time for the units currently being produced. Our average of 65 hours per unit is the average time needed for the 529th to the 614th units, which is much less than 76.25 hours per unit.

Workings for solution

A 90% learning curve applies because the cumulative average time per unit is 90% of what it was previously each time that cumulative total output doubles.

$Y = aX^b$, where $b = \log$ of the learning rate (as a proportion)/log of 2

With a 90% learning curve, $b = \log 0.9/\log 2 = -0.152$

(1)   X = 528,

The average labour hours per unit $= aX^{-0.152} = (200)(528)^{-0.152} = 77.124$

(2)   X = (528 + 86) = 614

The average labour hours per unit $= aX^{-0.152} = (200)(614)^{-0.152} = 75.375$

Total output Units	Average time Hours	Total time per unit Hours
614	75.375	46,280
528	77.124	40,721
86		5,559

The average time per unit for the 86 units produced in the period should be 5,559/86 = 64.64 hours, say 65 hours per unit.

Suggested solution

(a)   The standard overhead rate per hour = $150,903/(86 × 65 hours) = $27

	Estimated cost per V8ll $
Material cost	250
Labour cost (65 hours × $10 per hour)	650
Overheads (65 hours × $27 per hour)	1,755
Estimated cost per unit	2,655

(b)   **Usefulness**

(i)   Where there is a learning effect, it would be inaccurate and unrealistic to estimate labour times and labour costs without taking this effect into account.

(ii)   It is particularly important where the learning effect applies to labour which makes up a large proportion of total costs of production and sales.

(iii)   Accurate estimates of labour times are needed for efficient capacity scheduling and competitive pricing, if prices are set on a cost plus basis.

(c)   **Limitations**

(i)   An accurate estimate of labour times depends on reliable estimates of both of the following:

(1)   The learning rate
(2)   Estimated output in the period

There will almost certainly be some margin of error in the estimated times.

(ii)   The learning effect does not apply in all situations. When a product is long established, the learning effect will have worn off, and standard times per unit will be constant. The learning effect will not be significant in capital intensive operations.

Now try these questions from the Practice Question Bank	*Number*	*Marks*	*Time*
	Q10 Objective test questions	10	18 mins
	Q11 Dench	10	18 mins
	Q12 Life cycle costing	10	18 mins

PRICING STRATEGIES

 Although pricing is no longer viewed as being the most important decision made by the sales and marketing teams, it is still important for **profit-making purposes** and hence the company's survival. It is a **highly competitive tool**, particularly in markets where **product differentiation** is dominant.

This chapter focuses not only on **pricing decisions** but also on **pricing strategies**. The pricing strategy adopted will depend heavily on the **type of market** in which the product is being sold and the product's position in its **life cycle**.

The chapter begins with a look at factors that influence the pricing decision and moves on to pricing to **maximise profits**. As we move through the chapter, we will consider **cost-based approaches** to pricing, followed by pricing strategies that are appropriate in particular circumstances.

This is quite a long chapter with a lot of material in it. Read through it slowly, making sure you understand each concept before moving on.

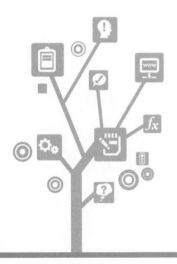

topic list	learning outcomes	syllabus references	ability required
1 Demand	C2(a)	C2(a)(i)	analysis
2 Other issues that influence pricing decisions	C2(a)	C2(a)(i)	analysis
3 Deriving the demand curve	C2(a)	C2(a)(i)	analysis
4 The profit-maximising price/output level	C2(a)	C2(a)(i)	analysis
5 Full cost-plus pricing	C2(a)	C2(a)(i)	analysis
6 Marginal cost-plus (mark-up) pricing	C2(a)	C2(a)(i)	analysis
7 Pricing based on mark-up per unit of limiting factor	C2(a)	C2(a)(i)	analysis
8 Pricing strategies for new products	C2(a)	C2(a)(ii)	analysis
9 Other pricing strategies	C2(a)	C2(a)(ii)	analysis

Chapter Overview

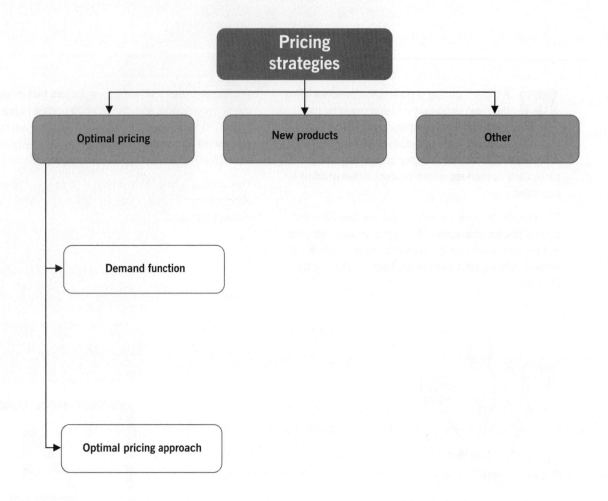

1 Demand

Introduction

In the first sections of this chapter you will be learning about the many issues that need to be considered in decisions about the price which can be charged for a product or service. The first issues relate to demand.

1.1 Issue 1: the relationship between price and demand

There are two extremes in the relationship between price and demand.

A supplier can **sell a certain quantity, Q, at any price** (as in graph (a)). Demand is totally unresponsive to changes in price and is said to be **completely inelastic**.

Alternatively, **demand might be limitless at a certain price** P (as in graph (b)), but there would be no demand above price P and there would be little point in dropping the price below P. In such circumstances, demand is said to be **completely elastic**.

(a)   (b)

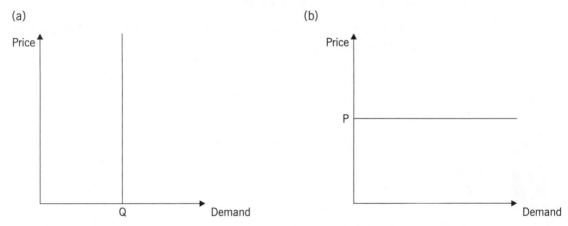

A more **normal situation** is shown below. The **downward sloping** demand curve shows the inverse relationship between unit selling price and sales volume. As one rises, the other falls. Demand is **elastic** because demand will increase as prices are lowered.

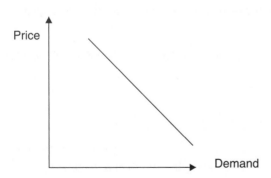

1.1.1 Price elasticity of demand (η)

KEY TERM

PRICE ELASTICITY OF DEMAND (η), which is a measure of the extent of change in market demand for a good in response to a change in its price, is measured as:

$$\frac{\text{The change in quantity demanded, as a \% of demand}}{\text{The change in price, as a \% of the price}}$$

Since the demand goes up when the price falls, and goes down when the price rises, the elasticity has a negative value, but it is usual to ignore the minus sign.

Example: Price elasticity of demand

The price of a good is $1.20 per unit and annual demand is 800,000 units. Market research indicates that an increase in price of 10 pence per unit will result in a fall in annual demand of 75,000 units. What is the price elasticity of demand?

Solution

Annual demand at $1.20 per unit is 800,000 units.

Annual demand at $1.30 per unit is 725,000 units.

% change in demand $= (75,000/800,000) \times 100\% = 9.375\%$
% change in price $= (10p/120p) \times 100\% = 8.333\%$
Price elasticity of demand $= (-9.375/8.333) = -1.125$

Ignoring the minus sign, price elasticity is 1.125.

The demand for this good, at a price of $1.20 per unit, would be referred to as **elastic** because the **price elasticity of demand is greater than 1**.

1.1.2 Elastic and inelastic demand

The value of demand elasticity may be anything from zero to infinity.

KEY TERM

Demand is referred to as INELASTIC if the absolute value is less than 1 and ELASTIC if the absolute value is greater than 1.

Exam skills

Think about what this means.

(a) Where demand is inelastic, the quantity demanded falls by a smaller percentage than the percentage increase in price.

(b) Where demand is elastic, demand falls by a larger percentage than the percentage rise in price.

1.1.3 Price elasticity and the slope of the demand curve

Generally, **demand curves slope downwards**. Consumers are willing to buy more at lower prices than at higher prices. In general, **elasticity** will **vary** in value **along the length of a demand curve**.

(a) If a downward sloping demand curve becomes **steeper** over a particular range of quantity, then demand is becoming **more inelastic**.

(b) A **shallower** demand curve over a particular range indicates **more elastic** demand.

The ranges of price elasticity at different points on a downward sloping straight line demand curve are illustrated in the diagram below.

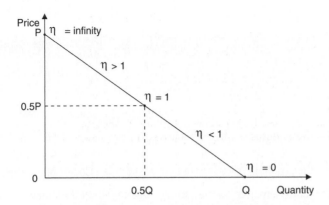

(a)   At **higher prices** on a straight line demand curve (the **top** of the demand curve), **small percentage price reductions** can bring **large percentage increases in quantity** demanded. This means that **demand is elastic** over these ranges, and **price reductions** bring **increases in total expenditure** by consumers on the commodity in question.

(b)   At **lower prices** on a straight line demand curve (the **bottom** of the demand curve), **large percentage price reductions** can bring **small percentage increases in quantity**. This means that **demand is inelastic** over these price ranges, and **price increases** result in **increases in total expenditure**.

1.1.4 Two special values of price elasticity

(a)   **Demand is perfectly inelastic ($\eta = 0$).** There is **no change in quantity** demanded, **regardless of the change in price**. The demand curve is **a vertical straight line** (as in graph (a) in Section 1.1).

(b)   **Perfectly elastic demand ($\eta = \infty$).** Consumers will want to **buy an infinite amount**, but **only up to a particular price level**. Any price increase above this level will reduce demand to zero. The demand curve is a **horizontal straight line** (as in graph (b) in Section 1.1).

1.1.5 Elasticity and the pricing decision

In practice, organisations will have only a rough idea of the shape of their demand curve: there will only be a limited amount of data about quantities sold at certain prices over a period of time **and**, of course, factors other than price might affect demand. Because any conclusions drawn from such data can only give an indication of likely future behaviour, management skill and expertise are also needed. Despite this limitation, an **awareness of the concept of elasticity can assist management with pricing decisions**.

(a)   (i)   With **inelastic demand, increase prices** because revenues will increase and total costs will reduce (because quantities sold will reduce).

        (ii)   With **elastic demand**, increases in price will bring decreases in revenue and decreases in price will bring increases in revenue. Management therefore have to **decide** whether the **increase/decrease in costs will be less than/greater than the increases/decreases in revenue**.

(b)   In situations of **very elastic demand**, overpricing can lead to massive drops in quantity sold and hence profits, whereas underpricing can lead to costly inventory outs and, again, a significant drop in profits. **Elasticity must therefore be reduced by creating a customer preference which is unrelated to price** (through advertising and promotion).

(c)   In situations of **very inelastic demand**, customers are **not sensitive to price. Quality, service, product mix and location** are therefore **more important** to a firm's pricing strategy.

(d)   In practice, the **prices** of many products, such as consumer durables, need to **fall** over time if demand is to rise. **Costs** must therefore **fall by the same percentage to maintain margins.**

1.1.6 Determining factors

Factors that determine the degree of elasticity	Detail
The price of the good	
The price of other goods	For two types of good the market demand is interconnected.
	(a) **Substitutes**, so that an increase in demand for one version of a good is likely to cause a decrease in demand for others. Examples include rival brands of the same commodity (like Coca-Cola and Pepsi-Cola).
	(b) **Complements**, so that an increase in demand for one is likely to cause an increase in demand for the other (eg cups and saucers).
Income	A rise in income gives households more to spend and they will want to buy more goods. However, this phenomenon does not affect all goods in the same way.
	(a) Normal goods are those for which a rise in income increases the demand.
	(b) Inferior goods are those for which demand falls as income rises, such as cheap clothes.
	(c) For some goods demand rises up to a certain point and then remains unchanged, because there is a limit to which consumers can or want to consume. Examples are basic foodstuffs such as salt and bread.
Tastes and fashions	A change in fashion will alter the demand for a good, or a particular variety of a good. Changes in taste may stem from psychological, social or economic causes. There is an argument that tastes and fashions are created by the producers of products and services. There is undeniably some truth in this, but the modern focus on responding to customers' needs and wants suggests otherwise.
Expectations	Where consumers believe that prices will rise or that shortages will occur they will attempt to inventory up on the product, thereby creating excess demand in the short term.
Obsolescence	Many products and services have to be replaced periodically.
	(a) Physical goods are literally 'consumed'. Carpets become threadbare, glasses get broken, foodstuffs get eaten, children grow out of clothes.
	(b) Technological developments render some goods obsolete. Manual office equipment has been largely replaced by electronic equipment, because it does a better job, more quickly, quietly, efficiently and effectively.
Size of the market	The larger the market, the more inelastic the demand for the product in broad terms. For example, the demand for bread is relatively inelastic, whereas that for speciality bread such as olive ciabatta may be more elastic.
Necessities	Demand for basic items such as milk, toilet rolls and bread is, on the whole, price inelastic.

1.2 Issue 2: demand and the market

Economic theory suggests that the volume of **demand** for a good in **the market as a whole** is influenced by a variety of variables.

- The price of the good
- The price of other goods
- Expectations
- Obsolescence

- Tastes and fashion
- The perceived quality of the product
- The size and distribution of household income

1.3 Issue 3: demand and the individual firm

1.3.1 Product life cycle

KEY TERM

PRODUCT LIFE CYCLE is 'The period which begins with the initial product specification, and ends with the withdrawal from the market of both the product and its support. It is characterised by defined stages including research, development, introduction, maturity, decline and abandonment'.

(CIMA Official Terminology)

The typical product life cycle can be represented in graphical form:

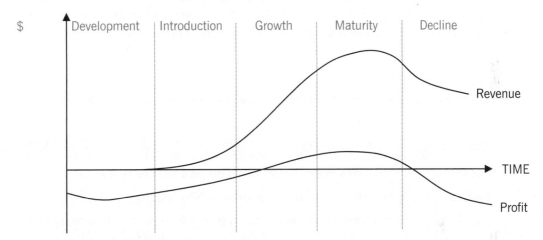

The four phases are described in more detail below:

Phase	Description
Introduction	The product is introduced to the market. Heavy capital expenditure will be incurred on product development and perhaps on the purchase of new non-current assets and building up inventory. On its launch, the product will earn some revenue, but initial demand is likely to be small. Potential customers will be unaware of the product or service, and more advertising spend may be needed to bring it to the attention of the market.
Growth	The product gains a bigger market as demand builds up. Sales revenues increase and the product begins to make a profit. The initial costs of the investment in the new product are gradually recovered.
Maturity	Eventually, growth in demand for the product will slow down and it will enter a period of relative maturity. It will continue to be profitable. The product may be modified or improved, as a means of sustaining demand.
Saturation and decline	At some stage, the market will have bought enough of the product and it will therefore reach 'saturation point'. Demand will fall. For a while, the product will still be profitable despite falling sales, but eventually it will become a loss-maker and this is the time when the organisation should stop selling the product, and so then its life cycle should reach its end.

The life expectancy of a product will influence the pricing decision. **Short-life products** must be quite **highly priced** so as to give the manufacturer a chance to **recover their investment** and **make a worthwhile** return. This is why fashion goods and new high technology goods, for example, tend to have high prices.

The current tendency is towards shorter product life cycles. Notwithstanding this observation, the **life cycles** of different products may **vary in terms of length of phases, overall length and shape**.

(a)   Fashion products have a very short life and so do high technology products because they become rapidly outdated by new technological developments.

(b)   **Different versions of the same product may have different life cycles**, and consumers are often aware of this. For example, the prospective buyer of a new car is more likely to purchase a recently introduced Ford than a Vauxhall that has been on the market for several years, even if there is nothing to choose in terms of quality and price.

1.3.2 Quality

One firm's product may be perceived to be better quality than another's, and may in some cases actually be so, if it uses sturdier materials, goes faster or does whatever it is meant to do in a 'better' way. Other things being equal, **the better quality good will be more in demand** than other versions.

1.3.3 Marketing

You may be familiar with the 'four Ps' of the marketing mix, all of which influence demand for a firm's goods.

Ps	Details
Price	This refers to the price at which the product is being sold.
Product	This refers to the particular product being analysed.
Place **(or Distribution)**	This refers to the place where a good can be, or is likely to be, purchased. • If a good is difficult to obtain, potential buyers will turn to substitutes. • Some goods only have a local appeal.
Promotion	This refers to the various means by which firms draw attention to their products and services. • A good brand name is a strong influence on demand. • Demand can be stimulated by a variety of promotional tools, such as free gifts, money off, shop displays, direct mail and media advertising.

In recent years, **emphasis** has been placed, especially in marketing, on the importance of **non-price factors in demand**. Thus the roles of product quality, promotion, personal selling and distribution and, in overall terms, brands, have grown. While it can be relatively easy for a competitor to copy a price cut, at least in the short term, it is much **more difficult to copy a successful brand image**.

Some larger organisations go to considerable effort to estimate the demand for their products or services at differing price levels; in other words, they produce estimated demand curves. A **knowledge of demand curves can be very useful**.

For example, a large transport company such as Stagecoach might be considering an increase in bus fares. The effect on total revenues and profit of the fares increase could be estimated from a **knowledge of the demand for transport services at different price levels**.

If an increase in the price per ticket caused a large fall in demand (that is, if demand were price-elastic), total revenues and profits would fall, whereas a fares increase when demand is price-inelastic would

boost total revenue and, since a transport authority's costs are largely fixed, would probably boost total profits too.

Section summary

Demand is normally **elastic** because demand will increase as prices are lowered.

Price elasticity of demand is a measure of the extent of change in market demand for a good in response to a change in its price.

If **demand** is **elastic**, a reduction in price would lead to a rise in total sales revenue. If **demand** is **inelastic**, a reduction in price would lead to a fall in total sales revenue.

The **volume of demand for one organisation's goods rather than another's** is influenced by three principal factors: product life cycle, quality and marketing.

2 Other issues that influence pricing decisions

Introduction

This section follows on from Section 1 by covering additional issues that influence pricing decisions, including competition, quality, price sensitivity and the market in which an organisation operates.

2.1 Issue 4: markets

The price that an organisation can charge for its products will be determined to a greater or lesser degree by the market in which it operates. Here are some familiar terms that might feature as background for a question or that you might want to use in a written answer.

KEY TERMS

(a) PERFECT COMPETITION: many buyers and many sellers all dealing in an identical product. Neither producer nor user has any market power and both must accept the prevailing market price.

(b) MONOPOLY: one seller who dominates many buyers. The monopolist can use their market power to set a profit-maximising price.

(c) MONOPOLISTIC COMPETITION: a large number of suppliers offer similar, but not identical, products. The similarities ensure elastic demand, whereas the slight differences give some monopolistic power to the supplier.

(d) OLIGOPOLY: where relatively few competitive companies dominate the market. Whilst each large firm has the ability to influence market prices, the unpredictable reaction from the other giants makes the final industry price indeterminate. CARTELS are often formed.

| Question 4.1 | Markets |

Learning outcome C2(a)

A cartel is often formed in which type of market?

2.2 Issue 5: competition

In established industries dominated by a few major firms, it is generally accepted that a price initiative by one firm will be countered by a price reaction by competitors. In these circumstances, prices tend to be fairly **stable**, unless pushed upwards by inflation or strong growth in demand.

If a rival cuts its prices in the expectation of increasing its market share, a firm has several options.

(a)   It will **maintain its existing prices** if the expectation is that only a small market share would be lost, so that it is more profitable to keep prices at their existing level. Eventually, the rival firm may drop out of the market or be forced to raise its prices.

(b)   It may **maintain its prices but respond with a non-price counter-attack**. This is a more positive response, because the firm will be securing or justifying its current prices with a product change, advertising, or better back-up services.

(c)   It may **reduce its prices**. This should protect the firm's market share so that the main beneficiary from the price reduction will be the consumer.

(d)   It may **raise its prices and respond with a non-price counter-attack**. The extra revenue from the higher prices might be used to finance an advertising campaign or product design changes. A price increase would be based on a campaign to emphasise the quality difference between the firm's own product and the rival's product.

2.2.1 Fighting a price war

Peter Bartram (*Financial Management,* March 2001) suggested a number of ways to fight a price war.

(a)   **Sell on value, not price**, where value is made up of service, response, variety, knowledge, quality, guarantee and price

(b)   **Target service, not product market niches**, to build in the six non-price factors in (a) above

(c)   **Use 'package pricing' to attract customers**

CASE STUDY

Computer retailers such as PC World have beaten discounters by offering peripherals, discounted software and extended warranties as part of their more expensive packages.

(d)   **Make price comparisons difficult**. Terrestrial and mobile phone companies offer a bewildering variety of rates and discount offers which disguise the core price and make comparisons almost impossible.

(e)   **Build up key accounts**, as it is cheaper to get more business from an existing customer than to find a new one. Customer profitability analysis, covered in Chapter 1, is important here.

(f)   **Explore new pricing models**. E-business provides opportunities to use new pricing models.

   (i)   Online auctions for a wide range of products are carried out on certain websites.

   (ii)   Other websites use a 'community shopping' pricing model, where the price of an item falls as more people buy it.

   (iii) Marginal cost pricing is used on certain websites to get rid of inventory such as unsold theatre tickets and holidays.

CASE STUDY

Budget airlines such as EasyJet vary the price of a ticket depending on how early the traveller books.

2.3 Other issues

Issue	Explanation/example
Price sensitivity	This will vary amongst purchasers. Those that can pass on the cost of purchases will be the least sensitive and will therefore respond more to other elements of perceived value. For example, the business traveller will be more concerned about the level of service and quality of food in looking for a hotel than price, provided that it fits the corporate budget. In contrast, the family on holiday are likely to be very price sensitive when choosing an overnight stay.
Price perception	This is the way customers react to prices. For example, customers may react to a price increase by buying more. This could be because they expect further price increases to follow (they are 'stocking up').
Compatibility with other products	A typical example is operating systems on computers, for which a user would like to have a wide range of compatible software available. For these types of product there is usually a **cumulative effect on demand**. The more people who buy one of the formats, the more choice there is likely to be of software for that format. This in turn is likely to influence future purchasers. The owner of the rights to the preferred format will eventually find little competition and will be able to charge a premium price for the product.
Competitors	An organisation, in setting prices, sends out signals. Competitors are likely to react to these signals in some way. In some industries (such as petrol retailing) pricing moves in unison; in others, price changes by one supplier may initiate a price war, with each supplier undercutting the others. Competition is discussed in more detail below.
Competition from substitute products	These are products which could be transformed for the same use or which might become desirable to customers at particular price levels. For example, train travel comes under competition as the quality, speed and comfort of coach travel rises. Similarly, if the price of train travel rises, it comes under competition from cheaper coach travel and more expensive air travel.
Suppliers	If an organisation's suppliers notice a price rise for the organisation's products, they may seek a rise in the price for their supplies to the organisation on the grounds that it is now able to pay a higher price.
Inflation	In periods of inflation the organisation may need to change prices to reflect increases in the prices of supplies and so on. Such changes may be needed to keep relative (real) prices unchanged.
Quality	In the absence of other information, customers tend to judge quality by price. Thus a price change may send signals to customers concerning the quality of the product. A price rise may indicate improvements in quality; a price reduction may signal reduced quality, for example through the use of inferior components.
Incomes	In times of rising incomes, price may become a less important marketing variable compared with product quality and convenience of access (distribution). When income levels are falling and/or unemployment levels rising, price will become a much more important marketing variable.

Section summary

As well as demand, a **range of other issues influence pricing decisions**, including the market in which an organisation operates, competition, quality and price sensitivity.

3 Deriving the demand curve

Introduction

The demand curve shows the relationship between the price charged for a product and the subsequent demand for that product. This section shows how a demand curve is derived. Don't be put off by the equations – work through the examples slowly and make sure you are comfortable with working with the equations before moving on.

3.1 Demand curve equations

LEARN

Formulae to learn

When demand is linear the **equation for the demand curve is P = a − bx**

Where P = the selling price
x = the quantity demanded at that price
a = theoretical maximum price. If price is set at 'a' or above, demand will be zero
b = the change in price required to change demand by one unit
a and b are constants and are calculated as follows:

$$a = \$ (\text{current price}) + \left(\frac{\text{Current quantity at current price}}{\text{Change in quantity when price changed by } \$b} \times \$b \right)$$

$$b = \frac{\text{Change in price}}{\text{Change in quantity}} \quad \text{(it is the gradient of line)}$$

You need to learn these formulae.

Example: Deriving the demand curve

The current price of a product is $12. At this price the company sells 12,000 items a month. One month the company decides to raise the price to $13, but only 9,500 items are sold at this price. Determine the demand equation.

Solution

STEP **1**   **Find the gradient of the line (b)**

Using the formula above, this can be shown as:

$$b = \frac{\$1}{2,500} = 0.0004$$

STEP 2

Extract figures from the question

The **demand equation** can now be determined as P = a – bx

b = 0.0004

x = 12,000 (number of units sold at current selling price)

P = a – (0.0004 × 12,000)

12 = a – 4.80

a = 16.80

∴P = 16.80 – 0.0004x

STEP 3

Check your equation

We can check this by substituting $12 and $13 for P.

12 = 16.80 – 0.0004x = 16.80 – (0.0004 × 12,000)
13 = 16.80 – 0.0004x = 16.80 – (0.0004 × 9,500)

Example: Profit maximisation and the demand curve

Maximum demand for JL's product is 110,000 units per annum. Demand will reduce by 50 units for every $1 increase in the selling price. JL has calculated that the profit-maximising level of sales for the coming year will be 42,000 units.

Required

Calculate the profit-maximising selling price for the product.

Solution

Using the demand equation P = a – bx

P = selling price

x = the quantity demanded at that price

a,b = constants

Maximum demand is achieved when the product is free (when P = 0).

When price = 0, demand (x) = 110,000   0 = a – 110,000b (i)

When price = 1, demand (x) = 109,950   1 = a – 109,950b (ii)

Subtract (i) from (ii)   1 = 50b

                                          b = 0.02

Substitute in (i)   a = 110,000 × 0.02

                                             = 2,200

The demand equation for the product is therefore P = 2,200 – 0.02x

When x = 42,000 units   P = 2,200 – (0.02 × 42,000)
                                  = 1,360

Therefore, the profit-maximising selling price is $1,360 per unit.

Question 4.2 | Profit maximisation

Learning outcomes C2(a)

Maximum demand for AL's product is 8,000 units per annum. Demand will reduce by 50 units for every $1 increase in the selling price.

AL has calculated that the profit-maximising selling price for the coming year will be $10.

What is the profit-maximising sales level in units?

Section summary

When demand is linear the **equation for the demand curve** is **P = a − bx**

Where P = the selling price
 x = the quantity demanded at that price
 a = theoretical maximum price. If price is set at 'a' or above, demand will be zero
 b = the change in price required to change demand by one unit

a and b are constants and are calculated as follows:

$$a = \$ \text{(current price)} + \left(\frac{\text{Current quantity at current price}}{\text{Change in quantity when price changed by \$b}} \times \$b \right)$$

$$b = \frac{\text{Change in price}}{\text{Change in quantity}} \quad \text{(it is the gradient of line)}$$

You need to learn these formulae.

---

4 The profit-maximising price/output level

Introduction

The overall objective of an organisation should be **profit maximisation**. In this section we look at how the profit-maximising price and output levels can be derived. Remember that, in microeconomic theory, profits are maximised when marginal revenue = marginal cost.

4.1 Microeconomic theory and profit maximisation

Microeconomic theory suggests that as output increases, the marginal cost per unit might rise (due to the law of diminishing returns) and, whenever the firm is faced with a downward sloping demand curve, the **marginal revenue per unit will decline**.

Eventually, a level of output will be reached where the **extra cost** of making one extra unit of output is greater than the **extra revenue** obtained from its sale. It would then be unprofitable to make and sell that extra unit.

Profits will continue to be maximised only up to the output level where marginal cost has risen to be exactly equal to the marginal revenue.

Profits are maximised using marginalist theory when **marginal cost (MC) = marginal revenue (MR)**.

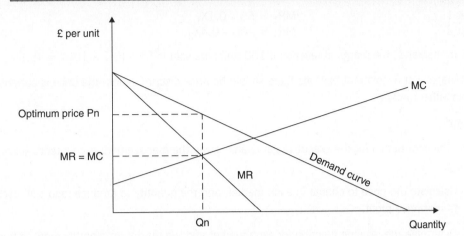

Profits are **maximised** at the point where **MC = MR**, ie at a volume of Qn units. If we add a demand curve to the graph, we can see that at an output level of Qn, the sales price per unit would be Pn.

It is important to make a clear distinction in your mind between the **sales price** and **marginal revenue**. In this example, the optimum price is Pn, but the marginal revenue is much less. This is because the 'additional' sales unit to reach output Qn has only been achieved by reducing the unit sales **price** from an amount higher than Pn for all the units to be sold, not just the marginal extra one. The increase in sales volume is therefore partly offset by a reduction in unit price; hence MR is lower than Pn.

4.2 Determining the profit-maximising selling price: using equations

The **optimal selling price** can be determined using equations (ie when MC = MR).

You could be **provided with equations for marginal cost and marginal revenue** and/or have to **devise them from information** in the question. By **equating the two equations** you can determine the optimal price. Remember, **marginal cost** is the **extra cost of producing one extra unit; marginal revenue** is the **extra revenue from producing one extra unit**. **Marginal revenue may not be the same as** the **price** charged for all units up to that demand level, as to increase volumes the price may have to be reduced. The following example provides an illustration.

Example: MC = MR

MOC makes and sells a copyrighted, executive game for two distinct markets, in which it has a monopoly. The fixed costs of production per month are $20,000 and variable costs per unit produced, and sold, are $40. (The monthly sales can be thought of as X, where $X = X_1 + X_2$, with X_1 and X_2 denoting monthly sales in their respective markets.) Detailed market research has revealed the demand functions in the markets to be as follows, with prices shown as P_1, P_2.

Market 1: $P_1 = 55 - 0.05X_1$
Market 2: $P_2 = 200 - 0.2X_2$

(**Note**. These formulae are simply **linear equations**. They show how the price (P) can be determined for a given level of demand (X). So in market 1, at a level of demand of 100, the price (P) will be $55 - (0.05 \times 100) = 50$.)

From these, the management accountant has derived that the marginal revenue functions in the two markets are as follows.

Market 1: $MR_1 = 55 - 0.1X_1$

Market 2: $MR_2 = 200 - 0.4X_2$

(**Note**. In market 1, the marginal revenue if 100 units are sold is $55 - (0.1 \times 100) = 45$.)

The management accountant believes there should be price discrimination; the price is currently $50 per game in either market.

Required

Analyse the information for the executive game and, given the management accountant's belief, do the following.

(a)   Calculate the price to charge in each market, and the quantity to produce (and sell) each month, to maximise profit.

(b)   Determine the revenue function for each market and the maximum monthly profit in total.

(c)   Calculate and comment on the change in total profitability and prices.

Solution

(a)   In both markets, **marginal cost = variable cost per unit = $40**

Profit is maximised when **marginal revenue = marginal cost**.

Market 1

$55 - 0.1X_1$ $= 40$

$0.1X_1$ $= 15$

X_1 $= 15/0.1 = 150$

and price $P_1 = 55 - (0.05 \times 150) = \$47.5$.

Hence the price in market 1 should be $47.50 per unit and 150 units should be produced.

Market 2

$200 - 0.4X_2$ $= 40$

$0.4X_2$ $= 160$

X_2 $= 160/0.4 = 400$

and price $P_2 = 200 - (0.2 \times 400) = \$120$.

Hence the price in market 2 should be $120 per unit and 400 units should be produced.

Total number of items to be produced per month is 550.

(b)   **Revenue = unit price × number of units sold**

Market 1

Revenue $= P_1X_1 = 55X_1 - 0.05X_1^2$

Market 2

Revenue $= P_2X_2 = 200X_2 - 0.2X_2^2$

From (a), profit is maximised when

$X_1 = 150$ and $X_2 = 400$

$P_1 = 47.5$ and $P_2 = 120$

At maximum profit:

Total revenue = $(47.5 \times 150) + (120 \times 400) = \$55,125$

Total costs = $20,000 + (40 \times 550) = \$42,000$

Total maximum monthly profit = $\$13,125$

(c)   Currently the price is $50 in both markets.

Market 1 $50 = 55 - 0.05X_1$
                $0.05X_1 = 55 - 50 = 5$
                $X_1 = 5/0.05 = 100$

Market 2 $50 = 200 - 0.2X_2$
                $0.2X_2 = 200 - 50 = 150$
                $X_2 = 150/0.2 = 750$

Therefore the **total number of units** = $100 + 750 = 850$.

Total revenue = $\$50 \times 850 = \$42,500$.

Total cost = $20,000 + (40 \times 850) = \$54,000$.

So the game **currently makes a loss** of $11,500.

Hence, if the prices are changed to $47.50 in market 1 and $120 in market 2, the company can expect to turn a monthly loss of $11,500 into a profit of $13,125.

You will be provided with equations representing MC and MR if they are needed. Note, however, that if a question states that the extra cost of producing one extra item is $20, say, you will be expected to realise that the MC is $20. Likewise, if you are told that **100 units are sold for $10 each**, but **101 can only be sold for $9.99**, the **MR of the 101st item is (101 × $9.99) – (100 × $10) = $8.99**.

Question 4.3	Deriving an MR equation from the demand curve

Learning outcomes C2(a)

AB has used market research to determine that if a price of $250 is charged for product G, demand will be 12,000 units. It has also been established that demand will rise or fall by 5 units for every $1 fall/rise in the selling price. The marginal cost of product G is $80.

Required

If marginal revenue = $a - 2bx$ when the selling price (P) = $a - bx$, calculate the profit-maximising selling price for product G.

4.3 Determining the profit-maximising selling price: visual inspection of a tabulation of data

KEY POINT

The **optimum selling price** can also be determined using tabulation, graphs and gradients.

To determine the profit-maximising selling price:

(a)   Work out the **demand curve** and hence the **price** and the **total revenue** (PQ) at various levels of demand

(b)   Calculate **total cost** and hence **marginal cost** at each level of demand

(c)   Finally calculate **profit** at each level of demand, thereby determining the price and level of demand at which profits are maximised

Question 4.4   Tabulation approach to find profit-maximising price

Learning outcomes C2(a)

An organisation operates in a market where there is imperfect competition so that, to sell more units of output, it must reduce the sales price of all the units it sells. The following data is available for prices and costs.

Total output Units	Sales price per unit (AR) $	Average cost of output (AC) $ per unit
0	–	–
1	504	720
2	471	402
3	439	288
4	407	231
5	377	201
6	346	189
7	317	182
8	288	180
9	259	186
10	232	198

The total cost of zero output is $600.

Required

Complete the table below to determine the output level and price at which the organisation would maximise its profits, assuming that fractions of units cannot be made.

Units	Price $	Total revenue $	Marginal revenue $	Total cost $	Marginal cost $	Profit $
0						
1						
2						
3						
4						
5						
6						
7						
8						
9						
10						

4.4 Determining the profit-maximising selling price: graphical approach

The diagrams below show that **profits are maximised** at the point where the **vertical distance** between the total revenue curve and the total costs curve is at a **maximum** (which is fairly obvious if you think about it, since profits are maximised when the difference between cost and revenue is maximised). This profit-maximising demand level also **corresponds** to the point at which the **MC and MR curves intersect**, as we would expect. Notice how the profit-maximising price can be read off from the demand curve.

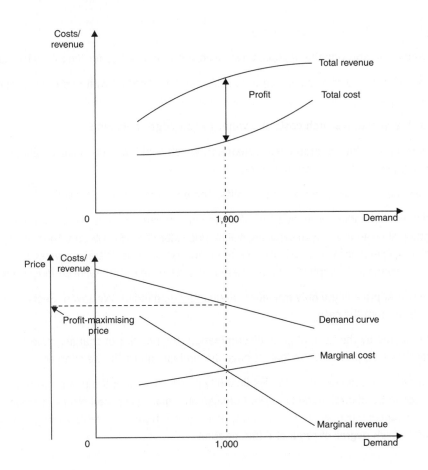

4.5 Determining the profit-maximising selling price: using gradients

Suppose we were to draw **tangents** to the total revenue and total cost curves at the **points at which profit is maximised**. As you can see, the gradients of these tangents **are the same**.

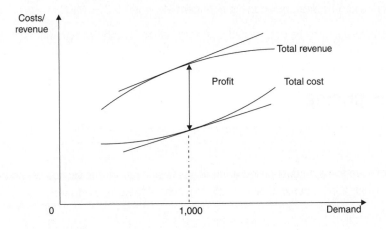

The **gradient of the total cost curve** is the **rate at which total cost changes with changes in volume**, which is simply **marginal cost**. Likewise, the **gradient of the total revenue curve** is the **rate at which total revenue changes with changes in volume**, which is the **marginal revenue**. At the **point of profit maximisation**, the two gradients are **equal** and hence, once again, **MC = MR**.

4.6 Optimum pricing in practice

There are problems with applying the approach described above in practice for the following reasons.

(a) It assumes that the demand curve and total costs can be **identified with certainty**. This is unlikely to be so.

(b) It ignores the **market research costs of** acquiring knowledge of demand.

(c) It assumes the firm has **no production constraint**, which could mean that the equilibrium point between supply and demand cannot be reached.

(d) It assumes the objective is **to maximise profits**. There may be other objectives.

CASE STUDY

Microsoft dominates the market for many types of computer software, but this domination was not achieved by setting short-term profit-maximising selling prices for the MS-DOS and Windows operating systems. By offering cheap licences to PC manufacturers for use of these operating systems, Microsoft word processing, spreadsheet, graphics and database packages have become almost industry-standard.

(e) It assumes that **price is the only influence** on quantity demanded. We saw in Sections 1 and 2 that this is far from the case.

(f) It is **complicated by** the issue of **price discrimination** (the practice of charging different unit selling prices for the same product). We look at price discrimination later in the chapter.

(g) Although there are arguments for the **applicability** of the concept of the profit-maximising unit selling price in **traditional markets** where **homogenous, mass-produced** products are in **continuous supply** (such as public transport), the **modern trend** is towards **short product life cycles** and a **high degree of product differentiation**.

Section summary

Profits are maximised using marginalist theory when **marginal cost (MC) = marginal revenue (MR)**.

The **optimal selling price** can be determined using equations (ie when MC = MR).

The **optimum selling price** can also be determined using tabulation, graphs and gradients.

5 Full cost-plus pricing

Introduction

In the next two sections we focus on cost-based approaches to pricing. In this section we concentrate on full cost-plus pricing which adds a percentage onto the full cost of the product to arrive at the selling price.

5.1 Reasons for its popularity

In practice cost is one of the most important influences on price. Many firms base price on simple **cost-plus rules** (costs are estimated and then a mark-up is added in order to set the price). A study by Lanzilotti gave a number of **reasons** for the **predominance of this method**.

(a)   Planning and use of scarce capital resources are easier.

(b)   Assessment of divisional performance is easier.

(c)   It emulates the practice of successful large companies.

(d)   Organisations fear government action against 'excessive' profits.

(e)   There is a tradition of production rather than of marketing in many organisations.

(f)   There is sometimes tacit collusion in industry to avoid competition.

(g)   Adequate profits for shareholders are already made, giving no incentive to maximise profits by seeking an 'optimum' selling price.

(h)   Cost-based pricing strategies based on internal data are easier to administer.

(i)   Over time, cost-based pricing produces stability of pricing, production and employment.

KEY TERM

FULL COST-PLUS PRICING is a method of determining the sales price by calculating the full cost of the product and adding a percentage mark-up for profit.

5.2 Setting full cost-plus prices

The 'full cost' may be a fully absorbed production cost only, or it may include some absorbed administration, selling and distribution overhead.

A business might have an idea of the percentage profit margin it would like to earn, and so might **decide on an average profit mark-up** as a general guideline for pricing decisions. This would be particularly **useful for** businesses that carry out a large amount of **contract work or jobbing work**, for which individual job or contract prices must be quoted regularly to prospective customers. However, the percentage profit **mark-up does not have to be rigid and fixed**, but can be varied to suit the circumstances. In particular, the percentage mark-up can be varied to suit demand conditions in the market.

Question 4.5	Cost-plus pricing

Learning outcome C2(a)

A product's full cost is $4.75 and it is sold at full cost plus 70%. A competitor has just launched a similar product selling for $7.99.

Required

Fill in the gap in the sentence below.

The cost-plus percentage will need to be reduced by...... %.

Example: Full cost-plus pricing

Markup has begun to produce a new product, Product X, for which the following cost estimates have been made.

	$
Direct materials	27
Direct labour: 4 hours at $5 per hour	20
Variable production overheads: machining, ½ hour at $6 per hour	3
	50

Production fixed overheads are budgeted at $300,000 per month and, because of the shortage of available machining capacity, the company will be restricted to 10,000 hours of machine time per month. The absorption rate will be a direct labour rate, however, and budgeted direct labour hours are 25,000 per month. It is estimated that the company could obtain a minimum contribution of $10 per machine hour on producing items other than product X.

The direct cost estimates are not certain as to material usage rates and direct labour productivity, and it is recognised that the estimates of direct materials and direct labour costs may be subject to an error of ± 15%. Machine time estimates are similarly subject to an error of ± 10%.

The company wishes to make a profit of 20% on full production cost from product X.

Required

Ascertain the full cost-plus based price.

Solution

Even for a relatively 'simple' cost-plus pricing estimate, some problems can arise, and certain assumptions must be made and stated. In this example, we can identify two problems.

(a)   Should the opportunity cost of machine time be included in cost or not?
(b)   What allowance, if any, should be made for the possible errors in cost estimates?

Different assumptions could be made.

(a)   **Exclude machine time opportunity costs: ignore possible costing errors**

	$
Direct materials	27.00
Direct labour (4 hours)	20.00
Variable production overheads	3.00
Fixed production overheads (at $\frac{£300,000}{25,000}$ = $12 per direct labour hour)	48.00
Full production cost	98.00
Profit mark-up (20%)	19.60
Selling price per unit of product X	117.60

(b)   **Include machine time opportunity costs: ignore possible costing errors**

	$
Full production cost as in (a)	98.00
Opportunity cost of machine time: contribution forgone (½ hour × $10)	5.00
Adjusted full cost	103.00
Profit mark-up (20%)	20.60
Selling price per unit of product X	123.60

(c)   **Exclude machine time opportunity costs but make full allowance for possible underestimates of cost**

	$	$
Direct materials	27.00	
Direct labour	20.00	
	47.00	
Possible error (15%)	7.05	
		54.05
Variable production overheads	3.00	
Possible error (10%)	0.30	
		3.30
Fixed production overheads (4 hours × $12)	48.00	
Possible error (labour time) (15%)	7.20	
		55.20
Potential full production cost		112.55
Profit mark-up (20%)		22.51
Selling price per unit of product X		135.06

(d)   **Include machine time opportunity costs and make a full allowance for possible underestimates of cost**

	$
Potential full production cost as in (c)	112.55
Opportunity cost of machine time:	
potential contribution forgone (½ hr × $10 × 110%)	5.50
Adjusted potential full cost	118.05
Profit mark-up (20%)	23.61
Selling price per unit of product X	141.66

Using different assumptions, we could arrive at any of 4 different unit prices in the range $117.60 to $141.66.

5.3 Problems with and advantages of full cost-plus pricing

There are several serious **problems** with relying on a full cost-plus approach to pricing.

(a)   It **fails to recognise** that, since demand may be determining price, **there will be a profit-maximising combination of price and demand**.

(b)   There may be a need to **adjust prices to market and demand conditions**.

(c)   **Budgeted output volume** needs to be established. Output volume is a key factor in the overhead absorption rate.

(d)   A **suitable basis for overhead absorption** must be selected, especially where a business produces more than one product.

However, it is a **quick, simple and cheap** method of pricing which can be delegated to junior managers (which is particularly important with jobbing work where many prices must be decided and quoted each day) and, since the size of the profit margin can be varied, a decision based on a price in excess of full cost should ensure that a company working at normal capacity will **cover all of its fixed costs and make a profit**.

Example: Full cost-plus versus profit-maximising prices

Tiger has budgeted to make 50,000 units of its product, timm. The variable cost of a timm is $5 and annual fixed costs are expected to be $150,000.

The financial director of Tiger has suggested that a mark-up of 25% on full cost should be charged for every product sold. The marketing director has challenged the wisdom of this suggestion, and has produced the following estimates of sales demand for timms.

Price per unit ($)	9	10	11	12	13
Demand (units)	42,000	38,000	35,000	32,000	27,000

Required

(a) Calculate the profit for the year if a full cost-plus price is charged.
(b) Calculate the profit for the year if a profit-maximising price is charged.

Assume in both (a) and (b) that 50,000 units of timm are produced regardless of sales volume.

Solution

The full cost per unit comprises $5 of variable costs plus $3 of fixed costs ($8 in total). A 25% mark-up on this cost gives a selling price of $10 per unit so that sales demand would be 38,000 units. (Production is given as 50,000 units.) **Profit using absorption costing** would be as follows.

	$	$
Sales		380,000
Costs of production (50,000 units)		
Variable (50,000 × $5)	250,000	
Fixed (50,000 × $3)	150,000	
	400,000	
Less increase in inventory (12,000 units × 8)	(96,000)	
Cost of sales		304,000
Profit		76,000

Profit using marginal costing instead of absorption costing, so that fixed overhead costs are written off in the period they occur, would be as follows. (The 38,000 unit demand level is chosen for comparison.)

	$
Contribution (38,000 × $(10 − 5))	190,000
Fixed costs	150,000
Profit	40,000

Since the company cannot go on indefinitely producing an output volume in excess of sales volume, this profit figure is more indicative of the profitability of timms in the longer term.

A **profit-maximising price** is one which gives the greatest net (relevant) cash flow, which in this case is the **contribution-maximising price**.

Price $	Unit contribution $	Demand Units	Total contribution $
9	4	42,000	168,000
10	5	38,000	190,000
11	6	35,000	210,000
12	7	32,000	224,000
13	8	27,000	216,000

The profit maximising price is $12, with annual sales demand of 32,000 units.

This example shows that a **cost-plus based price is unlikely to be the profit-maximising price**, and that a **marginal costing approach**, calculating the total contribution at a variety of different selling prices, will be **more helpful** for establishing what the profit-maximising price ought to be.

Section summary

In **full cost-plus pricing** the sales price is determined by calculating the full cost of the product and then adding a percentage mark-up for profit. The most important criticism of full cost-plus pricing is that it fails to recognise that since sales demand may be determined by the sales price, there will be a profit-maximising combination of price and demand.

6 Marginal cost-plus (mark-up) pricing

Introduction

This section follows on from Section 5 by looking at marginal cost-plus pricing. Whereas a full cost-plus approach to pricing draws attention to net profit and the net profit margin, a marginal (variable) cost-plus approach to pricing **draws attention to gross profit** and the **gross profit margin**, or **contribution**.

MARGINAL COST-PLUS PRICING/MARK-UP PRICING is a method of determining the sales price by adding a profit margin onto either marginal cost of production or marginal cost of sales.

Question 4.6	Marginal cost pricing

Learning outcome C2(a)

A product has the following costs.

	$
Direct materials	5
Direct labour	3
Variable overheads	7

Fixed overheads are $10,000 per month. Budgeted sales per month are 400 units to allow the product to break even.

Required

Fill in the blank in the sentence below.

The mark-up which needs to be added to **marginal** cost to allow the product to break even is ...... %.

6.1 The advantages and disadvantages of a marginal cost-plus approach to pricing

The main advantages are as follows.

(a)   It is a **simple and easy** method to use.

(b)   The **mark-up percentage can be varied**, and so mark-up pricing can be adjusted to reflect demand conditions.

(c) It **draws management attention to contribution**, and the effects of higher or lower sales volumes on profit. In this way, it helps to create a better awareness of the concepts and implications of marginal costing and cost-volume-profit analysis. For example, if a product costs $10 per unit and a mark-up of 150% is added to reach a price of $25 per unit, management should be clearly aware that every additional $1 of sales revenue would add 60 pence to contribution and profit.

(d) In practice, mark-up pricing is used in businesses **where there is a readily identifiable basic variable cost**. Retail industries are the most obvious example, and it is quite common for the prices of goods in shops to be fixed by adding a mark-up (20% or 33.3%, say) to the purchase cost.

There are, of course, drawbacks to marginal cost-plus pricing.

(a) Although the **size** of the mark-up can be varied in accordance with demand conditions, it **does not ensure that sufficient attention is paid to demand conditions, competitors' prices and profit maximisation**.

(b) It **ignores fixed overheads** in the pricing decision, but the sales price must be sufficiently high to ensure that a profit is made after covering fixed costs.

Section summary

Marginal cost-plus pricing involves adding a profit margin to the marginal cost of production/sales. A marginal costing approach is more likely to help with identifying a profit-maximising price.

---

7 Pricing based on mark-up per unit of limiting factor

Introduction

This short section demonstrates how to calculate a price based on mark-up per unit of a limiting factor.

Example: Mark-up per unit of limiting factor

Suppose that a company provides a window cleaning service to offices and factories. Business is brisk, but the company is restricted from expanding its activities further by a shortage of window cleaners. The workforce consists of 12 window cleaners, each of whom works a 35-hour week. They are paid $4 per hour. Variable expenses are $0.50 per hour. Fixed costs are $5,000 per week. The company wishes to make a contribution of at least $15 per hour.

The minimum charge per hour for window cleaning would then be as follows.

	$ per hour
Direct wages	4.00
Variable expenses	0.50
Contribution	15.00
Charge per hour	19.50

The company has a total workforce capacity of (12 × 35) 420 hours per week, and so total revenue would be $8,190 per week, contribution would be (420 × $15) $6,300, leaving a profit after fixed costs of $1,300 per week.

Section summary

Another approach to pricing might be taken when a **business is working at full capacity and is restricted by a shortage of resources** from expanding its output further. By deciding what target profit it would like to earn, it could **establish a mark-up per unit of limiting factor**.

8 Pricing strategies for new products

Introduction

When a new product is launched, it is essential that the company gets the pricing strategy correct, otherwise the wrong message may be given to the market (if priced too cheaply) or the product will not sell (if the price is too high). This section looks at how to approach pricing for new products to ensure a smooth launch.

Two pricing strategies for **new** products are **market penetration pricing** and **market skimming pricing**.

KEY POINT

8.1 Tabulation

Suppose that Novo is about to launch a new product with a variable cost of $10 per unit. The company has carried out market research (at a cost of $15,000) to determine the potential demand for the product at various selling prices.

Selling price $	Demand Units
30	20,000
25	30,000
20	40,000

Its current capacity is for 20,000 units but additional capacity can be made available by using the resources of another product line. If this is done, the lost contribution from the other product will be $35,000 for each additional 10,000 units of capacity.

How could we **analyse this information** for senior management in a way that helps them to **decide on the product's launch price**?

Tabulation is the approach to use with a problem of this type.

Selling price $	Demand Units ('000)	Variable costs $'000	Opportunity costs $'000	Total costs $'000	Sales revenue $'000	Contribution $'000
30	20	200	–	200	600	400
25	30	300	35	335	750	415
20	40	400	70	470	800	330

The **optimum price to maximise short-term profits is $25**. However, it is quite possible that the aim will **not** be to maximise short-term profits, and a number of other strategies may be adopted, as discussed below.

The main **objections** to the approach described above are that it only **considers a limited range of prices** (what about charging $27.50?) and it **takes no account of the uncertainty of forecast demand**. However, allowance could be made for both situations by collecting more information.

Question 4.7   Pricing new products

Learning outcome C2(a)

JPM is just about to launch a new product.

Production capacity means that a maximum of 120 units can be manufactured each week and manufacture must be in batches of 10. The marketing department estimates that at a price of $120 no units will be sold but, for each $3 reduction in prices, 10 additional units per week will be sold.

Fixed costs associated with manufacturing the product are expected to be $6,000 per week. Variable costs are expected to be $40 per unit for the first 8 batches, but after that the unit variable cost of the products in the batch will be $2 more than those in the preceding batch.

Which is the most profitable level of output per week?

A   80 units

B   90 units

C   100 units

D   110 units

8.2 First on the market?

A new product pricing strategy will depend largely on whether a company's product or service is the first of its kind on the market.

(a)   If the **product is the first of its kind**, there will be **no competition** yet, and the company, for a time at least, will be a **monopolist**. Monopolists have more influence over price and are able to set a price at which they think they can maximise their profits. A monopolist's price is likely to be higher, and its profits bigger, than those of a company operating in a competitive market.

(b)   If the new product being launched by a company is **following a competitor's product** onto the market, the pricing strategy will be **constrained by what the competitor** is already doing. The new product could be given a higher price if its quality is better, or it could be given a price which matches the competition. Undercutting the competitor's price might result in a price war and a fall of the general price level in the market.

8.2.1 Market penetration pricing

MARKET PENETRATION PRICING is a policy of low prices when the product is first launched in order to obtain sufficient penetration into the market.

Circumstances in which a penetration policy may be appropriate.

(a)   If the firm wishes to **discourage new entrants** into the market

(b)   If the firm wishes to **shorten the initial period of the product's life cycle** in order to enter the growth and maturity stages as quickly as possible

(c)   If there are **significant economies of scale** to be achieved **from a high volume of output**, so that quick penetration into the market is desirable in order to gain unit cost reductions

(d)   If **demand is highly elastic** and so would respond well to low prices

Penetration prices are prices which aim to **secure a substantial share in a substantial total market**. A firm might therefore **deliberately build excess production capacity** and set its prices very low. As demand builds up, the spare capacity will be used up gradually and unit costs will fall; the firm might

even reduce prices further as unit costs fall. In this way, early losses will enable the firm to dominate the market and have the lowest costs.

8.2.2 Market skimming pricing

KEY TERM

MARKET SKIMMING PRICING involves charging high prices when a product is first launched and spending heavily on advertising and sales promotion to obtain sales.

As the product moves into the later stages of its life cycle, **progressively lower prices will be charged** and so the profitable 'cream' is skimmed off in stages until sales can only be sustained at lower prices.

The aim of market skimming is to **gain high unit profits early in the product's life**. High unit prices make it **more likely that competitors will enter the market** than if lower prices were to be charged.

Circumstances in which such a policy may be appropriate

(a)   Where the product is **new and different**, so that customers are prepared to pay high prices so as to be one up on other people who do not own it.

(b)   Where the **strength** of demand and the **sensitivity of demand** to price are **unknown**. It is better from the point of view of marketing to start by charging high prices and then reduce them if the demand for the product turns out to be price elastic, than to start by charging low prices and then attempt to raise them substantially if demand appears to be insensitive to higher prices.

(c)   Where **high prices** in the early stages of a product's life might **generate high initial cash flows**. A firm with liquidity problems may prefer market-skimming for this reason.

(d)   Where the firm **can identify different market segments** for the product, each prepared to pay progressively lower prices. If **product differentiation** can be introduced, it may be possible to continue to sell at higher prices to some market segments when lower prices are charged in others. This is discussed further below.

(e)   Where products may have a **short life cycle**, and so need to recover their development costs and make a profit relatively quickly.

Section summary

Two pricing strategies for **new** products are **market penetration pricing** and **market skimming pricing**.

Market penetration pricing is a policy of low prices when the product is first launched in order to obtain sufficient penetration into the market.

Market skimming pricing involves charging high prices when a product is first launched and spending heavily on advertising and sales promotion to attract customers.

9   Other pricing strategies

Introduction

This section looks at other pricing strategies that might be employed by organisations. There are quite a few strategies covered here, so make sure you understand the key points of each.

9.1 Product differentiation and price discrimination

PRICE DISCRIMINATION is the practice of charging different prices for the same product to different groups of buyers when these prices are not reflective of cost differences.

In certain circumstances, the **same product** can be sold at different prices to **different customers**. There are a number of bases on which such discriminating prices can be set.

Basis	Detail
By market segment	A cross-channel ferry company would market its services at different prices in England and France, for example. Services such as cinemas and hairdressers are often available at lower prices to pensioners and/or juveniles.
By product version	Many car models have **optional extras** which enable one brand to appeal to a wider cross-section of customers. The final price need not reflect the cost price of the optional extras directly: usually the top of the range model would carry a price much in excess of the cost of provision of the extras, as a prestige appeal.
By place	Theatre seats are usually sold according to their location so that patrons pay different prices for the same performance according to the seat type they occupy.
By time	This is perhaps the most popular type of price discrimination. Off-peak travel bargains, hotel prices and telephone charges are all attempts to increase sales revenue by covering variable but not necessarily average cost of provision. Railway companies are successful price discriminators, charging more to rush hour rail commuters whose demand is inelastic at certain times of the day.

Price discrimination can only be effective if a number of **conditions** hold.

(a)   The market must be **segmentable** in price terms, and different sectors must show different intensities of demand. Each of the sectors must be identifiable, distinct and separate from the others, and be accessible to the firm's marketing communications.

(b)   There must be little or **no** chance of a **black market** developing (this would allow those in the lower priced segment to resell to those in the higher priced segment).

(c)   There must be little or **no** chance that **competitors** can and will undercut the firm's prices in the higher priced (and/or most profitable) market segments.

(d)   The cost of segmenting and **administering** the arrangements should not exceed the extra revenue derived from the price discrimination strategy.

9.1.1 'Own label' pricing: a form of price discrimination

Many supermarkets and multiple retail stores sell their 'own label' products, often at a lower price than established branded products. The supermarkets or multiple retailers do this by entering into arrangements with manufacturers, to supply their goods under the 'own brand' label.

9.2 Premium pricing

This involves making a product **appear 'different'** through **product differentiation** so as **to justify a premium price**. The product may be different in terms of, for example, quality, reliability, durability, after-sales service or extended warranties. Heavy advertising can establish brand loyalty, which can help to sustain a premium, and premium prices will always be paid by those customers who blindly equate high price with high quality.

9.3 Product bundling

Product bundling is a variation on price discrimination which involves **selling a number of products or services as a package at a price lower than the aggregate of their individual prices**. For example, a hotel might offer a package that includes the room, meals, use of leisure facilities and entertainment at a combined price that is lower than the total price of the individual components. This might encourage customers to buy services that they might otherwise not have purchased.

The **success** of a bundling strategy depends on the expected **increase in sales volume** and **changes in margin**. Other cost changes, such as in product handling, packaging and invoicing costs, are possible. **Longer-term issues**, such as competitors' reactions, must also be considered.

9.4 Pricing with optional extras

The decision here is very similar to that for product bundling. It rests on whether the **increase in sales revenue from the increased price that can be charged** is **greater** than the **increase in costs** required to incorporate extra features. Not all customers will be willing to pay a higher price for additional features if they do not want or need those features.

9.5 Loss leader pricing

A **loss leader** is when a company sets a very low price for one product intending to make customers buy other products in the range which carry higher profit margins. An example is selling inkjet printers at a relatively low price whilst selling the print cartridges at a higher profit margin. People will buy many of the high-profit items but only one of the low-profit items, yet they are 'locked in' to the former by the latter.

9.6 Using discounts

Reasons for using discounts to adjust prices:

- To get rid of perishable goods that have reached the end of their shelf life
- To sell off seconds
- Normal practice (eg antique trade)
- To increase sales volumes during a poor sales period without dropping prices permanently
- To differentiate between types of customer (wholesale, retail and so on)
- To get cash in quickly

9.7 Controlled prices

Many **previously nationalised industries** now operate within the private sector and are **overseen by an industry regulator** (such as OFCOM for telecommunications).

Regulators tend to concentrate on **price** so that these near monopolies cannot exploit their position (although the regulators are also concerned with quality of service/product).

If a **price is regulated**, the **elasticity of demand is zero**: 'small' customers pay less than they otherwise would, whereas 'large' customers pay more than in a competitive environment.

Prices have become **more flexible in recent years**, however:

(a)   Introduction of discounted price for very large customers
(b)   Entry of other companies into the market

Question 4.8   Pricing strategies

Learning outcome C2(a)

As management accountant to a group of companies manufacturing footwear, you have been asked to consider the following two subjects that are to be discussed at the next group pricing committee meeting.

(a)   The possibility of differential pricing for different sizes of shoes

(b)   The levels of prices at which contracts with a large multiple retailer for 'own label' shoes might be negotiated

Required

Describe briefly the major topics under each of the above headings that you would include in the agenda for discussion.

Section summary

Product differentiation may be used to make products appear to be different. **Price discrimination** is then possible.

Price discrimination is the practice of charging different prices for the same product to different groups of buyers when these prices are not reflective of cost differences.

Chapter Summary

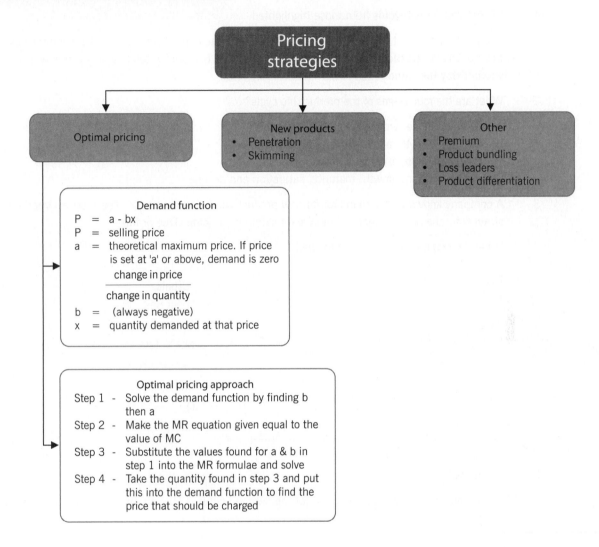

Pricing strategies

Optimal pricing

New products
- Penetration
- Skimming

Other
- Premium
- Product bundling
- Loss leaders
- Product differentiation

Demand function
$P = a - bx$
P = selling price
a = theoretical maximum price. If price is set at 'a' or above, demand is zero

$$\frac{\text{change in price}}{\text{change in quantity}}$$

b = (always negative)
x = quantity demanded at that price

Optimal pricing approach
Step 1 - Solve the demand function by finding b then a
Step 2 - Make the MR equation given equal to the value of MC
Step 3 - Substitute the values found for a & b in step 1 into the MR formulae and solve
Step 4 - Take the quantity found in step 3 and put this into the demand function to find the price that should be charged

Quick Quiz

1   Choose the correct words from those highlighted.

    The price elasticity of demand for a particular good at the current price is 1.2. Demand for this good at this price is (1) **elastic/inelastic**. If the price of the good is reduced, total sales revenue will (2) **rise/fall/stay the same**.

2   What are the four stages of the product life cycle?

    A   Appearance, growth, maturity, saturation
    B   Birth, growth, adolescence, old age
    C   Introduction, expansion, maturity, death
    D   Introduction, growth, maturity, saturation and decline

3   A company knows that demand for its new product will be highly elastic. The most appropriate pricing strategy for the new product will be market-skimming pricing. True or false?

4   Label the graph with the terms provided.

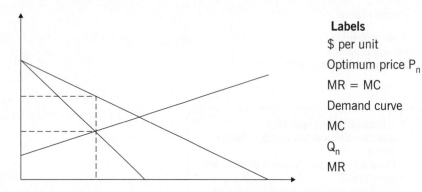

Labels
$ per unit
Optimum price P_n
MR = MC
Demand curve
MC
Q_n
MR

5   Fill in the blanks.

    When demand is linear, the equation for the demand curve is P = a – bx

    where

    P = ...

    x = ...

    a = ...

    b = ...

    The constant a is calculated as $ (....................) + ($\dfrac{\text{............................}}{\text{.............................}}$ × $b)

6   At the point of profit maximisation, the gradients of the total cost curve and total revenue curve are the same in absolute terms, but one is positive, one is negative. True or false?

7   Fill in the blanks.

    (a)   One of the problems with relying on a full cost-plus approach to pricing is that it fails to recognise that since price may be determining demand, there will be a .... combination of .... and ....

    (b)   An advantage of the full cost-plus approach is that, because the size of the profit margin can be varied, a decision based on a price in excess of full cost should ensure that a company working at .... capacity will cover .... and make a ....

8   A theatre offers a special deal whereby two show tickets and pre-theatre dinner can be purchased as a package for a reduced price. This pricing strategy is usually referred to as:

A   Loss leader pricing
B   Optional extras
C   Product bundling
D   Price discrimination

9   Pricing based on mark-up per unit of limiting factor is particularly useful if an organisation is not working to full capacity. True or false?

10   Fill in the blank.

The .... price is the price at which an organisation will break even if it undertakes particular work.

11   Choose the correct word from those highlighted.

Market-**skimming/penetration** pricing should be used if an organisation wishes to discourage new entrants into a market.

12   'Own label' pricing is a form of psychological pricing. True or false?

13   If a price is regulated, the elasticity of demand is:

A   −1
B   0
C   1
D   Infinity

Answers to Quick Quiz

1   (1) elastic, (2) rise

2   D. Learn them!

3   False. Market penetration pricing would be more appropriate.

4

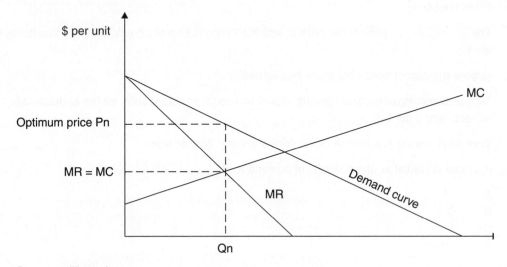

5   P   = selling price

     x   = quantity demanded at that price

     a   = price at which demand will be nil (theoretical maximum price)

     b   = $\dfrac{\text{change in price}}{\text{change in quantity}}$ Gradient of line. Represents the change in price required to change demand by 1 unit.

     The constant a is calculated as $ (current price) + $\left(\dfrac{\text{Current quantity at current price}}{\text{Change in quantity when price changed by }\$b} \times \$b \right)$

6   False. The gradients are exactly the same.

7   (a)   profit-maximising combination of price and demand

     (b)   working at normal capacity will cover all of its fixed costs and make a profit

8   C   Product bundling involves selling a number of products or services as a package at a price lower than the aggregate of their individual prices.

9   False. It is useful if the organisation is working at full capacity.

10   Minimum

11   Market penetration

12   False. It is a form of price discrimination.

13   B. The elasticity of demand is zero.

Answers to Questions

4.1 Markets

The correct answer is **an oligopoly**.

4.2 Profit maximisation

Using the demand equation $P = a - bx$

Maximum demand is achieved when the product is free (when $P = 0$)

When price = 0, demand (x) = 8,000	$0 = a - 8,000b$ (i)
When price = 1, demand (x) = 7,950	$1 = a - 7,950b$ (ii)
Subtract (i) from (ii)	$1 = 50b$
	$b = 0.02$
Substitute in (i)	$a = 8,000 \times 0.02$
	$= 160$

The demand equation for the product is therefore $P = 160 - 0.02x$

When price = $10	$\$10 = 160 - (0.02x)$
	$x = 7,500$

The profit-maximising sales level is 7,500 units.

4.3 Deriving an MR equation from the demand curve

$b = \dfrac{1}{5} = 0.2$

$a = \$250 + (12,000 \times 0.2) = \$2,650$

Profits are maximised when MC = MR, ie when $80 = a - 2bx$

$80 = 2,650 - 0.4x$, $\therefore 0.4x = 2,650 - 80$, $\therefore x = (2,650 - 80) / 0.4$, $\therefore x = 6,425$

Profit-maximising demand	$= 6,425$
$\therefore$ Profit-maximising price	$= \$(2,650 - 0.2 \times 1,285)$
	$= \$1,365$

4.4 Tabulation approach to find profit-maximising price

Profit is maximised at 7 units of output and a price of $317, when MR is most nearly equal to MC.

Units	Price $	Total revenue $	Marginal revenue $	Total cost $	Marginal cost $	Profit $
0	0	0	0	600	–	(600)
1	504	504	504	720	120	(216)
2	471	942	438	804	84	138
3	439	1,317	375	864	60	453
4	407	1,628	311	924	60	704
5	377	1,885	257	1,005	81	880
6	346	2,076	191	1,134	129	942
7	317	2,219	143	1,274	140	945
8	288	2,304	85	1,440	166	864
9	259	2,331	27	1,674	234	657
10	232	2,320	(11)	1,980	306	340

4.5 Cost-plus pricing

The correct answer is that the cost-plus percentage will need to be reduced by 2%.

Profits = $(7.99 – 4.75) = $3.24

Mark-up = ($3.24/$4.75) × 100% = 68%

∴ % needs to be reduced by (70 – 68)% = 2%

4.6 Marginal cost pricing

The correct answer is $166^2/_3\%$.

Breakeven point is when total contribution equals fixed costs.

At breakeven point, $10,000 = 400 (price – $15)

∴ $25 = price – $15
∴ $40 = price
∴ Mark-up = ((40 – 15) /15) × 100% = $166^2/_3\%$

4.7 Pricing new products

The correct answer is C.

Note that we cannot use the profit-maximisation model because of the non-linear relationships involved.

Units		Total variable costs $	Selling price per unit $	Total sales revenue $	Total contribution $
80	(× $40)	3,200	96*	7,680	4,480
90	(× $42)	3,780	93	8,370	4,590
100	(× $44)	4,400	90	9,000	4,600
110	(× $46)	5,060	87	9,570	4,510
120	(× $48)	5,760	84	10,080	4,320

*$120 – (8 × $3)

4.8 Pricing strategies

(a)   **Differential pricing for different sizes of shoes**

(i)   **Cost differences**
If the differential pricing is to allow for differences in cost, are these cost differences sufficient to justify significant price differentials?

(ii)   **Administration costs**
Consideration should be given to the increased cost of administering a differential price structure.

(iii)   **Custom and practice**
If it is accepted practice to charge differential prices for shoes, the company may be missing an opportunity to increase profits.

(iv)   **Reaction of retailers**
Retailers may not react favourably because their own pricing policy will become more complicated and time consuming.

(v)   **Effect on demand**
If higher prices are to be charged for larger shoes, what effect will this have on demand and profits?

(vi) **Competitors' actions**

If competitors are not already practising differential pricing, will they follow our lead? If not, what will be the effect on demand and profits?

(vii) **Differential pricing for marketing purposes**

If, instead of pricing according to cost, the company wishes to offer lower prices for the more popular sizes, will the extra demand justify the reduction in price?

(b) **Prices for own-label shoes**

(i) **Capacity available**

The available capacity will dictate whether or not marginal pricing can be used. It would not be advisable to use marginal pricing if this displaces full-price work.

(ii) **The effect on other business**

Will the sales of own-label shoes affect the demand for our other ranges? If lower prices are offered to the multiple retailer, will other customers start to demand similar reductions?

(iii) **The terms of the negotiated contract**

The company must ensure that they will have the flexibility to change prices if costs fluctuate.

(iv) **The cost of increased working capital**

An expansion in output will result in increased working capital. Will the retailers expect us to hold inventories for them and how much credit will they require? These facts must be evaluated and taken into account in the pricing policy.

(v) **Exclusive designs**

Will the retailer require exclusive designs, or can cost savings be achieved by using the same designs for our own range of footwear?

Now try these questions from the Practice Question Bank

Number	Marks	Time
Q13 Objective test questions	10	18 mins
Q14 PN motor components	10	18 mins
Q15 DX	10	18 mins
Q16 Plastic tools	10	18 mins
Q17 Costs and pricing	10	18 mins
Q18 Hilly plc	4	8 mins

CONTROL AND PERFORMANCE MANAGEMENT OF RESPONSIBILITY CENTRES

Part B

214

DECISION MAKING IN RESPONSIBILITY CENTRES

 This chapter follows on from your CIMA P1 studies of budgeting and focuses on how budgets can be used for control purposes.

Budgetary control is the comparison of actual results with budgeted results. **Variances** are calculated to identify the differences between actual and budgeted results and these differences are reported to management so that appropriate **action** can be taken.

Such an approach relies on a system of **flexible** (as opposed to fixed) budgets. We look at the difference between the two types in **Section 2. Flexible budgets**

are vital for both **planning and control. Section 2** shows how they are constructed and **Section 4** looks at their use in the overall **budgetary control process**.

The chapter then considers the **behavioural implications** of operating a budgetary control system. As in all studies of human behaviour, it is difficult to draw concrete conclusions. There is, however, one point which is agreed: **budgeting is more than a mathematical technique**.

The chapter concludes with a review of the criticisms of budgeting and the recommendations of the advocates of '**Beyond Budgeting**'.

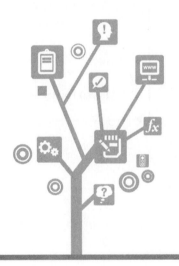

topic list	learning outcomes	syllabus references	ability required
1 Responsibility centres	B1(b), B3(a)	B1(b)(i), B3(a)(i), (ii)	application
2 Fixed and flexible budgets	B1(a)	B1(a)(i)	analysis
3 Preparing flexible budgets	B1(a)	B1(a)(i)	analysis
4 Flexible budgets and budgetary control	B1(a), (b)	B1(a)(i), (b)(i)	application
5 Behavioural implications of budgeting	B2(c)	B2(c)(i)	analysis
6 Budget participation	B2(c)	B2(c)(i)	analysis
7 The use of budgets as targets	B2(c)	B2(c)(i)	analysis
8 Budgets and motivation	B2(c)	B2(c)(i)	analysis
9 Beyond Budgeting	B2(c)	B2(c)(ii)	analysis

Chapter Overview

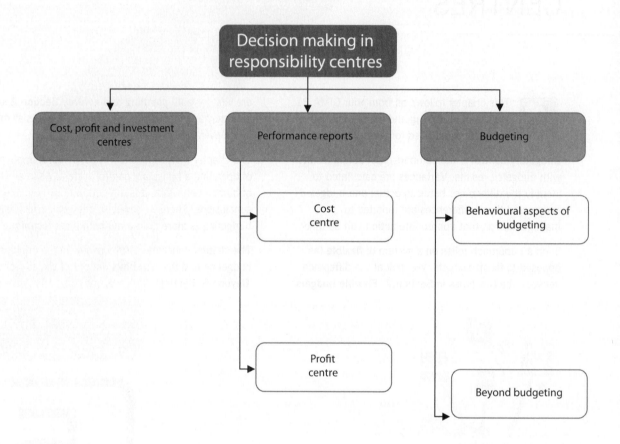

1 Responsibility centres

Introduction

This section focuses on the responsibility centre business model. Make sure you familiarise yourself with the different categories of responsibility centre and what they can control (costs, profit, investment).

1.1 Divisionalisation

In general, a large organisation can be **structured in one of two ways: functionally** (all activities of a similar type within a company, such as production, sales, research, are under the control of the appropriate departmental head) or **divisionally** (split into divisions in accordance with the products or services made or provided).

Divisional managers are therefore responsible for all operations (production, sales and so on) relating to their product, the functional structure being applied to each division. It is possible, of course, that only part of a company is divisionalised and activities such as administration are structured centrally on a functional basis with the responsibility of providing services to **all** divisions.

1.2 Decentralisation

In general, a **divisional structure will lead to decentralisation** of the decision-making process and divisional managers may have the freedom to set selling prices, choose suppliers, make product mix and output decisions and so on. Decentralisation is, however, a matter of degree, depending on how much freedom divisional managers are given.

1.3 Advantages of divisionalisation

(a)   Divisionalisation can **improve** the **quality of decisions** made because divisional managers (those taking the decisions) know local conditions and are able to make more informed judgements. Moreover, with the personal incentive to improve the division's performance, they ought to take decisions in the division's best interests.

(b)   **Decisions should be taken more quickly** because information does not have to pass along the chain of command to and from top management. Decisions can be made on the spot by those who are familiar with the product lines and production processes and who are able to react to changes in local conditions quickly and efficiently.

(c)   The authority to act to improve performance should **motivate divisional managers**.

(d)   Divisional organisation **frees top management** from detailed involvement in day to day operations and allows them to devote more time to strategic planning.

(e)   Divisions provide **valuable training grounds for future members of top management** by giving them experience of managerial skills in a less complex environment than that faced by top management.

(f)   In a large business organisation, the central head office will not have the management resources or skills to direct operations closely enough itself. Some authority must be delegated to local operational managers.

1.4 Disadvantages of divisionalisation

(a) A danger with divisional accounting is that the business organisation will divide into a number of self-interested segments, each acting at times against the wishes and interests of other segments. Decisions might be taken by a divisional manager in the best interests of his own part of the business, but against the best interest of other divisions and possibly against the interests of the organisation as a whole.

A task of **head office** is therefore to try to **prevent dysfunctional decision making** by individual divisional managers. To do this, head office must reserve some power and authority for itself so that divisional managers cannot be allowed to make entirely independent decisions. A **balance** ought to be kept **between decentralisation** of authority, to provide incentives and motivation, **and retaining centralised authority**, to ensure that the organisation's divisions are all working towards the same target, to the benefit of the organisation as a whole (in other words, **retaining goal congruence** among the organisation's separate divisions).

KEY TERM

GOAL CONGRUENCE 'In a control system is the state which leads individuals or groups to take actions which are in their self-interest and also in the best interest of the entity'.   (*CIMA Official Terminology*)

(b) It is claimed that the **costs of activities that are common** to all divisions, such as running the accounting department, **may be greater** for a divisionalised structure than for a centralised structure.

(c) **Top management**, by delegating decision making to divisional managers, may **lose control**, since they are not aware of what is going on in the organisation as a whole. (With a good system of performance evaluation and appropriate control information, however, top management should be able to control operations just as effectively.)

1.5 Responsibility accounting

KEY TERM

RESPONSIBILITY ACCOUNTING is a system of accounting that segregates revenue and costs into areas of personal responsibility in order to monitor and assess the performance of each part of an organisation.

The creation of divisions allows for the operation of a system of responsibility accounting. There are a number of types of responsibility accounting unit or responsibility centre that can be used within a system of responsibility accounting.

In the weakest form of **decentralisation** a system of cost centres might be used. As decentralisation becomes stronger, the responsibility accounting framework will be based around profit centres. In its **strongest form investment centres are used**.

Type of responsibility centre	Manager has control over ...	Principal performance measures
Cost centre	Controllable costs	Variance analysis Efficiency measures
Revenue centre	Revenues only	Revenues
Profit centre	Controllable costs Sales prices (including transfer prices)	Profit
Investment centre	Controllable costs Sales prices (including transfer prices) Output volumes Investment in non-current assets and working capital	Return on investment Residual income Other financial ratios

1.6 Cost centres

A cost centre manager is responsible for, and has control over, the costs incurred in the cost centre. The manager has **no responsibility for earning revenues** or for **controlling the assets and liabilities of the centre**.

Cost centre organisations can be relatively easy to establish because, as you will recall from your earlier studies, a cost centre is any part of the organisation to which costs can be separately attributed. A cost centre **forms the basis for building up cost records** for cost measurement, budgeting and control.

Functional departments such as production, personnel and marketing might be treated as cost centres and made responsible for their costs.

A performance report for a cost centre might look like this.

	Budgeted costs (original) $	Budgeted costs (flexed) $	Actual costs $	Variance $
COST CENTRE X				
PERFORMANCE REPORT FOR THE PERIOD				
Budgeted activity: (units)				
Actual activity: (units)				
Material costs				
Labour costs				
Variable overhead costs				
Depreciation costs				
etc				

Two important points to note about this report are as follows.

(a) The report should include **only controllable costs**, although, as we have seen, there is a case for also providing information on certain **uncontrollable costs**. However, there should be a **clear distinction** in the report between controllable costs and uncontrollable costs.

(b) The actual costs are compared with a budget that has been **flexed to the actual activity level achieved**. This approach provides better information, for the purposes of both control and motivation as we will see later in this chapter.

The use of flexible budget information is appropriate for control comparisons in production cost centres, but the costs attributed to **discretionary cost centres** are more difficult to control. Examples of discretionary cost centres include advertising, research and development and training cost centres. Management has a **significant amount of discretion** as to the amount to be budgeted for the particular activity in question.

Moreover, there is no optimum relationship between the inputs (as measured by the costs incurred) and the outputs achieved. **Fixed budgets** must be used for the control of discretionary costs.

Question 5.1   Responsibility accounting

Learning outcome B2(c)

Explain the meaning and importance of controllable costs, uncontrollable costs and budget cost allowance in the context of a system of responsibility accounting.

1.7 Revenue centres

The manager of a revenue centre is responsible only for raising revenue but has no responsibility for forecasting or controlling costs. An example of a revenue centre might be a sales centre.

Revenue centres are often used for control purposes in not-for-profit organisations such as charities. For example, a revenue centre manager may have responsibility for revenue targets **within an overall fundraising exercise**, but that manager does not control the costs incurred. Such responsibility would pass to a more senior manager to whom the revenue centre manager reports.

1.8 Profit centres

KEY TERM

A PROFIT CENTRE is a part of a business accountable for both costs and revenues.

For a profit centre organisation structure to be established, it is necessary to identify units of the organisation to which both revenues and costs can be separately attributed. Revenues might come from sales of goods and services to **external customers**, or from goods and services **provided to other responsibility centres within the organisation**. These internal 'sales' are charged at a notional selling price or **transfer price**. We will return to look at transfer prices in detail in Chapter 7.

A profit centre's performance report, in the same way as that for a cost centre, would identify separately the controllable and non-controllable costs. A profit centre performance report might look like this.

PROFIT CENTRE Y			
STATEMENT OF PROFIT OR LOSS FOR THE PERIOD			
	Budget	*Actual*	*Variance*
	$'000	$'000	$'000
Sales revenue	X	X	
Variable cost of sales	(X)	(X)	
Contribution	X	X	
Directly attributable/controllable fixed costs			
Salaries	X	X	
Stationery costs	X	X	
	etc	etc	
	(X)	(X)	
Gross profit (directly attributable/controllable)	X	X	
Share of uncontrollable costs (eg head office costs)	(X)	(X)	
Net profit	X	X	

Again, the budget for the sales revenue and variable cost of sales will be **flexed according to the activity level achieved**.

The variances could be analysed in further detail for the profit centre manager.

Notice that three different 'profit levels' are highlighted in the report.

(a)   Contribution, which is within the control of the profit centre manager

(b)   Directly attributable gross profit, which is also within the manager's control

(c)   Net profit, which is after charging certain uncontrollable costs and which is therefore not controllable by the profit centre manager

1.9 Attributable costs and controllable costs

In the example of profit centre Y we have assumed that all attributable costs are controllable costs. Although this is usually the case, some care is needed before this assumption is made.

In responsibility accounting, an attributable cost is **a cost that can be specifically identified with a particular responsibility centre**. No arbitrary apportionment is necessary to share the cost over a number of different responsibility centres.

You can see, therefore, that **most attributable costs will be controllable costs**. An example of an attributable fixed cost is the salary of the supervisor working in a particular responsibility centre.

However, think about the depreciation of the equipment in profit centre Y. This is certainly **attributable to the profit centre**, but is it a controllable cost? The answer is probably 'no'. It is unlikely that the manager has control over the level of investment in equipment in profit centre Y, otherwise the centre would be classified as an investment centre.

Therefore it might be necessary to include a third measure of 'profit' in our performance report, which would be the controllable profit before the deduction of those costs which are attributable to the profit centre, but which are not controllable by the profit centre manager.

Exam alert

If an assessment question requires you to prepare a performance report for a responsibility centre, read the information carefully to distinguish controllable attributable and non-controllable costs, and then state clearly any assumptions you need to make in order to distinguish between them.

1.10 Investment centres

KEY TERM

An INVESTMENT CENTRE is a 'Profit centre with additional responsibilities for capital investment and possibly for financing, and whose performance is measured by its return on investment'.

(CIMA Official Terminology)

Where a manager of a division or strategic business unit is **allowed some discretion about the amount of investment undertaken** by the division, assessment of results by profit alone (as for a profit centre) is clearly inadequate. The profit earned must be related to the amount of capital invested. Such divisions are sometimes called investment centres for this reason. Performance is measured by **return on capital employed (ROCE)**, often referred to as **return on investment (ROI)** and other subsidiary ratios, or by **residual income (RI)**.

Managers of **subsidiary companies will often be treated as investment centre** managers, accountable for profits and capital employed. Within each subsidiary, the major divisions might be treated as profit centres, with each divisional manager having the authority to decide the prices and output volumes for the products or services of the division. Within each division, there will be departmental managers,

section managers and so on, who can all be treated as cost centre managers. All managers should receive regular, periodic performance reports for their own areas of responsibility.

The amount of **capital employed** in an investment centre should consist only of **directly attributable non-current assets and working capital (net current assets)**.

(a)   Subsidiary companies are often required to remit spare cash to the central treasury department at group head office, and so directly attributable working capital would normally consist of inventories and receivables less payables, but minimal amounts of cash.

(b)   If an investment centre is apportioned a share of head office non-current assets, the amount of capital employed in these assets should be recorded separately because it is not directly attributable to the investment centre or controllable by the manager of the investment centre.

Section summary

There are a number of advantages and disadvantages to **divisionalisation**. The principal disadvantage is that it can lead to dysfunctional decision making and a lack of goal congruence.

Responsibility accounting is the term used to describe decentralisation of authority, with the performance of the decentralised units measured in terms of accounting results.

With a system of responsibility accounting there are three types of **responsibility centre: cost centre, profit centre and investment centre**.

2 Fixed and flexible budgets

Introduction

This section is a reminder of the differences between fixed and flexible budgets. You should know about fixed and flexible budgets from your earlier studies.

2.1 Fixed budgets

The master budget prepared before the beginning of the budget period is known as the **fixed** budget. By the term 'fixed', we do not mean that the budget is kept unchanged. Revisions to a fixed master budget will be made if the situation so demands. The term 'fixed' means the following.

(a)   The budget is prepared on the basis of an **estimated volume of production** and an **estimated volume of sales**, but no plans are made for the event that actual volumes of production and sales may **differ** from budgeted volumes.

(b)   When **actual volumes** of production and sales during a control period (month or four weeks or quarter) are achieved, a fixed budget is **not adjusted** (in retrospect) to represent a new target for the new levels of activity.

The major purpose of a fixed budget lies in its use at the **planning** stage, when it seeks to define the broad objectives of the organisation.

KEY TERM

A FIXED BUDGET is 'A budget set prior to the control period, and not subsequently changed in response to changes in activity or costs or revenues. It may serve as a benchmark in performance evaluation'.

(CIMA Official Terminology)

Fixed budgets (in terms of a **pre-set expenditure limit**) are also useful for **controlling any fixed cost**, and **particularly non-production fixed costs** such as advertising, because such costs should be unaffected by changes in activity level (within a certain range).

2.2 Flexible budgets

KEY TERM

A FLEXIBLE BUDGET is a budget which, by recognising different cost behaviour patterns, is designed to change as volume of activity changes.

Two uses of flexible budgets

(a) **At the planning stage**. For example, suppose that a company expects to sell 10,000 units of output during the next year. A master budget (the fixed budget) would be prepared on the basis of these expected volumes. However, if the company thinks that output and sales might be as low as 8,000 units or as high as 12,000 units, it may prepare **contingency** flexible budgets, at volumes of, say, 8,000, 9,000, 11,000 and 12,000 units, and then assess the possible outcomes.

(b) **Retrospectively**. At the end of each control period, flexible budgets can be used to compare actual results achieved with what results should have been under the circumstances. Flexible budgets are an essential factor in budgetary control.

   (i) Management needs to know about how good or bad actual performance has been. To provide a measure of performance, there must be a yardstick (budget/ standard) against which actual performance can be measured.

   (ii) Every business is dynamic, and actual volumes of output cannot be expected to conform exactly to the fixed budget. Comparing actual costs directly with the fixed budget costs is meaningless.

   (iii) For useful control information, it is necessary to compare actual results at the actual level of activity achieved against the results that should have been expected at this level of activity, which are shown by the flexible budget.

Section summary

Fixed budgets remain unchanged regardless of the level of activity; **flexible budgets** are designed to flex with the level of activity.

Flexible budgets are prepared using marginal costing and so mixed costs must be split into their fixed and variable components (possibly using the **high/low method**).

Flexible budgets should be used to show what costs and revenues should have been for the actual level of activity. Differences between the flexible budget figures and actual results are **variances**.

---

3 Preparing flexible budgets

Introduction

This section focuses on how to prepare flexible budgets. Again, this is something that should be familiar from your previous studies, but make sure you work through the example to reacquaint yourself with the process.

Knowledge brought forward from earlier studies

The preparation of flexible budgets:

- The first step in the preparation of a flexible budget is the determination of **cost behaviour patterns**, which means deciding whether costs are fixed, variable or semi-variable.

- Fixed costs will remain constant as activity levels change.

- For non-fixed costs, divide each cost figure by the related activity level. If the cost is a **linear variable cost**, the cost per unit will remain constant. If the cost is a **semi-variable cost**, the unit rate will reduce as activity levels increase.

- Split semi-variable costs into their fixed and variable components using the **high/low method** or the **scattergraph method**.

- Calculate the **budget cost allowance** for each cost item as budget cost allowance = budgeted fixed cost* + (number of units produced/sold × variable cost per unit)**.

  * nil for totally variable cost ** nil for fixed cost

KEY TERM

The BUDGET COST ALLOWANCE / FLEXIBLE BUDGET is the budgeted cost ascribed to the level of activity achieved in a budget centre in a control period. It comprises variable costs in direct proportion to volume achieved and fixed costs as a proportion of the annual budget.

Example: Fixed and flexible budgets

Suppose that Gemma expects production and sales during the next year to be 90% of the company's output capacity, that is, 9,000 units of a single product. Cost estimates will be made using the high-low method and the following historical records of cost.

Units of output/sales	Cost of sales Yen
9,800	44,400
7,700	38,100

The company's management is not certain that the estimate of sales is correct, and has asked for flexible budgets to be prepared at output and sales levels of 8,000 and 10,000 units. The sales price per unit has been fixed at Y5.

Required

Prepare appropriate budgets.

Solution

If we assume that within the range 8,000 to 10,000 units of sales, all costs are fixed, variable or mixed (in other words, there are no stepped costs, material discounts, overtime premiums, bonus payments and so on), the fixed and flexible budgets would be based on the estimate of fixed and variable cost.

		Yen
Total cost of 9,800 units	=	44,400
Total cost of 7,700 units	=	38,100
Variable cost of 2,100 units	=	6,300

The variable cost per unit is Yen 3.

		Yen
Total cost of 9,800 units	=	44,400
Variable cost of 9,800 units (9,800 × Yen 3)	=	29,400
Fixed costs (all levels of output and sales)	=	15,000

The fixed budgets and flexible budgets can now be prepared as follows.

	Flexible budget 8,000 units Yen	Fixed budget 9,000 units Yen	Flexible budget 10,000 units Yen
Sales (× Yen 5)	40,000	45,000	50,000
Variable costs (× Yen 3)	24,000	27,000	30,000
Contribution	16,000	18,000	20,000
Fixed costs	15,000	15,000	15,000
Profit	1,000	3,000	5,000

3.1 The need for flexible budgets

We have seen that flexible budgets may be prepared in order to plan for variations in the level of activity above or below the level set in the fixed budget. It has been suggested, however, that since many cost items in modern industry are fixed costs, the value of flexible budgets in planning is dwindling.

(a) In many manufacturing industries, plant costs (depreciation, rent and so on) are a very large proportion of total costs, and these tend to be fixed costs.

(b) Wage costs also tend to be fixed, because employees are generally guaranteed a basic wage for a working week of an agreed number of hours.

(c) With the growth of service industries, labour (wages or fixed salaries) and overheads will account for most of the costs of a business, and direct materials will be a relatively small proportion of total costs.

Flexible budgets are nevertheless necessary and, even if they are not used at the planning stage, they must be used for variance analysis.

Section summary

The **budget cost allowance/flexible budget** is the budgeted cost ascribed to the level of activity achieved in a budget centre in a control period. It comprises variable costs in direct proportion to volume achieved and fixed costs as a proportion of the annual budget.

4 Flexible budgets and budgetary control

Introduction

Flexible budgets are essential for control purposes. They represent the expected revenues, costs and profits for the actual units produced and sold and are then compared to actual results to determine any differences (or variances). Variances should already be familiar to you from your P1 studies – in this section we show how flexible budgets can be used to identify potential control issues.

KEY TERM

Budgetary control is carried out via a MASTER BUDGET 'devolved to responsibility centres, allowing continuous monitoring of actual results versus budget, either to secure by individual action the budget objectives or to provide a basis for budget revision'.   *(CIMA Official Terminology)*

In other words, individual managers are held responsible for investigating differences between budgeted and actual results, and are then expected to take corrective action or amend the plan in the light of actual events.

It is therefore vital to ensure that valid comparisons are being made. Consider the following example.

Example: Flexible budgets and budgetary control

Penny manufactures a single product, the Darcy. Budgeted results and actual results for May are as follows.

	Budget	Actual	Variance
Production and sales of the Darcy (units)	7,500	8,200	
	$	$	$
Sales revenue	75,000	81,000	6,000 (F)
Direct materials	22,500	23,500	1,000 (A)
Direct labour	15,000	15,500	500 (A)
Production overhead	22,500	22,800	300 (A)
Administration overhead	10,000	11,000	1,000 (A)
	70,000	72,800	2,800 (A)
Profit	5,000	8,200	3,200 (F)

Note. (F) denotes a favourable variance and (A) an unfavourable or adverse variance.

In this example, the variances are meaningless for the purposes of control. All costs were higher than budgeted but the volume of output was also higher; it is to be expected that actual variable costs would be greater those included in the fixed budget. However, it is not possible to tell how much of the increase is due to **poor cost control** and how much is due to the **increase in activity**.

Similarly, it is not possible to tell how much of the increase in sales revenue is due to the increase in activity. Some of the difference may be due to a difference between budgeted and actual selling price, but we are unable to tell from the analysis above.

For control purposes we need to know the answers to questions such as the following.

* Were actual costs higher than they should have been to produce and sell 8,200 Darcys?
* Was actual revenue satisfactory from the sale of 8,200 Darcys?

Instead of comparing actual results with a fixed budget which is based on a different level of activity to that actually achieved, the correct approach to budgetary control is to compare actual results with a budget which has been **flexed** to the actual activity level achieved.

Suppose that we have the following estimates of the behaviour of Penny's costs:

(a) Direct materials and direct labour are variable costs.

(b) Production overhead is a semi-variable cost, the budgeted cost for an activity level of 10,000 units being $25,000.

(c) Administration overhead is a fixed cost.

(d) Selling prices are constant at all levels of sales.

Solution

The **budgetary control analysis** should therefore be as follows.

	Fixed budget	Flexible budget	Actual results	Variance
Production and sales (units)	7,500	8,200	8,200	
	$	$	$	$
Sales revenue	75,000	82,000 (W1)	81,000	1,000 (A)
Direct materials	22,500	24,600 (W2)	23,500	1,100 (F)
Direct labour	15,000	16,400 (W3)	15,500	900 (F)
Production overhead	22,500	23,200 (W4)	22,800	400 (F)
Administration overhead	10,000	10,000 (W5)	11,000	1,000 (A)
	70,000	74,200	72,800	1,400 (F)
Profit	5,000	7,800	8,200	400 (F)

Workings

1   Selling price per unit = $75,000 ÷ 7,500 = $10 per unit
     Flexible budget sales revenue = $10 × 8,200 = 482,000

2   Direct materials cost per unit = $22,500 ÷ 7,500 = $3
     Budget cost allowance = $3 × 8,200 = $24,600

3   Direct labour cost per unit = $15,000 ÷ 7,500 = $2
     Budget cost allowance = $2 × 8,200 = $16,400

4   Variable production overhead cost per unit = $(25,000 – 22,500) ÷ (10,000 – 7,500)
     = $2,500 ÷ 2,500 = $1 per unit

     ∴ Fixed production overhead cost = $22,500 – (7,500 × $1) = $15,000

     ∴ Budget cost allowance = $15,000 + (8,200 × $1) = $23,200

5   Administration overhead is a fixed cost and hence budget cost allowance = $10,000

Comment

(a)   In selling 8,200 units, the expected profit should have been not the fixed budget profit of $5,000,
       but the flexible budget profit of $7,800. Instead actual profit was $8,200 ie $400 more than we
       should have expected.

       One of the reasons for this improvement is that, given output and sales of 8,200 units, the cost of
       resources (material, labour etc) was $1,400 lower than expected.

       In Paper P1 you saw how these total cost variances can be analysed to reveal how much of the
       variance is due to lower resource prices and how much is due to efficient resource usage.

(b)   The sales revenue was, however, $1,000 less than expected because a lower price was charged
       than budgeted.

       We know this because flexing the budget has eliminated the effect of changes in the volume sold,
       which is the only other factor that can affect sales revenue. You have probably already realised
       that this variance of $1,000 (A) is a **selling price variance**.

       The lower selling price could have been caused by the increase in the volume sold (to sell the
       additional 700 units, the selling price had to fall below $10 per unit). We do not know if this is
       the case, but without flexing the budget we could not know that a different selling price to that
       budgeted had been charged. Our initial analysis above had appeared to indicate that sales revenue
       was ahead of budget.

The difference of $400 between the flexible budget profit of $7,800 at a production level of 8,200 units
and the actual profit of $8,200 is due to the net effect of cost savings of $1,400 and lower than expected
sales revenue (by $1,000).

The difference between the original budgeted profit of $5,000 and the actual profit of $8,200 is the total
of the following.

(a)   The savings in resource costs/lower than expected sales revenue (a net total of $400 as indicated
       by the difference between the flexible budget and the actual results).

(b)   The effect of producing and selling 8,200 units instead of 7,500 units (a gain of $2,800 as
       indicated by the difference between the fixed budget and the flexible budget). This is the **sales
       volume contribution variance**.

A **full variance analysis statement** would be as follows.

	$	$
Fixed budget profit		5,000
Variances		
Sales volume	2,800 (F)	
Selling price	1,000 (A)	
Direct materials cost	1,100 (F)	
Direct labour cost	900 (F)	
Production overhead cost	400 (F)	
Administration overhead cost	1,000 (A)	
		3,200 (F)
Actual profit		8,200

If management believes that any of the variances are large enough to justify it, they will investigate the reasons for their occurrence to see whether any corrective action is necessary.

4.1 Flexible budgets, control and computers

The production of flexible budget control reports is an area in which computers can provide invaluable assistance to the cost accountant, calculating flexed budget figures using fixed budget and actual results data and hence providing detailed variance analysis. For control information to be of any value, it must be produced quickly: speed is one of the many advantages of computers.

4.2 Flexible budgets using ABC data

Instead of flexing budgets according to the number of units produced or sold, in an ABC environment it is possible to use **more meaningful bases for flexing the budget**. The budget cost allowance for each activity can be determined according to the number of **cost drivers**.

Suppose the budget for a production department for a given period is as follows.

	$
Wages	220,000
Materials	590,000
Equipment	20,000
Power, heat and light	11,000
	841,000

This budget gives little indication of the link between the level of activity in the department and the costs incurred, however.

Suppose the activities in the department have been identified as sawing, hammering, finishing, reworking and production reporting. The budget might therefore be restated as follows.

Activities	*Cost driver*	*Budgeted cost per unit of cost driver* $	*Budgeted no of cost drivers*	*Budget* $
Sawing	Number of units sawed	50.00	5,000	250,000
Hammering	Number of units hammered together	10.00	35,000	350,000
Finishing	Number of sq metres finished	0.50	400,000	200,000
Reworking	Number of items reworked	12.40	2,500	31,000
Production reporting	Number of reports	400.00	25	10,000
				841,000

Advantages of this approach

(a)   Costs classified as fixed in the first budget can now be seen to be variable and hence can be more
        readily controlled.

(b)   The implications of increases/decreases in levels of activity are immediately apparent. For example,
        if acceptable quality levels were raised, requiring an additional 200 units per annum to be
        reworked, budgeted costs would increase by 200 × $12.40 = $2,480.

A **flexible budget** would be prepared as follows.

	Actual no of cost drivers	Budgeted cost per unit of cost driver $	Flexed budget $	Actual cost $	Variance $
Sawing	6,000	50.00	300,000	297,000	3,000 (F)
Hammering	40,000	10.00	400,000	404,000	4,000 (A)
Finishing	264,400	0.50	132,200	113,200	19,000 (F)
Reworking	4,500	12.40	55,800	56,100	300 (A)
Production reporting	30	400.00	12,000	13,700	1,700 (A)
			900,000	884,000	16,000 (F)

4.3 The link between standard costing and budget flexing

The calculation of standard cost variances and the use of a flexed budget to control costs and revenues
are **very similar in concept**.

For example, a direct material total variance in a standard costing system is calculated by **comparing the
material cost that should have been incurred for the output achieved, with the actual cost that was
incurred**.

Exactly the same process is undertaken when a budget is flexed to provide a basis for comparison with
the actual cost: **the flexible budget cost allowance for material cost is the same as the cost that should
have been incurred for the activity level achieved**. In the same way as for standard costing, this is then
compared with the actual cost incurred in order to practise control by comparison.

However, there are differences between the two techniques.

(a)   **Standard costing variance analysis is more detailed**. The total material cost variance is analysed
        further to determine how much of the total variance is caused by a difference in the price paid for
        materials (the material price variance) and how much is caused by the usage of material being
        different from the standard (the material usage variance). In flexible budget comparisons only total
        cost variances are derived.

(b)   **For a standard costing system to operate, it is necessary to determine a standard unit cost for all
        items of output**. All that is required to operate a flexible budgeting system is an understanding of
        the cost behaviour patterns and a measure of activity to use to flex the budget cost allowance for
        each cost element.

Section summary

Budgetary control is based around a system of **budget centres**. Each centre has its own budget which is
the responsibility of the **budget holder**.

4.4 Budget control systems – key features

KEY TERM

A BUDGET CENTRE is 'A section of an entity for which control may be exercised through budgets prepared'.
(CIMA Official Terminology)

Budgetary control is based around a system of budget centres. Each budget centre will have its own budget and a manager will be responsible for managing the budget centre and ensuring that the budget is met.

The **selection of budget centres** in an organisation is therefore a **key first step in setting up a control system**. What should the budget centres be? What income, expenditure and/or capital employment plans should each budget centre prepare? And how will measures of performance for each budget centre be made?

A well-organised system of control should have the following features.

Feature	Explanation
A hierarchy of budget centres	If the organisation is quite large, a hierarchy is needed. Subsidiary companies, departments and work sections might be budget centres. Budgets of each section would then be consolidated into a departmental budget, departmental budgets in turn would be consolidated into the subsidiary's budget and the budgets of each subsidiary would be **combined into a master budget** for the group as a whole.
Clearly identified responsibilities for achieving budget targets	Individual managers should be made responsible for achieving the budget targets of a particular budget centre.
Responsibilities for revenues, costs and capital employed	Budget centres should be organised so that all the revenues earned by an organisation, all the costs it incurs and all the capital it employs are made the responsibility of someone within the organisation, at an appropriate level of authority in the management hierarchy.

Budgetary control and budget centres are therefore part of the overall system of **responsibility accounting** within an organisation.

4.5 The controllability principle

Care must be taken to distinguish between controllable costs and uncontrollable costs in variance reporting. The **controllability principle** is that managers of responsibility centres should only be held accountable for costs over which they have **some influence**. From a **motivation** point of view this is important because it can be very demoralising for managers who feel that their performance is being judged on the basis of something over which they have no influence. It is also important from a **control** point of view, in that control reports should ensure that information on costs is reported to the manager who is able to take action to control them.

4.6 Controllable and uncontrollable costs

KEY TERM

A CONTROLLABLE COST is a 'Cost which can be controlled, typically by a cost, profit or investment centre manager'.
(CIMA Official Terminology)

Responsibility accounting attempts to associate costs, revenues, assets and liabilities with the managers most capable of controlling them. As a system of accounting, it therefore distinguishes between **controllable** and **uncontrollable** costs.

Most **variable costs** within a department are thought to be **controllable in the short term** because managers can influence the efficiency with which resources are used, even if they cannot do anything to raise or lower price levels.

A cost which is not controllable by a junior manager might be controllable by a senior manager. For example, there may be high direct labour costs in a department caused by excessive overtime working. The junior manager may feel obliged to continue with the overtime to meet production schedules, but their senior may be able to reduce costs by hiring extra full-time staff, thereby reducing the requirements for overtime.

A cost which is not controllable by a manager in one department may be controllable by a manager in another department. For example, an increase in material costs may be caused by buying at higher prices than expected (controllable by the purchasing department) or by excessive wastage (controllable by the production department) or by a faulty machine producing rejects (controllable by the maintenance department).

Some costs are **non-controllable**, such as increases in expenditure items due to inflation. Other costs are **controllable, but in the long term rather than the short term**. For example, production costs might be reduced by the introduction of new machinery and technology, but in the short term, management must attempt to do the best they can with the resources and machinery at their disposal.

4.6.1 The controllability of fixed costs

It is often assumed that all fixed costs are non-controllable in the short run. This is not so.

(a)   **Committed fixed costs** are those costs arising from the possession of plant, equipment, buildings and an administration department to **support the long-term needs of the business**. These costs (depreciation, rent, administration salaries) are largely **non-controllable in the short term** because they have been committed by longer-term decisions affecting longer-term needs. When a company decides to cut production drastically, the long-term committed fixed costs will be reduced, but only after redundancy terms have been settled and assets sold.

(b)   A **discretionary cost** is a cost whose amount, within a particular time period, is **determined by**, and can be **altered by**, the **budget holder**. **Discretionary fixed costs**, such as advertising and research and development costs, are incurred as a result of a top management decision, but could be **raised or lowered at fairly short notice** (irrespective of the actual volume of production and sales).

4.6.2 Controllability and apportioned costs

Managers should only be held accountable for costs over which they have some influence. This may seem quite straightforward in theory, but it is not always so easy in practice to distinguish controllable from uncontrollable costs. **Apportioned overhead costs provide a good example**.

Example: Apportioned costs

Suppose that a manager of a production department in a manufacturing company is made responsible for the costs of his department. These costs include **directly attributable overhead items**, such as the costs of indirect labour employed and indirect materials consumed in the department. The department's overhead costs also include an apportionment of costs from other cost centres, such as rent and rates for the building it shares with other departments and a share of the costs of the maintenance department.

Should the production manager be held accountable for any of these apportioned costs?

Solution

(a)   Managers should not be held accountable for costs over which they have no control. In this example, apportioned rent and rates costs would not be controllable by the production department manager.

(b)   Managers should be held accountable for costs over which they have some influence. In this example, it is the responsibility of the maintenance department manager to keep maintenance costs within budget, but their costs will be partly variable and partly fixed, and the variable cost element will depend on the volume of demand for their services. If the production department's staff treat their equipment badly, we might expect higher repair costs, and the production department manager should therefore be made accountable for the repair costs that his department makes the maintenance department incur on its behalf.

(c)   Charging the production department with some of the costs of the maintenance department prevents the production department from viewing the maintenance services as 'free services'. Over-use would be discouraged and the production manager is more likely to question the activities of the maintenance department, possibly resulting in a reduction in maintenance costs or the provision of more efficient maintenance services.

4.6.3 Controllability and dual responsibility

Quite often a particular cost might be the **responsibility of two or more managers**. For example, raw materials costs might be the responsibility of the purchasing manager (prices) and the production manager (usage). A **reporting system must allocate responsibility appropriately**. The purchasing manager must be responsible for any increase in raw materials prices, whereas the production manager should be responsible for any increase in raw materials usage.

Exam skills

You can see that there are **no clear-cut rules** as to which costs are controllable and which are not. Each situation and cost must be reviewed separately and a decision taken according to the control value of the information and its behavioural impact.

4.7 Budgetary control reports

If the **budget holders** (managers of budget centres) are to attempt to meet budgets, they must receive regular budgetary control reports so that they can monitor the budget centre's operations and take any necessary control action.

The **amount of detail** included in reports will **vary** according to the needs of management. In general terms, there should be **sufficient detail** within the reports to **motivate the individual manager to take the most appropriate action** in all circumstances. A form of **exception reporting** can be used for **top management**, reports just detailing significant variances.

Section summary

A **budget centre** is defined in *CIMA Official Terminology* as 'A section of an entity for which control may be exercised through budgets prepared'.

Responsibility accounting is a system of accounting that segregates revenue and costs into areas of personal responsibility in order to monitor and assess the performance of each part of an organisation.

Controllable costs are those which can be influenced by the budget holder. **Uncontrollable costs** cannot be so influenced.

5 Behavioural implications of budgeting

Introduction

Although the principal purpose of a budgetary control system is to assist in planning and control, it can also have an effect on the behaviour of those directly affected by the budget. This section looks at how budgets can affect employees' behaviour and motivation.

5.1 Budgets and the provision of control information

The purpose of a budgetary control system is to assist management in **planning and controlling** the resources of their organisation by providing **appropriate control information**. The information will only be valuable, however, if it is **interpreted correctly** and used purposefully by managers **and** employees.

The correct use of control information therefore depends not only on the **content** of the information itself but also on the **behaviour** of its recipients. This is because control in business is exercised by people. Their attitude to control information will colour their views on what they should do with it and a number of behavioural problems can arise.

(a)   The **managers who set the budget** or standards are **often not the managers** who are then made **responsible for achieving budget targets**.

(b)   The **goals of the organisation as a whole**, as expressed in a budget, **may not coincide with the personal aspirations of individual managers**.

(c)   **Control is applied at different stages by different people**. A supervisor might get weekly control reports, and act on them; his superior might get monthly control reports, and decide to take different control action. Different managers can get in each other's way, and resent the interference from others.

5.2 Budgeting and standards

How demanding should a standard be? Should the standard represent perfect performance or easily attainable performance? There are four types of standard.

KEY TERMS

An **ideal standard** is a standard which can be attained under perfect operating conditions: no wastage, no inefficiencies, no idle time, no breakdowns.

An **attainable standard** is a standard which can be attained if production is carried out efficiently, machines are properly operated and/or materials are properly used. Some allowance is made for wastage and inefficiencies.

A **current standard** is a standard based on current working conditions (current wastage, current inefficiencies).

A **basic standard** is a long-term standard which remains unchanged over the years and is used to show trends.

The **different types of standard have a number of advantages and disadvantages**.

(a)   **Ideal standards** can be seen as **long-term targets** but are not very useful for day to day control purposes.

(b)   **Ideal standards cannot be achieved**. If such standards are used for budgeting, an allowance will have to be included to make the budget realistic and attainable.

(c) **Attainable standards** can be used for **product costing**, cost control, inventory valuation, estimating and as a basis for budgeting.

(d) **Current standards** or attainable standards provide the **best basis for budgeting**, because they represent an achievable level of productivity.

(e) Current standards **do not attempt to improve** on current levels of efficiency.

(f) **Current standards** are useful during **periods when inflation is high**. They can be set on a month by month basis.

(g) **Basic standards** are used to show **changes in efficiency or performance** over a long period of time. They are perhaps the least useful and least common type of standard in use.

5.3 Motivation

Motivation is what makes people behave in the way that they do. It comes from **individual attitudes** or group attitudes. Individuals will be motivated by **personal desires and interests**. These may be in line with the objectives of the organisation, and some people 'live for their jobs'. Other individuals see their job as a chore, and their motivations will be unrelated to the objectives of the organisation they work for.

It is therefore vital that the goals of management and the employees harmonise with the goals of the organisation as a whole. This is known as **goal congruence**. Although obtaining goal congruence is essentially a behavioural problem, **it is possible to design and run a budgetary control system which will go some way towards ensuring that goal congruence is achieved**. Managers and employees must therefore be favourably disposed towards the budgetary control system so that it can operate efficiently.

The management accountant should therefore try to ensure that employees have positive attitudes towards **setting budgets, implementing budgets** (that is, putting the organisation's plans into practice) and feedback of results (**control information**).

5.3.1 Poor attitudes when setting budgets

If managers are involved in preparing a budget, poor attitudes or hostile behaviour towards the budgetary control system can begin at the **planning stage**.

(a) Managers may **complain that they are too busy** to spend much time on budgeting.

(b) They may **build 'slack' into their expenditure estimates**.

(c) They may argue that **formalising a budget plan on paper is too restricting** and that managers should be allowed flexibility in the decisions they take.

(d) They may set budgets for their budget centre and **not co-ordinate** their own plans with those of other budget centres.

(e) They may **base future plans on past results**, instead of using the opportunity for formalised planning to look at alternative options and new ideas.

On the other hand, **managers may not be involved in the budgeting process**. Organisational goals may not be communicated to them and they might have their budget decided for them by senior management or an administrative decision. It is **hard for people to be motivated to achieve targets set by someone else**.

5.3.2 Poor attitudes when putting plans into action

Poor attitudes also arise **when a budget is implemented**.

(a) Managers might **put in only just enough effort** to achieve budget targets, without trying to beat targets.

(b) A formal budget might **encourage rigidity and discourage flexibility**.

(c)   **Short-term planning** in a budget **can draw attention away from the longer-term consequences** of decisions.

(d)   There might be **minimal co-operation and communication** between managers.

(e)   Managers will often try to make sure that they **spend up to their full budget allowance, and do not overspend**, so that they will not be accused of having asked for too much spending allowance in the first place.

(f)   Particularly in **service departments and public sector organisations**, where performance is assessed by comparing actual and budget spending, managers may consider the **budget** as a **sum of money that has to be spent**. A manager of a local authority department might be given an annual budget of $360,000. The manager knows that he will be punished for spending more than $360,000 but that if he spends less than $300,000 his budget will probably be reduced next year, leading to a loss of status and making his job more difficult next year. To ensure he does not overspend, he may spend $26,000 a month for 11 months of the year (by reducing the provision of the department's service), building up a contingency fund of (11 × $4,000) $44,000 to be used in case of emergencies. In the final month of the year he would then need to spend ($(44,000 + 30,000)) $74,000 to ensure his whole budget was used (perhaps by using extra labour and/or high-quality materials). The manager's **behaviour** has therefore been **distorted by the control system**.

5.3.3 Poor attitudes and the use of control information

The **attitude of managers towards the accounting control information** they receive **might reduce the information's effectiveness**.

(a)   Management accounting control reports could well be seen as having a relatively **low priority** in the list of management tasks. Managers might take the view that they have more pressing jobs on hand than looking at routine control reports.

(b)   Managers might **resent control information**; they may see it as **part of a system of trying to find fault with their work**. This resentment is likely to be particularly strong when budgets or standards are imposed on managers without allowing them to participate in the budget-setting process.

(c)   If budgets are seen as **pressure devices** to push managers into doing better, control reports will be resented.

(d)   Managers **may not understand the information** in the control reports, because they are unfamiliar with accounting terminology or principles.

(e)   Managers might have a **false sense of what their objectives should be**. A production manager might consider it more important to maintain quality standards regardless of cost. He would then dismiss adverse expenditure variances as inevitable and unavoidable.

(f)   **If there are flaws in the system of recording actual costs**, managers will dismiss control information as unreliable.

(g)   **Control information** might be **received weeks after the end of the period to which it relates**, in which case managers might regard it as out of date and no longer useful.

(h)   Managers might be **held responsible for variances outside their control**.

It is therefore obvious that accountants and senior management should try to implement systems that are acceptable to budget holders and which produce positive effects.

5.3.4 Pay as a motivator

Many researchers agree that **pay can be an important motivator**, when there is a formal link between higher pay (or other rewards, such as promotion) and achieving budget targets. Individuals are likely to work harder to achieve budget if they know that they will be rewarded for their successful efforts. There are, however, problems with using pay as an incentive.

(a)   A serious problem that can arise is that **formal reward and performance evaluation systems can encourage dysfunctional behaviour**. Many investigations have noted the tendency of managers to pad their budgets either in anticipation of cuts by superiors or to make the subsequent variances more favourable. And there are numerous examples of managers making decisions in response to performance indices, even though the decisions are contrary to the wider purposes of the organisation.

(b)   The targets must be challenging, but fair, otherwise individuals will become dissatisfied. **Pay can be a demotivator as well as a motivator!**

Section summary

Used correctly, a budgetary control system can **motivate**, but it can also produce undesirable **negative reactions**.

6 Budget participation

Introduction

It has been argued that **participation** in the budgeting process **will improve motivation** and so will improve the quality of budget decisions and the efforts of individuals to achieve their budget targets. This section looks at different budget styles and how they affect the participation process.

KEY TERM

There are basically two ways in which a budget can be set: from the TOP DOWN (imposed budget) or from the BOTTOM UP (participatory budget).

6.1 Imposed style of budgeting

KEY TERM

An IMPOSED/TOP-DOWN BUDGET is a 'Budgeting process where budget allowances are set without permitting the ultimate budget holders to have the opportunity to participate in the budgeting process'.

(CIMA Official Terminology)

In this approach to budgeting, **top management prepare a budget with little or no input from operating personnel**, which is then imposed upon the employees who have to work to the budgeted figures.

The times when imposed budgets are effective:

- In newly formed organisations
- In very small businesses
- During periods of economic hardship
- When operational managers lack budgeting skills
- When the organisation's different units require precise co-ordination

There are, of course, advantages and disadvantages to this style of setting budgets.

(a)   **Advantages**

     (i)   Strategic plans are likely to be incorporated into planned activities.

     (ii)   They enhance the co-ordination between the plans and objectives of divisions.

     (iii)   They use senior management's awareness of total resource availability.

     (iv)   They decrease the input from inexperienced or uninformed lower-level employees.

     (v)   They decrease the period of time taken to draw up the budgets.

(b)   **Disadvantages**

   (i)   There is dissatisfaction, defensiveness and low morale amongst employees. It is hard for people to be motivated to achieve targets set by somebody else.

   (ii)   The feeling of team spirit may disappear.

   (iii) The acceptance of organisational goals and objectives could be limited.

   (iv)   The feeling of the budget as a punitive device could arise.

   (v)   Managers who are performing operations on a day to day basis are likely to have a better understanding of what is achievable.

   (vi)   Unachievable budgets could result if consideration is not given to local operating and political environments. This applies particularly to overseas divisions.

   (vii) Lower-level management initiative may be stifled.

6.2 Participative style of budgeting

KEY TERM

PARTICIPATIVE/BOTTOM-UP BUDGETING is a 'Budgeting process where all budget holders have the opportunity to participate in setting their own budgets'.   (*CIMA Official Terminology*)

In this approach to budgeting, **budgets are developed by lower-level managers who then submit the budgets to their superiors**. The budgets are based on the lower-level managers' perceptions of what is achievable and the associated necessary resources.

Question 5.2   Participative budgets

Learning outcome B2(c)

In what circumstances might participative budgets **not** be effective?

A   In centralised organisations
B   In well-established organisations
C   In very large businesses
D   During periods of economic affluence

Advantages of participative budgets

*   They are based on information from employees most familiar with the department.
*   Knowledge spread among several levels of management is pulled together.
*   Morale and motivation is improved.
*   They increase operational managers' commitment to organisational objectives.
*   In general they are more realistic.
*   Co-ordination between units is improved.
*   Specific resource requirements are included.
*   Senior managers' overview is mixed with operational-level details.
*   Individual managers' aspiration levels are more likely to be taken into account.

Disadvantages of participative budgets

*   They consume more time.
*   Changes implemented by senior management may cause dissatisfaction.
*   Budgets may be unachievable if managers are not qualified to participate.
*   They may cause managers to introduce budgetary slack and budget bias.
*   They can support 'empire building' by subordinates.
*   An earlier start to the budgeting process could be required.
*   Managers may set 'easy' budgets to ensure that they are achievable.

6.3 Negotiated style of budgeting

KEY TERM

A **NEGOTIATED BUDGET** is a 'Budget in which budget allowances are set largely on the basis of negotiations between budget holders and those to whom they report'.   (*CIMA Official Terminology*)

At the two extremes, budgets can be dictated from above or simply emerge from below but, in practice, different levels of management often agree budgets by a process of negotiation. In the imposed budget approach, operational managers will try to negotiate with senior managers the budget targets that they consider to be unreasonable or unrealistic. Likewise, senior management usually review and revise budgets presented to them under a participative approach through a process of negotiation with lower-level managers. **Final budgets are therefore most likely to lie between what top management would really like and what junior managers believe is feasible.** The budgeting process is hence a **bargaining process** and it is this bargaining which is of vital importance, **determining whether the budget is an effective management tool or simply a clerical device**.

6.4 Budget slack

KEY TERM

BUDGET SLACK is the 'Intentional overestimation of expenses and/or underestimation of revenues during the budget setting'.   (*CIMA Official Terminology*)

In the process of preparing budgets, managers might **deliberately overestimate costs and underestimate sales**, so that they will not be blamed in the future for overspending and poor results.

In controlling actual operations, managers must then **ensure that their spending rises to meet their budget**, otherwise they will be 'blamed' for careless budgeting.

Budget bias can **work in the other direction**, too. It has been noted that, after a run of mediocre results, some managers **deliberately overstate revenues and understate cost estimates**, no doubt feeling the need to make an immediate favourable impact by promising better performance in the future. They may merely delay problems, however, as the managers may well be censured when they fail to hit these optimistic targets.

Yet again, this is an example of **control systems distorting the processes they are meant to serve**.

Section summary

There are basically two ways in which a budget can be set: from the **top down** (**imposed** budget) or from the **bottom up** (**participatory** budget). Many writers refer to a third style (**negotiated**).

Budget slack occurs when managers deliberately underestimate sales or overestimate costs to avoid being blamed for future poor results.

---

7 The use of budgets as targets

Introduction

Once decided, budgets become targets. As targets, they can motivate managers to achieve a high level of performance. This section looks at the extent to which managers can be motivated by budget targets and the challenges of ensuring the correct level of difficulty of these targets.

7.1 Setting the target

(a)   There is likely to be a **demotivating** effect where an **ideal standard** of performance is set, because adverse efficiency variances will always be reported.

(b)   A **low standard of efficiency** is also **demotivating**, because there is no sense of achievement in attaining the required standards, and there will be no impetus for employees to try harder to do better than this.

(c)   A **budgeted level of attainment** could be 'normal': that is, the **same as the level that has been achieved in the past**. Arguably, this level will be **too low**. It might **encourage budgetary slack**.

7.2 Aspiration levels

It has been argued that **each individual has a personal 'aspiration level'**. This is a level of performance in a task with which the individual is familiar, which the individual undertakes for himself to reach. This aspiration level might be quite challenging and, if individuals in a work group all have similar aspiration levels, it should be possible to incorporate these levels within the official operating standards.

Some care should be taken, however, in applying this.

(a)   If a manager's **tendency to achieve success is stronger than the tendency to avoid failure**, budgets with **targets of intermediate levels of difficulty** are the most motivating and stimulate a manager to better performance levels. Budgets which are either too easy to achieve or too difficult are demotivating, and managers given such targets achieve relatively low levels of performance.

(b)   A manager's **tendency to avoid failure might be stronger than the tendency to achieve success**. (This is likely in an organisation in which the budget is used as a pressure device on subordinates by senior managers.) Managers might then be discouraged from trying to achieve budgets of intermediate difficulty and tend to avoid taking on such tasks, resulting in poor levels of performance, worse than if budget targets were either easy or very difficult to achieve.

7.3 A case for two budgets?

It has been suggested that in a situation where budget targets of an intermediate difficulty **are** motivating, such targets ought to be set if the purpose of budgets is to motivate. However, although budgets which are set for **motivational purposes** need to be stated in terms of **aspirations rather than expectations**, budgets for planning and decision purposes need to be stated in terms of the **best available estimate** of expected actual performance. The **solution** might therefore be to have **two budgets**:

(a)   A **budget for planning and decision making based on reasonable expectations**

(b)   A second **budget for motivational purposes**, with **more difficult targets of performance** (that is, targets of an intermediate level of difficulty)

These two budgets might be called an **'expectations budget'** and an **'aspirations budget'** respectively.

Section summary

In certain situations it is useful to prepare an **expectations budget** (for planning and decision-making purposes) and an **aspirations budget** (to act as a motivational tool).

8   Budgets and motivation

Introduction

We have seen that budgets serve many purposes, but in some instances their purposes can conflict and have an effect on management behaviour. This section examines the need for strategies and methods to deal with the resulting tensions and conflict.

8.1 Is motivation from budgets ever possible?

Can performance measures and the related budgetary control system ever **motivate managers** towards achieving the organisation's goals?

(a)   Accounting measures of performance **can't provide a comprehensive assessment** of what a person has achieved for the organisation.

(b)   It is unfair as it is usually **impossible to segregate controllable and uncontrollable components of performance**.

(c)   Accounting **reports tend to concentrate on short-term achievements**, to the exclusion of the long-term effects.

(d)   Many accounting **reports try to serve several different purposes**, and in trying to satisfy several needs actually satisfy none properly.

8.2 Support from senior management

The management accountant does not have the authority to do much on their own to improve hostile or apathetic attitudes to control information. There has to be support, either from senior management or from budget centre managers.

(a)   **How senior management can offer support:**

    (i)   Making sure that a **system of responsibility accounting is adopted**

    (ii)   Allowing **managers to have a say in formulating their budgets**

    (iii)   Offering **incentives** to managers who meet budget targets

    (iv)   Not regarding budgetary control information as a way of apportioning blame

(b)   **Budget centre managers should accept their responsibilities**. In-house training courses could be held to encourage a collective, co-operative and positive attitude among managers.

8.3 Support from the management accountant

The management accountant can offer support in the following ways.

(a)   **Develop a working relationship with operational managers**, going out to meet them and discussing the control reports

(b)   **Explain the meaning of budgets and control reports**

(c)   **Keep accounting jargon in these reports to a minimum**

(d)   Make **reports clear and to the point**, for example using the principle of reporting by exception

(e)   Provide control information with a **minimum of delay**

(f)   **Make control information as useful as possible**, by distinguishing between directly attributable and controllable costs, over which a manager should have influence, and apportioned or fixed costs, which are unavoidable or uncontrollable

(g)   Make sure that **actual costs are recorded accurately**

(h)   Ensure that **budgets are up to date**, either by having a system of rolling budgets, or else by updating budgets or standards as necessary, and ensuring that standards are 'fair' so that control information is realistic

Question 5.3

Behavioural aspects of budget participation

Learning outcome B2(c)

Discuss the behavioural aspects of participation in the budgeting process and any difficulties you might envisage.

Section summary

There are no ideal solutions to the conflicts caused by the operation of a budgetary control system. Management and the management accountant have to develop their own ways of dealing with them, taking into account their organisation, their business and the personalities involved.

---

9 Beyond Budgeting

Introduction

This section looks at the arguments put forward by the Beyond Budgeting Round Table that traditional budgeting should be abandoned.

9.1 Criticisms of budgeting

In our discussion of the budgetary planning process, we have come across many difficulties with budgets and criticisms of how they are used in organisations. The discussion on behavioural issues in this chapter should help you to appreciate the real danger that budgets can cause unintended dysfunctional behaviour that needs to be guarded against in organisations.

The Beyond Budgeting Round Table (BBRT), an independent research collaborative, proposes that budgeting, as most organisations practise it, should be abandoned. Their website at www.bbrt.org lists the following ten criticisms of budgeting as put forward by Hope and Fraser in *Beyond Budgeting* (1st edition, Harvard Business School Press, 2003).

(a) **Budgets are time consuming and expensive**. Even with the support of computer models it is estimated that the budgeting process uses up to 20% to 30% of senior executives' and financial managers' time.

(b) **Budgets provide poor value to users**. Although surveys have shown that some managers feel that budgets give them control, a large majority of financial directors wish to reform the budgetary process because they feel that finance staff spend too much time on 'lower value added activities'.

(c) **Budgets fail to focus on shareholder value**. Most budgets are set on an incremental basis as an acceptable target agreed between the manager and the manager's superior. Managers may be rewarded for achieving their short-term budgets and will not look to the longer term or take risks, for fear of affecting their own short-term results.

(d) **Budgets are too rigid and prevent fast response**. Although most organisations do update and revise their budgets at regular intervals as the budget period proceeds, the process is often too slow compared with the pace at which the external environment is changing.

(e) **Budgets protect rather than reduce costs**. Once a manager has an authorised budget, they can spend that amount of resource without further authorisation. A 'use it or lose it' mentality often develops, so that managers will incur cost unnecessarily. This happens especially towards the end

of the budget period in the expectation that managers will not be permitted to carry forward any
unused resource into the budget for next period.

(f)   **Budgets stifle product and strategy innovation**. The focus on achieving the budget discourages
managers from taking risks in case this has adverse effects on their short-term performance.
Managers do not have the freedom to respond to changing customer needs in a fast-changing
market because the activity they would need to undertake is not authorised in their budget.

(g)   **Budgets focus on sales targets rather than customer satisfaction**. The achievement of short-term
sales forecasts becomes the focus of most organisations. However, this does not necessarily result
in customer satisfaction. The customer may be sold something **inappropriate to their needs**, as in
recent years in the UK financial services industry. Alternatively, if a manager has already met the
sales target for a particular period, they might try to **delay sales to the next period**, in order to give
themselves a 'head start' towards achieving the target for the next period. Furthermore, there is an
incentive towards the end of a period, if a manager feels that the sales target is not going to be
achieved for the period, to **delay sales until the next period**, and thus again have a head start
towards achieving the target for the next period. All of these actions, focusing on sales targets
rather than customer satisfaction, will have a detrimental effect on the organisation in the longer
term.

(h)   **Budgets are divorced from strategy**. Most organisations monitor the monthly results against the
short-term budget for the month. What is needed instead is a system of monitoring the longer-term
progress against the organisation's strategy.

(i)   **Budgets reinforce a dependency culture**. The process of planning and budgeting within a
framework devolved from senior management perpetuates a culture of dependency. Traditional
budgeting systems, operated on a centralised basis, do not encourage a culture of **personal
responsibility**.

(j)   **Budgets lead to unethical behaviour**. For example, we have seen in this chapter a number of
opportunities for dysfunctional behaviour, such as **building slack into the budget** in order to create
an easier target for achievement.

9.2 Beyond Budgeting (BB) concepts

Two fundamental concepts underlie the Beyond Budgeting (BB) approach.

(a)   **Use adaptive management processes rather than the more rigid annual budget**. Traditional
annual plans tie managers to predetermined actions which are not responsive to current situations.
Managers should instead be planning on a **more adaptive**, rolling basis, but with the focus on cash
forecasting rather than purely on cost control. Performance is monitored against world-class
benchmarks, competitors and previous periods.

(b)   **Move towards devolved networks rather than centralised hierarchies**. The emphasis is on
encouraging a culture of personal responsibility by delegating decision making and performance
accountability to line managers.

Beyond Budgeting model

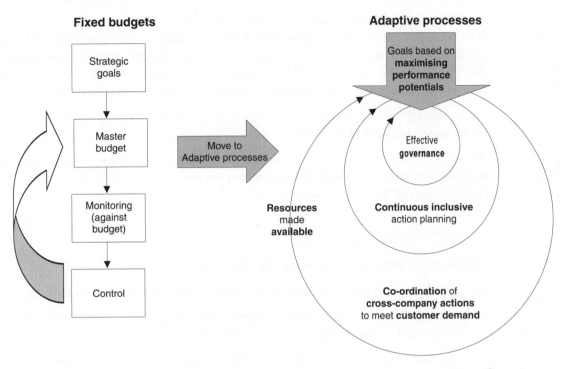

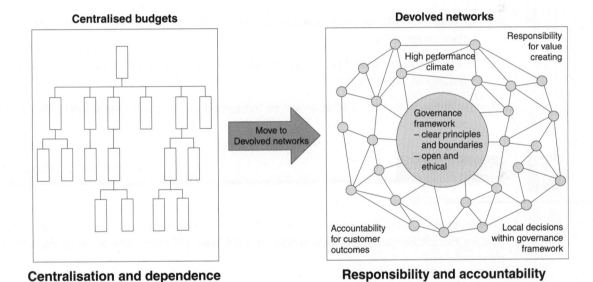

Centralisation and dependence   **Responsibility and accountability**

(Adapted from www.bbrt.org)

9.3 Adaptive management processes

An adaptive management process **does not tie a manager to the achievement of a fixed target** but
instead expects managers to deliver **continuous performance improvement in response to changing
conditions**. Planning is undertaken on a continuous, participative basis.

Evaluation of a manager's performance is based on **relative improvement** and this evaluation is carried
out using a **range of relative performance indicators with hindsight**, ie taking account of the conditions
under which the manager was operating.

Managers are **given the resources** they need as they are required and horizontal **cross-company activities
are co-ordinated** to respond to customer demand.

9.4 Devolved organisations

In a devolved organisation, managers are enabled and encouraged to make their own local decisions in order to achieve results, **within a governance framework based on clear principles and boundaries**. Managers are not restricted to a specific agreed plan but **can use their own initiative and local knowledge** to achieve the organisation's goals. They are expected to make decisions that create value and are fully **accountable for customer satisfaction** and for **achieving a high level of relative success**.

The emphasis in information systems is on openness and 'one truth' throughout the organisation, thus **encouraging ethical behaviour** that is beneficial to the organisation.

The ability of managers to act immediately, without the restriction of a fixed plan, but **with clear principles and values and within strategic boundaries** enables the organisation to respond quickly to identified opportunities and threats.

9.5 BB implementation

A BB implementation should incorporate the following six main principles.

(a)   The responsibilities of managers within an organisation should be clearly defined.

(b)   Managers should be given goals and targets which are based on key performance indicators and benchmarks. These targets should be linked to shareholder value.

(c)   Managers should be given a degree of freedom to make decisions. A BB organisation chart should be 'flat'.

(d)   Responsibility for decisions that generate value should be placed with 'front line teams' in line with the concept of TQM.

(e)   Front line teams should be made responsible for relationships with customers, associate businesses and suppliers.

(f)   Information support systems should be transparent and align with the activities that managers are responsible for.

Question 5.4	In defence of traditional budgeting

Learning outcome B2(c)

Identify **three** criticisms that are levelled at the traditional budgeting process by advocates of techniques that are 'Beyond Budgeting' and explain how the traditional budgeting process can be adapted to address these criticisms.

Section summary

The **Beyond Budgeting Round Table**, an independent research collaborative, have proposed that traditional budgeting should be abandoned. They have published ten main criticisms of the traditional process.

The two fundamental concepts of the **BB** approach are the use of **adaptive management processes** rather than fixed annual budgets and a move to a more decentralised way of managing the business with a culture of personal responsibility.

Chapter Summary

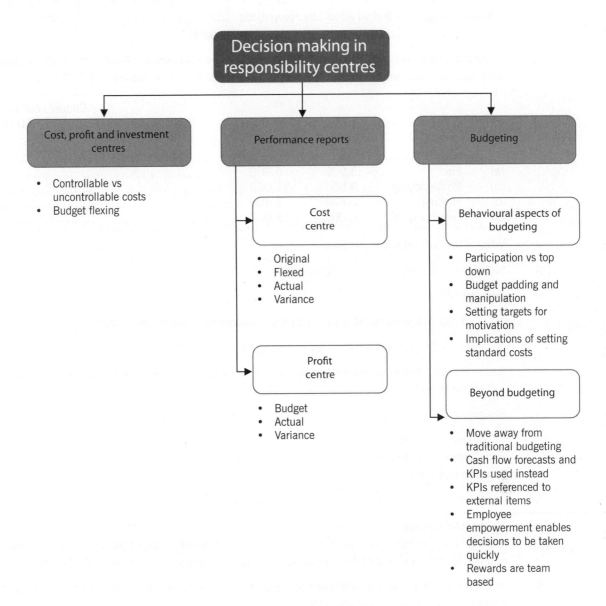

Quick Quiz

1   Fill in the blanks.

      A flexible budget is a budget which, by recognising ...., is designed
to................................. as the level of activity changes.

2   An extract of the costs incurred at two different activity levels is shown. Classify the costs according to
their behaviour patterns and show the budget cost allowance for an activity of 1,500 units.

		1,000 units $	2,000 units $	Type of cost	Budget cost allowance for 1,500 units $
(a)	Fuel	3,000	6,000	....	....
(b)	Photocopying	9,500	11,000	....	....
(c)	Heating	2,400	2,400	....	....
(d)	Direct wages	6,000	8,000	....	....

3   What is the controllability principle?

4   Match the descriptions to the budgeting style.

      Description

      (a)   Budget allowances are set without the involvement of the budget holder.

      (b)   All budget holders are involved in setting their own budgets.

      (c)   Budget allowances are set on the basis of discussions between budget holders and those to whom
they report.

      Budgeting style

      Negotiated budgeting
      Participative budgeting
      Imposed budgeting

5   Choose the appropriate words from those highlighted.

      An **expectations/aspirations** budget would be most useful for the purposes of planning and decision
making based on reasonable expectations, whereas an **aspirations/expectations** budget is more
appropriate for improving motivation by setting targets of an intermediate level of difficulty.

6   In the context of a balanced scorecard approach to performance measurement, to which of the four
perspectives does each measure relate?

	Performance measure	*Perspective*
(a)	Time taken to develop new products	....
(b)	Percentage of on-time deliveries	....
(c)	Average set-up time	....
(d)	Return on capital employed	....

7   Choose the appropriate words from those highlighted.

      The correct approach to budgetary control is to compare **actual/budgeted** results with a budget that has
been flexed to the **actual/budgeted** level of activity.

8   Not all fixed costs are non-controllable in the short term. True or false?

9   What is goal congruence (in terms of organisational control systems)?

   A   When the goals of management and employees harmonise with the goals of the organisation as a whole

   B   When the goals of management harmonise with the goals of employees

   C   When the work-related goals of management harmonise with their personal goals

   D   When an organisation's goals harmonise with those of its customers

10   For each organisation there is an ideal solution to the conflicts caused by the operation of a budgetary control system and it is the responsibility of the management accountant to find that solution. True or false?

11   Which of the following is **not** consistent with the concepts of the Beyond Budgeting approach?

   A   Continuous forecasting
   B   Participative planning
   C   Centralised decision making
   D   Relative performance measures

12   Which of the following definitions is/are correct?

   1   An imposed budget is a budget which, by recognising different cost behaviour patterns, is designed to change as the volume of activity changes.

   2   Bottom-up budgeting is a process where all budget holders have the opportunity to participate.

   A   Neither are correct.
   B   Definition 1 only is correct.
   C   Definition 2 only is correct.
   D   Both definitions are correct.

Answers to Quick Quiz

1   cost behaviour patterns

     flex or change

2   (a)   Variable $4,500
     (b)   Semi-variable $10,250
     (c)   Fixed $2,400
     (d)   Semi-variable $7,000

3   The principle that managers should only be held responsible for costs that they have direct control over

4   (a)   Imposed budgeting
     (b)   Participative budgeting
     (c)   Negotiated budgeting

5   expectations
     aspirations

6   (a)   Learning
     (b)   Customer
     (c)   Internal
     (d)   Financial

7   actual
     actual

8   True. Discretionary fixed costs can be raised or lowered at fairly short notice.

9   A

10   False. There are no ideal solutions. Management and the management accountant have to develop their
     own ways of dealing with the conflicts, taking into account the organisation, the business and the
     personalities involved.

11   C

12   C   Definition 1 refers to a flexible budget.

Answers to Questions

5.1 Responsibility accounting

In a system of responsibility accounting costs and revenues are **segregated into areas of personal responsibility** in order to monitor and assess the performance of each part of an organisation.

Controllable costs are those costs which are within the control of the manager of a responsibility centre, whereas uncontrollable costs are **outside the control** of the centre manager.

A budget cost allowance is the **cost that should be incurred** in a responsibility centre **for the actual activity level that was achieved**. It is the flexible budget cost that is obtained by flexing the variable cost allowance in line with changes in the level of activity.

All three items are important from the point of view of **control** and **motivation**.

Better cost control is achieved if those areas that a manager can control (controllable costs) are **highlighted separately** from those costs that the manger cannot control (uncontrollable costs). Better cost control is also achieved through **more meaningful variances** that are obtained by comparing a realistic flexible budget cost allowance with the actual results that were achieved.

Motivation of managers is improved if uncontrollable items are analysed separately, since otherwise they will feel they are **being held accountable for something over which they have no control**. Similarly, the realistic flexible budget of comparison is more likely to have a positive motivational impact because a **more meaningful** comparative measure of actual performance is obtained.

5.2 Participative budgets

A participative budget is likely to be least effective in a centralised organisation. An imposed budget will be more effective in such an organisation.

5.3 Behavioural aspects of budget participation

The level of participation in the budgeting process can vary from zero participation to a process of group decision making. There are a number of behavioural aspects of participation to consider.

(a)   **Communication**. Managers cannot be expected to achieve targets if they do not know what those targets are. Communication of targets is made easier if managers have participated in the budgetary process from the beginning.

(b)   **Motivation**. Managers are likely to be better motivated to achieve a budget if they have been involved in compiling it, rather than having a dictatorial budget imposed on them.

(c)   **Realistic targets**. A target must be achievable and accepted as realistic if it is to be a motivating factor. A manager who has been involved in setting targets is more likely to accept them as realistic. In addition, managers who are close to the operation of their departments may be more aware of the costs and potential savings in running it.

(d)   **Goal congruence**. One of the best ways of achieving goal congruence is to involve managers in the preparation of their own budgets, so that their personal goals can be taken into account in setting targets.

        Although participative budgeting has many advantages, difficulties might also arise.

(e)   **Pseudo-participation**. Participation may not be genuine, but merely a pretence at involving managers in the preparation of their budgets. Managers may feel that their contribution is being ignored, or that the participation consists of merely obtaining their agreement to a budget which has already been decided. If this is the case, then managers are likely to be more demotivated than if there is no participation at all.

(f) **Co-ordination**. If participative budgeting is well managed it can improve the co-ordination of the preparation of the various budgets. There is, however, a danger that too many managers will become involved so that communication becomes difficult and the process complex.

(g) **Training**. Some managers may not possess the necessary skill to make an effective contribution to the preparation of their budgets. Additional training may be necessary, with the consequent investment of money and time. It may also be necessary to train managers to understand the purposes and advantages of participation.

(h) **Slack**. If budgets are used in a punitive fashion for control purposes, then managers will be tempted to build in extra expenditure to provide a 'cushion' against overspending. It is easier for them to build in slack in a participative system.

5.4 In defence of traditional budgeting

Three criticisms that could be addressed by adapting the traditional budgeting process are as follows.

(a) Budgets are time consuming and expensive.
(b) Budgets protect rather than reduce costs.
(c) Budgets focus on sales targets rather than customer satisfaction.

The traditional budgeting process can be operated in a fashion that addresses these criticisms as follows.

(a) **Budgets are time consuming and expensive.**

A traditional budgeting system need not be more expensive and time consuming than the adaptive management process advocated as a 'Beyond Budgeting' concept. Managers need to appreciate that the cost of obtaining information should not exceed the benefit to be derived from it. A culture of '**sufficiently accurate**' should be encouraged in budget managers and they should understand that their task is to quantify the costs to be incurred in their area **in order to achieve the organisation's strategy**. This does not necessitate a separate forecast for every paperclip and staple, down to the nearest penny, but budgets can instead be prepared to the nearest thousand or to the nearest million, depending on the size of the organisation.

(b) **Budgets protect rather than reduce costs.**

The attitude of senior managers needs to change in order to prevent unnecessary expenditure and slack being built into the budget. If a budget manager has not used all of their allocated budget resource during a period, they should not expect to lose that resource in the next period. **Each manager should be able to request the resource needed to achieve the organisation's strategy**, regardless of the expenditure incurred in the latest period or the amount that was included in the original budget. Thus a 'use it or lose it' culture can be avoided.

Slack can also be avoided by **using budgetary control reports in a less punitive and rigid manner**. If managers believe they are going to be admonished for exceeding the budget expenditure or they are not going to be allowed more resource than stated in their original budget, then they will build in slack at the planning stage in order to provide some leeway.

(c) **Budgets focus on sales targets rather than customer satisfaction.**

The punitive use of budgetary control reports will again aggravate this situation. Managers must be given the opportunity to justify any sales shortfalls and should not be penalised for any shortfalls that are beyond their control. The use of **non-financial performance measures** combined with the financial budgetary control reports will assist in moving managers' focus away from the sales targets. For example, managers' performance could be assessed on a combination of sales targets and the level of customer satisfaction achieved.

Now try these questions from the Practice Question Bank

Number	Marks	Time
Q19 Objective test questions	10	18 mins
Q20 Responsibility accounting	5	9 mins
Q21 Budgets and people	12	22 mins
Q22 Divisional performance	15	27 mins
Q23 B and C	30	54 mins
Q24 Pasta division	30	54 mins

PERFORMANCE MEASUREMENT

Performance measurement and evaluation is important as it allows management to determine how well the company is doing in comparison both with previous years and with competitors.

It is important that the performance of an organisation is monitored, and this is most commonly done by calculating a number of ratios. Non-financial performance indicators are important too and these are covered in Section 6.

topic list	learning outcomes	syllabus references	ability required
1 Financial performance indicators (FPIs)	B2(a)	B2(a)(i)	application
2 Return on investment (ROI)	B2(a)	B2(a)(i)	application
3 ROI and decision making	B2(a)	B2(a)(i)	application
4 Residual income (RI)	B2(a)	B2(a)(i)	application
5 Economic value added (EVA®)	B2(a)	B2(a)(i)	application
6 Non-financial performance indicators (NFPIs)	B2(b)	B2(b)(i)	application
7 The balanced scorecard	B2(b)	B2(b)(ii)	analysis
8 Benchmarking	B2(a)	B2(a)(ii), (iii)	application
9 Not-for-profit organisations	B2(a)	B2(a)(ii)	application

Chapter Overview

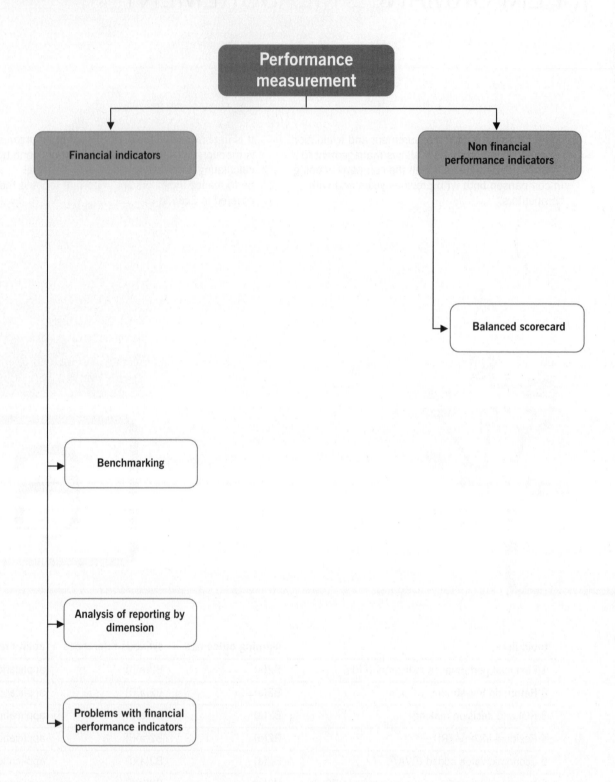

1 Financial performance indicators (FPIs)

Introduction

This section covers the ways in which performance can be measured using financial performance indicators. Make sure you can interpret the ratios as well as calculate them!

1.1 Setting the scene

KEY POINT

Financial performance indicators analyse profitability, liquidity and risk.

Financial indicators (or **monetary** measures) include the following.

Measure	Example
Profit	Profit is the commonest measure of all. Profit maximisation is usually cited as the main objective of most business organisations: 'ICI increased pre-tax profits to $233m'; 'General Motors ... yesterday reported better-than-expected first-quarter net income of $513m. Earnings improved $680m from the first quarter of last year when GM lost $167m.'
Revenue	'The US businesses contributed $113.9m of total group turnover of $409m.'
Costs	'Sterling's fall benefited pre-tax profits by about $50m while savings from the cost-cutting programme instituted in 1991 were running at around $100m a quarter'; 'The group interest charge rose from $48m to $61m.'
Share price	'The group's shares rose 31p to 1,278p despite the market's fall.'
Cash flow	'Cash flow was also continuing to improve, with cash and marketable securities totalling $8.4bn on March 31, up from $8bn at December 31.'

Note that the monetary amounts stated are **only given meaning in relation to something else**. Financial results should be compared against a **yardstick** such as:

- Budgeted **sales**, **costs** and **profits**

- **Standards** in a standard costing system

- The **trend** over time (last year/this year, say)

- The results of **other parts of the business**

- The results of **other businesses**

- The **economy** in general

- **Future potential** (for example, the performance of a new business may be judged in terms of nearness to breaking even)

Exam skills

Knowledge of how to calculate and interpret key ratios is a weak point for many students. Make sure it is one of your strong points.

1.2 Profitability

A company should of course be profitable, and there are obvious checks on **profitability**.

(a)   Whether the company has made a profit or a loss on its ordinary activities
(b)   By how much this year's profit or loss is bigger or smaller than last year's profit or loss

It is probably better to consider separately the profits or losses on exceptional items if there are any. Such gains or losses should not be expected to occur again, unlike profits or losses on normal trading.

Question 6.1			Profitability

Learning outcome B2(a)

A company has the following summarised statements of profit or loss for two consecutive years.

	Year 1 $	Year 2 $
Turnover	70,000	100,000
Less cost of sales	42,000	55,000
Gross profit	28,000	45,000
Less expenses	21,000	35,000
Net profit	7,000	10,000

Although the net profit margin is the same for both years at 10%, the gross profit margin is not.

Year 1 $\frac{28,000}{70,000} = 40\%$ Year 2 $\frac{45,000}{100,000} = 45\%$

Is this good or bad for the business?

Profit on ordinary activities before taxation is generally thought to be a **better** figure to use than profit after taxation, because there might be unusual variations in the tax charge from year to year which would not affect the underlying profitability of the company's operations.

Another profit figure that should be calculated is **profit before interest and tax (PBIT)**. This is the amount of profit which the company earned **before having to pay interest to the providers of loan capital**. By providers of loan capital, we usually mean longer-term loan capital, such as debentures and medium-term bank loans, which will be shown in the balance sheet as 'Payables: amounts falling due after more than one year'. This figure is of particular importance to bankers and lenders.

PBIT = profit on ordinary activities before taxation + interest charges on long-term loan capital

1.2.1 Sales margin

KEY TERM

SALES MARGIN is turnover less cost of sales.

Look at the following examples.

(a)

Wyndeham Press, a printer	20X5 $'000
Turnover	89,844
Cost of sales	(60,769)
Gross profit	29,075
Distribution expenses	(1,523)
Administrative expenses	(13,300)
Goodwill amortisation	(212)
Operating profit (15.6%)	14,040
(Interest etc)	

Cost of sales comprises **direct material** cost, such as paper, and **direct labour**. Distribution and administrative expenses include depreciation. **Sales margin = 32%.**

Sales margin at least shows the contribution that is being made, especially when direct variable costs are very significant.

(b)

Arriva, a bus company	20X4
	$m
Turnover	1,534.3
Cost of sales	1,282.6
Gross profit	251.7
Net operating expenses	133.8
Operating profit (7.7%)	117.9

Sales margin = 16%. Clearly a higher percentage of costs are operating costs.

(c)   **Lessons to be learnt**

(i)   Sales margin as a measure is **not really any use in comparing different industries**.

(ii)   Sales margin is **influenced** by the level of **fixed costs**.

(iii)   **Trends** in sales margin are of interest. A falling sales margin suggests an organisation has not been able to pass on input price rises to customers.

(iv)   **Comparisons** with similar companies are of interest. If an organisation has a lower sales margin than a similar business, this suggests problems in controlling input costs.

In short, the value of sales margin as a measure of performance depends on the **cost structure** of the industry and the **uses** to which it is put.

1.2.2 Earnings per share (EPS)

Earnings per share (EPS) is a convenient measure as it shows how well the shareholder is doing.

EPS is widely used as a **measure of a company's performance**, especially in **comparing** results over a period **of several years**. A company must be able to sustain its earnings in order to pay dividends and reinvest in the business so as to achieve future growth. Investors also look for **growth in the EPS** from one year to the next.

EARNINGS PER SHARE (EPS) is defined as the profit attributable to each equity (ordinary) share.

KEY TERM

Question 6.2	EPS

Learning outcome B2(a)

Walter Wall Carpets made profits before tax in 20X8 of $9,320,000. Tax amounted to $2,800,000.

The company's share capital is as follows.

	$
Ordinary share (10,000,000 shares of $1)	10,000,000
8% preference shares	2,000,000
	12,000,000

Required

Calculate the EPS for 20X8.

EPS on its own does not really tell us anything. It must be seen **in context**.

(a) EPS is used for comparing the results of a company **over time**. Is its EPS growing? What is the rate of growth? Is the rate of growth increasing or decreasing?

(b) EPS should not be used blindly to compare the earnings of one company with another. For example, if A plc has an EPS of 12c for its 10,000,000 10c shares and B plc has an EPS of 24c for its 50,000,000 25c shares, we must take account of the numbers of shares. When **earnings are used to compare one company's shares with another**, this is done **using the P/E ratio or perhaps the earnings yield**.

(c) If EPS is to be a reliable basis for comparing results, it **must be calculated consistently**. The EPS of one company must be directly comparable with the EPS of others, and the EPS of a company in one year must be directly comparable with its published EPS figures for previous years. Changes in the share capital of a company during the course of a year cause problems of comparability.

(d) EPS is a figure based on past data, and it is easily manipulated by changes in accounting policies and by mergers or acquisitions. **The use of the measure in calculating management bonuses makes it particularly liable to manipulation**. The attention given to EPS as a performance measure by City analysts is arguably disproportionate to its true worth. Investors should be more concerned with **future earnings**, but of course estimates of these are more difficult to reach than the readily available figure.

1.2.3 Profitability and return: the return on capital employed (ROCE)

It is impossible to assess profits or profit growth properly without relating them to the amount of funds (the capital) employed in making the profits. An important profitability ratio is therefore **return on capital employed (ROCE)**, which states the profit as a **percentage of the amount of capital employed**.

$$\text{RETURN ON CAPITAL EMPLOYED} = \frac{\text{PBIT}}{\text{Capital employed}}$$

CAPITAL EMPLOYED = Shareholders' funds **plus** 'payables: amounts falling due after more than one year' **plus** any long-term provisions for liabilities and charges

= Total assets less current liabilities

What does a company's ROCE tell us? What should we be looking for? There are three **comparisons** that can be made.

(a) The change in ROCE from **one year to the next**

(b) The ROCE being earned by **other companies**, if this information is available

(c) A comparison of the ROCE with **current market borrowing rates**

   (i) What would be the cost of extra borrowing to the company if it needed more loans, and is it earning an ROCE that suggests it could make high enough profits to make such borrowing worthwhile?

   (ii) Is the company making an ROCE which suggests that it is making profitable use of its current borrowing?

1.2.4 Analysing profitability and return in more detail: the secondary ratios

We may analyse the ROCE, to find out why it is high or low, or better or worse than last year. There are two factors that contribute towards an ROCE, both related to turnover.

(a)   **Profit margin**. A company might make a high or a low profit margin on its sales. For example, a company that makes a profit of 25c per $1 of sales is making a bigger return on its turnover than another company making a profit of only 10c per $1 of sales.

(b)   **Asset turnover**. Asset turnover is a measure of how well the assets of a business are being used to generate sales. For example, if two companies each have capital employed of $100,000, and company A makes sales of $400,000 a year, but company B only makes sales of $200,000 a year, company A is making a higher turnover from the same amount of assets. This means company A will make a higher ROCE than company B. Asset turnover is expressed as 'x times' so that assets generate x times their value in annual turnover. Here, company A's asset turnover is 4 times and company B's is 2 times.

Profit margin and asset turnover together explain the ROCE, and if the ROCE is the primary profitability ratio, these other two are the secondary ratios. The relationship between the three ratios is as follows.

Profit margin   ×   **asset turnover**   =   **ROCE**

$$\frac{\text{PBIT}}{\text{Sales}} \quad \times \quad \frac{\text{Sales}}{\text{Capital employed}} \quad = \quad \frac{\text{PBIT}}{\text{Capital employed}}$$

It is also worth noting the **change in turnover** from one year to the next. Strong sales growth will usually indicate volume growth as well as turnover increases due to price rises, and volume growth is one sign of a prosperous company.

Asset turnover can also be calculated with any category of asset, such as non-current assets, if required.

1.3 Liquidity

Profitability and also debt, or gearing, are important aspects of a company's performance. Neither, however, directly addresses the key issue of liquidity. A company needs liquid assets so that it can meet its debts when they fall due.

KEY TERM

LIQUIDITY is the amount of cash a company can obtain quickly to settle its debts (and possibly to meet other unforeseen demands for cash payments too).

1.3.1 Liquid assets

Liquid funds include:

(a)   Cash

(b)   Short-term investments for which there is a ready market, such as investments in shares of other companies (NB **not** subsidiaries or associates)

(c)   Fixed-term deposits with a bank or building society, for example six-month deposits with a bank

(d)   Trade receivables

(e)   Bills of exchange receivable

Some assets are more liquid than others. Inventories of goods are fairly liquid in some businesses. Inventories of finished production goods might be sold quickly, and a supermarket will hold consumer goods for resale that could well be sold for cash very soon. Raw materials and components in a manufacturing company have to be used to make a finished product before they can be sold to realise cash, and so they are less liquid than finished goods. Just how liquid they are depends on the speed of inventory turnover and the length of the production cycle.

Non-current assets are not liquid assets. A company can sell off non-current assets, but unless they are no longer needed, or are worn out and about to be replaced, they are necessary to continue the company's operations. Selling non-current assets is certainly not a solution to a company's cash needs and so, although there may be an occasional non-current asset item which is about to be sold off, probably

because it is going to be replaced, it is safe to disregard non-current assets when measuring a company's liquidity.

In summary, **liquid assets are current asset items that will or could soon be converted into cash, and cash** itself. Two common definitions of liquid assets are **all current assets** or **all current assets with the exception of inventories**.

The main source of liquid assets for a trading company is sales. A company can obtain cash from sources other than sales, such as the issue of shares for cash, a new loan or the sale of non-current assets. But a company cannot rely on these at all times and, in general, obtaining liquid funds depends on making sales and profits.

1.3.2 The current ratio

The **current ratio** is the standard test of liquidity.

$$\text{CURRENT RATIO} = \frac{\text{Current assets}}{\text{Current liabilities}}$$

A company should have enough current assets that give a promise of 'cash to come' to meet its commitments to pay its current liabilities. Obviously, a ratio in **excess of 1** should be expected. In practice, a ratio comfortably in excess of 1 should be expected, but what is 'comfortable' varies between different types of businesses.

Companies are not able to convert all their current assets into cash very quickly. In particular, some manufacturing companies might hold large quantities of raw material inventories, which must be used in production to create finished goods. Finished goods might be warehoused for a long time, or sold on lengthy credit. In such businesses, where inventory turnover is slow, most inventories are not very liquid assets, because the cash cycle is so long. For these reasons, we calculate an additional liquidity ratio, known as the quick ratio or acid test ratio.

1.3.3 The quick ratio

$$\text{QUICK RATIO or ACID TEST RATIO} = \frac{\text{Current assets less inventories}}{\text{Current liabilities}}$$

This ratio should ideally be **at least 1** for companies with a **slow inventory turnover**. For companies with a **fast inventory turnover**, a quick ratio can be **less than 1** without indicating that the company is in cash flow difficulties.

Do not forget the other side of the coin. The current ratio and the quick ratio can be higher than they should be. A company with large volumes of inventories and receivables might be overinvesting in working capital, and so tying up more funds in the business than it needs to. This would suggest poor management of receivables or inventories by the company.

1.3.4 The accounts receivable payment period

ACCOUNTS RECEIVABLE DAYS or ACCOUNTS RECEIVABLE PAYMENT PERIOD

$$= \frac{\text{Trade receivables}}{\text{Credit sales turnover}} \times 365 \text{ days}$$

This is a rough measure of the average length of time it takes for a company's accounts receivable to pay what they owe.

The trade accounts receivable are not the **total** figure for accounts receivable in the statement of financial position, which includes prepayments and non-trade accounts receivable. The trade accounts receivable figure will be itemised in an analysis of the total accounts receivable, in a note to the accounts.

The estimate of accounts receivable days is only approximate.

(a)   The **statement of financial position value** of accounts receivable might be **abnormally high** or low compared with the 'normal' level the company usually has. This may apply especially to smaller companies, where the size of year-end accounts receivable may largely depend on whether a few customers or even a single large customer pay just before or just after the year end.

(b)   Turnover in the statement of profit or loss excludes sales tax, but the accounts receivable figure in the statement of financial position includes sales tax. We are not strictly comparing like with like.

1.3.5 The inventory turnover period

$$\text{INVENTORY DAYS} = \frac{\text{Inventory}}{\text{Cost of sales}} \times 365 \text{ days}$$

This indicates the average number of days that items of inventory are held for. As with the average accounts receivable collection period, this is only an approximate figure, but one which should be reliable enough for finding changes over time.

A lengthening inventory turnover period indicates:

(a)   A **slowdown** in **trading**, or

(b)   A **build-up** in **inventory levels**, perhaps suggesting that the investment in inventories is becoming excessive

If we add together the inventory days and the accounts receivable days, this should give us an indication of how soon inventory is convertible into cash, thereby giving a further indication of the **company's liquidity**.

1.3.6 The accounts payable payment period

$$\text{ACCOUNTS PAYABLE PAYMENT PERIOD} = \frac{\text{Average trade payables}}{\text{Credit purchases or Cost of sales}} \times 365 \text{ days}$$

The accounts payable payment period often helps to assess a company's liquidity; an increase in accounts payable days is often a sign of a lack of long-term finance or poor management of current assets, resulting in the use of extended credit from suppliers, increased bank overdraft and so on.

All the ratios calculated above will **vary by industry**; hence **comparisons** of ratios calculated with other similar companies in the same industry are important.

Question 6.3   Liquidity and working capital ratios

Calculate liquidity and working capital ratios from the accounts of a manufacturer of products for the
construction industry, and comment on the ratios.

	20X8 $m	20X7 $m
Turnover	2,065.0	1,788.7
Cost of sales	1,478.6	1,304.0
Gross profit	586.4	484.7
Current assets		
Inventories	119.0	109.0
Receivables (note 1)	400.9	347.4
Short-term investments	4.2	18.8
Cash at bank and in hand	48.2	48.0
	572.3	523.2
Payables: amounts falling due within one year		
Loans and overdrafts	49.1	35.3
Corporation taxes	62.0	46.7
Dividend	19.2	14.3
Payables (note 2)	370.7	324.0
	501.0	420.3
	$m	$m
Net current assets	71.3	102.9
Notes		
1 Trade receivables	329.8	285.4
2 Trade payables	236.2	210.8

1.4 Reporting a performance evaluation

Once business performance has been analysed using FPIs, the next stage is to report the performance
evaluation.

A business may report an evaluation using any of the following approaches.

(a)   **Horizontal analysis**

Horizontal analysis involves a **line by line comparison** of one set of data with another; for example,
comparing current year financial statements with those of the previous year. Expressing year on
year movements in percentage terms can help to highlight areas where further analysis is required.

(b)   **Trend analysis**

Trend analysis is horizontal analysis **extended** over a **greater period of time**. For example,
comparing financial statements over the past 5 years may reveal that, on average, company
turnover increased at a rate of 5% per annum.

(c)   **Vertical analysis**

Vertical analysis is a method in which data is expressed **as a percentage of a total account
balance** within the financial statements. For example, cash, accounts receivable and inventory are
likely to be expressed as a percentage of total assets within the statement of financial position.
This type of analysis can provide an insight into the liquidity position and financial condition of a
company.

Section summary

Financial performance indicators analyse profitability, liquidity and risk.

A company can be profitable but at the same time get into cash flow problems. Liquidity ratios (**current** and **quick**) and **working capital turnover ratios** give some idea of a company's liquidity.

A business may report an evaluation using **horizontal** analysis, **trend** analysis or **vertical** analysis.

2   Return on investment (ROI)

Introduction

Return on investment (ROI) is usually used to monitor the performance of an investment centre. This section looks at how ROI is measured – make sure you understand the concepts before moving on.

2.1 A definition

Return on investment (ROI) is generally regarded as the **key performance measure**. The main reason for its **widespread use** is that it **ties in directly with the accounting process**, and is identifiable from the statement of profit or loss and statement of financial position. However, it does have limitations, as we will see later in this chapter.

KEY TERM

RETURN ON INVESTMENT (ROI) (or RETURN ON CAPITAL EMPLOYED (ROCE)) shows how much profit has been made in relation to the amount of capital invested and is calculated as (profit/capital employed) × 100%.

For example, suppose that a company has two investment centres, A and B, which show results for the year as follows.

	A $	B $
Profit	60,000	30,000
Capital employed	400,000	120,000
ROI	15%	25%

Investment centre A has made double the profits of investment centre B, and in terms of profits alone has therefore been more 'successful'. However, B has achieved its profits with a much lower capital investment, and so has earned a much higher ROI. This suggests that B has been a more successful investment than A.

2.2 Measuring ROI

ROI can be measured in different ways.

2.2.1 Profit after depreciation as a percentage of net assets employed

This is probably the **most common method**, but it does present a problem. If an investment centre maintains the same annual profit, and keeps the same assets without a policy of regular replacement of non-current assets, its ROI will increase year by year as the assets get older. This **can give a false impression of improving performance over time**.

For example, the results of investment centre X, with a policy of straight-line depreciation of assets over a five-year period, might be as follows.

Year	Non-current assets at cost $'000	Depreciation in the year $'000	NBV (mid year) $'000	Working capital $'000	Capital employed $'000	Profit $'000	ROI
0	100			10	110		
1	100	20	90	10	100	10	10.0%
2	100	20	70	10	80	10	12.5%
3	100	20	50	10	60	10	16.7%
4	100	20	30	10	40	10	25.0%
5	100	20	10	10	20	10	50.0%

This table of figures shows that an investment centre can **improve its ROI** year by year simply **by allowing its non-current assets to depreciate**. There could be a **disincentive to** investment centre managers to **reinvest in new or replacement assets** because the centre's ROI would initially probably fall.

Question 6.4

ROI calculation (1)

Learning outcome B2(a)

A new company has non-current assets of £460,000 which will be depreciated to nil on a straight-line basis over 10 years. Net current assets will consistently be £75,000, and annual profit will consistently be £30,000. ROI is measured as return on net assets.

Required

Calculate the company's ROI in years 2 and 6.

A further disadvantage of measuring ROI as profit divided by net assets is that, for similar reasons, it is not **easy to compare** fairly the **performance of investment centres**.

For example, suppose that we have two investment centres, P and Q.

	Investment centre P $	Investment centre P $	Investment centre Q $	Investment centre Q $
Working capital		20,000		20,000
Non-current assets at cost	230,000		230,000	
Accumulated depreciation	170,000		10,000	
Net book value		60,000		220,000
Capital employed		80,000		240,000
Profit		$24,000		$24,000
ROI		30%		10%

Investment centres P and Q have the same amount of working capital, the same value of non-current assets at cost, and the same profit. But P's non-current assets have been depreciated by a much bigger amount (presumably P's non-current assets are much older than Q's) and so P's ROI is three times the size of Q's ROI. The conclusion might therefore be that P has performed much better than Q. This comparison, however, would not be 'fair', because the **difference in performance might be entirely attributable to the age of their non-current assets**.

The arguments for using net book values for calculating ROI

(a)   It is the **'normally accepted'** method of calculating ROI.

(b)   Organisations are continually buying new non-current assets to replace old ones that wear out and so, on the whole, the **total net book value** of all non-current assets together **will remain fairly constant** (assuming nil inflation and nil growth).

2.2.2 Profit after depreciation as a percentage of gross assets employed

Instead of measuring ROI as return on net assets, we could measure it as return on gross assets. This would **remove the problem of ROI increasing over time as non-current assets get older**.

If a company acquired a non-current asset costing $40,000, which it intends to depreciate by $10,000 p.a. for 4 years, and if the asset earns a profit of $8,000 p.a. after depreciation, ROI might be calculated on net book values or gross values, as follows.

Year	Profit	NBV (mid-year value)	ROI based on NBV	Gross value	ROI based on gross value
	$	$		$	
1	8,000	35,000	22.9%	40,000	20%
2	8,000	25,000	32.0%	40,000	20%
3	8,000	15,000	53.3%	40,000	20%
4	8,000	5,000	160.0%	40,000	20%

The ROI based on **net book value** shows an **increasing trend over time**, simply because the asset's value is falling as it is depreciated. The ROI based on gross book value suggests that the asset has **performed consistently** in each of the four years, which is probably a more valid conclusion.

Question 6.5	ROI calculation (2)

Learning outcome B2(a)

Repeat **Question 6.4: ROI calculation (1)**, measuring ROI as return on gross assets.

However, using gross book values to measure ROI has its **disadvantages**. Most important of these is that measuring ROI as return on gross assets ignores the age factor, and **does not distinguish between old and new assets**.

(a) **Older non-current assets** usually **cost more to repair and maintain**, to keep them running. An investment centre with old assets may therefore have its profitability reduced by repair costs, and its ROI might fall over time as its assets get older and repair costs get bigger.

(b) **Inflation** and **technological change alter the cost of non-current assets**. If one investment centre has non-current assets bought 10 years ago with a gross cost of £1 million, and another investment centre, in the same area of business operations, has non-current assets bought very recently for £1 million, the quantity and technological character of the non-current assets of the two investment centres are likely to be very different.

2.2.3 Constituent elements of the investment base

Although we have looked at how the investment base should be valued, we need to consider its appropriate constituent elements.

(a) If a **manager's performance is being evaluated**, only those **assets** which can be **traced directly to the division** and are **controllable by the manager should be included**. Head office assets or investment centre assets controlled by head office should not be included. So, for example, only those cash balances actually maintained within an investment centre itself should be included.

(b) If it is **the performance of the investment centre that is being appraised, a proportion of the investment in head office assets would need to be included** because an investment centre could not operate without the support of head office assets and administrative backup.

2.2.4 Profits

We have looked at how to define the asset base used in the calculations, but what about profit? If the **performance of the investment centre manager is being assessed**, it should seem reasonable to **base profit on the revenues and costs controllable by the manager** and exclude service and head office costs except those costs specifically attributable to the investment centre. If it is the **performance of the investment centre that is being assessed, however, the inclusion of general service and head office costs would seem reasonable**.

2.2.5 Tangible and intangible assets

The management accountant is free to capitalise or expense intangible assets. When significant expenditure on an **intangible asset** (such as an advertising campaign) which is expected to provide future benefits is expensed, profits will be reduced and ROI/RI artificially depressed. In the future, the investment should produce significant cash inflows and the ROI/RI will be artificially inflated. **Such expenditure** should therefore be **capitalised so as to smooth out performance measures and eradicate the risk of drawing false conclusions from them**. The calculation of economic value added (EVA®), which we will learn about later in Section 5 of this chapter, does just this.

A **comparison of the performance of manufacturing divisions and service divisions** should be **treated with caution**. The majority of a **manufacturing division's assets** will be **tangible** and therefore are **automatically capitalised**, whereas the treatment of a **service division's** mostly **intangible assets** is **open to interpretation**.

2.2.6 Massaging the ROI

If a manager's large bonus depends on ROI being met, the manager may feel pressure to massage the measure. The **asset base** of the ratio can be **altered** by **increasing/decreasing payables and receivables** (by **speeding up or delaying payments and receipts**).

Section summary

The performance of an investment centre is usually monitored using either or both of **return on investment (ROI)** (also known as return on capital employed (ROCE)) and **residual income (RI)**.

There is no generally agreed method of calculating ROI and it can have **behavioural implications** and lead to dysfunctional decision making when used as a guide to investment decisions. It focuses attention on short-run performance, whereas investment decisions should be evaluated over their full life.

3 ROI and decision making

Introduction

This section is a continuation of Section 2 and looks at how ROI can be used in decision making.

3.1 New investments

If investment centre performance is judged by ROI, we should expect that the managers of investment centres will probably decide to undertake new capital investments **only if these new investments are likely to increase the ROI of their centre**.

Suppose that an investment centre, A, currently makes a return of 40% on capital employed. The manager of centre A would probably only want to undertake new investments that promise to yield a return of 40% or more, otherwise the investment centre's overall ROI would fall.

For example, if investment centre A currently has assets of $1,000,000 and expects to earn a profit of $400,000, how would the centre's manager view a new capital investment which would cost $250,000 and yield a profit of $75,000 p.a.?

	Without the new investment	With the new investment
Profit	$400,000	$475,000
Capital employed	$1,000,000	$1,250,000
ROI	40%	38%

The **new investment** would **reduce the investment centre's ROI** from 40% to 38%, and so the investment centre manager would probably decide **not to undertake** the new investment.

If the group of companies of which investment centre A is a part has a target ROI of, say, 25%, the new investment would presumably be seen as **beneficial for the group as a whole**. But even though it promises to yield a return of 75,000/250,000 = 30%, which is above the group's target ROI, it would still make investment centre A's results look worse. The manager of investment centre A would, in these circumstances, be motivated to do not what is best for the organisation as a whole, but what is **best for their division**.

ROI should not be used to guide investment decisions, but there is a difficult motivational problem. If management performance is measured in terms of ROI, any decisions which benefit the company in the long term but which reduce the ROI in the immediate short term would reflect badly on the manager's reported performance. In other words, **good investment decisions would make a manager's performance seem worse than if the wrong investment decision were taken instead**.

3.2 Extended example: ROI and decision making

At the end of 20X3, Division S (part of a group) had a book value of non-current assets of $300,000 and net current assets of $40,000. Net profit before tax was $64,000.

The non-current assets of Division S consist of 5 separate items, each costing $60,000, which are depreciated to zero over 5 years on a straight-line basis. On 31 December of each of the past years, Division S has bought a replacement for the asset that has just been withdrawn and it proposes to continue this policy. Because of technological advances, the asset manufacturer has been able to keep his prices constant over time. The group's cost of capital is 15%.

Required

Assuming that, except where otherwise stated, there are no changes in the above data, deal with the following separate situations.

(a) Division S has the opportunity of an investment costing $60,000, and yielding an annual profit of $10,000.

   (i) Calculate its new ROI if the investment were undertaken.

   (ii) State whether the manager of Division S would recommend that the investment be undertaken.

(b) Division S has the opportunity of selling, at a price equal to its written-down book value of $24,000, an asset that currently earns $3,900 p.a.

   (i) Calculate its new ROI if the asset were sold.
   (ii) State whether the manager of Division S would recommend the sale of the asset.

Solution in general

The question does not state whether capital employed should include a valuation of non-current assets at gross historical cost or at net book value. It is assumed that net book value is required. It is also assumed that the non-current asset which has just been bought as a replacement on 31 December 20X3 has not been depreciated at all.

Exam skills

It is worth stating assumptions such as these at the start of a solution to questions of this sort.

The gross book value of the 5 non-current asset items is 5 × $60,000 = $300,000.

	$
Net book value of asset just bought on 31.12.X3	60,000
NBV of asset bought 1 year earlier	48,000
NBV of asset bought 2 years earlier	36,000
NBV of asset bought 3 years earlier	24,000
NBV of asset bought 4 years earlier	12,000
NBV of all 5 non-current assets at 31.12.X3	180,000
Net current assets	40,000
Total capital employed, Division S	220,000

Solution to part (a)

Part (i)

Begin with a comparison of the existing ROI (which is presumably the typical ROI achieved each year under the current policy of asset replacement) and the ROI with the new investment.

Existing ROI = (64/220) × 100% = 29.1%

For the ROI with the new investment it is assumed that the full asset cost of $60,000 should be included in the capital employed, although the asset will obviously be depreciated over time. It is also assumed that the additional profit of $10,000 is net of depreciation charges.

ROI with new investment = ((64 + 10)/(220 + 60)) × 100% = 26.4%

If the investment centre manager based his investment decisions on whether an investment would increase or reduce his ROI, he would not want to make the additional investment. This investment has a **marginal ROI** of (10/60) × 100% = 16.7%, which is **above the group's cost of capital but below Division S's current ROI** of 29.1%. Making the investment would therefore lower the division's average ROI.

Part (ii)

This example **illustrates the weakness of ROI as a guide to investment decisions**. An investment centre manager might want an investment to show a good ROI from year 1, when the new investment has a high net book value. In the case of Division S, the average net book value of the asset over its full life will be 50% of $60,000 = $30,000, and so the average ROI on the investment over time will be ($10,000/$30,000) × 100% = 33.3%, which is greater than the cost of capital.

Presumably, however, the Division S manager would not want to wait so long to earn a good ROI and wants to protect his division's performance in the short run as well as the long run. Therefore he would not recommend that the investment be undertaken.

Solution to part (b)

Part (b) of the question deals with a disinvestment proposal, compared to an acquisition in part (a). The same basic principles apply.

The **ROI if the asset is sold** is ((64 − 3.9)/(220 − 24)) × 100% = 30.7%

This compares favourably with the division's current average ROI of 29.1%, and so if the manager of Division S made his divestment decisions on the basis of ROI, he would **presumably decide to get rid of the asset**.

However, the decision would be misguided, because **decisions should not be based on the short-term effects on ROI**.

The asset which would be sold earns an ROI of (3.9/24) × 100% = 16.3%, which is higher than the group's cost of capital, but lower than the Division S average.

On the assumption that the asset would earn $3,900 after depreciation for the 2 remaining years of its life, its ROI next year would be (3.9/12) × 100% = 32.5%, which again is higher than the cost of capital.

Exam alert

You could be asked to discuss the conflict that may arise between NPV and ROI in an investment decision.

Section summary

If investment centre performance is judged by ROI, we would expect that the managers of these centres would undertake new capital investments only if these new investments increase the centre's ROI.

4 Residual income (RI)

Introduction

Residual income (RI) can also be used to measure the performance of investment centres. However, it has a number of weaknesses that make it less preferable than ROI as a performance measure. This section focuses on how to calculate RI and compares it to ROI. Make sure you know the strengths and weaknesses of this measure, as well as how to calculate it.

4.1 Calculating RI

An alternative way of measuring the performance of an investment centre, instead of using ROI, is residual income (RI). **RI is a measure of the centre's profits after deducting a notional or imputed interest cost**.

(a)   The centre's profit is **after deducting depreciation** on capital equipment.

(b)   The imputed cost of capital might be the organisation's cost of borrowing or its weighted average cost of capital.

KEY TERM

RESIDUAL INCOME (RI) is 'Profit minus a charge for capital employed in the period'.

(CIMA Official Terminology)

Question 6.6   RI

Learning outcome B2(a)

A division with capital employed of $400,000 currently earns an ROI of 22%. It can make an additional investment of $50,000 for a 5-year life with nil residual value. The average net profit from this investment would be $12,000 after depreciation. The division's cost of capital is 14%.

What are the residual incomes before and after the investment?

4.2 The advantages and weaknesses of RI compared with ROI

The advantages of using RI

(a)   RI will **increase** when investments earning above the cost of capital are undertaken and investments earning below the cost of capital are eliminated.

(b)   RI is **more flexible**, since a different cost of capital can be applied to investments with **different risk** characteristics.

The **weakness** of RI is that it **does not facilitate comparisons** between investment centres, nor **does it relate the size of a centre's income to the size of the investment**.

4.3 RI versus ROI: marginally profitable investments

RI will increase if a new investment is undertaken which earns a profit in excess of the imputed interest charge on the value of the asset acquired. RI will go up even if the investment only just exceeds the imputed interest charge, and this means that 'marginally profitable' investments are likely to be undertaken by the investment centre manager.

In contrast, when a manager is judged by ROI, a marginally profitable investment would be less likely to be undertaken because it would reduce the average ROI earned by the centre as a whole.

Example: RI and decision making

In the previous example in Section 3.2, **whereas ROI would have worsened with the new investment opportunity (part (a)) and improved with the disinvestment (part (b)), RI would have done the opposite** – improved with the new investment and worsened with the disinvestment.

The figures would be:

(a)   *Part (a)*

	Without new investment $	Investment $	With new investment $
Profit before notional interest	64,000	10,000	74,000
Notional interest (15% of $340,000)	51,000	9,000*	60,000
	13,000	1,000	14,000

*15% of $60,000

If the manager of Division S were **guided by RI** into making decisions, he would **approve the new investment**.

(b)   *Part (b)*

	Without disinvestment $	*Disinvestment* $	*With disinvestment* $
Profit before notional interest	64,000	3,900	60,100
Notional interest	51,000	3,600 *	47,400
Residual income	13,000	300	12,700

*15% of $24,000

If the investment centre manager is guided by RI, he would decide to **keep the asset** instead of selling it off.

RI **does not always point to the right investment decision**. However, RI is **more likely than ROI to improve when managers make correct investment/divestment decisions**, and so is probably a 'safer' basis than ROI on which to measure performance.

Example: ROI vs RI

Suppose that Department H has the following profit, assets employed and an imputed interest charge of 12% on operating assets.

	$	$
Operating profit	30,000	
Operating assets		100,000
Imputed interest (12%)	12,000	
Return on investment		30%
Residual income	18,000	

Suppose now that an additional investment of $10,000 is proposed, which will increase operating income in Department H by $1,400. The effect of the investment would be:

	$	$
Total operating income	31,400	
Total operating assets		110,000
Imputed interest (12%)	13,200	
Return on investment		28.5%
Residual income	18,200	

If the Department H manager is made responsible for the department's performance, he would **resist the new investment if he were to be judged on ROI**, but would **welcome the investment if he were judged according to RI**, since there would be a marginal increase of $200 in RI from the investment, but a fall of 1.5% in ROI.

The marginal investment offers a return of 14% ($1,400 on an investment of $10,000), which is above the 'cut-off rate' of 12%. Since the original ROI was 30%, the marginal investment will reduce the overall divisional performance. Indeed, any marginal investment offering an accounting rate of return of less than 30% in the year would reduce the overall performance.

Exam skills

ICS questions on RI may focus on the sort of behavioural aspects of investment centre measurement that we have discussed above, for example why it is considered necessary to use RI to measure performance rather than ROI, and why RI might influence an investment centre manager's investment decisions differently.

You should also be able to discuss other methods of assessment alongside ROI and RI. These may include EVA® (see Section 5), the balanced scorecard (see Section 7), other non-financial measures, controllable profit and cash generated.

Section summary

RI can sometimes give results that avoid the **behavioural** problem of **dysfunctionality**. Its weakness is that it does not facilitate comparisons between investment centres, nor does it relate the size of a centre's income to the size of the investment.

5 Economic value added (EVA®)

Introduction

The final performance measure we are going to look at is economic value added (EVA®). The calculation is similar to that for RI so make sure you don't get them mixed up!

LEARN

EVA® is an alternative absolute performance measure. It is similar to RI and is calculated as follows.

EVA® = net operating profit after tax (NOPAT) less capital charge

where the capital charge = weighted average cost of capital × net assets

5.1 Calculating EVA®

Economic value added (EVA®) is a registered trade mark owned by Stern Stewart & Co. It is a specific type of RI calculated as follows.

EVA® = net operating profit after tax (NOPAT) less capital charge

where the capital charge = weighted average cost of capital × net assets

You can see from the formula that the calculation of EVA® is very similar to the calculation of RI.

The calculation of EVA® is different to RI because the net assets used as the basis of the imputed interest charge are usually valued at their **replacement cost** and are **increased by any costs that have been capitalised** (see below).

There are also differences in the way that NOPAT is calculated compared with the profit figure that is used for RI, as follows.

(a)   Costs which would normally be treated as expenses, but which are considered within an EVA® calculation as **investments building for the future**, are added back to NOPAT to derive a figure for 'economic profit'. These costs are included instead as assets in the figure for net assets employed, ie as investments for the future. Costs treated in this way include items such as **goodwill, research and development expenditure and advertising costs**.

(b)   Adjustments are sometimes made to the depreciation charge, whereby accounting depreciation is added back to the profit figures, and **economic depreciation** is subtracted instead to arrive at NOPAT. Economic depreciation is a charge for the fall in asset value due to wear and tear or obsolescence.

(c)   Any lease charges are excluded from NOPAT and added in as a part of capital employed.

Another point to note about the calculation of NOPAT, which is the same as the calculation of the profit figure for RI, is that **interest** is excluded from NOPAT because interest costs are taken into account in the capital charge.

Example: Calculating EVA®

An investment centre has reported operating profits of $21 million. This was after charging $4 million for the development and launch costs of a new product that is expected to generate profits for 4 years. Taxation is paid at the rate of 25% of the operating profit.

The company has a risk adjusted weighted average cost of capital of 12% per annum and is paying interest at 9% per annum on a substantial long-term loan.

The investment centre's non-current asset value is $50 million and the net current assets have a value of $22 million. The replacement cost of the non-current assets is estimated to be $64 million.

Required

Calculate the investment centre's EVA® for the period.

Solution

Calculation of NOPAT

	$m
Operating profit	21.00
Taxation @ 25%	(5.25)
	15.75
Add back development costs	4.00
Less one year's amortisation of development costs ($4m/4)	(1.00)
NOPAT	18.75

Calculation of economic value of net assets

	$m
Replacement cost of net assets ($22 million + $64 million)	86
Add back investment in new product to benefit future	3
Economic value of net assets	89

Calculation of EVA®

The capital charge is based on the **weighted average cost of capital**, which takes account of the cost of share capital as well as the cost of loan capital. Therefore the correct interest rate is 12%.

	$m
NOPAT	18.75
Capital charge (12% × $89 million)	(10.68)
EVA®	8.07

5.2 Advantages of EVA®

The advantages of EVA® include the following.

(a)   Maximisation of EVA® will create real wealth for the shareholders.

(b)   The adjustments within the calculation of EVA® mean that the measure is based on figures that are closer to cash flows than accounting profits. Hence EVA® may be **less distorted by the accounting policies selected**.

(c)   The EVA® measure is an absolute value which is easily understood by non-financial managers.

(d)   If management are assessed using performance measures based on traditional accounting policies, they may be unwilling to invest in areas such as advertising and development for the future because **such costs will immediately reduce the current year's accounting profit**. EVA® recognises such costs as investments for the future and thus they do not immediately reduce the EVA® in the year of expenditure.

5.3 Disadvantages of EVA®

EVA® does have some drawbacks.

(a)   It is still a **relatively short-term measure** which can encourage managers to focus on short-term performance.

(b)   EVA® is based on historical accounts which may be of **limited use as a guide to the future**. In practice, also, the influences of accounting policies on the starting profit figure may not be completely negated by the adjustments made to it in the EVA® model.

(c)   Making the necessary adjustments can be problematic, as sometimes a **large number of adjustments** are required.

(d)   Investment centres which are larger in size may have larger EVA® figures for this reason. **Allowance for relative size** must be made when comparing the relative performance of investment centres.

| Question 6.7 | Calculating EVA® |

Learning outcome B2(a)

Division D operates as an investment centre. The book value of the non-current assets is $83,000 but their replacement value is estimated to be $98,000. Working capital in the division has a value of $19,000.

Latest operating profits for the division were $18,500, after charging historical cost depreciation of $8,100 and the costs of a major advertising campaign which amounted to $6,000. The advertising campaign is expected to boost revenues for two years.

An economic depreciation charge for the period would have been $12,300.

The risk adjusted weighted cost of capital for the company is 11% per annum.

Required

Calculate the EVA® for Division D. Ignore taxation.

Section summary

EVA® is an alternative absolute performance measure. It is similar to RI and is calculated as follows.

EVA® = net operating profit after tax (NOPAT) less capital charge

where the capital charge = weighted average cost of capital × net assets

EVA® and RI are similar because both result in an absolute figure which is calculated by subtracting an imputed interest charge from the profit earned by the investment centre. However, there are differences as follows.

(a)   The profit figures are calculated differently. EVA® is based on an **'economic profit'** which is derived by making a series of adjustments to the accounting profit.

(b)   The notional capital charges use **different bases for net assets**. The replacement cost of net assets is usually used in the calculation of EVA®.

6 Non-financial performance indicators (NFPIs)

Introduction

As well as evaluating performance using financial performance indicators, companies can use non-financial indicators. This section focuses on the different types of non-financial indicators and how they can be used for performance evaluation.

6.1 Increased emphasis on NFPIs

KEY TERM

NON-FINANCIAL PERFORMANCE INDICATORS (NFPIS) are 'measures of performance based on non-financial information that may originate in, and be used by, operating departments to monitor and control their activities without any accounting input'.   (*CIMA Official Terminology*)

There has been a growing emphasis on NFPIs for a number of reasons.

(a)   **Concentration on too few variables**. If performance measurement systems focus entirely on those items which can be expressed in monetary terms, managers will concentrate on only those variables and ignore other important variables that cannot be expressed in monetary terms.

(b)   **Lack of information on quality**. Traditional responsibility accounting systems do not provide information on the quality or relative importance of operations.

(c)   **Changes in cost structures**. Modern technology can require massive investment and product life cycles have got shorter. A greater proportion of costs are sunk and a large proportion of costs are designed into a product/service before production/delivery. By the time the product/service is produced/delivered, it is therefore too late to effectively control costs.

(d)   **Changes in competitive environment**. Financial measures do not convey the full picture of a company's performance, especially in a modern business environment. They are also open to distortion by the effect of market forces and by the choice of accounting policy.

(e)   **Changes in manufacturing environment**. New manufacturing techniques and technologies focus on minimising throughput times, inventory levels and set-up times, but managers can reduce the costs for which they are responsible by increasing inventory levels through maximising output. If a performance measurement system focuses principally on costs, managers may concentrate on cost reduction and ignore other important strategic manufacturing goals.

(f)   **NFPIs are a better indicator of future prospects**. Financial indicators tend to focus on the short term and are largely historical. They can give a positive message based on results in the immediate past, but problems may be looming. For example, falling quality will ultimately damage profitability.

6.2 The value of NFPIs

Unlike traditional variance reports, NFPIs can be provided **quickly** for managers, per shift, daily or even hourly as required. They are likely to be easy to calculate, and easier for non-financial managers to **understand** and therefore to **use effectively**.

The beauty of non-financial indicators is that **anything can be compared** if it is **meaningful** to do so. The measures should be **tailored** to the circumstances so that, for example, number of coffee breaks per 20 pages of Study Text might indicate to you how hard you are studying!

Many suitable measures combine elements from the chart shown below. The chart is not intended to be prescriptive or exhaustive.

Errors/failure	Time	Quantity	People
Defects	Second	Range of products	Employees
Equipment failures	Minute	Parts/components	Employee skills
Warranty claims	Hour	Units produced	Customers
Complaints	Shift	Units sold	Competitors
Returns	Cycle	Services performed	Suppliers
Stockouts	Day	kg/litres/metres	
Lateness/waiting	Month	m^2/m^3	
Misinformation	Year	Documents	
Miscalculation		Deliveries	
Absenteeism		Enquiries	

Traditional measures derived from these lists like 'kg (of material) per unit produced' or 'units produced per hour' are fairly obvious, but what may at first seem a fairly **unlikely combination** may also be very revealing. 'Absenteeism per customer', for example, may be of no significance at all or it may reveal that a particularly difficult customer is being avoided, and hence that some action is needed.

There is clearly a need for the information provider to work more closely with the managers who will be using the information to make sure that their needs are properly understood. The measures used are likely to be **developed and refined over time**. It may be that some will serve the purpose of drawing attention to areas in need of improvement but will be of no further relevance once remedial action has been taken. A flexible, responsive approach is essential.

Exam alert

Be prepared to explain a number of NFPIs that a business could use.

Learning outcome B2(b)

Using the above chart, develop five non-financial indicators for your organisation or one that you know
well, and explain how each might be useful.

6.3 NFPIs in relation to employees

One of the many criticisms of traditional accounting performance measurement systems is that they **do
not measure the skills, morale and training of the workforce**, which can be as **valuable to an
organisation as its tangible assets**. For example, if employees have not been trained in the manufacturing
practices required to achieve the objectives of the new manufacturing environment, an organisation is
unlikely to be successful.

Employee attitudes and morale can be measured by **surveying** employees. Education and skills levels,
promotion and training, absenteeism and labour turnover for the employees for which each manager is
responsible can also be monitored.

6.4 Performance measurement in a total quality management (TQM) environment

As you know from Chapter 1, **total quality management** (TQM) embraces every activity of a business.
Therefore, performance measures cannot be confined to the production process but must also cover the
work of sales, distribution and administration departments, the efforts of external suppliers, and the
reaction of external customers.

In many cases the measures used will be non-financial ones. They may be divided into three types.

(a)   **Measuring the quality of incoming supplies.** Quality control should include procedures for
        acceptance and inspection of goods inwards and measurement of rejects.

(b)   **Monitoring work done as it proceeds.** 'In-process' controls include statistical process controls and
        random sampling, and measures such as the amount of scrap and reworking in relation to good
        production. Measurements can be made by product, by worker or work team, by machine or
        machine type, by department, or whatever is appropriate.

(c)   **Measuring customer satisfaction.** This may be monitored in the form of letters of complaint,
        returned goods, penalty discounts, claims under guarantee, or requests for visits by service
        engineers. Some companies adopt a more proactive approach to monitoring customer satisfaction
        by surveying their customers on a regular basis. They use the feedback to obtain an index of
        customer satisfaction which is used to identify quality problems before they affect profits.

6.5 Quality of service

Service quality is measured principally by **qualitative measures**, as you might expect, although some
quantitative measures are used by some businesses.

(a)   If it were able to obtain the information, a retailer might use number of lost customers in a period
        as an indicator of service quality.

(b)   Lawyers use the proportion of time spent with clients.

6.5.1 Measures of customer satisfaction

You have probably filled in **questionnaires** in restaurants or on planes without realising that you were completing a customer attitude survey for input to the organisation's management information system.

Other possible measures of customer satisfaction include:

(a)   Market research on customer preferences and customer satisfaction with specific product features
(b)   Number of defective units supplied to customers as a percentage of total units supplied
(c)   Number of customer complaints as a percentage of total sales volume
(d)   Percentage of products which fail early or excessively
(e)   On-time delivery rate
(f)   Average time to deal with customer queries
(g)   New customer accounts opened
(h)   Repeat business from existing customers

Section summary

Changes in cost structures, the competitive environment and the manufacturing environment have led to an **increased use of non-financial performance indicators** (NFPIs).

NFPIs can usefully be applied to **employees** and product/service **quality**.

7 The balanced scorecard

Introduction

Another approach to performance measurement is the use of what is called a 'balanced scorecard', which is the subject of this section.

KEY TERM

The **BALANCED SCORECARD APPROACH** is an 'Approach to the provision of information to management to assist strategic policy formulation and achievement. It emphasises the need to provide the user with a set of information which addresses all relevant areas of performance in an objective and unbiased fashion. The information provided may include both financial and non-financial elements, and cover areas such as profitability, customer satisfaction, internal efficiency and innovation.'   (*CIMA Official Terminology*)

7.1 The four perspectives

The balanced scorecard focuses on **four different perspectives**, as follows.

Perspective	Question	Explanation
Customer	What do existing and new customers value from us?	Gives rise to targets that matter to customers: cost, quality, delivery, inspection, handling and so on.
Internal	What processes must we excel at to achieve our financial and customer objectives?	Aims to improve internal processes and decision making.
Innovation and learning	Can we continue to improve and create future value?	Considers the business's capacity to maintain its competitive position through the acquisition of new skills and the development of new products.
Financial	How do we create value for our shareholders?	Covers traditional measures such as growth, profitability and shareholder value but set through talking to the shareholder or shareholders direct.

Performance targets are set once the key areas for improvement have been identified, and the balanced scorecard is the **main monthly report**.

The scorecard is '**balanced**' in the sense that managers are required to **think in terms of all four perspectives**, to **prevent improvements being made in one area at the expense of** another.

7.1.1 Types of measures

The types of measure which may be monitored under each of the four perspectives include the following. The list is not exhaustive but it will give you an idea of the possible scope of a balanced scorecard approach. The measures selected, particularly within the internal perspective, will vary considerably with the type of organisation and its objectives.

Perspective	Measures	
Customer	• New customers acquired • Customer complaints	• On-time deliveries • Returns
Internal	• Quality control rejects • Average set-up time	• Speed of producing management information
Innovation and learning	• Labour turnover rate • Percentage of revenue generated by new products and services • Average time taken to develop new products and services	
Financial	• Return on capital employed • Cash flow	• Revenue growth • Earnings per share

Broadbent and Cullen (in Berry, Broadbent and Otley, eds, *Management Control*, 1995) identify the following **important features** of this approach.

- It looks at both **internal and external matters** concerning the organisation.
- It is **related to the key elements of a company's strategy**.
- **Financial and non-financial measures** are linked together.

The balanced scorecard approach may be particularly useful for performance measurement in organisations that are unable to use simple profit as a performance measure. For example, the **public sector** has long been forced to use a **wide range of performance indicators**, which can be formalised with a balanced scorecard approach.

7.2 Example

An example of how a balanced scorecard might appear is offered below.

Balanced scorecard

Financial perspective

GOALS	MEASURES
Survive	Cash flow
Succeed	Monthly sales growth and operating income by division
Prosper	Increase market share and ROI

Customer perspective

GOALS	MEASURES
New products	Percentage of sales from new products
Responsive supply	On-time delivery (defined by customer)
Preferred supplier	Share of key accounts' purchases
	Ranking by key accounts
Customer partnership	Number of cooperative engineering efforts

Internal business perspective

GOALS	MEASURES
Technology capability	Manufacturing configuration vs competition
Manufacturing excellence	Cycle time
	Unit cost
	Yield
Design productivity	Silicon efficiency
	Engineering efficiency
New product introduction	Actual introduction schedule vs plan

Innovation and learning perspective

GOALS	MEASURES
Technology leadership	Time to develop next generation of products
Manufacturing learning	Process time to maturity
Product focus	Percentage of products that equal 80% sales
Time to market	New product introduction vs competition

Question 6.9

Balanced scorecard

Learning outcome B2(b)

Spotlight Productions has in the past produced just one fairly successful product. Recently, however, a new version of this product has been launched. Development work continues to add a related product to the product list. Given below are some details of the activities during the month of November.

Units produced	– existing product	25,000
	– new product	5,000
Cost of units produced	– existing product	$375,000
	– new product	$70,000
Sales revenue	– existing product	$550,000
	– new product	$125,000
Hours worked	– existing product	5,000
	– new product	1,250
Development costs		$47,000

Required

(a)   Suggest and calculate performance indicators that could be calculated for each of the four
      perspectives on the balanced scorecard.

(b)   Suggest how this information would be interpreted.

Exam alert

Be prepared to discuss the implementation of the balanced scorecard for the specific industry or non profit
making organisation (NGO) required by the question.

7.3 Problems

As with all techniques, problems can arise when the balanced scorecard is applied.

Problem	Explanation
Conflicting measures	Some measures in the scorecard, such as research funding and cost reduction, may naturally conflict. It is often difficult to determine the balance which will achieve the best results.
Selecting measures	Not only do appropriate measures have to be devised but the number of measures used must be agreed. Care must be taken that the impact of the results is not lost in a sea of information.
Expertise	Measurement is only useful if it initiates appropriate action. Non-financial managers may have difficulty with the usual profit measures. With more measures to consider, this problem will be compounded.
Interpretation	Even a financially trained manager may have difficulty in putting the figures into an overall perspective.
Too many measures	The ultimate objective for commercial organisations is to maximise profits or shareholder wealth. Other targets should offer a guide to achieving this objective and not become an end in themselves.

Section summary

The **balanced scorecard approach** to the provision of information focuses on four different perspectives:
customer, financial, internal, and innovation and learning.

8 Benchmarking

Introduction

Analysing performance by a single comparison of data (eg current year vs prior year) can be difficult.
Benchmarking is another type of comparison exercise through which an organisation attempts to improve
performance. The idea is to seek the best available performance against which the organisation can
monitor its own performance.

KEY TERM

'BENCHMARKING is the establishment, through data gathering, of targets and comparators, through whose use relative levels of performance (and particularly underperformance) can be identified. By the adoption of identified best practices it is hoped that performance will improve.' *(CIMA Official Terminology)*

CIMA identified three distinct approaches to benchmarking in *CIMA Insider*.

Type	Description
Metric benchmarking	The practice of **comparing appropriate metrics** to identify possible areas for improvement.
	For example, IT investment as a percentage of total assets may be compared across different departments within the same company to identify areas of the company where additional investment is required.
Process benchmarking	The practice of **comparing processes with a partner** as part of an improvement process. For example, a distributor of personal computers may analyse a competitor's supply chain function in the hope of identifying successful elements of the process that it can use to its advantage.
Diagnostic benchmarking	The practice of **reviewing the processes of a business** to identify those which indicate a problem and offer a potential for improvement.
	For example, a company may critically assess each element of the value chain and conclude that there is potential for improvement within the marketing and sales function.

8.1 Obtaining information

Financial information about competitors is **easier** to acquire than non-financial information. Information about **products** can be obtained from **reverse engineering** (buying a competitor's products and dismantling them in order to understand their content and configuration), **product literature**, **media comment** and **trade associations** in order to undertake **competitive benchmarking** against successful competitors.

Information about **processes** (how an organisation deals with customers or suppliers) is more **difficult to find**.

Such information can be obtained through the following channels.

(a)   In **intra-group benchmarking**, groups of companies in the same industry agree to pool data on their processes. The processes are benchmarked against each other and an 'improvement taskforce' is established to undertake **strategic benchmarking** to **identify** and transfer 'best practice' to all members of the group.

(b)   In **inter-industry benchmarking**, a non-competing business with similar processes is identified and asked to participate in a **functional benchmarking** exercise. The participants in the scheme are able to benefit from the experience of the other and establish 'best practice' in their common business processes.

It is also possible to undertake **internal benchmarking** against other units or departments in the same organisation.

8.2 Why use benchmarking?

8.2.1 For setting standards

Benchmarking allows **attainable standards** to be established following the examination of both **external and internal information**. These standards are most commonly established in the form of key performance indicators. If these standards and indicators are **regularly reviewed** in the light of information gained through benchmarking exercises, they can become part of a programme of **continuous improvement** by becoming increasingly demanding.

8.2.2 Other reasons

(a)   Its **flexibility** means that it can be used in both the public and private sector and by people at different levels of responsibility.

(b)   Cross-comparisons (as opposed to comparisons with similar organisations) are more likely to expose radically **different ways of doing things**.

(c)   It is an **effective method** of **implementing change**, people being involved in identifying and seeking out different ways of doing things in their own areas.

(d)   It identifies the **processes** to improve.

(e)   It helps with **cost reduction**.

(f)   It improves the **effectiveness** of **operations**.

(g)   It delivers services to a **defined standard**.

(h)   It provides a **focus** on **planning**.

(i)   It can provide early **warning** of **competitive disadvantage**.

(j)   It should lead to a greater incidence of **team working** and **cross-functional learning**.

Benchmarking works, it is claimed, for the following reasons.

(a)   The **comparisons** are **carried out** by the **managers** who have to live with any changes implemented as a result of the exercise.

(b)   Benchmarking focuses on improvement in key areas and sets targets which are challenging but 'achievable'. What is **really** achievable can be discovered by examining what others have achieved. Managers are therefore able to accept that they are not being asked to perform miracles.

8.3 Benchmarking – the disadvantages

There are a number of potential disadvantages that businesses should consider prior to performing a benchmarking exercise.

(a)   Businesses may experience difficulties in deciding **which activities** to benchmark.
(b)   Businesses may find it difficult to **identify the 'best in class'** for each activity.
(c)   It is often difficult to **persuade other organisations** to share information.
(d)   Successful practices in one organisation **may not transfer** successfully to another.
(e)   There is a risk of **drawing incorrect conclusions** from inappropriate comparisons.

Exam alert

You could be asked to discuss the advantages and disadvantages of benchmarking.

8.4 Reporting by dimension

A company can use segment reporting to analyse performance using internal information. The larger the organisation, the more useful this information may be. Reporting can also be done by product or channel, where products can be found with sufficient comparability for the information to be relevant.

The benefits and limitations of reporting by dimension include the following:

Benefits	Limitations
• Different segments have **different risks, returns, rates of growth and future prospects**. Without information on these segments, decision makers would be unable to identify these differences and it would be impossible to properly assess the performance and position of the entity.	• There may be **problems with comparability** if an organisation fails to compare segments or products with sufficient similarities. This may lead to incorrect conclusions being drawn.
• The availability of the information may identify inefficiencies in some areas of the business, which can be addressed by comparison to more profitable products or segments. It therefore promotes the sharing of information in the organisation.	• The 'management' approach of segment identification is **subjective** and, therefore, open to manipulation.
• The information is internal and therefore is readily available to decision makers.	• Certain expenses, assets and liabilities **cannot be allocated** to segments or products, reducing the usefulness of the segment analysis.

Section summary

Benchmarking is an attempt to identify best practices and to achieve improved performance by comparison of operations.

9 Not-for-profit organisations (NGOs)

Introduction

It is not only profit-making organisations whose performance is evaluated. Not-for-profit organisations (NGOs) are expected to account for how their funds are used and are assessed on their efficiency, effectiveness and economy in handling these funds.

Some organisations are set up with a prime objective which is not related to making profits. Charities and government organisations are examples. These organisations exist to pursue non-financial aims, such as providing a service to the community. However, there will be financial constraints which limit what any organisation can do.

(a)   A not-for-profit organisation (NGO) needs finance to pay for its operations, and the major financial constraint is the amount of funds that it can obtain from its donors (its customers).

(b)   Having obtained funds, an NGO will use the funds to help its 'clients', for example by alleviating suffering. It should seek to use the funds in three ways (sometimes known as 'the three Es'):

- **Economically** – that is, not spending $2 when the same thing can be bought for $1
- **Efficiently** – getting the best use out of what the money is spent on
- **Effectively** – spending funds so as to achieve the organisation's objectives

Section summary

Not-for-profit organisations are assessed on the **effectiveness**, **efficiency** and **economy** with which they use their funds.

Chapter Summary

Performance
measurement

Financial indicators

- ROI = $\dfrac{\text{Divisional Profit}}{\text{Divisional Investment}} \times 100$
- Only projects which increase the existing ROI should be undertaken

Residual income = Divisional profit less imputed interest (investment × cost of capital)

- Projects with a positive residual income should be undertaken

EVA = Economic profit (NOPAT)
less capital charge (net assets × cost of capital)

Accounting profit adjusted for:
- Economic depreciation
- Advertising/development costs
Net assets are valued at replacement cost

Benchmarking

A business will adopt best practice in order to improve its own performance
- Internal
- External or competitive
- Reverse engineering
- Intra-group
- Inter-industry

Analysis of reporting by dimension

- Segment
- Product
- Channel

Problems with financial performance indicators

- Monetary indicator only
- Focus on past
- Only part of the picture
- Short-term measure

Non-financial performance indicators

- Can measure anything
- Quantitative and qualitative
- Gather information on key areas eg quality, customers, employees
- Good indicator of future prospects
- Can provide too much information
- Can forget overall goal

Balanced scorecard

Enables focus on both internal and external factors and on key elements of business strategy

Four dimensions are:
- Customer
- Internal
- Financial
- Innovation and learning

BPP
LEARNING MEDIA

Quick Quiz

1   Give five examples of a financial performance measure.

- ....
- ....
- ....
- ....
- ....

2   Choose the correct words from those highlighted.

In general, a current ratio **in excess of 1/less than 1/approximately zero** should be expected.

3   Choose the correct words from those highlighted.

ROI based on profits as a % of net assets employed will (1) **increase/decrease** as an asset gets older and its book value (2) **increases/reduces**. This could therefore create a(n) (3) **incentive/disincentive** to investment centre managers to reinvest in new or replacement assets.

4   An investment centre with capital employed of $570,000 is budgeted to earn a profit of $119,700 next year. A proposed non-current asset investment of $50,000, not included in the budget at present, will earn a profit next year of $8,500 after depreciation. The company's cost of capital is 15%. What is the budgeted ROI and residual income for next year, both with and without the investment?

	ROI	Residual income
Without investment	....	....
With investment	....	....

5   'The use of residual income in performance measurement will avoid dysfunctional decision making because it will always lead to the correct decision concerning capital investments.' True or false?

6   Choose the correct words from those highlighted.

If accounting ROI is used as a guideline for investment decisions, it **should be/should not be** looked at over the full life of the investment. In the short term, the accounting ROI is likely to be **high/low** because the net book value of the asset will be **high/low**.

7   EVA® is calculated as operating profit less a capital charge. True or false?

8   Company H has reported annual profits for 20X7 of $83.4m. This is after charging $8.3m for development costs of a new product that is expected to last for the current year and two more years. The cost of capital is 12% per annum. Fixed assets have a historical cost of $110m and the replacement cost of these fixed assets at the beginning of the year is $156m. The assets have been depreciated at 10% per year and the company has working capital of $25.2m. Ignoring the effect of taxation, what is the EVA® of the company?

Answers to Quick Quiz

1   • Profit
    • Revenue
    • Costs

    • Share price
    • Cash flow

2   in excess of 1

3   (a)   increase
    (b)   reduces
    (c)   disincentive

4
	ROI	Residual income
Without investment	21.0%	$34,200
With investment	20.7%	$35,200

5   False

6   should be
    low
    high

7   False. EVA® = NOPAT less a capital charge

8

	$m
Profit	83.40
Add	
Current depreciation (110 × 10%)	11.00
Development costs (8.3 × 2/3)	5.53
Less	
Replacement depreciation (156 × 10%)	(15.60)
	84.33
Less cost of capital (W1)	(20.54)
EVA®	63.79

W1   *Cost of capital charge*

Fixed assets (156 – 15.6)	140.40	
Working capital	25.20	
Development costs	5.53	
	171.13	× 12% = 20.54

Answers to Questions

6.1 Profitability

An increased profit margin must be good because this indicates a wider gap between selling price and cost of sales. Given that the net profit ratio has stayed the same in the second year, however, expenses must be rising. In year 1 expenses were 30% of turnover, whereas in year 2 they were 35% of turnover. This indicates that administration, selling and distribution expenses or interest costs require tight control.

Percentage analysis of profit between year 1 and year 2

	Year 1 %	Year 2 %
Cost of sales as a % of sales	60	55
Gross profit as a % of sales	40	45
	100	100
Expenses as a % of sales	30	35
Net profit as a % of sales	10	10
Gross profit as a % of sales	40	45

6.2 EPS

	$
Profits before tax	9,320,000
Less tax	2,800,000
Profits after tax	6,520,000
Less preference dividend (8% of $2,000,000)	160,000
Earnings	6,360,000
Number of ordinary shares	10,000,000
EPS	63.6c

6.3 Liquidity and working capital ratios

	20X8	20X7
Current ratio	572.3/501.0 = 1.14	523.2/420.3 = 1.24
Quick ratio	453.3/501.0 = 0.90	414.2/420.3 = 0.99
Receivables' payment period (days)	329.8/2,065.0 × 365 = 58	285.4/1,788.7 × 365 = 58
Inventory turnover period (days)	119.0/1,478.6 × 365 = 29	109.0/1,304.0 × 365 = 31
Payables' turnover period (days)	236.2/1,478.6 × 365 = 58	210.8/1,304.0 × 365 = 59

As a manufacturing group serving the construction industry, the company would be expected to have a comparatively lengthy receivables' turnover period, because of the relatively poor cash flow in the construction industry. It is clear that the company compensates for this by ensuring that it does not pay for raw materials and other costs before they have sold their inventories of finished goods (hence the similarity of receivables' and payables' turnover periods).

The company's current ratio is a little lower than average but its quick ratio is better than average and very little less than the current ratio. This suggests that inventory levels are strictly controlled, which is reinforced by the low inventory turnover period. It would seem that working capital is tightly managed, to avoid the poor liquidity which could be caused by a high receivables' turnover period and comparatively high payables.

6.4 ROI calculation (1)

Year 2	$	Year 6	$
Non-current assets at net book value	368,000	Non-current assets at net book value	184,000
Current assets	75,000	Current assets	75,000
	443,000		259,000

$$\frac{\$30,000}{\$443,000} \times 100 = 6.8\%$$ $$\frac{\$30,000}{\$259,000} \times 100 = 11.6\%$$

Year 2 – 6.8%
Year 6 – 11.6%

6.5 ROI calculation (2)

Year 2 – 5.6%

Year 6 – 5.6%

6.6 RI

	Before investment $	After investment $
Divisional profit ($400,000 × 22%)	88,000	100,000
Imputed interest		
(400,000 × 0.14)	56,000	
(450,000 × 0.14)		63,000
Residual income	32,000	37,000

6.7 Calculating EVA®

	$
Operating profit	18,500
Add back historical cost depreciation	8,100
Less economic depreciation	(12,300)
Add back advertising costs	6,000
Less amortisation of advertising costs ($6,000/2)	(3,000)
NOPAT (ignoring taxation)	17,300
Replacement value of non-current assets	98,000
Working capital	19,000
Add investment in advertising to benefit next year	3,000
Economic value of net assets	120,000
NOPAT	17,300
Capital charge (11% × $120,000)	13,200
EVA®	4,100

6.8 NFPIs

Here are five indicators, showing you how to use the chart, but there are many other possibilities.

(a)   Services performed late vs total services performed
(b)   Total units sold vs total units sold by competitors (indicating market share)
(c)   Warranty claims per month
(d)   Documents processed per employee
(e)   Equipment failures per 1,000 units produced

Don't forget to explain how the ones that you chose might be useful.

6.9 Balanced scorecard

(a)   **Customer**

- Percentage of sales represented by new products $\quad = s \times 100$
$\quad = 18.5\%$

Internal

- Productivity – existing product
$$= \frac{25,000 \text{ units}}{5,000 \text{ units}}$$
$= 5 \text{ units per hour}$

        – new product
$$= \frac{5,000 \text{ units}}{1,250 \text{ units}}$$
$= 4 \text{ units per hour}$

- Unit cost – existing product
$$= \frac{\$375,000}{25,000 \text{ units}} = \$15 \text{ per unit}$$

        – new product
$$= \frac{\$70,000}{5,000 \text{ units}} = \$14 \text{ per unit}$$

Financial

- Gross profit – existing product
$$= \frac{\$550,000 - 375,000}{\$550,000}$$
$= 32\%$

        – new product
$$= \frac{\$125,000 - 70,000}{\$125,000}$$
$= 44\%$

Innovation and learning

- Development costs as % of sales
$$= \frac{\$47,000}{\$675,000}$$
$= 7\%$

(b)   Using a range of performance indicators will allow Spotlight Productions to look at the success of the new product in wider terms than just its profitability. For example, productivity is lower for the new product than the existing product, so managers may wish to examine the processes involved in order to make improvements. Sales of the new product look very promising but some additional measure of customer satisfaction could provide a better view of long-term prospects.

**Now try these questions from
the Practice Question Bank**

Number	Marks	Time
Q25 Objective test questions	10	18 mins
Q26 Balanced scorecard	5	9 mins
Q27 MPL	30	54 mins

TRANSFER PRICING

 We looked at responsibility accounting in Chapter 5. In this chapter we look at how a transfer pricing system can work in responsibility centres.

Sections 1 and 2 provide you with a **framework** for transfer pricing. **Sections 3 to 8** cover the **various** **approaches** to transfer pricing required in particular circumstances.

The key points have been highlighted in the section summaries. Make sure you are happy with each point before moving on.

topic list	learning outcomes	syllabus references	ability required
1 The basic principles of transfer pricing	B3(b), (c)	B3(b)(i),(ii), (c)(i)-(iii)	analysis
2 General rules	B3(b), (c)	B3(i)-(v)	analysis
3 The use of market price as a basis for transfer prices	B3(b), (c)	B3(i)-(v)	analysis
4 Transfer pricing with an imperfect external market	B3(b), (c)	B3(i)-(v)	analysis
5 Transfer pricing when there is no external market for the transferred item	B3(b), (c)	B3(i)-(v)	analysis
6 Transfer pricing and changing costs/prices	B3(b), (c)	B3(i)-(v)	analysis
7 Identifying the optimal transfer price	B3(b), (c)	B3(i)-(v)	analysis
8 Negotiated transfer prices	B3(b), (c)	B3(i)-(v)	analysis
9 International transfer pricing	B3 (b), (c)	B3(i)-(v)	analysis

Chapter Overview

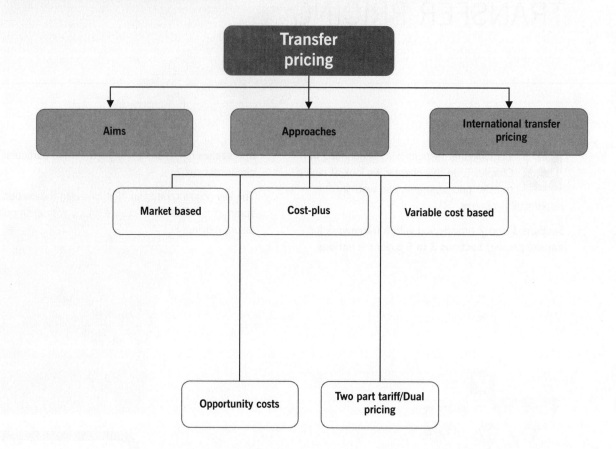

1   The basic principles of transfer pricing

Introduction

This section introduces the important topic of transfer pricing with a summary of the basic principles.
Make sure you understand the main points before moving on, as this section forms the basis for the rest
of the chapter.

1.1 What is a transfer price?

KEY TERM

A TRANSFER PRICE is the 'Price at which goods or services are transferred between different units of the
same company'.   (*CIMA Official Terminology*)

Transfer pricing is used when divisions of an organisation need to charge other divisions of the same
organisation for goods and services they provide to them. For example, subsidiary A might make a
component that is used as part of a product made by subsidiary B of the same company, but that can
also be sold to the external market, including makers of rival products to subsidiary B's product. There will
therefore be two sources of revenue for A.

(a)   External sales revenue from sales made to other organisations

(b)   Internal sales revenue from sales made to other responsibility centres within the same
      organisation, valued at the transfer price

1.2 Main uses of transfer prices

1.2.1 Evaluation of divisional managers' performance

Transfer prices will be a **cost** for the **division receiving the goods** and a **revenue** for the division **supplying
the goods**. Just as managers are assessed on their management of costs from external suppliers, they are
also assessed on their **ability to control internal costs**. This can lead to disputes between divisional
managers as they try to protect their own interests and achieve optimal performance of their own
divisions.

1.2.2 To achieve the overall organisational goals

Also known as **goal congruence**, transfer prices in theory should be set to ensure that **organisational goals**
(such as profit maximisation) **are achieved**. Although divisional managers are being assessed on their own
division's performance, their overall objective should be to ensure that their behaviour supports the
achievement of organisational goals. Transfer prices should be set at a level that **encourages 'trade'**
between divisions, rather than driving divisional managers to purchase the goods from external suppliers.

1.2.3 To preserve divisional autonomy

Divisional autonomy refers to the right of a division to govern itself; that is, the **freedom to make
decisions without consulting a higher authority first and without interference from a higher body**.

Transfer prices are particularly appropriate for **profit centres** because if one profit centre does work for
another, the size of the transfer price will affect the costs of one profit centre and the revenues of another.

1.3 Problems with transfer pricing

1.3.1 Maintaining the right level of divisional autonomy

This problem echoes one of the problems of divisionalisation.

A task of **head office** is to try to **prevent dysfunctional decision making** by individual profit centres. To do this, head office must reserve some power and authority for itself and so **profit centres cannot be allowed to make entirely autonomous decisions**.

Just how much authority head office decides to retain will vary according to the circumstances. **A balance** should be kept **between divisional autonomy** to provide incentives and motivation, and **retaining centralised authority** to ensure that the organisation's profit centres are all working towards the same target, the benefit of the whole organisation (in other words, the divisions should **retain goal congruence**).

1.3.2 Ensuring divisional performance is measured fairly

Profit centre managers tend to put their own profit performance above everything else. Since profit centre performance is measured according to the profit they earn, no profit centre will want to do work for another and incur costs without being paid for it. Consequently, profit centre managers are likely to dispute the size of transfer prices with each other, or disagree about whether or not one profit centre should do work for another. Transfer prices **affect behaviour and decisions** by profit centre managers.

1.3.3 Ensuring corporate goals are met

These goals could be strategic or financial in nature. Strategic goals could involve market share for a product, where one division is making supplies to the competitor of another division.

Financial goals could be organisation wide, such as minimising the overall tax liability, or divisional, such as how much work should be transferred between divisions and how many sales the division should make to the external market. For this, there is presumably a **profit-maximising level of output and sales for the organisation as a whole**. However, unless each profit centre also maximises its own profit at this same level of output, there will be inter-divisional disagreements about output levels and the profit-maximising output will not be achieved.

1.3.4 The ideal solution

Ideally a transfer price should be set at a level that overcomes these problems.

(a)   The transfer price should provide an 'artificial' selling price that enables the **transferring division to earn a return for its efforts**, and the receiving division to incur a cost for benefits received.

(b)   The transfer price should be set at a level that enables **profit centre performance** to be **measured 'commercially'**. This means that the transfer price should be a fair commercial price.

(c)   The transfer price, if possible, should encourage profit centre managers to agree on the amount of goods and services to be transferred, which will also be at a level that is consistent with the aims of the organisation as a whole, such as **maximising company profits**.

In practice it is difficult to achieve all three aims.

| Question 7.1 | Benefits of transfer pricing |

Learning outcome B3(b)

The transfer pricing system operated by a divisional company has the potential to make a significant contribution towards the achievement of corporate financial objectives.

Required

Explain the potential benefits of operating a transfer pricing system within a divisionalised company.

Section summary

Transfer prices are a way of promoting **divisional autonomy**, ideally without prejudicing the **measurement of divisional performance** or discouraging **overall corporate profit maximisation**.

Transfer prices should be set at a level which ensures that **profits for the organisation as a whole are maximised**.

2   General rules

Introduction

This section highlights the boundaries within which transfer prices should fall to make them acceptable to both the supplying and receiving divisions.

2.1 Minimum and maximum prices

KEY POINT

The **limits within which transfer prices should fall** are as follows.

- **The minimum.** The sum of the supplying division's marginal cost and opportunity cost of the item transferred.

- **The maximum.** The lowest market price at which the receiving division could purchase the goods or services externally, less any internal cost savings in packaging and delivery.

The **minimum** results from the fact that the **supplying division will not agree to transfer if the transfer price is less than the marginal cost + opportunity cost of the item transferred** (because if it were, the division would incur a loss).

The **maximum** results from the fact that the **receiving division will buy the item at the cheapest price possible**.

Example: General rules

Division X produces product L at a marginal cost per unit of $100. If a unit is transferred internally to Division Y, $25 contribution is forgone on an external sale. The item can be purchased externally for $150.

- **The minimum**. Division X will not agree to a transfer price of less than $(100 + 25) = $125 per unit.

- **The maximum**. Division Y will not agree to a transfer price in excess of $150.

The difference between the two results ($25) represents the savings from producing internally as opposed to buying externally.

2.1.1 Opportunity cost

The **opportunity cost** included in determining the lower limit will be one of the following.

(a) The maximum contribution forgone by the supplying division **in transferring internally rather than selling goods externally**

(b) The contribution forgone by not using the same facilities in the producing division for their next best alternative use

If there is **no external market** for the item being transferred, and **no alternative uses for** the division's facilities, the **transfer price = standard variable cost of production**.

If there is an **external market** for the item being transferred and **no alternative, more profitable use** for the facilities in that division, the **transfer price = the market price**.

Exam alert

An ICS question could ask you to discuss the appropriateness of a company's transfer pricing policy.

Section summary

The **limits within which transfer prices should fall** are as follows.

- **The minimum**. The sum of the supplying division's marginal cost and opportunity cost of the item transferred.

- **The maximum**. The lowest market price at which the receiving division could purchase the goods or services externally, less any internal cost savings in packaging and delivery.

3 The use of market price as a basis for transfer prices

Introduction

This is the first of five sections that explain the various approaches to setting transfer prices. Make sure you follow the example and are aware of the pros and cons of market price as a basis for transfer price.

3.1 When should market price be used as the transfer price?

If an external market exists for the product being transferred (and there is unsatisfied demand externally), the ideal transfer price will be the market price.

KEY POINT

> If **variable costs and market prices are constant**, regardless of the volume of output, a **market-based transfer price** is the ideal transfer price.
>
> If a **perfect external market** exists, **market price** is the **ideal** transfer price.

If an **external market price exists** for transferred goods, profit centre managers will be aware of the price they could obtain or the price they would have to pay for their goods on the external market, and they would inevitably **compare** this price **with the transfer price**.

The external market is also sometimes known as the **intermediate market**.

Example: Transferring goods at market value

A company has two profit centres, A and B. A sells half of its output on the open market and transfers the other half to B. Costs and external revenues in an accounting period are as follows.

	A $	B $	Total $
External sales	8,000	24,000	32,000
Costs of production	12,000	10,000	22,000
Company profit			10,000

Required

What are the consequences of setting a transfer price at market value?

Solution

If the transfer price is at market price, A would be happy to sell the output to B for $8,000.

	A $	A $	B $	B $	Total $
Market sales		8,000		24,000	32,000
Transfer sales		8,000		–	
		16,000		24,000	
Transfer costs		–	8,000		
Own costs	12,000		10,000		22,000
		12,000		18,000	
Profit		4,000		6,000	10,000

The **transfer sales of A are self-cancelling with the transfer cost of B**, so that the total profits are unaffected by the transfer items. The transfer price simply spreads the total profit between A and B.

Consequences

(a)   A earns the same profit on transfers as on external sales. B must pay a commercial price for transferred goods, and both divisions will have their profit measured in a fair way.

(b)   A will be indifferent about selling externally or transferring goods to B because the profit is the same on both types of transaction. B can therefore ask for and obtain as many units as it wants from A.

A **market-based** transfer price therefore seems to be the **ideal** transfer price.

3.2 Adjusted market price

Internal transfers are often **cheaper** than external sales, with **savings** in selling and administration costs, bad debt risks and possibly transport/delivery costs. It would therefore seem reasonable for the **buying division to expect a discount** on the external market price. The transfer price might be slightly less than market price, so that **A and B could share the cost savings** from internal transfers compared with external sales. It should be possible to reach agreement on this price and on output levels with a minimum of intervention from head office.

3.3 The merits of market value transfer prices

3.3.1 Divisional autonomy

In a decentralised company, divisional managers should have the **autonomy** to make output, selling and buying **decisions which appear to be in the best interests of the division's performance**. (If every division optimises its performance, the company as a whole must inevitably achieve optimal results.) Thus a **transferor division should be given the freedom to sell output on the open market**, rather than to transfer it within the company.

'Arm's length' transfer prices, which give profit centre managers the freedom to negotiate prices with other profit centres as though they were independent companies, will tend to result in a market-based transfer price.

3.3.2 Corporate profit maximisation

In most cases where the transfer price is at market price, **internal transfers** should be **expected**, because the **buying division** is likely to **benefit** from a better quality of service, greater flexibility and dependability of supply. **Both divisions** may **benefit** from cheaper costs of administration, selling and transport. A market price as the transfer price would therefore **result in decisions which would be in the best interests of the company or group as a whole**.

3.4 The disadvantages of market value transfer prices

Market value as a transfer price does have certain **disadvantages**.

(a)   The **market price may be a temporary one**, induced by adverse economic conditions, or dumping, or the market price might depend on the volume of output supplied to the external market by the profit centre.

(b)   A transfer price at market value might, under some circumstances, **act as a disincentive to use up any spare capacity** in the divisions. A price based on incremental cost, in contrast, might provide an incentive to use up the spare resources in order to provide a marginal contribution to profit.

(c)   Many products **do not have an equivalent market price** so that the price of a similar, but not identical, product might have to be chosen. In such circumstances, the option to sell or buy on the open market does not really exist.

(d)   There might be an **imperfect external market** for the transferred item, so that if the transferring division tried to sell more externally, it would have to reduce its selling price.

Section summary

If **variable costs and market prices are constant**, regardless of the volume of output, a **market-based transfer price** is the ideal transfer price.

If a **perfect external market** exists, **market price** is the **ideal** transfer price.

4 Transfer pricing with an imperfect external market

Introduction

This section focuses on how transfer prices are set when there is an imperfect external market for the product being transferred. The main problem in this situation is that there may be no external market on which a price can be based.

4.1 Problems with having an imperfect external market

Cost-based approaches to transfer pricing are often used in practice, because in practice the following conditions are common.

(a) There is **no external market** for the product that is being transferred (see Section 5).

(b) Alternatively, although there is an external market, it is an **imperfect** one because the market price is affected by such factors as the amount that the company setting the transfer price supplies to it, or because there is only a limited external demand. We cover this situation in this section.

In either case there will **not be a suitable market price** upon which to base the transfer price. Another basis must therefore be used.

4.2 Transfer prices based on full cost

Under this approach, unsurprisingly, the **full cost** (including fixed production overheads absorbed) that has been incurred by the supplying division in making the intermediate product is charged to the receiving division. If a **full cost plus approach** is used, a **profit margin is also included** in this transfer price.

Example: Transfer prices based on full cost

Suppose a company has two profit centres, A and B. A can only sell half of its maximum output of 800 units externally because of limited demand. It transfers the other half of its output to B which also faces limited demand. Costs and revenues in an accounting period are as follows.

	A $	B $	Total $
External sales	8,000	24,000	32,000
Costs of production in the division	13,000	10,000	23,000
Profit			9,000

Division A's costs included fixed production overheads of $4,800 and fixed selling and administration costs of $1,000.

There are no opening or closing inventories. It does not matter, for this illustration, whether marginal costing or absorption costing is used. For the moment, we shall ignore the question of whether the current output levels are profit-maximising and congruent with the goals of the company as a whole.

If the transfer price is at full cost, A in our example would have 'sales' to B of $6,000 (($13,000 – 1,000) × 50%). Selling and administration costs are not included, as these are not incurred on the internal transfers. This would be a cost to B, as follows.

	$	A $	$	B $	Company as a whole $
Open market sales		8,000		24,000	32,000
Transfer sales		6,000		–	
Total sales, inc transfers		14,000		24,000	
Transfer costs			6,000		
Own costs	13,000		10,000		23,000
Total costs, inc transfers		13,000		16,000	
Profit		1,000		8,000	9,000

The **transfer sales of A are self-cancelling with the transfer costs of B** so that total profits are **unaffected by the transfer items**. The transfer price simply spreads the total profit of $9,000 between A and B.

The obvious **drawback** to the transfer price at cost is that **A makes no profit** on its work, and the manager of Division A would much prefer to sell output on the open market to earn a profit, rather than transfer to B, regardless of whether or not transfers to B would be in the best interests of the company as a whole. Division A needs a profit on its transfers in order to be motivated to supply B; therefore transfer pricing at cost is inconsistent with the use of a profit centre accounting system.

4.2.1 Sub-optimal decisions

Note, also, that as the level of transfer price increases, its effect on Division B could lead to sub-optimalisation problems for the organisation as a whole.

Example: Sub-optimal decisions

For example, suppose Division B could buy the product from an outside supplier for $10 instead of paying $15 ($6,000/(800/2)) to Division A. This transfer price would therefore force Division B to buy the product externally at $10 per unit, although it could be manufactured internally for a variable cost of $(13,000 – 4,800 – 1,000)/800 = $9 per unit.

Although Division B (the buying division) would save $15 – 10) = $5 per unit by buying externally, the organisation as a whole would lose $400 as follows.

	Per unit $
Marginal cost of production	9
External purchase cost	10
Loss if buy-in	1

The overall loss on transfer/purchase of 400 units is therefore 400 × $1 = $400.

This loss of $1 per unit assumes that any other use for the released capacity would produce a benefit of less than $400. If the 400 units could also be sold externally for $20 per unit, the optimal decision for the organisation as a whole would be to buy in the units for Division B at $10 per unit.

	Per unit $
Market price	20
Marginal cost	9
Contribution	11
Loss if buy-in	(1)
Incremental profit	10

The overall incremental profit would therefore be 400 × $10 = $4,000.

4.3 Transfer prices based on full cost plus

If the transfers are at cost plus a margin of, say, 10%, A's sales to B would be $6,600 ($13,000 –
1,000) × 50% × 1.10).

	A			B	Total
	$	$	$	$	$
Open market sales		8,000		24,000	32,000
Transfer sales		6,600		–	
		14,600		24,000	
Transfer costs			6,600		
Own costs	13,000		10,000		23,000
		13,000		16,600	
Profit		1,600		7,400	9,000

Compared to a transfer price at cost, **A gains some profit** at the expense of B. However, A makes a bigger
profit on external sales in this case because the profit mark-up of 10% is less than the profit mark-up on
open market sales. The choice of 10% as a profit mark-up was arbitrary and unrelated to external market
conditions.

The transfer price **fails on all three criteria** (divisional autonomy, performance measurement and
corporate profit measurement) for judgement.

(a)   Arguably, the transfer price does not give A fair revenue or charge B a reasonable cost, and so their
profit **performance is distorted**. It would certainly be unfair, for example, to compare A's profit with
B's profit.

(b)   Given this unfairness, it is likely that the **autonomy** of each of the divisional managers is **under
threat**. If they cannot agree on what is a fair split of the external profit, a decision will have to be
imposed from above.

(c)   It would seem to give A an incentive to sell more goods externally and transfer less to B. This may
or **may not be in the best interests of the company as a whole**.

In fact we can demonstrate that the method is **flawed from the point of view of corporate profit
maximisation**. Division A's total production costs of $12,000 include an element of fixed costs. Half of
Division A's total production costs are transferred to Division B. However, from the point of view of
Division B, the cost is entirely variable.

The cost per unit to A is $15 ($12,000 ÷ 800) and this includes a fixed element of $6 ($4,800 ÷ 800),
while Division B's own costs are $25 ($10,000 ÷ 400) per unit, including a fixed element of $10 (say).
The **total variable cost is really** $9 + $15 = **$24**, but from Division **B's point of view** the **variable cost** is
$15 + $(25 – 10) = **$30**. This means that Division B will be unwilling to sell the final product for less
than $30, whereas any price above $24 would make a contribution to overall costs. Thus, if external
prices for the final product fall, B might be tempted to cease production.

4.4 Transfer prices based on variable or marginal cost

A variable or marginal cost approach entails charging the variable cost (which we assume to be the same as the marginal cost) that has been incurred by the supplying division to the receiving division. As above, we shall suppose that A's cost per unit is $15, of which $6 is fixed and $9 variable.

	A $	A $	B $	B $	Company as a whole $	Company as a whole $
Market sales		8,000		24,000		32,000
Transfer sales		3,600		–		
		11,600		24,000		
Transfer costs	–		3,600			
Own variable costs	7,200		6,000		13,200	
Own fixed costs	5,800		4,000		9,800	
Total costs and transfers		13,000		13,600		23,000
(Loss)/Profit		(1,400)		10,400		9,000

4.4.1 Divisional autonomy, divisional performance measurement and corporate profit maximisation

(a)   This result is **deeply unsatisfactory for the manager of Division A**, who could make an additional $4,400 ($(8,000 – 3,600)) profit if no goods were transferred to Division B, but all were sold externally.

(b)   Given that the manager of Division A would prefer to transfer externally, **head office** are likely to have to **insist** that internal transfers are made.

(c)   For the company overall, external transfers only would cause a large fall in profit, because Division B could make no sales at all.

Point to note. Suppose no more than the current $8,000 could be earned from external sales and the production capacity used for production for internal transfer would remain idle if not used. Division A would be indifferent to the transfers at marginal cost as they do not represent any benefit to the division.

If more than the $8,000 of revenue could be earned externally (ie Division A could sell more externally than at present), Division A would have a strong disincentive to supply B at marginal cost.

4.5 Dual pricing

One of the problems with a variable cost approach to transfer pricing is that the selling division will not cover its fixed costs.

Dual pricing, as the name suggests, results in **different prices** being used by the selling and buying divisions. The selling division will use a price that will allow it to report a **reasonable profit** (usually the external market price if there is one). The buying division will be charged with the **variable cost**.

The difference between the two prices will be debited to a group account which will then be cancelled out when divisional results are consolidated to arrive at the group profit.

However, despite its advantages, dual pricing is not widely used in practice for the following reasons.

(a)   Head office will need to be notified of each transaction to ensure that it is accounted for correctly. This is likely to take a considerable amount of time and may require a separate accounting function to be set up.

(b)   Dual pricing is a complicated system to operate when many goods are being transferred between a number of different divisions.

(c)   By continually reporting transactions to head office, managers of divisions may feel that they are not being given the freedom to run their division as they see fit.

(d) If total cost plus pricing is used due to market prices collapsing, it could be argued that managers of the supplying division are being 'protected' from tough market conditions.

4.6 Two-part tariff system

A two-part tariff system can be used to ensure that the selling division's fixed costs are covered. Transfer prices are set at variable cost and once a year there is a **transfer of a fixed fee as a lump sum payment to the supplying division**, representing an allowance for its fixed costs.

This method risks sending the message to the supplying division that it need not control its fixed costs, however, because the company will subsidise any inefficiencies.

Section summary

If transfer prices are set at variable cost with an imperfect external market, the supplying division does not cover its fixed costs. **Dual pricing** or a **two-part tariff system** can be used in an attempt to overcome this problem.

If **transfers** are made at actual cost instead of **standard cost**, there is no incentive for the supplying division to control costs, as they can all be passed on to the receiving division.

5 Transfer pricing when there is no external market for the transferred item

Introduction

There may be instances when there is no external market for the item being transferred. This section focuses on how to set an appropriate transfer price in such circumstances. Note the argument that profit centre accounting might not even be appropriate in this situation.

5.1 What is the appropriate transfer price?

KEY POINT

When there is **no external market** for the item being transferred, the transfer price should be **greater than or equal to** the variable cost in the **supplying division**, but **less than or equal to** the selling price minus variable costs (net marginal revenue) in the **receiving division**.

If there is **no similar item sold on an external market**, and if the **transferred item** is a **major product of the transferring division**, there is a strong argument that **profit centre accounting is a waste of time**. Profit centres cannot be judged on their commercial performance because there is no way of estimating what a fair revenue for their work should be. It would be more appropriate, perhaps, to treat the transferring division as a cost centre, and to judge performance on the basis of cost variances.

If **profit centres are established**, in the **absence of a market price**, the **optimum transfer price is likely to be one based on standard cost plus**, but only provided that the **variable cost per unit and selling price per unit are unchanged at all levels of output**. A standard cost plus price would motivate divisional managers to increase output and to reduce expenditure levels.

Example: Standard cost plus as a transfer price in the absence of an external market

Motivate has two profit centres, P and Q. P transfers all its output to Q. The variable cost of output from P is $5 a unit, and fixed costs are $1,200 a month. Additional processing costs in Q are $4 a unit for variable costs, plus fixed costs of $800 a month. Budgeted production is 400 units a month, and the output of Q sells for $15 a unit.

Required

Determine the range of prices from which the transfer price (based on standard full cost plus) should be selected, in order to motivate the managers of both profit centres to both increase output and reduce costs.

Solution

Any transfer price based on standard cost plus will motivate managers to cut costs, because favourable variances between standard costs and actual costs will be credited to the division's profits. Managers of each division will also be willing to increase output (above the budget) provided that it is profitable to do so.

(a) The **manager of P** will **increase output if the transfer price exceeds the variable cost** of $5 a unit.

(b) The **manager of Q** will **increase output if the transfer price is less than the difference between the fixed selling price ($15)** and the **variable costs** in **Q** itself. This amount of $11 ($15 – $4) is sometimes called **net marginal revenue**.

The range of prices is therefore between $5.01 and $10.99.

Check:

Suppose the transfer price is $9. With absorption based on the budgeted output of 400 units, what would divisional profits be if output and sales are 400 units and 500 units?

Overheads per unit are $1,200/400. The full cost of sales is $(5 + 3) = $8 in Division P. In Division Q, full cost is $(4 + 2) = $6, plus transfer costs of $9.

(a) At 400 units:

	P $	Q $	Total $
Sales	–	6,000	6,000
Transfer sales	3,600	–	
Transfer costs	–	(3,600)	
Own full cost of sales	(3,200)	(2,400)	(5,600)
	400	0	400
Under-/over-absorbed overhead	0	0	0
Profit/(loss)	400	0	400

(b) At 500 units:

	P $	Q $	Total $
Sales	–	7,500	7,500
Transfer sales	4,500	–	–
Transfer costs	–	(4,500)	–
Own full cost of sales	(4,000)	(3,000)	(7,000)
	500	0	500
Over-absorbed overhead	300	200	500
Profit/(loss)	800	200	1,000

Increasing output improves the profit performance of both divisions and the company as a whole, and so decisions on output by the two divisions are likely to be **goal congruent**.

Section summary

When there is **no external market** for the item being transferred, the transfer price should be **greater than or equal to** the variable cost in the **supplying division** but **less than or equal to** the selling price minus variable costs (net marginal revenue) in the **receiving division**.

6 Transfer pricing and changing costs/prices

Introduction

This section is related to Section 5, in that it considers the situation where there is no external market for the transferred item **and** changing costs/prices for the final product. Note the differences in preferred transfer prices between the two sections.

6.1 No external market for the transferred item

KEY POINT

When there is no external market for the transferred item and changing costs/prices for the final output, the transfer price should be greater than or equal to the marginal cost in the supplying division, but less than or equal to the net marginal revenue in the receiving division.

If **cost behaviour patterns change** and the **selling price** to the **external market (for the receiving division's product)** is **reduced at higher levels of output**, there will be a **profit-maximising level of output**: to produce more than an 'optimum' amount would cause reductions in profitability.

Under such circumstances, the ideal transfer price is one which would motivate profit centre managers to produce at the optimum level of output, and neither below nor above this level.

Example: The profit-maximising transfer price

MCMR has two divisions, S and T. There is no external intermediate market and so S transfers all its output to T, which finishes the work. Costs and revenues at various levels of capacity are as follows.

Output Units	S costs $	T revenues $	T costs $	T net revenues $	Profit $
600	600	3,190	240	2,950	2,350
700	700	3,530	280	3,250	2,550
800	840	3,866	336	3,530	2,690
900	1,000	4,180	400	3,780	2,780
1,000	1,200	4,480	480	4,000	2,800 *
1,100	1,450	4,780	580	4,200	2,750
1,200	1,800	5,070	720	4,350	2,550

* Company profits are maximised at $2,800 with output of 1,000 units. But if we wish to select a transfer price in order to establish S and T as profit centres, what transfer price would motivate the managers of S and T together to produce 1,000 units, no more and no less?

Discussion and Solution

The transfer price will act as revenue to S and as a cost to T.

(a) **S will continue to produce more output until** the costs of additional production exceed the transfer price revenue; that is, where the **marginal cost exceeds the transfer price**.

(b) **T will continue to want to receive more output from S until** its net revenue from further processing is not sufficient to cover the additional transfer price costs; that is, where its **net marginal revenue is less than the transfer price**.

Output Units	Division S marginal costs $	Division T net marginal revenues $
600	–	–
700	100	300
800	140	280
900	160	250
1,000	200	220
1,100	250	200
1,200	350	150

Since S will continue to produce more output if the transfer price exceeds the marginal cost of production, a **price of at least $200 per 100 units ($2 per unit) is required to 'persuade' the manager of S to produce as many as 1,000 units**. A price in excess of $250 per 100 units would motivate the manager of S to produce 1,100 units or more.

By a similar argument, T will continue to want more output from S if the net marginal revenues exceed the transfer costs from S. **If T wants 1,000 units, the transfer price must be less than $220 per 100 units**. However, if the transfer price is lower than $200 per 100 units, T will ask for 1,100 units from S in order to improve its divisional profit further.

Summary

(a) The total company profit is maximised at 1,000 units of output.

(b) Division S will want to produce 1,000 units, no more and no less, if the transfer price is between $200 and $250 per 100 units, or $2 and $2.50 per unit.

(c) Division T will want to receive and process 1,000 units, no more and no less, if the transfer price per unit is between $2 and $2.20.

(d) A transfer price must therefore be selected in the **range $2.00 to $2.20 per unit** (exclusive).

Question 7.2

Transfer pricing and changing costs/prices (no external market)

Learning outcome B3(b)

Explain how the following figures are calculated, or arrived at.

(a) Example 6.1 – T net revenues
(b) Example 6.1 Discussion and solution (b) – Division S marginal costs
(c) Example 6.1 Discussion and solution (b) – Division T net marginal revenue
(d) Example 6.1 – a transfer price of $2.10 per unit

6.2 With an external market for the transferred item

6.2.1 Imperfect external market

KEY POINT

Where there is an **imperfect external market** for the transferred item and changing costs/prices for the final output, the **transfer price** should again **fall between marginal cost in the supplying division and net marginal revenue in the receiving division**.

The approach is essentially the same as the one shown above, except that the supplying division may also have income, and so its marginal revenue needs to be taken into account.

Example: Profit maximisation with an imperfect external market

IMP makes hand-built sports cars. The company has two divisions, M and N. The output of Division M can either be sold externally or transferred to Division N which turns it into a version for the US. Due to competition from Japanese car makers, the US market is giving poor returns at present. Cost and marginal revenues at various levels of output are as follows.

Cars produced	M Total cost $'000	M Marginal cost $'000	M Marginal revenue $'000	N Net marginal revenue $'000
1	18	18	20 (1)	18 (2)
2	26	8	16 (3)	12 (4)
3	35	9	12 (5)	6
4	45	10	8 (6) will not be built	0
5	56	11	4	(6)
6	68	12	0	(12)
7	81	13	(4)	(18)
8	95	14	(8)	0

You are required to determine the optimal output level.

Solution

(a)   In this situation, for any individual car, **marginal revenue will be received by Division M *or* net marginal revenue will be received by Division N. The same car cannot be sold twice!**

(b)   Marginal revenue is the extra amount received for each additional car sold into M's market (or net marginal revenue is the extra amount for additional cars in N's market). Thus the marginal revenue for three cars in M's market is $12,000 only if all three cars have been sold in M's market. If three are produced but one is sold in N's market, the marginal revenue for M for the other two is $16,000.

(c)   For each car produced a decision must therefore be made as to which market to sell it in, and this will be done according to which market offers the higher marginal revenue.

(d)   As shown by the numbers in brackets, the first car is sold in M's market, the second in N's, the third in M's, and the fourth and fifth in either. By the time six cars have been produced and shared out between the two markets, the marginal cost has risen to $12,000. This is greater than the marginal revenue obtainable from either market ($8,000 in M, $6,000 in N).

(e)   The sixth car will therefore not be built. Division M will produce five units and sell three cars itself and transfer two to Division N. The transfer price must be more than $11,000 to meet M's marginal cost, but less than $12,000, otherwise Division N will not buy it.

We now need to consider whether the profit-maximising transfer price should be set using the same approach if **supplies of the transferred item are limited**.

6.3 Maximising profits when the transferred item is in short supply

KEY POINT

Where there is a **capacity constraint** resulting in short supplies of the product, a transfer price based on matching marginal cost and marginal revenue **will not encourage** corporate profit maximisation.

Suppose that one month Division M suffered a two-week strike and was only able to produce two cars. If it follows normal policy and transfers the second to Division N, its own results for the month will be as follows.

		$'000
Sales	– own	20
	– transfers	11
		31
Total cost		26
		5

However, if Division M keeps the second car and sells both in its own market, it will earn $36,000 in total ($20,000 + $16,000), increasing its own divisional profit by $5,000.

From the point of view of the company this is a bad decision. If the second car is transferred to Division N, it can be sold for $18,000. Overall revenue and profit will increase by $2,000 (($18,000 – 16,000)).

The only way to be sure that a profit-maximising transfer policy will be implemented is to **dictate the policy from the centre**.

6.3.1 Perfect external market

The approach is the same as that used for an imperfect external market, except that marginal revenue for the supplying division is constant at the market price for all volumes of output.

6.4 Profit maximisation with a perfect external market

KEY POINT

When there is a **perfect external market for the transferred item** and **changing costs/prices** for the final output, profits are maximised when **market price** is used on the transfer price.

We will use the example of IMP again, but this time the market price achieved by M is $10,000. The costs and marginal revenues at various levels of output are as follows.

Cars produced	M Total cost $'000	M Marginal cost $'000	M Marginal revenue $'000	N Net marginal revenue $'000
1	18	18	10 (3)	18 (1)
2	26	8	10 (4)	12 (2)
3	35	9	10	6
4	45	10	10	0
5	56	11	10	(6)
6	68	12	10	(12)
7	81	13	10	(18)
8	95	14	10	0

Marginal cost is greater than marginal revenue in both markets by car five, so four cars will be built, two sold by M and two transferred to be sold by N. As seen earlier, the market price will be the transfer price.

| Question 7.3 | Profit-maximising transfer price |

Learning outcome B3(b)

Divisions J and A are in M Group. Division J manufactures part N. Three units of part N are used in product Z manufactured by Division A. Division J has no external customers for part N. Division J transfers part N to Division A at variable cost ($35 per part) plus 50%. The variable cost to Division A of manufacturing product Z is $50 per unit. This $50 does not include the cost of part N transferred from Division J.

Division A can sell the following number of units of product Z, earning the associated levels of marginal revenue.

Units sold	1	2	3	4
Marginal revenue	$270	$240	$210	$180

How many units of product Z should management of Division A sell if they wish to maximise divisional profit?

Section summary

When there is **no external market for the transferred item** and changing costs/prices for the final output, the **transfer price** should be **greater than or equal to the marginal cost in the supplying division** but **less than or equal to the net marginal revenue in the receiving division**.

Where there is an **imperfect external market** for the transferred item and changing costs/prices for the final output, the **transfer price** should again **fall between marginal cost in the supplying division and net marginal revenue in the receiving division**.

Where there is a **capacity constraint** resulting in short supplies of the product, a transfer price based on matching marginal cost and marginal revenue **will not encourage** corporate profit maximisation.

Where there is a **perfect external market for the transferred item** and **changing costs/prices** for the final output, profits are maximised when **market price** is used on the transfer price.

7 Identifying the optimal transfer price

Introduction

Throughout the chapter we have been leading up to the following guiding rules for identifying the optimal transfer price. This section focuses on how to determine this price.

7.1 The optimal transfer price

(a)   The **ideal transfer price** should **reflect the opportunity cost** of sale to the supply division and the opportunity cost to the buying division. Unfortunately, full information about opportunity costs may not be easily obtainable in practice.

(b)   Where a **perfect external market price exists and unit variable costs and unit selling prices are constant**, the **opportunity cost** of transfer will be **external market price** or **external market price less savings in selling costs**.

(c)   In the **absence of a perfect external market price for the transferred item, but when unit variable costs are constant**, and the **sales price per unit of the end product is constant**, the **ideal transfer**

price should reflect the opportunity cost of the resources consumed by the supply division to make and supply the item and so should be at standard **variable cost + opportunity cost of making the transfer**.

(d)   When **unit variable costs and/or unit selling prices are not constant**, there will be a **profit-maximising level of output** and the **ideal transfer price** will only be found by sensible **negotiation** and careful **analysis**.

    (i)   Establish the output and sales quantities that will optimise the profits of the company or group as a whole.

    (ii)   Establish the transfer price at which both profit centres would maximise their profits at this company-optimising output level.

There may be a range of prices within which both profit centres can agree on the output level that would maximise their individual profits and the profits of the company as a whole. Any price within the range would then be 'ideal'.

Question 7.4	Optimal transfer prices

Learning outcome B2(b)

You should try to learn the above rules, and refer back to the appropriate part of the chapter if you are not sure about any point. Read through the rules again and then answer these questions.

(a)   In what situation should the transfer price be the external market price?

(b)   How should the transfer price be established when there are diseconomies of scale and prices have to be lowered to increase sales volume?

(c)   What is the ideal transfer price?

(d)   In what circumstances should the transfer price be standard variable cost + the opportunity cost of making the transfer?

Note. There is no solution at the end of the chapter for this question. The solution can be found in the rules in Section 7.1 above.

Section summary

There are various rules involved in the determination of the optimal transfer price. Make sure you read transfer pricing questions carefully to ensure you recommend the correct price.

8   Negotiated transfer prices

Introduction

As transfer prices are often difficult to determine, divisional managers may negotiate appropriate prices with each other. This section looks at the implications of negotiated transfer prices.

8.1 Negotiating a transfer price

A transfer price based on opportunity cost is often difficult to identify, for lack of suitable information about costs and revenues in individual divisions.

In this case it is likely that transfer prices will be set by means of negotiation. The agreed price may be finalised from a mixture of accounting arithmetic, politics and compromise.

(a)   A negotiated price might be based on market value, but with some reductions to allow for the internal nature of the transaction, which saves external selling and distribution costs.

(b)   Where one division receives near-finished goods from another, a negotiated price might be based on the market value of the end product, minus an amount for the finishing work in the receiving division.

8.2 Behavioural implications

Even so, inter-departmental **disputes** about transfer prices are likely to arise and these may need the **intervention or mediation of head office** to settle the problem. Head office management may then **impose a price** which maximises the profit of the company as a whole. On the other hand, head office management might restrict their intervention to the **task of keeping negotiations in progress** until a transfer price is eventually settled. The **more head office has to impose** its own decisions on profit centres, the less **decentralisation of authority** there will be and the **less effective the profit centre system** of accounting will be for **motivating** divisional managers.

Section summary

If divisional managers are allowed to **negotiate transfer prices** with each other, the agreed price may be finalised from a mixture of **accounting arithmetic, negotiation and compromise**.

9   International transfer pricing

Introduction

When products are transferred internally between divisions based in different countries, the transfer pricing problem becomes even less clear cut. This section looks at the various problems encountered with international transfer pricing, including currency and taxation issues.

9.1 Factors to be considered

Factor	Explanation
Exchange rate fluctuation	The value of a transfer of goods between profit centres in different countries could depend on fluctuations in the currency exchange rate.
Taxation in different countries	If tax on profits is 20% in Country A and 50% of profits in Country B, a company will presumably try to 'manipulate' profits (by raising or lowering transfer prices or invoicing the subsidiary in the high-tax country for 'services' provided by the subsidiary in the low-tax country) so that profits are maximised for a subsidiary in Country A, by reducing profits for a subsidiary in Country B.
	Artificial attempts to reduce tax liabilities could, however, upset a country's tax officials if they discover it and may lead to a penalty. Many tax authorities have the power to modify transfer prices in computing tariffs or taxes on profit, although a genuine arm's length market price should be accepted.
	There are three methods the tax authorities can use to determine an arm's length price.

Factor	Explanation
	The **comparable price method (also known as comparable uncontrolled price, or CUs)** involves setting the arm's length price based on the price of similar products (usually the market price). This is the preferred method where possible.
	The **resale price method** involves setting the arm's length price based on the price paid for a final product by an independent party and a suitable mark-up (to allow for the seller's expenses and profit) is deducted. This method is often used for the transfer of goods to distributors where good are sold on with little further processing.
	The **cost-plus method** involves obtaining an arm's length gross margin and applying it to the seller's manufacturing costs.
	Many countries have double taxation agreements that mean that a company will pay tax on a transaction in only one country. If a tax authority determines that a company has set an unrealistic transfer price and has paid less tax than is due, the company would then pay tax in both countries, plus any applicable penalties.
	A mitigation against this is an Advanced Pricing Agreement, entered into with both of the tax authorities involved.
	We shall work through an example on international transfer pricing and taxation later in this chapter.
Import tariffs/customs duties	Country A imposes an import tariff of 20% on the value of goods imported. A multinational company has a subsidiary in Country A which imports goods from a subsidiary in Country B. The company would minimise costs by keeping the transfer price to a minimum.
Exchange controls	If a country imposes restrictions on the transfer of profits from domestic subsidiaries to foreign multinationals, the restrictions on the transfer can be overcome if head office provides some goods or services to the subsidiary and charges exorbitantly high prices, disguising the 'profits' as sales revenue, and transferring them from one country to the other. The ethics of such an approach should, of course, be questioned.
Anti-dumping legislation	Governments may take action to protect home industries by preventing companies from transferring goods cheaply into their countries. They may do this, for example, by insisting on the use of a fair market value for the transfer price.
Competitive pressures	Transfer pricing can be used to enable profit centres to match or undercut local competitors.
Repatriation of funds	By inflating transfer prices for goods sold to subsidiaries in countries where inflation is high, the subsidiaries' profits are reduced and funds repatriated, thereby saving their value.
Minority shareholders	Transfer prices can be used to reduce the amount of profit paid to minority shareholders by artificially depressing a subsidiary's profit.

9.2 The pros and cons of different transfer pricing bases

(a) A transfer price at **market value** is usually encouraged by the tax and customs authorities of both host and home countries as they will receive a **fair share of the profits** made but there are **problems** with its use.

(i)   Prices for the same product may **vary considerably** from one country to another.

(ii)   Changes in exchange rates, local taxes and so on can result in **large variations in selling price**.

(iii)   A division will want to set its prices in relation to the supply and demand conditions present in the country in question to ensure that it can compete in that country.

(b)   A transfer price at **cost** is usually acceptable to tax and customs authorities since it provides some indication that the transfer price approximates to the real cost of supplying the item and because it indicates that they will therefore receive a fair share of tax and tariff revenues. Cost-based approaches do not totally remove the suspicion that the figure may have been massaged because the choice of the type of cost (full actual, full standard, actual variable, marginal) can alter the size of the transfer price.

(c)   In a multinational organisation, **negotiated** transfer prices may result in overall sub-optimisation because no account is taken of factors such as differences in tax and tariff rates between countries.

Question 7.5   International transfer pricing

Learning outcome B3

RBN is a UK parent company with an overseas subsidiary. The directors of RBN wish to transfer profits from the UK to the overseas company. They are considering changing the level of the transfer prices charged on goods shipped from the overseas subsidiary to UK subsidiaries and the size of the royalty payments paid by UK subsidiaries to the overseas subsidiary.

In order to transfer profit from the UK to the overseas subsidiary should the manager of RBN increase or decrease the transfer prices and the royalty payments?

Question 7.6   More international transfer pricing

Learning outcome B3

LL Multinational transferred 4,000 units of product S from its manufacturing division in the US to the selling division in the UK in the year to 31 December.

Each unit of S cost $350 to manufacture, the variable cost proportion being 75%, and was sold for £600. The UK division incurred marketing and distribution costs of £8 per unit. The UK tax rate was 30% and the exchange rate £ = $1.5.

If the transfers were at variable cost, what was the UK division's profit after tax?

Example: International transfer pricing and taxation

Division W, which is part of the XYZ group, is based in country A and has the capacity to manufacture 100,000 units of product B each year. The variable cost of producing a unit of B is $15 and the division can sell 85,000 units externally per annum at $25 per unit.

Division D is part of the same group and is based in country L. Division D purchases 40,000 units of product B each year from O (which is not part of XYZ group), which is also based in country L. D pays a dollar equivalent of $20 per unit.

If division D were to purchase product B from division W, division W would set a transfer price of $22. Given that there are no selling costs involved in transferring units to division D, this would give division W the same contribution on internal and external sales.

Division W would give priority to division D and so the orders from some external customers would not be met.

Required

Determine from whom division D should purchase product B in each of the following circumstances if the aim is to maximise group profit.

(a)   The tax rate in country A is 30% and the tax rate in country L is 40%.
(b)   The tax rate in country A is 60% and the tax rate in country L is 15%.

You may assume that changes in contribution can be used as a basis of calculating changes in tax charges and that division D is able to absorb any tax benefits from the profit it generates on other activities.

Solution

We need to consider the relevant costs, which are the changes in contribution and tax paid.

	$'000	(a)	(b)
Current position			
D buys 40,000 units from O @ $20 per unit	(800)		
These purchases reduce D's tax liability by			
$800,000 × 40%		320	
$800,000 × 15%			120
W sells 85,000 units @ $(25 – 15) = $10			
contribution per unit	850		
W's tax on this contribution			
$850,000 × 30%		(255)	
$850,000 × 60%			(510)
If D buys from W			
D buys 40,000 units @ $22 per unit	(880)		
These purchases reduce D's tax liability by			
$880,000 × 40%		352	
$880,000 × 15%			132
W sells 100,000 units @ $10 contribution per unit	1,000,000		
W's tax on this contribution			
$1,000,000 × 30%		(300)	
$1,000,000 × 60%			(600)

Summary			
		(a)	(b)
If D switches to W			
Decrease in D's contribution			
$((880) – (800))		(80)	(80)
Decrease in D's tax liability			
$(352 – 320)		32	
$(132 – 120)			12
Increase in W's contribution			
$(1,000,000 – 850,000)		150	150
Increase in W's tax liability			
$((300) – (255))		(45)	
$((600) – (510))			(90)
Net gain to XYZ group		57	(8)

∴ Division D should purchase from division W to maximise group profit in scenario (a) but from O in scenario (b).

Exam skills

The figures in the summary above are calculated by deducting the cash flow arising in the current position from the cash flows if D buys from W.

9.3 Currency management

When subsidiaries in different countries trade with each other it will be necessary to **decide which currency will be used for the transfer price**.

If the transfer price is set in one of the subsidiaries' home currencies and there is a movement in the exchange rate then one of the subsidiaries will make a **loss on exchange of foreign currencies**.

Example: Transfer prices and exchange rate losses

A subsidiary in the UK sells product P to a US subsidiary. Details are as follows.

	Per unit
Transfer price	$21
Cost incurred in UK subsidiary	£9

At the date that the transfer price was agreed the exchange rate was £1 = $1.50.

The US subsidiary incurs additional costs of $3 per unit to convert product P for sale in the US, at a selling price of $29 per unit.

Due to a weakening of the dollar against the pound, the exchange rate is now £1 = $1.80.

Required

Calculate the effect of the change in exchange rate on the profit per unit earned by each subsidiary, if the agreed transfer price was fixed in terms of:

(a)   Dollars   (b)   Pounds sterling

Solution

When exchange rate is £1 = $1.50

	UK subsidiary £ per unit	US subsidiary $ per unit
Selling price of product ($21 ÷ 1.50)	14	29
Costs incurred in subsidiary – internal	(9)	(3)
– transfer		(21)
Profit per unit	5	5

When exchange rate is £1 = $1.80. Transfer price fixed in dollars ($21)

	UK subsidiary £ per unit	US subsidiary $ per unit
Selling price of product ($21 ÷ 1.80)	11.67	29
Costs incurred in subsidiary – internal	(9.00)	(3)
– transfer		(21)
Profit per unit	2.67	5

When exchange rate is £1 = \$1.80. Transfer price fixed in pounds sterling

	UK subsidiary £ per unit		US subsidiary \$ per unit
Selling price of product	14		29.00
Costs incurred in subsidiary – internal	(9)		(3.00)
– transfer		(£14 × 1.80)	(25.20)
Profit per unit	5		0.80

Thus the weakening dollar had a detrimental effect on the UK subsidiary when the transfer price was fixed in dollars, but a detrimental effect to the UK subsidiary when the transfer price was fixed in pounds sterling.

As well as having a **behavioural impact**, this could affect the **taxation of the whole group**. If a particular currency weakens, as in this example, then the selection of the correct currency for the transfer price can ensure that currency translation losses occur in the subsidiary which pays the higher rate of taxation.

Exam skills

If you find transfer pricing difficult then try to make sure that you understand the basic principles. Remember that individual managers want to maximise their own profit and this may not be in the best interests of the company as a whole. There must be a system in place which provides an equal distribution of profit between divisions, motivates divisional managers and promotes goal congruence. You can usually use your common sense to calculate this in an exam question.

Section summary

Problems associated with currency exchange rates, taxation, import tariffs, exchange control, anti-dumping legislation and competitive pressures arise **with transfer pricing in multinational companies**.

Chapter Summary

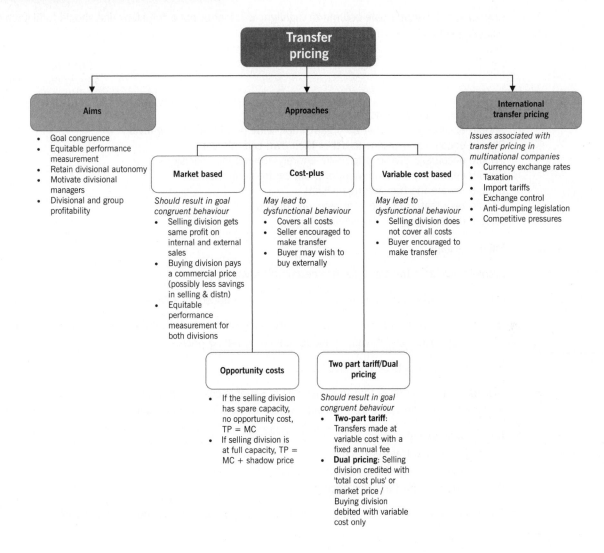

Transfer pricing

Aims

- Goal congruence
- Equitable performance measurement
- Retain divisional autonomy
- Motivate divisional managers
- Divisional and group profitability

Approaches

Market based

Should result in goal congruent behaviour
- Selling division gets same profit on internal and external sales
- Buying division pays a commercial price (possibly less savings in selling & distn)
- Equitable performance measurement for both divisions

Cost-plus

May lead to dysfunctional behaviour
- Covers all costs
- Seller encouraged to make transfer
- Buyer may wish to buy externally

Variable cost based

May lead to dysfunctional behaviour
- Selling division does not cover all costs
- Buyer encouraged to make transfer

International transfer pricing

Issues associated with transfer pricing in multinational companies
- Currency exchange rates
- Taxation
- Import tariffs
- Exchange control
- Anti-dumping legislation
- Competitive pressures

Opportunity costs

- If the selling division has spare capacity, no opportunity cost, TP = MC
- If selling division is at full capacity, TP = MC + shadow price

Two part tariff/Dual pricing

Should result in goal congruent behaviour
- **Two-part tariff:** Transfers made at variable cost with a fixed annual fee
- **Dual pricing:** Selling division credited with 'total cost plus' or market price / Buying division debited with variable cost only

Quick Quiz

1   Put ticks in the appropriate column to highlight whether or not a transfer price should fulfil each of the following criteria.

	Criteria should be fulfilled	Criteria should not be fulfilled
Should encourage dysfunctional decision making		
Should encourage output at an organisation-wide profit-maximising level		
Should encourage divisions to act in their own self-interest		
Should encourage divisions to make entirely autonomous decisions		
Should enable the measurement of profit centre performance		
Should reward the transferring division		
Should be a reasonable cost for receiving division		
Should discourage goal congruence		

2   Fill in the gaps.

Market value as a transfer price has certain disadvantages.

(a)   The market price might be ...., induced by adverse economic conditions, say.

(b)   There might be an .... external market, so that if the transferring division tried to sell more externally, it would have to reduce its selling price.

(c)   Many products do not have ....

3   Division P transfers its output to Division Q at variable cost. Once a year P charges a fixed fee to Q, representing an allowance for P's fixed costs. This type of transfer pricing system is commonly known as:

A   Dual pricing
B   Negotiated transfer pricing
C   Opportunity cost based transfer pricing
D   Two-part tariff transfer pricing

4   Profits are maximised when marginal cost is equal to marginal revenue. True or false?

5   Choose the correct words from those highlighted.

When transfer prices are based on opportunity costs, opportunity costs are either the (1) **contribution/profit** forgone by the (2) **receiving/supplying** division in transferring (3) **internally/externally** rather than (4) **selling externally/transferring internally**, or the (5) **profit/contribution** forgone by not using the relevant facilities for their (6) **next best/cheapest/most profitable** alternative use.

6   Choose the correct words from those highlighted.

Taxation on profits in country C is charged at a higher rate than in country D. When goods are transferred from a subsidiary in country C to a subsidiary in country D it would be beneficial, from the point of view of the whole organisation, to charge a (1) **higher/lower** transfer price so that the total taxation cost for the organisation is (2) **higher/lower**.

7   Choose the correct words from those highlighted.

The more head office has to impose its own decisions on profit centres, the **more/less** decentralisation of authority there will be and the **more/less** effective the profit centre system of accounting will be for motivating divisional managers.

Answers to Quick Quiz

1

	Criteria should be fulfilled	Criteria should not be fulfilled
Should encourage dysfunctional decision making		✓
Should encourage output at an organisation-wide profit-maximising level	✓	
Should encourage divisions to act in their own self-interest		✓
Should encourage divisions to make entirely autonomous decisions		✓
Should enable the measurement of profit centre performance	✓	
Should reward the transferring division	✓	
Should be a reasonable cost for receiving division	✓	
Should discourage goal congruence		✓

2 (a) temporary
     (b) imperfect
     (c) an equivalent market price

3 D

4 True

5 (1) contribution
     (2) supplying
     (3) internally
     (4) selling externally
     (5) contribution
     (6) next best

6 (1) lower
     (2) lower

7 less
     less

Answers to Questions

7.1 Benefits of transfer pricing

Potential benefits of operating a transfer pricing system within a divisionalised company include the following.

(a) It can lead to **goal congruence** by motivating divisional managers to make decisions, which improve divisional profit and improve profit of the organisation as a whole.

(b) It can prevent **dysfunctional decision making** so that decisions taken by a divisional manager are in the best interests of their own part of the business, other divisions and the organisation as a whole.

(c) Transfer prices can be set at a level that enables divisional performance to be measured 'commercially'. A transfer pricing system should therefore report a level of divisional profit that is a **reasonable measure of the managerial performance** of the division.

(d) It should ensure that **divisional autonomy** is not undermined. A well-run transfer pricing system helps to ensure that a balance is kept between divisional autonomy, to provide incentives and motivation, and centralised authority, to ensure that the divisions are all working towards the same target, to the benefit of the organisation as a whole.

7.2 Transfer pricing and changing costs/prices (no external market)

(a) T revenues minus T costs
(b) S costs for 700 units minus S costs for 600 units (and so on)
(c) T net revenues for 700 units minus T net revenues for 600 units (and so on)
(d) See Example 7.2 Discussion and solution

This exercise is to make sure that you were following the argument.

7.3 Profit-maximising transfer price

Variable cost of parts for Division A's product Z = $35 \times 3 = \$105$

Transfer price = $\$105 \times 150\% = \$157.50$

Division A's variable cost per unit of Z = $50

Total variable/marginal cost to division A = $207.50

Division A will sell until marginal cost = marginal revenue.

It will therefore sell 3 units.

7.4 Optimal transfer prices

See Section 7.1 for the answer to this question.

7.5 International transfer pricing

To increase the overseas subsidiary's profit, the **transfer price needs to be higher** (since it is the overseas subsidiary doing the selling) and the **royalty payments** by the UK subsidiaries to the overseas subsidiary company **should also be higher**. Both would add to the overseas subsidiary's revenue without affecting its costs.

7.6 More international transfer pricing

	£
External sales (£600 × 4,000)	2,400,000
Variable cost (transfer price of ($350 × 75%/$1.5) × 4,000)	700,000
Marketing and distribution costs (£8 × 4,000)	32,000
Profit before tax	1,668,000
Tax at 30%	500,400
Profit after tax	1,167,600

Now try the question from the Practice Question Bank

Number	Marks	Time
Q28 Objective test questions	10	18 mins
Q29 Transfer pricing	30	54 mins

LONG-TERM DECISION MAKING

Part C

PROJECT APPRAISAL

 In this chapter we will be examining the appraisal of **projects** which involve the **outlay of capital**.

We begin the chapter with an overview of the **investment decision-making process** in **Sections 1 and 2. Section 3 addresses some of the non-financial considerations in long-term decisions**, before moving on to examine two capital investment appraisal techniques, the straightforward **payback method (Section 4)** and the slightly more involved **accounting rate of return method (Section 5)**.

In Sections 6, 7, 8 and 9 we turn our attention to methods based on discounted cash flow (DCF) techniques, namely net present value (NPV), internal rate of return (IRR) and discounted payback. **Sections 8 and 10** cover issues that could be examined in discursive questions.

In the final two sections of the chapter we **incorporate the effects into inflation and tax in investment appraisal**.

Section 11 looks at inflation and Section 12 looks at tax.

topic list	learning outcomes	syllabus references	ability required
1 The process of investment decision making	C1(b)	C1(b)(i)	analysis
2 Post audit	C1(b)	C1(b)(i)	analysis
3 Non-financial considerations in long-term decisions	C1(a)	C1(a)(ii)	analysis
4 The payback method	C1(c)	C1(c)(i)	analysis
5 The accounting rate of return (ARR) method	C1(c)	C1(c)(i)	analysis
6 The net present value (NPV) method	C1(a)	C1(a)(i)	analysis
7 The internal rate of return (IRR) method	C1(c)	C1(c)(i)	analysis

topic list	learning outcomes	syllabus references	ability required
8 NPV and IRR compared	C1(c)	C1(c)(i)	analysis
9 Discounted payback	C1(c)	C1(c)(i)	analysis
10 DCF: additional points	C1(a)	C1(a)(i)	analysis
11 Allowing for inflation	C1(a)	C1(a)(i)	analysis
12 Allowing for taxation	C1(a)	C1(a)(i)	analysis

Chapter Overview

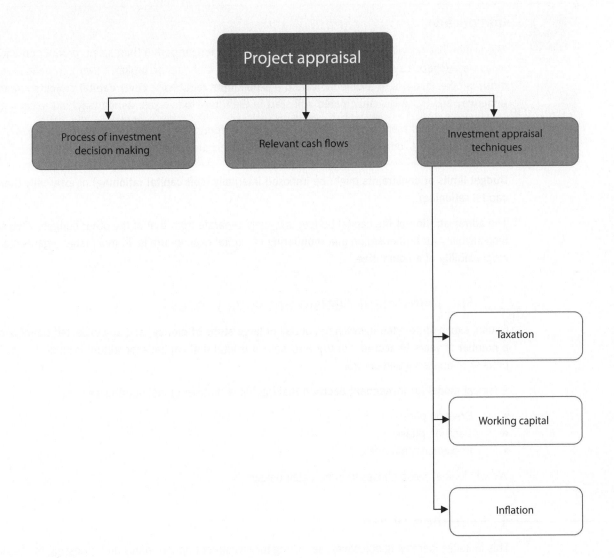

1   The process of investment decision making

1.1 Creation of capital budgets

Introduction

The capital budget will normally be **prepared to cover a longer period than sales, production and resource budgets**, say from three to five years, although it should be **broken down** into periods matching those of other budgets. It should indicate the expenditure required to cover **capital projects already underway** and those it is **anticipated will start** in the three- to five-year period (say) of the capital budget.

The budget should therefore be based on the current production budget, future expected levels of production and the long-term development of the organisation, and industry, as a whole.

Budget limits or constraints might be imposed internally (**soft capital rationing**) or externally (**hard capital rationing**).

The **administration of** the capital budget is usually separate from that of the other budgets. Overall responsibility for **authorisation and monitoring** of capital expenditure is, in most large organisations, the **responsibility of a committee**.

1.2 The investment decision-making process

Capital expenditure often involves the outlay of **large sums of money**, and any expected **benefits may take a number of years to accrue**. For these reasons it is vital that capital expenditure is subject to a rigorous process of appraisal and control.

A typical **model for investment decision making** has a number of distinct phases.

*   Creation phase
*   Decision phase
*   Implementation phase

We will look at these phases in more detail below.

1.3 Creation phase

This includes identifying objectives, searching for investment opportunities and assessing the business environment.

Investment opportunities **do not just appear** out of thin air. They **must be created**.

An organisation must set up a **mechanism that scans the environment for potential opportunities and gives an early warning of future problems**. A technological change that might result in a drop in sales might be picked up by this scanning process, and steps should be taken immediately to respond to such a threat.

Ideas for investment might come from those working in technical positions. A factory manager, for example, could be well placed to identify ways in which expanded capacity or new machinery could increase output or the efficiency of the manufacturing process. Innovative ideas, such as new product lines, are more likely to come from those in higher levels of management, given their strategic view of the organisation's direction and their knowledge of the competitive environment.

The overriding feature of any **proposal** is that it should be **consistent with the organisation's overall strategy to achieve its objectives**.

1.4 Decision phase

This phase involves listing the possible alternatives and carrying out financial analysis. Then a go/no go decision is made.

The financial analysis will involve the **application of the organisation's preferred investment appraisal techniques**. We will be studying these techniques in detail in this chapter. In many projects some of the financial implications will be extremely difficult to quantify, but every effort must be made to do so, in order to have a formal basis for planning and controlling the project.

Go/no go decisions on projects may be **made at different levels within the organisational hierarchy**, depending on three factors.

(a)　The type of investment
(b)　Its perceived riskiness
(c)　The amount of expenditure required

1.5 Implementation phase

This phase includes approving capital investment proposals and reviewing capital investment decisions, usually by way of a post-completion audit. We will look at this in more detail in the next section.

1.6 Other considerations

1.6.1 Qualitative issues

Financial analysis of capital projects is obviously vital because of the amount of money involved and the length of time for which it is tied up. However, a consideration of qualitative issues is also relevant to the decision (ie factors which are difficult or impossible to quantify). Qualitative issues would be considered in the **initial screening stage (decision phase)**, for example in reviewing the project's 'fit' with the organisation's overall objectives and whether it is a mandatory investment. There is a very wide range of other qualitative issues that may be relevant to a particular project.

(a)　What are the implications of not undertaking the investment, eg adverse effect on staff morale, loss of market share?

(b)　Will acceptance of this project lead to the need for further investment activity in future?

(c)　What will be the effect on the company's image?

(d)　Will the organisation be more flexible as a result of the investment, and better able to respond to market and technology changes?

Section summary

A typical **model for investment decision making** has three phases.

- Creation phase
- Decision phase
- Implementation phase

2 Post audit

Introduction

The post-completion audit is a **forward-looking** rather than a backward-looking technique. It seeks to **identify general lessons** to be learned from a project.

KEY TERM

A POST-COMPLETION AUDIT (PCA) is 'An objective independent assessment of the success of a capital project in relation to plan. Covers the whole life of the project and provides feedback to managers to aid the implementation and control of future projects'.

(*CIMA Official Terminology*)

2.1 Why perform a post-completion appraisal (PCA) or audit?

(a)   The **threat** of the PCA will **motivate managers** to work to achieve the promised benefits from the project.

(b)   If the audit takes place before the project life ends, and if it finds that the benefits have been less than expected because of management inefficiency, steps can be taken to **improve efficiency**. Alternatively, it will **highlight those projects which should be discontinued**.

(c)   It can help to **identify** managers who have been **good performers** and those who have been poor performers.

(d)   It might identify weaknesses in the forecasting and estimating techniques used to evaluate projects, and so should help to **improve** the discipline and quality of **forecasting** for future investment decisions.

(e)   Areas where improvements can be made in methods which should help to achieve **better results in general from capital investments** might be revealed.

(f)   The **original estimates may be more realistic** if managers are aware that they will be monitored, but PCAs **should not be unfairly critical**.

2.2 Which projects should be audited?

A reasonable **guideline** might be to **audit all projects above a certain size, and a random selection of smaller projects**.

A PCA does not need to focus on all aspects of an investment, but should **concentrate on those aspects which have been identified as particularly sensitive or critical to the success of a project**. The most important thing to remember is that PCAs are time consuming and costly, and so **careful consideration should be given to the cost-benefit trade-off** arising from the PCA results.

2.3 When should projects be audited?

If the audit is carried out too soon, the information may not be complete. On the other hand, if the audit is too late then management action will be delayed and the usefulness of the information is greatly reduced.

There is no correct answer to the question of when to audit, although research suggests that in practice most companies perform the PCA **approximately one year after the completion of the project**.

2.4 Who performs a PCA?

Because it can be very difficult to evaluate an investment decision completely objectively, it is generally appropriate to **separate responsibility** for the **investment decision** from that for the **PCA**. Line management involved in the investment decision should therefore not carry out the PCA. To avoid conflicts of interest, **outside experts** could even be used.

2.5 Problems with PCA

(a) There are many **uncontrollable factors** which are outside management control in long-term investments, such as environmental changes.

(b) It **may not be possible** to **identify separately the costs and benefits** of any particular project.

(c) PCA can be a **costly** and **time-consuming** exercise.

(d) Applied punitively, PCA exercises may lead to **managers becoming over-cautious** and unnecessarily **risk averse**.

(e) The **strategic effects** of a capital investment project **may take years** to materialise and it may in fact **never be possible** to identify or quantify them effectively.

Despite the growth in popularity of PCAs, you should bear in mind the possible **alternative** control processes.

(a) **Teams** could manage a project from beginning to end, control being used **before** the project is started and **during** its life, rather than at the end of its life.

(b) **More time could be spent choosing projects** rather than checking completed projects.

Section summary

A **post audit** cannot reverse the decision to incur the capital expenditure, because the expenditure has already taken place, but it does have a certain control value.

3 Non-financial considerations in long-term decisions

Introduction

As well as financial considerations, any decision support information provided to management should also incorporate **non-financial considerations**.

Here are some examples.

(a) **Impact on employee morale**. Most investments affect employees' prospects, sometimes for the better, sometimes for the worse. A new cafeteria for employees would have a favourable impact, for example.

(b) **Impact on the community**. This is a particularly important consideration if the investment results in loss of jobs, more jobs or elimination of small businesses.

(c) **Impact on the environment**. The opening of a new mine, the development of products which create environmentally harmful waste and so on, all have an impact on the environment. This can affect an organisation's image and reputation and hence its long-term growth and survival prospects. Some of these environmental effects can also impact directly on project cash flows

because organisations have to pay fines, incur legal costs, incur disposal and cleanup costs and so on.

(d) **Ethical issues**. Some investments might be legal but might not be in line with the ethics and code of conduct demanded by various stakeholder groups.

(e) **Learning**. Many investments, particularly those which advance an organisation's technology, provide opportunities for learning. For example, investment in new computerised equipment to revolutionise a production process would enable an organisation to better use highly technical production methods.

Section summary

Management must also consider the non-financial implications of their decisions.

4 The payback method

Introduction

Now that we have discussed all the stages involved in the capital budgeting process, we will return to study in detail the stage that many managers consider to be the most important: the financial appraisal. We will begin with what is probably the most straightforward appraisal technique: the payback method.

KEY TERM

PAYBACK is 'The time required for the cash inflows from a capital investment project to equal the cash outflows'.

(CIMA Official Terminology)

When **deciding between two or more competing projects**, the usual decision is to **accept the one with the shortest payback**.

Payback is often used as a **'first screening method'**. By this, we mean that when a capital investment project is being subjected to financial appraisal, the first question to ask is: 'How long will it take to pay back its cost?' The organisation might have a target payback, and so it would reject a capital project unless its payback period were less than a certain number of years.

However, a project should not be evaluated on the basis of payback alone. Payback should be a **first** screening process, and if a project gets through the payback test, it ought **then to be evaluated with a more sophisticated project appraisal technique**.

You should note that when payback is calculated, we take **profits before depreciation**, because we are trying to estimate the **cash** returns from a project and profit before depreciation is likely to be a **rough approximation of cash flows**.

4.1 Why is payback alone an inadequate project appraisal technique?

Look at the figures below for two mutually exclusive projects (this means that only one of them can be undertaken).

	Project P	Project Q
Capital cost of asset	$60,000	$60,000
Profits before depreciation		
Year 1	$20,000	$50,000
Year 2	$30,000	$20,000
Year 3	$40,000	$5,000
Year 4	$50,000	$5,000
Year 5	$60,000	$5,000

Project P pays back in year 3 (about one-quarter of the way through year 3). Project Q pays back halfway through year 2. **Using payback alone** to judge projects, **Project Q would be preferred. But the returns from Project P over its life are much higher than the returns from Project Q.** Project P will earn total profits before depreciation of $200,000 on an investment of $60,000, whereas Project Q will earn total profits before depreciation of only $85,000 on an investment of $60,000.

Question 8.1	Payback

Learning outcome C1(c)

An asset costing $120,000 is to be depreciated over 10 years to a nil residual value. Profits after depreciation for the first 5 years are as follows.

Year	$
1	12,000
2	17,000
3	28,000
4	37,000
5	8,000

How long is the payback period to the nearest month?

A   3 years 7 months
B   3 years 6 months
C   3 years
D   The project does not pay back in 5 years

4.2 Disadvantages of the payback method

There are a number of serious drawbacks to the payback method.

(a)   It **ignores the timing of cash flows** within the payback period, the cash flows after the end of the payback period and therefore the total project return.

(b)   It **ignores the time value of money** (a concept incorporated into more sophisticated appraisal methods). This means that it does not take account of the fact that $1 today is worth more than $1 in one year's time. An investor who has $1 today can either consume it immediately or alternatively can invest it at the prevailing interest rate, say 10%, to get a return of $1.10 in a year's time.

There are also other disadvantages.

(a)   The method is unable to distinguish between projects with the same payback period.

(b)   The choice of any cut-off payback period by an organisation is arbitrary.

(c)   It may lead to excessive investment in short-term projects.

(d)   It takes account of the risk of the timing of cash flows but does not take account of the variability of those cash flows.

4.3 Advantages of the payback method

The use of the payback method does have advantages, especially as an initial screening device.

(a)   Long payback means **capital is tied up**.
(b)   Focus on early payback can **enhance liquidity**.
(c)   **Investment risk is increased** if payback is longer.

(d)   **Shorter-term forecasts** are likely to be **more reliable**.
(e)   The calculation is **quick** and **simple**.
(f)   Payback is an **easily understood** concept.

Section summary

The **payback method** looks at how long it takes for a project's net cash inflows to equal the initial investment.

5   The accounting rate of return (ARR) method

Introduction

The accounting rate of return (ARR) method (also called the return on capital employed (ROCE) method or the return on investment (ROI) method) of appraising a project is to estimate the accounting rate of return that the project should yield. If it exceeds a target rate of return, the project will be undertaken.

KEY TERM

The CIMA OFFICIAL TERMINOLOGY definition is $\dfrac{\text{Average annual profit from investment} \times 100}{\text{Average investment}}$

Unfortunately there are several different definitions of ARR.

$$\text{ARR} = \frac{\text{Estimated total profits}}{\text{Estimated initial investment}} \times 100\% \quad \textbf{or}$$

$$\text{ARR} = \frac{\text{Estimated average profits}}{\text{Estimated initial investment}} \times 100\%$$

KEY POINT

There are arguments in favour of each of these definitions. The most important point is, however, that the **method selected should be used consistently**. For **examination** purposes, we recommend the **first definition** (CIMA's definition) unless the question clearly indicates that some other one is to be used.

Note that this is the only appraisal method that we will be studying that **uses profit** instead of cash flow. If you are not provided with a figure for profit, **assume that net cash inflow minus depreciation equals profit**.

Example: the accounting rate of return

A company has a target accounting rate of return of 20% (using the CIMA definition above), and is now considering the following project.

Capital cost of asset	$80,000
Estimated life	4 years
Estimated profit before depreciation	
Year 1	$20,000
Year 2	$25,000
Year 3	$35,000
Year 4	$25,000

The capital asset would be depreciated by 25% of its cost each year, and will have no residual value.

Required

Assess whether the project should be undertaken.

Solution

The annual profits after depreciation, and the mid-year net book value of the asset, would be as follows.

Year	Profit after depreciation $	Mid-year net book value $	ARR in the year %
1	0	70,000	0
2	5,000	50,000	10
3	15,000	30,000	50
4	5,000	10,000	50

As the table shows, the ARR is low in the early stages of the project, partly because of low profits in year 1 but mainly because the NBV of the asset is much higher early on in its life. The project does not achieve the target ARR of 20% in its first 2 years, but exceeds it in years 3 and 4. Should it be undertaken?

When the **ARR from a project varies from year to year**, it makes sense to **take an overall or 'average' view of the project's return**. In this case, we should look at the return over the four-year period.

	$
Total profit before depreciation over four years	105,000
Total profit after depreciation over four years	25,000
Average annual profit after depreciation	6,250
Original cost of investment	80,000
Average net book value over the four-year period ((80,000 + 0)/2)	40,000

The project would not be undertaken because its ARR is 6,250/40,000 = 15.625% and so it would fail to yield the target return of 20%.

5.1 The ARR and the comparison of mutually exclusive projects

The ARR method of capital investment appraisal can also be used to compare two or more projects which are mutually exclusive. The project with the highest ARR would be selected (provided that the expected ARR is higher than the company's target ARR).

Question 8.2	The ARR and mutually exclusive projects

Learning outcome C1(c)

Arrow wants to buy a new item of equipment. Two models of equipment are available, one with a slightly higher capacity and greater reliability than the other. The expected costs and profits of each item are as follows.

	Equipment item X	Equipment item Y
Capital cost	$80,000	$150,000
Life	5 years	5 years
Profits before depreciation	$	$
Year 1	50,000	50,000
Year 2	50,000	50,000
Year 3	30,000	60,000
Year 4	20,000	60,000
Year 5	10,000	60,000
Disposal value	0	0

ARR is measured as the average annual profit after depreciation, divided by the average net book value of the asset.

Equipment item Y should be selected if the company's target ARR is 30%. True or false?

5.2 The drawbacks and advantages to the ARR method of project appraisal

The ARR method has the serious **drawback** that it **does not take account of the timing of the profits from a project**. Whenever capital is invested in a project, money is tied up until the project begins to earn profits which pay back the investment. Money tied up in one project cannot be invested anywhere else until the profits come in. Management should be aware of the benefits of early repayments from an investment, which will provide the money for other investments.

There are a number of other disadvantages.

(a)　It is **based on accounting profits** which are **subject to a number of different accounting treatments**.

(b)　It is a **relative measure** rather than an absolute measure and hence **takes no account of the size of the investment**.

(c)　**It takes no account of the length of the project**.

(d)　Like the payback method, it **ignores the time value of money**.

There are, however, **advantages** to the ARR method.

(a)　It is quick and **simple** to calculate.

(b)　It involves a **familiar concept** of a percentage return.

(c)　Accounting profits can be **easily calculated from financial statements**.

(d)　It **looks at the entire project life**.

(e)　Managers and investors are accustomed to thinking in terms of profit, and so an appraisal method which **employs profit** may therefore be more **easily understood**.

Question 8.3	Payback and ARR

Learning outcome C1(c)

A company is considering two capital expenditure proposals. Both proposals are for similar products and both are expected to operate for four years. Only one proposal can be accepted.

The following information is available.

| | Profit/(loss) after depreciation | |
| | Proposal A | Proposal B |
	$	$
Initial investment	46,000	46,000
Year 1	6,500	4,500
Year 2	3,500	2,500
Year 3	13,500	4,500
Year 4	(1,500)	14,500
Estimated scrap value at the end of year 4	4,000	4,000

Depreciation is charged on the straight-line basis.

Required

(a)   Calculate the following for both proposals.

   (i)   The payback period to one decimal place
   (ii)   The return on capital employed on **initial investment**, to one decimal place

(b)   Give two advantages of each of the methods of appraisal used in (a) above.

Section summary

The accounting rate of return has several different definitions but the *CIMA Official Terminology* definition is $\dfrac{\text{Average annual profit from investment} \times 100\%}{\text{Average investment}}$

Exam skills

Make sure you are happy with the payback method and the ARR as they could earn you easy marks in the OT assessment.

---

6   The net present value (NPV) method

6.1 Discounting

Introduction

Compounding means that, as interest is earned, it is added to the original investment and starts to earn interest itself. Discounting is the reverse of compounding. These concepts were covered in CIMA C03 *Fundamentals of Business Maths*, so should not be completely new to you.

Suppose that a company has $10,000 to invest, and wants to earn a return of 10% (compound interest) on its investments. This means that if the $10,000 could be invested at 10%, the value of the investment with interest would build up as follows.

(a)   After 1 year $10,000 × (1.10)   = $11,000
(b)   After 2 years $10,000 × (1.10)^2   = $12,100
(c)   After 3 years $10,000 × (1.10)^3   = $13,310

and so on.

This is **compounding**. The formula for the future value of an investment plus accumulated interest after n time periods is $V = X(1 + r)^n$

where   V   is the future value of the investment with interest

   X   is the initial or 'present' value of the investment

   r   is the compound rate of return per time period, expressed as a proportion (so 10% = 0.10, 5% = 0.05 and so on)

   n   is the number of time periods

Discounting starts with the future value (a sum of money receivable or payable at a future date), and converts the future value to a **present value**, which is the cash equivalent now of the future value.

For example, if a company expects to earn a (compound) rate of return of 10% on its investments, how much would it need to invest now to have the following investments?

(a) $11,000 after 1 year
(b) $12,100 after 2 years
(c) $13,310 after 3 years

The answer is $10,000 in each case, and we can calculate it by discounting.

The **discounting formula** to calculate the present value (X) of a future sum of money (V) at the end of n time periods is $X = V/(1+r)^n$.

(a)   After 1 year, $11,000 \times 1/1.10 = \$10,000$
(b)   After 2 years, $12,100 \times 1/1.10^2 = \$10,000$
(c)   After 3 years, $13,310 \times 1/1.10^3 = \$10,000$

KEY TERM

PRESENT VALUE is 'The cash equivalent now of a sum of money receivable or payable at a future date'.

(*CIMA Official Terminology*)

The **timing of cash flows is taken into account by discounting them**. The effect of discounting is to **give a bigger value per $1 for cash flows that occur earlier**: $1 earned after one year will be worth more than $1 earned after 2 years, which in turn will be worth more than $1 earned after 5 years, and so on.

Question 8.4	Present value calculation

Learning outcome C1(b)

Spender expects the cash inflow from an investment to be $40,000 after 2 years and another $30,000 after 3 years. Its target rate of return is 12%.

Required

Fill in the blank in the sentence below.

The present value of these future returns is $.................. .

Question 8.5	Meaning of present value

Learning outcome C1(b)

Look back at the detail of the question above and then fill in the gaps in the paragraph below.

The present value of the future returns, discounted at ......, is .... This means that if Spender can invest now to earn a return of .... on its investments, it would have to invest .... now to earn .... after 2 years plus .... after 3 years.

KEY TERM

DISCOUNTED CASH FLOW (DCF) is 'The discounting of the projected net cash flows of a capital project to ascertain its present value. The methods commonly used are:

- yield, or internal rate of return (IRR), in which the calculation determines the return in the form of a percentage;

- net present value (NPV), in which the discount rate is chosen and the present value is expressed as a sum of money;

- discounted payback, in which the discount rate is chosen, and the payback is the number of years required to repay the original investment.'

(*CIMA Official Terminology*)

We will be looking at these methods in the remainder of this chapter.

KEY POINT

DCF looks at the **cash flows** of a project, **not the accounting profits**. Like the payback technique of investment appraisal, DCF is concerned with liquidity, not profitability. Cash flows are considered because they show the costs and benefits of a project when they actually occur. For example, the capital cost of a project will be the original cash outlay, and not the notional cost of depreciation, which is used to spread the capital cost over the asset's life in the financial accounts.

6.2 The net present value (NPV) method

KEY TERM

NET PRESENT VALUE (NPV) is 'The difference between the sum of the projected discounted cash inflows and outflows attributable to a capital investment or other long-term project'. (*CIMA Official Terminology*)

The NPV method therefore **compares the present value of all the cash inflows** from a project **with the present value of all the cash outflows** from a project. The **NPV** is thus calculated as the **PV of cash inflows minus the PV of cash outflows**.

(a)   If the **NPV is positive**, it means that the present value of the cash inflows from a project is greater than the present value of the cash outflows. The **project should therefore be undertaken**.

(b)   If the **NPV is negative**, it means that the present value of cash outflows is greater than the present value of inflows. The **project should therefore not be undertaken**.

(c)   If the **NPV is exactly zero**, the present value of cash inflows and cash outflows are equal and the **project will be only just worth undertaking**.

Example: NPV

Slogger has a cost of capital of 15% and is considering a capital investment project, where the estimated cash flows are as follows.

Year	Cash flow $
0 (ie now)	(100,000)
1	60,000
2	80,000
3	40,000
4	30,000

Required

Calculate the NPV of the project, and assess whether it should be undertaken.

Solution

Year	Cash flow $	Discount factor 15%	Present value $
0	(100,000)	1.000	(100,000)
1	60,000	$1/(1.15) = 0.870$	52,200
2	80,000	$1/1.15^2 = 0.756$	60,480
3	40,000	$1/1.15^3 = 0.658$	26,320
4	30,000	$1/1.15^4 = 0.572$	17,160
			NPV = $\overline{56,160}$

(**Note**. The **discount factor for any cash flow 'now' (time 0) is always 1**, whatever the cost of capital.)

The **PV of cash inflows exceeds the PV of cash outflows** by $56,160, which means that the project will earn a DCF yield in excess of 15%. It should therefore be **undertaken**.

6.3 Timing of cash flows: conventions used in discounted cash flow (DCF)

Discounting reduces the value of future cash flows to a present value equivalent and so is clearly concerned with the timing of the cash flows. As a general rule, the following guidelines should be applied.

(a)   A cash outlay to be incurred at the beginning of an investment project ('now') occurs in time 0. The present value of $1 now, in time 0, is $1 regardless of the value of the discount rate r. This is common sense. (Note that it is usual to assume that year 0 is a day, ie the first day of a project. Year 1 is the last day of the first year.)

(b)   A cash flow which occurs during the course of a time period is assumed to occur all at once at the end of the time period (at the end of the year). Receipts of $10,000 during time period 1 are therefore taken to occur at the end of time period 1.

(c)   A cash flow which occurs at the beginning of a time period is taken to occur at the end of the previous time period. Therefore a cash outlay of $5,000 at the beginning of time period 2 is taken to occur at the end of time period 1.

6.4 Discount tables for the PV of $1

The discount factor that we use in discounting is $1/(1+r)^n = (1+r)^{-n}$. Instead of having to calculate this factor every time, we can use **tables**. Discount tables for the present value of $1, for different **integer** values of r and n, are **shown in the Appendix at the back of this Study Text** and **will be provided in the exam**. Use these tables to work out your own solution to the following question.

Question 8.6	NPV

Learning outcome C1(b)

LCH manufactures product X which it sells for $5 per unit. Variable costs of production are currently $3 per unit, and fixed costs 50c per unit. A new machine is available which would cost $90,000 but which could be used to make product X for a variable cost of only $2.50 per unit. Fixed costs, however, would increase by $7,500 per annum as a direct result of purchasing the machine. The machine would have an expected life of 4 years and a resale value after that time of $10,000. Sales of product X are estimated to be 75,000 units per annum. LCH expects to earn at least 12% per annum from its investments.

Required

Choose the appropriate words in the sentence below from those highlighted.

LCH **should purchase/should not purchase** the machine.

Exam alert

Discount tables are provided in the assessment, but they cover only integer values of r. If you need to use a discount rate of, say, 10.5%, you would need to use the discounting formula.

6.5 Annuities

KEY TERM

An **ANNUITY** is a constant cash flow from year to year.

In the previous exercise, the calculations could have been simplified for years 1–3 as follows.

$$
\begin{aligned}
& 30{,}000 \times 0.893 \\
+\;& 30{,}000 \times 0.797 \\
+\;& 30{,}000 \times 0.712 \\
\hline
=\;& 30{,}000 \times 2.402
\end{aligned}
$$

Where there is a **constant cash flow from year to year** (in this case $30,000 per annum for years 1–3) it is quicker to calculate the present value by adding together the discount factors for the individual years. These total factors could be described as 'same cash flow per annum' factors, **'cumulative present value' factors** or **'annuity' factors**. They are **shown in the table for cumulative PV of $1 factors which is shown in the Appendix at the back of this Study Text** (2.402, for example, is in the column for 12% per annum and the row for year 3). If you have not used them before, check that you can understand annuity tables by trying this question.

Question 8.7	Delayed annuity

Learning outcome C1(b)

What is the present value of $2,000 costs incurred each year from years 3–6 when the cost of capital is 5%?

A $6,300
B $6,434
C $6,000
D $4,706

The annuity tables only show the annuity factors for whole number rates. If you wanted to find the annuity factor for a rate such as 6.5% over, say, 3 years, you would have to use the formula given on the formula sheet.

$$
PV = \frac{1}{r}\left[1 - \frac{1}{[1+r]^n}\right] = \frac{1}{0.065}\left[1 - \frac{1}{[1+0.065]^3}\right] = 2.648
$$

Exam alert

As well as incorporating the use of annuity tables, the example which follows includes **working capital requirements**. Take note of how this is dealt with, as such a feature could well be a complicating factor in an OT or ICS question.

Example: NPV including use of annuity tables

Elsie is considering the manufacture of a new product which would involve the use of both a new machine (costing $150,000) and an existing machine, which cost $80,000 two years ago and has a current net book value of $60,000. There is sufficient capacity on this machine, which has so far been under-utilised. Annual sales of the product would be 5,000 units, selling at $32 per unit. Unit costs would be as follows.

	$
Direct labour (4 hours at $2 per hour)	8
Direct materials	7
Fixed costs including depreciation	9
	24

The project would have a 5-year life, after which the new machine would have a net residual value of $10,000. Because direct labour is continually in short supply, labour resources would have to be diverted from other work which currently earns a contribution of $1.50 per direct labour hour. The fixed overhead absorption rate would be $2.25 per hour ($9 per unit) but actual expenditure on fixed overhead would not alter. Working capital requirements would be $10,000 in the first year, rising to $15,000 in the second year and remaining at this level until the end of the project, when it will all be recovered.

Required

Assess whether the project is worthwhile, given that the company's cost of capital is 20%. Ignore taxation.

Solution

The relevant cash flows are as follows.

		$
Year 0	Purchase of new machine	150,000
Years 1–5	Contribution from new product (5,000 units × $(32 – 15))	85,000
	Less contribution forgone (5,000 × (4 × $1.50))	30,000
		55,000

The project requires $10,000 of working capital at the start of year 1 and a further $5,000 at the start of year 2. Increases in working capital reduce the net cash flow for the period to which they relate. When the working capital tied up in the project is 'recovered' at the end of the project, it will provide an extra cash inflow (for example customers will eventually pay up).

All other costs, which are past costs, notional accounting costs or costs which would be incurred anyway without the project, are not relevant to the investment decision.

The NPV is calculated as follows.

Year	Equipment $	Working capital $	Contribution $	Net cash flow $	Discount factor 20%	PV of net cash flow $
0	(150,000)	(10,000)		(160,000)	1.000	(160,000)
1		(5,000)		(5,000)	0.833	(4,165)
1–5			55,000	55,000	2.991	164,505
5	10,000	15,000		25,000	0.402	10,050
					NPV =	10,390

The NPV is positive and the project is worthwhile, although there is not much margin for error. Some risk analysis of the project is recommended.

6.6 Annual cash flows in perpetuity

KEY TERM

A **PERPETUITY** is an annuity that lasts forever.

It can sometimes be useful to calculate the **cumulative present value of $1 per annum** for every year in perpetuity (that is, **forever**).

When the cost of capital is r, the cumulative PV of $1 per annum in perpetuity is **$1/r**. For example, the PV of $1 per annum in perpetuity at a discount rate of 10% would be $1/0.10 = $10.

Similarly, the PV of $1 per annum in perpetuity at a discount rate of 15% would be $1/0.15 = $6.67 and at a discount rate of 20% it would be $1/0.20 = $5.

Question 8.8	Perpetuities

Learning outcome C1(b)

An organisation with a cost of capital of 14% is considering investing in a project costing $500,000 that would yield cash inflows of $100,000 p.a. in perpetuity.

Required

Choose the appropriate words from those highlighted in the sentence below.

The project **should be/should not be** undertaken.

You might well wonder what the use of cash flows is in perpetuity. This surely is an impractical and nonsensical notion? **Cash flows in perpetuity** do actually have **two practical uses**.

(a)   They are used in the calculation of a company's cost of capital.

(b)   They indicate the maximum value of the cumulative present value factor of $1 per annum. For example, we can say that the maximum present value of $1 p.a. for any period of time at a discount rate of 10% is $1/0.1 = $10. The longer the period of time under review, and the more years that are in the project period, the closer the cumulative PV factor of $1 p.a. will get to $10 at a 10% discount rate.

(i)   The PV factor of $1 p.a. at 10% for years 1 to 15 is $7.606.
(ii)   The PV factor of $1 p.a. at 10% for years 1 to 20 is $8.514.
(iii)   The PV factor of $1 p.a. at 10% for years 1 to 30 is $9.427.
(iv)   The PV factor of $1 p.a. at 10% for years 1 to 50 is $9.915.

As you can see, the cumulative PV gets closer to the limit of $10 as time progresses and the limit has almost been reached by year 50, and even by year 30. Knowing what the limit is might help with project analysis when capital projects extend over a long period of time and certainly it can provide a very useful yardstick and 'ready-reckoner' for managers who must carry out DCF evaluations as a regular part of their job.

6.7 Changing discount rates

This is best illustrated using an example.

Example: changing discount rates

G Co expects its cost of capital to increase over the next four years as follows.

Year 1	11%
Year 2	12%
Year 3	14%
Year 4	16%

Calculate the discount factor that should be used for each year.

Solution

The discount factor for year 1 is taken from the tables as normal. Then the discount factor for year 2 is the year 1 discount factor divided by (1 + the discount rate for year 2).

Year		Discount factor
0		1
1	From tables =	0.901
2	0.901/1.12 =	0.804
3	0.804/1.14 =	0.705
4	0.705/1.16 =	0.608

6.8 Net terminal value (NTV)

KEY TERM

NET TERMINAL VALUE (NTV) is the cash surplus remaining at the end of a project after taking account of interest and capital repayments.

The NTV discounted at the cost of capital will give the NPV of the project.

Example: the net terminal value

A project has the following cash flows.

Year	$
0	(5,000)
1	3,000
2	2,600
3	6,200

The project has an NPV of $4,531 at the company's cost of capital of 10% (workings not shown).

Required

Calculate the net terminal value of the project.

Solution

The net terminal value can be determined directly from the NPV, or by calculating the cash surplus at the end of the project.

Assume that the $5,000 for the project is borrowed at an interest rate of 10% and that cash flows from the project are used to repay the loan.

	$
Loan balance outstanding at beginning of project	5,000
Interest in year 1 at 10%	500
Repaid at end of year 1	(3,000)
Balance outstanding at end of year 1	2,500
Interest year 2	250
Repaid year 2	(2,600)
Balance outstanding year 2	150
Interest year 3	15
Repaid year 3	(6,200)
Cash surplus at end of project	6,035

The net terminal value is $6,035.

Check:

NPV = $6,035 × 0.751 (discount factor for year 3) = $4,532

Allowing for the rounding errors caused by three-figure discount tables, this is the correct figure for the NPV.

6.9 Assumptions in the NPV model

(a) Forecasts are assumed to be certain.

(b) Information is assumed to be freely available and costless.

(c) The discount rate is a measure of the opportunity cost of funds which ensures wealth maximisation for **all** individuals and companies.

Exam alert

Make sure you know the strengths and weaknesses of the method.

Question 8.9	Non-standard discount factors

Learning outcome C1(b)

A project has the following forecast cash flows.

Year	$
0	(280,000)
1	149,000
2	128,000
3	84,000
4	70,000

Using two decimal places in all discount factors, what is the net present value of the project at a cost of capital of 16.5%?

A $27,906   B $29,270   C $32,195   D $33,580

6.10 Non-annual compounding

Interest may be compounded **daily**, **weekly**, **monthly** or **quarterly**.

For example, $10,000 invested for 5 years at an interest rate of 2% per month will have a final value of $10,000 × (1 + r)^n = $10,000 × (1 + 0.02)^{60} = $32,810. Notice that n relates to the number of periods (5 years × 12 months) that r is compounded.

6.11 Effective annual rate of interest

The non-annual compounding interest rate can be converted into an effective annual rate of interest. This is also known as the **APR** (annual percentage rate) which lenders such as banks and credit companies are required to disclose.

LEARN

Effective annual rate of interest: $(1 + R) = (1 + r)^n$

Where   R is the effective annual rate

r is the period rate

n is the number of periods in a year

Example: The effective annual rate of interest

Calculate the effective annual rate of interest (to two decimal places) of:

(a)   1.5% per month, compound
(b)   4.5% per quarter, compound
(c)   9% per half year, compound

Solution

(a) $1 + R = (1 + r)^n$

$1 + R = (1 + 0.015)^{12}$

$R = 1.1956 - 1$

$= 0.1956$

$= 19.56\%$

(b) $1 + R = (1 + 0.045)^4$

$R = 1.1925 - 1$

$= 0.1925$

$= 19.25\%$

(c) $1 + R = (1 + 0.09)^2$

$R = 1.1881 - 1$

$= 0.1881$

$= 18.81\%$

Section summary

Discounting starts with the future value (a sum of money receivable or payable at a future date), and converts the future value to a **present value**, which is the cash equivalent now of the future value.

The **discounting formula** to calculate the present value (X) of a future sum of money (V) at the end of n time periods is $X = V/(1+r)^n$.

The **NPV method of project appraisal** is to accept projects with a positive NPV.

An **annuity** is a constant cash flow for a number of years.

A **perpetuity** is a constant cash flow forever.

7 The internal rate of return (IRR) method

Introduction

The internal rate of return (IRR) method of project appraisal is to calculate the exact DCF rate of return which the project is expected to achieve; in other words, the rate at which the NPV is zero.

If the expected rate of return (the IRR yield or DCF yield) exceeds a target rate of return, the project would be worth undertaking (ignoring risk and uncertainty factors).

KEY TERM

The INTERNAL RATE OF RETURN (IRR) is 'The annual percentage return achieved by a project, at which the sum of the discounted cash inflows over the life of the project is equal to the sum of the discounted cash outflows'.   (*CIMA Official Terminology*)

Without a computer or calculator program, an estimate of the IRR is made using either a graph or a hit and miss technique known as the interpolation method.

7.1 Graphical approach

The easiest way to estimate the IRR of a project is to **find the project's NPV at a number of costs of capital** and **sketch a graph of NPV against discount rate**. You can then use the sketch to estimate the **discount rate at which the NPV is equal to zero (the point where the curve cuts the axis)**.

Example: graphical approach

A project might have the following NPVs at the following discount rates.

Discount rate %	NPV $
5	5,300
10	2,900
15	(1,700)
20	(3,200)

This could be sketched on a graph as follows.

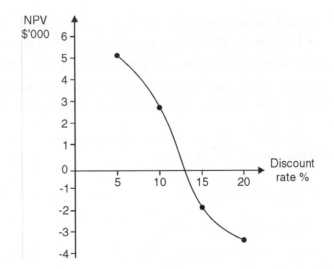

The IRR can be **estimated as 13%**. The NPV should then be **recalculated using this interest rate**. The resulting NPV **should be equal to, or very near, zero. If it is not, additional NPVs at different discount rates should be calculated, the graph resketched and a more accurate IRR determined**.

7.2 Interpolation method

If we were to draw a graph of a 'typical' capital project, with a negative cash flow at the start of the project, and positive net cash flows afterwards up to the end of the project, we could draw a graph of the project's NPV at different costs of capital. It would look like this.

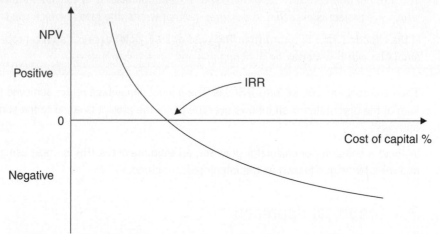

If we determine **a cost of capital where the NPV is slightly positive, and another cost of capital where it is slightly negative**, we can **estimate the IRR – where the NPV is zero – by drawing a straight line between the two points** on the graph that we have calculated.

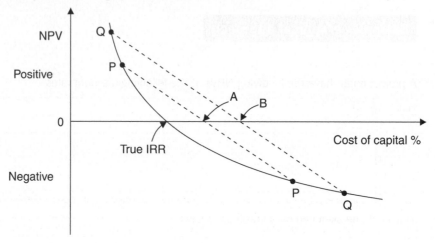

- If we **establish the NPVs at the two points P**, we would estimate the **IRR** to be at **point A**.
- If we **establish the NPVs at the two points Q**, we would estimate the **IRR** to be at **point B**.

The **closer our NPVs are to zero, the closer our estimate will be to the true IRR**.

The **interpolation method assumes that the NPV rises in linear fashion between the two NPVs close to 0**. The real rate of return is therefore assumed to be on a straight line between the two points at which the NPV is calculated.

The **IRR interpolation formula** to apply is:

$$IRR = A + \left[\frac{P}{P-N} \times (B-A) \right]\%$$

where A is the (lower) rate of return

      B is the (higher) rate of return

      P is the NPV at A

      N is the NPV at B

Note that N doesn't have to be negative but if it is then we effectively end up adding, in the denominator.

Example: the IRR method and interpolation

A company is trying to decide whether to buy a machine for $80,000 which will save costs of $20,000 per annum for 5 years and which will have a resale value of $10,000 at the end of year 5.

Required

If it is the company's policy to undertake projects only if they are expected to yield a DCF return of 10% or more, ascertain using the IRR method whether this project should be undertaken.

Solution

The first step is to calculate two net present values, both as close as possible to zero, using rates for the cost of capital which are whole numbers. One NPV should be positive and the other negative.

Choosing rates for the cost of capital which will give an NPV close to zero (ie rates which are close to the actual rate of return) is a hit and miss exercise, and several attempts may be needed to find satisfactory rates. **As a rough guide**, try starting at a **return figure which is about two-thirds or three-quarters of the ARR**.

Annual depreciation would be $(80,000 – 10,000)/5 = $14,000.

The **ARR** would be (20,000 – depreciation of 14,000)/(½ of (80,000 + 10,000)) = 6,000/45,000 = 13.3%.

Two-thirds of this is 8.9% and so we can start by trying 9%.

Try 9%

Year	Cash flow $	PV factor 9%	PV of cash flow $
0	(80,000)	1.000	(80,000)
1–5	20,000	3.890	77,800
5	10,000	0.650	6,500
		NPV =	4,300

This is **fairly close to zero**. It is also **positive**, which means that the **real rate of return** is **more than 9%**. We can use 9% as one of our two NPVs close to zero, although for greater accuracy we should try 10% or even 11% to find an NPV even closer to zero if we can. As a guess, it might be worth trying 12% next, to see what the NPV is.

Try 12%

Year	Cash flow $	PV factor 12%	PV of cash flow $
0	(80,000)	1.000	(80,000)
1–5	20,000	3.605	72,100
5	10,000	0.567	5,670
		NPV =	(2,230)

This is **fairly close to zero** and **negative**. The **real rate of return** is therefore **greater than 9%** (positive NPV of $4,300) but **less than 12%** (negative NPV of $2,230).

Note. If the first NPV is positive, choose a higher rate for the next calculation to get a negative NPV. If the first NPV is negative, choose a lower rate for the next calculation.

So, IRR $= 9 + \left[\dfrac{4,300}{4,300 + 2,230} \times (12 - 9) \right] \% = 10.98\%$, say 11%

If it is company policy to undertake investments which are expected to yield 10% or more, this project would be undertaken.

 Question 8.10   IRR

Learning outcome C1(b)

The project shown below should be accepted if the company requires a minimum return of 17%. True or false?

Time		$
0	Investment	(4,000)
1	Receipts	1,200
2	Receipts	1,410
3	Receipts	1,875
4	Receipts	1,150

7.3 The IRR of an annuity

Suppose an investment now of $100,000 will produce inflows of $30,000 each year over the next 4 years. We know that the IRR is the discount rate which produces an NPV of zero. **At the IRR (rate r) the PV of inflows must therefore equal the PV of outflows.**

∴ $100,000 = PV of $30,000 for years 1 to 4 at rate r

∴ $100,000 = (cumulative PV factor for years 1 to 4 at rate r) × $30,000

∴ $100,000/$30,000 = cumulative PV factor for years 1 to 4 at rate r

∴ 3.333 = cumulative PV factor for years 1 to 4 at rate r

We can now **look in cumulative PV tables along the line for year 4 to find a discount factor which corresponds to 3.333. The corresponding rate is the IRR**. The nearest figure is 3.312 and so the IRR of the project is approximately 8%.

7.4 The IRR of a perpetuity

Suppose an investment of $25,000 will produce annual cash flows in perpetuity of $2,000. Using the **same reasoning** as in Section 2.3:

$25,000 = PV of $2,000 in perpetuity

∴ $25,000 = $2,000/r (where r = IRR)

∴ $r = \dfrac{\$2,000}{\$25,000} = 0.08 = 8\%$

 Question 8.11   NPV and IRR

Learning outcome C1(b)

The VWXYZ Company produces a variety of high-quality garden furniture and associated items, mostly in wood and wrought iron.

There is potential to expand the business. The directors have identified three main options for a four-year plan.

(a)   Expand its flourishing retail outlet to include all products

(b)   Branch out into mail order

(c)   Produce greenhouses and conservatories

These options would require initial expenditure of (a) $75,000, (b) $120,000 or (c) $200,000. The best information on year-end cash flows is as follows.

	Year 1 $'000	Year 2 $'000	Year 3 $'000	Year 4 $'000
(a)	40	50	50	50
(b)	50	60	80	100
(c)	50	100	150	150

Required

(a)   Using the data on expansion plans, evaluate the three investment options using the net present value (NPV) technique, assuming the cost of capital to be 10%, and recommend, with reasons, one option.

(b)   Find the approximate internal rate of return (IRR) of your choice in (a) above.

Section summary

The **IRR method of project appraisal** is to accept projects which have an IRR (the rate at which the NPV is zero) that exceeds a target rate of return. The IRR can be estimated either from a graph or using interpolation.

The **IRR interpolation formula** to apply is:

$$IRR = A + \left[\frac{P}{P-N} \times (B-A) \right]\%$$

where   A is the (lower) rate of return
         B is the (higher) rate of return
         P is the NPV at A
         N is the NPV at B

8   NPV and IRR compared

Introduction

Unfortunately there are several disadvantages as well as advantages to the IRR method. Managers should always bear these in mind.

8.1 Advantages of IRR method

(a)   The main advantage is that the information it provides is more **easily understood** by managers, especially non-financial managers. 'The project will be expected to have an initial capital outlay of $100,000, and to earn a yield of 25%. This is in excess of the target yield of 15% for investments' is easier to understand than 'The project will cost $100,000 and have an NPV of $30,000 when discounted at the minimum required rate of 15%'.

(b)   A **discount rate does not have to be specified** before the IRR can be calculated. A hurdle discount rate is simply required to which the IRR can be compared.

8.2 Disadvantages of IRR method

(a)   If managers were given information about both **ROCE (or ROI) and IRR**, it might be easy to get their relative **meaning and significance mixed up**.

(b)   It **ignores the relative size of investments**. Both projects below have an IRR of 18%.

	Project A $	Project B $
Cost, year 0	350,000	35,000
Annual savings, years 1–6	100,000	10,000

Clearly, project A is bigger (ten times as big) and so more 'profitable', but if the only information on which the projects were judged were to be their IRR of 18%, project B would be made to seem just as beneficial as project A, which is not the case.

(c)   **When discount rates are expected to differ over the life of the project, such variations can be incorporated easily into NPV calculations, but not into IRR calculations**, and an **adjustment** can be made to the **discount rate** used in NPV calculations to include an allowance for project **risk**.

(d)   There are **problems** with using the IRR **when the project has non-conventional cash flows** (see Section 8.3) or when **deciding between mutually exclusive projects** (see Section 8.4).

'In spite of all the efforts to convince managers that the net present value (NPV) is the "correct" method of investment appraisal to use, recent research shows that they continue to prefer the internal rate of return (IRR). And, although a number of modified versions of the IRR have been developed, they too have been condemned by some academics even though such modifications are an improvement on the conventional IRR. No single investment appraisal technique will give the right answer in all investment situations, however, and the NPV is no exception. This is reflected again in recent research which shows that companies now use a greater number of financial appraisal techniques than in the past, but with no consensus on the actual combination. This increase in usage has been attributed to the increase in computer software that is now readily available to perform the basic calculations of the various financial appraisal techniques such as payback (PB), accounting rate of return (ARR), IRR, and NPV.'

Lefley and Morgan, 'The NPV profile – a creative way of looking at the NPV', *Management Accounting*,
June 1999

8.3 Non-conventional cash flows

The projects we have considered so far have had **conventional cash flows (an initial cash outflow followed by a series of inflows)** and in such circumstances the NPV and IRR methods give the same accept or reject decision. When flows vary from this they are termed non-conventional. The following project has non-conventional cash flows.

Year	Project X
	$'000
0	(1,900)
1	4,590
2	(2,735)

Project X above has two IRRs as shown by the diagram which follows.

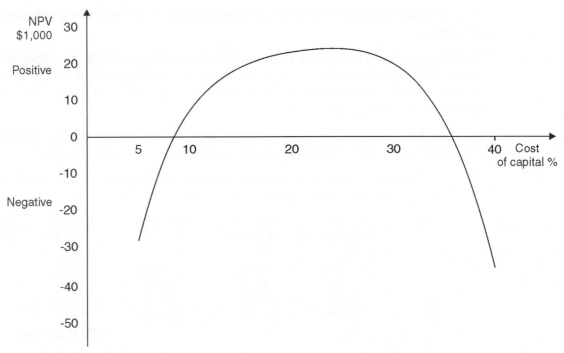

Suppose that the required rate of return on project X is 10% but that the IRR of 7% is used to decide whether to accept or reject the project. The project would be rejected since it appears that it can only yield 7%. The diagram shows, however, that **between rates of 7% and 35% the project should be accepted**. Using the IRR of 35% would produce the correct decision to accept the project. **Lack of knowledge of multiple IRRs** could therefore lead to serious **errors in the decision** of whether to accept or reject a project.

In general, if the sign of the net cash flow changes in successive periods (inflow to outflow or vice versa), it is possible for the calculations to produce **as many IRRs as there are sign changes**.

The use of the **IRR** is therefore **not recommended** in circumstances in which there are **non-conventional cash flow patterns** (unless the decision maker is aware of the existence of multiple IRRs). The NPV method, on the other hand, gives clear, unambiguous results whatever the cash flow pattern.

8.4 Mutually exclusive projects

The IRR and NPV methods give conflicting rankings as to which project should be given priority. Let us suppose that a company with a cost of capital of 16% is considering two mutually exclusive options, Option A and Option B. The cash flows for each are as follows.

Year		Option A $	Option B $
0	Capital outlay	(10,200)	(35,250)
1	Net cash inflow	6,000	18,000
2	Net cash inflow	5,000	15,000
3	Net cash inflow	3,000	15,000

The NPV of each project is calculated below.

Year	Discount factor	Option A Cash flow $	Present value $	Option B Cash flow $	Present value $
0	1.000	(10,200)	(10,200)	(35,250)	(35,250)
1	0.862	6,000	5,172	18,000	15,516
2	0.743	5,000	3,715	15,000	11,145
3	0.641	3,000	1,923	15,000	9,615
		NPV =	+ 610	NPV =	+ 1,026

The **DCF yield (IRR) of Option A is 20%, while the yield of Option B is only 18%** (workings not shown).

On a **comparison of NPVs, Option B would be preferred**, but on a **comparison of IRRs, Option A would be preferred**.

The preference should go to Option B. This is because the **differences in the cash flows** between the two options, when discounted at the cost of capital of 16%, show that the present value of the incremental benefits from **O**ption B compared with **O**ption A exceeds the PV of the incremental costs. This can be restated in the following ways.

(a)   The **NPV of the differential cash flows (Option B cash flows minus Option A cash flows) is positive**, and so it is worth spending the extra capital to get the extra benefits.

(b)   The **IRR of the differential cash flows exceeds the cost of capital 16%**, and so it is worth spending the extra capital to get the extra benefits.

Year	Option A cash flow $	Option B cash flow $	Difference $	Discount factor 16%	Present value of difference $
0	(10,200)	(35,250)	(25,050)	1.000	(25,050)
1	6,000	18,000	12,000	0.862	10,344
2	5,000	15,000	10,000	0.743	7,430
3	3,000	15,000	12,000	0.641	7,692
				NPV of difference	416

The **NPV of the difference**, not surprisingly, **is also the difference between the NPV of Option A ($610) and the NPV of Option B ($1,026).**

The **IRR of the differential cash flows** (see working below) **is approximately 17%.**

The NPV at 16% is $416. Applying a discount rate of 20%:

$	20%	$	
−25,050	1.000	−25,050	
12,000	0.833	9,996	
10,000	0.694	6,940	
12,000	0.579	6,948	−1,166

IRR = 16% + [(416/416 + 1166) × (20% − 16%)] = 17.05%.

It must be stressed that the investment represented by (B − A) is a notional one, but the inflows from this notional project would be enjoyed by the company if Option B were accepted and would be lost if Option A were accepted.

Mutually exclusive investments do not have to be considered over equal time periods. For example, suppose an organisation has two investment options, one lasting two years and one lasting four years. The two options can be compared and the one with the highest NPV chosen. If, however, the investment is an asset which is required for four years, the organisation will have to reinvest if it chooses the two-year option. In such circumstances the investment options should be compared over a similar period of time. We will be looking at how to do this in Chapter 9.

8.5 Reinvestment assumption

An assumption underlying the **NPV method** is that any net cash **inflows generated** during the life of the project will be **reinvested** elsewhere **at the cost of capital** (that is, the discount rate). The **IRR method**, on the other hand, **assumes** these **cash flows** can be **reinvested** elsewhere to earn a **return** equal to the **IRR** of the original project.

In the example in Section 8.4, the **NPV method** assumes that the cash inflows of $6,000, $5,000 and $3,000 for Option A will be reinvested at the cost of capital of **16%** whereas the **IRR** method assumes

they will be reinvested at **20%**. If the IRR is considerably higher than the cost of capital, this is an unlikely assumption. In theory, a firm will have accepted all projects which provide a return in excess of the cost of capital and any other funds which become available can only be reinvested at the cost of capital. (This is the assumption implied in the NPV rule.) If the assumption is not valid, the IRR method overestimates the real return.

8.6 Modified internal rate of return (MIRR)

The modified internal rate of return (MIRR) overcomes the problem of the **reinvestment assumption** and the fact that **changes in the cost of capital over the life of the project** cannot be incorporated in the IRR method.

Consider a project requiring an initial investment of $24,500, with cash inflows of $15,000 in years 1 and 2 and cash inflows of $3,000 in years 3 and 4. The cost of capital is 10%.

If we calculate the IRR:

Year	Cash flow $	Discount factor 10%	Present value $	Discount factor 25%	Present value $
0	(24,500)	1.000	(24,500)	1.000	(24,500)
1	15,000	0.909	13,635	0.800	12,000
2	15,000	0.826	12,390	0.640	9,600
3	3,000	0.751	2,253	0.512	1,536
4	3,000	0.683	2,049	0.410	1,230
			5,827		(134)

$$IRR = 10\% + \left[\frac{5,827}{5,827 + 134} \times (25\% - 10\%) \right] = 24.7\%$$

Remember that the MIRR is calculated on the basis of **investing the inflows** at the **cost of capital**.

The table below shows the **values of the inflows if they were immediately reinvested at 10%**. For example, the $15,000 received at the end of year 1 could be reinvested for 3 years at 10% p.a. (multiply by $1.1 \times 1.1 \times 1.1 = 1.331$).

Year	Cash inflows $	Interest rate multiplier	Amount when reinvested $
1	15,000	1.331	19,965
2	15,000	1.21	18,150
3	3,000	1.1	3,300
4	3,000	1.0	3,000
			44,415

The total cash outflow in year 0 ($24,500) is compared with the possible inflow at year 4, and the resulting figure of 24,500/44,415 = 0.552 is the discount factor in year 4. By looking along the year 4 row in present value tables you will see that this gives a return of 16%. This means that the $44,415 received in year 4 is equivalent to $24,500 in year 0 if the discount rate is 16%.

Alternatively, instead of using discount tables, we can calculate the MIRR as follows.

$$\text{Total return} = \frac{44,415}{24,500} = 1.813$$

$$MIRR = \sqrt[4]{1.813} - 1$$

$$= 1.16 - 1$$

$$= 16\%$$

In theory the MIRR of 16% will be a **better measure** than the IRR of 24.7%.

8.6.1 Advantages of MIRR

MIRR has the advantage of IRR that it assumes the **reinvestment rate** is the **company's cost of capital**. IRR assumes that the reinvestment rate is the IRR itself, which is usually untrue.

In many cases where there is conflict between the NPV and IRR methods, the MIRR will give the same indication as NPV, which is the **correct theoretical method**. This helps when explaining the appraisal of a project to managers, who often find the concept of rate of return easier to understand than that of net present value.

8.6.2 Disadvantages of MIRR

However, MIRR, like all rate of return methods, suffers from the problem that it may lead an investor to reject a project which has a **lower rate of return** but, because of its size, generates a **larger increase in wealth**.

In the same way, a **high-return** project with a **short life** may be preferred over a **lower-return** project with a longer life.

Section summary

When compared with the NPV method, the **IRR method** has a number of **disadvantages**.

- It ignores the relative size of investments.

- There are problems with its use when a project has non-conventional cash flows or when deciding between mutually exclusive projects.

- Discount rates which differ over the life of a project cannot be incorporated into IRR calculations.

The MIRR is calculated on the basis of investing the inflows at the cost of capital.

---

9 Discounted payback

Introduction

Payback can be combined with DCF and a **discounted payback period** calculated.

KEY TERM

The DISCOUNTED PAYBACK PERIOD (DPP) is the time it will take before a project's cumulative NPV turns from being negative to being positive.

For example, if we have a cost of capital of 10% and a project with the cash flows shown below, we can calculate a discounted payback period.

Year	Cash flow $	Discount factor 10%	Present value $	Cumulative NPV $
0	(100,000)	1.000	(100,000)	(100,000)
1	30,000	0.909	27,270	(72,730)
2	50,000	0.826	41,300	(31,430)
3	40,000	0.751	30,040	(1,390)
4	30,000	0.683	20,490	19,100
5	20,000	0.621	12,420	31,520
		NPV =	31,520	

The DPP is early in year 4.

A company can set a target DPP, and choose not to undertake any projects with a DPP in excess of a certain number of years, say five years.

9.1 Advantages and disadvantages of DPP

The approach has **all the perceived advantages of the payback period** method of investment appraisal: it is easy to understand and calculate, and it provides a focus on liquidity where this is relevant. In addition, however, it **also takes into account the time value of money**. It therefore bridges the gap between the theoretically superior NPV method and the regular payback period method.

However, it does differ from NPV in that the discount rate used is the **unadjusted cost of capital**, whereas NPV often uses an **adjusted rate to reflect project risk and uncertainty**.

Because the DPP approach takes the time value of money into consideration, it **produces a longer payback period** than the non-discounted payback approach, and **takes into account more of the project's cash flows**.

Another advantage it has over traditional payback is that it has a **clear accept or reject criterion**. Using payback, acceptance of a project depends on an arbitrarily determined cut-off time. Using DPP, a project is acceptable if it pays back within its lifetime.

DPP still shares one disadvantage with the payback period method: **cash flows which occur after the payback period are ignored** (although, as the DPP is longer than the payback period, fewer of these are ignored).

9.2 Discounted payback index (DPBI) or profitability index

This is a measure of the number of times a project recovers the initial funds invested, something that is particularly important if funds are scarce.

$$\text{DPBI} = \frac{\text{Present value of net cash inflows}}{\text{Initial cash outlay}}$$

The higher the figure, the greater the returns. A DPBI less than 1 indicates that the present value of the net cash inflows is less than the initial cash outlay.

Alternatively the index might be shown as:

$$\frac{\text{PV of project}}{\text{Initial outlay}}$$

This form of the index is known as the **profitability index** and shows the NPV per $1 invested in a project. As we will see in a later chapter, it is particularly useful if investment funds are limited and choices have to be made between different investment options.

9.3 NPV profile

It has been suggested that instead of just relying on the NPV as an absolute figure, a **wider profile** of the capital investment should be provided. This profile should include not only the **NPV**, but also the **DPB**, **DPBI** and a **marginal growth rate (MGR)**. (The MGR is a measure of the project's rate of net profitability.) This enables management to take into consideration any liquidity restrictions that an organisation may have and allows them to be more flexible in their general approach to capital investment appraisal, as they can place different emphasis on different parts of the profile to suit particular situations.

Section summary

The **discounted payback period (DPP)** is the time it will take before a project's cumulative NPV turns from being negative to being positive.

$$\text{Discounted payback index} = \frac{\text{Present value of net cash inflows}}{\text{Initial cash outlay}}$$

10 DCF: additional points

Introduction

One of the principal advantages of the DCF appraisal method is that it takes account of the **time value of money**.

10.1 The time value of money

DCF is a project appraisal technique that is based on the concept of the time value of money, that $1 earned or spent sooner is worth more than $1 earned or spent later. Various reasons could be suggested as to **why a present $1 is worth more than a future $1**.

(a) **Uncertainty.** The business world is full of risk and uncertainty and, although there might be the promise of money to come in the future, it can never be certain that the money will be received until it has actually been paid. This is an important argument, and risk and uncertainty must always be considered in investment appraisal. But this argument does not explain why the discounted cash flow technique should be used to reflect the time value of money.

(b) **Inflation.** Because of inflation, it is common sense that $1 now is worth more than $1 in the future. It is important, however, that the problem of inflation should not be confused with the meaning of DCF, and the following points should be noted.

    (i) If there were no inflation at all, discounted cash flow techniques would still be used for investment appraisal.

    (ii) Inflation, for the moment, has been completely ignored.

    (iii) It is obviously necessary to allow for inflation.

(c) **An individual attaches more weight to current pleasures than to future ones, and would rather have $1 to spend now than $1 in a year's time**. Individuals have the choice of consuming or investing their wealth and so the return from projects must be sufficient to persuade individuals to prefer to invest now. Discounting is a measure of this time preference.

(d) Money is invested now to make profits (more money or wealth) in the future. **Discounted cash flow techniques** can therefore be used to **measure** either of two things.

    (i) **What alternative uses of the money would earn (NPV method)** (assuming that money can be invested elsewhere at the cost of capital)

    (ii) **What the money is expected to earn (IRR method)**

10.2 Advantages of DCF methods of appraisal

Taking account of the time value of money (by discounting) is one of the principal advantages of the DCF appraisal method. Other advantages include:

(a) The method uses all cash flows relating to the project.

(b)   It allows for the timing of the cash flows.

(c)   There are universally accepted methods of calculating the NPV and IRR.

10.3 A comparison of the ARR and NPV methods

Managers are often judged on the return on investment (ROI) of their division or business unit. They will only want to **invest in projects that increase divisional ROI** but on occasion such a strategy **may not correspond** with the **decision** that would be arrived at if **NPV** were used to appraise the investment.

For example, suppose that Division M is considering an investment of $200,000, which will provide a net cash inflow (before depreciation) of $78,000 each year for the 4 years of its life. It is group policy that investments must show a minimum return of 15%.

As the working below shows, using NBV at the start of each year and depreciating on a straight-line basis to a nil residual value, in year 1 the ROI would be below the target rate of return of 15%. If management were to take a **short-term view** of the situation, the **investment would be rejected if** using the **ROI** measure. This is despite the fact that the investment's **NPV is positive** and that in **years 2 to 4** the **ROI** is **greater** than the **target** rate of return.

	Years			
	1	*2*	*3*	*4*
	$	$	$	$
NBV of investment at start of year	200,000	150,000	100,000	50,000
Cash flow (before depreciation)	78,000	78,000	78,000	78,000
Less depreciation	(50,000)	(50,000)	(50,000)	(50,000)
Net profit	28,000	28,000	28,000	28,000
ROI	14.00%	18.67%	28.00%	56.00%

NPV = –$200,000 + ($78,000 × 2.855) = $22,690.

10.4 Future cash flows: relevant costs

KEY POINT

The **cash flows to be considered** in investment appraisal are those which arise as a consequence of the investment decision under evaluation. When comparing two decision options, they are the expected future cash flows that differ between the alternatives.

It therefore follows that any costs incurred **in the past**, or any **committed costs** which will be **incurred regardless** of whether or not an investment is undertaken, are **not relevant cash flows**. They have occurred, or will occur, whatever investment decision is taken.

To a management accountant, it might be apparent that the annual profits from a project can be calculated as the **incremental contribution earned minus any incremental fixed costs** which are cash items of expenditure (ie ignoring depreciation and so on).

There are, however, other cash flows to consider. These might include the following.

(a)   The extra **taxation** that will be payable on extra profits, or the reductions in tax arising from capital allowances or operating losses in any year. We cover this topic later in this chapter.

(b)   The **residual value or disposal value of equipment at the end of its life, or its disposal cost**.

(c)   **Working capital**. If a company invests $20,000 in working capital and earns cash profits of $50,000, the net cash receipts will be $30,000. Working capital will be released again at the end of a project's life, and so there will be a cash inflow arising out of the eventual realisation into cash of the project's inventory and receivables in the final year of the project.

Finance-related cash flows, on the other hand, are normally **excluded** from DCF project appraisal exercises because the discounting process takes account of the time value of money; that is, the opportunity cost of investing the money in the project. The cash inflow from, say, a loan could be

included but then the cash outflows of the interest payments and the loan repayment would also have to be included. These flows would all be discounted at the cost of capital (which we assume is the same as the cost of the loan) and they would reduce to a zero NPV. They would therefore have had no **effect on the NPV** and are thus deemed **irrelevant** to the appraisal.

Finance-related cash flows are **only relevant if they incur a different rate of interest from that which is being used as the discount rate**. For example, a company may be offered a loan at a preferential rate below that which it uses for its discount rate and so the inclusion and discounting of the loan's cash flows produces a differential NPV.

10.5 The discount rate

Throughout our study of DCF techniques we have been using the same discount rate across all years of the project under consideration, on the assumption that the cost of capital will remain the same over the life of the project. There are a range of factors that influence the cost of capital, however, including inflation and interest rates, and these can fluctuate widely over fairly short periods of time. An organisation may therefore wish to **use different discount rates at different points over the life of a project** to reflect this. This is **possible if NPV and discounted payback methods of appraisal are being used**, but IRR and ARR methods are based on a single rate.

Another problem is **deciding on the correct rate in the first place**. This is difficult enough in year 1 of a project's life, but even more problematic five years later, say, because of economic changes and so on.

Section summary

One of the principal advantages of the DCF appraisal method is that it takes account of the **time value of money**.

11   Allowing for inflation

Introduction

As the **inflation rate increases so will the minimum return required by an investor**. For example, you might be happy with a return of 5% in an inflation-free world, but if inflation was running at 15% you would expect a considerably greater yield.

Example: inflation (1)

An organisation is considering investing in a project with the following cash flows.

Time	Actual cash flows
	$
0	(15,000)
1	9,000
2	8,000
3	7,000

The organisation requires a minimum return of 20% under the present and anticipated conditions. Inflation is currently running at 10% a year, and this rate of inflation is expected to continue indefinitely. Should the organisation go ahead with the project?

Let us first look at the organisation's required rate of return. Suppose that it invested $1,000 for one year on 1 January, then on 31 December it would require a minimum return of $200. With the initial investment of $1,000, the total value of the investment by 31 December must therefore increase to

$1,200. During the course of the year the purchasing value of the dollar would fall due to inflation. We can restate the **amount received on 31 December in terms of the purchasing power of the dollar at 1 January** as follows.

Amount received on 31 December in terms of the value of the dollar at 1 January $= \dfrac{\$1,200}{(1.10)^1} = \$1,091$

In terms of the value of the dollar at 1 January, the organisation would make a profit of $91 which represents a rate of return of 9.1% in **'today's money' terms**. This is known as the **real rate of return**. The required rate of 20% is a **money rate of return** (sometimes called a **nominal rate of return**).

(a)   The **money rate** measures the **return in terms of the dollar**, which is, of course, **falling in value**.

(b)   The **real rate** measures the return in **constant price level** terms.

The two rates of return and the inflation rate are linked by an equation.

LEARN

$(1 + \text{money rate}) = (1 + \text{real rate}) \times (1 + \text{inflation rate})$

where all the rates are expressed as proportions.

In our example, $(1 + 0.20) = (1 + 0.091) \times (1 + 0.10) = 1.20$

We must decide **which rate** to use for discounting, the **money rate** or the **real rate**. The rule is as follows.

(a)   If the cash flows are expressed in terms of the **actual number of dollars** that will be received or paid on the various future dates, we **use the money rate for discounting**. (Money cash flows should be discounted at a money discount rate.)

(b)   If the cash flows are expressed in terms of the **value of the dollar at time 0 (that is, in constant price level terms), we use the real rate.** (Real cash flows should be discounted at a real discount rate.)

The **cash flows** given in the previous example are expressed **in terms of the actual number of dollars** that will be received or paid at the relevant dates. We should, therefore, **discount** them using the **money rate of return**.

Time	Cash flow $	Discount factor 20%	PV $
0	(15,000)	1.000	(15,000)
1	9,000	0.833	7,497
2	8,000	0.694	5,552
3	7,000	0.579	4,053
			2,102

The project has a positive NPV of $2,102.

The future **cash flows** can be **re-expressed** in terms of the **value of the dollar at time 0** as follows, given inflation at 10% a year.

Time	Actual cash flow $	Cash flow at time 0 price level		$
0	(15,000)			(15,000)
1	9,000	$9,000 \times \dfrac{1}{1.10}$	=	8,182
2	8,000	$8,000 \times \dfrac{1}{(1.10)^2}$	=	6,612
3	7,000	$7,000 \times \dfrac{1}{(1.10)^3}$	=	5,259

The cash flows expressed in terms of the value of the dollar at time 0 can now be **discounted using the real rate** of 9.1%.

Time	Cash flow $	Discount factor 9.1%	PV $
0	(15,000)	1.00	(15,000)
1	8,182	$\dfrac{1}{1.091}$	7,500
2	6,612	$\dfrac{1}{(1.091)^2}$	5,555
3	5,259	$\dfrac{1}{(1.091)^3}$	4,050
		NPV	2,105

The NPV is the same as before (and the present value of the cash flow in each year is the same as before) apart from rounding errors with a net total of $3.

11.1 The advantages and misuses of real values and a real rate of return

Although it is recommended that **companies should discount money values at the money cost of capital**, there are some advantages of using real values discounted at a real cost of capital.

(a)   **When all costs and benefits rise at the same rate of price inflation, real values are the same as current day values**, so that no further adjustments need be made to cash flows before discounting. In contrast, when money values are discounted at the money cost of capital, the prices in future years must be calculated before discounting can begin.

(b)   The Government or nationalised industries might prefer to set a real return as a target for investments, as being more suitable to their particular situation than a commercial money rate of return.

11.2 Costs and benefits which inflate at different rates

Not all costs and benefits will rise in line with the general level of inflation. In such cases, we can **apply the money rate** to inflated values to determine a project's NPV.

Example: inflation (2)

RR is considering a project which would cost $5,000 now. The annual benefits, for 4 years, would be a fixed income (ie not affected by inflation) of $2,500 a year, plus other savings of $500 a year in year 1, rising by 5% each year because of inflation. Running costs will be $1,000 in the first year, but would increase at 10% each year because of inflating labour costs. The general rate of inflation is expected to be 7½% and the organisation's required money rate of return is 16%. Is the project worthwhile? Ignore taxation.

Solution

The cash flows at inflated values are as follows.

Year	Fixed income $	Other savings $	Running costs $	Net cash flow $
1	2,500	500	1,000	2,000
2	2,500	525	1,100	1,925
3	2,500	551	1,210	1,841
4	2,500	579	1,331	1,748

The NPV of the project is as follows.

Year	Cash flow $	Discount factor 16%	PV $
0	(5,000)	1.000	(5,000)
1	2,000	0.862	1,724
2	1,925	0.743	1,430
3	1,841	0.641	1,180
4	1,748	0.552	965
			+ 299

The NPV is positive and the project would seem therefore to be worthwhile.

Question 8.12	Investment appraisal and inflation

Learning outcome C1(b)

An investment requires an immediate cash outflow of $120,000. It will have zero residual value at the end of four years. The annual cost inflow will be $40,000. The cost of capital is 10% and the annual inflation rate is 3%.

What is the maximum monetary cost of capital for this project to remain viable (to the nearest %)?

A   16%   C   10%

B   13%   D   7%

11.3 Deflation

Deflation may have an effect on business decision making. Businesses may be put off making long-term decisions such as the purchase of assets because they may fall in value. It may also be difficult for businesses to reduce costs, for example employee wages, during a period of deflation. Sales, however, may fall in the short term as customers wait for prices to fall.

Exam skills

A discursive question could ask you to explain what a money rate is or what a real rate is and how they would be used to calculate an NPV.

Section summary

Inflation is a feature of all economies, and it must be accommodated in investment appraisal.

(1 + money rate) = (1 + real rate) × (1 + inflation rate)

where all the rates are expressed as proportions.

Money cash flows should be discounted at a money discount rate.

Real cash flows (ie adjusted for inflation) should be discounted at a real discount rate.

12 Allowing for taxation

Introduction

Taxation is a major practical consideration for businesses. It is vital to take it into account in making decisions.

Payments of tax, or reductions in the capital of tax that has to be paid, are **relevant cash flows** and so the amounts connected with a project ought to be included in the DCF appraisal.

12.1 Introduction to the calculation of taxation in capital projects

The calculation of taxation in relation to capital projects may seem daunting at first. However, there is a method using simple steps which you could follow. This breaks the calculation down into manageable elements.

(a)   Calculate the **total** cost of any new asset.

(b)   Calculate WDA for each year and multiply by the tax rate to give the tax saving.

(c)   Half of tax saving is a benefit in the year in question, half in the following year.

(d)   Calculate a balancing allowance or charge on the sale of the asset

      (i)   If sales price > reducing balance ⇒ balancing charge (increases taxable profit)

      (ii)   If sales price < reducing balance ⇒ balancing allowance (reduces taxable profit)

(e)   Effect of the balancing charge/allowance (which is calculated as amount × tax rate) is felt half in the year in which the asset is sold and half in the following year.

(f)   Include in the appraisal: tax on WDAs and balancing allowance/charge, net cash inflows due to project (ie taxable profits) and tax on these net cash inflows.

12.2 Corporation tax

Under the UK system, corporation tax is **payable** by large companies **quarterly**.

•   In the **seventh and tenth months** of the year in which the profit is earned
•   In the **first and fourth months** of the following year

This simply means that **half the tax is payable in the year in which the profits are earned** and **half in the following year**.

Example: payment of corporation tax

If a project increases taxable profits by $10,000 in year 2, there will be tax payments of $10,000 × 30% × 50% = $1,500 in both year 2 and in year 3 (assuming a tax rate of 30%). It is these tax payments (that are a direct result of the project) that need to be included in a DCF analysis.

KEY POINT

Note that **net cash flows from a project** should be considered as the **taxable profits** arising from the project (unless an indication is given to the contrary).

12.3 Capital allowances/writing down allowances (WDAs)

Remember that depreciation is a way of charging the cost of plant and machinery against financial accounting profits over a number of periods (thereby reducing profits). Similarly, writing down allowances (WDAs) or capital allowances (sometimes called tax allowable depreciation) are a way of charging the cost of plant and machinery against taxable profits over a number of periods, thereby **reducing taxable profits and hence the tax payable**.

The **reduction in tax payable** (to be included in the DCF analysis) = **amount of WDA × tax rate**.

As half the tax on profit is paid in the year to which the profits relate, and half in the following year, the **benefit of the WDA** is also felt **half in the year to which it relates** and **half in the following year**.

The rate at which the allowance is given will always be provided in the question, although it is more than likely to be 25% on a reducing balance basis.

Example: WDAs

Suppose an organisation purchases plant costing $80,000. The rate of corporation tax is 30% and WDAs are given on a 25% reducing balance basis. Here are the WDAs and reductions in tax payable for years 1 to 4.

| | Reducing balance | Tax saved | Benefit received | | | |
| | | | Yr 1 | Yr 2 | Yr 3 | Yr 4 |
	$	$	$	$	$	$
Purchase price	80,000					
Yr 1 WDA (25%)	(20,000)	6,000	3,000	3,000		
Value at start year 2	60,000					
Yr 2 WDA (25%)	(15,000)	4,500		2,250	2,250	
Value at start year 3	45,000					
Yr 3 WDA (25%)	(11,250)	3,375			1,687	1,688
Value at start year 4	33,750					
Yr 4 WDA (25%)	(8,438)	2,531				1,266
Value at start year 5	25,312					

Points to note

(a)   The tax saved is 30% of the WDA.
(b)   Half of the tax saved is a benefit in the year in question, half in the following year.

Exam alert

Note that 'tax depreciation and the resulting cash flows' means the WDAs, the tax saved and the benefits received, as shown in the example above.

You should always make the following assumptions unless told otherwise.

- The organisation in question generates enough profit from other projects to absorb any tax benefits in the year to which they relate.

- Assume the organisation has elected to use **'short life' asset treatment**. This means that the asset is kept separate from the general pool of the organisation's assets provided it is sold within five years of purchase.

You also need to be sure that you **start off with the correct balance** on which to calculate the capital allowances. For example, in addition to the original capital costs of a machine, it may be possible to claim capital allowances on the costs of installation, such as the labour and overhead costs of removing an old machine, levelling the area for the new machine and/or altering part of a building to accommodate the new machine. Remember to **state** your **assumptions** concerning this type of item.

KEY POINT

Assumptions about capital allowances could be simplified in an exam question. For example, you might be told that capital allowances can be claimed at the rate of 25% of cost on a straight-line basis (that is, over four years), or a question might refer to 'tax allowable depreciation', so that the capital allowances equal the depreciation charge.

12.4 Balancing allowances and balancing charges

Suppose an organisation sells an item of plant in year 3 at a price which differs from the reducing balance amount **before year 3 WDAs** are included.

(a)   If the **selling price is greater than the reducing balance amount**, the difference between the two is treated as a **taxable profit (balancing charge)**.

(b)   If the **selling price is less than the reducing balance amount**, the difference between the two is treated as a **reduction in tax payable (balancing allowance)**.

'Short-life' asset treatment means any balancing allowance/charge should be dealt with in the year of sale.

Example: balancing allowances/charges

If, in the example above, the plant is sold during year 4 for $20,000, there will be a balancing allowance of $(33,750 − 20,000) = $13,750, being the difference between the reducing balance amount at the end of year 3 / beginning of year 4 and the selling price.

This allowance results in a reduction in tax paid of $13,750 × 30% = $4,125, the benefits of which are received in years 4 and 5.

Here is the full calculation.

	Reducing balance $	Tax saved $	Yr 1 $	Yr 2 $	Yr 3 $	Yr 4 $	Yr 5 $
				Benefits received			
Purchase price	80,000						
Yr 1 WDA (25%)	(20,000)	6,000	3,000	3,000			
	60,000						
Yr 2 WDA (25%)	(15,000)	4,500		2,250	2,250		
	45,000						
Yr 3 WDA (25%)	(11,250)	3,375			1,687	1,688	
	33,750						
Yr 4 sales price	20,000						
Balancing allowance	13,750	4,125				2,062	2,063

If the asset had been sold for $40,000, however, there would be a **balancing charge** of $(40,000 − 33,750) = $6,250, being the difference between the reducing balance amount at the end of year 3/beginning of year 4 and the selling price.

This charge has to be included in year 4 taxable profits, resulting in an **increase in tax paid** of $6,250 × 30% = $1,875, which must be paid half in year 4 and half in year 5.

Let's now look at how to integrate all of this into a DCF appraisal.

Example: taxation

An organisation is considering whether or not to purchase an item of machinery costing $40,000. It would have a life of 4 years, after which it would be sold for $5,000. The machinery would create annual cost savings of $14,000.

The machinery would attract writing down allowances of 25% on the reducing balance basis. A balancing allowance or charge would arise on disposal. The rate of corporation tax is 30%. Tax is payable quarterly in the seventh and tenth months of the year in which the profit is earned and in the first and fourth months of the following year. The after-tax cost of capital is 8%.

Should the machinery be purchased?

Solution

WDAs and balancing charges/allowances

We begin by calculating the WDAs and balancing charge/allowance.

Year		Reducing balance $
0	Purchase	40,000
1	WDA	10,000
	Value at start of year 2	30,000
2	WDA	7,500
	Value at start of year 3	22,500
3	WDA	5,625
	Value at start of year 4	16,875
4	Sale	5,000
	Balancing allowance	11,875

Calculate tax savings/payments

Having calculated the allowances each year, the **tax savings** can be computed. The tax savings affect two years, the year for which the allowance is claimed and the following year.

Year of claim	Allowance $	Tax saved $	Tax saving				
			Yr 1 $	Yr 2 $	Yr 3 $	Yr 4 $	Yr 5 $
1	10,000	3,000	1,500	1,500			
2	7,500	2,250		1,125	1,125		
3	5,625	1,688			844	844	
4	11,875	3,562	–	–	–	1,781	1,781
	35,000 *		1,500	2,625	1,969	2,625	1,781

* Net cost $(40,000 – 5,000) = $35,000

These tax savings relate to capital allowances. We must also take the **tax effects of the annual savings** of $14,000 into account.

The savings increase taxable profit (costs are lower) and so extra tax must be paid. Each saving of $14,000 will lead to extra tax of $14,000 × 30% × 50% = $2,100 in the year in question and the same amount in the following year.

Calculate NPV

The **net cash flows and the NPV** are now calculated as follows.

Year	Equipment $	Savings $	Tax on savings $	Tax saved on capital allowances $	Net cash flow $	Discount factor 8%	Present value of cash flow $
0	(40,000)				(40,000)	1.000	(40,000)
1		14,000	(2,100)	1,500	13,400	0.926	12,408
2		14,000	(4,200)	2,625	12,425	0.857	10,648
3		14,000	(4,200)	1,969	11,769	0.794	9,345
4	5,000	14,000	(4,200)	2,625	17,425	0.735	12,807
5			(2,100)	1,781	(319)	0.681	(217)
							4,991

The NPV is positive and so the purchase appears to be worthwhile.

12.5 An alternative and quicker method of calculating tax payments or savings

In the above example, the tax computations could have been combined, as follows.

Year	1 $	2 $	3 $	4 $	5 $
Cost savings	14,000	14,000	14,000	14,000	
Capital allowance	10,000	7,500	5,625	11,875	
Taxable profits	4,000	6,500	8,375	2,125	
Tax (paid)/received at 30%	(1,200)	(1,950)	(2,512)	(638)	
Yr of (payment)/saving	(600)	(600)			
		(975)	(975)		
			(1,256)	(1,256)	
				(319)	(319)
(Payment)/saving	(600)	(1,575)	(2,231)	(1,575)	(319)

The net cash flows would then be as follows.

Year	Equipment $	Savings $	Tax $	Net cash flow $
0	(40,000)			(40,000)
1		14,000	(600)	13,400
2		14,000	(1,575)	12,425
3		14,000	(2,231)	11,769
4	5,000	14,000	(1,575)	17,425
5			(319)	(319)

The net cash flows are exactly the same as calculated previously in Step 3 above.

12.6 Taxation and DCF

The effect of taxation on capital budgeting is theoretically quite simple. Organisations must pay tax, and the effect of undertaking a project will be to increase or decrease tax payments each year. These **incremental tax cash flows should be included in the cash flows** of the project for discounting to arrive at the project's NPV.

When **taxation is ignored** in the DCF calculations, the **discount rate** will reflect the **pre-tax rate of return** required on capital investments. When **taxation is included** in the cash flows, a **post-tax required rate** of return should be used.

Question 8.13

Taxation

Learning outcome C1(b)

An organisation is considering the purchase of an item of equipment, which would earn profits before tax of $25,000 a year. Depreciation charges would be $20,000 a year for 6 years. Capital allowances would be $30,000 a year for the first 4 years. Corporation tax is at 30%.

Assume that tax payments occur half in the same year as the profits giving rise to them, half in the following year, and there is no balancing charge or allowance when the machine is scrapped at the end of the sixth year.

Required

Fill in the blanks below.

The net cash inflows of the project after tax in the first six years are:

Year 1 .... Year 4 ....

Year 2 .... Year 5 ....

Year 3 .... Year 6 ....

Question 8.14

Taxation and cash flow

Learning outcome C1(b)

An organisation is considering the purchase of a machine for $150,000. It would be sold after 4 years for an estimated realisable value of $50,000. By this time capital allowances of $120,000 would have been claimed. The rate of corporation tax is 30%.

The cash flow arising as a result of the tax implications of the sale of the machine at the end of the four years is:

A $6,000 inflow
B $6,000 outflow
C $15,000 outflow
D $20,000 outflow

12.7 Sensitivity analysis and taxation

To carry out **sensitivity analysis** when taxation is relevant, **use after-tax cash flows**.

Look back at the example in Section 12.4 called Taxation. Suppose you were required to calculate the sensitivity of the project to changes in the annual cost savings.

To do this you have to calculate (as before) (**NPV of project/PV of annual cost savings**) × 100% but both figures must be **after-tax figures**.

We therefore need to calculate the PV of the savings.

Year	Savings $	Tax on savings $	Net cash flow $	Discount factor 8%	Present value $
1	14,000	(2,100)	11,900	0.926	11,019
2	14,000	(4,200)	9,800	0.857	8,399
3	14,000	(4,200)	9,800	0.794	7,781
4	14,000	(4,200)	9,800	0.735	7,203
		(2,100)	(2,100)	0.681	(1,430)
					32,972

The overall NPV of the project is $4,991 and so the sensitivity is therefore (4,991/32,972) × 100% = 15.14%.

Don't forget that when carrying out sensitivity analysis, we need to **consider the cash flows affected by the variables under consideration**. So if you were asked to examine the sensitivity of a project to **price**, you would need to calculate the post-tax PV of revenue (as a change in selling price affects revenue and hence revenue is the cash flow affected), whereas sensitivity to **volume** would require the calculation of post-tax contribution (as a change in volume affects revenue and variable costs and hence contribution can be used as the cash flow affected).

12.8 Summary

(a) Calculate the **total** cost of any new asset.

(b) Calculate WDA for each year and multiply by the tax rate to give the tax saving. **See example in 12.3 called WDAs.**

(c) Half of tax saving is a benefit in the year in question, half in the following year. **See example in 12.3 called WDAs.**

(d) Calculate a balancing allowance or charge on the sale of the asset. **See example in 12.4 called Balancing allowances/charges.**

    (i)   If sales price > reducing balance ⇒ balancing charge (increases taxable profit)

    (ii)   If sales price < reducing balance ⇒ balancing allowance (reduces taxable profit)

(e) Effect of the balancing charge/allowance (which is calculated as amount × tax rate) is felt half in the year in which the asset is sold and half in the following year. **See example in 12.4 called Balancing allowances/charges.**

(f) Include in the appraisal: tax on WDAs and balancing allowance/charge, net cash inflows due to project (ie taxable profits) and tax on these net cash inflows. **See example in 12.4 called Taxation and Section 12.5**.

| Question 8.15 | Tax effects |

Learning outcome C1(b)

Describe the potential major effects of taxation on capital investment decisions.

Section summary

Taxation is a major practical consideration for businesses. It is vital to take it into account in making decisions.

Under the UK system, corporation tax is **payable** by large companies **quarterly**.

- In the **seventh and tenth months** of the year in which the profit is earned
- In the **first and fourth months** of the following year

Capital allowances/WDAs reduce taxable profits and hence tax payable.

If **taxation is ignored** in the project cash flows, the discount rate should be the **pre-tax** cost of capital. When **taxation is included** in the cash flows, the **after-tax** cost of capital should be used.

To carry out **sensitivity analysis** when taxation is relevant, **use after-tax cash flows**.

Chapter Summary

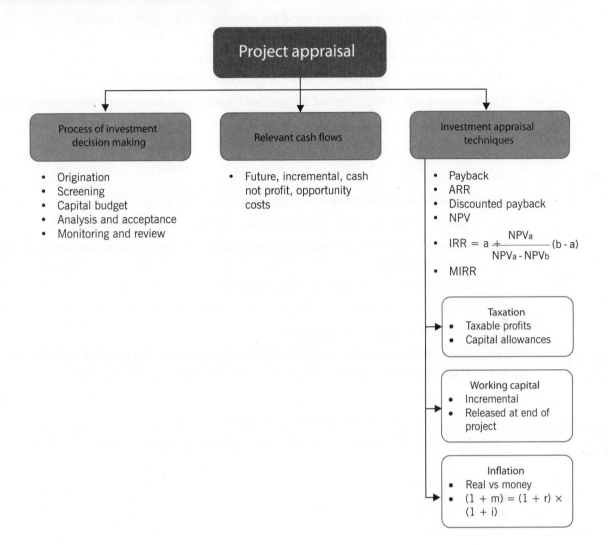

Project appraisal

Process of investment decision making

- Origination
- Screening
- Capital budget
- Analysis and acceptance
- Monitoring and review

Relevant cash flows

- Future, incremental, cash not profit, opportunity costs

Investment appraisal techniques

- Payback
- ARR
- Discounted payback
- NPV
- $IRR = a + \dfrac{NPV_a}{NPV_a - NPV_b}(b - a)$
- MIRR

Taxation
- Taxable profits
- Capital allowances

Working capital
- Incremental
- Released at end of project

Inflation
- Real vs money
- $(1 + m) = (1 + r) \times (1 + i)$

Quick Quiz

1   Fill in the blanks in these statements about the advantages of the payback method.

    (a)   Focus on early payback can enhance ....

    (b)   Investment risk is .... if payback is longer.

    (c)   ....–term forecasts are likely to be more reliable.

2   The accounting rate of return method of investment appraisal uses accounting profits before depreciation charges.

    True   ☐

    False   ☐

3   Which of the following statements about post-completion audit is correct?

    A   Size should not be used as a guide as to which projects should be audited.

    B   Managers should perceive that every capital expenditure project has a chance of being the subject of a detailed audit.

    C   All capital expenditure projects should be audited.

    D   In general, projects should be audited approximately one week after completion.

4   Choose the correct words from those highlighted.

    (a)   The imposition of internal capital budget constraints is known as **hard/soft** capital rationing.

    (b)   **Hard/soft** capital rationing occurs when external capital budget limits are set.

5   Fill in the blank.

    The average net book value of an asset is calculated as ....

6   Applied punitively, PCA exercises may lead to managers becoming risk seekers.

    True   ☐

    False   ☐

7   Fill in the blanks.

    The recommended definition of ARR is: $\dfrac{................}{................} \times 100\%$

8   In a discounted cash flow exercise, what is the discount factor (to 3 decimal places) for year 4 when the cost of capital is 11.5%?

    A 0.647   B 0.115   C 3.587   D 1.546   E 0.721

9   What is the present value of a cash inflow of $3,000 each year from years 1 to 5, when the required return on investment is 12%?

    A $15,000   B $16,800   C $13,393   D $9,111   E $10,815

10   With a cost of capital of 13%, what is the present value of $2,500 received every year in perpetuity?

    A $2,825   B $17,563   C $2,212   D $28,736   E None of these options

11   For a certain project, the net present value at a discount rate of 15% is $3,670, and at a rate of 18% the net present value is negative at ($1,390). What is the internal rate of return of the project?

    A 15.7%   B 16.5%   C 16.6%   D 17.2%   E None of these options

12   Tick the correct box to indicate whether or not the following items are included in the cash flows when determining the net present value of a project.

Included   Not included

(a)   The disposal value of equipment at the end of its life

(b)   Depreciation charges for the equipment

(c)   Research costs incurred prior to the appraisal

(d)   Interest payments on the loan to finance the investment

13   At what point on the graph below is the project's IRR?

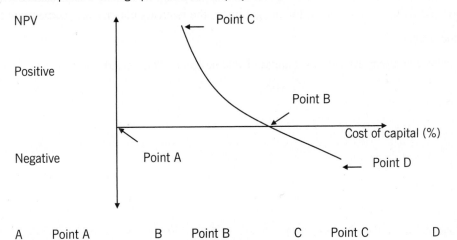

A   Point A   B   Point B   C   Point C   D   Point D

14   Choose the correct word from those highlighted.

When there are non-conventional cash flow patterns, the **IRR/NPV** method is not recommended.

15   Fill in the blanks.

DPBI = $\dfrac{\text{.........................}}{\text{.........................}}$

16   Fill in the blank in the sentence below.

The present value of $1,000 in contribution earned each year from years 1 to 10, when the required return on investment is 11%, is $................ .

17   Fill in the gaps.

The relationship between the money rate of return, the real rate of return and the rate of inflation is

(1 + ... rate) = (1 + ... rate) × (1 + ... rate).

18   The money cost of capital is 11%. The expected annual rate of inflation is 5%. What is the real cost of capital?

A 16.6%   B 6.0%   C 16.0%   D None of these options

19   A company wants a minimum real return of 3% a year on its investments. Inflation is expected to be 8% a year. What is the company's minimum money cost of capital?

A 4.9%   B 11.24%   C 5%   D 11%

20   A company is appraising an investment that will save electricity costs. Electricity prices are expected to rise at a rate of 15% per annum in future, although the general inflation rate will be 10% per annum. The money cost of capital for the company is 20%. What is the appropriate discount rate to apply to the forecast actual money cash flows for electricity?

A 20.0%   B 22.0%   C 26.5%   D 32.0%

21 Choose the correct words from those highlighted.

Capital allowances are used to (1) **increase/reduce** taxable profits, and the consequent reduction in a tax payment should be treated as a (2) **cash saving/cash payment** arising from the acceptance of a project.

Writing down allowances are generally allowed on the cost of (3) **materials and labour/plant and machinery** at the rate of (4) **25%/30%** on a (5) **straight-line/reducing balance** basis.

When the plant is eventually sold, the difference between the sales price and the reducing balance amount will be treated as a (6) **taxable profit/tax allowable loss** if the sales price exceeds the reducing balance, and as a (7) **taxable profit/tax allowable loss** if the reducing balance exceeds the sales price.

The cash saving on the capital allowances (or the cash payment for a charge) is calculated by (8) **multiplying/dividing** the allowances (or charge) by (9) the **reducing balance rate/corporation tax rate**.

22 Fill in the blanks.

The sensitivity of a project's NPV to changes in volume can be determined using:

(......................./.......................) × 100%

Answers to Quick Quiz

1   (a)   liquidity   (b)   increased   (c)   shorter

2   False. It uses accounting profits after depreciation.

3   B. This should improve the overall capital expenditure decision-making process.

4   (a)   soft   (b)   hard

5   (Capital cost + disposal value)/2

6   False. They are likely to become unnecessarily risk averse.

7   $$\frac{\text{Average annual profit from investment}}{\text{Average investment}} \times 100\%$$

8   A $1/(1 + 0.115)^4 = 0.647$

9   E $\$3,000 \times 3.605 = \$10,815$

10   E $\$2,500/0.13 = \$19,231$

11   D $15\% + \{(3,670/[3,670 + 1,390]) \times 3\%\} = 17.2\%$

12   (a)   Included

     (b)   Not included (non-cash)

     (c)   Not included (past cost)

     (d)   Not usually included, unless the loan incurs a different rate of interest from that which is being used as the discount rate

13   B. The IRR is the rate (cost of capital) at which the NPV is zero.

14   IRR

15   $$\text{DPBI} = \frac{\text{Sum of net discounted cash inflows}}{\text{Initial cash outlay}}$$

16   The PV of $1,000 earned each year from year 1 to 10 when the required earning rate of money is 11% is calculated as follows.

     $\$1,000 \times 5.889 = \$5,889$

17   (1 + money rate) = (1 + real rate) × (1 + inflation rate)

18   D $1.11/1.05 = 1.057$. The real cost of capital is 5.7%.

19   B $1.03 \times 1.08 = 1.1124$. The money cost of capital is 11.24%.

20   A   The money rate of 20% is applied to the money cash flows.

21   (1)   reduce   (4)   25%   (7)   tax allowable loss
     (2)   cash saving   (5)   reducing balance   (8)   multiplying
     (3)   plant and machinery   (6)   taxable profit   (9)   corporation tax rate

22   (Overall project NPV/PV of contribution) × 100%

Answers to Questions

8.1 Payback

The correct answer is A.

Profits before depreciation should be used.

Year	Profit after depreciation $'000	Depreciation $'000	Profit before depreciation $'000	Cumulative profit $'000
1	12	12	24	24
2	17	12	29	53
3	28	12	40	93
4	37	12	49	142
5	8	12	20	

$$\therefore \text{ Payback period } = 3 \text{ years} + \left(\frac{(120-93)}{(142-93)} \times 12 \text{ months} \right)$$

$$= 3 \text{ years 7 months}$$

8.2 The ARR and mutually exclusive projects

The correct answer is that X should be selected and so the statement is false.

	Item X $	Item Y $
Total profit over life of equipment		
Before depreciation	160,000	280,000
After depreciation	80,000	130,000
Average annual profit after depreciation	16,000	26,000
Average investment = (capital cost + disposal value)/2	40,000	75,000
ARR	40%	34.7%

Both projects would earn a return in excess of 30%, but since **item X would earn a bigger ARR, it would be preferred to item Y**, even though the profits from Y would be higher by an average of $10,000 a year.

8.3 Payback and ARR

(a)   Depreciation must first be **added** back to the **annual profit figures**, to arrive at the annual cash flows.

$$\text{Depreciation} = \frac{\text{Initial investment } \$46,000 - \text{scrap value } \$4,000}{4 \text{ years}}$$

$$= \$10,500 \text{ p.a.}$$

Adding $10,500 per annum to the profit figures produces the cash flows for each proposal.

	Proposal A		Proposal B	
	Annual	Cumulative	Annual	Cumulative
Year	cash flow	cash flow	cash flow	cash flow
	$	$	$	$
0	(46,000)	(46,000)	(46,000)	(46,000)
1	17,000	(29,000)	15,000	(31,000)
2	14,000	(15,000)	13,000	(18,000)
3	24,000	9,000	15,000	(3,000)
4	9,000	18,000	25,000	22,000
4	4,000	22,000	4,000	26,000

(i)   *Proposal A*   *Proposal B*

$$\text{Payback period} = 2 + \left(\frac{15,000}{24,000} \times 1 \text{ year}\right) \quad \text{Payback period} = 3 + \left(\frac{3,000}{25,000} \times 1 \text{ year}\right)$$

$$= 2.6 \text{ years} \quad\quad\quad\quad\quad\quad = 3.1 \text{ years}$$

(ii)   The return on capital employed (ROCE) is calculated using the accounting profits given in the question.

Proposal A   Average profit   = $(6,500 + 3,500 + 13,500 – 1,500)/4
                                   = $22,000/4 = $5,500

                  ROCE $= \dfrac{\$5,500}{\$46,000} \times 100\% = 12.0\%$

Proposal B   Average profit   = $(4,500 + 2,500 + 4,500 + 14,500)/4
                                   = $26,000/4 = $6,500

                  ROCE $= \dfrac{\$6,500}{\$46,000} \times 100\% = 14.1\%$

(b)   Two advantages of each of the methods of appraisal can be selected from the following.

Payback period

(i)   It is simple to calculate
(ii)   It preserves liquidity by preferring early cash flows
(iii)   It uses cash flows instead of more arbitrary accounting profits
(iv)   It reduces risk by preferring early cash flows

Return on capital employed

(i)   It uses readily available **accounting profits**
(ii)   It is **understood** by **non-financial managers**
(iii)   It is a measure used by **external analysts** which should be monitored by the company

---

8.4 Present value calculation

The correct answer is $53,240

Year	Cash flow $	Discount factor 12%	Present value $
2	40,000	$\dfrac{1}{(1.12)^2} = 0.797$	31,880
3	30,000	$\dfrac{1}{(1.12)^3} = 0.712$	21,360
		Total PV	53,240

8.5 Meaning of present value

The correct answer is: The present value of the future returns, discounted at **12%**, is **$53,240**. This means that if Spender can invest now to earn a return of **12%** on its investments, it would have to invest **$53,240** now to earn **$40,000** after 2 years plus **$30,000** after 3 years.

8.6 NPV

The correct answer is that LCH should purchase the machine.

Savings are 75,000 × ($3 – $2.50) = $37,500 per annum.

Additional costs are $7,500 per annum.

Net cash savings are therefore $30,000 per annum. (Remember, depreciation is not a cash flow and must be ignored as a 'cost'.)

The first step in calculating an NPV is to establish the relevant costs year by year. The relevant cash flows are all future cash flows arising as a direct consequence of the decision, which should be taken into account.

It is assumed that the machine will be sold for $10,000 at the end of year 4.

Year	Cash flow $	PV factor 12%	PV of cash flow $
0	(90,000)	1.000	(90,000)
1	30,000	0.893	26,790
2	30,000	0.797	23,910
3	30,000	0.712	21,360
4	40,000	0.636	25,440
		NPV =	+7,500

The **NPV is positive** and so the project is expected to **earn more than 12%** per annum and is therefore **acceptable**.

8.7 Delayed annuity

The correct answer is B.

The PV of $2,000 in costs each year from years 3 to 6 when the cost of capital is 5% per annum is calculated as follows.

$$\$2,000 \times \left[\begin{array}{l} \text{PV of \$1 per annum for years 1-6 at 5\%} = 5.076 \\ \text{Less PV of \$1 per annum for years 1-2 at 5\%} = \underline{1.859} \\ \text{PV of \$1 per annum for years 3-6} \qquad = \underline{\underline{3.217}} \end{array} \right]$$

PV = $2,000 × 3.217 = $6,434

If you chose Option A, you performed the calculation $2,000 × 105% × 3 years. You need to use a discount factor.

If you chose Option C, you simply took the sum of $2,000 paid annually for 3 years.

If you chose Option D, you deducted the cumulative discount factor for years 1 to 3 instead of the factor for years 1 and 2 from that for years 1 to 6.

8.8 Perpetuities

The correct answer is: The project should be undertaken.

Year	Cash flow $	Discount factor 14%	Present value $
0	(500,000)	1.00	(500,000)
1–∞	100,000	1/0.14 = 7.14	714,000
		Net present value	214,000

The NPV is positive and so the project should be undertaken.

8.9 Non-standard discount factors

The correct answer is D.

There are no present value tables for 16.5%, therefore you need to calculate your own discount factors, using discount factor = $1/(1 + r)^n$ where r = cost of capital and n = number of years.

Year		16.5% factor	Cash flow $	Present value $
0		1.00	(280,000)	(280,000)
1	$\dfrac{1}{(1 + 0.165)}$	0.86	149,000	128,140
2	$\dfrac{1}{(1 + 0.165)^2}$	0.74	128,000	94,720
3	$\dfrac{1}{(1 + 0.165)^3}$	0.63	84,000	52,920
4	$\dfrac{1}{(1 + 0.165)^4}$	0.54	70,000	37,800
			Net present value	33,580

8.10 IRR

The IRR is 15% and so the statement is false.

The total receipts are $5,635 giving a total profit of $1,635 and average profits of $409. The average investment is $2,000. The ARR is $409 ÷ $2,000 = 20%. Two-thirds of the ARR is approximately 14%. The initial estimate of the IRR that we shall try is therefore 14%.

Time	Cash flow $	Try 14% Discount factor 14%	PV $	Try 16% Discount factor 16%	PV $
0	(4,000)	1.000	(4,000)	1.000	(4,000)
1	1,200	0.877	1,052	0.862	1,034
2	1,410	0.769	1,084	0.743	1,048
3	1,875	0.675	1,266	0.641	1,202
4	1,150	0.592	681	0.552	635
		NPV	83	NPV	(81)

The **IRR must be less than 16%, but higher than 14%**. The NPVs at these two costs of capital will be used to estimate the IRR.

Using the **interpolation formula**

$$IRR = 14\% + \left[\frac{83}{83+81} \times \left(16\% - 14\%\right)\right] = 15.01\%$$

The IRR is, in fact, exactly 15%.

The project should be **rejected** as the **IRR is less than the minimum return demanded**.

8.11 NPV and IRR

(a)   **Option A – Expand retail outlet**

Year	Cash flow $'000	Discount factor 10%	NPV $'000
0	(75)	1.000	(75.00)
1	40	0.909	36.36
2	50	0.826	41.30
3	50	0.751	37.55
4	50	0.683	34.15
			74.36

Option B – Mail order

Year	Cash flow $'000	Discount factor 10%	NPV $'000
0	(120)	1.000	(120.00)
1	50	0.909	45.45
2	60	0.826	49.56
3	80	0.751	60.08
4	100	0.683	68.30
			103.39

Option C – Greenhouses and conservatories

Year	Cash flow $'000	Discount factor 10%	NPV $'000
0	(200)	1.000	(200.00)
1	50	0.909	45.45
2	100	0.826	82.60
3	150	0.751	112.65
4	150	0.683	102.45
			143.15

Option C gives the highest NPV and therefore this should be chosen.

(b)   The NPV for option C is quite high relative to the initial investment and the IRR is therefore probably considerably higher than 10%.

Try 30%

Year	Cash flow $'000	Discount factor 30%	NPV $'000
0	(200)	1.000	(200.00)
1	50	0.769	38.45
2	100	0.592	59.20
3	150	0.455	68.25
4	150	0.350	52.50
			18.40

Try 40%

Year	Cash flow $'000	Discount factor 40%	NPV $'000
0	(200)	1.000	(200.0)
1	50	0.714	35.7
2	100	0.510	51.0
3	150	0.364	54.6
4	150	0.260	39.0
			(19.7)

$$\text{IRR} = 30\% + \left[\frac{18.4}{18.4+19.7} \times 10\right]\% = 34.83\%$$

8.12 Investment appraisal and inflation

The correct answer is A.

The rate required is the IRR (the rate at which the project breaks even).

Let the rate = r

∴ $120,000 = PV of $40,000 for years 1 to 4 at rate r

∴ $120,000 = (cumulative PV factor for years 1 to 4 at rate r) × $40,000

∴ $120,000/$40,000 = cumulative PV factor for years 1 to 4 at rate r

∴ 3.000 = cumulative PV factor for years 1 to 4 at rate r

In cumulative PV tables this corresponds to a rate of approximately 12.5% over 4 years.

∴ The real cost of capital to give an NPV of zero = 12.5%

Substituting in the formula, with X = monetary cost of capital:

$$\frac{(1+X)}{1.03} - 1 = 0.125$$

∴ X = 15.875%

Option B is the real cost of capital. Option C is the current cost of capital. Option D is the difference between the current cost of capital and the rate of inflation.

8.13 Taxation

The correct answer is:

Year 1 $42,750   Year 4 $40,500
Year 2 $40,500   Year 5 $36,000
Year 3 $40,500   Year 6 $31,500

	Years 1–4 $	Years 5–6 $
Profit before tax	25,000	25,000
Add back depreciation	20,000	20,000
Net cash inflow before tax	45,000	45,000
Less capital allowance	30,000	0
	15,000	45,000
Tax at 30%	4,500	13,500

	Yr 1 $	Yr 2 $	Yr 3 $	Yr 4 $	Yr 5 $	Yr 6 $	Yr 7 $
Tax on yr 1 profit	2,250	2,250					
Tax on yr 2 profit		2,250	2,250				
Tax on yr 3 profit			2,250	2,250			
Tax on yr 4 profit				2,250	2,250		
Tax on yr 5 profit					6,750	6,750	
Tax on yr 6 profit						6,750	6,750
	2,250	4,500	4,500	4,500	9,000	13,500	6,750
Net cash inflow before tax	45,000	45,000	45,000	45,000	45,000	45,000	
Net cash inflow after tax	42,750	40,500	40,500	40,500	36,000	31,500	

8.14 Taxation and cash flow

The correct answer is B.

There will be a balancing charge on the sale of the machine of $(50,000 – (150,000 – 120,000)) = $20,000. This will give rise to a tax payment of 30% × $20,000 = $6,000.

If you chose A you got the calculations correct but the direction of the cash flow was wrong.

Option C is 30% taxation on the estimated sales value. The revenue from the actual sale is not taxed directly, but any remaining balancing charge will be taxable.

If you chose option D you forgot to calculate the 30% corporation tax on the balancing charge of $20,000.

8.15 Tax effects

Taxation can affect investment decisions in various ways.

(a) The existence of taxation will **reduce the returns** and **mitigate the costs** of projects.

(b) The arrangements for paying tax will determine by how much tax payments are **discounted** in the investment appraisal. It will be significant whether tax is payable in the year profits are earned or in the following year.

(c) Tax is payable on **taxable profits that relate to the investment**, which are not necessarily the same as the **cash flows**. There may be **timing differences between expenditure being accrued** for accounting and tax purposes, and payment being made.

(d) Taxation arrangements are complicated by the availability of **capital allowances**, which allow businesses to write off the costs of non-current assets against taxable profit. Businesses need to consider for what types of asset claims can be made and the **timing** of allowances, as this will again affect by how much allowances are discounted. This may determine when an asset is purchased; it may be advantageous to purchase an asset just before the end of a tax year, and thus claim capital allowances a year earlier than would be the case if the asset was purchased early in the new tax year.

(e) If the effects of taxation are included in the investment appraisal, a **post-tax rate of return** should be used.

Now try the question from the Practice Question Bank

Number	Marks	Time
Q30 Objective test questions	10	18 mins
Q31 Webber design	25	45 mins
Q32 X	10	18 mins
Q33 Research director	10	18 mins
Q34 Alphabet Ltd	10	18 mins
Q35 PPA	10	18 mins
Q36 Payback	10	18 mins
Q37 Two projects	10	18 mins
Q38 NPV and IRR	10	18 mins
Q39 HP	25	45 mins

FURTHER ASPECTS OF DECISION MAKING

In this chapter, we examine some further **applications of discounted cash flow (DCF)** techniques. An enterprise may be faced with more investment opportunities than it can finance with the capital available, and we look first at how **capital rationing** may affect the investment decision.

We then examine various techniques that can be used to deal with complications in investment decisions. The **equivalent annual cost** method can be used when maintenance costs are an important element in an investment decision. **Real option theory** can be used to assist when organisations have to or can make further decisions after the initial investment decision.

topic list	learning outcomes	syllabus references	ability required
1 Capital rationing	C1(b), (c)	C1(b)(i), (c)(ii)	analysis
2 Equivalent annual cost	C1(b)	C1(b)(ii)	analysis
3 Real options	C1(b)	C1(b)(iii)	analysis

Chapter Overview

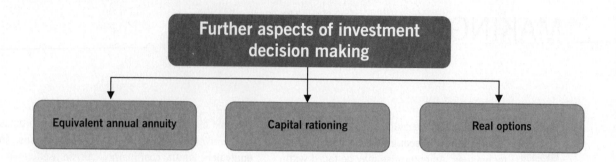

1   Capital rationing

Introduction

We saw in the last chapter that the decision rule with DCF techniques is to accept all projects which result in positive NPVs when discounted at the company's cost of capital. If an entity suffers capital rationing, it will not be able to enter into all projects with positive NPVs because there is not enough capital for all the investments. In this section we look at techniques to deal with this problem.

KEY TERM

CAPITAL RATIONING is a restriction on an organisation's ability to invest capital funds, caused by an internal budget ceiling being imposed on such expenditure by management (**soft capital rationing**), or by external limitations being applied to the company, as when additional borrowed funds cannot be obtained (**hard capital rationing**).   (*CIMA Official Terminology*)

If an organisation is in a capital rationing situation it will not be able to invest in all available projects which have positive NPVs because there is not enough capital for all of the investments. Capital is a **limiting factor**.

1.1 Soft and hard capital rationing

Capital rationing may be necessary in a business due to **internal factors** (soft capital rationing) or **external factors** (hard capital rationing).

Soft capital rationing may arise for one of the following reasons.

(a)   Management may be **reluctant to issue additional share capital** because of concern that this may lead to outsiders gaining control of the business.

(b)   Management may be **unwilling to issue additional share capital** if it will lead to a dilution of earnings per share.

(c)   Management may **not want to raise additional debt capital** because they do not wish to be committed to large fixed interest payments.

(d)   There may be a desire within the organisation to **limit investment** to a level that can be financed solely from retained earnings.

(e)   **Capital expenditure budgets** may restrict spending.

Note that whenever an organisation adopts a policy that restricts funds available for investment, such a policy may be less than optimal as the organisation may reject projects with a positive NPV and forgo opportunities that would have enhanced the market value of the organisation.

Hard capital rationing may arise for one of the following reasons.

(a)   Raising money through the stock market may not be possible if **share prices are depressed**.

(b)   There may be **restrictions on bank lending** due to government control.

(c)   Lending institutions may consider an organisation to be too **risky** to be granted further loan facilities.

(d)   The **costs** associated with making small issues of capital may be too great.

1.2 Divisible and non-divisible projects

(a)   **Divisible projects** are those which can be undertaken completely or in fractions. Suppose that Project A is divisible and requires the investment of $15,000 to achieve an NPV of $4,000. $7,500 invested in Project A will earn an NPV of ½ × $4,000 = $2,000.

(b)   **Indivisible projects** are those which must be undertaken completely or not at all. It is not possible to invest in a fraction of the project.

You may also encounter **mutually exclusive** projects when one, and only one, of two or more choices of project can be undertaken.

1.3 Single period rationing with divisible projects

With **single period capital rationing**, investment funds are a limiting factor in the current period. The total return will be maximised if management follows the decision rule of maximising the return per unit of the limiting factor. They should therefore **select those projects whose cash inflows have the highest present value per $1 of capital invested**. In other words, rank the projects according to their **profitability index**.

$$\text{Profitability index} = \frac{\text{NPV of project}}{\text{Initial cash outflow}}$$

Exam skills

The cash outflow should be in the year in which capital is rationed. This may not be Year 0 so make sure you read the question carefully.

Example: Single period rationing with divisible projects

Short O'Funds has capital of $130,000 available for investment in the forthcoming period, at a cost of capital of 20%. Capital will be freely available in the future. Details of six projects under consideration are as follows. All projects are independent and divisible. Which projects should be undertaken and what NPV will result?

Project	Investment required $'000	Present value of inflows at 20% $'000
P	40	56.5
Q	50	67.0
R	30	48.8
S	45	59.0
T	15	22.4
U	20	30.8

Solution

The first step is to rank the projects according to the return achieved from the limiting factor of investment funds.

Project	PV inflows $'000	Investment $'000	PV per $1 invested $	Ranking
P	56.5	40	1.41	4
Q	67.0	50	1.34	5
R	48.8	30	1.63	1
S	59.0	45	1.31	6
T	22.4	15	1.49	3
U	30.8	20	1.54	2

The available funds of $130,000 can now be allocated.

Project	Investment $'000		PV $'000
R	30		48.8
U	20		30.8
T	15		22.4
P	40		56.5
Q (balance)	25	(½)	33.5
	130	Maximum PV =	192.0

Project S should not be undertaken and only half of project Q should be undertaken.

The resulting total NPV generated will be 192.0 − 130 = $62,000.

Note that the PI can be used as a project appraisal method in its own right. The decision rule to apply will be to accept all projects with a PI greater than one (in which case, PV inflows > initial investment, ie NPV > 0).

1.3.1 Advantages of the PI method

(a)   Similar to the NPV method, usually **giving the same result** on **individual projects**.

(b)   Can be used to rank divisible projects in conditions of **capital rationing**.

1.3.2 Disadvantages of the PI method

(a)   PI indicates **relative returns** and is not an absolute measure.

(b)   The PI method may **rank projects incorrectly** (If cash is not rationed, it is preferable to look at the NPV, which is an absolute measure).

(c)   **Establishing** what is the **initial investment** may **not be straightforward** (the PI method works well only if the project has an outflow of cash at time 0, followed by cash inflows which may be at various times).

1.4 Single period rationing with non-divisible projects

If the projects are **not divisible** then the method shown in the last paragraph may not result in the optimal solution. Another complication which arises is that there is likely to be a small amount of **unused capital** with each combination of projects. The best way to deal with this situation is to use **trial and error** and test the NPV available from different combinations of projects. This can be a laborious process if there are a large number of projects available. We will continue with the previous example to demonstrate the technique.

Example: Single period rationing with non-divisible projects

Short O'Funds now discovers that funds in the forthcoming period are actually restricted to $95,000. The directors decide to consider projects P, Q and R only. They wish to invest only in whole projects, but surplus funds can be invested. Which combination of projects will produce the highest NPV at a cost of capital of 20%?

Solution

The investment combinations we need to consider are the various possible pairs of Projects P, Q and R.

Projects	Required investment $'000	PV of inflows $'000	NPV from projects $'000
P and Q	90	123.5	33.5
P and R	70	105.3	35.3
Q and R	80	115.8	35.8

Highest NPV – undertake Projects Q and R and invest the unused funds of $15,000 externally.

Question 9.1

Capital rationing

Learning outcome: C1(c)

Bijoux is choosing which investment to undertake during the coming year. The following table has been prepared, summarising the main features of available projects.

Project	Cash outlays		Cash receipts	
	Time 0 €'000	Time 1 €'000	Time 1 €'000	Time 2 €'000
Diamond	24	60	24	96
Sapphire	48	42	48	66
Platinum	60	42	12	138
Emerald	48	18	12	90
Quartz	36	48	24	96

There will be no cash flows on any of the projects after time 2. All projects are regarded as being of equal risk. Bijoux uses only equity sources of finance at an estimated cost of 20% per annum.

The cash flows given above represent estimated results for maximum possible investment in each project; lower levels of investment may be undertaken, in which case all cash flows will be reduced in proportion.

Required

Prepare calculations to identify the optimal set of investment assuming that capital available is limited to €120,000 at time 0, and €240,000 at time 1; assume that the Platinum Project and the Emerald Project are mutually exclusive. (**Hint**. Firstly check in which years capital rationing occurs.)

1.5 Practical methods of dealing with capital rationing

A company may be able to limit the effects of capital rationing and exploit new opportunities.

(a)   It might **seek joint venture partners** with which to share projects.

(b)   As an alternative to direct investment in a project, the company may be able to consider a **licensing** or **franchising agreement** with another enterprise, under which the licensor/franchisor company would receive royalties.

(c)   It may be possible to **contract** out parts of a project to reduce the initial capital outlay required.

(d)   The company may seek **new** alternative **sources of capital** (subject to any restrictions which apply to it), for example:

    (i)   Venture capital

    (ii)   Debt finance secured on project assets

    (iii)   Sale and leaseback of property or equipment

(iv) Grant aid
(v) More effective capital management
(vi) Delay a project to a later period

Section summary

- **Capital rationing** may occur due to internal factors (**soft** capital rationing) or external factors (**hard** capital rationing).

- When capital rationing occurs in a **single period, divisible** projects are ranked in terms of a **profitability index**.

- **Trial and error NPV calculations** should be used to rank **indivisible projects**.

2 Equivalent annual cost

Introduction

When an asset is being replaced with an identical asset, the equivalent annual cost method is a technique which can be used to determine the **best time** to replace the asset.

When an investment is being evaluated in terms of annual running costs, it may be appropriate to convert the capital cost into an **annualised cost** at the company's cost of capital. For example, when the capital expenditure is only a relatively small feature of a project and annual running costs are a much more significant item, annual profitability is the key factor in the decision.

EXAM

$$\text{Equivalent annual cost} = \frac{\text{PV of costs over n years}}{\text{n year annuity factor}}$$

(a) **'PV of costs'** is the **purchase cost**, minus the present value of any subsequent disposal proceeds at the end of the item's life.

(b) The **n-year annuity factor is** at the company's cost of capital, for the number of years of the item's life.

Example: Annualised cost

A project is being considered which would involve a capital expenditure of $500,000 on equipment. The annual running costs and benefits would be as follows.

	$	$
Revenues		450,000
Costs		
Depreciation	100,000	
Other	300,000	
		400,000
Profit		50,000

The equipment would have a 5-year life, and no residual value, and would be financed by a loan at 12% interest per annum. Using annualised figures, assess whether the project is a worthwhile undertaking. Ignore risk and taxation.

Solution

The annualised capital cost of the equipment is as follows.

$$\frac{\$500,000}{\text{PV of \$1 per annum for yrs 1 to 5 at 12\%}} = \frac{\$500,000}{3.605} = \$138,696$$

Annual profit = \$450,000 − \$138,696 − \$300,000 = \$11,304

Depreciation is ignored because it is a notional cost and has already been taken into account in the annualised cost.

The project is a worthwhile undertaking, but only by about \$11,000 a year for 5 years.

2.1 Equivalent annual cost and asset replacement

The annualised cost method can be used to assess when and how frequently an asset should be replaced with another asset.

The equivalent annual cost method is the quickest method to use in a period of no inflation.

Calculate the **present value of costs** for each **replacement cycle** over **one cycle only**.

These costs are not comparable because they refer to different time periods, whereas replacement is continuous.

Turn the present value of costs for each replacement cycle into an **equivalent annual cost** (an annuity).

The equivalent annual cost is calculated as follows.

$$\frac{\text{The PV of cost over one replacement cycle}}{\text{The cumulative present value factor for the number of years in the cycle}}$$

For example, if there are three years in the cycle, the denominator will be the present value of an annuity for three years (eg at 10% would be 2.487).

Example: Replacement of an identical asset

James operates a machine which has the following costs and resale values over its four-year life.

Purchase cost: \$25,000

	Year 1 $	Year 2 $	Year 3 $	Year 4 $
Running costs (cash expenses)	7,500	11,000	12,500	15,000
Resale value (end of year)	15,000	10,000	7,500	2,500

The organisation's cost of capital is 10%. You are required to assess how frequently the asset should be replaced.

Solution

 Calculate the present value of costs for each replacement cycle over one cycle.

	Replace every year		Replace every 2 years		Replace every 3 years		Replace every 4 years	
Year	Cash flow $	PV at 10% $	Cash flow $	PV at 10% $	Cash flow $	PV at 10% $	Cash flow $	PV at 10% $
0	(25,000)	(25,000)	(25,000)	(25,000)	(25,000)	(25,000)	(25,000)	(25,000)
1	7,500	6,818	(7,500)	(6,818)	(7,500)	(6,818)	(7,500)	(6,818)
2			(1,000)	(826)	(11,000)	(9,086))	(11,000)	(9,086)
3					(5,000)	(3,755)	(12,500)	(9,388)
4							(12,500)	(8,538)
PV of cost over one replacement cycle	(18,182)		(32,644)		(44,659)		(58,830)	

STEP 2 Calculate the equivalent annual cost.

We use a discount rate of 10%.

(a)   Replacement every year:

Equivalent annual cost = $\dfrac{\$(18{,}182)}{0.909}$ = $(20,002)

(b)   Replacement every two years:

Equivalent annual cost = $\dfrac{\$(32{,}644)}{1.736}$ = $(18,804)

(c)   Replacement every three years:

Equivalent annual cost = $\dfrac{\$(44{,}659)}{2.487}$ = $(17,957)

(d)   Replacement every four years:

Equivalent annual cost = $\dfrac{\$(58{,}830)}{3.170}$ = $(18,558)

The optimum replacement policy is the one with the lowest equivalent annual cost, every three years.

2.2 Equivalent annual annuity

The equivalent annual annuity = $\dfrac{\text{NPV of project}}{\text{Annuity factor}}$

For example, a Project A with an NPV of $3.75m and a duration of 6 years, given a discount rate of 12%, will have an equivalent annual annuity of $\dfrac{3.75}{4.111}$ = 0.91. An alternative Project B with an NPV of $4.45m and a duration of 7 years will have an equivalent annual annuity of $\dfrac{4.45}{4.564}$ = 0.98.

This method is a useful way to compare projects with **unequal lives**.

3 Real options

Introduction

Real options theory is an attempt to incorporate real-life uncertainty and flexibility into the capital investment decision. A major capital investment may not always be set in stone.

Real options attempt to incorporate **flexibility** to adapt decisions in response to unexpected market developments. It is argued that traditional methods such as NPV fail to accurately capture the economic value of investments in an environment of widespread uncertainty and rapid change. The real options method applies **financial options theory** to quantify the value of this flexibility.

Call and put options are covered later in your studies. An understanding of their meaning will help here, but remember we are talking about capital investment projects, not currency and interest rate options.

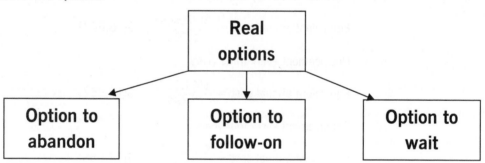

3.1 Option to follow-on

A follow-on option is a strategic option when the investment opportunity leads to follow-on wealth-generating opportunities. For example, buying new equipment could enable an organisation to develop experience and skills with the latest technology, which may allow opportunities that would otherwise have been unavailable.

This is equivalent to a **call option**.

3.2 Option to abandon

An abandonment option refers to the ability to abandon the project at a certain stage in its life. If large sums are being spent, and prospects do not appear healthy, an abandonment option may be available. If the benefit streams from a project are highly **uncertain**, an option to abandon the project if things go wrong could be highly valuable. The **riskiness** of the project is reduced and the expected NPV increased.

This type of option is affected, for example, by the type of equipment needed for the project and the terms on which the equipment is acquired. If equipment is readily resalable, this gives a more valuable abandonment option than if the equipment is highly specialised with no prospective secondhand purchasers.

This is equivalent to a **put option**.

3.3 Option to wait

An option to wait is a **timing option** which allows resolution of uncertainty. Investments are rarely 'now or never' opportunities, but we do need to consider the cash flows forgone in the period of postponement. The cost of this is balanced against the value of waiting.

For example, the possibility of 'doing nothing for a year' may be more valuable than a stated alternative because it will allow the **resolution of the uncertainty** surrounding legislation or to see if development status is granted on land.

This is equivalent to a **call option**.

3.4 Valuing real options

Real options can add value to projects, and should be taken into account in investment appraisal. Although the **valuation is difficult**, even a rough estimate is better than no estimate at all. Option theory provides a means for businesses to take into account:

(a)   **Initial costs and benefits**
(b)   The **present value of future benefits** and costs
(c)   The **variability of future benefits** and costs
(d)   The **timescale** directors are allowed to make the decision
(e)   The **cost of capital**

3.5 Numerical example of real options

Libby Co is considering a 3-year project that has an initial cost of $10,000. Depending on the economic cycle, the cash flows will either be $6,000 per year or $3,000 per year. There is a 60% probability that the cash flows will be $6,000 per year. The cost of capital is 10%.

This means that there is an expected cash flow per year of (6,000 × 0.6) + (3,000 × 0.4) = $4,800.

The NPV of this project is therefore:

Year	Cash flow $	Discount factor	Present value $
0	(10,000)	1.000	(10,000)
1–3	4,800	2.487	11,938
			1,938

Wait option

However, suppose that economic conditions after the first year are expected to remain the same for the **foreseeable future**. This means that Libby Co could wait one year to see which scenario occurs and then launch the project. This would give the following NPVs.

Best case

Year	Cash flow $	Discount factor	Present value $
1	(10,000)	0.909	(9,090)
2–4	6,000	2.261*	13,566
			4,476

Worst case

Year	Cash flow $	Discount factor	Present value $
1	(10,000)	0.909	(9,090)
2–4	3,000	2.261*	6,783
			(2,307)

* 4-year annuity factor – 1 year = 3.170 – 0.909 = 3.170 – 0.909 = 2.261

There is considerable value in the option to wait, in this case, because the NPV is increased by $4,476 – $1,938 = $2,538 as the downside risk is **eliminated** by waiting, as in the worst-case scenario the project would not commence.

Abandonment option

Alternatively, if the project is started now, there may be the option to abandon the project after one year when the machinery used can be sold for $6,000.

This option would create the following possibilities at the end of year 1.

Year (T_0 is now end of first year, when the decision is taken)	Cash flow $	Discount factor	Present value $
0	6,000	1.000	6,000
1	(6,000)	0.909	(5,454)
2	(6,000)	0.826	(4,956)
			(4,410)

Year	Cash flow $	Discount factor	Present value $
0	6,000	1.000	6,000
1	(3,000)	0.909	(2,727)
2	(3,000)	0.826	(2,478)
			795

This shows that if the cash flows are only $3,000 per year, then the abandonment option should be taken as this has a positive NPV.

The abandonment option can then be incorporated into the NPV of the project as follows.

The expected value of the cash flows can be calculated as follows (including the scrap value for abandoning the project).

	Year 1			Year 2			Year 3	
Probability	$	EV	Probability	$	EV	Probability	$	EV
0.6	6,000	3,600	0.6	6,000	3,600	0.6	6,000	3,600
0.4	9,000	3,600	0.4	–	–	0.4	–	–
		7,200			3,600			3,600

The NPV would then be

Year	Cash flow $	Discount factor	Present value $
0	(10,000)	1.000	(10,000)
1	7,200	0.909	6,545
2	3,600	0.826	2,974
3	3,600	0.751	2,704
			2,223

The option to abandon has increased the overall NPV by $2,223 – $1,938 = $285.

Section summary

Options theory can be applied to capital investments and can be used when managers are deciding whether to **wait, abandon** a project or make **follow-on** investments.

Chapter Summary

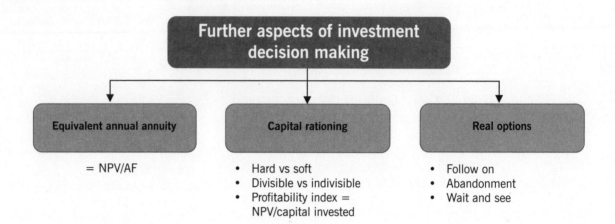

Quick Quiz

1   **Hard capital rationing** occurs when a restriction on an organisation's ability to invest capital funds is caused by an internal budget ceiling imposed by management.

   True ☐

   False ☐

2   Profitability index (PI) $= \dfrac{(1)}{(2)}$

   What are (1) and (2)?

3   Equivalent annual cost $= \dfrac{\text{PV of costs over n years}}{\text{n year annuity factor}}$

   Explain briefly what is meant by:

   (a)   PV of costs

   (b)   n year annuity factor

   Data for questions 4 and 5

   Four projects, K, L, M and N, are available to a company facing a shortage of capital over the next year; the maximum capital available is $100,000. Capital is expected to be freely available thereafter. None of the projects can be delayed.

	Project			
	K	L	M	N
Capital required in next year ($'000)	30	15	45	60
NPV ($'000)	90	60	150	120

4   What will be the best NPV attainable (to the nearest $'000) assuming that the projects are divisible?

   A $312

   B $356

   C $320

   D $270

5   What will be the best NPV attainable (to the nearest $'000) assuming that the projects are indivisible (ie cannot be done in part)?

   A $210

   B $300

   C $270

   D $320

Answers to Quick Quiz

1   1   False. This describes **soft** capital rationing.

2   (1)   Present value of cash inflows
    (2)   Initial investment

3   (a)   The purchase cost, minus the present value of any subsequent disposal proceeds at the end of the item's life

    (b)   The annuity factor at the company's cost of capital, for the number of years of the item's life

4   C

	NPV per $ invested	Ranking
K	3.0	3
L	4.0	1
M	3.3	2
N	2.0	4

After funding K, L and M $90,000 has been spent, leaving $10,000 to finance 10/60 = 16.67% of N.

So the total NPV will be 100% of projects K, L and M   =   90 + 60 + 150 = 300

also 16.67% of project N   =   0.1667 × 120 = 20

Giving a total of $320,000

5   B

Affordable combinations	Total NPV	Ranking
K + L + M	90 + 60 + 150 = **300**	1
K + N	90 + 120 = 210	2

Answers to Questions

9.1 Capital rationing

Optimal investments for Bijoux

First we need to determine in which year(s) capital is rationed, taking account of the fact that only one of the Platinum and Emerald projects will be undertaken.

	Cash flows with Platinum		Cash flows with Emerald	
Project	Time 0 €'000	Time 1 €'000	Time 0 €'000	Time 1 €'000
Diamond	(24)	(36)	(24)	(36)
Sapphire	(48)	6	(48)	6
Platinum	(60)	(30)		
Emerald			(48)	(6)
Quartz	(36)	(24)	(36)	(24)
Total	(168)	(84)	(156)	(60)
Capital available	120	240	120	240

To rank the projects the basic PI as previously defined cannot be used as this would ignore outlays at time 1. One option would be to use a PI defined as $\frac{PV\ of\ inflows}{PV\ of\ outlays}$ but this is not entirely appropriate as capital is not rationed at time 1.

An alternative, used here, is to use a PI defined as $\frac{NPV\ project}{Initial\ capital\ invested}$

It is therefore concluded that effective capital rationing exists only at time 0, ie a single period of capital rationing.

Project	Cash flows 0 €'000	1 €'000	2 €'000	PV of cash flows @ 20% 0 €'000	1 €'000	2 €'000	NPV €'000	PI	Rank
Diamond	(24)	(36)	96	(24)	(30.0)	66.6	12.6	0.525	1
Sapphire	(48)	6	66	(48)	5.0	45.8	2.8	0.058	5
Platinum	(60)	(30)	138	(60)	(25.0)	95.8	10.8	0.180	4
Emerald	(48)	(6)	90	(48)	(5.0)	62.5	9.5	0.198	3
Quartz	(36)	(24)	96	(36)	(20.0)	66.6	10.6	0.294	2

In time 0 with only €100,000 available, projects would be introduced in order of profitability as shown.

Platinum without Emerald

Project	Proportion accepted %	Funds used at time 0 €'000	Total NPV €'000
Diamond	100	24	12.6
Quartz	100	36	10.6
Platinum	100	60	10.8
Sapphire	Nil	NIL	NIL
Funds utilised and available		120	34.0

Emerald without Platinum

Project	Proportion accepted %	Funds used at time 0 €'000	Total NPV €'000
Diamond	100	24	12.6
Quartz	100	36	10.6
Emerald	100	48	9.5
Sapphire	25	12	0.7
Funds utilised and available		120	33.4

Platinum without Emerald is to be preferred as it yields a higher NPV.

Note. Platinum is selected in preference to Emerald even though it has a lower profitability index.

This is because the choice is effectively between investing €60,000 in Platinum with an NPV of €10,800 (PI = 0.18) or a package containing a €48,000 investment in Emerald and a €12,000 investment in Sapphire with a combined NPV of €10,200. This package has a profitability index of only 0.17 and is therefore rejected.

Now try the question from the Practice Question Bank	Number	Marks	Time
	Q40 Objective test questions	10	18 mins
	Q41 Fund restrictions	12	22 mins
	Q42 ANT	25	45 mins

MANAGEMENT CONTROL AND RISK

Part D

MANAGEMENT CONTROL AND RISK

 In this chapter we look at methods of assessing risk and uncertainty for short-term decision making.

Section 1 contains a general discussion of risk and uncertainty.

Sections 2 to 8 describe the various methods of analysing uncertainty and risk using probability. You need to understand the merits and limitations of these methods for your exam. The uncertainty about the future outcome from taking a decision can sometimes be reduced by obtaining more information first about what is likely to happen.

Sections 9 to 11 explore the areas of risk management, ethics and corporate social responsibility.

In Sections 12 to 16 we look at information systems and some of the risks associated with those systems.

In the final section we look at the concept of Big Data and its effects on the management of risk.

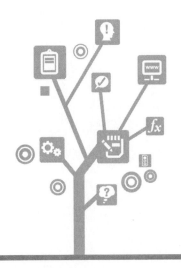

topic list	learning outcomes	syllabus references	ability required
1 The nature of risk	D2(a)	D2(a)(i), (ii), (iii)	analysis
2 Sensitivity analysis	D1(a)	D1(a)(i)	application
3 Probability analysis and expected values (EV)	D1(a)	D1(a)(ii)	application
4 Data tables	D1(b)	D1(b)(ii)	analysis
5 The maximin, maximax and minimax regret bases for decision making	D1(b)	D1(b)(ii)	analysis
6 Using the standard deviation to measure risk	D1(b)	D1(b)(ii)	analysis
7 Decision trees	D1(b)	D1(b)(iii)	analysis
8 The value of perfect information	D1(b)	D1(b)(ii)	analysis
9 Risk management	D2(a)	D2(a)(ii), (iii)	analysis
10 Business ethics and CSR	D2(a)	D2(a)(iv)	analysis

topic list	learning outcomes	syllabus references	ability required
11 Ethics and control systems	D2(a)	D2(a)(iv)	analysis
12 Information systems	D2(b)	D2(b)(i)	analysis
13 Types of information system	D2(b)	D2(b)(i)	analysis
14 The value of information	D2(b)	D2(b)(i)	analysis
15 Evaluating information systems	D2(b)	D2(b)(i)	analysis
16 Operational risks of information systems	D2(b)	D2(b)(i)	analysis
17 Big Data	D2(b)	D2(b)(ii)	analysis

Chapter Overview

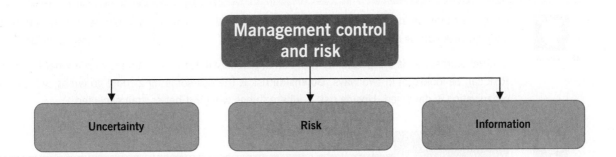

1 The nature of risk

Introduction

In this section we introduce some basic definitions of risk, explain the difference between risk and uncertainty and emphasise the important links between risk and return.

KEY TERM

RISK is a condition in which there exists a quantifiable dispersion in the possible outcomes from any activity. Risk can be classified in a number of ways. *(CIMA Official Terminology)*

In other words, risk is the possibility that actual results will turn out differently from what is expected. Risk can be looked at in two ways. **Downside** risk is the risk something could go wrong and the organisation is damaged. **Upside** risk is where things work out better than expected.

Question 10.1	Risks

Learning outcome D2 (a)

What sort of risks might an organisation face?

1.1 Categories of risk

KEY TERMS

FUNDAMENTAL RISKS are those that affect society in general, or broad groups of people, and are beyond the control of any one individual. For example, there is the risk of atmospheric pollution which can affect the health of a whole community, but which may be quite beyond the power of an individual within it to control.

PARTICULAR RISKS are risks over which an individual may have some measure of control. For example, there is a risk attached to smoking and we can control that risk by refraining from smoking.

SPECULATIVE RISKS are those from which either good (upside risks) or harm (downside risks) may result. A business venture, for example, presents a speculative risk because either a profit or loss can result.

PURE RISKS are those whose only possible outcome is harmful. The risk of damage to property by fire is a pure risk because no gain can result from it.

There are various types of risk that exist in business and in life generally.

1.2 Negative risks

A simple view of risk would see it in negative terms, as **downside risk**. Risk management would involve minimising the chances that adverse events will happen. However, it may **not be possible to eliminate negative risks** without undermining the whole basis on which the business operates or without incurring excessive costs and insurance premiums. Therefore there is likely to be a level of residual or remaining risk which is simply not worth eliminating.

1.3 Benefits of risk management

However, there are some benefits to be derived from the management of risk, possibly at the expense of profits, such as:

- **Predictability** of **cash flows**
- **Well-run systems**
- **Limitation of the impact** of potentially **bankrupting events**
- **Increased confidence** of shareholders and other investors

1.4 Risk and uncertainty

A complication in dealing with risks is the level of uncertainty involved. Ultimately risk assessment may be able to tell you the **possible outcomes**, and the **chances** that each outcome will occur. All that is unknown is the actual outcome. Uncertainty, however, means that you do not know the possible outcomes and/or the chances of each outcome occurring. It may arise from a lack of information about input/output relationships or the environment within which the business operates.

1.5 Risk and return

Businesses may be willing to **tolerate a higher level of risk** provided they receive **a higher level of return**. Indeed, a willingness to take certain risks in order to seize new opportunities may be **essential for business success**. Shareholders who themselves ultimately bear the risk of a business may welcome some risk taking.

Under this view a business should:

- **Reduce risk** where possible and necessary, but not eliminate all risks
- **Maximise the returns** that are possible given the levels of risk

1.6 Risk taking and reduction

Boards therefore should not just focus on managing negative risks; they should also seek to **limit uncertainty** and to **manage speculative risks and opportunities** in order to **maximise positive outcomes and hence shareholder value**.

Boards should consider the factors that determine **shareholder valuations** of the company, the **risks** associated with these and the ways in which shareholders would like the **risks to be managed**.

Most risks must be managed to some extent, and some should be sought to be eliminated as being outside the scope of the remit of the management of a business. For example, a business in a high-tech industry, such as computing, which evolves rapidly within ever-changing markets and technologies, has to accept high risks in its research and development activities; but should it also be speculating on interest and exchange rates within its treasury activities?

Risk management under this view is an integral part of strategy, and involves analysing what the key value drivers are in the organisation's activities, and the risks tied up with those value drivers. In its Risk Management Standard, the Institute of Risk Management linked in key value drivers with major risk categories.

Since risk and return are linked, one consequence of focusing on achieving or maintaining high profit levels may mean that the organisation bears a large amount of risk. The decision to bear these risk levels may not be conscious, and may go well beyond what is considered desirable by shareholders and other stakeholders.

1.7 Risk attitude

Because risk management is bound up with strategy, how organisations deal with risk will be determined not only by events and the information available about events, but also by **management perceptions or appetite** to take risk. These factors will also influence risk **culture**, the values and practices that influence how an organisation deals with risk in its day to day operations.

KEY TERM

RISK APPETITE is the amount of risk that an organisation is prepared to accept in pursuit of its objectives. It is based on:

- Risk attitude – the overall views of the board, whether the board is risk averse or risk seeking
- Risk capacity – the amount of risk that the organisation can bear

Because of its significance, the **board** should be responsible for **determining risk appetite**.

Section summary

Risks can be classified according to **whom** they affect, whether their outcomes will be **beneficial** or **adverse**, and the **area** of an organisation's **affairs affected**.

In an **uncertain situation** there is not sufficient information for the outcome to be predicted with statistical confidence.

2 Sensitivity analysis

Introduction

In general risky projects are those whose future cash flows, and hence the project returns, are likely to be variable – the greater the variability, the greater the risk. The problem of **risk is more acute with capital investment decisions** than other decisions because estimates of costs and benefits might be for up to 20 years ahead, and such long-term estimates can at best be approximations. Sensitivity analysis is one method of assessing the risk associated with a project.

2.1 Why are projects risky?

A decision about whether or not to go ahead with a project is based on expectations about the future. Forecasts of cash flows (whether they be inflows or outflows) that are likely to arise following a particular course of action are made. These forecasts are made, however, on the basis of what is expected to happen given the present state of knowledge and the future is, by definition, uncertain. Actual cash flows are almost certain to differ from prior expectations. It is this **uncertainty about a project's future income and costs that gives rise to risk in business generally and investment activity in particular**.

2.2 Using sensitivity analysis

Sensitivity analysis is one method of analysing the risk surrounding a capital expenditure project and enables an assessment to be made of how responsive the project's NPV is to changes in the variables that are used to calculate that NPV.

The NPV could depend on a number of uncertain independent variables.

- Estimated selling price
- Estimated sales volume
- Estimated cost of capital
- Estimated initial cost

- Estimated operating costs
- Estimated benefits
- Estimated length of project

2.3 The margin of error approach to sensitivity analysis

The **margin of error approach to sensitivity analysis** assesses how responsive the project's NPV (or payback period or ARR) is to changes in the variables used to calculate that NPV (or payback period or ARR).

This basic approach involves **calculating the project's NPV under alternative assumptions to determine how sensitive it is to changing conditions, thereby indicating those variables to which the NPV is most sensitive (critical variables)** and the **extent to which those variables may change before the investment decision would change** (ie a **positive NPV becoming a negative NPV**).

Once these critical variables have been identified, management should review them to assess whether or not there is a strong possibility of events occurring which will lead to a change in the investment decision. Management should also pay particular attention to controlling those variables to which the NPV is particularly sensitive, once the decision has been taken to accept the investment.

KEY POINT

The sensitivity of an NPV computation to changes in a variable that affects the cash flows is

$$\frac{\text{NPV of project}}{\text{PV of cash flow affected}} \times 100\%$$

Example: sensitivity analysis

KE, which has a cost of capital of 8%, is considering a project. The 'most likely' cash flows associated with the project are as follows.

	Year	0 $'000	1 $'000	2 $'000
Initial investment		(7,000)		
Variable costs			(2,000)	(2,000)
Cash inflows (650,000 units at $10 per unit)			6,500	6,500
Net cash flows		(7,000)	4,500	4,500

Required

Measure the sensitivity of the project to changes in variables.

Solution

The PVs of the cash flow are as follows.

Year	Discount factor 8%	PV of initial investment $'000	PV of variable costs $'000	PV of cash inflows $'000	PV of net cash flow $'000
0	1.000	(7,000)			(7,000)
1	0.926		(1,852)	6,019	4,167
2	0.857		(1,714)	5,571	3,857
		(7,000)	(3,566)	11,590	1,024

The project has a positive NPV and would appear to be worthwhile. The **changes in cash flows which would need to occur for the project to only just break even (and hence be on the point of being unacceptable) are as follows**.

(a)   **Initial investment**. The initial investment can rise by $1,024,000 before the investment breaks even. The initial investment may therefore increase by (1,024/7,000) × 100% = 14.6%.

(b)   **Sales volume**. Sales volume affects the level of variable costs and the level of cash inflows. We know that the PV of cash inflows less the PV of variable costs (ie PV of contribution) will have to fall to $7m for the NPV to be zero. The PV of contribution can therefore fall by ((1,024/(11,590 – 3,566)) × 100%) = 12.8% before the project breaks even.

(c)   **Selling price**. The PV of cash inflows can fall by $1,024,000 before the investment breaks even. On the assumption that sales volumes remain the same, the selling price can therefore fall by $((1,024/11,590) \times 100\%) = 8.8\%$ before the project just breaks even.

(d)   **Variable costs**. The PV of variable costs can rise by $1,024,000 before the investment breaks even. Variable costs may therefore increase by $(1,024/3,566) \times 100\%) = 28.7\%$.

(e)   **Cost of capital/IRR**. We need to calculate the IRR of the project. Let us try discount rates of 15% and 20%.

Year	Net cash flow $'000	Discount factor 15%	PV $'000	Discount factor 20%	PV $'000
0	(7,000)	1.000	(7,000)	1.000	(7,000)
1	4,500	0.870	3,915	0.833	3,749
2	4,500	0.756	3,402	0.694	3,123
			NPV = 317		NPV = (128)

$$IRR = 0.15 + [(317/(317 + 128)) \times (0.20 - 0.15)] = 18.56\%$$

The **cost of capital** can therefore increase by 132% before the NPV becomes negative.

Alternatively the **IRR** can fall by $(18.56\% - 8\%)/18.56\% = 57\%$ before the project would be rejected on the basis of IRR.

The elements to which the NPV appears to be **most sensitive** are the **selling price** followed by the **sales volume**, and it is therefore important for management to pay particular attention to these factors so that they can be carefully monitored.

Given this information, it might be possible to **re-engineer** the project in some way so as to **alter its risk/return profile**. For example, customers might be prepared to contract for a $9.75 fixed selling price, but guarantee to buy the 650,000 units. Obviously the NPV would drop, but a major source of uncertainty affecting project viability would be eliminated.

Question 10.2
Sensitivity analysis

Learning outcome D1(a)

NU has a cost of capital of 8% and is considering a project with the following 'most-likely' cash flows.

Year	Purchase of plant $	Running costs $	Savings $
0	(7,000)		
1		2,000	6,000
2		2,500	7,000

Required

Fill in the blanks in the sentences below about the sensitivity of the project to changes in the levels of expected costs and savings.

(a)   Plant costs would need to .... by a PV of $........ or ....% for the project to break even.

(b)   Running costs would need to .... by a PV of $.......... or ....% for the project to break even.

(c)   Savings would need to .... by a PV of $.......... or ....% for the project to break even.

Alternatively you can **change each variable** affecting the NPV of a project in turn **by a certain percentage** and **recalculate the NPV** to determine whether the project is more vulnerable to changes in some key variables than it is to changes in others.

2.3.1 Sensitivity analysis and payback

This would involve determining by how much profit could change in particular years before the decision to accept/not accept was no longer valid.

For example, suppose Project B requires initial capital expenditure of $250,000 and that profits before depreciation from the project are likely to be $80,000 in year 1, $100,000 in year 2 and $140,000 in year 3. The payback period is therefore 2½ years. If the target payback is three years, Project B would be accepted. For Project B to be rejected:

(a)   The initial expenditure would have to increase by at least $70,000 (or 28%)
(b)   The profits in year 1 would need to fall by at least $70,000 (or 87.5%)
(c)   The profits in year 2 would need to fall by at least $70,000 (or 70%)
(d)   The profits in year 3 would need to fall by at least $70,000 (or 50%)

The project is therefore most sensitive to changes in the initial capital expenditure and year 3 profits.

2.3.2 Sensitivity analysis and ARR

Suppose CC has a target ARR of 20% and is considering project D.

	$
Total profit before depreciation over five years	120,000
Total profit after depreciation over five years	40,000
Average annual profit after depreciation	8,000
Original cost of investment	64,000
Residual value of investment	nil
Average net book value over the 5-year period ((64,000 + 0)/2)	32,000

The project's ARR is ($8,000/$32,000) × 100% = 25% and so it would be acceptable.

For project D to be rejected:

(a)   Average annual profit after depreciation would need to fall by at least $1,600 to $6,400 (a fall of 20%)

(b)   The original cost of the investment would need to increase by at least $16,000 to $80,000 (an increase of 25%)

(c)   The residual value of the investment would need to increase by at least $16,000 to $16,000 (an infinite rise from the original $0)

The project is therefore most sensitive to changes in average annual profit.

2.3.3 Weaknesses of the margin of error approach to sensitivity analysis

(a)   The method requires that changes in each key variable are isolated, but management is more interested in the combination of the effects of changes in two or more key variables. Looking at factors in isolation is unrealistic since they are often interdependent.

(b)   Sensitivity analysis does not examine the probability that any particular variation in costs or revenues might occur.

2.4 Diagrammatic approach to sensitivity analysis

We can use a **graph** either to **show how sensitive a project is to changes in a key variable** or to **compare the sensitivities of two or more projects to changes in a key variable**.

Suppose that an organisation wishes to compare two machines (A and B), both of which produce product X. The machines' initial costs, annual fixed running costs and variable cost of producing one unit of product X are different. Annual demand for product X varies unpredictably between 0 and 10,000 units.

The selling price of product X is regulated by government and so is fixed at a certain level, whatever the demand.

The NPV of investments in machines A and B at the highest and lowest demand levels are as follows.

	NPVs	
Demand p.a. Units	Machine A $'000	Machine B $'000
0	(1)	(4)
10,000	8	11

If we plot these four points we can **see how the NPV changes as demand for product X changes**. Note that the NPV does not change in a linear fashion with changes in other variables, but **we can plot straight lines to approximate to the curvilinear behaviour** that would be evident if we calculated the NPV at more demand levels.

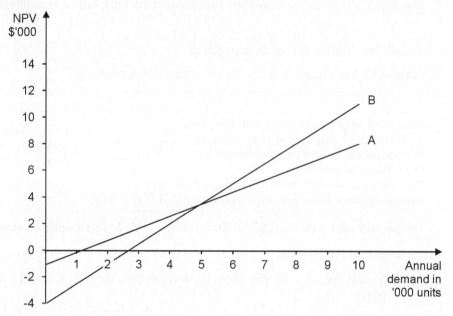

(a)   The two lines cross at demand of 5,000 units, so **Machine B returns a higher NPV in 50% of the possible outcomes that could arise**.

(b)   On the other hand, Machine A crosses the horizontal axis at around 1,100 units. This means that in **approximately 89% of the possible outcomes, Machine A would produce a positive NPV**. Contrast this with Machine B, where only about 73% of outcomes result in a positive NPV.

(c)   The point at which the **two lines cross** is the point at which the **two machines are equally viable**.

2.5 Sensitivity to changes in discount rate

In all our examples we have assumed, for simplicity, a constant rate of interest. Changes in interest rates can be easily accommodated in NPV and discounted payback calculations, but they are not so easily incorporated into IRR or ARR calculations since an IRR or ARR reflects an average rate of return over a project's life. In **periods of great discount rate volatility** the **NPV method should** therefore **be used**.

In situations of **non-conventional cash flows**, a graph can help show the sensitivity of projects to changes in discount rates. Take the following two projects with non-conventional cash flows.

Time	Project Y $'000	Project Z $'000
0	1,920	1,700
1	(4,800)	(4,800)
2	3,000	3,300
NPV @ 10%	$34,800	$62,600

If the projects were **mutually exclusive Project Z would be chosen. If interest rates were not likely to be stable, however, the graph below would illustrate the relative sensitivity of the projects**. (This kind of graph can be sketched by calculating the NPV of the projects at various discount rates, but the calculations have not been shown here.)

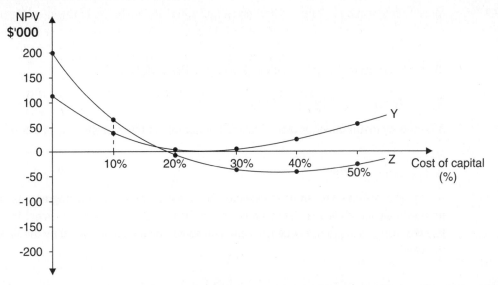

The graph shows that Project **Y will remain profitable at any interest rate**, but Project **Z would not be worthwhile if interest rates increased beyond about 18%** (unless they then increased to something over 50%). Therefore if one wished to avoid all risk, Project Y would be favourable.

2.6 Limitation of sensitivity analysis

One of the **assumptions** commonly made by decision makers in conditions of uncertainty is that the **probability distribution of possible project outcomes is grouped symmetrically around a mean and most likely outcome**. The outcomes close to this mean are assumed to be more likely than ones far from it. And many business projects do exhibit this tendency.

The **problem with sensitivity analysis**, however, is that it tends to **focus on ranges** of possible outcomes **without considering the probabilities of different results within those ranges**. It is possible that outcomes at one end of the range are far more likely to occur than outcomes around the central point.

In the scenario illustrated in the graph in Section 2.4, if low levels of demand were more likely than demand in excess of 5,000 units, Machine A would be preferred.

Sensitivity analysis does identify areas which are critical to success, but it does not point to the correct decision directly.

Section summary

Sensitivity analysis is one method of analysing the risk surrounding a capital expenditure project and enables an assessment to be made of how responsive the project's NPV is to changes in the variables that are used to calculate that NPV.

The **margin of error approach to sensitivity analysis** assesses how responsive the project's NPV (or payback period or ARR) is to changes in the variables used to calculate that NPV (or payback period or ARR).

3 Probability analysis and expected values (EVs)

3.1 Histograms and probability distributions

3.1.1 Frequency distributions

A **frequency distribution** (or **table**) records the number of times each value of a variable occurs.

3.1.2 Histograms

A frequency distribution can be represented pictorially by means of a **histogram**. As you should remember from your earlier studies, a histogram is a chart that looks like a bar chart except that the bars are joined together. On a histogram, frequencies are represented by the area covered by the bars (not the height of the bars).

3.1.3 Probability distributions

If we convert the frequencies in the following frequency distribution table into proportions, we get a **probability distribution**.

Marks out of 10 (statistics test)	Number of students (Frequency distribution)	Proportion or probability (Probability distribution)
0	0	0.00
1	0	0.00
2	1	0.02 (1/50)
3	2	0.04
4	4	0.08
5	10	0.20
6	15	0.30
7	10	0.20
8	6	0.12
9	2	0.04
10	0	0.00
	50	1.00

KEY TERM

A PROBABILITY DISTRIBUTION is an analysis of the proportion of times each particular value occurs in a set of items.

A **graph of the probability distribution** would be the same as the graph of the frequency distribution (histogram), but with the **vertical axis marked in proportions** rather than in numbers.

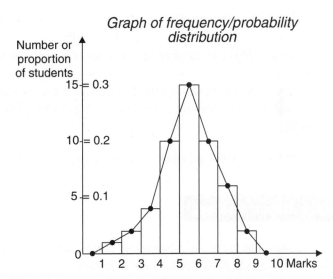

Graph of frequency/probability distribution

(a)   The area under the curve in the frequency distribution represents the total number of students whose marks have been recorded, 50 people.

(b)   **The area under the curve in a probability distribution is 100%, or 1** (the total of all the probabilities).

3.2 Expected values

Knowledge brought forward from earlier studies

Probability

- **Mutually exclusive outcomes** are outcomes where the occurrence of one of the outcomes excludes the possibility of any of the others happening.

- **Independent events** are events where the outcome of one event in no way affects the outcome of the other events.

- **Dependent** or **conditional** events are events where the outcome of one event depends on the outcome of the others.

- The **addition laws** for two events, A and B, are as follows.

  P(A or B) = P(A) + P(B) when A and B have mutually exclusive outcomes
  P(A or B) = P(A) + P(B) – P(A and B) when A and B are independent events

- The **multiplication laws** for two events, A and B, are as follows.

  P(A and B) = 0 when A and B have mutually exclusive outcomes
  P(A and B) = P(A) * P(B) when A and B are independent events
  P(A and B) = P(A) * P(B| A) = P(B) * P(A| B) when A and B are dependent/conditional events

Although the outcome of a decision may not be certain, sometimes probabilities can be assigned to the various possible outcomes from an analysis of previous experience.

Where probabilities are assigned to different outcomes, it is common to evaluate the worth of a decision as the expected value (EV), or weighted average, of these outcomes.

KEY TERM

EXPECTED VALUE (EV) is 'The financial forecast of the outcome of a course of action multiplied by the probability of achieving that outcome. The probability is expressed as a value ranging from 0 to 1'.

(CIMA Official Terminology)

LEARN

The **expected value** of an opportunity is equal to the sum of the probabilities of an outcome occurring multiplied by the return expected if it does occur:

> $$EV = \Sigma \, px$$
>
> where p is the probability of an outcome occurring and x is the value (profit or cost) of that outcome.

If a decision maker is faced with a number of alternative decisions, each with a range of possible outcomes, the optimum decision will be the one which gives the highest **expected value** (EV = Σpx). This is **Bayes' strategy**.

KEY TERM

The choice of the option with the highest EV is known as BAYES' STRATEGY.

Example: Bayes' strategy

Suppose a manager has to choose between mutually exclusive options A and B, and the probability distributions of the profits of both options are as follows.

Option A		Option B	
Probability	Profit $	Probability	Profit $
0.8	5,000	0.1	(2,000)
0.2	6,000	0.2	5,000
		0.6	7,000
		0.1	8,000

The EV of profit of each option would be measured as follows.

Probability		Option A profit $		EV of profit $	Probability		Option B profit $		EV of profit $
0.8	×	5,000	=	4,000	0.1	×	(2,000)	=	(200)
0.2	×	6,000	=	1,200	0.2	×	5,000	=	1,000
		EV	=	5,200	0.6	×	7,000	=	4,200
					0.1	×	8,000	=	800
							EV	=	5,800

In this example, since it offers a higher EV of expected profit, Option B would be selected in preference to A, unless further risk analysis is carried out.

Question 10.3

EV calculations

Learning outcomes D1(b)

A manager has to choose between mutually exclusive options A, B, C and D and the probable outcomes of each option are as follows.

Option A		Option B		Option C		Option D	
Probability	Cost $	Probability	Cost $	Probability	Cost $	Probability	Cost $
0.1	30,000	0.5	21,000	0.29	15,000	0.03	14,000
0.1	60,000	0.5	20,000	0.54	20,000	0.30	17,000
0.1	80,000			0.17	30,000	0.35	21,000
0.7	5,500					0.32	24,000

All options will produce an income of $30,000.

Which option should be chosen?

A	Option A		C	Option C
B	Option B		D	Option D

3.2.1 Limitations of EVs

Referring back to the example in Section 3.2 called Bayes' strategy, we decided on a preference for B over A on the basis of EV. Note, however, that A's worst possible outcome is a **profit** of $5,000, whereas B might incur a **loss** of $2,000 (although there is a 70% chance that profits would be $7,000 or more, which would be more than the best profits from option A).

Since the **decision must be made once only** between A and B, the EV of profit (which is merely a weighted average of all possible outcomes) has severe limitations as a decision rule by which to judge preference, as it **ignores the range of outcomes** and their **probabilities**. **Utility theory** can help overcome this problem.

EVs are more **valuable** as a guide to decision making where they refer to **outcomes which will occur many times over**.

- The probability that so many customers per day will buy a tin of peaches
- The probability that a call centre will receive so many phone calls per hour

Utility theory attaches weights to the sums of money involved depending on the person's attitude to risk.

3.3 EVs and elementary risk analysis

Where some analysis of risk is required when probabilities have been assigned to various outcomes, an elementary, but extremely useful, form of risk analysis is a form of the worst possible/most likely/best possible analysis.

Example: elementary risk analysis

Skiver has budgeted the following results for the coming year.

Sales Units	Probability	EV of sales Units
30,000	0.3	9,000
40,000	0.4	16,000
50,000	0.3	15,000
		40,000

The budgeted sales price is $10 per unit, and the expected cost of materials is as follows.

Cost per unit of output $	Probability	EV $
4	0.2	0.8
6	0.6	3.6
8	0.2	1.6
		6.0

Materials are the only variable cost. All other costs are fixed and are budgeted at $100,000.

The **EV of profit** is $60,000.

	$
Sales (EV 40,000 units) at $10 each	400,000
Variable costs (40,000 × $6)	240,000
Contribution	160,000
Fixed costs	100,000
Profit	60,000

The table below shows the total contribution depending on the level of sales and the material cost per unit.

Contribution table

		Sales units		
		30,000	40,000	50,000
Material cost per unit	$4 (contribution = $6)	$180,000	$240,000	$300,000
	$6 (contribution = $4)	$120,000	$160,000	$200,000
	$8 (contribution = $2)	$60,000	$80,000	$100,000

Given that fixed costs are $100,000, you can see from the table that Skiver will make a **loss** if material costs are $8 per unit **and** sales are **either** 30,000 p.a. **or** 40,000 p.a. The chance that one **or** other of these events will occur is 14%, as calculated below.

Sales	Probability	Material cost	Probability	Joint probabilities
30,000 units	0.3	$8	0.2	0.06
40,000 units	0.4	$8	0.2	0.08
		Combined probabilities		0.14

However, there is also a chance that sales will be 50,000 units and material will cost $4, so that contribution would be $300,000 in total and profits $200,000. This is the **best possible outcome** and it has a 0.3 × 0.2 = 0.06 or 6% probability of occurring.

A **risk-averse** decision maker might feel that a 14% chance of making a loss was unacceptable, whereas a **risk seeker** would be attracted by the 6% chance of making $200,000 profit. The **risk-neutral** decision maker would need to consider the EV of profit of $60,000.

3.4 EVs and more complex risk analysis

As we have seen, EVs can be used to compare two or more mutually exclusive alternatives: the alternative with the most favourable EV of profit or cost would normally be preferred. However, **alternatives can also be compared** by looking at the **spread of possible outcomes**, and the **probabilities** that they will occur. The technique of drawing up **cumulative probability tables** can be helpful, as the following example shows.

Example: mutually exclusive options and cumulative probability

QRS is reviewing the price that it charges for a major product line. Over the past 3 years the product has had sales averaging 48,000 units per year at a standard selling price of $5.25. Costs have been rising steadily over the past year and the company is considering raising this price to $5.75 or $6.25. The sales manager has produced the following schedule to assist with the decision.

Price	$5.75	$6.25
Estimates of demand (units)		
Pessimistic estimate (probability 0.25)	35,000	10,000
Most likely estimate (probability 0.60)	40,000	20,000
Optimistic estimate (probability 0.15)	50,000	40,000

Currently the unit cost is estimated at $5.00, analysed as follows.

	$
Direct material	2.50
Direct labour	1.00
Variable overhead	1.00
Fixed overhead	0.50
	5.00

The cost accountant considers that the most likely value for unit variable cost over the next year is $4.90 (probability 0.75) but that it could be as high as $5.20 (probability 0.15) and it might even be as low as $4.75 (probability 0.10). Total fixed costs are currently $24,000 p.a., but it is estimated that the corresponding total for the ensuing year will be $25,000 with a probability of 0.2, $27,000 with a probability of 0.6, $30,000 with a probability of 0.2. (Demand quantities, unit costs and fixed costs can be assumed to be statistically independent.)

Required

Analyse the foregoing information in a way which you consider will assist management with the problem, give your views on the situation and advise on the new selling price. Calculate the expected level of profit that would follow from the selling price that you recommend.

Solution

In this example, there are two mutually exclusive options, a price of $5.75 and a price of $6.25. Sales demand is uncertain, but would vary with price. Unit contribution and total contribution depend on sales price and sales volume, but total fixed costs are common to both options. Clearly, it makes sense to begin looking at EVs of contribution and then to think about fixed costs and profits later.

(a)   A probability table can be set out for each alternative, and an EV calculated, as follows.

Price $5.75

Sales demand Units	Probability (a)	Variable cost per unit $	Probability (b)	Unit cont'n $	Total cont'n $'000	Joint proba-bility* (a × b)	EV of cont'n $'000
35,000	0.25	5.20	0.15	0.55	19.25	0.0375	0.722
		4.90	0.75	0.85	29.75	0.1875	5.578
		4.75	0.10	1.00	35.00	0.0250	0.875
40,000	0.60	5.20	0.15	0.55	22.00	0.0900	1.980
		4.90	0.75	0.85	34.00	0.4500	15.300
		4.75	0.10	1.00	40.00	0.0600	2.400
50,000	0.15	5.20	0.15	0.55	27.50	0.0225	0.619
		4.90	0.75	0.85	42.50	0.1125	4.781
		4.75	0.10	1.00	50.00	0.0150	0.750
						EV of contribution	33.005

The EV of contribution at a price of $5.75 is $33,005.

* Remember to check that the joint probabilities sum to 1.

Alternative approach

An alternative method of calculating the EV of contribution is as follows.

EV of contribution	=	EV of sales revenue − EV of variable costs

EV of sales revenue =   EV of sales units × selling price
= ((35,000 × 0.25) + (40,000 × 0.60) + (50,000 × 0.15)) × $5.75
= 40,250 × $5.75 = $231,437.50

EV of variable costs =   EV of sales units × EV of unit variable costs

= 40,250 × (($5.20 × 0.15) + ($4.90 × 0.75) + ($4.75 × 0.10))
= 40,250 × $4.93
= $198,432.50

∴ EV of contribution = $(231,437.50 − 198,432.50) = $33,005

This method is quicker and simpler, but an extended table of probabilities will help the risk analysis when the two alternative selling prices are compared.

Price $6.25

Sales demand Units	Probability (a)	Variable cost per unit $	Probability (b)	Unit cont'n $	Total cont'n $'000	Joint proba- bility (a × b)	EV of cont'n $'000
10,000	0.25	5.20	0.15	1.05	10.50	0.0375	0.394
		4.90	0.75	1.35	13.50	0.1875	2.531
		4.75	0.10	1.50	15.00	0.0250	0.375
20,000	0.60	5.20	0.15	1.05	21.00	0.0900	1.890
		4.90	0.75	1.35	27.00	0.4500	12.150
		4.75	0.10	1.50	30.00	0.0600	1.800
40,000	0.15	5.20	0.15	1.05	42.00	0.0225	0.945
		4.90	0.75	1.35	54.00	0.1125	6.075
		4.75	0.10	1.50	60.00	0.0150	0.900
						EV of contribution	27.060

The EV of contribution at a price of $6.25 is $27,060.

(b)   The EV of **fixed costs** is $27,200.

Fixed costs $	Probability	EV $
25,000	0.2	5,000
27,000	0.6	16,200
30,000	0.2	6,000
		27,200

(c)   **Conclusion**

On the basis of EVs alone, a price of $5.75 is preferable to a price of $6.25, since it offers an EV of contribution of $33,005 and so an EV of profit of $5,805, whereas a price of $6.25 offers an EV of contribution of only $27,060 and so an EV of loss of $140.

Additional information

A comparison of cumulative probabilities would add to the information for risk analysis. The cumulative probabilities can be used to compare the **likelihood of earning a total contribution of a certain size with each selling price**.

Refer back to the two probability tables above. You should be able to read the probabilities and related total contributions straight from each table.

The table below shows that no matter whether fixed costs are $25,000, $27,000 or $30,000, the **probability of at least breaking even** is much higher with a price of $5.75 than with a price of $6.25. The only reason for favouring a price of $6.25 is that there is a better **probability of earning bigger profits** (a contribution of $50,000 or more), and so although a risk-averse decision maker would choose a price of $5.75, a risk-seeking decision maker might gamble on a price of $6.25.

Probability of total contribution of at least $	Price $5.75 Probability	Workings	Price $6.25 Probability	Workings
15,000	1.0000		0.7750	(1 – 0.0375 – 0.1875)
20,000	0.9625	(1 – 0.0375)	0.7500	(0.775 – 0.025)
25,000	0.8725	(0.9625 – 0.09)	0.6600	etc
27,000	0.8725		0.6600	
30,000	0.6625	(0.8725 – 0.1875 – 0.0225)	0.2100	
35,000	0.2125	etc	0.1500	
40,000	0.1875		0.1500	
50,000	0.0150		0.1275	
60,000	0.0000		0.0150	

3.5 The advantages and disadvantages of point estimate probabilities

A **point estimate probability** means an estimate of the **probability of particular outcomes occurring**. In the previous example, there were point estimate probabilities for **variable costs** ($5.20 or $4.90 or $4.75) but in **reality**, the **actual** variable cost per unit **might be any amount**, from below $4.75 to above $5.20. Similarly, point estimate probabilities were given for period fixed costs ($25,000 or $27,000 or $30,000), but in reality, actual fixed costs might be any amount between about $25,000 and $30,000.

This is a disadvantage of using point estimate probabilities: they can be **unrealistic**, and can only be an **approximation** of the risk and uncertainty in estimates of costs or sales demand.

In spite of their possible disadvantages, point estimate probabilities can be very helpful for a decision maker.

(a)   They provide some estimate of risk, which is probably **better than nothing**.

(b)   **If there are enough point estimates** they are likely to be a **reasonably good approximation of** a continuous probability distribution.

(c)   Alternatively, it can be **assumed** that point estimate probabilities **represent a range** of values, so that if we had the probabilities for variable cost per unit, say, of $5.20, $4.90 and $4.75, we could assume that those actually represent probabilities for the ranges, say, $5.05 to $5.30, and $4.82 to $5.04 and $4.70 to $4.81.

Section summary

If a decision maker is faced with a number of alternative decisions, each with a range of possible outcomes, the optimum decision will be the one which gives the highest **expected value** (EV = Σpx). This is **Bayes' strategy**.

The calculation of **joint probabilities** and **cumulative probabilities** adds to the information for risk analysis.

4 Data tables

Introduction

Data tables are often produced using spreadsheet packages and show the effect of changing the values of variables.

A **one-way or one-input data table shows the effect of a range of values of one variable**. For example, it might show the effect on profit of a range of selling prices. A **two-way or two-input data table shows the results of combinations of different values of two key variables**. The effect on contribution of combinations of various levels of demand and different selling prices would be shown in a two-way data table.

Any combination of variable values can therefore be changed and the **effects monitored**.

Example: a one-way data table

Suppose a company has production costs which it would expect to be in the region of $5m were it not for the effects of inflation. Economic forecasts for the inflation rate in the coming year range from 2% to 10%. Profit (before inflation is taken into account) is expected to be $475,000.

By using a spreadsheet package and with three or four clicks of the mouse, the data table below is produced. This shows the effects of different levels of inflation on production costs and profit.

		Production costs $'000	Profit $'000
	2%	5,100	375
	3%	5,150	325
Inflation rate	4%	5,200	275
	5%	5,250	225
	6%	5,300	175
	7%	5,350	125
	8%	5,400	75
	9%	5,450	25
	10%	5,500	(25)

So if inflation were to be 7%, the company could expect production costs to be in the region of $5,350,000 and profit to be about $125,000 ($(475,000 − (7% × $5m)).

Example: two-way data table

Suppose now that the company mentioned in the example above is not sure that its production costs will be $5m. They could be only $4.5m or they could be up to $5.5m.

We therefore need to examine the effects of both a range of rates of inflation and three different production costs on profit, and so we need a two-way data table as shown below.

Two-way data table showing profit for a range of rates of inflation and production costs

| | | Production costs | | |
		$4,500,000 $'000	$5,000,000 $'000	$5,500,000 $'000
	2%	385	375	365
	3%	340	325	310
Inflation rate	4%	295	275	255
	5%	250	225	200
	6%	205	175	145
	7%	160	125	90
	8%	115	75	35
	9%	70	25	(20)
	10%	25	(25)	(75)

So if production costs were $5,500,000 and the rate of inflation was 4%, the profit should be $255,000 ($(475,000 − (4% × $5,500,000)).

4.1 Data tables and probability

If a probability distribution can be applied to either or both of the variables in a data table, a revised table can be prepared to provide improved management information.

Example: data tables and probability

Estimates of levels of demand and unit variable costs, with associated probabilities, for product B are shown below. Unit selling price is fixed at $100.

Levels of demand

Pessimistic	Probability of 0.4	10,000 units
Most likely	Probability of 0.5	12,500 units
Optimistic	Probability of 0.1	13,000 units

Unit variable costs

Optimistic	Probability of 0.3	$20
Most likely	Probability of 0.4	$30
Pessimistic	Probability of 0.3	$35

Required

Produce a two-way data table showing levels of contribution that incorporates information about both the variables and the associated probabilities.

Solution

Table of total contributions

The shaded area on this table shows the possible total contributions and the associated joint probabilities.

Demand Probability			10,000 0.4	12,500 0.5	13,000 0.1
Unit variable cost	Probability	Unit contribution			
$20	0.3	$80	$800,000 0.12	$1,000,000 0.15	$1,040,000 0.03
$30	0.4	$70	$700,000 0.16	$875,000 0.20	$910,000 0.04
$35	0.3	$65	$650,000 0.12	$812,500 0.15	$845,000 0.03

Section summary

Data tables are often produced using spreadsheet packages and show the effect of changing the values of variables.

5 The maximin, maximax and minimax regret bases for decision making

Introduction

The **assumption** made so far in this chapter has been that when there is a decision to make, and probabilities of the various outcomes have been estimated, the decision maker should **prefer the option with the highest EV of profit.**

For **once-only decisions**, this choice of option with the best EV does not necessarily make sense. It provides one rational basis for decision making, but it is not the only rational basis.

There are several other ways of making a choice, including the following.

(a) **Playing safe**, and **choosing the option with the least damaging results if events were to turn out badly**

(b) Looking for the **best outcome**, no matter how small the chance that it might occur

(c) Looking at the opportunity loss when we choose an option but come to regret it

(d) **Balancing the EV of profit against the risk**, measured as the **standard deviation of variations in possible profit around the EV** (we cover this in Section 6)

The 'play it safe' basis for decision making is referred to as the **maximin basis**. This is short for '**maximise the minimum achievable profit**'. (It might also be called '**minimax**' which is short for '**minimise the maximum potential cost or loss**'.) Maximin decisions are taken by **risk-averse** decision makers.

A basis for making decisions by looking for the best outcome is known as the **maximax basis**, short for '**maximise the maximum achievable profit**'. (It can also be called the **minimin cost rule** – minimise the minimum costs or losses.) Maximax decisions are taken by **risk-seeking** decision makers.

The 'opportunity loss' basis for decision making is known as **minimax regret**.

Example: maximin decision basis

Suppose that a manager is trying to decide which of three mutually exclusive projects to undertake. Each of the projects could lead to varying net profits which are classified as outcomes I, II and III. The manager has constructed the following **pay-off table or matrix** (a **conditional profit table**).

Project	Net profit if outcome turns out to be		
	I	*II*	*III*
A	$50,000	$65,000	$80,000
B	$70,000	$60,000	$75,000
C	$90,000	$80,000	$55,000
Probability	0.2	0.6	0.2

Required

Decide which project should be undertaken.

Solution

If the project with the **highest EV of profit** were chosen, this would be Project C.

Outcome	Probability	Project A EV $	Project B EV $	Project C EV $
I	0.2	10,000	14,000	18,000
II	0.6	39,000	36,000	48,000
III	0.2	16,000	15,000	11,000
		65,000	65,000	77,000

However, if the **maximin criterion** were applied the assessment would be as follows.

Project selected	The worst outcome that could happen	Profit $
A	I	50,000
B	II	60,000
C	III	55,000

By **choosing Project B**, we are **'guaranteed' a profit of at least $60,000**, which is more than we would get from Projects A or C if the worst outcome were to occur for them. (We want the maximum of the minimum achievable profits.)

The decision would therefore be to **choose Project B**.

The main **weakness** of the maximin basis for decision making is that it **ignores the probabilities** that **various different outcomes might occur**, and so in this respect it is not as good as the EV basis for decision making.

Example: maximax

Here is a payoff table showing the profits that will be achieved depending upon the action taken (D, E or F) and the circumstances prevailing (I, II or III).

		Profits Actions		
		D	E	F
	I	100	80	60
Circumstances	II	90	120	85
	III	(20)	10	85
Maximum profit		100	120	85

Action E would be chosen if the maximax rule is followed.

Criticisms of this approach would be that it ignores probabilities and that it is over-optimistic.

5.1 Minimax regret

Minimax regret considers the extent to which we might come to regret an action we had chosen.

Regret for any combination of action and circumstances	=	Payoff for **best** action in those circumstances	−	Payoff of the action **actually taken** in those circumstances

An alternative term for regret is **opportunity loss**. We may apply the rule by considering the maximum opportunity loss associated with each course of action and choosing the course which offers the smallest maximum. If we choose an action which turns out not to be the best in the actual circumstances, we have lost an opportunity to make the extra profit we could have made by choosing the best action.

Example: minimax regret

A manager is trying to decide which of three mutually exclusive projects to undertake. Each of the projects could lead to varying net costs which the manager calls outcomes I, II and III. The following payoff table or matrix has been constructed.

| Project | Outcomes (Net profit) | | |
| | I | II | III |
	(Worst)	(Most likely)	(Best)
A	50	85	130
B	70	75	140
C	90	100	110

Which project should be undertaken?

Solution

A table of regrets can be compiled, as follows, showing the amount of profit that might be forgone for each project, depending on whether the outcome is I, II or III.

| | Outcome | | | Maximum |
	I	II	III	
Project A	40 *	15 ***	10	40
Project B	20 **	25	0	25
Project C	0	0	30	30

* 90–50   ** 90–70   *** 100–85   etc

The **maximum regret** is 40 with Project A, 25 with Project B and 30 with Project C. The lowest of these 3 maximum regrets is 25 with B, and so Project B would be selected if the minimax regret rule is used.

Section summary

The maximin basis means maximise the minimum achievable profit.

The maximax basis means maximise the maximum achievable profit.

The minimax regret basis means minimise the maximum regrets.

6   Using the standard deviation to measure risk

Introduction

Risk can be measured by the possible variations of outcomes around the expected value. One useful measure of such variations is the **standard deviation of the expected value**.

LEARN

The standard deviation is $s = \sqrt{\Sigma p(x - \bar{x})^2} = \sqrt{variance}$

where $\bar{x}$ is the EV of profit

   x represents each possible profit

   p represents the probability of each possible profit

The decision maker can then **weigh up the EV of each option against the risk** (the standard deviation) that is **associated with it**.

Example: measuring risk

The management of RC is considering which of two mutually exclusive projects to select. Details of each project are as follows.

	Project S		Project T	
Probability	Profit $'000		Probability	Profit $'000
0.3	150		0.2	(400)
0.3	200		0.6	300
0.4	250		0.1	400
			0.1	800

Required

Determine which project seems preferable, S or T.

Solution

On the basis of EVs alone, T is marginally preferable to S, by $15,000.

	Project S			Project T	
Probability	Profit $'000	EV $'000	Probability	Profit $'000	EV $'000
0.3	150	45	0.2	(400)	(80)
0.3	200	60	0.6	300	180
0.4	250	100	0.1	400	40
			0.1	800	80
	EV of profit	205		EV of profit	220

Project T is more risky, however, offering the prospect of a profit as high as $800,000 but also the possibility of a loss of $400,000.

One measure of this risk is the **standard deviation of the EV of profit**.

(a) **Project S**

Probability p	Profit x $\$'000$	$x - \overline{x}$	$p(x - \overline{x})^2$
0.3	150	−55	907.5*
0.3	200	−5	7.5
0.4	250	45	810.0
		Variance	1,725.0

* $0.3 \times (-55)^2$

Standard deviation = $\sqrt{1,725}$ = 41.533 = $\$41,533$

(b) **Project T**

Probability p	Profit x $\$'000$	$x - \overline{x}$	$p(x - \overline{x})^2$
0.2	(400)	−620	76,880
0.6	300	80	3,840
0.1	400	180	3,240
0.1	800	580	33,640
		Variance	117,600

Standard deviation = $\sqrt{117,600}$ = 342.929 = $\$342,929$

If the management are **risk averse**, they might therefore **prefer Project S** because, although it has a smaller EV of profit, the possible profits are subject to less variation.

The **risk associated with Project T can be compared with the risk associated with Project S** if we calculate the **coefficient of variation** for each project: the **ratio of the standard deviation of each project to its EV**.

	Project S	Project T
Standard deviation	$\$41,533$	$\$342,929$
EV of profit	$\$205,000$	$\$220,000$
Coefficient of variation (standard deviation/EV of profit)	0.20	1.56

Question 10.4	Using the standard deviation to measure risk

Learning outcome D1(b)

Fill in the blank in the sentence below.

On the basis of the information below a 'risk-averse' decision maker would choose project ....

Project A		Project B	
Estimated net cash flow $\$$	Probability	Estimated net cash flow $\$$	Probability
		1,000	0.2
2,000	0.3	2,000	0.2
3,000	0.4	3,000	0.2
4,000	0.3	4,000	0.2
		5,000	0.2

Learning outcome D1(b)

Frame is considering which of two mutually exclusive projects, A or B, to undertake. There is some uncertainty about the running costs with each project, and a probability distribution of the NPV for each project has been estimated, as follows.

	Project A			Project B	
NPV $'000	Probability		NPV $'000	Probability	
−20	0.15		+5	0.2	
+10	0.20		+15	0.3	
+20	0.35		+20	0.4	
+40	0.30		+25	0.1	

Required

Choose the correct words from those highlighted in the sentence below.

The organisation should choose **Project A/Project B** if management are risk averse.

Section summary

Risk can be measured by the possible variations of outcomes around the expected value. One useful measure of such variations is the **standard deviation of the expected value**.

7 Decision trees

Introduction

A probability problem such as 'what is the probability of throwing a six with one throw of a die?' is fairly straightforward and can be solved using the basic principles of probability.

More complex probability questions, although solvable using the basic principles, require a clear logical approach to ensure that all possible choices and outcomes of a decision are taken into consideration. **Decision trees** are a useful means of interpreting such probability problems.

KEY TERM

A DECISION TREE is 'A pictorial method of showing a sequence of interrelated decisions and their expected outcomes. Decision trees can incorporate both the probabilities of, and values of, expected outcomes, and are used in decision-making.' *(CIMA Official Terminology)*

Exactly how does the use of a decision tree permit a clear and logical approach?

- All the possible **choices** that can be made are shown as **branches** on the tree.
- All the possible **outcomes** of each choice are shown as **subsidiary branches** on the tree.

7.1 Constructing a decision tree

There are two stages in preparing a decision tree.

- Drawing the tree itself to show all the choices and outcomes
- Putting in the numbers (the probabilities, outcome values and EVs)

Every **decision tree starts** from a **decision point** with the **decision options** that are currently being considered.

(a) It helps to identify the **decision point**, and any subsequent decision points in the tree, with a symbol. Here, we shall use a **square shape**.

(b) There should be a **line**, or **branch**, for each **option** or **alternative**.

It is conventional to draw decision trees from left to right, and so a decision tree will start as follows.

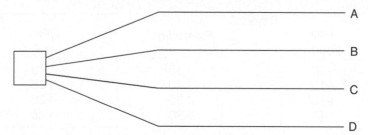

The **square** is the **decision point**, and A, B, C and D represent **four alternatives** from which a choice must be made (such as buy a new machine with cash, hire a machine, continue to use existing machine, raise a loan to buy a machine).

If the outcome from any choice is certain, the branch of the decision tree for that alternative is complete.

If the outcome of a particular choice is uncertain, the various possible outcomes must be shown.

We show the various possible outcomes on a decision tree by inserting an **outcome point** on the **branch** of the tree. Each possible outcome is then shown as a **subsidiary branch**, coming out from the outcome point. The probability of each outcome occurring should be written onto the branch of the tree which represents that outcome.

To distinguish decision points from outcome points, **a circle will be used as the symbol for an outcome point**.

In the example above, there are two choices facing the decision maker, A and B. The outcome if A is chosen is known with certainty but, if B is chosen, there are two possible outcomes, high sales (0.6 probability) or low sales (0.4 probability).

When several outcomes are possible, it is usually simpler to show two or more stages of outcome points on the decision tree.

 Example: several possible outcomes

A company can choose to launch a new product XYZ or not. If the product is launched, expected sales and expected unit costs might be as follows.

Sales		Unit costs	
Units	Probability	$	Probability
10,000	0.8	6	0.7
15,000	0.2	8	0.3

(a) The decision tree could be drawn as follows.

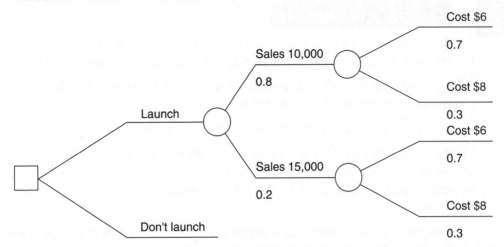

(b) The layout shown above will usually be easier to use than the alternative way of drawing the tree, which is as follows.

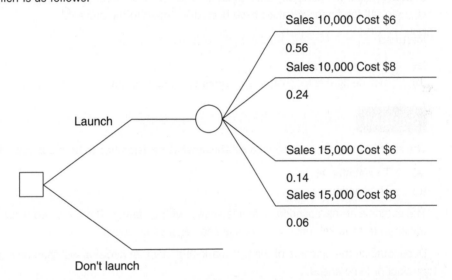

Sometimes, a **decision taken now** will lead to **other decisions to be taken in the future**. When this situation arises, the decision tree can be drawn as a **two-stage tree**, as follows.

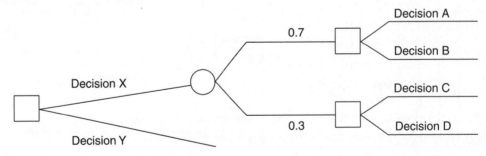

In this tree, either a choice between A and B or else a choice between C and D will be made, depending on the outcome which occurs after choosing X.

The decision tree should be in **chronological order** from **left to right**. When there are two-stage decision trees, the first decision in time should be drawn on the left.

Example: a decision tree

Beethoven has a new wonder product, the vylin, of which it expects great things. At the moment the company has two courses of action open to it, to test market the product or abandon it.

If the company test markets it, the cost will be $100,000 and the market response could be positive or negative with probabilities of 0.60 and 0.40.

If the response is positive, the company could either abandon the product or market it full scale.

If it markets the vylin full scale, the outcome might be low, medium or high demand, and the respective net gains/(losses) would be (200), 200 or 1,000 in units of $1,000 (the result could range from a net loss of $200,000 to a gain of $1,000,000). These outcomes have probabilities of 0.20, 0.50 and 0.30 respectively.

If the result of the test marketing is negative and the company goes ahead and markets the product, estimated losses would be $600,000.

If, at any point, the company abandons the product, there would be a net gain of $50,000 from the sale of scrap. All the financial values have been discounted to the present.

Required

(a)   Draw a decision tree.
(b)   Include figures for cost, loss or profit on the appropriate branches of the tree.

Solution

The starting point for the tree is to **establish what decision has to be made now**. What are the options?

(a)   To test market
(b)   To abandon

The outcome of the 'abandon' option is known with certainty. There are two possible outcomes of the option to test market, positive response and negative response.

Depending on the outcome of the test marketing, another decision will then be made, to abandon the product or to go ahead.

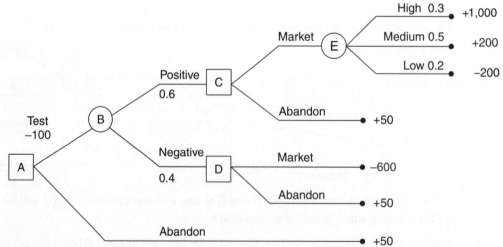

7.2 Evaluating the decision with a decision tree

Rollback analysis evaluates the EV of each decision option. You have to work from right to left and calculate EVs at each outcome point.

The EV of each decision option can be evaluated, using the decision tree to help with keeping the logic on track. The basic rules are as follows.

(a) We start on the **right-hand side** of the tree and **work back** towards the left-hand side and the current decision under consideration. This is sometimes known as the **'rollback' technique** or **'rollback analysis'**.

(b) Working from **right to left**, we calculate the **EV of revenue, cost, contribution or profit** at each outcome point on the tree.

In the example above, the right-hand-most outcome point is point E, and the EV is as follows.

	Profit	Probability	
	x	p	px
	$'000		$'000
High	1,000	0.3	300
Medium	200	0.5	100
Low	(200)	0.2	(40)
		EV	360

This is the EV of the decision to market the product if the test shows a positive response. It may help you to write the EV on the decision tree itself, at the appropriate outcome point (point E).

(a) **At decision point C**, the **choice** is as follows.

    (i) Market, EV = +360 (the EV at point E)
    (ii) Abandon, value = +50

The choice would be to market the product, and so the EV at decision point C is +360.

(b) **At decision point D**, the **choice** is as follows.

    (i) Market, value = –600
    (ii) Abandon, value = +50

The choice would be to abandon, and so the EV at decision point D is +50.

The second-stage decisions have therefore been made. If the original decision is to test market, the company will market the product if the test shows a positive customer response, and will abandon the product if the test results are negative.

The evaluation of the decision tree is completed as follows.

(a) **Calculate the EV at outcome point B.**

       0.6 × 360   (EV at C)
  +   0.4 × 50   (EV at D)
  =   216 + 20 = 236.

(b) **Compare the options at point A**, which are as follows.

    (i) Test: EV = EV at B minus test marketing cost = 236 – 100 = 136
    (ii) Abandon: Value = 50

The choice would be to test market the product, because it has a **higher EV of profit**.

Question 10.6

Simple decision tree

Learning outcome D1(b)

Consider the following diagram.

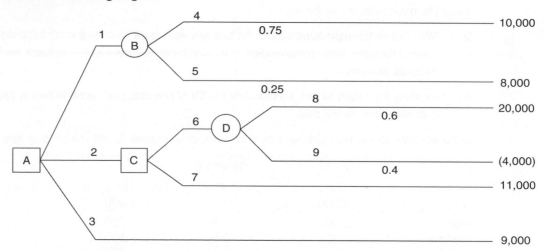

If a decision maker wished to maximise the value of the outcome, which options should be selected?

A   Option 2 and option 7
B   Option 3
C   Option 1 and option 4
D   Option 2, option 6 and option 8

Evaluating decisions by using **decision trees has a number of limitations**.

(a)   The time value of money may not be taken into account.

(b)   Decision trees are not very suitable for use in complex situations.

(c)   The outcome with the highest EV may have the greatest risks attached to it. Managers may be reluctant to take risks which may lead to losses.

(d)   The probabilities associated with different branches of the 'tree' are likely to be estimates, and possibly unreliable or inaccurate.

Section summary

Decision trees are diagrams which illustrate the choices and possible outcomes of a decision.

Rollback analysis evaluates the EV of each decision option. You have to work from right to left and calculate EVs at each outcome point.

8   The value of perfect information

Introduction

The **value of perfect information** is the difference between the EV of profit with perfect information and the EV of profit without perfect information. Imperfect information is better than no information at all, but could be wrong in its prediction of the future.

PERFECT INFORMATION removes all doubt and uncertainty from a decision, and enables managers to make decisions with complete confidence that they have selected the optimum course of action.

8.1 The value of perfect information

If we **do not have perfect information** and we must choose between two or more decision options, we would select the decision option which offers the **highest EV** of profit. This option will not be the best decision under all circumstances. There will be some probability that what was really the best option will not have been selected, given the way actual events turn out.

With **perfect information**, the **best decision option will always be selected**. The profits from the decision will depend on the future circumstances which are predicted by the information; nevertheless, the EV of profit with perfect information should be higher than the EV of profit without the information.

The **value of perfect information** is **the difference between these two EVs**.

Example: the value of perfect information

The management of Ivor Ore must choose whether to go ahead with either of two mutually exclusive projects, A and B. The expected profits are as follows.

	Profit if there is strong demand	Profit/(loss) if there is weak demand
Project A	$4,000	$(1,000)
Project B	$1,500	$500
Probability of demand	0.3	0.7

Required

(a)   Ascertain what the decision would be, based on expected values, if no information about demand were available.

(b)   Calculate the value of perfect information about demand.

Solution

STEP 1

If there were **no information** to help with the decision, the project with the higher EV of profit would be selected.

Probability	Project A		Project B	
	Profit	EV	Profit	EV
	$	$	$	$
0.3	4,000	1,200	1,500	450
0.7	(1,000)	(700)	500	350
		500		800

Project B would be selected.

This is clearly the better option if demand turns out to be weak. However, if demand were to turn out to be strong, Project A would be more profitable. There is a 30% chance that this could happen.

STEP 2

Perfect information will indicate for certain whether demand will be weak or strong. If demand is forecast as 'weak', Project B would be selected. If demand is forecast as 'strong', Project A would be selected, and perfect information would improve the profit from $1,500, which would have been earned by selecting B, to $4,000.

Forecast demand	Probability	Project chosen	Profit	EV of profit
			$	$
Weak	0.7	B	500	350
Strong	0.3	A	4,000	1,200
		EV of profit with perfect information		1,550

STEP 3

	$
EV of profit without perfect information (ie if Project B is always chosen)	800
EV of profit with perfect information	1,550
Value of perfect information	750

Provided that the information does not cost more than $750 to collect, it would be worth having.

Question 10.7

Decision based on EV of profit

Learning outcome D1(b)

Watt Lovell must decide at what level to market a new product, the urk. The urk can be sold nationally, within a single sales region (where demand is likely to be relatively strong) or within a single area. The decision is complicated by uncertainty about the general strength of consumer demand for the product, and the following conditional profit table has been constructed.

		Demand		
		Weak	Moderate	Strong
		$	$	$
Market	nationally (A)	(4,000)	2,000	10,000
	in one region (B)	0	3,500	4,000
	in one area (C)	1,000	1,500	2,000
Probability		0.3	0.5	0.2

Option B should be selected, based on EVs of profit. True or false?

Question 10.8

Learning outcome D1(b)

Using the information in your answer to the question above (Decision based on EV of profit), fill in the blank in the sentence below.

The value of information about the state of demand is $.......... .

8.2 Perfect information and decision trees

When the option exists to obtain information, the decision can be shown, like any other decision, in the form of a decision tree, as follows. We will suppose, for illustration, that the cost of obtaining perfect information is $400.

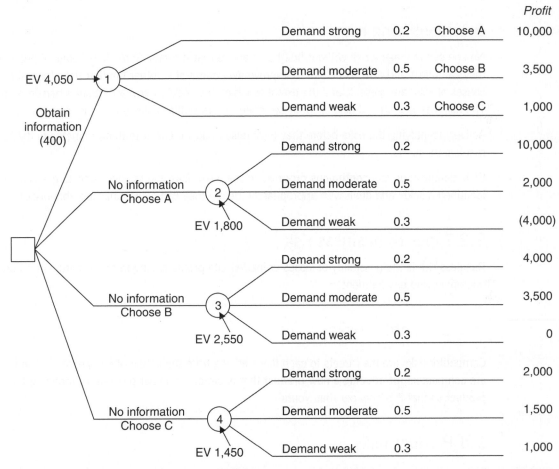

The decision would be to obtain perfect information, since the EV of profit is $4,050 – $400 = $3,650.

Exam skills

You should check carefully that you understand the logic of this decision tree and that you can identify how the EVs at outcome boxes 1, 2, 3 and 4 have been calculated.

> ## Section summary
> **Perfect information** is guaranteed to predict the future with 100% accuracy. **Imperfect information** is better than no information at all, but could be wrong in its prediction of the future.
>
> The **value of perfect information** is the difference between the EV of profit with perfect information and the EV of profit without perfect information.

9 Risk management

> ## Introduction
> We now move on to consider what organisations can do to deal with the risks they are facing.

9.1 Identifying risk

No one can manage a risk without first being aware that it exists. Some knowledge of perils, what items they can affect and how, is helpful to improve awareness of whether **familiar risks** (potential sources and causes of loss) are present, and the extent to which they could harm a particular person or organisation. The risk manager should also keep an eye open for **unfamiliar risks** which may be present.

Actively identifying the risks before they crystallise makes it easier to think of methods that can be used to manage them.

Risk identification is a **continuous process**, so that new risks and changes affecting existing risks may be identified quickly and dealt with appropriately, before they can cause unacceptable losses.

9.2 Types of business risk

Business risk is the possibility of losses or inadequate profits arising from the nature of an organisation's operations and environment.

9.3 Competitor risks

Competitor risks are the threats to cash flows arising from the action of competitors. Obvious examples are competitors **introducing a new product** that is better than your product, or **reducing the price of their product** so that it is cheaper than yours.

9.4 Product risks

Product risks are risks that revenues from existing products will fall or that new product launches will be unsuccessful. These can arise from a variety of sources. A **change in customer tastes** could mean that products become less fashionable.

Product risks will include the risks of financial loss due to producing a poor-quality product. These include the need to **compensate dissatisfied customers**, possible **loss of sales** if the product has to be withdrawn from the market or because of loss of reputation (see below) and the need for **expenditure on improved quality control procedures**.

Other risks connected with products would be **poor branding and marketing strategies**.

9.5 Commodity risks

9.5.1 Supply risks

Supply risks include the **risks of disruption to operations** due to a **shortage of necessary supplies**. These may only be temporary. However, longer-term shortages, for example a worldwide shortage of a particular raw material, may be classified as strategic, since they force a change in business strategy into producing different products or changing the mix of raw materials in the products. Another example of supply risks would be **substandard supplies** disrupting the production process or affecting demand.

9.5.2 Commodity price risks

Large or unexpected fluctuations in the price of a commodity can cause significant problems for businesses that provide that commodity or for which the commodity is a key resource. An example is the risk to road haulage companies of changes in the price of fuel.

9.6 Environmental and social risks

Environmental risk is a term used in different senses. It can be defined as the risk to cash flows arising from changes in the business environment within which the organisation trades. This includes the PEST factors – a variety of political, economic, social and technological issues (many of which are discussed in detail below).

Alternatively, environmental risk can mean the risks arising from the impact of the organisation on the **natural environment or the natural environment upon the organisation** (for example the impact of extreme weather conditions).

Much business activity takes place at some cost to the environment. A 1998 IFAC report identified several examples of how businesses impact on the environment:

- Depletion of natural resources
- Noise and aesthetic impacts
- Residual air and water emissions
- Long-term waste disposal (exacerbated by excessive product packaging)
- Uncompensated health effects
- Change in the local quality of life (through for example the impact of tourism)

9.7 CIMA's risk management cycle

CIMA's suggested approach to risk management is illustrated in the diagram below.

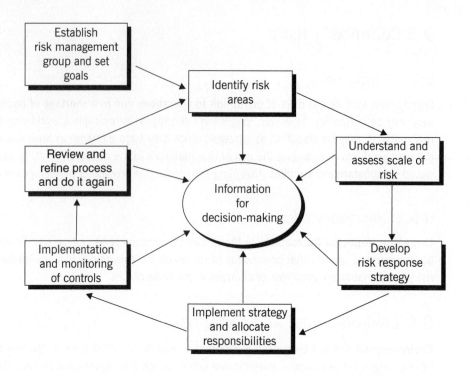

9.8 Risk mapping

This stage involves using the results of a risk assessment to group risks into risk families. One way of doing this severity/frequency matrix (also known as a likelihood/consequences matrix) is as follows.

Severity

		Low	High
Frequency	Low	Loss of small suppliers	Loss of senior or specialist staff Loss of sales to competitor Loss of sales due to macroeconomic factors
	High	Loss of lower-level staff	Loss of key customers Failure of computer systems

This **profile** can then be used to set **priorities** for risk mitigation.

9.9 Managing risk using the TARA framework

In this section we shall consider **risk portfolio management**, the various ways in which organisations can try to mitigate risks or indeed consider whether it will be worthwhile for them to accept risks.

Risk response can be linked into the severity/frequency matrix, and also the organisation's **appetite** for risk taking. In order to deal with risk, organisations will consider the following **TARA** framework.

		Severity	
		Low	*High*
Frequency	*Low*	**Accept** Risks are not significant. Keep under view, but costs of dealing with risks unlikely to be worth the benefits.	**Transfer** Insure risk or implement contingency plans. Reduction of severity of risk will minimise insurance premiums.
	High	**Control or reduce** Take some action, eg enhanced control systems to detect problems or contingency plans to reduce impact.	**Abandon or avoid** Take immediate action, eg change major suppliers or abandon activities.

9.9.1 Abandonment

A company may deal with risk by **abandoning** operations, for example operations in politically volatile countries where the risks of loss (including loss of life) are considered to be too great or the costs of security are considered to be too high.

CASE STUDY

Toyota responded to concerns over the safety of its cars by recalling millions of models worldwide during 2009 and 2010. Sales of a number of models were suspended in the US. Although Toyota's actions aimed to resolve risks to health and safety, it may have been less effective in mitigating the risks to its reputation. Commentators highlighted an initial reluctance to admit the problem and poor communication of what it intended to do to regain control of the situation. The impact threatened car sales and share price, with investors reluctant to hold Toyota shares because of the level of uncertainty involved.

9.9.2 Control of risk

Often risks can be controlled or reduced, but not avoided altogether. This is true of many business risks, where the risks of launching new products can be reduced by market research, advertising and so on.

Many businesses undertake **hazardous activities** where there is a risk of injury or loss of life (for example on an oil rig, factory or farm). These risks cannot be avoided completely. However, they have to be **reduced to an acceptable level** by incurring the costs of risk mitigation – installing protective shielding, issuing safety equipment like hats or protective glasses. The level of risk mitigation is a trade-off between cost and the risk's likelihood and impact. Businesses will also, of course, need to comply with the law.

Methods of controlling risk over the whole organisation include **risk diversification** and **hedging** risks; both involve turning the multiple risks an organisation faces to its advantage by limiting or countering the impact of individual risks.

Contingency planning

Contingency planning involves identifying the **post-loss needs** of the business, **drawing up plans** in advance and **reviewing them regularly** to take account of changes in the business. The process has three basic constituents.

Information	How, for example, do you turn off the sprinklers once the fire is extinguished? All the information that will need to be available during and after the event should be gathered in advance.
Responsibilities	The plan should lay down what is to be done by whom.
Practice	A full-scale test may not always be possible; simulations, however, should be as realistic as possible and should be taken seriously by all involved. The results of any testing should be monitored so that amendments can be made to the plan as necessary.

Loss control

Control of losses also requires careful advance planning. There are two main aspects to good loss control, the physical and the psychological.

(a)   There are **many physical devices** that can be installed to minimise losses when harmful events actually occur. Sprinklers, fire extinguishers, escape stairways, burglar alarms and machine guards are obvious examples.

(b)   The key psychological factors are **awareness** and **commitment**. Every person in the business should be made aware that losses are possible and that they can be controlled. Commitment to loss control can be achieved by making individual managers **accountable for** the losses under their control. Staff should be encouraged to draw attention to any aspects of their job which make losses possible.

Procedural approach to risk control

A procedural approach to risk control sees it as being built on adherence to regulations, codes and operating procedures:

- **Rules and regulations** include statute and corporate governance guidance, such as the UK Corporate Governance Code.

- **Other codes** include professional and organisation ethical codes.

- **Procedures** include detailed authorisation or operating procedures.

This approach is likely to be particularly characteristic of a bureaucratic organisation.

Risk pooling and diversification

Risk pooling and diversification involves using portfolio theory to reduce overall risk levels. You may well remember that portfolio theory is an important part of an organisation's financial strategy, but its principles can be applied to non-financial risks as well.

Risk pooling or diversification involves creating a **portfolio of different risks** based on a number of events, which are co-ordinated so that if some turn out well, others will turn out badly and the average outcome will be neutral. What an organisation has to do is to avoid having all its risks **positively correlated**, which means that everything will turn out **extremely well** or **extremely badly**.

One means of diversification may be **geographical diversification** across countries at different stages of the trade cycle. The business may also **diversify its product base**, aiming to produce products that are at different stages of their product life cycle. Alternatively it could **expand the portfolio of its business activities** by taking over businesses operating at other stages of its supply chain (forward or backward integration), or developing activities that complement or compete with the current portfolio (horizontal integration).

Although diversification sounds good in theory, the company could find it bears significant additional risks if it moves into a new country. The company may have **insufficient expertise** in the product or geographical markets into which it diversifies. It may be vulnerable to competition from other companies which focus on a specific market or product type. Businesses often find it difficult to compete effectively

in many different areas and wide diversification may make them much more difficult to manage. Also, in terms of the Ansoff matrix that you have come across in other papers, diversification is seen as the highest risk strategy of the possible product-market strategies.

A further argument against diversification by companies is that their shareholders have the option of diversifying their portfolio of shares held and can do so more efficiently than the companies.

| Question 10.9 | Controls |

Learning outcome D2(a)

To demonstrate how controls are an important part of managing risks, we list below a number of the important risks that a business may well face. See if you can suggest some appropriate controls.

Risks		Example controls
Business process	Business processes not aligned with strategic objectives	
Staff departure	Strategy and operations disrupted by key staff leaving	
Resource wastage	Employee time being wasted on unproductive activities	
Investor	Investors losing confidence in the way the company is run and selling their shares	
Staff behaviour	Staff behaving in a way that is not compatible with the ethos of the organisation	
Employee error	Employee error causing loss of key resources to the business	
Technology access	Unauthorised persons gaining access to computer systems	
Fraud	Monies or assets being stolen	
Investment	Loss-making investments being made	
Foreign exchange transaction	Having to pay more on a future transaction because of adverse exchange rate movements	
Political	Operations or revenues being disrupted by political activity	
Information	Taking the wrong decisions due to inadequate information	
Information disruption	Disruption to operations caused by failures of information technology	
Systems development	Unreliable systems that are not in accordance with user needs being developed	

9.9.3 Risk acceptance

Risk acceptance or retention is where the organisation bears the risk itself. If an unfavourable outcome occurs, it will suffer the full loss. Risk retention is inevitable to some extent. However good the organisation's risk identification and assessment processes are, there will always be some unexpected risk. Other reasons for risk retention are that the risk is considered to be **insignificant** or the **cost of avoiding** the risk is considered to be too great, set against the potential loss that could be incurred.

The decision of whether to retain or transfer risks depends first on whether there is anyone to transfer a risk to. The answer is more likely to be 'no' for an individual than for an organisation. In the last resort, organisations usually have customers to pass their risks or losses to, up to a point, and individuals do not.

You must remember that risk acceptance is a **conscious decision** to take no action to counter the risk. Risk acceptance and ignoring risk are **not** the same. Risks accepted should generally be **low frequency, low severity risks**.

An organisation can ignore risks of any degree of seriousness. If it does so, it may suffer some nasty surprises.

9.9.4 Transfer of risk

Alternatively, risks can be transferred – to other internal departments or externally to suppliers, customers or **insurers**. Risk transfer can even be to the state.

Decisions to transfer should not be made without careful consideration. A decision not to rectify the design of a product, because rectification could be as expensive as paying claims from disgruntled customers, is in fact a decision to transfer the risk to the customers without their knowledge. The decision may not take into account the possibility of courts awarding exemplary damages to someone injured by the product, to discourage people from taking similar decisions in the future.

Risk sharing

Risks can be partly held and partly transferred to someone else. An example is an insurance policy, where the insurer pays any losses incurred by the policyholder above a set amount.

Risk-sharing arrangements can be very significant in business strategy. For example, in a **joint venture** arrangement each participant's risk can be limited to what it is prepared to bear.

Section summary

Methods of dealing with risk include **abandonment, reduce, acceptance** and **transfer**, which should be remembered as the TARA framework.

10 Business ethics and CSR

Introduction

Ethical and **social responsibility** are two key areas in which businesses have adopted non-financial objectives, taking into account stakeholder needs and interests, partly in response to political and consumer pressure. Contemporary thinking is that **shareholders' wealth and ethics need not be mutually exclusive**.

KEY TERMS

ETHICS are the moral principles by which people act or do business.

SOCIAL RESPONSIBILITY comprises those values and actions which the organisation is not obliged to adopt for business reasons, which it adopts for the good and wellbeing of stakeholders within and outside the organisation.

10.1 Why be socially responsible?

Social responsibility is concerned with the impact that an organisation has on stakeholders and on the wider community.

Managers need to take into account the effect of organisational outputs into the market and the wider **social community**, for several reasons.

(a)   The modern **marketing concept** says that in order to survive and succeed, organisations must satisfy the needs, wants and values of customers and potential customers. Communication and education have made people much more aware of issues such as the environment, the exploitation of workers, product safety and consumer rights. Therefore an organisation may have to be seen to be responsible in these areas in order to retain public support for its products.

(b)   There are skill shortages in the labour pool and employers must compete to attract and retain high-quality employees. If the organisation gets a reputation as a socially responsible employer, it will find it easier to do this than if it has a poor '**employer brand**'.

(c)   A business itself is a **social system**, not just an economic machine (Mintzberg). Organisations rely on the society and local community, of which they are a part, for access to facilities, business relationships, media coverage, labour, supplies, customers and so on. Organisations that acknowledge their responsibilities as part of the community may find that many areas of their operation are facilitated.

(d)   Social responsibility recognises **externalities**: the costs imposed by businesses on other people (but not included in the costing of their products and activities). For example, it is recognised that industrial pollution is bad for health.

(e)   Law, regulation and Codes of Practice **impose** certain social responsibilities on organisations, in areas such as employment protection, equal opportunities, environmental care, health and safety, product labelling and consumer rights. There are financial and operational **penalties** for organisations which fail to comply.

The **stakeholder view** of organisations emphasises that they are not solely 'self-interested': other parties have an interest or 'stake' in the performance and practices of an organisation.

The stakeholder approach acknowledges that such parties have a **legitimate interest** – and may also have **influence** over the organisation. (Workers can withhold labour; customers can withhold business.) The objectives of the organisation should therefore take into account the needs and claims of influential stakeholder groups.

10.2 Areas of social responsibility

The perceived social responsibilities of a business, depending on the nature of its operations, may include the following matters.

(a)   The impact of its operations on the **natural environment**

(b)   Its **human resource management policies**: for example, the hiring and promotion of people from minority groups, policies on sexual harassment, refusal to exploit cheap labour in developing countries

(c)   Non-reliance on contracts with **adverse political connotations**: sustainable business practices in developing countries, compliance with sanctions imposed by the international community and so on

(d)   **Charitable support** and activity in the local community or in areas related to the organisation's field of activity

(e)   **Above-minimum (legal) standards** of workplace health and safety, product safety and labelling, and so on

Question 10.10

Learning outcome D2a

See if you can come up with examples of socially responsible activities, in line with (a) to (e) above.

10.3 Limits of corporate social responsibility

According to Milton Friedman and Elaine Sternberg, 'the social responsibility of business is profit maximisation': in other words, the only responsibility of a **business** organisation, as opposed to a public sector one, is to maximise wealth for its owners over the long term.

(a)   Business profits are shareholders' wealth. Spending on other objectives **not** related to shareholders' wealth maximisation is irresponsible.

(b)   The public interest is served because the state levies taxes: the state is a better arbiter of the public interest than a business.

(c)   Without the discipline of shareholders, managers will simply favour their own pet interests. 'Managers who are accountable to everyone are accountable to none.'

'Consequently, the only justification for social responsibility is **enlightened self interest**' (Friedman) on the part of the organisation. Socially responsible behaviour should be pursued for its **benefits** in employee recruitment, retention and commitment; customer retention; and public relations.

10.4 Ethics

The meanings of the words 'ethics' and 'morals' are similar and difficult to distinguish. For example, the Concise Oxford Dictionary offers the following two definitions:

(a)   **Morals** are 'standards of behaviour or principles of right and wrong'.
(b)   **Ethics** are 'the moral principles governing or influencing conduct'.

Morals or ethics will also differ depending on the beliefs, value systems and norms of a particular society or culture. So, ethics might be considered to be **a system of behaviour which is deemed acceptable in the society or context under consideration**.

Blanchard and Peale suggest that, when faced with an ethical dilemma, individuals should ask themselves three questions:

(a)   Is it legal?

(b)   Is it balanced? (ie is it fair to all parties involved?)

(c)   Is it right? This is often related to your instinctive feeling about it. How would you feel if others knew you had taken this decision?

Ethics are a feature of business, as well as life, and managers are regularly faced with ethical issues. Examples might include the setting of fair pay and working conditions; non-exploitation of people or countries; honest advertising; effects of consuming products (eg tobacco or alcohol); and the management of redundancies.

Organisations may take a number of steps to assist management and others in dealing with ethics and making ethical decisions. These could include:

(a)   Developing corporate ethical codes
(b)   Setting up sustainability policies and strategies
(c)   An analysis of the impact on the environment and on society of the activities of the organisation
(d)   Building social responsibility into the organisation's strategy generation and planning systems

10.5 Business ethics

An organisation may have values to do with non-discrimination, fairness and integrity. It is very important that managers understand:

(a)   The importance of ethical behaviour

(b)   The differences in what is considered ethical behaviour in different cultures

Theorist Elaine Sternberg suggests that two **ethical values** are particularly pertinent for business, because without them business could not operate at all.

(a)   **Ordinary decency**. This includes respect for property rights, honesty, fairness and legality.

(b)   **Distributive justice**. This means that organisational rewards should be proportional to the contributions people make to organisational ends. The supply and demand for labour will influence how much a person is actually paid but, if that person is worth employing and the job worth doing, then the contribution will justify the expense.

Business ethics in a **global marketplace** are, however, far from clear cut. If you are working outside the UK, you will need to develop – in line with whatever policies your organisation may have in place – a kind of 'situational' ethic to cover various issues.

(a)   **Gifts** may be construed as bribes in Western business circles, but are indispensable in others.

(b)   Attitudes to **women** in business vary according to ethnic traditions and religious values.

(c)   The use of **cheap labour** in very poor countries (eg through offshoring) may be perceived as 'development' – or as 'exploitation'.

(d)   The expression and nature of **agreements** vary according to cultural norms.

A business may operate on principles which strive to be:

(a)   Ethical and legal (eg The Body Shop)

(b)   Unethical but legal (eg arms sales to repressive regimes)

(c)   Ethical but illegal (eg publishing stolen documents on government mismanagement)

(d)   Unethical and illegal (eg the drugs trade, employing child labour)

10.5.1 Applying ethical principles

There are two basic approaches to the **management of ethics** in organisations.

(a)   A **compliance-based approach** seeks to ensure compliance with law, regulation and rules of behaviour. It is based on the communication of clear rules, procedures and guidelines which must be adhered to in given circumstances. Behaviour is monitored and infringements of ethical codes are subject to disciplinary action.

(b)   An **integrity-based approach** seeks to support members of the organisation in making their own ethical decisions in any situation they encounter. It is based on the communication and reinforcement of ethical values, and the creation of frameworks within which ethical issues and dilemmas can be freely discussed and resolved.

Using an integrity-based approach, a firm can embed ethical values in its culture and systems in the following ways.

(a)   Include **value statements** in corporate culture, policy and codes of practice. (Professional staff should also be encouraged to adhere to the ethical codes of their professional bodies.)

(b)   Ensure that human resources **(HR) systems** (appraisal, training and rewards) are designed to support ethical behaviour.

(c)   Identify ethical objectives in the **mission statement**, as a public declaration of what the organisation stands for.

(d)   Establish **ethics committees** and discussion groups to encourage questioning and problem solving on ethical issues faced by staff.

(e)   Provide confidential channels for '**whistle-blowing**' if staff feel that colleagues or the organisation is behaving illegally or unethically.

(f)   Ensure that there is **top-down support** for, and modelling of, **ethical behaviour by managers**.

10.6 CIMA's Code of Ethics for professional accountants

If you are a CIMA registered student, you are subject to CIMA's Code of Ethics for professional accountants. You can find more detail about the code at www.cimaglobal.com/ethics. The preface to the code states that:

> 'As chartered management accountants, CIMA members (and registered students) throughout the world have a duty to observe the highest standards of conduct and integrity, and to uphold the good standing and reputation of the profession. They must also refrain from any conduct which might discredit the profession.'

CIMA's Code of Ethics is based on the International Federation of Accountants (IFAC) Code of Ethics.

Fundamental principles

(a)   **Integrity**

A professional accountant should be straightforward and honest in all professional and business relationships.

(b)   **Objectivity**

A professional accountant should not allow bias, conflict of interest or undue influence of others to override professional or business judgements.

(c)   **Professional competence and due care**

A professional accountant has a continuing duty to maintain professional knowledge and skill at the level required to ensure that a client or employer receives competent professional service based on current developments in practice, legislation and techniques. A professional accountant should act diligently and in accordance with applicable technical and professional standards when providing professional services.

(d)   **Confidentiality**

A professional accountant should respect the confidentiality of information acquired as a result of professional and business relationships and should not disclose any such information to third parties without proper and specific authority unless there is a legal or professional right or duty to disclose. Confidential information acquired as a result of professional and business relationships should not be used for the personal advantage of the professional accountant or third party.

(e)   **Professional behaviour**

A professional accountant should comply with relevant laws and regulations and should avoid any action that discredits the profession.

Conceptual framework

The conceptual framework sets out how **professional accountants** should comply with the fundamental principles. Specifically, they are required **to identify, evaluate and respond to threats to compliance with the fundamental principles**. When assessing the significance of a threat, they should take qualitative as well as quantitative factors into account.

There is a wide range of circumstances in which compliance with the fundamental principles may be threatened. Many **threats** fall into the following categories:

(a)   **Self-interest threats**, which may occur as a result of the financial or other interests of a professional accountant or of an immediate or close family member

(b)   **Self-review threats**, which may occur when a previous judgement needs to be re-evaluated by the professional accountant responsible for that judgement

(c)   **Advocacy threats**, which may occur when a professional accountant promotes a position or opinion to the point that subsequent objectivity may be compromised

(d)   **Familiarity threats**, which may occur when, because of a close relationship, a professional accountant becomes too sympathetic to the interests of others

(e)   **Intimidation threats**, which may occur when a professional accountant may be deterred from acting objectively by threats, actual or perceived

Safeguards that may eliminate or reduce such threats to an acceptable level include safeguards **created by the profession, legislation or regulation**, such as the following:

(a)   Educational, training and experience requirements for entry into the profession

(b)   Continuing professional development requirements

(c)   Corporate governance regulations

(d)   Professional standards

(e)   Professional or regulatory monitoring and disciplinary procedures

(f)   External review by a legally empowered third party of the reports, returns, communications or information produced by a professional accountant

Safeguards may also be found in the **work environment**. Examples include the following:

(a)   Effective, well-publicised complaints systems operated by the employing organisation, the profession or a regulator, which enable colleagues, employers and members of the public to draw attention to unprofessional or unethical behaviour

(b)   An explicitly stated duty to report breaches of ethical requirements

Section summary

Business ethics are the values underlying what an organisation understands by socially responsible behaviour.

There is pressure towards **corporate social responsibility (CSR)** from law and regulation, market forces and the stakeholder perspective.

11   Ethics and control systems

Introduction

This section gives more detail about some of the ways organisations promote ethical behaviour.

11.1 Compliance vs integrity-based approaches

Lynne Paine *(Harvard Business Review*, March–April 1994) suggests that there are two approaches to the management of ethics in organisations:

*   **Compliance**-based
*   **Integrity**-based

11.1.1 Compliance-based approach

A compliance-based approach is primarily designed to ensure that the company **acts within the letter of the law**, and that violations are prevented, detected and punished. Some organisations, faced with the legal consequences of unethical behaviours, take legal precautions such as those below.

- Compliance procedures to detect misconduct
- Audits of contracts
- Systems for employees to report criminal misconduct without fear of retribution
- Disciplinary procedures to deal with transgressions

Corporate compliance is limited in that it relates only to the law, but legal compliance is 'not an adequate means for addressing the full range of ethical issues that arise every day'. Furthermore, mere compliance with the law is no guide to **exemplary** behaviour.

11.1.2 Integrity-based programmes

'An integrity-based approach combines a concern for the law with an **emphasis on managerial responsibility** for ethical behaviour. Integrity strategies strive to define companies' guiding values, aspirations and patterns of thought and conduct. When integrated into the day-to-day operations of an organisation, such strategies can help prevent damaging ethical lapses, while tapping into powerful human impulses for moral thought and action.'

An integrity-based approach to ethics treats ethics as an issue of organisational culture.

The table below indicates some of the differences between the two main approaches.

	Compliance	Integrity
Ethos	Knuckle under to external standards	Choose ethical standards
Objective	Keep to the law	Enable legal and responsible conduct
Originators	Lawyers	Management, with lawyers, HR specialists etc
Methods (both include education, audits, controls, penalties)	Reduced employee discretion	Leadership, organisation systems
Behavioural assumptions	People are solitary self-interested beings	People are social beings with values
Standards	The law	Company values, aspirations (including law)
Staffing	Lawyers	Managers and lawyers
Education	The law, compliance system	Values, the law, compliance systems
Activities	Develop standards, train and communicate, handle reports of misconduct, investigate, enforce, oversee compliance	Integrate values into company systems, provide guidance and consultation, identify and resolve problems, oversee compliance

In other words, an integrity-based approach incorporates ethics into corporate culture and systems.

12   Information systems

Introduction

In this section, we consider what information is and why organisations need information. Information is needed for recording transactions, measuring performance, decision making, planning and control. We also look at the types of information (strategic, tactical and operational) and information systems.

12.1 Needs for information

KEY TERMS

DATA is the raw material for data processing. Data consists of numbers, letters and symbols and relates to facts, events and transactions. INFORMATION is data that has been processed in such a way as to be meaningful to the person who receives it.

An INFORMATION SYSTEM is 'an organisational and management solution, based on information technology, to any challenge posed by the environment'.

All organisations require information for a range of purposes, which are discussed below.

12.1.1 Planning

Planning requires knowledge of the available resources, possible timescales and the likely outcome under alternative scenarios. Information is required that helps **decision making**, and how to implement decisions taken.

12.1.2 Controlling

Once a plan is implemented, its actual performance must be controlled. Information is required to assess **whether it is proceeding as planned** or whether there is some unexpected deviation from the plan. It may consequently be necessary to take some form of corrective action.

12.1.3 Recording transactions

Information about **each transaction or event** is required. Reasons include:

(a)   Documentation of transactions can be used as **evidence** in a case of dispute.

(b)   There may be a **legal requirement** to record transactions, for example for accounting and audit purposes.

(c)   **Operational information** can be built up, allowing control action to be taken.

12.1.4 Performance measurement

Just as individual operations need to be controlled, so overall performance must be measured. **Comparisons against budget or plan** are able to be made. This may involve the collection of information on, for example, costs, revenues, volumes, timescale and profitability.

12.1.5 Decision making

Information is needed to optimise decision making for **strategic planning, management control** and **operational control**.

12.2 Data capture

Data capture refers to the media or input device from which the data is obtained. Data can be in:

*   **Machine form**, which uses IT to capture the data correctly, eg a bar code scanner; its advantages are speed, accuracy, large volume capabilities

*   **Human sensible form**, which requires human intervention for data to be input to an IT medium; its advantages are flexibility and ease of understanding

The data capture mechanism needs to be appropriate for the type of organisation. In addition, the quality of the output is **dependent** on the quality of input. In other words:

RUBBISH IN = RUBBISH OUT

12.3 Types of information

12.3.1 Strategic information

Strategic information is used to **plan** the **objectives** of the **organisation** and to **assess** whether the objectives are being met in practice. Such information includes overall profitability, the profitability of different segments of the business, future market prospects, the availability and cost of raising new funds, total cash needs, total manning levels and capital equipment needs.

Strategic information is:

*   Derived from both **internal and external** sources
*   **Summarised** at a high level
*   Relevant to the **long term**
*   Concerned with the **whole organisation**
*   Often prepared on an **'ad hoc'** basis
*   Both **quantitative and qualitative**
*   **Uncertain**, as the future cannot be accurately predicted

12.3.2 Tactical information

Tactical information is used when strategic decisions are implemented. It is used when decisions are made on **how the resources of the business should be employed**, to **monitor** how they are being and have been employed. Such information includes productivity measurements (output per hour), budgetary control reports, variance analysis reports, cash flow forecasts, staffing levels within a particular department of the organisation and short-term purchasing requirements.

Tactical information is:

*   Primarily generated internally (but may have a limited external component)
*   **Summarised at a lower level**
*   Relevant to the **short and medium term**
*   Concerned with **activities or departments**
*   Prepared **routinely and regularly**
*   Based on **quantitative** measures

12.3.3 Operational information

Operational information is used to ensure that **specific operational tasks** are planned and carried out as intended. It assists in controlling the day to day activities of an organisation and should be pushed upwards to assist in tactical decision making if necessary.

Operational information is:

- Derived from **internal** sources such as transaction recording methods

- **Detailed**, being the processing of raw data (eg transaction reports listing all transactions in a period)

- Relevant to the **immediate term**

- **Task-specific**

- Prepared very **frequently**

- Largely **quantitative**

13   Types of information system

Introduction

In this section we consider the different types of information system available to organisations, including Executive Support Systems, Management Information Systems and Decision Support Systems.

13.1 Input, processes and output

In this section we shall examine different types of information systems. You need to remember that the three component parts of a system are:

(a)   **Input.** The systems are only as good as the data that is fed into them. Remember – Rubbish In, Rubbish Out. The **data capture process**, the means by which source data enters the system, needs to be appropriate.

(b)   **Processes.** We shall examine what different systems do in the rest of this section.

(c)   **Output.** We shall discuss how system output – what systems produce – is assessed in the next section.

13.2 Systems requirements

A modern organisation requires a **wide range of systems** to hold, process and analyse information. We will now examine the various information systems used to serve organisational information requirements.

System level	System purpose
Strategic	To help senior managers with long-term planning. Their main function is to ensure changes in the external environment are matched by the organisation's capabilities.
Management	To help middle managers monitor and control. These systems check if things are working well or not. Some management level systems support non-routine decision making such as 'what if?' analyses.
Knowledge	To help knowledge and data workers design products, distribute information and perform administrative tasks. These systems help the organisation integrate new and existing knowledge into the business and to reduce the reliance on paper documents.
Operational	To help operational managers track the organisation's day to day operational activities. These systems enable routine queries to be answered, and transactions to be processed and tracked.

The major **types of information system** are discussed below.

13.3 Executive Support Systems (ESS)

KEY TERMS

An EXECUTIVE SUPPORT SYSTEM (ESS) or EXECUTIVE INFORMATION SYSTEM (EIS) pools data from internal and external sources and makes information available to senior managers in an easy to use form. An ESS helps senior managers make strategic, unstructured decisions.

An ESS should provide senior managers with easy access to key **internal and external** information such as market share and customer satisfaction. The system summarises and tracks strategically critical information, possibly drawn from internal MIS and DSS, but also including data from external sources eg competitors, legislation and external databases such as Reuters. Data will be summarised and often graphical, but have drill-down facilities to allow further detail to be accessed if required.

An ESS is likely to have the following **features**.

- Flexibility
- Quick response time
- Sophisticated data analysis and modelling tools

13.4 Strategic Enterprise Management Systems (SEMS)

KEY TERM

STRATEGIC ENTERPRISE MANAGEMENT SYSTEMS (SEMS) OR STRATEGIC INFORMATION SYSTEMS help organisations make high-level strategic decisions.

SEMS assist organisations in **setting strategic goals**, **measuring performance** in the light of those goals, and **measuring** and **managing intellectual capital**. They can also be a great help in **activity-based management**, which you will have covered in your earlier studies. By incorporating activity-based management, an SEMS can identify which areas of the business are really adding value and should receive investment.

13.5 Enterprise Resource Planning Systems (ERPS)

KEY TERM

The ENTERPRISE RESOURCE PLANNING SYSTEM (ERPS) is a software system designed to support and automate the business processes of medium and large enterprises. ERPS are accounting oriented information systems which aid in identifying and planning the enterprise wide resources needed to resource, make, account for and deliver customer orders. ERPS tend to incorporate a number of software developments such as the use of relational databases, object-oriented programming and open system portability.   *(CIMA Official Terminology)*

ERPS handle many aspects of operations including manufacturing, distribution, inventory, invoicing and accounting. They also cover **support functions** such as **human resource management** and **marketing**. **Supply chain management** software can provide links with **suppliers** and customer relationship management with **customers**.

ERPS thus operate **over the whole organisation** and **across functions**. All departments that are involved in operations or production are **integrated** into one system. Some ERPS software is custom-built, and often now ERPS software is written for organisations in particular industries. ERPS can be configured for organisations' needs and software adapted for circumstances. The data is made available in data warehouses, which can be used to produce **customised reports** containing data that is consistent across applications. They can **support performance measures** such as **balanced scorecard** and **strategic planning**.

ERPS should result in **lower costs** and lower **investment required** in assets. ERPS should increase **flexibility** and **efficiency of production**. Their disadvantages include cost, implementation time, and lack of scope for adaption to the demands of specific businesses. In addition, a **problem** with one function can affect all the other functions. ERPS linked in with supply chains can similarly be vulnerable to problems with any links in the chain, and switching costs may be high. The blurring of boundaries can also cause accountability problems.

13.6 Management Information Systems (MIS)

MANAGEMENT INFORMATION SYSTEMS (MIS) convert data from mainly internal sources (transaction processing systems) into information, often in a standard format (eg summary reports, exception reports). This information enables managers to make timely and effective decisions for planning, directing and controlling the activities for which they are responsible.

An MIS provides regular reports and (usually) online access to the organisation's current and historical performance, including information about financial performance and important non-financial information such as volume of deliveries and accuracy and timeliness of deliveries.

MIS usually transform data from underlying transaction processing systems into summarised files that are used as the basis for standard management reports.

MIS have the following characteristics:

- Support **structured** decisions at operational and management control levels
- Designed to report on **existing** operations
- Have **little analytical capability**
- Relatively **inflexible**
- Have an **internal** focus
- Not suitable for **strategic planning** and **decision making**

Exam alert

You may see the term **Management Information System** used as an umbrella term for **all information systems** within an organisation.

13.7 Decision Support Systems (DSS)

DECISION SUPPORT SYSTEMS (DSS) combine data and analytical models or data analysis tools to support decision making.

DSS are used by management to assist in making decisions on issues which are subject to high levels of uncertainty about the problem, the various **responses** which management could undertake or the likely **impact** of those actions.

DSS are intended to provide a wide range of alternative information gathering and analytical tools with a major emphasis upon **flexibility** and **user-friendliness**.

DSS have more analytical power than other systems, enabling them to analyse and condense large volumes of data into a form that helps managers make decisions, for example in spreadsheet form. The objective is to allow the manager to consider a number of **alternatives** and evaluate them under a variety of potential conditions.

13.8 Expert systems

An EXPERT SYSTEM is a computer program that stores information in a limited domain of knowledge to enable simple decisions to be made.

Expert system software uses a knowledge base that consists of facts, concepts and the relationships between them on a particular domain of knowledge, and uses pattern-matching techniques to 'solve' problems.

A simple business example programmed into a credit check may be: 'Don't allow credit to a person who has no credit history and has changed address twice or more within the last three years'.

Many financial institutions now use expert systems to process straightforward **loan applications**. The user enters certain key facts into the system such as the loan applicant's name and most recent addresses, their income and monthly outgoings, and details of other loans. The system will then:

(a) **Check the facts** given against its database to see whether the applicant has a good previous credit record

(b) **Perform calculations** to see whether the applicant can afford to repay the loan

(c) **Make a judgement** as to what extent the loan applicant fits the lender's profile of a good risk (based on the lender's previous experience)

(d) **Suggest a decision** based on the results of this processing

This is why it is now often possible to get a loan or arrange insurance **over the telephone**, whereas in the past it would have been necessary to go and speak to a bank manager or send details to an actuary and then wait for him or her to come to a decision.

An organisation can use an expert system when a number of conditions are met.

- The problem is **well defined**.
- Those using the expert system can **define the problem correctly**.
- The expert can define **rules** by which the problem can be solved.
- The investment in an expert system is **cost-justified**.

The knowledge base of an expert system must be kept up to date. Programming the necessary changes may be costly and time consuming.

Expert systems are not suited to high-level, complex, unstructured problems. These require information from a wide range of sources and human judgement, rather than using prescribed processes to obtain the information required to decide between a few known alternatives.

13.9 Knowledge Work Systems (KWS)

KEY TERMS

KNOWLEDGE WORK SYSTEMS (KWS) are information systems that facilitate the creation and integration of new knowledge into an organisation.

KNOWLEDGE WORKERS are people whose jobs consist of primarily creating new information and knowledge. They are often members of a profession such as doctors, engineers, lawyers and scientists.

KWS are information systems that facilitate the creation and integration of new knowledge into an organisation. They provide knowledge workers with tools such as:

- Analytical tools
- Powerful graphics facilities
- Communication tools
- Access to external databases
- A user-friendly interface

The workstations of knowledge workers are often designed for the specific tasks they perform. For example, a design engineer would require sufficient graphics power to manipulate 3-D Computer Aided Design (CAD) images; a financial analyst would require a powerful desktop computer to access and manipulate a large amount of financial data (an **investment workstation**).

Virtual reality systems are another example of KWS. These systems create computer-generated simulations that emulate real-world activities. Interactive software and hardware (eg special headgear) provide simulations so realistic that users experience sensations that would normally only occur in the real world.

13.10 Office Automation Systems (OAS)

KEY TERM

OFFICE AUTOMATION SYSTEMS (OAS) are computer systems designed to increase the productivity of data and information workers.

OAS support the major activities performed in a typical office such as document management, facilitating communication and managing data. Examples include:

- Word processing, desktop publishing, and digital filing systems
- Email, voicemail, videoconferencing, groupware, intranets, schedulers
- Spreadsheets, desktop databases

13.11 Transaction Processing Systems (TPS)

KEY TERM

A TRANSACTION PROCESSING SYSTEM (TPS) performs and records routine transactions.

TPS are used for **routine tasks** in which data items or transactions must be processed so that operations can continue. TPS support most business functions in most types of organisations. They include accounting systems such as the sales and purchase ledger and operational systems such as delivery tracking systems.

Section summary

Organisations require different **types of information system** to provide **different levels** of information in a range of **functional areas**.

Major types of Information Systems include: Executive Support Systems (**ESS**), Strategic Enterprise Management Systems (**SEMS**), Enterprise Resource Planning Systems (**ERPS**), Management Information Systems (**MIS**), Decision Support Systems (**DSS**), Knowledge Work Systems (**KWS**), Office Automation Systems (**OAS**) and Transaction Processing Systems (**TPS**).

14 The value of information

Introduction

In this section we look at the factors that make information valuable. We also briefly examine the use of enterprise analysis to identify the key elements and attributes of organisational data and information.

14.1 Factors that make information a valuable commodity

Information is now recognised as a valuable resource, and a **key tool in the quest for a competitive advantage**.

Easy **access** to information, the **quality** of that information and **speedy methods of exchanging** the information have become essential elements of business success.

Organisations that make **good use of information** in decision making, and which use new technologies to access, process and exchange information are likely to be **best placed to survive** in increasingly competitive world markets.

14.2 The value of obtaining information

In spite of its value in a general sense, information which is **obtained but not used** has no actual value to the person that obtains it. A decision taken on the basis of information received also has no actual value. It is only the **action taken** as a result of a decision which realises actual value for a company. An item of information that leads to an actual increase in profit of £90 is not worth having if it costs £100 to collect.

Businesses may also try to assess the costs of not having the information and also whether alternative (cheaper, more convenient) sources may be used instead.

14.3 Costs of information

IT costs include **hardware and software costs**, **implementation costs** associated with a new systems development and **day to day costs**, such as salaries and accommodation.

Many organisations invest large amounts of money in IS, but not always wisely. The unmanaged proliferation of IT is likely to lead to expensive mistakes. Two key benefits of IT, the ability to **share** information and the **avoidance of duplication**, are likely to be lost.

All IT expenditure should therefore require approval to ensure that it enhances rather than detracts from the overall information strategy.

Effective budgeting may be required to keep costs under control, particularly purchase of new equipment. An activity-based approach may be appropriate.

Question 10.11	Assessing the value of information

Learning outcome D2(b)

The value of information lies in the action taken as a result of receiving it. What questions might you ask in order to make an assessment of the value of information?

Section summary

The **cost and value** of information are often not easy to quantify – but attempts should be made to do so.

15 Evaluating information systems

Introduction

In this section, we look at the methods of evaluating information systems, such as cost-benefit analysis and balanced scorecard.

15.1 Why have an information strategy?

A strategy for IS and IT is **justified** on the grounds that IS/IT:

- Involves **high costs**
- Is **critical to the success** of many organisations
- Is now used as part of the commercial strategy in the battle for **competitive advantage**
- Impacts on **customer service**

- Affects **all levels of management**
- Affects the way **management information** is created and presented
- **Requires effective management** to obtain the maximum benefit
- Involves many **stakeholders** inside and outside the organisation

15.2 Cost-benefit analysis

Traditional cost-benefit investment appraisal methods such as net present value (NPV), internal rate of return and payback period can be used to evaluate computer systems.

However, NPV analysis may have to be used with care. If, for example, systems development is being proposed because of threats to the current situation, investment in systems should be compared not with the current situation but the **projected situation** if the threats are realised. It is also important to **collect all the costs** involved, including programming, training, **maintenance** and employee costs.

Cost-benefit analysis is most appropriate when **direct improvements** in productivity and performance are being sought. It should be possible to quantify benefits if efficiency and effectiveness are being pursued.

The main tangible costs will be **capital items, installation costs, development costs** and **changes in operational costs**.

15.3 Problems with cost-benefit analysis

The main problem with using traditional cost-benefit analysis to evaluate systems is that the costs and benefits tend to be derived from the accounting system. However, a very important aspect of investment in systems is **improving the quality** of **operational and control information** and this cannot **easily be measured in accounting terms**. For example, what cost can be placed on not having information? Other benefits, such as improved **responsiveness** and **flexibility**, may also be very difficult to measure.

The indirect benefits, **often strategic**, of better information are also very difficult to quantify. Organisations may find it very difficult to assess how much better information about customers has impacted upon customer service, or whether improved information about competitors yielded a competitive advantage. Internal benefits might include **improving the linkages** between **processes and activities**, **improved organisational performance** in areas other than those where the new systems are introduced, such as better customer service, and **intangible improvements**, such as improved staff morale or better decision making.

Possible methods for dealing with unquantifiable benefits include:

- Carry out the NPV analysis using alternative values for intangibles.

- Treat intangibles as options.

- Calculate the NPV for the quantifiable cash flows. If it is positive, accept the investment. If it is negative, calculate the value of intangibles to make the NPV zero and assess whether these values appear to be realistic.

There are also less tangible costs such as:

- **Switching costs** – reduced efficiency, staff discontent with change

- **Locking in costs** – being locked into a single supplier and not being able to take advantage of subsequent better offers from other suppliers

- **Opportunity costs** – the investment in IT meaning that other investments cannot be undertaken

15.4 Other methods

Along with financial analysis methods, other methods can be appropriate in different circumstances. These are discussed below.

15.4.1 Balanced scorecard

A balanced scorecard approach covering multiple goals is likely to be most appropriate if systems are meant to change fundamentally the way the organisation is **managed** by, for example, removing constraints or increasing flexibility. If improvements are to result in better forecasting or planning, changes in the organisational structure may also be required. You covered this approach in detail in Chapter 6, so refer back to it if necessary.

15.4.2 Strategic analysis

Use of a model to assess the impact of systems on competitive forces should be used if information systems are designed to help the organisation achieve **competitive advantage**.

15.4.3 Business case analysis

Business case analysis is helpful if systems are being used to **generate new business**. It needs to cover financial consequences, marketing and operational issues.

15.4.4 User requirements

Users' views are investigated in terms of their requirements, how much they will use the system and how much they are prepared to pay.

15.5 Technical and operational viability

As well as assessing viability in terms of financial value or benefits to the business, technical and operational issues must be considered carefully.

Technical issues	Operational issues
Availability of technology	Availability, reliability and clarity of data
Skills necessary to use technology	Strong operational procedures
Changes in risk profile	Level of support and commitment
Compatibility with existing systems	Human resource implications
The systems' number of users and transaction/data volumes	Impacts on external stakeholders

Question 10.12   New information system

Learning outcome D2(b)

NEST is a national furniture retailer operating from 12 large showrooms on retail parks close to the principal motorways. The present management information system was set up in 20X0 and since that time the business has expanded rapidly. A new project for the design and implementation of a new system to meet current and future needs will commence soon. There is some urgency as the present system frequently 'crashes', leaving staff with the problem of explaining delays to dissatisfied customers. Staff turnover among systems personnel is high.

Required

Write a memorandum to the Head of Systems to explain the need for a cost-benefit assessment of the proposed new system.

Section summary

Although **cost-benefit analysis** should be used to evaluate information systems, the **wider operational and control issues** mean that other methods such as the **balanced scorecard** should also be used.

As well as fulfilling financial criteria, systems must be **technically and operationally viable**.

The **IS/IT steering committee** makes decisions relating to the future use and development of IS/IT.

The **database administrator** is responsible for all data and information held within an organisation.

An **Information Centre (IC)** provides support for computer users within the organisation.

16 Operational risks of information systems

Introduction

In this section, we consider the various risks to information operations. These include physical factors, data and systems integrity, fraud, internet usage, data protection considerations and systems development.

16.1 Risks of physical damage

16.1.1 Natural threats

Fire is the **most serious hazard** to computer systems. Destruction of data can be even more costly than the destruction of hardware.

Water is a serious hazard. In some areas flooding is a natural risk, for example in parts of central London and many other towns and cities near rivers or coasts. Basements are therefore generally not regarded as appropriate sites for large computer installations.

Wind, rain and storms can all cause substantial **damage to buildings**. In certain areas the risks are greater, for example the risk of typhoons in parts of the Far East. Many organisations make heavy use of prefabricated and portable offices, which are particularly vulnerable. Cutbacks in maintenance expenditure may lead to leaking roofs or dripping pipes.

Lightning and electrical storms can play havoc with power supplies, causing power failures coupled with power surges as services are restored. Minute adjustments in power supplies may be enough to affect computer processing operations (characterised by lights which dim as the country's population turns on electric kettles following a popular television programme).

16.1.2 Human threats

Organisations may also be exposed to physical threats through the actions of humans. **Political terrorism** is the main risk, but there are also threats from individuals with **grudges**. Staff are a physical threat to computer installations, whether by spilling a cup of coffee over a desk covered with papers, or tripping and falling doing some damage to themselves and to an item of office equipment.

16.2 Risks to data and systems integrity

The **risks** include:

- Human error

    - Entering incorrect transactions
    - Failing to correct errors
    - Processing the wrong files
    - Failing to follow prescribed security procedures

- Technical error such as malfunctioning hardware or software and supporting equipment such as communication equipment, normal and emergency power supplies and air conditioning units

- Risks of data transfer, including loss and corruption of data, also interception and copying of data

- Commercial espionage

- Malicious damage

- Industrial action

These risks may be particularly significant because of the nature of computer operations. The **processing** capabilities of a computer are **extensive**, and enormous quantities of data are processed without human intervention, and so without humans knowing what is going on. Information on a computer file **can be changed** without leaving any physical trace of the change. In comparison, a change to a manual file would often involve leaving a trace – eg crossing out data on a card file to insert new data.

Increasing connectivity and the openness of computer networks in the global business environment exposes businesses to system and network failures and to cyber attack. In a study titled 'The Economic Impact of Cyber Attacks' the US Congressional Research Service reported that recent estimates of the total worldwide losses due to hostile attacks range from US$13 billion (for worms and viruses only) to US$226 billion (for all forms of attacks). The study also noted that cyber incidents had the effect of wiping 1% to 5% off the share price of targeted companies.

CASE STUDY

The IT Governance Institute in the US has published guidance on IT controls (*IT Control Objectives for Sarbanes-Oxley*) that aims to help businesses comply with the Sarbanes-Oxley legislation. The guidance therefore emphasises the role of information technology in the internal control system operating over disclosure and financial reporting. IT controls need to be changed as financial reporting processes change, and ensure **consistency** between different units.

16.3 Risks of fraud

Computer fraud usually involves the theft of funds by **dishonest use** of a computer system. The type of computer fraud depends on the point in the system at which the fraud is perpetrated.

(a) **Input fraud**

Data input is falsified; good examples are putting a **non-existent employee** on to the salary file, or a non-existent supplier on to the purchases file.

(b) **Processing fraud**

A programmer or someone who has broken into this part of the system may **alter a program**. For example, in a large organisation, a 'patch' might be used to change a program so that 10 pence was deducted from every employee's pay cheque and sent to a fictitious account to which the perpetrator had access. A 'patch' is a change to a program which is characterised by its speed and ease of implementation.

(c) **Output fraud**

Output documents may be **stolen or tampered with** and control totals may be altered. Cheques are the most likely document to be stolen, but other documents may be stolen to hide a fraud.

(d) **Fraudulent use of the computer system**

Employees may feel that they can use the computer system for their **own purposes** and this may take up valuable processing time. This is probably quite rare, but there was a case of a newspaper publisher's computer system being used by an employee to produce another publication!

16.3.1 Recent developments increasing the risk of fraud

Over the last few years there have been rapid developments in all aspects of computer technology and these have increased the opportunities that are available to commit a fraud. The most important of the recent developments are as follows.

(a) **Computer literacy**

The proportion of the population which is computer literate (including programming knowledge) is growing all the time. Once people know how to use a computer, the dishonest ones among them may attempt computer fraud.

(b) **Communications**

The use of public communication systems has increased the ability of people outside the organisation to break into the computer system. These 'hackers' could not have operated when access was only possible on site.

(c) **Reduction in internal checks and documentation**

The more computers are used, the fewer the tasks left to personnel to carry out. A consequence of this is often a **reduction** in the number of **internal checks** carried out for any transaction. As many data entries occur automatically, documentation is also reduced.

(d) **Real-time processing**

Immediate processing of transactions means **access** and **input** must be well controlled.

(e) **Technical change**

Improvements in the **quality of software** and the increase in **implementation of good software** has not kept pace with the improvements in hardware. Distributed systems and networks are very common. Many organisations now allow employees to connect their own tablet and/or smartphone device to the organisational network, usually via wireless network link (a trend sometimes referred to as 'bring your own device'). These developments reduce the amount of control that can be exercised over central databases and programs.

16.3.2 Other deliberate actions

Data and/or systems may be threatened by deliberate actions other than fraud, for example **commercial espionage**, **malicious damage** or **industrial action**.

16.4 Internet risks

Establishing organisational links to the internet brings numerous security dangers.

(a) Corruptions such as **viruses** on a single computer can spread through the network to all of the organisation's computers.

(b) **Disaffected employees** have much greater potential to do **deliberate damage** to valuable corporate data or systems because the network could give them access to parts of the system that they are not really authorised to use.

(c) If the organisation is linked to an external network, persons outside the company (**hackers**) may be able to get into the organisation's internal network, either to steal data or to damage the system.

(d) Employees may **download inaccurate information** or imperfect or **virus-ridden software** from an external network. For example, 'beta' (free trial) versions of forthcoming new editions of many major packages are often available on the internet, but the whole point about a beta version is that it is not fully tested and may contain bugs that could disrupt an entire system.

(e) Information transmitted from one part of an organisation to another may be **intercepted**. Data can be 'encrypted' (scrambled) in an attempt to make it unintelligible to eavesdroppers.

(f) The **communications link itself may break down or distort data**. The worldwide telecommunications infrastructure is improving thanks to the use of new technologies. There are communications 'protocols' governing the format of data and signals transferred.

16.4.1 Hacking

Hacking involves attempting to gain unauthorised access to a computer system, usually through telecommunications links.

Hackers require only limited programming knowledge to cause large amounts of damage. The fact that billions of bits of information can be transmitted in bulk over the public telephone network has made it **hard to trace** individual hackers, who can therefore make repeated attempts to invade systems. Hackers, in the past, have mainly been concerned with **copying** information, but a recent trend has been their desire to **corrupt it**.

Phone numbers and passwords can be guessed by hackers using **electronic phone directories** or number generators and by software which enables **rapid guessing** using hundreds of permutations per minute.

Default passwords are also available on some electronic bulletin boards and sophisticated hackers could even try to 'tap' messages being transmitted along phone wires (the number actually dialled will not be scrambled).

16.4.2 Viruses

KEY TERM

A VIRUS is a piece of software which infects programs and data and possibly damages them, and which replicates itself.

Viruses need an **opportunity to spread**. The programmers of viruses therefore place viruses in the kind of software which is most likely to be copied. This includes:

- Free software (for example from the internet).

- Pirated software (cheaper than original versions).

- Games software (wide appeal).

- **Email attachments**. Email has become the most common means of spreading the most destructive viruses. The virus is often held in an attachment to the email message. Recent viruses have been programmed to send themselves to all addresses in the user's electronic address book.

16.4.3 Denial of service attack

A fairly new threat, relating to internet websites and related systems, is the '**Denial of Service (DoS)**' attack. A DoS attack is characterised by an attempt by attackers to prevent legitimate users of a service from using that service. Examples include attempts to:

- 'Flood' or bombard a site or network, thereby preventing legitimate network traffic (major sites such as Amazon.com and Yahoo! have been targeted in this way)
- Disrupt connections between two machines, thereby preventing access to a service
- Prevent a particular individual from accessing a service

16.5 Data protection risks

16.5.1 Data protection legislation

In recent years, there has been a growing fear that the ever-increasing amount of **information** about individuals held by organisations could be misused. In particular, it was felt that an individual could easily be harmed by the existence of computerised data about him or her which was inaccurate or misleading and which could be **transferred to unauthorised third parties** at high speed and little cost. During the 1980s and 1990s individuals were therefore **given more protection** from organisations holding data about them.

16.5.2 Consequences of failure to comply with legislation

Organisations may be subject to sanctions if they breach individuals' rights.

(a) A data subject may seek **compensation** through the courts for damage and any associated distress caused by the **loss**, **destruction** or **unauthorised disclosure** of data about himself or herself or by **inaccurate data** about himself or herself.

(b) A data subject may apply to the courts for **inaccurate data** to be **put right** or even **wiped off** the data user's files altogether.

(c) A data subject may obtain **access** to personal data of which he or she is the subject. (This is known as the 'subject access' provision.) In other words, a data subject can ask to see his or her personal data that the data user is holding.

(d) A data subject can **sue** a data user for any **damage or distress** caused to him or her by personal data about him or her that is **incorrect** or **misleading** as to matter of **fact** (rather than opinion).

16.5.3 Compliance with data protection legislation

Measures could include the following.

- **Obtain consent from individuals** to hold any sensitive personal data you need.
- **Supply individuals** with a **copy of any personal data** you hold about them if so requested.
- Consider if you may need to **obtain consent** to **process personal data**.
- Ensure you **do not pass on personal data** to unauthorised parties.

16.6 Systems development risks

If systems development is not controlled properly, the following problems could develop:

- Unauthorised changes to systems
- Development of systems that do not provide required information for management decision making
- Programs being changed without adequate planning and testing
- Poor systems being allowed to become active
- Development of systems that are not flexible enough to cope with changes in circumstances
- Loss of confidence among managers, staff and customers
- Increased risk of fraud or problems with data protection legislation
- Excessive costs
- Lack of audit trail

16.7 Audit risks

Auditors may face a number of issues when auditing computer systems:

- Concentration of controls and lack of segregation of duties
- Lack of audit trail from originating document through to output
- Overwriting of data that the auditor requires

16.8 Risk assessment

As with other risks, a key part of IT risk assessment will be determining the **likelihood and consequences** of risks materialising. The US's Information Systems Audit and Control Association has published guidance suggesting that a number of factors will indicate that risks are significant:

Technology	Complex, unique, customised, developed in-house
People	Inexperience, lack of training, limited number of people, high staff turnover
Processes	Decentralised, multi-location, ad hoc
Past experience	History of problems including processing errors, system outages, data corruption
Financial reports	Direct significance, used for initiating and recording amounts in the financial reports

16.9 Combating risks and security

KEY TERM

SECURITY, in information management terms, means the protection of data from accidental or deliberate threats which might cause unauthorised modification, disclosure or destruction of data, and the protection of the information system from the degradation or non-availability of services.

Security refers to **technical** issues related to the computer system, psychological and **behavioural** factors in the organisation and its employees, and protection against the unpredictable occurrences of the **natural world**.

Security can be subdivided into a number of aspects.

Prevention	It is in practice impossible to prevent all threats cost effectively.
Detection	Detection techniques are often combined with prevention techniques: a log can be maintained of unauthorised attempts to gain access to a computer system.
Deterrence	As an example, computer misuse by personnel can be made grounds for disciplinary action.
Recovery	If the threat occurs, its consequences can be contained (for example checkpoint programs).
Correction	These ensure the vulnerability is dealt with (for example, by instituting stricter controls).
Avoidance	This might mean changing the design of the system.

We examine the controls to mitigate the risks to information operations in the remainder of this chapter.

CASE STUDY

The international security standard, ISO 17799 groups its recommendations under the following headings.

(a) **Business continuity planning**. This means that there should be measures to ensure that if major failures or disasters occur, the business will not be completely unable to function.

(b) **Systems access control**. This includes protection of information, information systems, networked services, detection of unauthorised activities and security when using the systems.

(c)   **Systems development and maintenance**. This includes steps to protect data in operational and application systems and ensuring that IT projects and support are conducted securely.

(d)   **Physical and environmental security**. Measures should be taken to prevent unauthorised access, damage and interference to business premises, assets, information and information facilities and prevention of theft.

(e)   **Compliance** with any relevant legal requirements and also with organisational policies in standards. There is no point in having them if they are not enforced.

(f)   **Personnel security**. This covers issues such as recruitment of trustworthy employees, and also reporting of security-related incidents. Training is particularly important, with the aim that users are aware of information security threats and concerns and are equipped to comply with the organisation's security policy.

(g)   **Security organisation**. It should be clear who has responsibility for the various aspects of information security. Additional considerations will apply if facilities and assets are accessed by third parties or responsibility for information processing has been outsourced.

(h)   **Computer and network management**. This includes ensuring continuity of operations and minimising the risk of systems failures, also protecting the integrity of systems and safeguarding information, particularly when exchanged between organisations. Particularly important is protection from viruses.

(i)   **Asset classification and control**. Information is an asset, just like a machine, building or a vehicle, and security will be improved if information assets have an 'owner', and are classified according to how much protection they need.

(j)   **Security policy**. A written document setting out the organisation's approach to information security should be available to all staff.

Section summary

Risks to data and systems include **physical risks** such as fire and water and **risks** through **human error or fraud**.

Internet links have resulted in additional risks including **hacking** and **viruses**.

Risks arising from **systems development** include the risks that the system will have **inadequate security**, and will **not meet the users' requirements**.

---

17 Big Data

Introduction

In this section, we look at the use of 'Big Data' in the management of risk.

17.1 What is 'Big Data'?

Big Data refers to the mass of data that society creates each year, extending far beyond the traditional financial and enterprise data created by companies. Sources of Big Data include social networking sites, internet search engines, and mobile devices.

17.1.1 The four Vs of Big Data

The main characteristics of Big Data are volume, velocity, variety, and veracity.

(a) **Volume**. The **scale of information** which can now be created and stored is staggering. Advancing technology has allowed **embedded sensors** to be placed **in everyday items** such as cars, video games and refrigerators. Mobile devices have led to an increasingly networked world where people's consumer preferences, spending habits, and even their movements can be recorded.

Advances in **data storage** technology as well as a fall in price of this storage has allowed for the captured data to be **stored for further analysis**.

(b) **Velocity**. Timeliness is a key factor in the usefulness of financial information to decision makers, and it is no different for the users of Big Data. One source of high-velocity data is Twitter, users of which are estimated to generate nearly 100,000 tweets every 60 seconds.

(c) **Variety**. Big Data consists of **both structured and unstructured data**. While the sources of data have grown, the software tools for **interpreting** the data have **not kept pace** with this change. **Structured** data consists of **traditional data** sets, such as financial transactions, while **unstructured** refers to the majority of information created by **social media sites**. The challenge is bringing together both structured and unstructured information to reveal new insights.

(d) **Veracity**. Another challenge to users of Big Data is keeping the information 'clean' and free from so-called noise, or **bias**. Due in part to the other three factors, it is **not possible to 'cleanse' the data**. While even unstructured data such as tweets can give an accurate view as to how an event or product is perceived, it **may not be useful in predicting sales** of a product. The **age profile and location** of the average Twitter user **may act as a bias**, therefore distorting the data collected.

17.2 Big Data and risk management

17.2.1 Increased data in risk forecasting

A company can **mitigate** a particular **risk depending on the level of information** available to it. Take, for example, a car company which offers financing to its customers. A credit score gives a good indication of the customer's ability to pay, in addition to their employment status.

Traditionally, there has not been any additional information available on which the car company can base its decision. Increasingly, such companies are seeking information such as specific spending traits in order to mitigate the risk of missed payments even further. Credit card analysis showing regular payments to betting agents, in addition to online registrations with different online gambling organisations, may give further insight into the consumer profile, and influence the car company in its decision on whether or not to grant credit.

17.2.2 Identifying risks in real time

Timeliness is an important characteristic of good-quality information. By **monitoring** the **reaction on social media** to products and services, companies can get **instant feedback** on new products, services and events. Effective **monitoring** of trends can be **used in supply chain management**. This information can therefore **minimise the risks** associated with carrying **too much** or **too little inventory**.

17.2.3 Identifying longer-term opportunities

Expansion into **new markets** has always contained a **high level of risk**, as companies had limited information to help predict consumer reaction to new products. The emergence of **Big Data** and the advent of internet shopping have **negated** the **influence of territorial borders**. Internet searches, financial transactions and social media trends can all be used to **predict consumer preference**.

17.3 Big Data concerns

Privacy: While Big Data can be a valuable 'asset' to a company, there are certain risks associated with Big Data. In addition to being beneficial for companies and customers, Big Data has the potential to harm individuals. The link between online and offline identity and who should control our data is a key question. Big Data is borderless, but cultural attitudes towards privacy are very different across the world. Concerns about whether or not governments are also gathering Big Data about individuals, including their own citizens, raises questions about the balance between the benefits and the infringement of rights.

Security: Companies using Big Data should ensure that they are not infringing the security of other organisations and their customers.

This also relates to people who are unaware of the security risks posed by their own actions, such as people who post their location on social media, revealing that they are on holiday, and are then targeted by robbers.

Intellectual property: such as the ownership of material posted onto social media and how it can be used. This is a particular point with respect to underage users.

Chapter Summary

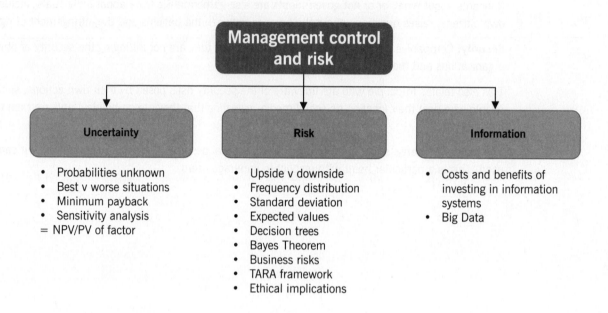

Management control and risk

Uncertainty
- Probabilities unknown
- Best v worse situations
- Minimum payback
- Sensitivity analysis
  = NPV/PV of factor

Risk
- Upside v downside
- Frequency distribution
- Standard deviation
- Expected values
- Decision trees
- Bayes Theorem
- Business risks
- TARA framework
- Ethical implications

Information
- Costs and benefits of investing in information systems
- Big Data

Quick Quiz

1   Sensitivity analysis allows for uncertainty in project appraisal by assessing the probability of changes in the decision variables.

   True ☐

   False ☐

2   A probability can be expressed as any value from –1 to +1.

   True ☐

   False ☐

3   A manager is trying to decide which of three mutually exclusive projects to undertake. Each of the projects could lead to varying net costs which the manager calls outcomes I, II and III. The following payoff table or matrix has been constructed.

	Outcomes (Net profit)		
Project	I (Worst)	II (Most likely)	III (Best)
A	60	70	120
B	85	75	140
C	100	120	135

   Using the minimax regret decision rule, decide which project should be undertaken.

4   If the decision maker is trying to maximise the figure, what figure would the decision maker choose at point B in the diagram below?

   A   40,000

   B   11,800

   C   13,900

   D   22,000

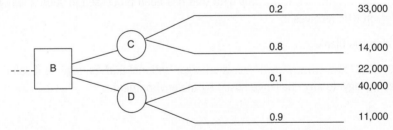

5   Given the probability distribution shown below, assign ranges of numbers in order to run a simulation model.

Probability	Numbers assigned	Probability	Numbers assigned
0.132	....	0.083	....
0.410	....	0.060	....
0.315	....		

6   Fill in the blanks.

   Standard deviation, $s = \sqrt{\rule{1.5cm}{0pt}}$

   where $\bar{x}$ is ...., x represents ...., p represents ....

7   AB can choose from five mutually exclusive projects. The projects will each last for one year only and their net cash inflows will be determined by the prevailing market conditions. The forecast net cash inflows and their associated probabilities are shown below.

Market conditions	Poor	Good	Excellent
Probability	0.20	0.40	0.40
	$'000	$'000	$'000
Project L	550	480	580
Project M	450	500	570
Project N	420	450	480
Project O	370	410	430
Project P	590	580	430

(a)   Based on the expected value of the net cash inflows, which project should be undertaken?

(b)   Calculate the value of perfect information about the state of the market.

8   Which of the following is not a category of threat identified in CIMA's guidance?

A   Advocacy

B   Confidentiality

C   Familiarity

D   Self-review

9   Fill in the blank. The temptation to manipulate .... information when preparing accounts is potentially a very serious ethical threat.

10   Give three examples of factors that may prevent a professional accountant from acting with sufficient expertise.

11   What fundamental principles should be observed by all CIMA members?

12   List five characteristics each of strategic information, tactical information and operational information.

13   Fill in the blank.

.... is data that has been processed in such a way as to be meaningful to the person who receives it.

14   Fill in the blank.

An .... is an organisational and management solution, based on information technology, to any challenge posed by the environment.

Answers to Quick Quiz

1   False. It does not assess the probability of changes in the decision variables.

2   False. Should be 0 to 1.

3   A table of regrets can be compiled, as follows, showing the amount of profit that might be forgone for each project, depending on whether the outcome is I, II or III.

	Outcome			Maximum
	I	*II*	*III*	
Project A	40 *	50	20	50
Project B	15 **	45	0	45
Project C	0	0	5	5

* 100–60   ** 100–85 etc

The **maximum regret** is 50 with project A, 45 with B and 5 with C. The lowest of these three maximum regrets is 5 with C, and so Project C would be selected if the minimax regret rule is used.

4   D   Choice between $((0.2 \times 33{,}000) + (0.8 \times 14{,}000)) = 17{,}800$ at C, 22,000,
         and $((0.1 \times 40{,}000) + (0.9 \times 11{,}000)) = 13{,}900$ at D.

5

Probability	Numbers assigned	Probability	Numbers assigned
0.132	000–131	0.083	857–939
0.410	132–541	0.060	940–999
0.315	542–856		

6   Standard deviation, $s = \sqrt{\Sigma p(x - \bar{x})^2}$

where $\bar{x}$ is the EV of profit, x represents each possible profit, p represents the probability of each possible profit

7   (a)

		EV $'000
Project L	$(550 \times 0.20 + 480 \times 0.40 + 580 \times 0.40)$	534
Project M	$(450 \times 0.20 + 500 \times 0.40 + 570 \times 0.40)$	518
Project N	$(420 \times 0.20 + 450 \times 0.40 + 480 \times 0.40)$	456
Project O	$(370 \times 0.20 + 410 \times 0.40 + 430 \times 0.40)$	410
Project P	$(590 \times 0.20 + 580 \times 0.40 + 430 \times 0.40)$	522

Project L has the highest EV of expected cash inflows and should therefore be undertaken.

(b)

Market condition	Probability	Project chosen	Net cash inflow	EV of net cash inflow $'000
Poor	0.20	P	590	118
Good	0.40	P	580	232
Excellent	0.40	L	580	232
EV of net cash inflows with perfect information				582
EV of net cash inflows without perfect information				534
Value of perfect information				48

8   B   Confidentiality

9   The temptation to manipulate **price-sensitive** information when preparing accounts is potentially a very serious ethical threat.

10
- Lack of time
- Lack of information
- Insufficient training
- Insufficient experience
- Insufficient education
- Inadequate resources

11
- Integrity
- Objectivity
- Professional competence and due care
- Confidentiality
- Professional behaviour

12

Strategic information	Tactical information	Operational information
Derived from both internal and external sources	Primarily generated internally (but may have a limited external component)	Derived from internal sources
Summarised at a high level	Summarised at a lower level	Detailed, being the processing of raw data
Relevant to the long term	Relevant to the short and medium term	Relevant to the immediate term
Concerned with the whole organisation	Concerned with activities or departments	Task-specific
Often prepared on an 'ad hoc' basis	Prepared routinely and regularly	Prepared very frequently
Both quantitative and qualitative	Based on quantitative measures	Largely quantitative
Uncertain, as the future cannot be predicted accurately		

13 **Information** is data that has been processed in such a way as to be meaningful to the person who receives it.

14 An **information system** is an organisational and management solution, based on information technology, to any challenge posed by the environment.

Answers to Questions

10.1 Risks

Make your own list, specific to the organisations that you are familiar with. Here is a list extracted from an article by Tom Jones, 'Risk Management' (Administrator, April 1993).

- Fire, flood, storm, impact, explosion, subsidence and other hazards

- Accidents and the use of faulty products

- Error: loss through damage or malfunction caused by mistaken operation of equipment or wrong operation of an industrial programme

- Theft and fraud

- Breaking social or environmental regulations

- Political risks (the appropriation of foreign assets by local governments, or of barriers to the repatriation of overseas profit)

- Computers: fraud, viruses and espionage

- Product tamper

- Malicious damage

10.2 Sensitivity analysis

The correct answer is:

(a) Plant costs would need to increase by a PV of $560, that is by (560/7,000) × 100% = 8% for the project to break even.

(b) Running costs would need to increase by a PV of $560, that is by (560/3,995) × 100% = 14% for the project to break even.

(c) Savings would need to fall by a PV of $560, that is by (560/11,555) × 100% = 4.8% for the project to break even.

The PVs of the cash flows are as follows.

Year	Discount factor 8%	PV of plant cost $	PV of running costs $	PV of savings $	PV of net cash flow $
0	1.000	(7,000)			(7,000)
1	0.926		(1,852)	5,556	3,704
2	0.857		(2,143)	5,999	3,856
		(7,000)	(3,995)	11,555	560

10.3 EV calculations

The correct answer is C.

A EV of cost = $20,850
    EV of profit = $9,150

C EV of cost = $20,250
    EV of profit = $9,750

B EV of cost = $20,500
    EV of profit = $9,500

D EV of cost = $20,550
    EV of profit = $9,450

C has the highest EV of profit.

10.4 Using the standard deviation to measure risk

The correct answer is project A.

The projects have the same EV of net cash flow ($3,000); therefore a risk-averse manager would choose the project with the smaller standard deviation of expected profit.

Project A

Cash flow	Probability	EV of cash flow	Cash flow minus EV of cash flow $(x - \bar{x})$	$p(x - \bar{x})^2$
$		$	$	$
2,000	0.3	600	−1,000	300,000
3,000	0.4	1,200	0	0
4,000	0.3	1,200	+1,000	300,000
		EV = 3,000		Variance = 600,000

Standard deviation = $\sqrt{600,000}$ = $775

Project B

Cash flow	Probability	EV of cash flow	Cash flow minus EV of cash flow $(x - \bar{x})$	$p(x - \bar{x})^2$
$		$	$	$
1,000	0.2	200	−2,000	800,000
2,000	0.2	400	−1,000	200,000
3,000	0.2	600	0	0
4,000	0.2	800	+1,000	200,000
5,000	0.2	1,000	+2,000	800,000
		EV = 3,000		Variance = 2,000,000

Standard deviation = $\sqrt{2,000,000}$ = $1,414

10.5 Standard deviation of the net present value

The correct answer is project B.

We can begin by calculating the EV of the NPV for each project.

	Project A				Project B	
NPV $'000	Prob	EV $'000	NPV $'000	Prob	EV $'000
−20	0.15	(3.0)	5	0.2	1.0
10	0.20	2.0	15	0.3	4.5
20	0.35	7.0	20	0.4	8.0
40	0.30	12.0	25	0.1	2.5
		18.0			16.0

Project A has a higher EV of NPV, but what about the risk of variation in the NPV above or below the EV? This can be measured by the standard deviation of the NPV.

The standard deviation of a project's NPV can be calculated as $\sqrt{\Sigma p(x - \bar{x})^2}$, where $\bar{x}$ is the EV of the NPV.

Project A, $\bar{x}$ = 18				Project B, $\bar{x}$ = 16			
x $'000	p	$x - \bar{x}$ $'000	$p(x-\bar{x})^2$	x $'000	p	$x - \bar{x}$ $'000	$p(x-\bar{x})^2$
−20	0.15	−38	216.6	5	0.2	−11	24.2
10	0.20	−8	12.8	15	0.3	−1	0.3
20	0.35	+2	1.4	20	0.4	+4	6.4
40	0.30	+22	145.2	25	0.1	+9	8.1
			$\overline{376.0}$				$\overline{39.0}$

Project A			Project B		
Standard deviation	=	$\sqrt{376}$	Standard deviation	=	$\sqrt{39.0}$
	=	19.391		=	6.245
	=	$19,391		=	$6,245

Although **Project A has a higher EV of NPV**, it also has a **higher standard deviation of NPV**, and so has **greater risk** associated with it.

Which project should be selected? Clearly it depends on the attitude to risk of the company's management. If management are **risk averse**, they will opt for the **less risky Project B**.

(If management were prepared **to take the risk of a low NPV in the hope of a high NPV**, they will opt for **Project A**.)

10.6 Simple decision tree

The correct answer is A.

The various outcomes must be evaluated using expected values.

EV at point B: (0.75 × 10,000) + (0.25 × 8,000) = 9,500
EV at point D: (0.6 × 20,000) + (0.4 × (4,000)) = 10,400
EV at point C: Choice between 10,400 and 11,000
EV at point A: Choice between B (9,500), C (10,400 or 11,000) and choice 3 (9,000).

If we are trying to maximise the figure, Option 2 and then Option 7 are chosen to give 11,000.

10.7 Decision based on EV of profit

The correct answer is Option B and so the statement is true.

Without perfect information, the option with the highest EV of profit will be chosen.

	Option A (National)		Option B (Regional)		Option C (Area)	
Probability	Profit $	EV $	Profit $	EV $	Profit $	EV $
0.3	(4,000)	(1,200)	0	0	1,000	300
0.5	2,000	1,000	3,500	1,750	1,500	750
0.2	10,000	2,000	4,000	800	2,000	400
		$\overline{1,800}$		$\overline{2,550}$		$\overline{1,450}$

Marketing regionally (option B) has the highest EV of profit, and would be selected.

10.8 Perfect information

The correct answer is $1,500.

If perfect information about the state of consumer demand were available, Option A would be preferred if the forecast demand is strong, and Option C would be preferred if the forecast demand is weak.

Demand	Probability	Choice	Profit $	EV of profit $
Weak	0.3	C	1,000	300
Moderate	0.5	B	3,500	1,750
Strong	0.2	A	10,000	2,000
EV of profit with perfect information				4,050
EV of profit, selecting option B				2,550
Value of perfect information				1,500

10.9 Controls

The risks chosen in the question are designed to illustrate how different types of control can be used to counter different risks. Important points from the list below include the following:

(a) Some controls are meant to **match exactly with specific risks**; for example the risk of a transaction in foreign exchange causing losses can be mitigated by undertaking an equal and opposite transaction designed to match the first.

(b) With other controls the matching is less obvious; these controls are designed to deal with the ways the **business is organised**, the way **decisions are taken** and the ways in which **employee performance** is **maximised**.

(c) Some controls are designed to **prevent** problems occurring in the first place; others to **detect** problems if they arise and **minimise their impact**.

(d) **Information** is key to control and decision making. Effective risk management depends on having the right type and level of information, including, but not only, management accounting information.

Risks		Example controls
Business process	Business processes not aligned with strategic objectives	The way the business is **structured**, particularly how much **central control** is exercised over operations
Staff departure	Strategy and operations disrupted by key staff leaving	**Human resource measures**, such as incentives to encourage staff and appraisals to monitor views and dissatisfaction
Resource wastage	Employee time being wasted on unproductive activities	**Management accounting systems**, enabling assessment of employee contribution and highlighting problem areas
Investor	Investors losing confidence in the way the company is run and selling their shares	**Corporate governance** arrangements ensuring board exercises proper stewardship over the company and communicates effectively with shareholders
Staff behaviour	Staff behaving in a way that is not compatible with the ethos of the organisation	Strong **control environment** highlighting the need for ethical behaviour and integrity
Employee error	Employee error causing loss of key resources to the business	**Control procedures** to **detect** errors before they cause loss, such as approval by senior staff and **training** to improve staff's abilities and **prevent** errors occurring
Technology access	Unauthorised persons gaining access to computer systems	**Internal audit detecting** unauthorised access and **failure** by the controls in place to stop unauthorised persons accessing systems

Risks		Example controls
Fraud	Monies or assets being stolen	**Fraud response plan** if fraud is detected or suspected
Investment	Loss-making investments being made	Use of **different financial measures** to provide extra perspectives on the investment
Foreign exchange transaction	Having to pay more on a future transaction because of adverse exchange rate movements	**Purchase an instrument** fixing the exchange rate used in the transaction
Political	Operations or revenues being disrupted by political activity	**Monitor** political situation; **negotiate with key stakeholders** (political parties)
Information	Taking the wrong decisions due to inadequate information	**Information systems** the organisation chooses providing quality of information needed for decision making
Information disruption	Disruption to operations caused by failures of information technology	Controls to **prevent** disruption occurring, such as **avoiding** placing IT in **vulnerable locations**, and **contingency plans** if disruption occurs
Systems development	Unreliable systems that are not in accordance with user needs being developed	A formal systems **development process** encompassing planning, testing and review

10.10 Socially responsible activities

Examples (our suggestions only) include:

(a)   The Body Shop (among others) not using animal testing for ingredients; Shell (as a **negative** example) being held responsible for environmental devastation in Nigeria's river deltas; recyclable packaging

(b)   British Airways' extension of married employees' benefits to homosexual partners; The Body Shop (again) building economic infrastructures in rural communities

(c)   Sanctions or boycotts of countries such as (in the past) South Africa or Iraq

(d)   Major supermarkets and retailers such as Waitrose often sponsor community facilities, charities and sporting events

(e)   Some organisations have very stringent quality standards, and immediate no-strings product recall policies

10.11 Assessing the value of information

(a)   What information is provided?
(b)   What is it used for?
(c)   Who uses it?
(d)   How often is it used?
(e)   Does the frequency with which it is used coincide with the frequency of provision?
(f)   What is achieved by using it?
(g)   What other relevant information is available which could be used instead?

An assessment of the value of information can be derived in this way, and the cost of obtaining it should then be compared against this value. On the basis of this comparison, it can be decided whether certain items of information are worth having. It should be remembered that there may also be intangible benefits which may be harder to quantify.

10.12 New information system

MEMORANDUM

To: Head of Systems
From: Accountant
Date: 24 July 20X4
Re: Cost-benefit assessment of the proposed new system

The primary purpose of the cost-benefit assessment is to ensure that the **benefits are greater** than the **costs**.

It is important to include both **capital and revenue costs** and to cover all of the setting up, running and maintenance expenses. Costs should include the following:

(a)   Hardware, software, computer room modifications, cabling and ancillary equipment (eg modems)

(b)   Set-up costs for analysis, design, specification, programming etc, file conversion; to training implementation and testing, staff recruitment

(c)   Ongoing costs: wages of systems staff, telecoms costs, power, consumables, further training, fallback facilities

(d)   Investment in training will be particularly important as part of a strategy to reduce staff turnover

Benefits are much harder to express quantitatively, but there are some that will be of particular value to NEST.

(a)   **Improved customer satisfaction**: a higher level of reliability of the system will increase customer confidence and goodwill and reduce customer complaints.

(b)   **Higher staff morale** will result from improved self-esteem and teamworking with the new reliable system.

(c)   The **saving of valuable time** spent resolving the consequences of current 'crashes'. This in turn may bring the further benefits of higher sales and improved inventory control.

(d)   **Improved decision making** based on high-quality information.

Capital investment appraisal techniques can help to evaluate the project, using payback period, accounting rate of return or discounted cash flow methods.

Whilst it is impossible to eliminate the risks associated with the project entirely, careful assessment of the costs and benefits will give the company confidence to proceed with the required new system.

Now try the question from the Practice Question Bank

Number	Marks	Time
Q43 Objective test questions	10	18 mins
Q44 Elsewhere	25	45 mins

APPENDIX:
MATHEMATICAL TABLES AND
EXAM FORMULAE

PRESENT VALUE TABLE

Present value of $1 ie $(1+r)^{-n}$ where r = interest rate, n = number of periods until payment or receipt.

Periods (n)	Interest rates (r)									
	1%	2%	3%	4%	5%	6%	7%	8%	9%	10%
1	0.990	0.980	0.971	0.962	0.952	0.943	0.935	0.926	0.917	0.909
2	0.980	0.961	0.943	0.925	0.907	0.890	0.873	0.857	0.842	0.826
3	0.971	0.942	0.915	0.889	0.864	0.840	0.816	0.794	0.772	0.751
4	0.961	0.924	0.888	0.855	0.823	0.792	0.763	0.735	0.708	0.683
5	0.951	0.906	0.863	0.822	0.784	0.747	0.713	0.681	0.650	0.621
6	0.942	0.888	0.837	0.790	0.746	0.705	0.666	0.630	0.596	0.564
7	0.933	0.871	0.813	0.760	0.711	0.665	0.623	0.583	0.547	0.513
8	0.923	0.853	0.789	0.731	0.677	0.627	0.582	0.540	0.502	0.467
9	0.914	0.837	0.766	0.703	0.645	0.592	0.544	0.500	0.460	0.424
10	0.905	0.820	0.744	0.676	0.614	0.558	0.508	0.463	0.422	0.386
11	0.896	0.804	0.722	0.650	0.585	0.527	0.475	0.429	0.388	0.350
12	0.887	0.788	0.701	0.625	0.557	0.497	0.444	0.397	0.356	0.319
13	0.879	0.773	0.681	0.601	0.530	0.469	0.415	0.368	0.326	0.290
14	0.870	0.758	0.661	0.577	0.505	0.442	0.388	0.340	0.299	0.263
15	0.861	0.743	0.642	0.555	0.481	0.417	0.362	0.315	0.275	0.239
16	0.853	0.728	0.623	0.534	0.458	0.394	0.339	0.292	0.252	0.218
17	0.844	0.714	0.605	0.513	0.436	0.371	0.317	0.270	0.231	0.198
18	0.836	0.700	0.587	0.494	0.416	0.350	0.296	0.250	0.212	0.180
19	0.828	0.686	0.570	0.475	0.396	0.331	0.277	0.232	0.194	0.164
20	0.820	0.673	0.554	0.456	0.377	0.312	0.258	0.215	0.178	0.149

Periods (n)	Interest rates (r)									
	11%	12%	13%	14%	15%	16%	17%	18%	19%	20%
1	0.901	0.893	0.885	0.877	0.870	0.862	0.855	0.847	0.840	0.833
2	0.812	0.797	0.783	0.769	0.756	0.743	0.731	0.718	0.706	0.694
3	0.731	0.712	0.693	0.675	0.658	0.641	0.624	0.609	0.593	0.579
4	0.659	0.636	0.613	0.592	0.572	0.552	0.534	0.516	0.499	0.482
5	0.593	0.567	0.543	0.519	0.497	0.476	0.456	0.437	0.419	0.402
6	0.535	0.507	0.480	0.456	0.432	0.410	0.390	0.370	0.352	0.335
7	0.482	0.452	0.425	0.400	0.376	0.354	0.333	0.314	0.296	0.279
8	0.434	0.404	0.376	0.351	0.327	0.305	0.285	0.266	0.249	0.233
9	0.391	0.361	0.333	0.308	0.284	0.263	0.243	0.225	0.209	0.194
10	0.352	0.322	0.295	0.270	0.247	0.227	0.208	0.191	0.176	0.162
11	0.317	0.287	0.261	0.237	0.215	0.195	0.178	0.162	0.148	0.135
12	0.286	0.257	0.231	0.208	0.187	0.168	0.152	0.137	0.124	0.112
13	0.258	0.229	0.204	0.182	0.163	0.145	0.130	0.116	0.104	0.093
14	0.232	0.205	0.181	0.160	0.141	0.125	0.111	0.099	0.088	0.078
15	0.209	0.183	0.160	0.140	0.123	0.108	0.095	0.084	0.074	0.065
16	0.188	0.163	0.141	0.123	0.107	0.093	0.081	0.071	0.062	0.054
17	0.170	0.146	0.125	0.108	0.093	0.080	0.069	0.060	0.052	0.045
18	0.153	0.130	0.111	0.095	0.081	0.069	0.059	0.051	0.044	0.038
19	0.138	0.116	0.098	0.083	0.070	0.060	0.051	0.043	0.037	0.031
20	0.124	0.104	0.087	0.073	0.061	0.051	0.043	0.037	0.031	0.026

CUMULATIVE PRESENT VALUE TABLE

This table shows the present value of $1 per annum, receivable or payable at the end of each year for

n years $\dfrac{1-(1+r)^{-n}}{r}$.

Periods (n)	1%	2%	3%	4%	5%	6%	7%	8%	9%	10%
1	0.990	0.980	0.971	0.962	0.952	0.943	0.935	0.926	0.917	0.909
2	1.970	1.942	1.913	1.886	1.859	1.833	1.808	1.783	1.759	1.736
3	2.941	2.884	2.829	2.775	2.723	2.673	2.624	2.577	2.531	2.487
4	3.902	3.808	3.717	3.630	3.546	3.465	3.387	3.312	3.240	3.170
5	4.853	4.713	4.580	4.452	4.329	4.212	4.100	3.993	3.890	3.791
6	5.795	5.601	5.417	5.242	5.076	4.917	4.767	4.623	4.486	4.355
7	6.728	6.472	6.230	6.002	5.786	5.582	5.389	5.206	5.033	4.868
8	7.652	7.325	7.020	6.733	6.463	6.210	5.971	5.747	5.535	5.335
9	8.566	8.162	7.786	7.435	7.108	6.802	6.515	6.247	5.995	5.759
10	9.471	8.983	8.530	8.111	7.722	7.360	7.024	6.710	6.418	6.145
11	10.368	9.787	9.253	8.760	8.306	7.887	7.499	7.139	6.805	6.495
12	11.255	10.575	9.954	9.385	8.863	8.384	7.943	7.536	7.161	6.814
13	12.134	11.348	10.635	9.986	9.394	8.853	8.358	7.904	7.487	7.103
14	13.004	12.106	11.296	10.563	9.899	9.295	8.745	8.244	7.786	7.367
15	13.865	12.849	11.938	11.118	10.380	9.712	9.108	8.559	8.061	7.606
16	14.718	13.578	12.561	11.652	10.838	10.106	9.447	8.851	8.313	7.824
17	15.562	14.292	13.166	12.166	11.274	10.477	9.763	9.122	8.544	8.022
18	16.398	14.992	13.754	12.659	11.690	10.828	10.059	9.372	8.756	8.201
19	17.226	15.679	14.324	13.134	12.085	11.158	10.336	9.604	8.950	8.365
20	18.046	16.351	14.878	13.590	12.462	11.470	10.594	9.818	9.129	8.514

Periods (n)	11%	12%	13%	14%	15%	16%	17%	18%	19%	20%
1	0.901	0.893	0.885	0.877	0.870	0.862	0.855	0.847	0.840	0.833
2	1.713	1.690	1.668	1.647	1.626	1.605	1.585	1.566	1.547	1.528
3	2.444	2.402	2.361	2.322	2.283	2.246	2.210	2.174	2.140	2.106
4	3.102	3.037	2.974	2.914	2.855	2.798	2.743	2.690	2.639	2.589
5	3.696	3.605	3.517	3.433	3.352	3.274	3.199	3.127	3.058	2.991
6	4.231	4.111	3.998	3.889	3.784	3.685	3.589	3.498	3.410	3.326
7	4.712	4.564	4.423	4.288	4.160	4.039	3.922	3.812	3.706	3.605
8	5.146	4.968	4.799	4.639	4.487	4.344	4.207	4.078	3.954	3.837
9	5.537	5.328	5.132	4.946	4.772	4.607	4.451	4.303	4.163	4.031
10	5.889	5.650	5.426	5.216	5.019	4.833	4.659	4.494	4.339	4.192
11	6.207	5.938	5.687	5.453	5.234	5.029	4.836	4.656	4.486	4.327
12	6.492	6.194	5.918	5.660	5.421	5.197	4.988	4.793	4.611	4.439
13	6.750	6.424	6.122	5.842	5.583	5.342	5.118	4.910	4.715	4.533
14	6.982	6.628	6.302	6.002	5.724	5.468	5.229	5.008	4.802	4.611
15	7.191	6.811	6.462	6.142	5.847	5.575	5.324	5.092	4.876	4.675
16	7.379	6.974	6.604	6.265	5.954	5.668	5.405	5.162	4.938	4.730
17	7.549	7.120	6.729	6.373	6.047	5.749	5.475	5.222	4.990	4.775
18	7.702	7.250	6.840	6.467	6.128	5.818	5.534	5.273	5.033	4.812
19	7.839	7.366	6.938	6.550	6.198	5.877	5.584	5.316	5.070	4.843
20	7.963	7.469	7.025	6.623	6.259	5.929	5.628	5.353	5.101	4.870

Probability

$A \cup B$ = A **or** B. $A \cap B$ = A **and** B (overlap). $P(B|A)$ = probability of B, **given** A.

Rules of addition

If A and B are **mutually exclusive**: $P(A \cup B) = P(A) + P(B)$

If A and B are **not** mutually exclusive: $P(A \cup B) = P(A) + P(B) - P(A \cap B)$

Rules of multiplication

If A and B are **independent**: $P(A \cap B) = P(A) * P(B)$

If A and B are **not** independent: $P(A \cap B) = P(A) * P(B|A)$

$E(X) = \sum (\text{probability} * \text{payoff})$

Descriptive statistics

Arithmetic mean

$$\bar{x} = \frac{\sum x}{n} \text{ or } \bar{x} = \frac{\sum fx}{\sum f} \text{ (frequency distribution)}$$

Standard deviation

$$SD = \sqrt{\frac{\sum (x - \bar{x})^2}{n}}$$

$$SD = \sqrt{\frac{\sum fx^2}{\sum f} - \bar{x}^2} \text{ (frequency distribution)}$$

Index numbers

Price relative = $100 * P_1 / P_0$

Quantity relative = $100 * Q_1 / Q_0$

Price: $\dfrac{\sum W \times P_1 / P_0}{\sum W} \times 100$ where W denotes weights

Quantity: $\dfrac{\sum W \times Q_1 / Q_0}{\sum W} \times 100$ where W denotes weights

Time series

Additive model: Series = Trend + Seasonal + Random
Multiplicative model: Series = Trend * Seasonal * Random

Financial mathematics

Compound Interest (Values and Sums)

Future Value of S, of a sum X, invested for n periods, compounded at r% interest:

$$S = X[1+r]^n$$

Annuity

Present value of an annuity of £1 per annum receivable or payable, for n years, commencing in one year, discounted at r% per annum:

$$PV = \frac{1}{r}\left[1 - \frac{1}{[1+r]^n}\right]$$

Perpetuity

Present value of £1 per annum, payable or receivable in perpetuity, commencing in one year discounted at r% per annum

$$PV = \frac{1}{r}$$

Learning curve

$$Y_x = aX^b$$

where Y_x = the cumulative average time per unit to produce X units

a = the time required to produce the first unit of output

X = the cumulative number of units

b = the index of learning

The exponent b is defined as the log of the learning curve improvement rate divided by log 2.

Inventory management

Economic Order Quantity

$$EOQ = \sqrt{\frac{2C_o D}{C_h}}$$

Where C_o = cost of placing an order

C_h = cost of holding one unit in inventory for one year

D = annual demand

PRACTICE QUESTION AND ANSWER BANK

What the examiner means

The very important table below has been prepared by CIMA to help you interpret exam questions.

Learning objectives	Verbs used	Definition
1 Knowledge What are you expected to know	• List • State • Define	• Make a list of • Express, fully or clearly, the details of/facts of • Give the exact meaning of
2 Comprehension What you are expected to understand	• Describe • Distinguish • Explain • Identify • Illustrate	• Communicate the key features of • Highlight the differences between • Make clear or intelligible/state the meaning of • Recognise, establish or select after consideration • Use an example to describe or explain something
3 Application How you are expected to apply your knowledge	• Apply • Calculate/ compute • Demonstrate • Prepare • Reconcile • Solve • Tabulate	• Put to practical use • Ascertain or reckon mathematically • Prove with certainty or to exhibit by practical means • Make or get ready for use • Make or prove consistent/compatible • Find an answer to • Arrange in a table
4 Analysis How you are expected to analyse the detail of what you have learned	• Analyse • Categorise • Compare and contrast • Construct • Discuss • Interpret • Prioritise • Produce	• Examine in detail the structure of • Place into a defined class or division • Show the similarities and/or differences between • Build up or compile • Examine in detail by argument • Translate into intelligible or familiar terms • Place in order of priority or sequence for action • Create or bring into existence
5 Evaluation How you are expected to use your learning to evaluate, make decisions or recommendations	• Advise • Evaluate • Recommend	• Counsel, inform or notify • Appraise or assess the value of • Propose a course of action

1 Restaurant   **18 mins**

Learning outcome: Revision

W has operated a restaurant for the last two years. Revenue and operating costs over the two years have been as follows.

	Year 1 $'000	*Year 2* $'000
Revenue	1,348,312	1,514,224
Operating costs		
Food and beverages	698,341	791,919
Wages	349,170	390,477
Other overheads	202,549	216,930

The number of meals served in year 2 showed an 8% increase on the year 1 level of 151,156. An increase of 10% over the year 2 level is budgeted for year 3.

All staff were given hourly rate increases of 6% last year (in year 2). In year 3 hourly increases of 7% are to be budgeted.

The inflation on 'other overheads' last year was 5%, with an inflationary increase of 6% expected in the year ahead.

Food and beverage costs are budgeted to average $5.14 per meal in year 3. This is expected to represent 53% of sales value.

Required

From the information given above, and using the high-low method of cost estimation, determine the budgeted expenditure on wages and other overheads for year 3.   **(10 marks)**

2 Objective test questions   **18 mins**

2.1   Which of the following is not a merit of activity based analysis?

    I   Activity based analysis recognises the complexity of modern business.

    II   Activity based analysis does not concern itself with all types of overhead cost.

    III   Some measure of arbitrary cost apportionment will still be required, even if such analysis is used.

    IV   Activity based analysis is based on the belief that it is always possible to improve.

    A   I only

    B   None of the above

    C   III and IV

    D   II, III and IV   **(2 marks)**

Data for questions 2.2 and 2.3

The following data relate to costs, output volume and cost drivers of Heighway Rubbery Ltd for June 20X1.

		Product P	Product Q	Product R	Total
1	Production and sales	3,000 units	2,000 units	1,500 units	
2	Direct production costs	$ per unit	$ per unit	$ per unit	
	Direct materials	12	11	8	$70,000
	Direct labour	3	6	2	$24,000
		15	17	10	$94,000
3	Labour hours per unit	½	1	⅓	
4	Machine hours per unit	2	1	2	
5	Number of production runs	8	2	10	20
6	Number of deliveries to customers	3	2	10	15
7	Number of production orders	30	5	15	50
8	Number of deliveries of materials into store	17	3	20	40
9	Production overhead costs				$
	Machining				71,500
	Set-up costs				10,500
	Materials handling (receiving)				35,000
	Packing costs (despatch)				22,500
	Engineering				25,500
					165,000

Indirect production overheads that are not driven by production volume are:

Item	Cost driver
Set-up costs	Production runs
Materials handling	Deliveries of materials
Packing	Deliveries to customers
Engineering	Production orders

2.2 What would be the full production cost per unit of product R if overheads are absorbed on the basis of direct labour hours?

   A $13.75

   B $23.75

   C $30.00

   D $51.25   **(2 marks)**

2.3 Calculate the full production cost per unit of product R using activity based costing and the cost drivers described above, with overheads that are driven by production volume absorbed on a machine hour basis.   **(2 marks)**

2.4 In activity based costing, what is a cost driver?

   A   An overhead cost that is incurred as a direct consequence of an activity

   B   Any direct cost element in a product's cost

   C   Any activity or product item for which costs are incurred

   D   Any factor which causes a change in the cost of an activity   **(2 marks)**

2.5 GK manufactures two products in its factory in Italy, the Romeo and the Romolo. Both products require the use of a machine in the factory, which has broken down on numerous occasions in recent months. It is currently operational for approximately 6,800 hours per annum. GK's management intends to replace the machine next year, but until then seeks advice as to which product to manufacture.

Information about the products is as follows.

	Romeo	Romolo
Selling price per unit	$120	$160
Direct material cost per unit	$50	$90
Variable conversion costs per unit	$35	$25
Time required on machine	0.65 hour	0.75 hour
Maximum demand	10,000	8,000

Using a throughput accounting approach, recommend which product GK should choose to manufacture first. **(2 marks)**

(Total = 10 marks)

3 ABC   18 mins

Learning outcome: A1(a)

(a) It is sometimes claimed that activity based costing (ABC) simply provides a **different** picture of product costs to traditional absorption costing, rather than a more accurate picture.

Explain the concepts that underlie ABC and discuss the claim above. **(5 marks)**

(b) Some advocates of ABC claim that it provides information which can be used for decision making. Critically appraise this view. **(5 marks)**

(Total = 10 marks)

4 ABC systems   18 mins

Learning outcome: A1(a)

'ABC systems are **resource-consumption models**. That is, they attempt to measure the cost of **using** resources, not the cost of **supplying** resources.'

Colin Drury, *Management Accounting Business Decisions*

Required

Discuss the statement above using figures, if you wish, to illustrate the points made. **(10 marks)**

5 Abkaber plc   54 mins

Learning outcome: A1(a)

Abkaber plc assembles three types of motorcycle at the same factory: the 50cc Sunshine; the 250cc Roadster and the 1000cc Fireball. It sells the motorcycles throughout the world. In response to market pressures Abkaber plc has invested heavily in new manufacturing technology in recent years and, as a result, has significantly reduced the size of its workforce.

Historically, the company has allocated all overhead costs using total direct labour hours, but is now considering introducing activity based costing (ABC). Abkaber plc's accountant has produced the following analysis.

	Annual output (units)	Annual direct labour Hours	Selling price ($ per unit)	Raw material cost ($ per unit)
Sunshine	2,000	200,000	4,000	400
Roadster	1,600	220,000	6,000	600
Fireball	400	80,000	8,000	900

The three cost drivers that generate overheads are:

Deliveries to retailers – the number of deliveries of motorcycles to retail showrooms

Set-ups – the number of times the assembly line process is re-set to accommodate a production run of a different type of motorcycle

Purchase orders – the number of purchase orders

The annual cost driver volumes relating to each activity and for each type of motorcycle are as follows:

	Number of deliveries to retailers	Number of set-ups	Number of purchase orders
Sunshine	100	35	400
Roadster	80	40	300
Fireball	70	25	100

The annual overhead costs relating to these activities are as follows:

	$
Deliveries to retailers	2,400,000
Set-up costs	6,000,000
Purchase orders	3,600,000

All direct labour is paid at $5 per hour. The company holds no inventories.

At a board meeting there was some concern over the introduction of activity based costing.

The finance director argued: 'I very much doubt whether selling the Fireball is viable but I am not convinced that activity based costing would tell us any more than the use of labour hours in assessing the viability of each product.'

The marketing director argued: 'I am in the process of negotiating a major new contract with a motorcycle rental company for the Sunshine model. For such a big order they will not pay our normal prices but we need to at least cover our incremental costs. I am not convinced that activity based costing would achieve this as it merely averages costs for our entire production'.

The managing director argued: 'I believe that activity based costing would be an improvement but it still has its problems. For instance if we carry out an activity many times surely we get better at it and costs fall rather than remain constant. Similarly, some costs are fixed and do not vary either with labour hours or any other cost driver.'

The chairman argued: 'I cannot see the problem. The overall profit for the company is the same no matter which method of allocating overheads we use. It seems to make no difference to me.'

Required

(a) Calculate the total profit on each of Abkaber plc's three types of product using each of the following methods to attribute overheads:

    (i) The existing method based upon labour hours

    (ii) Activity based costing   **(12 marks)**

(b) Write a report to the directors of Abkaber plc, as its management accountant. The report should:

    (i) Evaluate the labour hours and the activity based costing methods in the circumstances of Abkaber plc

(ii)   Examine the implications of activity based costing for Abkaber plc, and in so doing evaluate the issues raised by each of the directors   **(12 marks)**

(c)   In a manufacturing environment, activity based costing often classifies activities into unit, batch, product sustaining and facility sustaining. Explain these terms.   **(6 marks)**

Refer to your calculations in requirement (a) above where appropriate.   **(Total = 30 marks)**

6 CPA   18 mins

Learning outcome: A1(a)

As the management accountant of XY Ltd you have undertaken an analysis of the company's profitability in relation to the number of customers served. The results of your analysis are shown in the graph below.

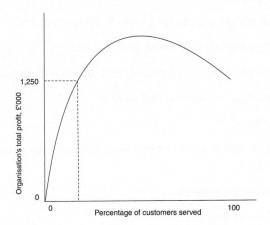

Required

Write a report to management which:

(a)   Explains the general concept that is encapsulated by the graph   **(4 marks)**

(b)   Advises management on the actions that are open to it to improve the profitability of the organisation   **(6 marks)**

(Total = 10 marks)

7 Just-in-time   45 mins

Learning outcome: A1(b)

Many organisations believe that a key element of just-in-time (JIT) systems is JIT production.

Required

(a)   Discuss five main features of a JIT production system.   **(20 marks)**
(b)   State the financial benefits of JIT.   **(5 marks)**

(Total = 25 marks)

8 Objective test questions

18 mins

8.1 A company makes and sells three products A, B and C. The products are sold in the proportions A:B:C = 1:1:4.

Monthly fixed costs are $55,100 and product details are as follows:

Product	Selling price $ per unit	Variable cost $ per unit
A	47	25
B	39	20
C	28	11

The company wishes to earn a profit of $43,000 next month. What is the required sales value of product A in order to achieve this target profit? **(2 marks)**

8.2 What are the primary activities of Porter's value chain for a manufacturing company?

A   Human resource management, information database and structure

B   Inward movement of materials, manufacture, marketing, distribution and after-sales service

C   R&D, design, production, marketing, distribution and service

D   Strategy, R&D, marketing and sales **(2 marks)**

8.3 Indicate which of the following methods can be used to move a currently attainable cost closer to target cost.

A   Using standard components wherever possible

B   Acquiring new, more efficient technology

C   Making staff redundant

D   Reducing the quality of the product in question **(2 marks)**

8.4 A mobile phone manufacturer, C Ltd, is planning to produce a new model. The potential market over the next year is 1,000,000 units.

C Ltd has the capacity to produce 400,000 units and could sell 100,000 units at a price of $50. Demand would double for each $5 fall in the selling price.

The company has an 80% cost experience curve for similar products. The cost of the first batch of 1,000 phones was $103,000.

A minimum margin of 25% is required.

Required

Calculate C Ltd's target cost per unit, to the nearest $. **(2 marks)**

8.5 Indicate whether or not the following aspects of 'value' should be considered in a value analysis exercise.

A   Sales value

B   Replacement value

C   Exchange value

D   Disposal value **(2 marks)**

(Total = 10 marks)

9 Cost reduction   45 mins

Learning outcome: A1(c)

It has been suggested that much of the training of management accountants is concerned with cost control whereas the major emphasis should be on cost reduction.

Required

(a)   Distinguish between cost control and cost reduction.   **(7 marks)**

(b)   Give **three** examples **each** of the techniques and principles used for (i) cost control and (ii) cost reduction.   **(8 marks)**

(c)   Discuss the proposition contained in the statement.   **(10 marks)**

                                                                (Total = 25 marks)

10 Objective test questions   18 mins

10.1   A company has produced the first batch of a new product which took 40 hours to manufacture. With an 80% learning curve, how long would it take to make the next 9 batches?   **(2 marks)**

10.2   The time taken to produce the first unit of a new product was 12 hours. By the time 4 units had been made, the average time per unit had dropped to 6 hours. What was the rate of learning experienced?   **(2 marks)**

10.3   KJ has recently developed a new product. It is usual for the workforce to experience an 80% learning effect as the work is repetitive. It takes 3 kg of material at $4/kg to produce each unit and variable overheads are expected to cost $2.50/hr. Labour is paid $8/hr.   **(2 marks)**

        If the first unit took 40 minutes to produce, what will be the expected cost of the fifth unit?

10.4   What are the four stages of the product life cycle?

        A   Introduction, growth, maturity, decline

        B   Growth, maturity, saturation, decline

        C   Introduction, growth, plateau, decline

        D   Growth, plateau, decline, obsolescence   **(2 marks)**

10.5   When are the bulk of a product's life cycle costs normally determined?

        A   At the design/development stage

        B   When the product is introduced to the market

        C   When the product is in its growth stage

        D   On disposal   **(2 marks)**

                                                                (Total = 10 marks)

11 Dench

18 mins

Learning outcome: A1(d)

Dench Manufacturing has received a special order from Sands Ltd to produce 225 components to be incorporated into Sands' product. The components have a high cost, due to the expertise required for their manufacture. Dench produces the components in batches of 15 and, as the ones required are to be custom-made to Sands' specifications, a 'prototype' batch was manufactured with the following costs:

		$
Materials		
	4 kg of A, $7.50/kg	30
	2 kg of B, $15/kg	30
Labour		
	20 hrs skilled, $15/hr	300
	5 hrs semi-skilled, $8/hr	40
Variable overhead		
	25 labour hours, $4/hr	100
		500

Additional information with respect to the workforce is noted below:

Skilled Virtually a permanent workforce that has been employed by Dench for a long period of time. These workers have a great deal of experience in manufacturing components similar to those required by Sands, and turnover is virtually non-existent.

Semi-Skilled Hired by Dench on an 'as needed' basis. These workers would have had some prior experience, but Dench management believe the level to be relatively insignificant. Past experience shows turnover rate to be quite high, even for short employment periods.

Dench's plans are to exclude the prototype batch from Sands' order. Management believes an 80% learning rate effect is experienced in this manufacturing process, and would like a cost estimate for the 225 components prepared on that basis.

Required

(a) Prepare the cost estimate, assuming an 80% learning rate is experienced. **(6 marks)**

(b) Briefly discuss some of the factors that can limit the use of learning curve theory in practice.

  (4 marks)

  (Total = 10 marks)

12 Life cycle costing

18 mins

Learning outcome: A1(c)

Explain life cycle costing and state what distinguishes it from more traditional management accounting techniques. **(10 marks)**

13 Objective test questions

18 mins

Data for questions 13.1 and 13.2

A firm has established that maximum demand for its product is 80,000 units per annum. When it reduced its prices by $20, demand rose by 1,600 units.

13.1 What is the demand function?

    A   P = 1,000 – 0.025x

    B   P = 1,000 – 0.0125x

    C   P = 50 – 0.025x

    D   P = 500 – 0.0125x   **(2 marks)**

13.2 What price should be set in order to sell 50,000 units?

    A $125

    B $225

    C $375

    D $500   **(2 marks)**

13.3 NRC Ltd makes and sells a single product, Z. The selling price and marginal revenue equations for product Z are as follows:

Selling price = $60 – $0.001x

Marginal revenue = $60 – $0.002x

The full cost of Z is $35 per unit. Fixed costs are $150,000 and it was originally budgeted to make 15,000 units.

In order to maximise profit, what should be the selling price per unit?   **(2 marks)**

13.4 Current demand for Orchard's product the Russet is 5,000 units each year; its selling price is $175. For every $10 that the selling price is increased by, demand for the Russet falls by 500 units. Marginal cost for the Russet is $65. What price will Orchard need to set in order to maximise profits?

    Note. If price P = a – bx then MR = a – 2bx.   **(2 marks)**

13.5 Off-peak travel bargains are an example of differential pricing using which base?

    A   Time

    B   Market segment

    C   Product version

    D   Place   **(2 marks)**

                                   (Total = 10 marks)

14 PN Motor Components   **18 mins**

Learning outcome: C2(a)

(a)   In an attempt to win over key customers in the motor industry and to increase its market share, PN Motor Components plc has decided to charge a price lower than its normal price for component WB47 when selling to the key customers who are being targeted. Details of component WB47's standard costs are as follows.

Standard cost data

	Component WB47 Batch size 200 units			
	Machine group 1 $	Machine group 7 $	Machine group 29 $	Assembly $
Materials (per unit)	26.00	17.00	–	3.00
Labour (per unit)	2.00	1.60	0.75	1.20
Variable overheads (per unit)	0.65	0.72	0.80	0.36
Fixed overheads (per unit)	3.00	2.50	1.50	0.84
	31.65	21.82	3.05	5.40
Setting-up costs per batch of 200 units	$10	$6	$4	–

Required

Compute the lowest selling price at which one batch of 200 units could be offered, and describe the other factors to consider when adopting such a pricing policy. **(6 marks)**

(b) The company is also considering the launch of a new product, component WB49A, and has provided you with the following information.

	Standard cost per box $
Variable cost	6.20
Fixed cost	1.60
	7.80

Market research – forecast of demand

Selling price ($)	13	12	11	10	9
Demand (boxes)	5,000	6,000	7,200	11,200	13,400

The company only has enough production capacity to make 7,000 boxes. However, it would be possible to purchase product WB49A from a sub-contractor at $7.75 per box for orders up to 5,000 boxes, and $7 per box if the orders exceed 5,000 boxes.

Required

Prepare and present a computation which illustrates which price should be selected in order to maximise profits. **(4 marks)**

(Total = 10 marks)

15 DX   18 mins

Learning outcome: C2(a)

DX manufactures a wide range of components for use in various industries. It has developed a new component, the U. It is the practice of DX to set a 'list' selling price for its components and charge this price to all customers. It sells its components directly to customers all over the UK and abroad.

DX has surplus capacity available to enable it to produce up to 350,000 units per year without any need to acquire new facilities or cut back on the production of other products.

Market research indicates that:

(a) If demand is 100,000 units or less, marginal revenue is $9 - 0.06x$, where x is demand in thousands of units

(b) If demand is above 100,000 units, marginal revenue is $10 - 0.08x$, where x is demand in thousands of units

BPP LEARNING MEDIA

Research into production costs indicates that the marginal costs for a unit of production in any given year are as follows.

(a) **Labour**. Initially $2.00 per unit but falling by 2.5p per unit for each extra 1,000 units produced, thus up to the first 1,000 units produced incurs a labour cost of $2,000, the second 1,000 incurs a labour cost of $1,975, the third 1,000 incurs a labour cost of $1,950 and so on until output reaches 80,000; output can be increased beyond 80,000 units per year without incurring any additional labour costs.

(b) **Materials**. 50p per unit constant at all levels of output.

(c) **Overhead**. Initially $1.00 per unit and remaining constant until output reaches 100,000 units per year; the overhead cost per unit of producing at above that level rises by 0.25p for each extra 1,000 units produced, thus the 101st thousand units produced incur an overhead cost of $1,002.50, the 102nd thousand units produced incur an overhead cost of $1,005 and so on.

Required

Calculate the output level that will maximise DX's profit from U production.   **(10 marks)**

16 Plastic tools   18 mins

Learning outcome: C2(a)

A small company is engaged in the production of plastic tools for the garden.

Subtotals on the spreadsheet of budgeted overheads for a year reveal the following.

	Moulding department	*Finishing department*	*General factory overhead*
Variable overhead $'000	1,600	500	1,050
Fixed overhead $'000	2,500	850	1,750
Budgeted activity			
Machine hours ('000)	800	600	
Practical capacity			
Machine hours ('000)	1,200	800	

For the purposes of reallocation of general factory overhead it is agreed that the variable overheads accrue in line with the machine hours worked in each department. General factory fixed overhead is to be reallocated on the basis of the practical machine hour capacity of the two departments.

It has been a long-standing company practice to establish selling prices by applying a mark-up on full manufacturing cost of between 25% and 35%.

A possible price is sought for one new product which is in a final development stage. The total market for this product is estimated at 200,000 units per annum. Market research indicates that the company could expect to obtain and hold about 10% of the market. It is hoped the product will offer some improvement over competitors' products, which are currently marketed at between $90 and $100 each.

The product development department have determined that the direct material content is $9 per unit. Each unit of the product will take two labour hours (four machine hours) in the moulding department and three labour hours (three machine hours) in finishing. Hourly labour rates are $5.00 and $5.50 respectively.

Management estimate that the annual fixed costs which would be specifically incurred in relation to the product are supervision $20,000, depreciation of a recently acquired machine $120,000 and advertising $27,000. It may be assumed that these costs are included in the budget given above. Given the state of development of this new product, management do not consider it necessary to make revisions to the budgeted activity levels given above for any possible extra machine hours involved in its manufacture.

Required

Prepare full cost and marginal cost information which may help with the pricing decision.   **(10 marks)**

17 Costs and pricing

18 mins

Learning outcome: C2(a)

(a) Comment on the cost information in question 16 above and suggest a price range which should be considered. **(5 marks)**

(b) Briefly explain the role of costs in pricing. **(5 marks)**

(Total = 10 marks)

18 Hilly plc

8 mins

Learning outcome: C2(a)

Hilly plc is a well-established manufacturer of high-quality goods. The company has recently developed a new product 'The Lauren' to complement its existing products.

Each Lauren requires 2 kilograms of material. Each kilogram costs $60.

The labour cost of manufacturing a 'Lauren' is estimated at $40 per unit.

Variable overheads are estimated to be $20 per unit.

The marketing director has estimated that at a selling price of $500 per Lauren, an annual sales volume of 500,000 would be achieved. He has further estimated that an increase/decrease in price of $20 will cause quantity demanded to decrease/increase by 25,000 units. He has provided you with the following formulae:

Price function: $P = a - bx$

Marginal revenue (MR) function: $= a - 2bx$

Where: a = the price at which demand would be nil

b = the amount by which the price falls for each stepped change in demand

Required

Calculate the profit-maximising output level for sales of 'The Lauren' and the price that should be charged. **(4 marks)**

19 Objective test questions

18 mins

19.1 Which of the following is/are purposes of flexible budgeting?

(i) To cope with different activity levels

(ii) To reward sales rather than production

(iii) To more meaningfully compare actual and budgeted costs

(iv) To show different results which may occur between different activity levels

A (i) only

B (i), (ii) and (iii)

C (i), (iii) and (iv)

D (i) and (iv) **(2 marks)**

19.2 Flexed budgets for the cost of hotel laundry based on occupancy percentages are shown below.

Occupancy	82%	94%
Laundry cost	$410,000	$429,200

During the period, the actual occupancy was 87% and the total laundry cost was $430,000.

The variance on laundry was:

A $5,000 adverse

B $12,000 adverse

C $5,000 favourable

D $12,000 favourable   **(2 marks)**

19.3 Which of the following definitions best describes the responsibility of an investment centre in a decentralised organisation?

A   Responsibility for the level of sales, production costs, collection of debts and payment of suppliers

B   Responsibility for the level of sales, production costs and treasury functions

C   Responsibility for the level of sales, production costs and purchase of new fixed assets

D   Responsibility for the level of production costs, treasury functions and collection of debtors and payment of suppliers   **(2 marks)**

19.4 One of the main reasons for adopting a decentralised rather than a centralised organisation structure is the:

A   Improved goal congruence between divisional manager and the goals of the organisation

B   Rapid response of management to environmental changes

C   Availability of less subjective measures of performance

D   Improved communication of information among the organisation's managers   **(2 marks)**

19.5 Which of the following items would be included in the calculation of controllable divisional profit before tax?

I   Sales to outside customers

II   Head office costs

III   Variable divisional expenses

IV   Controllable divisional fixed costs

A   IV only

B   II and III

C   I, III and IV

D   III and IV

E   II only   **(2 marks)**

                                                                        (Total = 10 marks)

20 Responsibility accounting   9 mins

Learning outcome: B1(a), B2(c)

Explain the importance of an established system of responsibility accounting in the construction of functional budgets that support the overall master budget.   **(5 marks)**

21 Budgets and people

22 mins

Learning outcome: B1(a), B3(a)

In his study of *The Impact of Budgets on People* Argyris reported inter alia the following comment by a financial controller on the practice of participation in the setting of budgets in his company.

'We bring in the supervisors of budget areas, we tell them that we want their frank opinion but most of them just sit there and nod their heads. We know they're not coming out with exactly how they feel. I guess budgets scare them.'

Required

Suggest reasons why managers may be reluctant to participate fully in setting budgets, and suggest also unwanted side effects which may arise from the imposition of budgets by senior management.

(12 marks)

22 Divisional performance

27 mins

Learning outcome: B1(a)

(a)   Compare and contrast the use of residual income and return on investment in divisional performance measurement, stating the advantages and disadvantages of each.   **(10 marks)**

(b)   Division Y of Chardonnay currently has capital employed of $100,000 and earns an annual profit after depreciation of $18,000. The divisional manager is considering an investment of $10,000 in an asset which will have a 10-year life with no residual value and will earn a constant annual profit after depreciation of $1,600. The cost of capital is 15%.

Calculate the following and comment on the results.

(i)   The return on divisional investment, before and after the new investment

(ii)   The divisional residual income before and after the new investment   **(5 marks)**

(Total = 15 marks)

23 B and C

54 mins

Learning outcome: B1(a), 3(a)

(a)   The following figures for the years ending 31 December 20X4 and 20X3 relate to the B and C divisions of Cordeline.

The return on capital employed (ROCE) figure is the basis for awarding a 20% bonus to the manager of B division (actual ROCE/target ROCE). The below target ROCE for C division has resulted in a zero bonus award to its manager.

	Division			
	B		C	
	20X4	20X3	20X4	20X3
	$'000	$'000	$'000	$'000
Sales	9,850	7,243	4,543	2,065
Profit before interest and taxes (PBIT)	1,336	1,674	924	363
Included in profit calculation:				
Depreciation for year	960	919	1,300	251
Net book value (NBV) of non-current assets*	5,540	6,000	7,700	2,600
Original cost of non-current assets	12,600	12,100	9,500	3,100
Replacement cost of non-current assets	25,000	24,500	9,750	3,350
New investment in non-current assets	500	750	6,400	2,400
Cost of capital	8%	8%	8%	8%
Return on capital employed**	24%	28%	12%	14%
Target return on capital	20%	20%	20%	20%

* Net book value is original cost less accumulated depreciation to date.

** Cordeline consider ROCE for bonus purposes to be PBIT as a % of NBV.

Required

Cordeline's board is meeting to review the company's management performance appraisal and reward system. Prepare a short paper for the board, drawing on the above information, which contains the following.

| (i) | An explanation of possible counter-productive behaviour resulting from using the current ROCE calculation for performance appraisal | **(14 marks)** |

| (ii) | A revised ROCE measure together with justification for your suggestion | **(6 marks)** |

| (b) | Briefly explain the advantages and disadvantages of divisionalisation. | **(10 marks)** |

(Total = 30 marks)

24 Pasta Division   54 mins

Learning outcome: B1(a), 3(a)

A well-established food manufacturing and distribution company, specialising in Italian food products, currently has an annual turnover in excess of $15 million. At present, the company has three production and distribution divisions, each responsible for specific product groups and a cost of capital of 15%.

The summary information of the pasta division relating to divisional assets and profitability is as follows.

Pasta division

This division produces a wide range of both dried and fresh pasta products which it sells to both the supermarket sector and the restaurant trade.

Last year the divisional figures were as follows.

	$m
Investment in non-current assets	1.5
Investment in working capital	1.0
Operating profit	0.5

The company is keen to ensure that each division operates as an autonomous profit-making unit to ensure efficiency prevails and motivation and competitiveness are maximised. Managers are given as much freedom as possible to manage their divisions. Divisional budgets are set at the beginning of each year and these are then monitored on a month by month basis. Divisional managers are rewarded in terms of divisional return on investment.

The company is currently considering expansion into a new but allied product range. This range consists of sauces and canned foods. Projected figures for the expansion into sauces and canned foods are:

	$m
Additional non-current assets required	0.75
Additional investment in working capital	0.35
Budgeted additional profit	0.198

The manager of the pasta division has produced successful results over the past few years for her division. She and her staff have enjoyed handsome bonuses on the basis of return on investment. The company has traditionally calculated return on investment as operating profit as a percentage of return on all net divisional assets, and bonuses are paid as a percentage on this basis. The board proposes that the pasta division will be responsible for the expansion into sauces and canned foods.

Required

(a) Calculate the return on investment for the division both before and after the proposed divisional expansion. **(5 marks)**

(b) Calculate the residual income for the division both before and after the proposed divisional expansion. **(5 marks)**

(c) Using return on investment as a performance measure, determine whether the divisional manager will be happy to accept the proposed expansion. Explain how your answer would differ if residual income was used as a performance measure instead of return on investment. **(5 marks)**

(d) Briefly outline the advantages and disadvantages of return on investment and residual income as divisional performance measures. **(8 marks)**

(e) Briefly explain the main features of Economic Value Added (EVA®) as it would be used to assess the performance of divisions. **(3 marks)**

(f) Briefly explain how the use of EVA® to assess divisional performance might affect the behaviour of divisional senior executives. **(4 marks)**

(Total = 30 marks)

25 Objective test questions

18 mins

25.1 Division X of Tina Pease Ltd produced the following results in the last financial year:

		$'000
Net profit		360
Capital employed:	fixed assets	1,500
	net current assets	100

For evaluation purposes all divisional assets are valued at original cost. The division is considering a project which will increase annual net profit by $25,000 but will require average stock levels to increase by $30,000 and fixed assets to increase by $100,000. Tina Pease Ltd imposes an 18% capital charge on its divisions.

Given these circumstances, will the evaluation criteria of return on investment (ROI) and residual income (RI) motivate Division X management to accept the project?

	ROI	RI
A	Yes	Yes
B	Yes	No
C	No	Yes
D	No	No

(2 marks)

25.2 Division W of Stoak Ltd produced the following results in the last financial year:

Net profit ($'000)   200
Gross capital employed ($'000)   1,000

For evaluation purposes all divisional assets are valued at original cost.

A proposed project will increase the division's net profit by $22,000, but will require gross assets to increase by $100,000. Stoak Ltd imposes a 20% capital charge on its divisions.

Will the evaluation criteria of return on investment (ROI) and residual income (RI) motivate division W's managers to accept the project?

	ROI	RI
A	Yes	Yes
B	Yes	No
C	No	Yes
D	No	No

(2 marks)

25.3 The following data have been extracted from a company's year-end accounts:

	$
Turnover	7,100,000
Gross profit	4,850,500
Operating profit	3,630,000
Non-current assets	4,500,000
Cash at bank	2,750,000
Short-term borrowings	950,000
Trade receivables	525,000
Trade payables	435,000

Calculate the following performance measures:

(i)   Operating profit margin

(ii)   Return on capital employed

(iii) Trade receivable days

(iv)   Current ratio   (2 marks)

25.4 Green division is one of many divisions in Colour plc. At its year end, the fixed assets invested in Green were $30 million, and the net current assets were $5 million. Included in this total was a new item of plant that was delivered three days before the year end. This item cost $4 million and had been paid for by Colour, which had increased the amount of long-term debt owed by Green by this amount.

The profit earned in the year by Green was $6 million before the deduction of $1.4 million of interest payable to Colour.

What is the most appropriate measure of ROI for the Green division?

A   13.1%

B   14.8%

C   17.1%

D   19.4%   (2 marks)

25.5 Division G has reported annual operating profits of $20.2 million. This was after charging $3 million for the full cost of launching a new product that is expected to last 3 years. Division G has a risk adjusted cost of capital of 11% and is paying interest on a substantial bank loan at 8%. The historical cost of the assets in Division G, as shown on its balance sheet, is $60 million, and the replacement cost has been estimated at $84 million.

Ignore the effects of taxation.

What would be the EVA® for Division G?

A $15.40 million

B $15.48 million

C $16.60 million

D $12.96 million   **(2 marks)**

(Total = 10 marks)

26 Balanced scorecard   9 mins

Learning outcome: B2(b)

For each perspective of the balanced scorecard, suggest ONE key performance indicator that could be monitored by a company that provides training courses to the general public, and explain why each might be a useful indicator.   **(5 marks)**

27 MPL   54 mins

Learning outcomes: B1(a), B2(b)

(a)   MPL is a company specialising in providing consultancy services to the catering industry. The operating statement for period 5 for the IT division is as follows. The division operates as a profit centre.

	Budget	Actual	Variance
Chargeable consultancy hours	2,400	2,500	100
	€	€	€
Central administration costs – fixed	15,000	15,750	750 (A)
Consultants' salaries – fixed	80,000	84,000	4,000 (A)
Casual wages – variable	960	600	360 (F)
Motor and travel costs – fixed	4,400	4,400	-
Telephone – fixed	600	800	200 (A)
Telephone – variable	2,000	2,150	150 (A)
Printing, postage & stationery – variable	2,640	2,590	50 (F)
Depreciation of equipment – fixed	3,200	3,580	380 (A)
Total costs	108,800	113,870	5,070 (A)
Fees charged	180,000	200,000	20,000 (F)
Profit	71,200	86,130	14,930 (F)

While the manager of the IT division is pleased that the actual profit exceeded the budget expectation, she is interested to know how this has been achieved. After the budget had been issued to her she had queried the meaning of variable costs and had been told that they were variable in direct proportion to chargeable consultancy hours.

Required

As the newly appointed management accountant, prepare a report addressed to the board of directors of MPL which:

(i)   Explains the present approach to budgeting adopted in MPL and discusses the advantages and disadvantages of involving consultants in the preparation of future budgets.   **(8 marks)**

(ii) Critically discusses the format of the operating statement for period 5. **(5 marks)**

(iii) Prepare an alternative statement for the profit centre which distinguishes clearly between controllable profit and attributable profit and which provides a realistic measure of the variances for the period. State any assumptions you make. **(7 marks)**

(b) Briefly explain the balanced scorecard approach and the problems that can arise when it is applied. **(10 marks)**

(Total = 30 marks)

28 Objective test questions   18 mins

28.1 In which of the following circumstances is there a strong argument that profit centre accounting is a waste of time with regards to transfer pricing?

A When the transferred item is also sold on an external market

B When the supplying division is based in a different country to head office

C If the transferred item is a major product of the supplying division

D If there is no similar product sold on an external market and the transferred item is a major product of the supplying division **(2 marks)**

28.2 During the year the Dutch manufacturing division of NTN plc transferred 6,000 units of Product C to the UK selling division.

Each unit cost €350 to manufacture and was sold for £650. The variable cost proportion was 75%. The UK division incurred marketing and distribution costs of £20 per unit. The UK tax rate was 30% and the exchange rate was £1 = €1.50. The transfers were at variable cost. What was the UK division's profit after tax on the sale of 6,000 units? **(2 marks)**

28.3 Transfer prices based on standard cost provide an incentive for the receiving division to control costs.
True or false?

The following data relates to questions 28.4 and 28.5

T plc manufactures a component D12, and two main products F45 and P67. The following details relate to each of these items.

	D12 $ per unit	F45 $ per unit	P67 $ per unit
Selling price	–	146.00	159.00
Material cost	10.00	15.00	26.00
Component D12 (bought-in price)		25.00	25.00
Direct labour	5.00	10.00	15.00
Variable overhead	6.00	12.00	18.00
Total variable cost per unit	21.00	62.00	84.00
	$ per annum	$ per annum	$ per annum
Fixed overhead costs			
Avoidable *	9,000	18,000	40,000
Non-avoidable	36,000	72,000	160,000
Total	45,000	90,000	200,000

* The avoidable fixed costs are product specific fixed costs that would be avoided if the product or component were to be discontinued.

28.4 Assuming that the annual demand for component D12 is 5,000 units and that T plc has sufficient capacity to make the component itself, the maximum price that should be paid to an external supplier for 5,000 components per year is:

A $105,000

B $114,000

C $141,000

D $150,000   **(2 marks)**

28.5 Assuming that component D12 is bought from an external supplier for $25.00 per unit, the number of units of product F45 that must be sold to cover its own costs without contributing to T plc's non-avoidable fixed costs is closest to:

A   188 units

B   214 units

C   228 units

D   261 units   **(2 marks)**

(Total = 10 marks)

29 Transfer pricing   54 mins

Learning outcome: B3(c)

(a)   Explain the potential benefits of operating a transfer pricing system within a divisionalised company.   **(6 marks)**

(b)   A company operates two divisions, Able and Baker. Able manufactures two products, X and Y. Product X is sold to external customers for $42 per unit. The only outlet for product Y is Baker.

Baker supplies an external market and can obtain its semi-finished supplies (product Y) from either Able or an external source. Baker currently has the opportunity to purchase product Y from an external supplier for $38 per unit. The capacity of division Able is measured in units of output, irrespective of whether product X, Y or combination of both are being manufactured. The associated product costs are as follows.

	X	Y
Variable costs per unit	32	35
Fixed overheads per unit	5	5
Total unit costs	37	40

Required

Using the above information, provide advice on the determination of an appropriate transfer price for the sale of product Y from division Able to division Baker under the following conditions.

(i)   When division Able has spare capacity and limited external demand for product X   **(3 marks)**

(ii)   When division Able is operating at full capacity with unsatisfied external demand for product X

          (4 marks)

(c)   A group has two companies, K, which is operating at just above 50% capacity and L, which is operating at full capacity (7,000 production hours).

L produces two products, X and Y, using the same labour force for each product. For the next year its budgeted capacity involves a commitment to the sale of 3,000 kg of Y, the remainder of its capacity being used on X. Direct costs of these two products are as follows.

	X		Y	
	$ per kg		$ per kg	
Direct materials	18		14	
Direct wages	15	(1 production hour)	10	(²/₃ production hour)

The company's overhead is $126,000 per annum relating to X and Y in proportion to their direct wages. At full capacity $70,000 of this overhead is variable. L prices its products with a 60% mark-up on its total costs.

For the coming year, K wishes to buy from L 2,000 kg of product X which it proposes to adapt and sell, as product Z, for $100 per kg. The direct costs of adaptation are $15 per kg. K's total fixed costs will not change, but variable overhead of $2 per kg will be incurred.

Required

As group management accountant, make the following recommendations.

(i)   The range of transfer prices, if any, at which 2,000 kg of product X should be sold to K

(ii)   The other points that should be borne in mind when making any recommendations about transfer prices in the above circumstances **(12 marks)**

(d)   Discuss briefly whether standard costs or actual costs should be used as the basis for cost-based transfer prices. **(5 marks)**

(Total = 30 marks)

30 Objective test questions   18 mins

30.1 Harston Ltd is to spend $60,000 on a machine which will have an economic life of 10 years and no residual value. Depreciation is to be charged using the straight-line method. Estimated operating cash flows are:

Year	$
1	– 2,000
2	+13,000
3	+20,000
4–6	+25,000 p.a.
7–10	+30,000 p.a.

What is the payback period (PB) and the average annual return on initial investment (ARR)?

	PB	ARR
A	5.47 years	37.67%
B	5.47 years	27.67%
C	4.16 years	37.67%
D	4.16 years	27.67%

(2 marks)

30.2 Lee is considering the following two investments that are mutually exclusive:

Project 1:   Initial outlay = $100,000
                     Scrap proceeds at end of project = $5,000
                     Profit receivable = $15,000 p.a. for 8 years

Project 2:   Initial outlay = $50,000
                     Scrap proceeds at end of project = $5,000
                     Cash flows receivable = $15,000 p.a. for 5 years

If Lee has a target Accounting Rate of Return of 20% based on average investment, determine which project(s) he would find acceptable. **(2 marks)**

30.3 Paisley proposes to purchase a machine costing $13,500. The machine will save labour costs of $7,000 per annum for 2 years and will then be sold for $5,000.

What is the IRR of the project? Ignore tax.

A   18.6%

B   23.3%

C   38.7%

D   Impossible to determine without a cost of capital   **(2 marks)**

30.4 A company has 31 March as its accounting year end. On 1 April 20X6 a new machine costing $2,000,000 is purchased. The company expects to sell the machine on 31 March 20X8 for $500,000.

The effective rate of corporation tax for the company is 35%. Writing down allowances are obtained at 25% on the reducing balance basis and a balancing allowance is available on disposal of the asset. Tax cash flows occur 12 months after the end of the accounting period in which the originating cash flows occurred. The company makes sufficient profits to obtain relief for capital allowances as soon as they arise.

If the company's cost of capital is 10% per annum, calculate the present value at 1 April 20X6 of the capital allowances (to the nearest thousand dollars).   **(2 marks)**

30.5 SPT Limited is commencing a project with an initial outlay of $50,000 on 1 January 20X0. It is estimated that the company will sell 1,000 items on 31 December 20X0 and at the end of each subsequent year until 31 December 20X2. The contribution per unit on 31 December 20X0 will be $33, and is expected to rise by 10% per year over the life of the project.

At the end of the project scrap sales are expected to realise a cash amount of $15,000. This will be received by the company on 31 December 20X2.

At an inflation rate of 10% p.a. the real cost of capital is 10% p.a.

To the nearest thousand dollars, what is the net present value of the project's cash flows at 1 January 20X0?

A $33,000

B $36,000

C $41,000

D $43,000   **(2 marks)**

(Total = 10 marks)

31 Webber Design   45 mins

Learning outcome: B1(a)

Webber Design had almost completed a specialised piece of equipment when it discovered that the customer who had commissioned the work had gone out of business. Another customer was found to be interested in this piece of equipment but certain extra features would be necessary.

The following data is provided in respect of the additional work.

Direct materials costing $2,500 would be required. Webber Design has these in stock but if not used to manufacture the specialised equipment they would be used on another contract in place of materials which would cost $4,500.

The company has three departments, welding, machining and assembly, within which the extra features would incur the following additional work to be undertaken. In the welding department one worker would be needed for three weeks. The wage rate is $280 per worker per week. The welding department is currently operating at only 50% of normal capacity, but two workers must be kept on the payroll to ensure that the department can respond instantly to any increase in demand.

Two workers would be needed for 5 weeks in the machining department, which is working normally and the wage rate is $240 per worker, per week.

The assembly department is always extremely busy. Its wage rate is $200 per worker, per week and is currently yielding a contribution of $5 per $1 of direct labour. The additional requirements for this job would be two workers for eight weeks.

Overtime would need to be sanctioned in order to finish the job for the customer. This would cost $1,500. Such costs are normally charged to production overhead.

Variable overhead is 15% of direct wages and a special delivery charge of $3,400 would be incurred. Fixed production overhead is absorbed in each department on the basis of a fixed percentage of direct wages as follows.

Welding at 120%
Machining at 80%
Assembly at 40%

The costs of the equipment as originally estimated and incurred so far are as follows.

	Original quotation $	Work to date $	Work to complete $
Direct materials	13,075	10,745	2,300
Direct wages	7,500	6,700	1,050
Variable overheads	1,125	1,050	150
Fixed production overhead	6,500	5,250	1,200
Fixed administration	1,250	1,050	200

The price to the original customer allowed for a profit margin of 20% on selling price. An advance payment of 15% of the price had been received on confirmation of the order.

If the work of the new customer is not carried out some of the materials in the original equipment would be used for another contract in place of materials that would have cost $4,000 but would need two workers' weeks in the machining department to make them suitable. The remaining materials would realise $5,200 as scrap. The design for the equipment, which would normally be included in the selling price, could be sold for $1,500.

Required

(a)   Calculate the minimum price that Webber Design should quote to the new customer.   **(10 marks)**

(b)   State any further considerations you think Webber Design should take into account in setting the price.   **(7 marks)**

(c)   Define 'relevant cost', 'opportunity cost' and 'discretionary cost', and state their use to management.
                                                                                                                (8 marks)

(Total = 25 marks)

32 X

18 mins

Learning outcome: B1(a)

X manufactures four liquids – A, B, C and D. The selling price and unit cost details for these products are as follows.

	A	B	C	D
	$/litre	$/litre	$/litre	$/litre
Selling price	100	110	120	120
Direct materials	24	30	16	21
Direct labour ($6/hour)	18	15	24	27
Direct expenses	–	–	3	–
Variable overhead	12	10	16	18
Fixed overhead (note 1)	24	20	32	36
Profit	22	35	29	18

Note 1. Fixed overhead is absorbed on the basis of labour hours, based on a budget of 1,600 hours per quarter.

During the next three months the number of direct labour hours is expected to be limited to 1,345. The same labour is used for all products.

The marketing director has identified the maximum demand for each of the four products during the next three months as follows.

A	200 litres	C	100 litres
B	150 litres	D	120 litres

These maximum demand levels include the effects of a contract already made between X and one of its customers, Y Ltd, to supply 20 litres of each of A, B, C and D during the next three months.

Required

Determine the number of litres of products A, B, C and D to be produced/sold in the next three months in order to maximise profits, and calculate the profit that this would yield.

Assume that no inventory is held at the beginning of the three months which may be used to satisfy demand in the period.

(10 marks)

33 Research director

18 mins

Learning outcome: B1(a)

After completing the production plan in question 32 above, you receive two memos.

The first is from the research director.

'New environmental controls on pollution must be introduced with effect from the start of next month to reduce pollution from the manufacture of product D. These will incur fixed costs of $6,000 per annum.'

The second memo is from the sales director.

'An overseas supplier has developed a capacity to manufacture products C and D on a sub-contract basis, and has quoted the following prices to X.'

C	$105/litre	D	$100/litre

Required

Using the information from **both** of these memos, state and quantify the effect (if any) on X's plans.

(10 marks)

34 Alphabet Ltd   **18 mins**

Learning outcome: B1(a)

Alphabet Ltd have received a proposal to manufacture 12,000 units of T over 12 months at a selling price of $3 per unit.

The following statement has been prepared:

	$	$
Sales revenue		36,000
Costs: Material X at historical cost	5,000	
Material Z at contract price	9,000	
Manufacturing labour	10,000	
Depreciation of machine	4,000	
Variable overheads @ 30c per unit	3,600	
Fixed overheads		
(absorbed @ 80% of manufacturing labour)	8,000	
		(39,600)
		(3,600)

Further information

1   Material X cannot be used or sold for any other product. It would cost $200 to dispose of the existing inventories.

2   Each unit of new production uses two kilos of material Z. The company has entered into a long-term contract to buy 24,000 kilos at an average price of 37.5c per kilo. The current price is 17.5c per kilo. This material is regularly used in the manufacture of the company's other products.

3   The machine which would be used to manufacture T was bought new 3 years ago for $22,000. It had an estimated life of 5 years with a scrap value of $2,000.

   If the new product is not manufactured the machine could be sold immediately for $7,000. If it is used for one year it is estimated that it could then be sold for $4,000.

4   The new product requires the use of skilled labour, which is scarce. If product T were not made this labour could be used on other activities, which would yield a contribution of $1,000.

Required

Prepare a statement of relevant costs and revenues and determine whether or not the proposal should be accepted.   **(10 marks)**

35 PPA   **18 mins**

Learning outcome: C1(b)

Discuss the advantages and disadvantages of post-project appraisal.   **(10 marks)**

36 Payback   **18 mins**

Learning outcome: C1(c)

Explain the uses, limitations and merits of the payback period method of investment appraisal.
                                                                              (10 marks)

37 Two projects

18 mins

Learning outcome: C1(c)

A company is considering which of two mutually exclusive projects it should undertake. The finance director thinks that the project with the higher NPV should be chosen whereas the managing director thinks that the one with the higher IRR should be undertaken, especially as both projects have the same initial outlay and length of life. The company anticipates a cost of capital of 10% and the net after tax cash flows of the projects are as follows.

Year	Project X $'000	Project Y $'000
0	–200	–200
1	35	218
2	80	10
3	90	10
4	75	4
5	20	3

Required

(a) Calculate the NPV and IRR of each project. **(6 marks)**

(b) Recommend, with reasons, which project you would undertake (if either). **(2 marks)**

(c) Explain the inconsistency in ranking of the two projects in view of the remarks of the directors.

(2 marks)

(Total = 10 marks)

38 NPV and IRR

18 mins

Learning outcome: C1(c)

Explain the uses, limitations and merits of the NPV and IRR methods of investment appraisal. **(10 marks)**

39 HP

45 mins

Learning outcome: C1(c)

HP is considering purchasing a new machine to alleviate a bottleneck in its production facilities. At present it uses an old machine which can process 200 units of product P per hour. HP could replace it with machine AB, which is product-specific and can produce 500 units an hour. Machine AB costs $500,000. If it is installed, two members of staff will have to attend a short training course, which will cost the company a total of $5,000. Removing the old machine and preparing the area for machine AB will cost $20,000.

The company expects demand for P to be 12,000 units per week for another 3 years. After this, early in the fourth year, the new machine would be scrapped and sold for $50,000. The existing machine will have no scrap value. Each P earns a contribution of $1.40. The company works a 40-hour week for 48 weeks in the year. HP normally expects a payback within 2 years, and its after-tax cost of capital is 10% per annum. The company pays corporation tax at 30% and receives writing down allowances of 25%, reducing balance. Corporation tax is payable quarterly, in the seventh and tenth months of the year in which the profit is earned, and in the first and fourth months of the following year.

Required

(a) Prepare detailed calculations that show whether machine AB should be bought, and advise the management of HP as to whether it should proceed with the purchase.

Make the following assumptions.

  (i) The company's financial year begins on the same day that the new machines would start operating, if purchased.

  (ii) The company uses discounted cash flow techniques with annual breaks only.

  (iii) For taxation purposes, HP's management will elect for short-life asset treatment for this asset. **(18 marks)**

(b) The investment decision in part (a) is a closely defined manufacturing one. Explain how a marketing or an IT investment decision might differ in terms of approach and assessment.

(7 marks)

(Total = 25 marks)

40 Objective test questions   18 mins

40.1 Identify three common types of 'real option' found in relation to capital projects. **(2 marks)**

40.2 What is an indivisible project? **(2 marks)**

40.3 Give three reasons why hard capital rationing may occur. **(2 marks)**

40.4 What is the best way to find the optimal solution in a situation of single period rationing with indivisible projects? **(2 marks)**

40.5 What is the best way to find the optimal solution in a situation of single period rationing with divisible projects? **(2 marks)**

(Total = 10 marks)

41 Fund restrictions   22 mins

Learning outcome: C1(c)

A company can invest in the following four projects. The timing and amounts of the cash flows are shown below.

	T_0 $'000	t_1 $'000	t_2 $'000	NPV (15%) $'000	IRR %
Project A	(150)	100	105	14.22	9
Project B	(200)	150	135	28.27	14
Project C		(175)	230	21.74	12
Project D	(300)	200	220	35.01	12

Required

(a) If the company has a present restriction of $450,000 for investment, calculate which projects it would invest in. Assume that all projects are divisible. **(5 marks)**

(b) If there are no fund restrictions and these four projects are mutually exclusive, explain with reasons which project the company should choose. **(2 marks)**

(c) Explain why capital rationing occurs. **(5 marks)**

(Total = 12 marks)

42 ANT

45 mins

Learning outcome: C1(b)

ANT, a multi-product company, is considering four investment projects, details of which are given below.

Development costs already incurred on the projects are as follows.

A	B	C	D
$	$	$	$
100,000	75,000	80,000	60,000

Each project will require an immediate outlay on plant and machinery, the cost of which is estimated as follows.

A	B	C	D
$	$	$	$
2,100,000	1,400,000	2,400,000	600,000

In all four cases the plant and machinery has a useful life of five years, at the end of which it will be valueless.

Unit sales per annum, for each project, are expected to be as follows.

A	B	C	D
150,000	75,000	80,000	120,000

Selling price and variable costs per unit for each project are estimated below.

	A	B	C	D
	$	$	$	$
Selling price	30.00	40.00	25.00	50.00
Materials	7.60	12.00	4.50	25.00
Labour	9.80	12.00	5.00	10.00
Variable overheads	6.00	7.00	2.50	10.50

The company charges depreciation on plant and machinery on a straight-line basis over the useful life of the plant and machinery. Development costs of projects are written off in the year that they are incurred. The company apportions general administration costs to projects at a rate of 5% of selling price. None of the above projects will lead to any actual increase in the company's administration costs.

Working capital requirements for each project will amount to 20% of the expected annual sales value. In each case this investment will be made immediately and will be recovered in full when the projects end in five years' time.

Funds available for investment are limited to $5,200,000. The company's cost of capital is estimated to be 18%.

Required

(a) Calculate the NPV of each project. **(12 marks)**

(b) Calculate the profitability index for each project and advise the company which of the new projects, if any, to undertake. You may assume that each of the projects can be undertaken on a reduced scale for a proportionate reduction in cash flows. Your advice should state clearly your order of preference for the four projects, what proportion you would take of any project that is scaled down, and the total NPV generated by your choice. **(5 marks)**

(c) Discuss the limitations of the profitability index as a means of dealing with capital rationing problems. **(8 marks)**

Ignore taxation. **(Total = 25 marks)**

43 Objective test question

18 mins

43.1 Which of the following methods can be used to help appraise risk in investment appraisal?

(i) Payback

(ii) Discounted payback

(iii) Expected net present value

(iv) Increase cost of capital for riskier projects

(v) Sensitivity analysis

A (i), (ii) and (iv)

B (i), (iii), (iv) and (v)

C (i), (ii), (iv) and (v)

D All the above **(2 marks)**

43.2 Three sales representatives – J, K and L – rate their (independent) chances of achieving certain levels of sales as follows:

Possible sales		$10,000	$20,000	$30,000
J	Probability	0.3	0.5	0.2
K	Probability	0.3	0.4	0.3
L	Probability	0.2	0.6	0.2

(For example, J rates her chances of selling $20,000 worth of business as '50-50' and K has a 30% chance of selling $30,000.)

On this evidence, the highest expected sales will be from:

A J alone

B K alone

C L alone

D K and L **(2 marks)**

43.3 Brain Ltd is considering launching a new product. Expected sales volumes (at a selling price of $5 per unit) and expected unit variable costs are as follows:

	Sales		Variable costs per unit	
Units	Probability	$	Probability
1,000	0.9	1.30	0.55
2,000	0.1	1.50	0.45

Fixed costs are expected to be $3,000. The company produces to order. What is the expected profit?

A $2,400

B $30

C $3,971

D $971 **(2 marks)**

Data for questions 43.4 and 43.5

Maisy has to decide how many birthday cakes should be baked each day. Daily demand ranges from 9 cakes to 12 cakes and each cake sold yields a positive contribution of $5. Unsold cakes yield a negative contribution of $3.

Maisy believes that unsatisfied demand has an opportunity cost of $2.

43.4 Calculate the number of cakes that Maisy should make each day assuming she uses:

(i)   Maximax decision rule

(ii)   Maximin decision rule

(iii)   Minimax regret decision rule   **(2 marks)**

43.5 Maisy now believes that the daily demand for cakes will have the following probabilities:

Demand Units	Probability
9	0.2
10	0.2
11	0.3
12	0.3

An independent market research company has agreed to provide Maisy, in advance, with details of the definite daily demand. This means that Maisy will always bake the correct number of cakes to satisfy daily demand.

If the information will cost $5 per day, advise Maisy whether she should obtain this information. You must justify your advice.   **(2 marks)**

(Total = 10 marks)

44 Elsewhere

45 mins

Learning outcomes: D1(b)

Rubbish Records Ltd is considering the launch of a new pop group, Elsewhere.

If the group is launched without further market research being carried out it is thought that demand for their records and the present value of profit earned from record sales will be as follows.

Demand	Probability	Present value of profit
		$'000
High	0.5	800
Medium	0.2	100
Low	0.3	(300)

It is possible, however, to commission a market research survey which will forecast either a successful or unsuccessful career for Elsewhere. The probability of an unsuccessful career is 0.3.

Probabilities of high, medium or low demand for Elsewhere's records under each of the two market research results are as follows.

	Demand		
	High	Medium	Low
Successful chart career	0.7	0.1	0.2
Unsuccessful chart career	0.1	0.3	0.6

So, for example, if the research indicated an unsuccessful chart career, then the probability of medium demand for the group's records would be 0.3.

The survey would cost $50,000.

Required

(a) Calculate the expected value of profit if Rubbish Records does not commission a market research survey. **(5 marks)**

(b) (i) Draw a decision tree to show the choices facing Rubbish Records. **(10 marks)**

    (ii) Briefly explain whether or not the record company should commission the survey. **(3 marks)**

(c) (i) Determine the maximum the company should pay for the survey (often referred to as the value of the imperfect information provided by the survey). **(2 marks)**

    (ii) Establish the disadvantages of using expected values and decision trees as decision-making tools. **(5 marks)**

(Total = 25 marks)

1 Restaurant

Wages

> **Top tip**. You need to work out the variable wages cost using the high-low method. There are only two years, so one is taken as 'high' and one as 'low'.

	Year 1	Year 2	Increase
Number of meals	151,156	(× 8%) 163,248	12,092
	$	$	$
Wages cost	349,170	390,477	41,307

We must account for inflation, however, by adjusting year 1 to year 2 costs. The figure used is the 6% hourly rate increase.

	$	$	$
$349,170 \times 106\% =$	370,120	390,477	20,357

In year 2, the variable wages cost of a meal is $\dfrac{\$20,357}{12,092} = \$1.68$

	$
Variable wages cost (year 2) ($1.68 × 163,248)	274,257
Fixed wages cost (year 2) (balance)	116,220
Total wages cost (year 2)	390,477

	$
So, in year 3, variable cost = (163,248 × 110%) meals × $1.68 × 107%	322,800
Fixed cost = $116,220 × 107%	124,355
Total wages cost (year 3)	447,155

Overheads

	Year 1	Year 2	Increase
Number of meals	151,156	163,248	12,092
	$	$	$
Overhead costs	202,549	216,930	14,381
Adjusting year 1 costs to year 2 cost (× 105%)	212,676	216,930	4,254

Variable overhead cost in year 2 is $\dfrac{\$4,254}{12,092} = \$0.352$ per meal

	$
∴ In year 2, variable overhead cost ($0.352 × 163,248)	57,463
Fixed overhead cost (balance)	159,467
Total overhead cost (year 2)	216,930
∴ In year 3, variable cost = (163,248 × 110%) meals × $0.352 × 106%	67,002
Fixed cost = $159,467 × 106%	169,035
Total overhead cost (year 3)	236,037

2 Objective test answers

2.1 D   **I**   This is a merit of activity based analysis, according to its proponents.

           II   Activity based analysis **is** concerned with all overhead costs, including the costs of non factory floor activities such as quality control and customer service. It therefore takes cost accounting beyond its traditional factory floor boundaries.

           III   Arbitrary cost apportionment may still be required at the pooling stage for items like rent and rates.

           IV   It is TQM that is based on this belief.

2.2 B

Direct labour hours	P	$3,000 \times \frac{1}{2}$	= 1,500
	Q	$2,000 \times 1$	= 2,000
	R	$1,500 \times \frac{1}{3}$	= 500
			4,000

Absorption rate for overhead   = $165,000 \div 4,000$
                               = $41.25 per direct labour hour.

Unit cost of R   = $ (8 + 2 + \frac{1}{3} \text{ of } 41.25) = $23.75

2.3   Overhead rates

Machining	$71,500 ÷ 11,000 machine hours	= $6.50 per machine hour
Set-up costs	$10,500 ÷ 20 production runs	= $525.00 per run
Materials handling	$35,000 ÷ 40 materials deliveries	= $875.00 per delivery
Packing costs	$22,500 ÷ 15 deliveries to customers	= $1,500.00 per delivery
Engineering	$25,500 ÷ 50 production orders	= $510.00 per order

Product R overhead costs		$
Machining	3,000 machine hours × $6.50	19,500
Set-up costs	10 production runs × $525.00	5,250
Materials handling	20 deliveries × $875.00	17,500
Packing costs	10 customer deliveries × $1,500.00	15,000
Engineering	15 production orders × $510.00	7,650
		64,900

Cost per unit of R		$
Direct materials		8.00
Direct labour		2.00
Overhead	($64,900 ÷ 1,500 units of R)	43.27
		53.27

2.4 D   A cost driver determines the size of the costs of an activity or causes the costs of an activity. For example, the costs of the despatching activity might be determined by the number of despatches and so the number of despatches would be the cost driver.

2.5

	Romeo	Romolo
Throughput per unit	($(120 − 50)) = $70	($(160 − 90)) = $70
÷ time on key resource	÷ 0.65 hr	÷ 0.75 hr
Return per hour	$108	$93
Ranking	1st	2nd

GK should manufacture product Romeo first.

3 ABC

> **Top tips.** Requirements such as these are just the sort of thing you might encounter as parts of questions in the exam. You are expected to be able to critically appraise the management accounting techniques and methods included in the syllabus so don't be afraid to be critical of a view used as the basis for a question.

(a)   **ABC** attempts to **relate all costs**, with the possible exception of facility sustaining costs, to **cost objects** such as products, services or customers. It does this by **collecting costs/resources** and **relating them to either primary or support activities via resource cost drivers. Support activity costs are then spread across primary activities.** Finally the **costs of the primary activities** are **related** to **cost units using activity cost drivers**.

It is likely that ABC will **provide a different picture of product costs than that produced using traditional absorption costing**. This is because different assumptions are made because the costs are spread across the activities, etc. As both methods make assumptions about the behaviour and cause of costs, it is impossible to say categorically that ABC results are more accurate than those produced using traditional absorption costing.

Nevertheless there are usually more activities than cost centres and this should make the process **more accurate**. Furthermore, it is **easier to justify the selection of cost driver rates** with ABC than the absorption rates used with traditional absorption costing. ABC also allows costs to be accumulated per batch or per number of products made, as well as per unit.

These factors all suggest that in most cases ABC will produce a more accurate answer.

(b)   Some commentators argue that only marginal costing provides suitable information for decision making. This is untrue. Marginal costing provides a crude method of differentiating between different types of cost behaviour by splitting costs into their variable and fixed elements. **Marginal costing** can only be used for **short-term decisions** and usually even these have longer-term implications which ought to be considered.

ABC spreads costs across products or other cost units according to a number of different bases. The analysis may show that one activity which is carried out for one or two products is expensive. If costs have been apportioned using the traditional method prior to this, the cost of this activity is likely to have been spread across all products, thus hiding the fact that the products using this activity may be loss making. If these costs are not completely variable costs but are, for example, batch costs, marginal costing would not have related them to the products at all. Therefore ABC can be used to make decisions about pricing, discontinuing products, and so on.

4 ABC systems

> **Top tips.** This old syllabus pilot paper question was not easy, in that you may have had difficulty in finding enough to write about to justify 10 marks. To get close to full marks you should expand your argument to include ABM.

To a certain extent Drury is correct when he states that ABC systems are resource-consumption models.

When ABC systems were first discussed companies were using other systems, usually absorption-based, for the purposes of inventory valuation. ABC analysis and supporting calculations would be carried out using actual data to see what the 'actual' costs of products were as a way of improving decision making and operational control.

In this retrospective context ABC starts with the processes of allocating costs to cost pools and determining an appropriate cost driver. For example, $250,000 may have been spent on labour and materials for the packing department which processed 25,000 customer orders. This results in a cost of $10 per order to trace back to products, where 'number of orders' is the identified cost driver.

Clearly, in this context, ABC is looking at the **cost of using resources** within the packing department.

Increasingly, however, companies are using ABC as their main costing system but as part of a broader system of **activity based management** (ABM). Here an **activity based budget** (ABB) will be prepared, using budgeted costs and levels of activity, and compared to the ABC figures over the period for the purposes of exercising control.

It is likely that when the ABB is being prepared it will start with expected sales volumes and from there consider what activities will be required in order to generate the required volume of product. Thus the example above would shift emphasis from 'we spent $250,000 in packing last year' to 'how much resource should we supply the packing department with so as to have them pack the expected volume?'. If the ABB is accurate then the ABB figure for packing will be the same as the figures obtained through ABC.

Hopefully companies that are using ABC are using it in the broader context of ABM so as to be able to obtain a broader range of benefits. Although ABC in isolation does focus on resource consumption, **ABM will consider both the consumption and the supply of resources.**

5 Abkaber plc

> **Top tips.** There is a lot of information in this question and in an exam situation you would probably make use of some of the 20 minutes' reading time. Make sure you show your workings clearly (cross-referencing if possible) – there are quite a few easy marks that can be picked up in part (a). In part (b) make sure your answer is in the form of a report, as specified in the question, and relate your answer to the company in the scenario.

(a)(i) **Existing method**

	Sunshine	Roadster	Fireball
	$	$	$
Direct labour ($5 per hr) (W1)	1,000,000	1,100,000	400,000
Materials (W2)	800,000	960,000	360,000
Overheads (at $24) (W3)	4,800,000	5,280,000	1,920,000
Total costs	6,660,000	7,340,000	2,680,000
Output (units)	2,000	1,600	400
	$	$	$
Selling price	4,000	6,000	8,000
Cost per unit (W4)	3,300	4,587.5	6,700
	700	1,412.5	1,300
	$	$	$
Total profit (output in units × profit/unit)	1,400,000	2,260,000	520,000

Total profit = $4,180,000

Workings

1   *Labour cost*

Sunshine   200,000 hours × $5 per hour =   1,000,000
Roadster   220,000 hours × $5 per hour =   1,100,000
Fireball   80,000 hours × $5 per hour =   400,000

2   *Material cost*

Sunshine   2,000 × 400 = 800,000
Roadster   1,600 × 600 = 960,000
Fireball   400 × 900 = 360,000

3   *Overhead per labour hour*

	$
Total overhead cost =	12,000,000
Total labour hours =	500,000 hours
Overhead per labour hour =	$\dfrac{\$12,000,000}{500,000} = \$24$

4   *Cost per unit*

Sunshine: $\dfrac{\text{Total costs}}{\text{Units produced}} = \dfrac{6,600,000}{2,000} = \$3,300$

Roadster: $\dfrac{\text{Total costs}}{\text{Units produced}} = \dfrac{7,340,000}{1,600} = \$4,587.50$

Fireball: $\dfrac{\text{Total costs}}{\text{Units produced}} = \dfrac{2,680,000}{400} = \$6,700$

(ii) **Activity based costing**

	Sunshine	Roadster	Fireball
	$	$	$
Direct labour ($5 per hr) (as (W1) above)	1,000,000	1,100,000	400,000
Materials (as (W2) above)	800,000	960,000	360,000
Overheads			
Deliveries (W5(a))	960,000	768,000	672,000
Set up costs (W5(b))	2,100,000	2,400,000	1,500,000
Purchase orders (W5(c))	1,800,000	1,350,000	450,000
	6,600,000	6,578,000	3,382,000
Output units	2,000	1,600	400
	$	$	$
Selling price	4,000	6,000	8,000
Cost per unit (W4)	3,330	4,111.25	8,455
Profit/(loss) per unit	670	1,888.75	(455)
Total profit/(loss)	$1,340,000	$3,022,000	($182,000)

Total profit = $4,180,000

Workings

5   *Overheads*

$\dfrac{\text{Overhead cost of deliveries to retailers}}{\text{Total number of deliveries}} = \dfrac{2,400,000}{250} = \$9,600$

$\dfrac{\text{Overhead cost of set - ups}}{\text{Total number of set - ups}} = \dfrac{6,000,000}{100} = \$60,000$

$\dfrac{\text{Overhead cost of purchase orders}}{\text{Total number of purchase orders}} = \dfrac{3,600,000}{800} = \$4,500$

5(a) *Deliveries overheads*

Sunshine	$9,600 × 100 =	$960,000
Roadster	$9,600 × 80 =	$768,000
Fireball	$9,600 × 70 =	$672,000

5(b) *Set-up cost overheads*

Sunshine	$60,000 × 35 =	$2,100,000
Roadster	$60,000 × 40 =	$2,400,000
Fireball	$60,000 × 25 =	$1,500,000

5(c) *Purchase order overheads*

Sunshine $4,500 × 400 = $1,800,000
Roadster $4,500 × 300 = $1,350,000
Fireball $4,500 × 100 = $450,000

(b) **REPORT**

To: Directors, Abkaber plc
From: Management accountant
Subject: The implications of activity based costing
Date: 12.12.X2

(i) **Labour hours and activity based costing allocation**

Labour hours

For the allocation of overheads on the basis of labour hours to be appropriate, there would need to be a direct relationship between overheads and labour hours. From the information available, this does not appear to be the case.

A traditional method of cost allocation, such as the one based on labour hours, was developed when an enterprise produced a narrow range of products which underwent similar operations and consumed similar proportions of overheads. Moreover, when such methods were being widely used, overhead costs were only a very small proportion of total costs, with direct labour and material costs accounting for the largest proportion of total costs.

Abkaber plc has invested in new technology and as a result has significantly reduced the size of its workforce. Direct labour costs now account for a relatively smaller proportion of total costs with overheads making up the highest single cost item. Allocation of overheads on the basis of labour costs would tend to allocate too great a proportion of overheads to the higher volume Sunshine than the lower volume Fireball, ignoring the fact that the lower volume product may require relatively more support services. It therefore seems likely that attributing overheads on the basis of labour hours may lead to inappropriate decisions.

Activity based costing

Activity based costing attempts to overcome this problem by identifying the factors which cause the costs of an organisation's major activities.

The idea behind activity based costing is that activities such as ordering, materials handling, deliveries and set-up cause costs. Producing goods creates demand for activities. Costs are assigned to a product on the basis of the product's consumption of activities.

Supporters of ABC argue that it is activities that generate costs, not labour hours.

The accuracy of any ABC system will depend on the appropriateness of the activities as cost drivers. Each cost driver selected should be appropriate to the overheads to which it relates. There should be a direct and proportionate relationship between the relevant overhead costs and the cost driver selected.

The labour hours costing system and ABC result in markedly different profit figures, especially with respect to the Fireball which appears profitable under the first system but loss making under ABC.

The reason for this is that, although the Fireball uses twice as many hours per unit as the Sunshine, its low output volume of only 400 units (compared with 2,000 units of Sunshine) means that a proportionately lower amount of overheads is absorbed.

Under activity based costing, the Fireball shows a loss because ABC recognises the relatively high set-up costs, deliveries and purchase orders.

(ii)   **Finance director's comments**

The finance director is questioning the viability of the Fireball, but doubts whether ABC provides more information than the labour hours costing method.

ABC helps the company focus on the fact that the low volumes of Fireball involve a disproportionate amount of set-up costs, deliveries and purchase orders, resulting in a relatively higher allocation of overheads.

It may be the case that a review of current activities relating to Fireball may reduce costs. There are also other, non-financial, considerations for continuing to produce the Fireball. As the most expensive of the three products, it may have brand value and help raise the reputation of the company as well as that of the other models.

Marketing director's comments

The marketing director is questioning the suitability of ABC in helping price a major new contract.

(1)   The accuracy of ABC depends on the appropriateness of the cost drivers identified. Although more appropriate than the labour hours allocation basis, for the type of one-off decision the marketing director needs to make, an incremental cost approach may be better.

(2)   There may be factors both financial and non-financial that ABC may not be able to capture. For example, there may be costs common to more than one product, interdependencies between costs and revenues, or interdependencies between the sales volumes of the different products.

The relationship between costs and activities is based on historic observations which may not be a reliable guide to the future.

Managing director's comments

The MD is correct to question the fact that ABC assumes that the cost per activity is constant. In practice, the existence of a learning curve may mean that the costs per activity are going down as the activity is repeated.

The MD is correct in questioning the inclusion of fixed costs which do not vary with either labour hours or any cost driver and thus show no cause and effect relationship under ABC.

Chairman's comments

As (i) and (ii) above illustrate, the overall profit under the two methods is the same. However, it would not be appropriate to dismiss the two approaches as irrelevant.

(1)   If the company carried inventory, then the method of cost allocation would affect the inventory valuation and consequently profit.

(2)   It is important to understand both the strengths and limitations of ABC as a decision-making tool. Although it may appear to be more appropriate than labour hours in the allocation of overheads, there are financial and non-financial factors that ABC does not capture. A decision to discontinue production of the Fireball should not be made without the consideration of these factors. These may include:

- Existence of a learning curve
- The inclusion of fixed costs that do not vary with level of activity
- Interdependencies of cost and revenues
- Interdependencies of sales of the three products

Further considerations

Abkaber plc will need to continue evaluating the activities identified and the relationship between cost drivers and overheads.

(c)   Unit level costs are costs that are driven by the number of units produced or delivered.

Batch costs are those costs which increase when a batch of items is made, for example set-up costs.

Product sustainability costs are costs that are incurred by the production/development of a product range. Advertising costs are often driven by the number of product lines.

Facility sustaining costs are not related to particular products but instead relate to maintaining the building and facilities, eg rent, rates.

6 CPA

Top tips. This is a fairly straightforward question. You can pick up marks straight away by using a report format as requested.

REPORT

To: Management of XY Ltd
From: Management accountant
Date: 20/05/X0

Title: **XY Ltd's profitability in relation to the number of our customers served**

1   **Concept encapsulated by the graph**

1.1   The graph illustrates what is often referred to as the 80:20 rule, that is that 80% of our profits are generated by a core 20% of our customer base.

2   **Application of the principle**

2.1   The same principle (known as Pareto analysis) can be applied in other spheres. For example, in information systems, 20% of systems design effort may provide systems meeting 80% of business requirements, with 80% of the effort being expended to meet the final 20% of requirements.

2.2   In the case of profitability in relation to the customer base, those 20% of customers who buy our standard product, pay invoices in full and on time and in all other respects conform to our procedures will be the ones who generate 80% of our profits. The other 80% of our customers will generate further costs through their non-compliance with our processes.

3   **Improving the profitability of the organisation**

3.1   To build upon the principles of the 80:20 rule there are a number of steps which can be taken.

3.2   **Conduct a survey of customer profitability.** It may be possible to identify specific customers who, as a result of particular requirements they have regarding the product they buy or special ordering or payment procedures they demand, are not being fully charged for the costs which they generate.

3.3   If this is the case a new selling price should be established which does cover the additional costs they generate and if they are not willing to pay this higher price it may be necessary to consider discontinuing supply. Although this may reduce sales revenues, it will increase profits because dealings with these customers are likely to be generating losses.

3.4   **Review internal processes.** It may be possible to align these more closely to those of our customers, thus increasing our overall profit.

3.5   The 20% most profitable customers need to be recognised and steps taken to ensure that they are retained and, if possible, sales to them are increased. Marketing need to ensure that these customers' needs are continually being identified and met. Investigations should be conducted to see whether it is possible to increase sales to these customers, for example by encouraging them to use XY Ltd as their sole supplier.

Signed: Management accountant

7 Just-in-time

> **Top tips**. In the exam you would probably only need to provide five (relevant) financial benefits in part (b) to gain the full five marks.

(a)   JIT production systems will include the following features.

Multiskilled workers

In a JIT production environment, production processes must be shortened and simplified. **Each product family is made in a work cell based on flowline principles**. The variety and complexity of work carried out in these work cells is increased (compared with more traditional processes), necessitating a group of dissimilar machines working within each work cell. **Workers must therefore be more flexible and adaptable, the cellular approach enabling each operative to operate several machines**. Operatives are trained to operate all machines on the line and undertake **routine preventative maintenance**.

Close relationships with suppliers

JIT production systems often go hand in hand with JIT purchasing systems. **JIT purchasing** seeks to **match the usage of materials with the delivery of materials** from external suppliers. This means that **material inventories can be kept at near-zero levels**. For JIT purchasing to be successful this requires the organisation to have confidence that the supplier will deliver on time, that the supplier will deliver materials of 100% quality, and that there will be no rejects, returns and hence no consequent production delays. The **reliability of suppliers is of utmost importance** and hence the company must **build up close relationships** with its suppliers. This can be achieved by doing **more business with fewer suppliers** and placing **long-term orders** so that the supplier is assured of sales and can produce to meet the required demand.

Machine cells

With JIT production, factory layouts must change to reduce movement of workers and products. Traditionally machines were grouped by function (drilling, grinding and so on). A part therefore had to travel long distances, moving from one part of the factory to the other, often stopping along the way in a storage area. All these are non value added activities that have to be reduced or eliminated. **Material movements between operations are therefore minimised by eliminating space between work stations and grouping machines or workers by product or component** instead of by type of work performed. Products can flow from machine to machine without having to wait for the next stage of processing or returning to stores. **Lead times and work in progress are thus reduced**.

Quality

Production management within a JIT environment seeks to both **eliminate scrap and defective units during production and avoid the need for reworking of units**. Defects stop the production line, thus creating rework and possibly resulting in a failure to meet delivery dates. Quality, on the other hand, reduces costs. Quality is assured by **designing products and processes with quality in mind, introducing quality awareness programmes and statistical checks on output quality**, providing **continual worker training** and implementing **vendor quality assurance programmes** to ensure that the correct product is made to the appropriate quality level on the first pass through production.

Set-up time reduction

If an organisation is able to **reduce manufacturing lead time** it is in a better position to **respond quickly to changes in customer demand**. Reducing set-up time is one way in which this can be done. Machinery set-ups are non value added activities which should be reduced or even eliminated. **Reducing set-up time** (and hence set-up costs) also makes the manufacture of **smaller batches more economical and worthwhile**; managers do not feel the need to spread the set-up costs over as many units as possible (which then leads to high levels of inventory). Set-up time can be reduced by the **use of one product or one product family machine cells**, by **training workers** or by the use of **computer integrated manufacturing (CIM)**.

(b)   JIT systems have a number of financial **benefits**.

- Increase in labour productivity due to labour being multiskilled and carrying out preventative maintenance

- Reduction of investment in plant space

- Reduction in costs of storing inventory

- Reduction in risk of inventory obsolescence

- Lower investment in inventory

- Reduction in costs of handling inventory

- Reduction in costs associated with scrap, defective units and reworking

- Higher revenue as a result of reduction in lost sales following failure to meet delivery dates (because of improved quality)

- Reduction in the costs of setting up production runs

- Higher revenues as a result of faster response to customer demands

8 Objective test answers

8.1   Contribution per unit

A $22
B $19
C $17

Weighted average contribution

($22 × 1) + ($19 × 1) + ($17 × 4)   = $109/6 = 18.17

To achieve $43,000 profit:

$$\frac{\text{Fixed costs + target profit}}{\text{W. av. Contribution/ unit}} = \frac{55,100 + 43,000}{18.17}$$

= 5,399

	Mix	B/E point
A	1	900
B	1	900
C	4	3,599
	6	5,399

Required sales of A

$900 \times \$47 = \$42,300$ revenue

8.2 B

8.3 A   Using standard components wherever possible – **can**

     B   Acquiring new, more efficient technology – **can**

     C   Making staff redundant – **can't**

     D   Reducing the quality of the product in question – **can't**

To make improvements towards the target cost, technologies and processes must be improved (**B**). The use of standard components is a way of improving the production process (**A**).

Making staff redundant will not improve technologies and processes (**C**).

Reducing the quality of the product in question does not do this either (**D**).

8.4   Target cost = selling price at capacity – 25% profit margin

Price	Demand
$	Units
50	100,000
45	200,000
40	400,000

∴ Target cost = $\$40 - (25\% \times \$40) = \$30$

8.5 A   Sales value – **no**

     B   Replacement value – **no**

     C   Exchange value – **yes**

     D   Disposal value – **no**

The four aspects of value to consider are cost, exchange, use and esteem.

9 Cost reduction

Top tips. Parts (a) and (b) shouldn't have given you major problems. Or did you find it difficult to think of three **cost control techniques**? As you will see from our answer, however, these include some of the principal **conventional management accounting techniques**, only it is not always usual to explicitly describe them as such!

Part (c) required a little more thought. Try to give **reasoned arguments** that look at **both sides** of the proposition. Don't be afraid to be vaguely critical of management accounting training, but be extremely polite about it, as we have been. Always provide some sort of **conclusion** to your discussion.

(a)   **Cost control** is the regulation of the costs of operating a business and is concerned with keeping costs within acceptable limits.

In contrast, **cost reduction** is a planned and positive approach to reducing expenditure. It starts with an assumption that current or planned cost levels are too high and looks for ways of reducing them without reducing effectiveness.

Cost control action ought to lead to a reduction in excessive spending (for example, when material wastage is higher than budget levels or productivity levels are below agreed standards). However, a cost reduction programme is directed towards reducing expected cost levels below current budgeted or standard levels.

Cost control tends to be carried out on a routine basis whereas cost reduction programmes are often ad hoc exercises.

(b) **Three examples of cost control techniques**

    (i)   **Budgetary control**. Cost control is achieved by setting predetermined absolute levels for expenditure. If flexible budgeting is used then the budget cost allowance can be flexed in line with changes in activity. Control action is taken if actual expenditure differs from planned expenditure by an excessive amount.

    (ii)   **Standard costing**. Designed to control unit costs rather than absolute levels of expenditure, the use of standard costing depends on the existence of a measurable output which is produced in standard operations. Control action is taken if the actual unit costs differ from standard unit costs by an excessive amount.

    (iii)   **Limits on authority to incur expenditure**. Many organisations restrict the authority for their managers to incur expenditure. For example a budget manager may have an overall budget for overheads in a period, but even within this budget the manager may be required to seek separate authorisation for individual items of expenditure which are above a certain amount.

Three examples of cost reduction techniques

    (i)   **Value analysis**. CIMA defines value analysis as 'a systematic inter-disciplinary examination of factors affecting the cost of a product or service, in order to devise means of achieving the specified purpose most economically at the required standard of quality and reliability.' The aim in a value analysis exercise is to eliminate unnecessary costs without reducing the use value, the esteem value or the exchange value of the item under consideration.

    (ii)   **Work study**. This is a means of raising the production efficiency of an operating unit by the reorganisation of work. The two main parts to work study are method study and work measurement. Method study is the most significant in the context of cost reduction. It looks at the way in which work is done and attempts to develop easier and more effective methods in order to reduce costs.

    (iii)   **Variety reduction**. This involves standardisation of parts and components which can offer enormous cost reduction potential for some manufacturing industries. Variety reduction can also be used to describe the standardisation or simplification of an organisation's product range.

(c) The **statement suggests** that the training of management accountants should place the major **emphasis on cost reduction**.

This is true to some extent because of the changes in the competitive environment and the globalisation of markets. In order to remain competitive an organisation must provide goods and services of the right quality at prices which are attractive to the customer.

The **Japanese** in particular view costs as a **target** which must be reached rather than as a limit on expenditure. They employ cost reduction techniques to bring costs down below a target price with the result that prices dictate costs and not vice versa.

If companies are to compete effectively then they must adopt a similar philosophy. The management accountant needs to be trained to provide information which is useful for cost planning and cost reduction. An emphasis on cost control might create a tendency to concentrate effort and resources on the mechanics of recording and reporting historic costs, rather than on the planning and reducing of future costs.

On the other hand it is **still necessary to control costs** and to record and report actual costs so that management can take control action if necessary. An efficient plan will ensure that the organisation is starting out with the most effective cost targets, but only by recording the actual

costs and comparing them with the targets will management know whether those targets have been achieved.

Despite the implied criticism of management accounting training, an increasing awareness of the need for a **more strategic approach to management accounting** does exist, both among trainee and qualified management accountants. Active discussion is also taking place on the need to adapt information systems to be more useful in an advanced manufacturing technology environment.

In **conclusion**, while there may be a case for a **slight change in emphasis** in the training of management accountants, this should not lead to the total abandonment of cost control principles and techniques.

10 Objective test answers

10.1 $y = ax^b$

$$b = \frac{\log 0.8}{\log 2} = -0.3219$$

$y = 40 \times 10^{-0.3219}$

$y = 19.062$ hours

Time for all 10 batches	191
10×19.062	
Less time for first batch	(40)
Time for 9 batches	151 hours

10.2

Units	Average time (hours)	
1	12	r
2		r
4	6	r

$12r^2 = 6$

$$r = \sqrt{\frac{6}{12}}$$

$r = 0.707$ r 70.7%

10.3 $y = ax^b$

$$b = \frac{\log 0.8}{\log 2} = -0.3219$$

$y = 40 \times 5^{-0.3219}$

$\quad = 23.825$ mins

Time for 5 units $= 23.825 \times 5 \quad = 119.13$

Time for 4 units

$\quad = 40 \times 4^{-0.3219}$

$\quad = 25.6$ mins x 4 units $\quad = \underline{102.40}$

Time for 5th unit $\quad\quad\quad\quad \underline{16.73}$

Cost		$
Materials	3 kg × $4/kg	12.00
Labour	16.73 mins × $\frac{8}{60}$	2.23
Variable overheads	16.73 mins × $\frac{2.50}{60}$	0.70
Total cost of 5th unit		14.93

10.4 A   Remember that not all products will follow this life cycle. The concept can only be applied in general.

10.5 A   The bulk of a product's life cycle costs will be determined at the design/development stage (being designed in at the outset during product and process design, plant installation and setting up of the distribution network).

11 Dench

> **Top tips**. Part (a) uses a table to calculate the cumulative average time per batch. This is based on output doubling (cumulative batches) and the time taken reducing by 0.80 for each doubling of batches. You can also use the formula $Y_x = aX^b$ to work out the cumulative average time per batch.

(a)   Cost estimate for 225 components is based upon the following assumptions:

    (1)   The first batch of 15 is excluded from the order (and total cost for first batch is likewise excluded); and

    (2)   The 80% learning rate only applies to the skilled workforce (and related variable overhead), due to their high level of expertise/low turnover rate.

Cumulative batches	Cumulative units	Total time (hours)	Cum. ave time/batch (hours)
1	15	20	20
2	30	32	16
4	60	51.2	12.8
8	120	81.92	10.24
16	240	131.072	8.192

Total cost for 16 batches (240 components):

		$
Material A:	$30/batch	480
Material B:	$30/batch	480
Labour:	Skilled 131.072 hr @ $15/hour	1,966
	Semi-skilled $40/batch	640
Variable O.H.:	131.072 hr @ $4/hour	524
	5 hr/batch at $4/hour	320
		4,410
Less cost for 1st batch (15 components)		(500)
... cost for 225 components		$3,910

(b)   The limited use of learning curve theory is due to several factors:

    (i)   The learning curve phenomenon is not always present.

    (ii)   It assumes stable conditions at work (eg of the labour force and labour mix) which will enable learning to take place. This is not always practicable (eg because of labour turnover).

    (iii)   It must also assume a certain degree of motivation amongst employees.

(iv)   Extensive breaks between production of items must not be too long, or workers will 'forget' and the learning process would have to begin all over again.

(v)   It is difficult to obtain enough accurate data to decide what the learning curve rate is.

(vi)   There will be a cessation to learning eventually, once the job has been repeated often enough.

12 Life cycle costing

> **Top tips**. See how we have set out our answer with two headings addressing the two requirements in the question.

Life cycle costs

Life cycle costs are the **costs incurred on products and services from their design stage, through development to market launch, production and sales, and their eventual withdrawal from the market**. A product's life cycle costs might therefore be classified as follows.

(a)   Acquisition costs (costs of research, design, testing, production and construction)

(b)   Product distribution costs (transportation and handling)

(c)   Maintenance costs (customer service, field maintenance and 'in-factory' maintenance)

(d)   Operation costs (the costs incurred in operations, such as energy costs, and various facility and other utility costs)

(e)   Training costs (operator and maintenance training)

(f)   Inventory costs (the cost of holding spare parts, warehousing and so on)

(g)   Technical data costs (cost of purchasing any technical data)

(h)   Retirement and disposal costs (costs occurring at the end of the product's life)

Life cycle costing versus traditional management accounting systems

(a)   **Traditional management accounting practice**

This is, in general, to report costs at the physical production stage of the life cycle of a product; costs are not accumulated over the entire life cycle. Such practice **does not, therefore, assess a product's profitability over its entire life but rather on a periodic basis**. Costs tend to be accumulated according to function; research, design, development and customer service costs incurred on all products during a period are totalled and recorded as a period expense.

(b)   **Life cycle costing**

(i)   Using **life cycle costing**, on the other hand, such **costs are traced to individual products over complete life cycles**. These accumulated costs are compared with the revenues attributable to each product and hence the **total profitability of any given product can be determined**. Moreover, by gathering costs for each product, the relationship between the choice of design adopted and the resulting marketing and production costs becomes clear.

(ii)   The **control function** of life cycle costing lies in the **comparison of actual and budgeted life cycle costs for a product**. Such comparisons allow for the refinement of future decisions about product design, lead to more effective resource allocation and show whether expected savings from using new production methods or technology have been realised.

Life cycle costing and AMT environments

Research has shown that, for organisations operating within an **advanced manufacturing technology environment**, approximately **90% of a product's life cycle cost is determined by**

decisions made early within the life cycle. In such an environment there is therefore a **need to ensure that the tightest cost controls are at the design stage**, because the majority of costs are committed at this point. This necessitates the need for a management accounting system that assists in the planning and control of a product's life cycle costs, which monitors spending and commitments to spend during the early stages of a product's life cycle and which recognises the reduced life cycle and the subsequent challenge to profitability of products produced in an AMT environment. Life cycle costing is such a system.

Summary

Life cycle costing **increases the visibility of costs such as those associated with research, design, development and customer service**, and also enables **individual product profitability to be more fully understood** by attributing all costs to products. As a consequence, more **accurate feedback** information is available **on the organisation's success or failure in developing new products. In today's competitive environment, where the ability to produce new and updated versions of products is of paramount importance to the survival of the organisation**, this information is vital.

13 Objective test answers

13.1 B   Using the formula P = a – bx,

$$B = \frac{\Delta price}{\Delta demand} = \frac{-20}{1,600}$$

$$= -0.0125$$

To find a: maximum demand is 80,000 units ie when P = 0

$$0 = a - 0.0125 \times 80,000$$

$$a = 1,000$$

$$\underline{P = \$1,000 - 0.0125x}$$

13.2 C   P = $1,000 – 0.0125x

$$P = \$1,000 - (0.0125 \times 50,000)$$

$$\underline{P = \$375}$$

13.3   Marginal cost $= \$35 - \dfrac{\$150,000}{15,000}$

$$= \$25$$

To maximise profit set

MR	=	MC
$60 – $0.002x	=	$25
x	=	17,500
Selling price	=	$60 – (0.001 × 17,500)
	=	$\underline{\$42.50}$

13.4   P = a – bx

b = 10/500 = 0.02

175 = a – 0.02 × 5,000

175 = a – 100

a = 275

P = 275 – 0.02x

Maximise profits when MR = MC

65 = a – 2bx

65 = 275 – 0.04x

210 = 0.04x

x = 5,250

P = a – bx

P = 275 – 0.02 × 5,250

P = 170

13.5 A Discriminating prices based on time attempt to increase sales revenue by covering variable but not necessarily average cost of provision.

14 PN Motor Components

> **Top tips.** In part (a) you should have disregarded the information about fixed costs. You should have taken into account the setting-up costs, however, as they do vary with the volume of production and so are marginal costs.
>
> Many candidates find the discussion parts of questions the most difficult and so don't worry if your list of 'factors' in part (a) is far shorter than ours.

(a)   The **lowest selling price** of one batch of 200 units is **one which covers the marginal cost of production**. This comprises the variable costs of materials, labour, overheads and setting up.

Marginal cost per unit calculation

	Machine group 1 $	Machine group 7 $	Machine group 29 $	Assembly $	Total $
Materials	26.00	17.00	–	3.00	46.00
Labour	2.00	1.60	0.75	1.20	5.55
Variable overheads	0.65	0.72	0.80	0.36	2.53
Setting-up costs (÷ 200)	0.05	0.03	0.02	–	0.10
	28.70	19.35	1.57	4.56	54.18

The lowest selling price per batch is therefore $54.18 × 200 = $10,836.

The calculations show that the marginal cost of one batch of 200 units is $10,836 and this is therefore the lowest possible price that can be offered. However, to sell at such a price would mean that the component would make no contribution to fixed costs and such costs must be covered if the company is to make a profit.

Other factors to be considered when adopting such a pricing policy include the following.

(i)   It is inappropriate to set prices with reference only to an organisation's internal cost structure. Of equal **importance** is the **wider market environment** and the **pricing strategy of competitors**.

(ii)   The organisation must **take into account the likely reaction of competitors**. For example, such a policy could trigger off a price war in which the company could lose more than it gains.

(iii) The organisation **cannot continue to sell at the minimum price indefinitely**. It must therefore decide its future plans for the component. Will it reduce costs or increase prices? It may, however, take longer than the organisation imagines to be able to charge the full price for the component.

(iv) The organisation should consider the approach to be taken if existing customers for the component discover the 'special price' being offered to other customers. **Will the organisation gain a few new customers at the expense of alienating existing valuable customers?**

(b) **We begin by calculating the contribution per unit at different sales prices and sales volumes.**

Outputs and sales up to 7,000 units

Total demand	Selling price $	Variable cost $	Contribution $
5,000 boxes	13.00	6.20	6.80
6,000 boxes	12.00	6.20	5.80
7,200 boxes	11.00	6.20	4.80
11,200 boxes	10.00	6.20	3.80
13,400 boxes	9.00	6.20	2.80

Outputs and sales above 7,000 units

Total demand	Supplied by sub-contractor	Selling price $	Variable cost $	Contribution $
7,200 boxes	200 boxes	11.00	7.75	3.25
11,200 boxes	4,200 boxes	10.00	7.75	2.25
13,400 boxes	6,400 boxes	9.00	7.00	2.00

The total contribution at different sales levels can now be found.

Selling price $	Demand $	Own boxes sold	Unit contrib'n $	Sub contr's boxes	Unit contrib'n $	Total contrib'n $
13.00	5,000	5,000	6.80	0		34,000
12.00	6,000	6,000	5.80	0		34,800
11.00	7,200	7,000	4.80	200	3.25	34,250
10.00	11,200	7,000	3.80	4,200	2.25	36,050
9.00	13,400	7,000	2.80	6,400	2.00	32,400

The calculations show that contribution and therefore profit are maximised at a selling price of $10 with sales of 11,200 boxes.

15 DX

> **Top tips**. The way to tackle this sort of question is to read through the information twice and then to formulate it mathematically, taking care to define your variables as you go. You should then find that you have condensed all the information into a few simple equations.

Profit will be maximised when marginal cost (MC) equals marginal revenue (MR).

Let x = the number of thousands of units sold

For values of x up to 80,

$$MC = 2 - 0.025x + 0.5 + 1$$
$$MC = 3.5 - 0.025x$$

For values of x between 80 and 100,

$$MC = 0.5 + 1 = 1.5$$

For values of x above 100,

$$MC = 0.5 + 1 + 0.0025(x - 100)$$
$$MC = 1.25 + 0.0025x$$

If the profit-maximising output is below 80,000 units, it is at

$$9 - 0.06x = 3.5 - 0.025x$$
$$5.5 = 0.035x$$
$$x = 157.14$$

This is above 80,000 units, so the profit-maximising output is not below 80,000 units.

If the profit-maximising output is between 80,000 and 100,000 units, it is at

$$9 - 0.06x = 1.5$$
$$7.5 = 0.06x$$
$$x = 125$$

This is above 100,000 units, so the profit-maximising output is not between 80,000 and 100,000 units.

The profit-maximising output is therefore at

$$10 - 0.08x = 1.25 + 0.0025x$$
$$8.75 = 0.0825x$$
$$x = 106.061$$

The profit-maximising output is 106,061 units.

16 Plastic tools

> **Top tips.** The techniques required in this question are extremely **straightforward** (calculation of overhead absorption rates for example) so beware of making a silly arithmetical error.

Calculation of overhead absorption rates

	Moulding dept $'000	Finishing dept $'000	General factory overhead $'000
Variable overhead			
Initial allocation	1,600	500	1,050
Reapportion general overhead (800:600)	600	450	(1,050)
Total variable overhead	2,200	950	–
Budgeted machine hours	800	600	
Variable overhead rate per hour	$2.75	$1.58	
	$'000	$'000	$'000
Fixed overhead			
Initial allocation	2,500	850	1,750
Reapportion general overhead (1,200:800)	1,050	700	(1,750)
Total fixed overhead	3,550	1,550	–
Budgeted machine hours	800	600	
Fixed overhead rate per hour	$4.44	$2.58	

Information to assist with the pricing decision

		$ per unit	$ per unit
Direct material			9.00
Direct labour:	moulding dept (2 × $5)	10.00	
	finishing dept (3 × $5.50)	16.50	
			26.50
Variable overhead:	moulding dept (4 × $2.75)	11.00	
	finishing dept (3 × $1.58)	4.74	
			15.74
Variable manufacturing cost			51.24
Fixed overhead:	moulding dept (4 × $4.44)	17.76	
	finishing dept (3 × $2.58)	7.74	
			25.50
Full manufacturing cost			76.74

A **full-cost plus price** will be **based on this cost** of $76.74 **plus a mark-up** of between 25% and 35%. Taking a high, low and average mark-up, the potential prices are as follows.

	25% mark-up $ per unit	30% mark-up $ per unit	35% mark-up $ per unit
Full manufacturing cost	76.74	76.74	76.74
Mark-up	19.19	23.02	26.86
Full cost-plus price	95.93	99.76	103.60

Certain incremental or specific fixed costs have been identified, however, and these should be borne in mind for a well-informed pricing decision.

Product cost based on incremental fixed costs

		$'000	$ per unit
Variable manufacturing cost			51.24
Incremental fixed costs:	supervision	20	
	depreciation	120	
	Advertising	27	
		167	
Incremental fixed cost per unit (÷ 20,000 (W))			8.35
Incremental total cost per unit			59.59

Working

Total market = 200,000 units per annum

Ten per cent market share = 20,000 units per annum

17 Costs and pricing

> **Top tips.** In part (a), there is a lot of information in question 16 that you can use when suggesting a suitable price range. Your **higher-level skills** are required, however. Make sensible comments on the various possible prices.
>
> The most important point to make in (b) is that **cost is not the only factor to consider** when setting prices, although of course it must be considered. This part of the question is only worth 5 marks, so you should only spend a maximum of **9 minutes** on it. It would have been very easy to wander from the point and discuss the various pricing approaches in detail.

(a)   The cost information provides a range of bases for a pricing decision.

Variable manufacturing cost

The variable manufacturing cost is $51.24 per unit. At a price below this level there would be no contribution to fixed overheads. Since the prevailing market price is between $90 and $100 each, such a low price might suggest that the product is of inferior quality.

Incremental total cost

The incremental total cost per unit is $59.59. Management must select a price above this level to be sure of covering all costs associated with this product. This unit rate depends on achieving an annual volume of 20,000 units.

Full manufacturing cost

The full manufacturing cost per unit is $76.74. A price based on this cost will ensure that all costs are covered in the long run, if the annual volume of 20,000 units is achieved. Since competitors' prices range between $90 and $100 it seems possible that the company can compete with a price calculated on a full cost-plus basis.

The range of prices suggested, using the company's usual mark-up of between 25% and 35%, is $95.93 to $103.60 per unit.

Given the current price range of the competitors' products and the fact that the product is expected to offer some improvement over competitors' products, a price towards the upper end of the suggested range would be appropriate.

(b)   In general, the **price charged** for a product should **exceed its cost**. There are a number of different cost-based approaches to pricing, however, and each is appropriate in different circumstances.

Full-cost plus pricing involves adding a profit margin to the fully absorbed total cost of a product. In certain situations, for example if an organisation has spare capacity, it may be appropriate to use **marginal cost** as the basis for pricing. Alternatively, if the lowest possible price is sought, perhaps for strategic reasons, a **minimum** price based on **relevant costs** may be used as the basis for a pricing decision. Management must not lose sight of the need to cover fixed costs in the long run, however.

Whichever cost basis is used, it is important to appreciate that a cost-based price merely provides a **starting point for informed management decisions and pricing negotiations**.

Cost is **only one of the factors to bear in mind** when making a price-setting decision. Other factors to consider will include the organisation's objectives, the market in which the organisation operates and the effect which price has on the volume of demand for its goods.

18 Hilly plc

Demand function $P = a - bx$

$b = 20/25{,}000 = 0.0008$

When $P = 500$, $x = 500{,}000$

∴ $500 = a - (500{,}000 \times 0.0008)$

∴ $500 = a - 400$

∴$a = 900$

Demand function is therefore

$P = 900 - 0.0008x$

Maximise profit when $MR = MC$

Marginal or variable cost per unit

	$ per unit
Material (2 kg × $60)	120
Labour	40
Variable overhead	20
Total variable cost per unit (MC)	180

The marginal revenue (MR) function is

MR	= a – 2bx
∴ 180	= 900 – (2 × 0.0008) x
∴ 720	= 0.0016x
∴ x	= 450,000 units

Substituting x = 450,000 in the demand function

P = 900 – (0.0008 × 450,000)
P = 540

The profit-maximising level of sales is 450,000 units at a price of $540 per unit.

19 Objective test answers

19.1 C

19.2 B

Use the high/low method:

	Occupancy	Cost
Highest activity level	94%	429,200
Lowest activity level	82%	410,000
	12%	19,200

Variable cost per occupancy % = 19,200 / 12 = 1,600

Total cost for 82%	410,000
Variable cost for 82% = 82 × $1,600 =	(131,200)
Fixed cost	278,800

Budget cost for 87% occupancy:

Fixed cost	278,800
Variable cost (87 × 1,600)	139,200
	418,000

Variance:	87% bed occupancy should have cost	418,000
	But did cost	(430,000)
		12,000 (A)

19.3 C An investment centre has responsibility for sales, production and investment in new fixed assets.

19.4 B Problems associated with a decentralised structure include the following:

(i)   A potential lack of goal congruence
(ii) Difficulty in setting a suitable measure of performance
(iii) Difficulties in communication between divisional managers

The advantage of decentralisation is the opportunity for a speedier response to factors due to the more detailed knowledge of divisional managers.

19.5 C Controllable divisional profit before tax is calculated as sales to outside customers + sales to other divisions – variable cost of goods sold – variable divisional expenses – controllable divisional fixed costs.

20 Responsibility accounting

Top tips. A good exam technique with this type of question is to quickly clarify all of the main technical terms at the beginning of your answer. But don't take too long on this; you have only nine minutes at the very most to write out your complete answer.

Responsibility accounting is a system of accounting that identifies **specific areas of responsibility** or budget centres for all costs incurred by or revenues earned by an organisation. **Functional budgets** are budgets prepared for **each department** or process within an organisation. These functional budgets are then summarised to produce the overall summary or master budget for the whole organisation.

The main function of the system of responsibility accounting is **to identify clear responsibilities** for preparing and achieving budget targets. An individual manager is made responsible for each budget centre and for ensuring that their budget co-ordinates with all others that are affected by or affect their own activities. **The budgeting process cannot begin without such a system of defined responsibilities.** If individual responsibilities are not clarified at the outset then there may be duplication of effort, some areas may be overlooked completely and managers would not know who to consult when they require information about specific areas of the business.

A clearly defined hierarchy of budget centres is necessary in order to **consolidate and co-ordinate the master budget for the whole organisation**. The hierarchy can consist of a responsibility centre for each section, department or subsidiary company. For example in a large group the budget for each section would be **summarised** into a **budget** for each **function**. The **functional budgets** in turn would be **summarised** or consolidated into the **subsidiary company's budget** and the individual subsidiaries' budgets would then be summarised into an overall master budget for the group.

The hierarchy of individual budget centres should be organised to ensure that all the revenues earned by an organisation, all the costs it incurs, and all the capital it employs are made the responsibility of someone within the organisation, at an appropriate level in the hierarchy.

21 Budgets and people

Top tips. This question covers a wide range of the possible issues that you could encounter. Make sure that you **deal with both parts** of the question (the reasons for reluctance and the side effects of imposed budgets). Beware, however, of writing down everything you can possibly think of which is remotely related to the behavioural aspects of management accounting.

There is one major **reason why managers may be reluctant to participate** fully in setting up budgets and that is a **lack of education in the purposes of the budgeting process**. The budget's major role is to communicate the various motivations that exist among management so that everybody sees, understands and co-ordinates the goals of the organisation.

Specific reasons for the reluctance of managers to participate are as follows.

(a) Managers view budgets as **too rigid a constraint on their decision making**. For example, a manager may be unable to sanction an item of expenditure if it has not been budgeted for. The natural reaction to this supposed restriction of their autonomy is resistance and self defence.

(b) Managers feel that the top management **goals expressed by the budget will interfere with their personal goals** (for example their desire to 'build an empire' with substantial resources under their control, large personal income and so on). A successful budgetary system will harmonise the budget goals with the managers' personal goals, but it is by no means easy to achieve a successful system.

(c)   Managers imagine that the purpose of budgets is to provide senior management with a **rod** with which to chastise those who do not stay within budget. They will be unwilling to help in the construction of such a rod.

(d)   Managers view the budgeting process as one in which they must **fight for a fair share** of the organisation's **resources** in competition with colleagues with other responsibilities.

(e)   Managers misinterpret the **control function** of the budgeting system to be a method whereby **blame** can be **attached**. By not participating in the budget setting process, they are able to blame an 'unattainable' or 'unrealistic' budget for any poor results they may have.

As a reaction to these uneducated notions, the behaviour of managers involved in budget preparation can conflict with the desires of senior management. Such behaviour is often described as **dysfunctional**; it is counter-productive because it is **not goal congruent**.

The **unwanted side effects** which may arise from the **imposition of budgets** by senior management (for example under an authoritative rather than a participative budgetary system) are examples of **dysfunctional behaviour** and include the following.

(a)   There may be a **reluctance to reduce costs** for fear that future budget allowances may be reduced as a consequence of successful cost cutting.

(b)   Managers may **spend up to their budget** in order to justify levels of expenditure. This is particularly the case in local government circles where there is a tendency to spend any available cash at the end of a financial year.

(c)   There may be **padding**, whereby managers request inflated allowances. In turn senior management may cut budgets where they suspect padding exists. Padding is sometimes called slack and represents the difference between the budget allowance requested and the realistic costs necessary to accomplish the objective.

(d)   In extreme cases of authoritative budgeting, the **'emotional' responses** of managers can be highly detrimental to the goals of the organisation, for example non-cooperation.

22 Divisional performance

> **Top tips.** Parts (a) and (b) require you to demonstrate knowledge you should have picked up directly from the text. No application skills are required at all in this instance.
>
> That being said, it is vital that you do not learn the advantages and disadvantages of ROI and RI in a parrot fashion as they underlie the very core of the chapter. You **must understand how and why ROI affects managerial behaviour**, for example. You are just as likely to get a written question on this area as a calculation-based one.
>
> The calculations required in (b) should not have caused you any problems.

(a)   The **residual income (RI)** for a division is calculated by deducting from the divisional profit an imputed interest charge, based on the investment in the division.

The **return on investment (ROI)** is the divisional profit expressed as a percentage of the investment in the division.

Both methods use the **same basic figure for profit and investment**, but **RI** produces an **absolute** measure whereas the **ROI** is expressed as a **percentage**.

Both methods suffer from **disadvantages** in measuring the profit and the investment in a division which include the following.

(i)   Assets must be valued consistently at historical cost or at replacement cost. Neither valuation basis is ideal.

(ii)   Divisions might use different bases to value inventory and to calculate depreciation.

(iii)   Any charges made for the use of head office services or allocations of head office assets to divisions are likely to be arbitrary.

In addition, **ROI** suffers from the following **disadvantages**.

(i)   Rigid adherence to the need to maintain ROI in the short term can discourage managers from investing in new assets, since average divisional ROI tends to fall in the early stages of a new investment. RI can overcome this problem by highlighting projects which return more than the cost of capital.

(ii)   It can be difficult to compare the percentage ROI results of divisions if their activities are very different: RI can overcome this problem through the use of different interest rates for different divisions.

(b)   (i)   **Return on divisional investment (ROI)**

	Before investment	After investment
Divisional profit	$18,000	$19,600
Divisional investment	$100,000	$110,000
Divisional ROI	18.0%	17.8%

The ROI will fall in the short term if the new investment is undertaken. This is a problem which often arises with ROI, as noted in part (a) of this solution.

(ii)   **Divisional residual income**

	Before investment	After investment
	$	$
Divisional profit	18,000	19,600
Less imputed interest: $100,000 \times 15\%$	15,000	
$110,000 \times 15\%$		16,500
Residual income	3,000	3,100

The residual income will increase if the new investment is undertaken. The use of residual income has highlighted the fact that the new project returns more than the cost of capital (16% compared with 15%).

23 B and C

> **Top tips.** Part (a)(i) requires both regurgitation of book knowledge and **application of the data provided** in the question to illustrate your answer. The examiner needs evidence that you can apply the techniques and principles you have learnt to particular scenarios.
>
> We suggested use of **ROCE based on gross book value of assets** in part (a)(ii) as this overcomes the counterproductive behaviour caused by the current approach.

Paper for board meeting to review the company's performance appraisal and reward system

(a)   (i)   Possible counter-productive behaviour resulting from using the current ROCE calculation for *performance appraisal*

Under the current method of performance appraisal, managers are judged on the basis of the ROCE that their divisions earn, the ROCE being calculated using the net book value of non-current assets. The use of **ROCE** as a method of appraising performance has **disadvantages**, whilst there are **additional disadvantages** of using ROCE **based** on the **net book value** of **non-current assets**.

(1) As managers are judged on the basis of the ROCE that their divisions earn each year, they are likely to be **motivated** into taking **decisions** which increase the division's **short-term ROCE** and rejecting projects which reduce the short-term ROCE even if the project is in excess of the company's target ROCE and hence is desirable from the company's point of view.

Suppose that the manager of B division was faced with a proposed project which had a projected return of 21%. He would be likely to reject the project because it would reduce his division's overall ROCE to below 24%. The investment would be desirable from Cordeline's point of view, however, because its ROCE would be in excess of the company's target ROCE of 20%. This is an example of sub-optimality and a **lack of goal congruence** in decision making.

(2) A similar misguided decision would occur if the manager of C division, say, was worried about the low ROCE of his division and decided to reduce his investment by **scrapping** some **assets** not currently being used. The **reduction** in both **depreciation** charge and **assets** would immediately **improve** the **ROCE**. When the assets were eventually required, however, the manager would then be **obliged** to buy **new equipment**.

(3) The current method bases the calculation of ROCE on the net book value of assets. If a division maintains the same annual profits and keeps the same asset without a policy of regular replacement of non-current assets, its **ROCE** will **increase** year by year as the **assets get older**. Simply by allowing its assets to depreciate a divisional manager is able to give a false impression of improving performance over time.

The level of new investment in non-current assets by C division was over 3 times that of B division in 20X3 and nearly 13 times that of B division in 20X4. B division is using old assets that have been depreciated to a much greater extent than those of C division and hence the basis of the ROCE calculation is much lower. Consequently it is able to report a much higher ROCE.

(4) The method used to calculate ROCE therefore also provides a **disincentive** to divisional mangers to **reinvest** in new or replacement **assets** because the division's ROCE would probably fall. From the figures provided it is obvious that C division has replaced assets on a regular basis, the difference between original and replacement costs of its assets being small. The manager of B division, on the other hand, has not replaced assets, there being a marked difference between original and replacement cost of the division's assets.

(5) A further disadvantage of measuring ROCE as profit divided by the net book value of assets is that it is **not easy** to **compare** fairly the **performance** of one **division** with another. Two divisions might have the same amount of working capital, the same value of non-current assets at cost and the same profit. But if one division's assets have been depreciated by a much bigger amount, perhaps because they are older, that division's ROCE will be bigger.

In some respects this is the case with B and C divisions. Both the profit and the original asset cost of C division are about the same proportion of B division's profit and original asset cost but the ROCE of B division is twice that of C division.

The use of ROCE per se and ROCE calculated using the net book value of assets therefore produces a number of examples of **counter-productive behaviour**.

(ii) *A revised ROCE measure*

Instead of using the net book value of non-current assets to calculate ROCE, it could be calculated using the **gross book value** of non-current assets. This would **remove** the problem of ROCE increasing over time as assets get older and will enable **comparisons** to be made more **fairly**.

Using the alternative method, the ROCE for the two divisions in the two years would be as follows.

B	20X3	13.8%
	20X4	10.6%
C	20X3	11.7%
	20X4	9.7%

Although B division still has a greater ROCE, the difference between the ROCE of the two divisions is much less.

(b) In general, a large organisation can be structured in one of two ways: functionally (all activities of a similar type within a company) or divisionally (split into divisions in accordance with the products or services made or provided).

Advantages of divisionalisation

(i) Divisionalisation can **improve** the **quality of decisions** made because divisional managers (those taking the decisions) know local conditions and are able to make more informed judgements. Moreover, with the personal incentive to improve the division's performance, they ought to take decisions in the division's best interests.

(ii) **Decisions should be taken more quickly** because information does not have to pass along the chain of command to and from top management. Decisions can be made on the spot by those who are familiar with the product lines and production processes and who are able to react to changes in local conditions quickly and efficiently.

(iii) The authority to act to improve performance should **motivate divisional managers**.

(iv) Divisional organisation **frees top management** from detailed involvement in day to day operations and allows them to devote more time to strategic planning.

(v) Divisions provide **valuable training grounds for future members of top management** by giving them experience of managerial skills in a less complex environment than that faced by top management.

(vi) In a large business organisation, the **central head office will not have the management resources or skills to direct operations closely enough itself**. Some authority must be delegated to local operational managers.

Disadvantages of divisionalisation

(i) A danger with divisional accounting is that the business organisation will divide into a number of self-interested segments, each acting at times against the wishes and interests of other segments. Decisions might be taken by a divisional manager in the best interests of his own part of the business, but against the best interest of other divisions and possibly against the interests of the organisation as a whole.

(ii) It is claimed that the **costs of activities that are common** to all divisions such as running the accounting department **may be greater** for a divisionalised structure than for a centralised structure.

(iii) **Top management**, by delegating decision making to divisional managers, may **lose control** since they are not aware of what is going on in the organisation as a whole. (With a good system of performance evaluation and appropriate control information, however, top management should be able to control operations just as effectively.)

24 Pasta Division

> **Top tips.** Remember to calculate the ROI and RI for both situations in parts (a) and (b). In part (c), you must relate your answer to the scenario and your answers to part (a) – you will get 'own figure' marks in the exam if your calculations are incorrect. Parts (d)–(f) are quite general but pay attention to the word 'briefly' in each case – don't be tempted to write pages and pages!

(a)

	Before expansion $m	Additions $m	After proposed expansion $m
Investment in non-current assets	1.5	+0.75	2.25
Investment in working capital	1.0	+0.35	1.35
Net divisional assets	2.5		3.60
Operating profit	0.5	+0.198	0.698
Return on investment	20.0%		19.4%

(b)

	Before expansion		After proposed expansion	
		$m		$m
Operating profit		0.500		0.698
Imputed interest on net divisional assets	($2.5m × 15%)	0.375	($3.6m × 15%)	0.540
Residual income		0.125		0.158

(c)   Using return on investment (ROI) as a performance measure, the divisional manager would not be happy to accept the proposed expansion. The ROI would reduce if the expansion went ahead, indicating a deterioration in the division's performance, and because bonuses are paid as a percentage on this basis, the manager would receive a lower bonus.

If residual income (RI) was used as a performance measure the manager would be happy to accept the proposed expansion. This is because the RI would increase as a result of the expansion. This indicates an improvement in the division's performance and so the manager would receive a higher bonus.

(d)   ROI has the obvious advantages of being compatible with accounting reports and is easier to understand.

There are a number of disadvantages associated with both ROI and RI, however.

- Both methods suffer from disadvantages in measuring profit (how should inventory be valued, how should arbitrary allocations of head office charges be dealt with) and investment (what basis to use).

- It is questionable whether a single measure is appropriate for measuring the complexity of divisional performance.

- If a division maintains the same annual profit, keeps the same assets without a policy of regular non-current asset replacement and values assets at net book value, ROI and RI will increase year by year as the assets get older, even though profits may be static. This can give a false impression of improving performance over time and acts to discourage managers from undertaking new investments.

In addition, ROI suffers from the following disadvantages.

- The need to maintain ROI in the short term can discourage managers from investing in new assets (since the average ROI of a division tends to fall in the early stages of a new investment) even if the new investment is beneficial to the group as a whole (because the investment's ROI is greater than the group's target rate of return). This focuses attention on short-run performance whereas investment decisions should be evaluated over their full life.

RI can help to overcome this problem of sub-optimality and a lack of goal congruence by highlighting projects which return more than the cost of capital.

- It can be difficult to compare percentage ROI results of divisions if their activities are very different. RI can overcome this problem through the use of different interest rates for different divisions.

There are also a number of disadvantages associated with RI: it does not facilitate comparison between divisions; neither does it relate the size of a division's income to the size of the investment. In these respects ROI is a better measure.

The disadvantages of the two methods have a number of behavioural implications. Managers tend to favour proposals that produce excellent results in the short term (to ensure their performance appears favourable) but which, because they have little regard for the later life of their division's projects, are possibly unacceptable in the longer term. They will therefore disregard proposals that are in the best interests of the group as a whole. ROI and RI can therefore produce dysfunctional decision making.

(e) The main features of Economic Value Added (EVA®) as it would be used to assess the performance of divisions:

EVA, like residual income (RI), is a performance measure expressed in absolute terms. It is based on the concept of net economic profit after tax less a deduction for an imputed interest charge.

The relationship between economic and accounting profit is explained below. The imputed interest charge is based on the company's weighted average cost of capital. The assets are at their replacement cost as explained below. The imputed interest charge is based on the company's weighted average cost of capital.

EVA = net operating economic profit after tax less capital charge where the capital charge = weighted average cost of capital × net assets

The weighted average cost of capital is based on the capital asset pricing model.

(f) How the use of EVA to assess divisional performance might affect the behaviour of divisional senior executives:

- It is argued that maximisation of the EVA® target will lead to managers maximising wealth for shareholders.

- The adjustments within the calculation of EVA mean that the measure is based on figures closer to cash flows than accounting profits. Hence, EVA is less likely to be distorted by the accounting policies selected.

- EVA, like RI, is an absolute measure, as compared to a relative one such as ROCE. As such it will not lead to sub-optimal decisions with respect to new investment as it is the absolute increase in shareholder value which is used as a criterion. The ROCE criterion might lead to sub-optimal decisions if new investment has a lower relative return than existing investment, even though it may result in higher shareholder value.

- EVA is based on **economic profit** which is derived by making a series of adjustments to **accounting profits**. Examples of such adjustments are set out below:

  - Accounting depreciation is added back to the profit figures and **economic depreciation** which seeks to reflect the fall in asset values is subtracted to arrive at economic profit.

  - Goodwill is amortised over its useful life.

  - Research and development and advertising expenditure written off are added back to profit and amortised over their useful lives (ie the period over which the benefit from this expenditure will accrue).

- The assets used for the calculation of EVA are valued at their replacement cost and not at their historic accounting cost. They are also increased by any costs that have been capitalised as a result of the above adjustments.

25 Objective test answers

25.1 C   Current ROI = $\dfrac{360}{1,600}$ = 22.5%

New ROI = $\dfrac{(360+25)}{(1,600+130)}$ = $\dfrac{385}{1,730}$ = 22.25% which is lower

Current RI in $'000 = 360 – (18% of 1,600) = 72

New RI in $'000 = 385 – (18% of 1,730) = 73.6, which is higher

25.2 A   Current ROI = $\dfrac{200}{1,000}$ = 20%

New ROI = $\dfrac{200 + 22}{1,000 + 100}$ = 20.18%   ... Yes

Current RI	= Profit	200
	Imputed interest (1,000 × 20%)	(200)
		0
New RI	= Profit (200 + 22)	222
	Imputed interest (1,100 × 20%)	(220)
		2 ... Yes

25.3   Operating profit margin = (Operating profit / Turnover) × 100%
= (3,630,000 / 7,100,000) × 100% = 51.1%

ROCE = (Operating profit / Capital employed) × 100%
= (3,630,000 / (4,500,000 + 2,750,000 + 525,000 – 950,000 – 435,000)) × 100%
= 56.8%

Receivable days = (Receivables / Sales) × 365
= (525,000 / 7,100,000) × 365 = 26.6 days

Current ratio = Current assets / Current liabilities
= (2,750,000 + 525,000) / (950,000 + 435,000) = 2.4 times

25.4 D   The ROI will exclude the $4m plant not available as an earning asset during the year. By excluding it from fixed assets we would also be excluding the increase in long-term debt owed to Green by a corresponding amount.

Fixed assets + net current assets = Capital + reserves + long-term loans

The components of the numerator in an ROI calculation should be consistent with the components of the denominator. In this case the profit used would be gross of interest incurred as the denominator includes both capital and reserves and long-term loans.

Thus ROI will be $6 million/($35 million – $4 million) = 19.4%

25.5 D   EVA = net operating profit after tax less capital charge. The launch costs should be spread over three years. Therefore the $3 million relating to these has to be added back to profit and $1 million relating to the current year should be deducted. The capital charge should be based on the replacement cost of the net assets multiplied by the risk adjusted cost of capital.

26 Balanced scorecard

Top tips. We have provided more than one measure for each perspective but you must **not** do this in the exam otherwise you will waste time. You may have thought of other measures that are just as useful but the two key points to remember is that your measures must be **measurable** and **useful**. There is no point in thinking up with the most wonderful item to be monitored if it would not be feasible to collect the relevant data. Also, once the performance indicator is reported to management it **must initiate appropriate action**. There is nothing to be gained by reporting information to managers that they will not be able to act upon.

You might find it difficult at times to decide in which perspective a certain measure belongs. Don't worry about this. There will often be overlap between the perspectives. If you think of a measure just try to put it into the most sensible category and try to ensure that your measures are not all too similar.

Don't forget to explain **why** each measure might be a useful indicator.

Performance indicators that might usefully be monitored by a training company include the following.

Customer perspective

- Number of customer complaints; monitors customer satisfaction
- Average time to complete a booking; monitors customer service

Innovation and learning perspective

- Training expenditure per employee; monitors ability to update staff and lecturer skills
- Percentage of revenue generated by new courses; monitors ability to maintain competitiveness by continual development

Internal perspective

- Number of courses cancelled due to lack of demand; monitors ability to publicise available courses adequately and forecast the demand in the training market
- Response time in producing management accounting information; monitors ability to maintain competitiveness by keeping management informed

Financial perspective

- Return on capital employed; monitors ability to create value for the shareholders
- Revenue growth; monitors ability to maintain market share

27 MPL

Top tips. The key point to note in the scenario detail is that budgets are issued to the responsibility centre managers, implying that an **imposed system** of budgeting is in place. Make sure that you do discuss the advantages **and disadvantages** of participation as requested in the question, as all too often students focus on just the advantages, seeing a participative approach as the panacea for all organisational ills.

In part (a)(iii) you will need to distinguish between controllable and uncontrollable costs. Attributable profit is the profit after all attributable costs have been deducted. Controllable profit is profit before deduction of uncontrollable costs.

(a)   (i)   REPORT

To: Board of Directors of MPL
From: Management accountant
Date: 23 April 20X0
Subject: Budgeting

This report considers our present approach to budgeting, including the appropriateness of the format of the opening statement currently prepared.

Present approach to budgeting

Given that the budgets are '**issued to**' budget holders, they clearly have very **little or no input to the budget process**. Budgets are **set centrally by senior management** and are **imposed** on managers without the managers participating in their preparation.

Although there are advantages to such an approach (for example, strategic plans are likely to be incorporated into planned activities, there is little input from inexperienced or uninformed employees and the period of time taken to draw up the budgets is shorter), **dissatisfaction, defensiveness and low morale** amongst employees who must work with the budgets is often apparent. The budget may be seen as a **punitive device** and **initiative may be stifled**. More importantly, however, it is **difficult for people to be motivated to achieve targets that have been set by somebody else**.

- **Targets** that are **too difficult** will have a **demotivating** effect because **adverse efficiency variances** will always be reported.

- **Easy targets** are also **demotivating** because there is **no sense of achievement** in attaining them.

- **Targets set at the same levels as have been achieved in the past** will be too low and might **encourage budgetary slack**.

Academics have argued that each individual has a **personal 'aspiration level'** which the individual undertakes for himself to reach, and so it may be more appropriate to adopt a **participative approach** to budgeting. Budgets would be developed by the budget holders and would be based on their perceptions of what is achievable and the associated necessary resources.

Managers are more likely to be **motivated** to achieve targets that they have set themselves and overall the budgets are likely to be more **realistic** (as senior management's overview of the business is mixed with operational level details and the expectations of both senior management and the budget holders are considered).

Allowing participation in the budget-setting process is **time consuming**, however, and can produce **budget bias**. It is generally assumed that the bias will operate in one direction only, consultants building **slack** into their budgets so targets are easy to achieve. But **bias can work in two directions**. Optimistic forecasts may be made with the intention of pleasing senior management, despite the risk of displeasing them when optimistic targets are not met.

(ii)   **Format of the operating statement**

The current format of the operating statement classifies costs as either fixed or variable in relation to the number of chargeable consultancy hours and compares expected costs for the budgeted number of chargeable consultancy hours with actual costs incurred.

For **control purposes**, however, there is little point in comparing costs and revenues for the budgeted numbers of chargeable hours with actual costs and revenues if budgeted and actual hours differ. Rather, the **costs that should have been incurred given the actual number of chargeable consultancy hours should be compared with the actual costs incurred**. Although fixed costs should be the same regardless of the hours charged, such a comparison requires **variable costs to be flexed** to the actual activity level. More appropriate **variances** could then be calculated and denoted as either **adverse or favourable**.

The report should also **distinguish** between those **costs** which are **controllable** by the profit centre manager and those which are **uncontrollable**. The manager's attention will then be focused on those variances for which they are responsible and which, if significant, require action.

(iii) **Assumptions**

(1) Central administration costs are not directly attributable to the profit centre and they are outside the control of the profit centre manager.

(2) Depreciation of equipment is an attributable cost, since it can be specifically identified with the profit centre. However, it is not a controllable cost since the profit centre manager has no control over investment decisions.

Revised operating statement for period 5

	Original budget	Flexed budget	Actual	Variance
Chargeable consultancy hours	2,400	2,500	2,500	100
	€	€	€	€
Fees charged	180,000	187,500	200,000	12,500 (F)
Variable costs				
Casual wages	960	1,000	600	400 (F)
Telephone	2,000	2,083	2,150	67 (A)
Printing, postage and stationery	2,640	2,750	2,590	160 (F)
	5,600	5,833	5,340	493 (F)
Contribution	174,400	181.667	194,660	12,993 (F)
Controllable fixed costs				
Consultant's salaries	80,000	80,000	84,000	4,000 (A)
Motor and travel costs	4,400	4,400	4,400	–
Telephone	600	600	800	200 (A)
	85,000	65,000	89,200	4,200 (A)
Controllable profit	89,400	96,667	105,460	8,793 (F)
Attributable uncontrollable fixed cost	3,200	3,200	3,580	380 (A)
Attributable profit	86,200	93,467	101,880	8,413 (F)
Uncontrollable fixed cost	15,000	15,000	15,750	750 (A)
Division net profit	71,200	78,467	86,130	(7,663) (F)

(b) The balanced scorecard approach was originally developed by Kaplan and Norton and consists of a variety of **indicators**, both **financial** and **non-financial**. It focuses on **four different perspectives**.

Customer

The balanced scorecard asks what existing and new customers value from us. This gives rise to targets that matter to customers such as cost, quality, delivery and inspection.

Internal

The balanced scorecard asks at what processes we must excel to achieve our financial and customer objectives. This aims to improve internal processes and decision making.

Innovation and learning

The balanced scorecard asks if we can continue to improve and create future value. This considers the business's capacity to maintain its competitive position through the acquisition of new skills and the development of new products.

Financial

The balanced scorecard asks how we can create value for our shareholders. This covers traditional measures such as growth, profitability and shareholder value but set through talking to the shareholder or shareholders direct.

The balanced scorecard approach is not without its problems.

Conflicting measures

Some measures in the scorecard such as research funding and cost reduction may naturally conflict. It is often difficult to determine the balance which will achieve the best results.

Selecting measures

Not only do appropriate measures have to be devised but the number of measures used must also be agreed. Care must be taken that the impact of the results is not lost in a sea of information.

Expertise

Measurement is only useful if it initiates appropriate action. Non-financial managers may have difficulty with the usual profit measures. With more measures to consider this problem will be compounded.

Interpretation

Even a financially trained manager may have difficulty in putting the figures into an overall perspective.

Too many measures

The ultimate objective for commercial organisations is to maximise profits or shareholder wealth. Other targets should offer a guide to achieving this objective and not become an end in themselves.

28 Objective test answers

28.1 D If there is no similar product sold on an external market and the transferred item is a major product of the supplying division.

28.2

	£
External sales (6,000 × £650)	3,900,000
Variable cost	
Transfer price of ((€350 × 75%)/€1.50) × 6,000	(1,050,000)
Marketing and distribution (£20 × 6,000)	(120,000)
Profit before tax	2,730,000
Tax at 30%	(819,000)
	1,911,000

28.3 False. They provide an incentive to the supplying division.

28.4 B   Maximum price = costs saved by not manufacturing the 5,000 components

         = (5,000 × variable cost per unit) + avoidable fixed costs

         = (5,000 × $21) + $9,000 = $114,000

28.5 B   Let X = required number of units

X must be such that:

Sales revenue ($146 × X) = F45's own costs

F45's own costs = (variable cost per unit × X) + avoidable fixed costs

∴ X occurs when $146X   = $62X + $18,000

$84X   = $18,000

X   =   214.29

Top tips. Alternatively you could use breakeven arithmetic.

Contribution per unit = $(146 − 62) = $84

∴ Breakeven point = $18,000/$84 = 214.29 units

---

29 Transfer pricing

Top tips. Part (a) is basic book knowledge so you should have been able to score at least four of the six marks. If you can answer **part (b)** successfully then there is every chance that you really understand transfer pricing. The reasoning required is not at all difficult but goes to the very **heart of the topic**. If you couldn't answer part (b) yourself, work through our answer really carefully until you understand what's going on.

The **first thing** to do in part (c)(i) is to **calculate** the **unit costs** and **selling price** of product X. We are told that overheads are apportioned to X and Y in proportion to direct wages. Since hourly rates for labour are the same for both products, the same results will be obtained by **apportioning** the **overheads** according to **labour hours**.

The **next step** is to work out **whether** or not the 2,000 kg of product **X** should be **sold** to **K**. This depends on whether product Z earns a **positive contribution** based on an appropriate **relevant** cost.

Finally, the range of transfer prices can be established. You will need to use your **common sense** in this part of the question in terms of suggesting an appropriate level of **variable costs** that may be **saved** with **internal** transfers.

As usual we have included a **discursive** requirement. We know that it is tempting just to read our answer and tell yourself that you would be able to reproduce something similar in the exam, but it doesn't work like that. You must **practise** these requirements as conscientiously as the numerical ones.

(a) **Potential benefits of operating a transfer pricing system within a divisionalised company**

(i)   It can lead to **goal congruence** by motivating divisional managers to make decisions, which improve divisional profit and improve profit of the organisation as a whole.

(ii)   It can prevent **dysfunctional decision making** so that decisions taken by a divisional manager are in the best interests of his or her own part of the business, other divisions and the organisation as a whole.

(iii)   Transfer prices can be set at a level that enables divisional performance to be measured 'commercially'. A transfer pricing system should therefore report a level of divisional profit that is a **reasonable measure of the managerial performance** of the division.

(iv)   It should ensure that **divisional autonomy** is not undermined. A well-run transfer pricing system helps to ensure that a balance is kept between divisional autonomy to provide incentives and motivation, and centralised authority to ensure that the divisions are all working towards the same target, the benefit of the organisation as a whole.

(b) (i) **Division Able has spare capacity and limited external demand for product X**

In this situation, the incremental cost to the company of producing product Y is $35. It costs division Baker $38 to buy product Y from the external market and so it is cheaper by $3 per unit to buy from division Able.

The **transfer price** needs to be fixed at a price **above $35** both to **provide** some **incentive** to division Able to supply division Baker and to provide some **contribution** towards fixed overheads. The transfer price must be **below $38** per unit, however, to **encourage** division Baker to **buy** from division Able rather than from the **external supplier**.

The transfer price should therefore be set in the range above $35 and below $38 and at a level so that both divisions, acting independently and in their own interests, would choose to buy from and sell to each other.

(ii) **Division Able is operating at full capacity with unsatisfied external demand for product X**

If division Able chooses to supply division Baker rather than the external market, the **opportunity cost** of such a decision must be incorporated into the transfer price.

For every unit of product Y produced and sold to division Baker, division Able will lose $10 ($(42 – 32)) in contribution due to not supplying the external market with product X. The relevant cost of supplying product Y in these circumstances is therefore $45 ($(35 + 10)). It is therefore in the interests of the company as a whole if division Baker sources product Y externally at the cheaper price of $38 per unit. Division Able can therefore continue to supply external demand at $42 per unit.

The company can ensure this happens if the transfer price of product Y is set above $38, thereby encouraging division Baker to buy externally rather than from division Able.

(c) (i) **Product X**

	$ per kg
Direct materials	18.00
Direct wages	15.00
Variable overhead (($70,000/7,000 hours) × 1 hr)	10.00
	43.00
Fixed overhead (($56,000/7,000 hours) × 1 hr)	8.00
	51.00
Profit mark-up 60%	30.60
Selling price	81.60

If product X is used by K in manufacturing product Z, the **opportunity cost** to the company is the sales revenue forgone, $81.60 per kg.

Relevant cost per kg of Z = $81.60 + $15 adaptation + $2 variable overhead
= $98.60

Contribution per kg of Z = $100 – $98.60 = $1.40 per kg

Product Z earns a positive contribution and therefore 2,000 kg of product X should be sold to K.

We can now consider the **transfer price**.

$81.60 would be the arm's length price at which a transfer could be made, and this price would make K aware of the full opportunity cost of using X to make product Z.

However, K may argue that certain variable costs may be saved with internal transfers, for instance packaging, credit control and transport costs. If these are, say, $3 per kg, then the transfer price could be reduced by $3 + 60% = $4.80, to, say, $(81.60 – 4.80) = $76.80.

K is also likely to be unhappy that L is taking a much larger profit mark-up, 60% compared with $1.40/$17 × 100% = 8.2% mark-up on K's costs.

However, it is unlikely that K can justify a substantial reduction in the transfer price, because of the opportunity costs involved.

The **suggested range of transfer prices** is therefore $76.80 to $81.60 per kg.

(ii)   **Other points which should be borne in mind when making any recommendations about transfer prices in these circumstances**

    (1)   What are the personal goals and aspirations of the individual managers, and the consequent motivational impact of any transfer price?

    (2)   Are there any other uses for L's and K's facilities?

    (3)   What will be the short-term and long-term effect on L's sales, if 2,000 kg of product X are withdrawn from the external market?

    (4)   What is the likely effect of the new product on the morale of K's staff, who must be aware of the current under-utilisation of capacity?

    (5)   What are the long-term prospects for product Z?

    (6)   Can the constraint on production hours in L be removed without any significant effect on unit costs?

    (7)   The forecast profit margin on Product Z is fairly small. It may therefore be risky to rely on this forecast for a new product.

(d)   **Actual cost versus standard cost**

When a transfer price is based on cost, **standard cost should be used**, not actual cost. A transfer at **actual cost** would give the **supplying division** no **incentive to control costs** because all of the costs could be passed on to the receiving division. **Actual cost** plus transfer prices might even **encourage** the manager of the supplying division to **overspend**, because this would increase divisional profit, even though the organisation as a whole (and the receiving division) suffers.

Standard cost based transfer prices should **encourage** the supplying division to become **more efficient** as any variances that arise would affect the results of the supplying division (as opposed to being passed on to the receiving division if actual costs were used).

The problem with the approach, however, is that it **penalises** the **supplying division** if the standard cost is **unattainable**, while it **penalises** the **receiving division** if it is **too easily attainable**.

30 Objective test answers

30.1   D   At the end of year 3 $31,000 repaid

∴ $29,000 left to repay

∴ Payback $= 4 + \dfrac{4}{25}$ years $= 4.16$ years

ROI $= \dfrac{\text{Average profit}}{\text{Investment}}$

$= \dfrac{\frac{1}{10}[226,000 - 60,000]}{60,000}$

$= \underline{27.67\%}$

30.2 **Project 1:**

Note. Profit was already given and so no adjustment was required for depreciation.

$$\text{ARR} = \frac{\$15,000}{\dfrac{\$(100,000 + 5,000)}{2}} = 28.6\%$$

Project 2:

$$\text{Profit after depreciation} = \$15,000 - \frac{(50,000 - 5,000)}{5}$$

$$= \$6,000$$

$$\text{ARR} = \frac{\$6,000}{\dfrac{\$(50,000 + 5,000)}{2}} = 21.8\%$$

Both projects have an ARR > 20% so both are acceptable.

30.3 **B**

Time	Cash $	DF 15%	PV $	DF 20%	PV $
0	(13,500)	1	(13,500)	1	(13,500)
1–2	7,000	1.626	11,382	1.528	10,696
2	5,000	0.756	3,780	0.694	3,470
			1,662		666

$$\text{IRR} = a + \frac{\text{NPV}_a}{\text{NPV}_a - \text{NPV}_b} \, (b-a)$$

$$= 15 + \frac{1,662}{1,662 - 666} \, (20 - 15)$$

$$= 15 + 8.34$$

$$= 23.3\%$$

30.4 Tax flows 12 months after end of AP means 1st tax saving by capital allowances in time 2 (claimed time 1).

	Flow	Tax	Time
time 1 claim	$\dfrac{\begin{array}{r}2,000,000\\500,000\end{array}}{1,500,000} \times 35\%$	175,000	t_2
time 2 claim for BA	$\dfrac{\begin{array}{r}1,000,000\\500,000\end{array}}{} \times 35\%$	350,000	t_3

$$\therefore \text{P} = (175,000 \times 0.826) + (350,000 \times 0.751)$$

$$= \underline{407,400}$$

30.5 **A**

Time	Flow ($)	DF	PV ($)
0	(50,000)		(50,000)
1–3	* 30,000 real	2.49	74,700
3	15,000 money 21%	0.56	8,400
			33,100

* Contribution per unit $33   31.12.00

                 = $30   1.1.00

Note. The catch in this question is that the $33 contribution is not in current price terms. It is a T1 value.

31 Webber Design

> **Top tips**. This is a relevant costing question so don't get led astray by the references to pricing.
>
> Part (c) is a standalone question that can be answered independently of the rest of the question. It also asks for **definitions** so you should be able to answer this using knowledge rather than application.

(a)   Incremental costs and revenues of altering equipment

	Note	Alter $	Scrap $	Difference $
Materials	1	4,500	–	4,500
Welding	2	–	–	–
Machining	2	–	–	–
Assembly	3	3,680	(16,000)	19,680
Overtime	4	1,500	–	1,500
Variable overhead	5	–	–	–
Delivery	6	3,400	–	3,400
Fixed overheads	7	–	–	–
Original costs	8	–	–	–
Advance	9	–	–	–
Original materials	10	–	(4,000)	4,000
Scrap	10	–	(5,200)	5,200
Design	10	–	(1,500)	1,500
				39,780

The minimum price to be charged is $39,780, but this is subject to clarification of a number of matters which could significantly affect the figure given. See the notes for details.

Notes

1   The cost of proceeding is the $4,500 which will have to be spent on materials for the other contract.

2   Although additional work is required in the welding and machining departments there is no indication that workers can be taken on or laid off at will: we assume that all workers involved in the alteration work will be paid their weekly wages whether or not the work proceeds.

3   Assembly department workers appear to be in short supply and they can generate $5 for every $1 of direct labour. By redeploying 2 workers for 8 weeks at $200 per worker the company will forgo $2 \times \$5 \times \$200 \times 8 = \$16,000$ contribution. Contribution is earned after having covered labour and variable overhead costs and therefore wages of $(2 \times 8 \times \$200) = \$3,200$ and variable overheads of 15% ($480) are also included in this case. Total reduced cost is $19,680.

4   Overtime is incurred as a direct result of the alteration work and will not be paid otherwise.

5   Variable overhead, like direct wages, will be incurred whatever decision is taken.

6   The special delivery charge is directly relevant to the new customer.

7   Fixed overheads do not change as a result of the decision to proceed and so no extra cost is included.

8   We do not know whether the 'additional work' is in place of or in addition to the work required to complete the equipment to the original specification. We do not know whether the completion costs are 'estimated' or already 'incurred'. We do not know whether direct wages costs are committed or not. Fixed costs are not relevant, since presumably they will not be saved whatever decision is taken.

None of the completion costs are included in our calculation but further information would have to be obtained before finalising the minimum price.

9   The advance can be calculated as follows.

	$
Original quotation – cost	29,450.00
– margin (20/80)	7,362.50
	36,812.50

Advance (15%) = $5,522

However, we do not know whether this is to be returned to the original customer or not – this will depend upon the terms of the contract. If it were returnable only in the event that the equipment were sold to another customer, it would be a relevant cost of proceeding; we have assumed that this is not the case.

10   Savings of $4,000 in materials (ignoring machining costs (see note 2)) would be made if the original equipment were scrapped, and disposal proceeds of $5,200 for other materials and $1,500 for the design would be forgone.

(b)   In addition to the queries raised in the notes above, Webber should consider the following matters in setting the price.

(i)   Whether any of the costs incurred to date can be recovered from the original customer under the terms of the contract

(ii)   If not, whether the price should attempt to recover costs incurred to date as well as future costs

(iii)   Whether repeat work is likely from the new customer, in which case it might be worthwhile to grant favourable terms on this order

(c)   Relevant costs are 'costs appropriate to a specific management decision'. They are future cash flows arising as a direct consequence of a decision.

Opportunity cost is 'the value of the benefit sacrificed when one course of action is chosen, in preference to an alternative'.

Discretionary cost is 'expenditure whose level is a matter of policy', for example advertising costs or research and development expenditure.

Relevant costs are (or should be) used by management to make decisions, as stated above. Opportunity costs are a type of relevant cost. The concept is particularly useful where resources are scarce. Discretionary costs do not have to be incurred in order to continue in business: it is thus useful to management to know which costs can be so classified where cost reductions are necessary or when budgeting.

32 X

Top tips. The ranking of the products is relatively straightforward, provided you adopt a systematic approach.

	A $/litre	B $/litre	C $/litre	D $/litre
Selling price	100	110	120	120
Variable cost	54	55	59	66
Contribution	46	55	61	54
Labour hours used per litre	3	2.5	4	4.5
Contribution per labour hour	$15.33	$22	$15.25	$12
Ranking	2	1	3	4

The available **labour hours** should be allocated **first** to the **contract already made** with Y Ltd. The **remaining hours** should then be allocated to **products according to this ranking**, and **subject to the maximum demand**.

	Product	Litres		Hours used	Cumulative hours used
Y Ltd	A, B, C, D	20 each	(× 14)	280	280
Ranking	B	130	(× 2.5)	325	605
	A	180	(× 3)	540	1,145
	C	50	(× 4)	200	1,345

Summary of recommended production for next three months

Product	Litres
A	200
B	150
C	70
D	20

Calculation of profit for next three months

Product		Contribution	
	Litres	$ per litre	$
A	200	46	9,200
B	150	55	8,250
C	70	61	4,270
D	20	54	1,080
Total contribution			22,800
Fixed overhead (see working)			12,800
Profit			10,000

Working

Calculation of fixed overhead per quarter

Using product A, fixed overhead per hour = $24/3 = $8 per hour

∴ Budgeted fixed overhead = 1,600 hours × $8 = $12,800

Note. The calculation of the hourly rate of $8 per hour could have been based on any of the four products.

33 Research director

> **Top tips**. The information provided changes the ranking compared with question 32, and so you will need to recalculate the production plan. Don't forget that the minimum quantity of D has to be produced.

Products **C and D** can both be **sold** for a **higher price than that offered by the overseas supplier**. The **unsatisfied demand** should therefore be **met** by using the **overseas supplier** next quarter.

	C	D
	$ per litre	$ per litre
External supplier's price	105	100
Internal variable cost of manufacture	59	66
Saving through internal manufacture	46	34
Labour hours used per litre	4	4.5
Saving per labour hour	$11.50	$7.56

Even when the extra cost of the pollution controls for product D is ignored, **it is therefore preferable to manufacture product C internally and purchase D from the overseas supplier**.

The capacity which would have been used to manufacture 20 litres of product D can now be allocated to product C (20 litres × 4.5 hours = 90 hours).

Summary of revised recommended production for the next three months

Product		Hours	Litres	Litres
A	Internal manufacture	600		200
B	Internal manufacture	375		150
C	Internal manufacture	370	92.5	
C	External purchase		7.5	100
D	External purchase			120
		1,345		570

Calculation of revised profit for next three months

Product			Contribution	
	Litres		$ per litre	$
A	200.0		46	9,200.00
B	150.0		55	8,250.00
C	92.5		61	5,642.50
	7.5	(120 – 105)	15	112.50
D	120.0	(120 – 100)	20	2,400.00
				25,605.00
Fixed overhead				12,800.00
Revised profit				12,805.00

Reasons that profit will increase by $2,805 per quarter are as follows.

(a)   Production of product D is subcontracted and the time saved is used on production of product C.

(b)   The additional fixed cost is not incurred because Product D production is subcontracted.

(c)   Maximum demand for products C and D can be met.

A number of factors should be considered, however, including the following.

(a)   The reliability of the supplier, which is particularly important in the case of an overseas supplier

(b)   The quality of supply

(c)   Any other sources of sub-contract supply

34 Alphabet Ltd

Sales revenue	(1)		36,000
Costs			
Material X	(2)	(200)	
Material Z	(3)	4,200	
Labour	(4)	11,000	
Variable overhead	(5)	3,600	
Depreciation	(6)	–	
Fixed overheads	(7)	–	
Lost scrap proceeds	(8)	3,000	
			(21,600)
Net Relevant Contribution			14,400

Conclusion: the proposal should be accepted as it makes a positive contribution of $14,400 based on relevant costs.

(1) Revenue earned as a result of producing and selling T.

(2) No other use for X in business, but $200 disposal costs are saved by using X to make Ts.

(3) Z is used in the business and will have to be replaced for $0.175 × 2 × 12,000 = $4,200.

Assuming inventories can be bought at this price.

(4) Opportunity cost of using labour = contribution foregone + cost of labour
= $1,000 + $10,000
= $11,000

(5) Variable overhead is only incurred when units are made.

∴ relevant cost = 12,000 × $0.30

(6) Depreciation is not a cash flow and ∴ not relevant.

(7) These fixed overheads will be incurred regardless of whether or not Ts are made, therefore cost is not relevant.

(8) If machine is used, instead of scrapped, the business loses $(7,000 – 4,000) of scrap proceeds.

However, the following non-financial factors also need to be considered:

(a) The likelihood of a more profitable proposal being received
(b) Whether repeat orders would be expected at the same price in future years
(c) Whether the company's present customers can be differentiated from this special order price

35 PPA

Top tips. Although a significant proportion of this answer is simply regurgitation of textbook knowledge, this **was** part of an old syllabus question and was worth 10 marks. Questions on this topic could well centre on such an appraisal's advantages and disadvantages.

What is post project appraisal and audit?

Post project appraisal and audit (PPAA) involves **measurement of the success of a capital expenditure project** in terms of **the realisation of anticipated benefits**. PPAA should cover the **implementation** of the project from authorisation to commissioning and **its technical and commercial performance** after commissioning. The information provided by the appraisal and audit can also be used by management as **feedback** to help with the implementation and control of future projects.

Advantages of PPAA

PPAA cannot reverse the decision to incur the capital expenditure, because the expenditure has already taken place. It does have **advantages in terms of control**, however.

(a) The threat of a PPAA will **motivate managers** to work to achieve the promised benefits from the project.

(b) If the audit takes place before the project life ends, and if it finds that the benefits have been less than expected because of management inefficiency, steps can be taken to **improve efficiency**. Alternatively, it will **highlight those projects which should be discontinued**.

(c) It can help to **identify** those managers who have been **good performers** and those who have been poor performers.

(d)   It might identify weaknesses in the forecasting and estimating techniques used to evaluate projects, and so should help to **improve** the discipline and quality of **forecasting** for future investment decisions.

(e)   Areas where improvements can be made in methods which should help to achieve **better results in general from capital investments** might be revealed.

(f)   The **original estimates may be more realistic** if managers are aware that they will be monitored, but PPAAs should not be unfairly critical.

Disadvantages of PPAA

There are a number of **problems** with PPAA.

(a)   There are many **uncontrollable factors** which are outside management control in long-term decisions, such as environmental changes.

(b)   It may **not be possible to identify separately** the costs and benefits of any particular project.

(c)   PPAA can be a **costly** and **time-consuming** exercise.

(d)   Applied punitively, PPAA may lead to **managers becoming overcautious and unnecessarily risk averse**.

(e)   The **strategic effects** of a capital investment project may **take years to materialise** and it may in fact never be possible to identify or quantify them effectively.

36 Payback

> **Top tip**. This is an easy question which you should be able to answer using material in the Study Text. Don't waffle and just put down the main points. Half a page will do for ten marks.

The payback period is the **time taken for the cash inflows from a project** to **equal the cash outflows**. A **maximum payback period may be set** and if the project's payback period exceeds this then it is not acceptable.

The payback method has the **advantage** of being **easily understood** and this may be important to the landowner who might not be a financial specialist. A further advantage is that it **focuses on early cash flows**, thereby **indicating projects likely to improve liquidity positions**. Again this may be important if the management does not wish to tie up cash any longer than necessary.

It is also claimed that the payback method **reduces risk by ignoring longer-term cash flows** occurring further into the future which may be subject to higher risk. The main risk element in a project might stem from the unpredictability of the weather. This risk does not increase in later years and so a shorter payback would not necessarily reduce this risk. There is, of course, a risk that demand could change in the future because of a fashion change or technological change. Use of a shorter payback period would reduce this risk, but it may not be as important as the unpredictability of the weather.

A **disadvantage** of payback is that it **ignores the timing of cash flows** within the payback period, the cash flows after the end of the payback period (which may sometimes be considerable) and therefore the total project return. It also **ignores the time value of money**. Furthermore, it is **unable to distinguish between projects with the same payback period**, the **choice of the payback period is arbitrary**, it may lead to excessive investment in short-term projects and it takes no account of the variability of cash flows. Finally, it **does not distinguish between investments of different sizes**.

37 Two projects

> **Top tips.** This is an easy, very useful question, covering some of the key issues and techniques.
>
> When calculating the **IRR by interpolation**, you should aim to work with a **positive NPV** and a **negative NPV**. If the **NPV** at the cost of capital is **positive**, you need to **use** a **higher** cost of capital for the next calculation so as to produce a **negative** NPV.
>
> If the NPV and IRR rules give **conflicting** results, it is generally accepted that the recommendation of the **NPV rule** should be **followed**.

(a) **Project X**

Year	Cash flow $'000	Disc factor 10%	PV $	Disc factor 20%	PV $
0	(200)	1.000	(200,000)	1.000	(200,000)
1	35	0.909	31,815	0.833	29,155
2	80	0.826	66,080	0.694	55,520
3	90	0.751	67,590	0.579	52,110
4	75	0.683	51,225	0.482	36,150
5	20	0.621	12,420	0.402	8,040
			29,130		(19,025)

IRR = 10% + [(29,130/(19,025 + 29,130)) × 10]% = 16.05%

NPV at 10% = $29,130

Project Y

Year	Cash flow $'000	Disc factor 10%	PV $	Disc factor 20%	PV $
0	(200)	1.000	(200,000)	1.000	(200,000)
1	218	0.909	198,162	0.833	181,594
2	10	0.826	8,260	0.694	6,940
3	10	0.751	7,510	0.579	5,790
4	4	0.683	2,732	0.482	1,928
5	3	0.621	1,863	0.402	1,206
			18,527		(2,542)

IRR = 10% + [(18,527/(18,527 + 2,542)) × 10]% = 18.8%

NPV at 10% = $18,527

(b) **Both** projects are **acceptable** because they generate a positive net present value at the company's cost of capital.

The company should **undertake project X**, because it has the **highest forecast net present value**. Although the internal rate of return for Y is greater, the NPV is generally accepted to be the better performance measure for maximising company wealth.

(c) The **inconsistency** in the ranking of the two projects – ie the conflicting results obtained with IRR and NPV – has **arisen because of the difference in timing of the cash flows** of the two projects. Project X cash flows occur mainly in the middle three years, whereas project Y generates most of its forecast cash flows in the first year, resulting in a higher IRR.

38 NPV and IRR

> **Top tips**. Make sure you get down the key points (those in bold) when you answer a short 10-mark question. You only have 18 minutes and expect to write round half a page.

(a)   **Net present value (NPV)**

This method **takes account of the timing of cash flows and the time value of the money** invested in the project. Future cash flows are discounted back to their present values. These present values are then summed to derive the NPV of the project. If the result is **positive** then the project is **acceptable**. If **two or more projects** are being compared then the **project with the higher NPV should be chosen**.

The major **difficulty** in calculating the NPV is in **determining the most appropriate discount rate** to use. An organisation may have alternative investment opportunities and the discount rate may be the expected return forgone on these investments. This is therefore the opportunity cost of capital. Alternatively an organisation may have raised a loan to cover the project in question, in which case the discount rate may be the interest rate payable on the loan.

A problem with the use of NPV relates to the **difficulty of explaining it** to a (possibly) non-financial manager. The NPV is **preferable to the payback period**, however, since it quantifies the effect of the timing of cash flows and it takes account of the different magnitudes of investments.

(b)   **Internal rate of return**

The internal rate of return (IRR) is the **discount rate which produces a zero net present value** when it is applied to a project's cash flows. If the IRR exceeds the cost of capital then the project is acceptable.

The IRR has the **advantage** of being **more easily understood** than the NPV and it does **take account of the time value of money**.

However, the IRR may be confused with the accounting return on capital employed and it **ignores the relative size of investments**. Furthermore, when cash flow patterns are non-conventional there **may be several IRRs**. More importantly, the IRR is **inferior to the NPV for ranking mutually exclusive projects** in order of preference.

Lastly, the IRR **assumes that cash flows from a project can be reinvested to earn a return equal to the IRR of the original project**. The organisation may not have this opportunity.

39 HP

> **Top tips**. In part (a) set out your proforma as we have done for the calculation of capital allowances and the tax effect of those allowances. This keeps workings clear. Do separate workings for payback and NPV as both of these are referred to in the question.

(a)   **Initial workings**

1   **Capital allowances**

	Tax @30%	Year 1	Year 2	Year 3	Year 4	Year 5
	$	$	$	$	$	$
Machine cost	520,000					
WDA year 1, 25%	130,000	39,000	19,500	19,500		
	390,000					
WDA year 2, 25%	97,500	29,250		14,625	14,625	
	292,500					
WDA year 3, 25%	73,125	21,938			10,969	10,969
	219,375					
Sale for scrap, year 4	50,000					
Balancing allowance	169,375	50,813				25,406	25,407
Tax payable on contribution (working 2)			(40,320)	(80,640)	(80,640)	(40,320)	
Tax relief on training costs ($5,000 × 30% × 0.5)			750	750			
Total tax recoverable/(payable)			(20,070)	(45,765)	(55,046)	(3,945)	25,407

2   **Incremental contribution**

Demand per week	12,000	units
Demand per hour (12,000/40)	300	units
Current capacity per hour	200	units
Incremental units per hour (300 – 200)	100	units
Contribution per unit	$1.40	
Hours available (40 hours × 48 weeks)	1,920	
Contribution per annum (100 × $1.40 × 1,920)	$268,800	
Tax @ 30%	$80,640	

Cash flows from profit

Year	Acquisition/ disposal	Contribution (W2)	Tax (W1)	Total cash flow	Discount factor	Present value
	$	$	$	$	10%	$
0	(525,000)			(525,000)	1.000	(525,000)
1		268,800	(20,070)	248,730	0.909	226,096
2		268,800	(45,765)	223,035	0.826	184,227
3		268,800	(55,046)	213,754	0.751	160,529
4	50,000		(3,945)	46,055	0.683	31,456
5			25,407	25,407	0.621	15,778
Net present value						93,086

Payback period

Year	Cash flow	Cumulative cash flow
	$	$
0	(525,000)	(525,000)
1	248,730	(276,270)
2	223,035	(53,235)
Payback period	= 2 years + ($53,235/$213,754)	
	= 2.25 years, or approximately 2 years 3 months	

The net present value (**NPV**) of the project is **positive** at $93,086 and on that basis it is recommended that the **project should go ahead** after consideration is given to the following.

(i)   The company expects a **payback within two years**. In this instance payback is only reached after approximately 2 years and 3 months but this should be overridden by the positive NPV.

(ii) The $50,000 **recoverable value** should be reconsidered in light of the fact that the current machine would be scrapped at a cost of $20,000.

(iii) Consideration should be given to **alternatives** such as working overtime on the old machine as a way of alleviating the bottleneck, thus eliminating the need for this investment.

(iv) It is noted that the new machine would be **operating at 60% capacity**. Is there an alternative machine with a capacity matched to our needs of 300 units per hour at a correspondingly lower price? Alternatively, are there actions we could take which would stimulate demand to be closer to our potential 500 unit capacity (assuming there would be no other bottlenecks) which would make this a more attractive investment?

(b) There are a number of **reasons why investment decision making will be different when the investment involves a marketing or IT project rather than tangible manufacturing equipment**.

(i) Although most projects will have specific outflows of cash in the investing period, neither IT nor marketing will necessarily give rise to the same sorts of **identifiable and easily measurable cash flows** as manufacturing equipment. In the case of marketing it may be possible to forecast an expected value of additional revenues as an estimate of future cash inflows, but for IT projects there may not be any easily attributable cash inflow.

(ii) The **estimation of the expected future** life of an IT investment is made difficult by the rapid rate of technological change in this area, and estimating the time that a marketing campaign's impact may be felt is even more problematic.

(iii) In terms of approach it is often recommended that NPV is used as a way of assessing IT investments. A **high discount factor** should be used to reflect the fact that any identified cash inflows are subject to a high risk of obsolescence.

(iv) It is possible that a **negative net present value** will be generated from an IT project. The investment decision will be based on management's assessment of whether the negative present value is a price worth paying for the intangible benefits of the system (increased user-friendliness, faster processing and so on).

(v) For marketing investments the decision-making approach will depend on the **value of marketing spend**.

(1) For small marketing campaigns it should be adequate merely to consider whether there are sufficient profits available to absorb the cost of the campaign and still leave an acceptable level of reported profit.

(2) For larger proposed expenditure an expected value of revenue increases should be calculated and compared to the campaign cost. The length of the campaign and its expected impact will often be so short that no discount factor will need to be applied to calculate the net present value of the campaign.

40 Objective test answers

40.1 (a) The option to make follow-on investments
   (b) The option to abandon a project
   (c) The option to wait before making an investment

40.2 A project that must be undertaken completely or not at all.

40.3 Any **three** of:

   (a) Raising money through the stock market may not be possible if share prices are depressed.
   (b) There are restrictions on lending due to government control.
   (c) Lending institutions may consider the organisation to be too risky.
   (d) The costs associated with making small issues of capital may be too great.

40.4   Use trial and error and test the NPV available from different project combinations.

40.5   Rank the projects according to their profitability index.

41 Fund restrictions

Top tips. In part (a) you should state any further assumptions that you make about the constraints on investment. The Profitability Index approach should be used. In part (c) it is helpful to consider the reasons why cash shortages may arise and to relate these to the capital budget constraints.

(a)   It is assumed that the **restriction on investment** applies to the total period under consideration, and that this **amount cannot be incremented** after period 0 by using funds generated from the projects selected earlier. The projects will be ranked using the profitability index (PI), which is calculated as the NPV per $1 invested.

Project	NPV	Investment	PI	Ranking
	$'000	$'000	$'000	
A	14.22	150	0.0948	4
B	28.27	200	0.1414	1
C	21.74	175	0.1242	2
D	35.01	300	0.1167	3

On this basis, the company should invest $200,000 in project B, $175,000 in project C, and the remaining $75,000 in project D. This will generate an expected NPV of $67,515.

(b)   If there are no fund restrictions and the projects are mutually exclusive, the company should select the project that has the **highest NPV** since this will make the greatest contribution to increasing the net worth of the business, and on this basis project D would be chosen.

(c)   A period of capital rationing is often associated with more general problems of cash shortage. Possible reasons for this include the following.

(i)   The business has become **loss making** and is unable to cover the depreciation charge. Since one purpose of the depreciation charge is to allow for the cost of the assets used in the profit and loss account, the implication is that there will be insufficient cash with which to replace these assets when necessary.

(ii)   High inflation may mean that even though the business is profitable in historical cost terms, it is still **failing to generate sufficient funds** to replace assets.

(iii)   If the business is growing it may face a **shortage of working capital** with which to finance expansion, and this may result in a period of capital rationing.

(iv)   If the business is seasonal or cyclical it may face **times of cash shortage** despite being fundamentally sound. In this situation, there may be a periodic need for capital rationing.

(v)   A large one-off item of expenditure such as a property purchase may mean that the company faces a **temporary shortage of cash** for further investment.

A further reason for capital rationing arises in the situation where the company has more investment opportunities available than the funds allocated to the capital budget permit. This means that projects must be ranked for investment, taking into account both financial and strategic factors.

42 ANT

> **Top tips.** A table setting out each element of unit cost is helpful. When doing the NPV calculations it is important to show them, but show them in a way that minimises the writing you have to do. If you were not able to fit your answer to (a) across the page, you could have stated the discount factors at the start of the answer and then done the calculations. Note also that we have taken the short cut of using annuity factors. Don't forget the 'reclaiming of working capital' in year 5.
>
> In (b) you are using **total inflows** to calculate the profitability index, not net present value. When setting out your workings a column on cumulative outlay should help you ensure you take the correct proportion of the partial project.
>
> (c) starts off by stating the **assumptions**, and then goes on to discuss **complications** in which the NPV approach could not be used.

(a)   The first step is to calculate the **annual contribution** from each project, together with the working capital cash flows. These cash flows, together with the initial outlay, can then be **discounted** at the **cost of capital** to arrive at the NPV of each project. Development costs already incurred are irrelevant. There are no additional administration costs associated with the projects, and depreciation is also irrelevant since it has no cash effect.

First, calculate annual contribution.

	A	B	C	D
Unit sales	150,000	75,000	80,000	120,000
	$	$	$	$
Selling price per unit	30.00	40.00	25.00	50.00
Material cost per unit	7.60	12.00	4.50	25.00
Labour cost per unit	9.80	12.00	5.00	10.00
Variable overheads per unit	6.00	7.00	2.50	10.50
	$'000	$'000	$'000	$'000
Sales per annum	4,500	3,000	2,000	6,000
Materials	1,140	900	360	3,000
Labour	1,470	900	400	1,200
Variable overheads	900	525	200	1,260
Annual contribution	990	675	1,040	540
	$'000	$'000	$'000	$'000
Working capital requirement (20% annual sales value)	900	600	400	1,200

It is assumed that working capital will be recovered at the end of year 5. The initial outlay will be made in year 0.

The NPV of each project can now be calculated.

Cash flows

Year	A Gross p.a. $'000	A Net $'000	B Gross p.a. $'000	B Net $'000	C Gross p.a. $'000	C Net $'000	D Gross p.a. $'000	D Net $'000	Discount factor 18%
0	(3,000)	(3,000)	(2,000)	(2,000)	(2,800)	(2,800)	(1,800)	(1,800)	1
1–4	990	2,663	675	1,816	1,040	2,798	540	1,453	2.690
5	1,890	826	1,275	557	1,440	629	1,740	760	0.437
		489		373		627		413	

(b)   The **profitability** index provides a **means** of **optimising the NPV** when there are more projects available which yield a positive NPV than funds to invest in them. The profitability index measures the ratio of the present value of **cash inflows** to the **initial outlay** and represents the NPV per $1 invested.

Project	PV of inflows $'000	Initial outlay $'000	Ratio	Ranking
A	3,489	3,000	1.163	4
B	2,373	2,000	1.187	3
C	3,427	2,800	1.224	2
D	2,213	1,800	1.229	1

Project D has the highest PI ranking and is therefore the first choice for investment. On this basis the funds available should be invested as follows.

Project	Initial outlay $'000	Total NPV $'000	% taken	Cumulative outlay $'000	Actual NPV $'000
D	1,800	413	100	1,800	413
C	2,800	627	100	4,600	627
B	2,000	373	30	5,200	112
A	3,000	491	0	5,200	0
Total NPV generated					1,152

(c) The profitability index (PI) approach can be applied only if the projects under consideration fulfil certain criteria, as follows.

(i) There is **only one constraint on investment**, in this case capital. The PI ensures that maximum return per unit of scarce resource (capital) is obtained.

(ii) **Each investment** can be **accepted** or **rejected** in its entirety or alternatively accepted on a partial basis.

(iii) The NPV generated by a given project is **directly proportional** to the percentage of the investment undertaken.

(iv) Each investment can only be **made once** and not repeated.

(v) The company's aim is to **maximise overall NPV**.

If **additional funds** are **available** but at a higher cost, then the simple PI approach cannot be used since it is not possible to calculate unambiguous individual NPVs.

If certain of the projects that may be undertaken are **mutually exclusive** then **sub-problems** must be **defined** and **calculations made** for different combinations of projects. This can become a very lengthy process. These assumptions place limitations on the use of the ratio approach. It is not appropriate to multi-constraint situations when linear programming techniques must be used. Each project must be infinitely divisible and the company must accept that it may need to undertake a small proportion of a given project. This is frequently not possible in practice. It is also very unlikely that there is a simple linear relationship between the NPV and the proportion of the project undertaken; it is much more likely that there will be discontinuities in returns.

Possibly a more serious constraint is the assumption that the company's only concern is to **maximise NPV**. It is possible that there may be long-term strategic reasons which mean that an investment with a lower NPV should be undertaken instead of one with a higher NPV, and the ratio approach takes no account of the relative degrees of risk associated with making the different investments.

43 Objective test answers

43.1 C Expected values produce an average long run outcome. Thus, they don't assess risk.

All other options help appraise risk, but they do not quantify it.

43.2 D The expected sales are given by

J: $10,000 \times 0.3 + 20,000 \times 0.5 + 30,000 \times 0.2 = 19,000$
K: $10,000 \times 0.3 + 20,000 \times 0.4 + 30,000 \times 0.3 = 20,000$
L: $10,000 \times 0.2 + 20,000 \times 0.6 + 30,000 \times 0.2 = 20,000$

43.3 D Expected sales quantity $= (1,000 \times 0.9) + (2,000 \times 0.1) = 1,100$
∴ Expected sales revenue $= 1,100 \times \$5 = \$5,500$
Expected unit cost $= (1.30 \times 0.55) + (1.50 \times 0.45) = \$1.39$
∴ Expected total variable costs $= \$1.39 \times 1,100 = \$1,529$

Profit calculation	$
Sales revenue	5,500
Less: variable costs	(1,529)
fixed costs	(3,000)
	971

43.4 Payoff table:

			Baked		
Demand	9	10	11	12
9	45	42	39	36
10	43	50	47	44
11	41	48	55	52
12	39	46	53	60

(i) Maximax 45 50 55 **60**
Bake 12 cakes

(ii) Maximin 39 **42** 39 39
Bake 10 cakes

(iii) Minimax regret – bake 11 cakes

			Opportunity cost		
Demand	9	10	11	12
9	-	3	6	9
10	7	-	3	6
11	14	7	-	3
12	21	14	7	-
Max regret	21	14	7	9
Minimax			7	

43.5

Demand	Probability	9	Division 10	11	12
9	0.2	45	42	39	36
10	0.2	43	50	47	44
11	0.3	41	48	55	52
12	0.3	39	46	53	60
	EV	41.6	46.6	49.6	49.6

With perfect information

		EV $
9	0.2 × 45	9.00
10	0.2 × 50	10.00
11	0.3 × 55	16.50
12	0.3 × 60	18.00
		53.50

VOPI = EV (with info) – EV (no info)

= 53.50 – 49.60

= $3.90

The information should not be purchased for $5, as it only has a value of $3.90.

44 Elsewhere

Top tips. This question is split into five parts so you have plenty of opportunity to earn marks. Part (a) uses information straight from the table in the question. Part (b) is a lot harder but you will need to practise these decision trees. Refer back to our tips in the chapter for drawing a tree if you have forgotten. Look at how we answered part (c)(i) as a simple equation.

(a)   The expected value of profit is calculated as follows.

Profit $'000	Probability	Expected profit $'000
800	0.5	400
100	0.2	20
(300)	0.3	(90)
		330

(b)   (i)

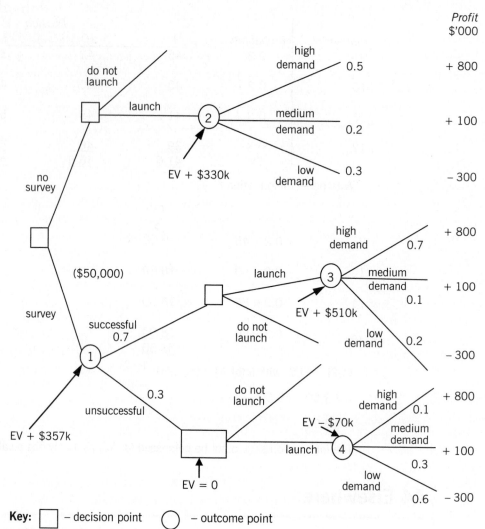

Key: ☐ – decision point   ◯ – outcome point

Expected value of profit

Profit	Probabilities outcome point			EV of profit outcome point		
	2	3	4	2	3	4
$'000				$'000	$'000	$'000
800	0.5	0.7	0.1	400	560	80
100	0.2	0.1	0.3	20	10	30
(300)	0.3	0.2	0.6	(90)	(60)	(180)
				330	510	(70)

(ii)   The record company should not commission the survey because the expected value of profit without the survey is $330,000. This is greater than the expected value of profit of $307,000 ($357,000 – $50,000) with the survey.

(c)   (i)   To find the maximum the company should pay for the survey, solve:

EV (survey) = EV (no survey)
$357K – survey cost = $330K

The maximum that the company should pay for this survey is $27,000.

(ii)   Whenever a decision is made when the outcome of the decision is uncertain, there will always be some doubt that the correct decision has been taken. If a decision is based on selecting the option with the highest EV of profit, it can be assumed that in the long run, that is, with enough repetition, the decision so selected will give the highest average profit.

But if the decision involves a once-only outcome, there will be a risk that in retrospect, it will be seen that the wrong decision was taken.

A decision tree is a simplified representation of reality, and it may omit some possible decision options, or it may simplify the possible outcomes. For example, in this question, 'success' and 'failure' are two extreme outcomes, whereas a variety of outcomes between success and failure may be possible. The decision tree is therefore likely to be a simplification of reality.

INDEX

Note. **Key terms** and their references are given in **bold**.

Notes

Notes

Notes

Notes

Notes

Notes

Review Form – Paper P2 Advanced Management Accounting (6/15)

Please help us to ensure that the CIMA learning materials we produce remain as accurate and user-friendly as possible. We cannot promise to answer every submission we receive, but we do promise that it will be read and taken into account when we update this Study Text.

Name: _____ Address: _____

_____

_____

How have you used this Study Text?
(Tick one box only)

☐ Home study (book only)

☐ On a course: college _____

☐ With 'correspondence' package

☐ Other _____

Why did you decide to purchase this Study Text? *(Tick one box only)*

☐ Have used BPP Texts in the past

☐ Recommendation by friend/colleague

☐ Recommendation by a lecturer at college

☐ Saw information on BPP website

☐ Saw advertising

☐ Other _____

During the past six months do you recall seeing/receiving any of the following?
(Tick as many boxes as are relevant)

☐ Our advertisement in *Financial Management*

☐ Our advertisement in *Pass*

☐ Our advertisement in *PQ*

☐ Our brochure with a letter through the post

☐ Our website www.bpp.com

Which (if any) aspects of our advertising do you find useful?
(Tick as many boxes as are relevant)

☐ Prices and publication dates of new editions

☐ Information on Text content

☐ Facility to order books off-the-page

☐ None of the above

Which BPP products have you used?

Text	☑	Passcard	☐
Kit	☐	i-Pass	☐

Your ratings, comments and suggestions would be appreciated on the following areas.

	Very useful	Useful	Not useful
Introductory section	☐	☐	☐
Chapter introductions	☐	☐	☐
Key terms	☐	☐	☐
Quality of explanations	☐	☐	☐
Case studies and other examples	☐	☐	☐
Exam skills and alerts	☐	☐	☐
Questions and answers in each chapter	☐	☐	☐
Chapter overview and summary diagrams	☐	☐	☐
Quick quizzes	☐	☐	☐
Question Bank	☐	☐	☐
Answer Bank	☐	☐	☐
Index	☐	☐	☐

	Excellent	Good	Adequate	Poor
Overall opinion of this Study Text	☐	☐	☐	☐

	Yes	No
Do you intend to continue using BPP products?	☐	☐

On the reverse of this page is space for you to write your comments about our Study Text We welcome your feedback.

The BPP Learning Media author team can be e-mailed at: cimaqueries@bpp.com

Please return this form to: CIMA Product Manager, BPP Learning Media Ltd, FREEPOST, London, W12 8BR

TELL US WHAT YOU THINK

Please note any further comments and suggestions/errors below. For example, was the text accurate, readable, concise, user-friendly and comprehensive?